Pradeep Ganguly
Clemson
12.10.76.

**Exchange
and Production
Theory in Use**

# Exchange
# and Production

# Theory in Use

## Armen A. Alchian
*University of California, Los Angeles*

## William R. Allen
*Texas A&M University*

Wadsworth Publishing Company, Inc.
Belmont, California

*8 9 10 — 80 79 78 77 76 75*

L. C. Cat. Card No.: 69-12366

*Printed in*
*the United States of America*

*This book has been printed on recycled paper.*

# Preface

This book is essentially the exchange and production analysis portion of our more inclusive text *University Economics*, with modifications, additions, and reordering of topics to make it self-contained. The book is designed for that portion of introductory and intermediate economics courses devoted to *microeconomics*—a short if somewhat misleading name for the analysis of exchange, production control, productive resource use, and pricing. That basic theory of pricing and exchange and production of particular goods is here exposited from its choice-theoretic foundations. And it is applied to a host of problems that we know from our teaching experience will interest students.

A few illustrations suggest the range of problems used in teaching students how to apply economic theory: types of competition permitted in seeking control over productive resources; the military draft; nonmarket exchange; racial discrimination; collegiate amateur and professional athletic cartels; military government cost-benefit analyses; water pollution and use; behavior of university administrators; TV advertising; public goods production and allocation; closed-market monopoly behavior and competition. These, and many more, help show that economic theory can help students to better understand the economic factors and forces determining their environment and to more effectively react to them. It should help students avoid many gross economic fallacies of everyday folklore.

A test of any theory or science is its ability to explain many events consistently. Economics passes that test. This book is an exposition of economic analysis at an introductory level, with emphasis on its empirical meaningfulness and validity. Students can easily learn the concepts and theorems, but application to and interpretation of real events is difficult to master. It has often been said, "They can parrot the theory, but they can't apply it to problems." To provide analytical competence, many illustrative applications are required. A major part of this text contains applications of the basic theorems.

The propriety of stressing the few fundamentals is evidenced by the statement of an economist, Alain A. Enthoven, Assistant Secretary of Defense:

> . . . the tools of analysis that we in Defense use are the simplest, most fundamental concepts of economic theory, combined with the simplest quantitative methods. The requirements for success in this line of work are a thorough understanding of and, if you like, belief in the relevance of such concepts as marginal products and costs in complex situations, combined with a good quantitative sense. The economic theory we are using is the theory most of us learned as sophomores. The reason Ph.D.'s are required is that many economists do not believe what they have learned until they have gone through graduate school and acquired a vested interest in marginal analysis. ("Economic Analysis in the Department of Defense," *American Economic Review*, Vol. 53 [May 1963], p. 422.)

Significant advances of the postwar years have been incorporated in the text. The theory covering choice, demand, exchange, and supply has been extended beyond the narrow, wealth-maximizing behavior in simple private-property markets. The analysis of cost, and its relation to various dimensions of output, has been modernized to include mass-production economies of industrial techniques, advancing economics beyond the mere classification of mutually exclusive possibilities to valid laws of costs. The role of information and the costs of acquiring it have been integrated into the analysis, explaining much pricing behavior as well as laying a foundation for analysis of fluctuations in national aggregates of employment and income.

The economic problems and economic analysis emphasized in this book were, beginning with the Deep Depression of the 1930s, almost ignored as interest turned to depressions and unemployment. Resurgence of concern with this portion of economics reflects two distinct factors. One probably has been the relatively negligible span of depression and recession in recent decades. Second, thirty years ago there was little understanding of the importance of the process in which the community responds to demand and supply shifts and approaches new equilibrating price and output patterns. For that reason, the theory of pricing and its application to exchange and production of individual goods and services were regarded as inapplicable to national income fluctuations. However, now the analysis of national income fluctuations is being more solidly built on the basic theory of pricing and exchange by explicitly incorporating the role of ascertaining and approaching prices and outputs appropriate to changed demand and supply conditions.

Perhaps the questions at the end of each chapter are the book's most unusual feature. Those are akin to questions typically found in chemistry, physics, and engineering texts. Instead of being cocktail conversation questions, they (1) reinforce the learning of concepts and principles, (2) develop a familiarity and ease in applying economic theory, (3) test the student's progress, and (4) stimulate exploration in slightly more advanced aspects not covered in the text. Most novel to economics, though not to texts in other sciences, is the inclusion of answers to half of the questions. (Answered questions are prefaced by a number in boldface type.) Answers serve two purposes: to guide and give the student confidence in his progress and to demonstrate that economic problems can have testable answers. Of course, questions that ask for one's preferences or beliefs admit of no uniquely correct answers. Answerable questions not answered in the text are answered in the Instructor's Manual.

Many examples and assertions in the text are not documented. Few students would refer to that documentation. In the Instructor's Manual, references are given to articles presenting applications of economic theory with factual and evidential material. These will enable the instructor to give more detail in classroom discussion.

So great has been the aid of the following in preparing this version that only with reluctance do we necessarily absolve them from blame for our errors: William Meckling, Donald Gordon, Karl Brunner, George Stigler, Jack Hirshleifer, Roland McKean, John Ashley, Henry Goldstein, Axel Leijonhufvud, George Hilton, Courtney Stone, Kenneth Clarkson, Earl Thompson, Wallace E. Oates, Daniel Orr, Laszlo Zsoldos, and Arline Alchian.

A Study Guide for *University Economics*, enabling the student to reinforce his learning, check his comprehension, and become acquainted with some extensions of the analysis, has been prepared by Richard Newcomb of Pennsylvania State University and David Ramsey of the University of Missouri; it is also useful for this text.

# Contents

# 5  Market Demand, Allocation, and Equilibrium Price   84

# 6  Applications of Demand Analysis to Market Pricing and Allocation   102

# 7  Price-Takers' and Price-Searchers' Markets   124

# 8  Nonclearing Market Prices   152

# Exchange
# and Production
# Theory in Use

# 1

## Scarcity, Competitive Behavior, and Economics

Two villains—nature and the rest of us people—dominate your life and prevent you from having all you want. Nature is niggardly: it provides fewer resources than we could use, and much of what is available is made useful only by hard work. As for the rest of us people, the problem stems not from malevolence; your wants and ours simply exceed what is available. Do not suppose that if we were less greedy, more would be within your grasp. For greed impels us to produce more, not only for ourselves, but, miraculously, more for you too— provided that productivity-inducing institutional arrangements exist.

Man wants more than is available and more than there is any prospect of obtaining. Some assert that we *could* satisfy our "needs" if only we were more efficient or worked harder or both. As a former government official has put it: "We have not had enough of anything, because we have not used fully the fantastic productive power which could provide us with enough of every-thing." "Enough" of *everything*? To satisfy *every* conceivable whim and desire? Of *every* person? It is a frustrating fact that the world is a poor place. Despite religious and philosophical exhortations to abandon natural desires for "more," our wants evidently are boundless: as soon as we have more of this, we want still more of it and also more of that . . . and that . . . and that . . . To say that we always want more is to say that man lives, even in the most affluent societies, in a state of *scarcity*.

An alternative explanation of man's material dilemma is that we *do* produce "enough" stuff in the aggregate, but—because of selfishness, inept planning, and poor taste—we turn out the wrong things: silly gadgets and cosmetics and over-large and too frequently remodeled automobiles instead of more symphony orchestras, better housing, art museums, and lunar explorations. But this expresses merely a preference for one collection of output *instead of* another basket. Planning would not avoid or vitiate scarcity. Indeed, in the blissful absence of scarcity, there would be no occasion to plan; with non-scarce resources, there would be no necessity to decide if productive services should be shifted between "silly" output and "wholesome" output. (What's in a name? Is it possible that the puritan would label as "silly" a product which the debonair would consider "wholesome"?)

A simple diagram dealing with two commodities, "guns" and "butter," can illustrate some features of scarcity. In Figure 1–1, society could produce a maximum quantity of $0P_1$ of guns if all available resources were directed to that end; alternatively, $0P_2$ of butter could be produced if there is no output of guns; and any combination of the commodities could be produced along line $P_1P_2$. Society can achieve a production point *on* or *inside* the $P_1P_2$ boundary line, but it cannot get *outside* that boundary, given its present productive powers and tastes for leisure. (1) A problem to be solved, some-how, by the socioeconomic organization is determining at what *point* to be on that boundary—that is, determining the total output *mix*. Point $A$ has more guns; $B$, more butter. Which will be chosen? (2) Will society produce an output combination as large as feasible? Or will it underproduce at a point *inside* the bounded area. Being inside may be the result of two kinds of inefficiency: (a) unnecessarily idle, unused resources or (b) misdirected, though fully employed, resources. (3) Growth is indicated in Figure 1–2 by an outward *shift* of the production-possibility boundary. This means society has become richer by acquiring improved technology or by more productive resources or both.

Even more is involved in the problem of scarcity. What determines how much *each* person produces and gets of that total? And what determines the particular *mix* of goods *he* consumes? These and more subtle issues, to be elaborated later, constitute the area of economic study.

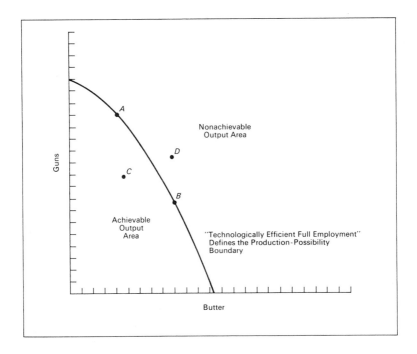

Figure 1–1
Scarcity, Efficiency, and Choice Illustrated by Production-Possibility Boundary

The curved line portrays largest combinations of amounts of guns and butter producible in the economy. Any point on the line (e.g., *A* or *B*) can be produced. No combination of guns and butter outside the curved line (e.g., point *D*) can be achieved by the economy given its productive powers and preference for leisure. Less would be produced if the productive resources were unemployed or used inefficiently—as, for example, indicated by point *C*. In some manner society selects a point on the boundary or inside it. The closer to full efficiency that the economy operates, the closer, by definition, it is to the production boundary. We shall be studying later the means for determining the output combination and efficiency of production.

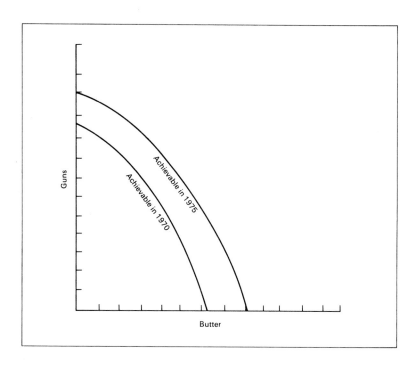

Figure 1–2
Growth of Economic Productive Powers of the Economy

A richer, more productive economy is represented by a production-possibility boundary that is higher and more to the right, as for 1975 compared to 1970. Growth can occur in several ways. A greater production-possibility boundary is usually induced by a larger labor force. (But does the output per person increase? That cannot be indicated by this diagram, which gives only the social totals.) Moving the frontier outward involves restricting consumption by saving either to create more productive goods or to invest in knowledge and inventions. (Problem: Suppose the two boundaries intersected. Which would represent greater productive power?)

### Competition

Competition always exists where there is scarcity. With scarcity there is only a choice among limited options, and we compete with each other for those options. Hence, in a society of more than one person, *scarcity implies competition.* There is only one way to avoid competition: according to the renowned practical philosopher, Arnold Palmer, "If you aren't competing, you're dead." And conversely.

You may have heard: "The free-enterprise, private-property system, because it is competitive, promotes antisocial, jungle behavior. It induces cheating, conformity, discrimination, and the dominance of the lowest quality, while discouraging humane behavior toward one's fellow men." But *competition*—whether it does, or necessarily must, yield dire consequences—is not unique to the free-enterprise, private-property system. *Competition exists in every social system.* It is a result of conflicts of interest in a world of scarcity—not of the social, cultural, or economic system within which we live. However, there are many forms of competition. We have some choice, even as individuals, about which form to rely on more heavily. Consider some, though it may seem like thinking of the unthinkable.

### Violence as a Form of Competition

Violence is an important mode of competition—that is, of resolving inter-personal conflicts of interests. Before rejecting violence as a means of competition, observe that it is highly respected and widely practiced—at least when applied successfully on a nationwide scale. When Caesar conquered Egypt, he was praised and honored by the Romans; had he instead roughed up a few people in Rome, he might have been damned as a ruffian and thief. When Alexander conquered the Near East, he was not regarded by the West as a gangster; neither was Charlemagne after he had conquered Europe. The white man acquired America from the native inhabitants by force. Lenin and his successors are not universally regarded in Russia as a line of gangsters. Nor is Franco regarded by all in Spain as merely a successful gangster who seized power by force. Nor Castro in Cuba, nor Nasser in Egypt.

This method is so effective that the application of violence or force is a jealously guarded monopoly of the national government. But we shall see that in certain areas of activity within a nation, violence or force is an accepted method of eliminating competitors—always, of course, for the good of the people as a whole, according to those who use it. Our street demonstrations and riots are sometimes regarded—even by college students—as appropriate forms of competition for access to political power and economic goods.

### Offers of Exchange as a Form of Competition

As an alternative to violence, mutual exchange is available as a solution—even though it, too, is sometimes classed as improper. As a matter of fact, a free-enterprise economic system—a system in which the bulk of property is privately owned—is a commonly used basis of competition. But let Adam Smith, the eighteenth-century British economist, comment:

> Man has almost constant occasion for the help of his brethren, and it is in vain for him to expect it from their benevolence only. He will be more likely to prevail if he can interest their self-love in his favor, and show them that it is for their own advantage to do for him what he requires of them. Whoever offers to another a bargain of any kind, proposes to do this: Give me that which I want, and you shall have this

which you want, is the meaning of every such offer; and it is in this manner that we obtain from one another the far greater part of those good offices which we stand in need of. It is not from the benevolence of the butcher, the brewer, or the baker, that we expect our dinner, but from their regard to their own interest. We address ourselves not to their humanity but to their self-love.

This book will investigate this kind of competition in great detail, but it will investigate the others, too, with possibly surprising implications.

### Other Types of Competition

Violence and exchange are only two of an enormous variety of interpersonal competitive techniques. The range of other common techniques can be suggested by a few examples.

Suppose you had to distribute 200 tickets to the Rose Bowl football game without selling them to the highest bidders. What forms of competition would you use in assigning priorities for deciding to whom to award the tickets? That is, what system of rationing or allocation would you use? If the authors of this book could set the rules, we would ask all applicants to send pictures, preferably in bathing suits. (Males need not apply.) We would select the prettiest 300—using our own standards of "prettiness"—and ask them to appear in our offices for interviews. Of these we would then select the most personable 200—using our own standards of "personality."

Certainly this pleasant system is discriminatory. *All* competition is discriminatory. That, indeed, is its purpose: to discriminate among the various claimants in deciding who gets what. Beauty and personality as competitive, discriminatory factors are generally accepted and applied widely every day. Men and women select mates, in part at least, according to beauty and personality. You and I allocate our money to the prettiest women for letting us see them perform in the movies. In fact, it is difficult to find many situations in which beauty is not a source of competitive advantage.

If you think beauty is an improper criterion, you might use the "first come, first served" method. For instance, you could insist that all the applicants run a race and give the tickets to the first 200 to arrive at the finish line. Sounds silly. If you simply replace the words "finish line" by "box office at the Rose Bowl," it is now realistic, but is it less silly? The only difference is that for Rose Bowl tickets there is no uniform starting time or place, so that some people start out a lot earlier and then camp right at the finish line. In any case, economic theory does *not* say that any particular form of competition is silly.

But is it fair? That depends on the circumstances and on what you mean by "fair"—it depends on the kind of competition *you* prefer. If you think "fair" means giving everyone an equal chance, would you want to give everyone an equal chance to operate on you for appendicitis, or to sing for you at a concert, or to teach you, or to be your wife, or to be the person you had to hire in your restaurant—or to whom you give Rose Bowl tickets? An equal chance could be provided by putting everyone's name (even those who did not take the time to apply for a ticket) on cards, then drawing 200 at random. That would be as equal a chance as possible, and nondiscriminatory. But, again, do you want to pick your mate that way? Do you want men selected for the armed forces that way? Obviously, "fair" or "preferred" does not mean "equal chance."

Before we leave this sampling of modes of competition, note a difficulty. After the goods (Rose Bowl tickets in this example) are initially distributed and rationed, what is to stop your selected recipients from handing the tickets on to other people, according to other preferred criteria? What is to prevent the prettiest girls from handing the tickets to the handsomest boys? It is extremely difficult to ensure that one's competitive selective criterion will in fact be the only criterion followed. Of course, he *might* tell all persons to whom he initially gives the tickets that they must go to the game themselves and not re-allocate the tickets in exchange for money or love. How he might enforce that condition, we leave to you.

### Competitive Criteria and Survival Traits

Nothing in economic theory suggests that any particular form of competition is "absurd." That evaluation rests on cultural and personal preferences. The first-come, first-served race to the box-office window, if used to parcel out food, would mean that the people best able to camp out or withstand the rigors of waiting in line would have the best prospects of survival and prosperity. In accordance with the classic theory of selective survival of the fittest, that type of person would prevail. And the institution of "camping out" would be characteristic of the economy. Instead, if food were parceled out to the tallest people, with short people getting the least, you can understand why the average height of the population would increase over time. And, alternatively, if beauty were rewarded, the beauty of women would increase—because women would make deliberate, conscious efforts to improve their beauty, and because the more beautiful would be more likely to survive. Or one might propose to allocate goods on the basis of forensics and personality, somewhat as we compete for political office. Under that system, the society would become noted for its articulate and personable people. Or resources could be given to those with the most talent for deception and misrepresentation; the reader can imagine the mores and dominant types that would evolve in that society. Or resources could go mainly to those who are best able to create goods and services. In that kind of society the more productive would be the wealthier and the dominant group.

Scarcity, Productive Activity, and Culture

In the wide gamut of economic problems of every society, there is, then, a pervasive, inescapable, inevitable pair: *scarcity and competition.* That is the starting point of our analysis, and behavioral consequences stemming directly or indirectly from it are our subject matter.

Since the fiasco in the Garden of Eden, most of what we want must be acquired through sweat, strain, and anxiety. Since we cannot have *all* of *everything* we want, we must *choose* how best to use available resources. What things shall we make and in what proportions? Under what institutions and laws? How and with what resources? Who will consume which goods and how much? How much shall we direct from current to future consumption?

These questions leave open the matter of precisely *who* is to make the decisions of what and how much to produce, how the production is to be done, and what goods to allocate to each person. To say simply that "we" do so does not identify who makes those detailed decisions, under what circumstances, and in response to what incentives and penalties. How is the diverse information about every person, his capabilities and preferences, to be collected and coordinated into decisions guiding *each* person? Is it to be done under the direction of an all-powerful economic czar with central planning? Is there any feasible alternative?

Not all systems for organizing production lead to equally efficient or productive results. *Appropriate* specialization in production combined with rational exchange of goods leads to a larger output and wealth than non-specialization (self-sufficiency) or inappropriate specialization. What are the characteristics of "appropriate" production, or efficient production (as it is called in economic jargon)? What institutional arrangements encourage that kind of productive activity? Kinds of property rights, rights of access to markets and rights to exchange goods and services, kind of money system used—all these are influential.

Whatever type of societal organization is used, what are the kinds of social and cultural behavior it will foster in people? Not many know much about these questions. Even a former President of the United States admitted that he felt unable to evaluate and refute charges that the private-property, open-market exchange (capitalist) system for organizing production and distribution was not only less efficient, but also bred more materialistic, less humanitarian, and inferior cultural traits than did socialism.

Economics, it is apparent, is concerned with fundamental, pervasive issues of society: What goods shall be produced? In what proportions? By whom and in what manner? For whose consumption? How much of current income shall be saved for the future? Who will suffer the losses of bad decisions? And to each of these questions should be appended, "According to *whose* preferences and by *whose* authority?" Finally, what are the social and cultural effects of the ways in which those questions are answered? Economics is a social science—a study of society.

## Our Economic Activities

Consider the awesome dimensions of the American community: a population of over 200,000,000 includes a labor force of 80,000,000 (one third of whom are women) and, through 11,000,000 business units (including 9,000,000 single proprietorships, 1,000,000 partnerships, and 1,000,000 corporations), annually produces goods and services worth almost $1,000,000,000,000— some 30 percent of the world total. Who designed and who now directs this vast production-and-distribution machine? In small and intimate matters, willy-nilly individual decision making may be tolerable, but to resolve the vital, over-all, aggregate problems, it seems that someone must be in charge.

But American economic activity is *not* directed, planned, or controlled by any economic czar—governmental or private. No person or group poses detailed questions of how the community is to use its resources, and no one imposes comprehensive answers to the questions. Yet such problems—large and small—somehow *are* solved daily. No particular person has been appointed to ensure that adequate food reaches every city each day and is allocated among competing claimants—and yet the people eat. No "big brother" oversees the multitudinous and infinitely varied operations of the economy and ensures that the essential functions are performed. The alternative to "big brother" evidently is not chaos and anarchy. An economic order does exist; some sort of control and direction does operate. Moreover, this mysterious system allows individuals and businesses to be essentially autonomous—and self-interested—agents (though subject to the constraints that define private property arrangements) and, at the same time, yields a viable and enviable degree of economic efficiency.

The individual, far from wrestling with grandiose problems of the universe, decides how much of his own wealth and income to expend for this or that, what kind of work to do to increase his wealth, and how much of his income to save. No farmer adds up the total demands for food in a city, comparing the total with the amount being shipped to the city, to make sure (because of his compassion) that adequate supplies will be available. Instead, with his individual interest and perspective, he asks, "Would I personally be richer or poorer if I shipped more or less?" No commission resolves issues of the "big picture" of the economy; instead, millions of us make decisions on our own "little pictures."

Although many of us successfully solve our personal problems, we may still be grossly ignorant about how our actions and laws affect the solutions to large problems that every society must solve. Comprehension of these larger problems requires understanding of economic theory, even if virtually no economic theory is required for our individual economic decisions. We can be sure that economic analysis is being ignored when any of the following incorrect assertions are proposed: the rationale of the capitalistic system requires a "harmony of interests"; customers must take what producers offer them; automation reduces available jobs; tariffs protect domestic wage earners from foreign labor; our otherwise unlimited productive capacity is curtailed by monopolistic capitalists who arbitrarily set prices high; unions protect workers from greedy employers; inflation hurts the wage earner and benefits the employer; social-security payments contributed by employers to their employees are paid for by the employers; private firms serve private interests while publicly owned agencies serve public interests; social conscience and civic sensitivity are or should be the main guides to business corporate behavior; unemployment occurs because not enough jobs are available or because some people are too shiftless and lazy; or American agriculture produces a surplus of wheat because it is so productive. And that is only a tiny sample!

### Three Attributes of Economic Analysis

To help understand what economics is, three of its methodological attributes should be clarified.

(1) Economic theory is "positive" or "non-normative." It does not give criteria for determining which consequence or type of behavior or economic policy is a good or better one—any more than physics tells whether gases are a "better" state of being than solids, or any more than medicine can tell whether you "ought" not to smoke and drink. Economics can tell only the consequences of certain conditions, policies, or choices. It is scarcely the proper role of the economist to sit on Mt. Olympus and decree what consequence is desirable or preferable to another.

(2) Economics explains what conditions will lead to what consequences. Economics yields conditional "if-A-then-B" propositions; it does not forecast that the A will occur—although some *economists* (as opposed to economics) may hazard such forecasts.

(3) A valid core of economic theory exists and is applicable to *all* economic systems and countries. There is *not* one special economic theory for capitalism and another for communism, although significant differences exist in the institutions and legal frameworks to which the theory is applied. For the present, it is sufficiently accurate to define capitalism as a system of exchangeable, private-property rights in goods and services, with the central government protecting and enforcing these rights. Private-property rights, in turn, can be defined as the rights of owners to choose the use of their goods and resources (including labor and time) as they see fit. If a rock is said to be my property and a piece of glass is yours, I have control over only the rock, and you over only the glass; for me to throw my rock through your glass

without your permission would violate your rights to use only your property as you see fit. In socialism, at the other extreme, rights to the uses of a good are not assigned to specified individuals but instead are divided among various people in government agencies, who decide about uses and consequences to be borne. This is a system of "government ownership."

Market exchange of property rights is applicable to a wider class of activity in a capitalistic private-property economy than it is in a socialistic society. This does not mean there is no market exchange in the latter; there is, of course, a great deal. However, the extent of and reliance on interpersonal market exchange is greater in a capitalistic system. In a socialist system, on the other hand, political power and exchange of *non*-privately held rights are used much more widely to solve the economic questions. If we were to devote primary attention to socialist systems, we would investigate much more fully political exchange, political decision making, and political competition.

Although applicable to all economic systems, historically economic theory has been more extensively applied to the analysis of capitalistic systems. More recently it has been applied to socialistic institutions.

In sum, economics studies the competitive and cooperative behavior of people in resolving conflicts of interest that arise because wants exceed what is available.

Introductory comments cannot adequately reveal what economics is or the richness of applications of economic theory. Only a study of economics can do that. Free societies and the open markets characterizing them *have* grown and prospered in the face of almost universal illiteracy about economic theory, so there *are* limits to the significance and usefulness of the formal study of economics. But give it a fair try, anyway. Economics does deal with things important on both a private and a social level; and attention to the principles of analysis can provide valuable experience in analyzing problems and utilizing evidence. Unless you fight it assiduously, it may well even be quite interesting.

## Summary

A cautionary note: do not use these summaries as quick learning devices for examinations. Instead treat them as listing in capsule, cryptic form the major ideas of the chapters. The statements do not always reveal the full content and significance of each idea.

1    Given the limitations of nature and the unlimited desires of man, scarcity is inevitable and pervasive.

2    People's desire for more goods leads to conflict of interests (competition). Scarcity and competition are inseparably paired.

3    A sensible person, instead of futilely complaining about the *existence* of competition, will devote his attention to the *alternative modes* of competition. He will see that different types of competition imply differing methods of ordering society or regulating the way people behave. It is not pertinent to ask, "How can we *eliminate* or *reduce* competition?" Ask instead: "What *kinds* of competition—or controls—are 'desirable' or 'undesirable'? What will make 'desirable' competition more viable, pervasive, and powerful; and what will make 'undesirable' competition ineffective?"

4    The preceding question involves three phases: (a) understanding the effects of different kinds of competitive behavior; (b) choosing—on some basis not derivable from economics—a criterion of "desirability"; (c) knowing what laws or institutions will affect the prevalence and effectiveness of each type of competition.

## Questions

Questions at the end of each chapter are a basic element in this book. Read each question, ponder it, and then read the answers at the end of the book. Questions numbered in bold type have answers at the end of this book. Do not skip the questions and answers; they contain some important ideas, applications, and interpretations you will find nowhere else in the book.

1    A recent book states (in essence) that: "We are trapped by the 'dismal science'—economics, which is dominated by the belief that the achievement of abundance is impossible and that the economic problem is still the distribution of scarce resources. This is nonsense. Abundance has arrived! The United States can produce so much that the basic problems are to see that the potential production is realized and distributed fairly and equitably." Are you inclined to agree or disagree? Why?

2    "If people were reasonable and acted with justice and good faith, there would be no strikes, no economic problems, and no wars." Do you agree? If so, why? If not, why not?

3    A more equal distribution of wealth is socially preferred to a less equal distribution."
a. Explain why you agree or disagree.
b. What is meant by "socially preferred," as contrasted to "individually preferred"?

4    What do you think is meant by a fair share? Do you think other people will agree with your interpretation? How does your interpretation compare with the idea of students getting "fair" grades?

5    What is nonsensical about the proposition "A good economic system maximizes the welfare of the maximum number of people"?

6    "Government monopolizes coercive violence." "Government is a social agency for resolving interpersonal conflict."
a. Are those two propositions correct and compatible statements of fact?
b. What evidence can you cite for your answer?

7    Name three honored statesmen who obtained their status by successfully competing in ability to use violence and who, had they failed, would have been punished for treason or crimes against mankind.

8    Evaluate the statement: "When property rights conflict with human rights, property rights must give way."

9    a. If you had the power to decide, what kinds of competition would you declare illegal?
b. What kinds of competition are made illegal by laws establishing price ceilings, minimum wages, fair-employment practices, pure food and drug standards, private-property rights, and by socialism?

10    a. What does "equality of opportunity" mean?
b. How could you determine whether it exists?
c. Is there equality of opportunity to get an $A$ in this course?
d. How would you make it equal, if it is not?
e. What is the difference between *increasing* opportunity and *equalizing* it?

11    Defend competition for admission to colleges on the basis of mental ability, athletic ability, good looks, residence, willingness to pay, alumni status of parents, color, sex, religious belief. All are used to some extent. Why?

12    a. What kinds of competition that are permissible in seeking political office are not permissible in private business?
b. What kinds of competition are permissible in seeking admission to college but not permissible in competition for grades in this course?
c. What kinds of competition are approved for business but not for admission to fraternities? Explain why.

13    As a group, which people do you think are most honest—politicians, businessmen, or teachers? What is your evidence? Can you think of any reasons why dishonesty would be more surely punished in one of these professions? Is there any reason to suspect that dishonesty, if successful, would be more rewarding in one rather than the others?

14    "Under socialism, cooperation will replace competition."
a. Do you believe the quoted proposition is correct?
b. What evidence can you cite to support your answer?
c. What is the difference between cooperation and competition?
d. Is there any difference between cooperation and coordination?

15    When a group of Russian officials toured American farms in 1960, they persistently asked who told the farmers how much to produce in order to supply the appropriate amounts of goods. The farmers said that no one told them, and the Russians were convinced that the farmers were concealing something. What would you have told the Russians?

16    Try to give a definition of "efficient" production, "scarcity," "shortage," "surplus," "needs." (Later, compare your definitions with those given in subsequent chapters.)

17    What is meant by specialization? Do you know anyone who does not specialize? Why do people specialize?

18    "The economy of the United States is directed by the capitalists concentrated in Wall Street." Evaluate this assertion now, and again when you have completed this course.

19    "Scarcity, competition, and discrimination are inextricably tied together. Any one implies the other two. Furthermore, to think of a society without these is to be a romantic dreamer." Do you agree? If so, why? If not, why not?

20    "Food is grown, harvested, sorted, processed, packed, transported, assembled in appropriately small bundles, and offered to consumers every day by individuals pursuing personal interests. No authority is responsible for seeing that these functions are performed and that the right amount of food is produced. Yet food is available every day. On the other hand, especially appointed authorities are responsible for seeing that such things as water, education, and electricity are made available. Is it not paradoxical that in the very areas where we consciously plan and control social output, we often find shortages and failure of service? References to classroom and water shortages are rife; but who has heard of a shortage of restaurants, churches, furniture, beer, shoes, or paper? Even further, is it not surprising that privately owned businesses, operating for the private gain of the owners, provide as good, if not better, service to patrons and customers as do the post office, schools, and other publicly owned enterprises? Furthermore, wouldn't you expect public agencies to be less discriminating according to race and creed than privately owned business? Yet the fact is that they are not." How do you explain these paradoxes?

21    What is meant by (a) the logical validity of a theory? (b) the empirical validity? (c) Does either imply the other?

22    The economic ideals of the Middle Ages were influenced by Christianity and by Aristotle's doctrines. Among those ideals were the following:

"(1) The purpose of economic activity is to provide goods and services for the community and to enable each member of society to live in security and freedom from want. Its purpose is not to furnish opportunity for the few to get rich at the expense of the many. Men who engage in business with the object of making as much money as possible are no better than pirates or robbers.

"(2) Every commodity has its 'just price,' which is equal to its cost of production. No merchant has a right to sell any article for more than this price plus a small charge for the service he renders in making goods available to the community. To take advantage of scarcity to boost the price or to charge all that the traffic will bear is to commit a mortal sin.

"(3) No man is entitled to any larger share of this world's goods than is necessary for his reasonable needs. Any surplus that may come into his possession is not rightfully his but belongs to Society. St. Thomas Aquinas, the greatest of all medieval philosophers, taught that if a rich man refuses to share his wealth with the poor, it is entirely justifiable that his surplus should be taken from him.

"(4) No man has a right to financial reward unless he engages in useful labor or incurs some actual risk in an economic venture. The taking of interest on loans where no genuine risk is involved constitutes the sin of usury.

"It would be foolish, of course, to suppose that these lofty ideals of an economic system largely devoid of the profit motive were ever carried out to perfection." (E. M. Burns, *Western Civilizations, Their History and Culture*, 5th ed. New York: W. W. Norton, 1958.)

What do you think of these ideals? Do you approve of them? Which ones? If you disagree with any, how would you express your ideal? After completing this course, answer these questions again.

23    The economic system is alleged to have an effect on the social and cultural characteristics that will be viable in a society. Among these characteristics are the patterns of speech, expression, religion, travel, marriage, divorce, inheritance, education, legal trials, art, literature, and music.

a. Do you believe that these characteristics are in any way different under capitalism than under socialism? Why?

b. Can you cite evidence for your answer?

24    "The free-enterprise, capitalist system is free in the sense that it involves no imposition of force or compulsion." Do you agree? Defend your answer.

25    The *Statistical Abstract of the United States*, published annually by the U. S. Department of Commerce, Bureau of the Census, is a standard summary of statistics on the social, political, and economic organization of the United States. It presents a myriad of data and also reveals

sources of data. Every college library has a copy. You are strongly urged to spend half an hour or so scanning the volume. For example, on page 133 of the 1966 edition you will find some data about faculty salaries. Do you think your instructor is underpaid or overpaid? After thinking about that for three minutes, compare faculty salaries with the information on pages 238–240 of that same edition about earnings in other industries.

# 2

## Some Behavior Postulates

Some basic concepts and postulates characterizing the behavior of people in the face of scarcity are presented in this chapter. These characterize *behavior* of people, not necessarily their thought processes. There is nothing presumptuous or absurd in basing analysis of human behavior on a few idealized concepts. Indeed, there is no alternative. This approach is the essence of science.

**Observation 1: The Unit of
Analysis Is the Individual**

The actions of groups, organizations, communities, nations, and societies can best be understood by focusing attention on the incentives and actions of members. When we speak of the goals and actions of the United States, we are really referring to the goals and actions of the *individuals* in the United States. A business, union, or family may be formed to further some common interest of the constituents, but group actions are still the results of decisions of individuals. Therefore, do not ask, "Why does the U.S. government, or General Motors, or some union, behave as it does?" Ask instead, "Why does the decision maker decide as he does?" The principles of economics are based on postulates about behavioral responses of individuals to changes in the environment.

**Observation 2: No Man Can
See the Future Perfectly**

Not all future events or outcomes of current actions are totally unpredictable, for laws of probability do predict the relative frequency of the outcome of a large series of trials. But, although probabilities may be computable or forecastable, accurate foreknowledge of the outcome of specific trials or events escapes our ken.

A changing, largely unpredictable future means that the usefulness or value of resources will change in unforeseen ways. Unavoidably and unpredictably, some resources will become more, and some less, valuable. As a tornado or earthquake destroys some resources, so psychological variables such as tastes and fashions, or biological factors such as age and health, destroy or create values in unexpected places and things. These profits and losses cannot be eliminated; they are thrust on somebody. If a city grows in one area and decays in another, who suffers the loss in usefulness (value) of the declining areas, and who reaps the gains in the growing areas? Upon whom *should* the profits and losses be thrust? The first question is one that economic theory can answer. The second is one that theory can help to answer by discerning (but not judging) some consequences of various methods of determining who will bear the unforeseen losses or gains. As long as uncertainty exists, the first question will persist and will receive some answer. The second may never be answered.

The word "good" means any desired entity, or goal. If having some of an entity is preferred to having none, then the entity is said to be a "good." Your idea of "goods" may differ from other people's. Maybe you think that cigarettes are not "goods" and that others would really be "better off" without them. Despite this possible difference of opinion, the term "goods" means no more than that some person—as *he* judges his situation—prefers to have some. All this is compactly summarized by saying that a good gives *utility* to someone.

It is useful to classify goods into *free* and *economic* goods. *Economic good* is the technical name for a *scarce good*. A good is scarce if, and only if, one prefers to have *more* of it than he has. Fresh chicken eggs are quantitatively more plentiful than bad eggs; but good eggs are scarce, while bad eggs are not. If a good, however desirable, is so abundant that one does not want *more* of it, it is a *free* good. Both free goods and economic goods provide utility, of course. But by definition *more* of a free good *adds* no utility. More of an economic good does. The classic case of a free good, to most of us most of the time, is air: we simply inhale, and there it is, without our sacrificing anything to obtain it. Generally, for each of us, *more* air than we now have would be of no value—that is, it would not *add* any utility. However, *fresh* air is an economic good to the astronaut, the deep-sea diver, and the city resident on a smoggy day. Hereafter we shall almost invariably use simply the word "good" when we mean "economic goods."

Beware of another usage of "free good." Often it is used to identify an *economic* good *distributed* at a *zero price*, even though the good is scarce, e.g., education, or streets, or books at the "free" public library. Just because a good distributed at a zero price to the recipient is called "free," it is not thereby so plentiful as not to be scarce. And to compound confusion, as we shall see later, distributing economic goods for "free" (at a zero price) paradoxically makes their scarcity seem even greater.

Often, it is incorrectly asserted that economics presumes an "economic man," whose sole interest is making more money or getting wealthier or improving just his own circumstances. Not so! Economics does *not* assume that men are motivated solely, or even primarily, by the desire to accumulate more wealth. Instead, economic theory assumes that man—in Karachi, Canton, or Kalamazoo—desires more of many other things as well: prestige, power, friends, love, respect, self-expression, talent, liberty, knowledge, good looks, leisure. Day to day, economic theory is usually applied to the production, sale, and consumption of goods with money expenditures via the market place. But economic theory does not ignore, let alone deny, that man is motivated by cultural and intellectual goods, and even by an interest in the welfare of other people—as we shall see.

---

[1] The Appendix to this chapter presents a graphic interpretation of these postulates.

Postulate 2. For Each Person,
Some Goods Are Scarce

Despite our work and sacrifices of leisure, we are unable to produce enough to satisfy *all* the wants of *all* people *all* the time. The desires of people for more goods exceed known bounds. They choose more if they can get it. Even affluent America is a society of scarcity. *Choices* among available opportunities are still required: better hi-fi equipment, wall-to-wall carpeting, walnut paneling, longer vacations. There are conflicting demands for more missiles, airplanes, hospitals, schools, highways, and houses—and for more foreign aid to buy peace and influence and to foster foreign economic growth. Nature simply has not provided enough to satiate the desires of every living being—not merely people, but also animals and plants, for they, too, are busily claiming all the earth.

Postulate 3. Substitution: A
Person Is Willing to Sacrifice
Some of Any Good to
Obtain More of Other Goods

Man does not wait until he has some specific level of food before he begins to care at all about clothes or shelter or freedom. He simultaneously wants some of *all* these things. Even in the poorest, most primitive societies, a good deal of effort is devoted to art, music, play, self-expression, and status, as well as to food and shelter. Man is willing to sacrifice *some* food for the sake of *more* leisure or friendship or prestige or art. A *bit* of friendship or prestige or love will in turn be forsaken for *some more* wealth or artistic accomplishment *There is no hierarchy of goods or of goals.*

The postulate of substitutability can be stated more precisely: "For *some more* of any good, a person is willing to sacrifice *some* of any one, or group, or other goods." Or, in reverse, "A person is willing to sacrifice *some bit* of any desired thing if he can obtain a *sufficient increase* in the amount of some other desired goods." It does not mean that he would sacrifice *all* of a good; but he will sacrifice *some* of a good for *more* of other goods.

Economics has a special measure of this substitutability. The *maximum* amount of some good that a person is willing to give up to get *one unit more* of some other specified good can be expressed as a ratio, or rate, of substitution. If you are willing to sacrifice a maximum of two bottles of Coke per month to get one more pack of cigarettes per month, your "subjective marginal consumption-substitution ratio" between Cokes and cigarettes is

$$\frac{2 \text{ bottles of Coke per month}}{1 \text{ pack of cigarettes per month}} = 2 \text{ Cokes per pack of cigarettes.}$$

If you did make an exchange at that rate, you would *not* reach a *preferred* situation, because the sacrifice of the two Cokes is just large enough exactly to offset the gain of one pack of cigarettes. If you had been able to exchange *less* than two Cokes for one more pack, you would have reached a preferred situation.

If we let the symbol ΔC denote the *change* in the amount of Cokes and ΔG the change in cigarettes, the ratio ΔC/ΔG measures the subjective rate of consumption-substitution between Cokes and cigarettes. That is, for the increase in cigarettes (ΔG), the decrease in Cokes (ΔC) is just exactly large enough to make one *indifferent* as to whether he makes the exchange. That ratio is sometimes called the "indifference rate of substitution." Given his pattern of tastes and his current stocks of goods, he is indifferent to the substitution of one more pack of cigarettes for that many Cokes.

This is a ratio of two *changes*: a *decrement* of one good and an *increment* of another. It is *not* the ratio between the *total* amounts of Cokes and cigarettes that the person happens to have. He may have twenty Cokes and twenty packs of cigarettes for the coming month. Given that amount of each, if he is indifferent to a substitution of *one more* pack for *two less* Cokes, his substitution ratio is 2/1—placing the *decrement in the numerator* and the increment in the denominator. A pack of cigarettes is worth two Cokes in his *personal* valuation. If the exchange is made, he then has eighteen Cokes and twenty-one cigarette packs—a combination that has the same utility to him as twenty of each.

To emphasize that we are dealing with a ratio between *small changes* in the goods, this "indifference ratio" is technically labeled the "*marginal* rate of substitution" between Cokes and cigarettes. It indicates the *subjective*, or *personal*, valuation (in terms of Cokes) assigned to cigarettes. Always placing the good being valued in the denominator and the good being paid in the numerator, we could say that the subjective or personal value placed on one more Coke is one-half pack of cigarettes: $\Delta G/\Delta C = 1/2$.

For our purposes, the *value* of a good to a person *is* the exchange rate, between that good and some other, at which he is indifferent whether the exchange is made. Value for any good is measured in terms of an amount of *some other economic good*. Value is not measured in terms of some psychic, psychological, or moral goodness or satisfaction.

Since people most frequently buy or sell goods for *money* the personal values are often expressed as a rate of exchange in terms of an amount of money for one unit of the good. However, for the moment we wish to look beyond money (a facilitator of exchange) to the goods themselves.

> Postulate 4. An Individual's Personal
> Valuation of Any Good Depends upon
> the Amount He Has of That Good; the
> More He Has, the Lower His Personal
> Value of the Good

The personal valuation a person places on goods is not entirely unpredictable. While it depends upon many things—such as past experience, education, general preference, and psychological traits—it is affected in a predictable way by the amounts of the goods he has. Since little can be said about the other factors affecting his personal valuation, we shall concentrate on the effect of the amounts possessed. In rough terms, the larger the amount of any good at his command, the lower its value to him—that is, the lower the value of another unit of that good. If my amount of $X$ were increased, with possession of all other goods held constant, then my personal valuation of another unit of $X$ would decrease. I would be willing to give up only smaller amounts $(\Delta Y)$ of any other good for an increment $(\Delta X)$ in $X$, the more of $X$ that I had at my command. That is, as the ratio $\Delta Y/\Delta X$ at which I am willing to acquire more $X$ decreases, the larger is the amount of $X$ that I have. This is sometimes known as the law of *diminishing* personal or subjective value.

### Postulate 5. Not All People Have Identical Preference Patterns

Although everyone's behavior corresponds to the first four postulates, no two people are alike in all characteristics. Diversity extends beyond talents, personality, initiative, responsibility, and appearance. One man's tastes are another man's prejudices; one's selectivity is another's discrimination. One person might value one more cigarette at two Cokes, while a second, even with the same amounts of various goods, might value it at three Cokes. This means that at the same given combination or "endowment" of various goods for each person, some people place a higher value on cigarettes relative to Cokes than do others. Or turning it around, the first person places a lower value on Cokes relative to cigarettes than does a second person. Furthermore, as a person has *different* combinations of goods, his personal values would be *changed*—as implied in proposition 4—and they would change in different degrees for different people. As one person got more cigarettes and fewer Cokes, his personal valuation of cigarettes (in terms of Cokes) might fall more rapidly than would the valuation of some other person in the same situation.

Resist the temptation to say, "Mr. A likes cigarettes less than Mr. B." There simply is no basis for comparing *intensity* of likes of two people for *one* good. Neither economics nor psychology has yet discovered a way validly to compare "absolute" likes of different people for a good on some psychic scale. Mr. A may put a value of two Cokes on one cigarette, and Mr. B's indifference ratio may be three Cokes for one cigarette. A puts a smaller *Coke* valuation on cigarettes than does B. But we have no way of knowing how much A and B like cigarettes without Cokes (or some other good) for reference. For all we know, A tingles at the mere thought of a cigarette (but he likes Cokes so well that he would give up only two Cokes to obtain one more cigarette) while B could easily swear off cigarettes (but Cokes make him burp, so he is willing to sacrifice as many as three of them for one more cigarette).

### Theorem and Proposition of Demand

These behavior postulates imply certain propositions relating the amount of a good a person will consume to the price of the good. First, it is necessary to distinguish between superior and inferior economic goods. A good is "superior" for a person if he would consume more of it when his *income* is larger (with the price of the good unchanged). A good is called "inferior" if he consumes less of it when his income increases, price unchanged. For example, if their incomes increase, most people will shift from dark bread, cotton socks, and rump roasts to lighter bread, wool socks, and better cuts of meat. Exactly when some *good shifts* from one category to another cannot be predicted. A very poor person's consumption of cotton socks might increase with his income, but at large incomes his consumption would shift toward wool. "Superior" and "inferior" labels are essentially ways of classifying the effects of income change on consumption. In economic jargon, if the "income effect is positive" for the consumption of a good, the good is called superior. If the income effect is negative, it is called inferior.

Imagine that the price of a superior good is reduced substantially. A person will certainly buy some more of this good *both* because (a) the price is now lower *relative* to other goods and because (b) the lower price in dollar terms means he can buy the old amount and have more income left to spend on this and other goods. The first effect of a lower price is the *relative* price effect, a "substitution effect" due to lower relative price; the second effect, that of the lower *absolute* dollar price, is called the "income effect." The more of his income he formerly spent on this good, the more that is now released, by the lower dollar price, for expenditure on other things *as well as* for more of this particular good. The fall in price of one good increases the amount of all goods he can now buy, and this is tantamount to an increase in his income. Both effects—the lower relative price and the released income—induce him to buy more of this good *if* it is a superior good. We now have our first implied *demand* proposition. *For a superior good, a reduction in price will increase the amount consumed (demanded) both because of the substitution effect (relative price reduction) and the income effect.*

But suppose the good is inferior. Again, a fall in the dollar price would induce the consumer to buy more since its costs are relatively lower, *but* this time the income effect works in the opposite direction. The released income will increase the person's real income power, inducing him to buy *less* of that inferior good. For an inferior good, a lower dollar price could reduce the amount of the good consumed when both effects are aggregated. This is more likely to happen the larger the portion of his income he was initially spending on that inferior good. However, these cases are very rare, indeed—so rare that well documented and verified cases are still to be discovered. Therefore, we shall assume for all goods, superior and inferior, that at a lower price more of the good is consumed—even though the contrary is conceptually possible for some inferior goods. Do not regard this demand proposition as applicable only between money costs and materialistic marketable goods. It applies between *all* goods, goals, or objectives.

If the price or cost of getting an A in this course were to rise from one hour to two hours of study per day, more students would choose to have lower grades and more time for other things. It could be objected that some student, particularly you, might still work hard enough to get an A even at that higher cost. Well and good. But what would you do if the cost of an A went up to six hours' study a day? To ten hours? There is always a *sufficiently higher* price of a good that will reduce the amount a person chooses to have (or demands). In general, for every person and for every good (material, psychic, moral, spiritual, intellectual, etc.), the higher the price of acquiring some of that good (where the cost can be some sacrifice of honesty, virtue, prestige, holiness, etc., and not necessarily just money), the less will he demand.

This, as we shall see later, is an extremely powerful proposition. In fact it is so powerful and directly useful, that it is called a "law"—*the law of demand.*

Rationality of Analysis versus
Rationality of People

If these postulates and observations seem trite, so much the better, for they form the bases of the economic analysis that we shall apply in deriving "explanations" of the real economic world. People may not be *aware* of these postulates, any more than parents are necessarily aware of the laws of genetics and sexual attraction. None of the present postulates requires that people have awareness of these propositions. The postulates assert simply that people display consistent and predictable patterns of responses to changes in their environment.

For example, the second postulate says that people prefer more to less goods. But so do many animals. In animals it is called the acquisitive *instinct*. In man we may call it a rationality. In fact, it may be instinctive in both. Or possibly millions of centuries ago, very early in the evolutionary stream, some species of pre-man manifested acquisitive behavior: collecting sticks, bones, food, or areas of land from which it kept out potential invaders. It may not have had any conscious reason for doing so, but nevertheless that behavior had high survival characteristics. Storing up food and territory enabled it to live longer and breed more prolifically. The survival value of that trait to the individual and to his species in the evolutionary selective process may have been a factor in the subsequent dominance of acquisitive species. Alternatively, you may believe that the acquisitive urge was instilled by God as punishment for man's fall from grace—a part of his original sinfulness. Man, by that acquisitive drive, is condemned to greed, work, and conflict. According to this position, he should seek to suppress that urge in order to live a "better" life. Or you may believe that since man has the capacity to think and foresee consequences, he has consciously decided that acquiring more goods is somehow "better" than having less.

Tolerant we can be with these interpretations, but economic theory does not imply that these drives, behaviors, or traits are taught and subtly imbued by the particular types of economic systems and institutions. These behavioral characteristics exist whether the economic system is capitalist, communist, or anarchist.

### Meaning of Self-Interest

Where in the preceding postulates is the assumption that man is interested only in his own wealth or welfare? It isn't there, and properly so. We did assume that man is greedy—meaning solely that he wants *command over more* rather than less goods. But a man may want control over more goods in order charitably to help others. It is not assumed that he is oblivious to other people or not solicitous of other people's welfare. Nor is he assumed to be concerned only with more wealth. If these assumptions had been made, the resultant theory would be immediately falsified by the fact that people do engage in charity, are solicitous of other people, do consider the effects of their behavior on other people, and do sacrifice marketable wealth for leisure, knowledge, and contemplation.

What *is* meant by "selfish" man is that he wants the right to choose among options that will affect his ensuing affairs. In short, the *right to make choices* about the future is a desired thing, an "economic good." However, like all other goods, the power to make choices among options that affect one's own and even other people's situations has its cost. Raise the cost, and less choice will be retained. Lower it, and more will be retained. Raise my salary enough, and I'll let you determine what kind of clothes I wear to work, or where I work, or how my retirement fund is invested.

### Utility-Maximizing Behavior

The preceding set of postulates is often called the "utility-maximizing" theory of human nature. Why? Is there something called "utility"—something like weight, height, wealth, or happiness—that people are trying to maximize? Not necessarily. The name originated during the early history of economic analysis. At that time it was popular to think that goods provided utility or usefulness in some psychological and measurable sense. But although that misleading psychological conception has been abandoned, the name "utility" has stuck. It is now simply an *indicator* for ranking options in accord with one's preferences. Thus, it is now a matter of convention to say that if a person chooses option $A$ rather than option $B$, option $A$ has more utility for him.

Saying that a person "maximizes" utility may seem an elaborate camouflage of our ignorance; for whatever a person does, could he not be said to be "maximizing his utility"? Yes, if we were unable to specify what entities are goods and goals and if we could not classify some situations according to higher or lower costs of acquiring goods. But we *can* make specifications of goods and relative costs and therefore can provide meaningful, refutable theorems. And we shall give several in this book. For the moment, consider a simple example. Saving lives may be a good. The more lives saved, the greater one's utility. Obviously it is tautological or irrefutable to say a person will save lives whenever he can. But consider two different situations. In one, he can save a life by jumping into a pond and pulling out a child; in the other, he must jump into a raging torrent with .99 probability of drowning himself. Now, what does utility-maximizing theory tell us? The probability with which people will jump into ponds is higher than for jumping into torrents.

Another, more mundane example is the trade off between work and leisure. Both income and leisure contribute to a higher utility. The utility-maximizing theorem says that the amount of leisure a person takes is not set at a minimum in order to maximize wealth from work. The person will choose a mixture of income and of leisure so as to maximize his utility rather than maximize his income or wealth. No one maximizes his income at the sacrifice of absolutely all his leisure nor does everyone work at the highest paying job regardless of the working conditions. Some trade income for more pleasant (utility-contributing) surroundings.

## Functional Analysis in Economics

A great deal of analysis in economics—and in other areas—is couched in terms of functions. A *function* is a relationship between two or more entities. A functional relationship is said to exist between caloric intake and weight, between force and speed, between height and weight, between age and baldness, between smoking and incidence of cardiovascular disease, and between wealth and higher education. Sometimes one entity is related to a group of other entities. Weight can be related to height and to girth and thus can be called a function of height and girth. To speak of weight as a function of height and girth does not mean that there is necessarily a cause-and-effect relationship from height and girth to weight. A functional relationship asserts that knowledge about the magnitudes of one set of entities will yield information about the magnitude of some other entity.

It is customary also to refer to one set of the variables as the explanatory or independent variables and the remaining one as the dependent or explained variables. This does not mean that the dependent or explained variable is causally dependent. Thus, one could regard education as a variable dependent on wealth in the sense that we can estimate more accurately the extent of one's formal education if his wealth is known; it does not have to mean that the extent of his wealth determined how much education he did obtain. The extent of his education may, in fact, have determined how much wealth he later earned. Regardless of whether the causation works in one direction or the other or even in both directions, to call one of the variables the independent, or explanatory, variable means only that a knowledge of the magnitude of that variable enables one to know the other variable with a greater degree of precision.

The functional relationship between the explained variable and an explanatory variable is said to be *positive* if an increase (decrease) in one is accompanied by an increase (decrease) in the other; it is a *negative* function if larger magnitudes of one are associated with smaller magnitudes of the other.

Finally, use of a functional relationship between *two* variables does not mean that the explanatory variable is the *only* or even the most important variable that affects the explained variable, or that other unspecified variables are assumed absent. An increase in caloric intake implies a gain in weight, even though an increase in caloric intake accompanied by increased physical activity may result in a weight decrease. There is still a positive relationship between caloric intake and weight, because—regardless of other factors—the weight will be greater than it would have been if caloric intake had not been increased. The expression "other things being the same" is merely a crude way of *concentrating attention* on the relationship between two particular variables, even though other explanatory variables may be pertinent and changing in magnitude. Take the assertion "If I give you $10, you will be richer—other things being the same." This is not falsified if other things change. For instance, if you lose $100 elsewhere, you are richer than if I had not given you the $10.

## Summary

This chapter presented some postulates about the nature of economic theory and about certain features of human "nature" that are at the foundations of economic theory. These are not an exhaustive catalog of the properties of human behavior in the face of scarcity, but they are particularly significant for present purposes.

Observations

1. The unit of analysis is the individual.
2. No man can foresee the future perfectly.

Postulates

1. Each person seeks a multitude of goods.

2. For each person, some goods are scarce.

3. A person is willing to sacrifice some of any good in order to obtain more of some other good.

4. The more one has of any good, the lower his personal marginal valuation of it.

5. Not all people have identical preference patterns.

Superior (inferior) goods to a person are those of which he will consume more (less) with an increase in income. For superior goods a lower price will increase the rate of consumption. For inferior goods a lower price will lead to a smaller rate of consumption *if* the income effect dominates the substitution effect; this seems to be a rare case.

Rationality in analysis should not be taken to mean that the people being analyzed are animate calculating machines. Self-interest is the desire to have the right to make those choices that will affect one's own circumstances. Utility-maximizing behavior is a name for behavior in accord with the postulates. Functional analysis does not require cause and effect, nor does it mean that the identified and analyzed factors are assumed to be the only entities that affect or are related to each other.

### Appendix: Preference Maps and Utility Lines

The postulates characterizing the economically relevant attributes of human behavior can be described by graphs called preference maps.

In Figure 2–1, point $A$ denotes a combination of two goods, $X$ and $Y$. The amount of $X$ in that combination is measured by the horizontal distance to the right from the vertical axis, and the amount of $Y$ by the vertical distance upward from the horizontal axis. Point $B$ denotes a different combination of goods $X$ and $Y$ that might be available. It contains more $X$, but no more $Y$, than does combination $A$. We know this because it lies directly to the right of point $A$. On the other hand, combination $C$ contains more $Y$ than point $A$, but no more $X$. It lies directly above $A$.

According to our postulates, the combination denoted by point $B$ is preferred to that of point $A$; also, point $C$ is preferred to point $A$. We mean that, if offered a choice between options $A$ and $B$, our person would choose $B$, since it has more $X$ and no less $Y$. The preference of $B$ over $A$ means that $X$ is an economic good. Similarly we assert he would choose $C$ over $A$, which means that $Y$ is an economic good.

To indicate his preference pattern or ordering, we could arbitrarily assign some number to point $B$, say 76, and assign a smaller number to point $A$, say 49. A point assigned a higher number is preferred to a point assigned a lower number. We shall arbitrarily attach the name "utility" to that preference indicator. Perhaps the name "preference" or "choice index" would be better, but the convention of economics dictates the name "utility."

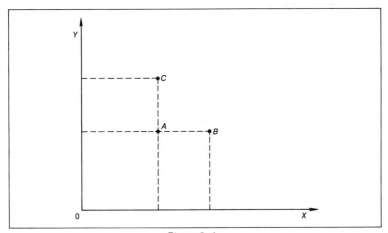

**Figure 2–1**
Combination of Goods *X* and *Y*

Points *A, B, C* denote different combinations of *X* and *Y*. The combination denoted by *B* has more *X* and the same amount of *Y* as the combination at *A*. *C* has more of *Y*. If point *B* is preferred to *A*, *X* is an economic good. Similarly, if point *C* is preferred to *A*, *Y* is an economic good. (Why?) If *B* is not preferred to *A*, *X* is either a free good or a "bad" (rather than a "good"). But we have defined *X* and *Y* to be goods and, in particular, economic goods. How could you portray diagrammatically the personal value of a unit of *X* at point *A*? Would it be greater or less than at *B*? At *C*? (See Figure 2–2 for the answers.)

Now consider Figure 2–2. A curved line labeled $U_1 U_1$ runs through point *B*. At point *B* is a little triangle, the length of whose vertical side measures the decrement of *Y*, $\Delta Y$, that would be the *most* our person would be willing to sacrifice to get the small increment (horizontal side) of *X*, $\Delta X$, given that the person initially was at the combination *B*. The ratio of $\Delta Y$ to $\Delta X$, $\Delta Y/\Delta X$, is indicated by the *slope* of the hypotenuse of that triangle; that slope *is* the slope of the curved line $U_1 U_1$ at *B*. The flatter that slope, the less is the decrement, $\Delta Y$, that our person is willing to sacrifice for the increment $\Delta X$ of *X*. The less is $\Delta Y/\Delta X$, the less is the value of an *X* (in terms of *Y*) and the greater is the value of a *Y* (in terms of *X*). Remember that the personal value of a unit of any good *is* simply the amount of his "equally preferred" change of some other good. The slope at point *A* is steeper than at *B* (with reference to the *X* axis). This means the value of an *X* at combination *A* is greater than the value of an *X* at *B*.

The slope of the line through point *C* is steeper than at *A*. The value of a unit of *X* is greater (in terms of *Y*) at *C* than at *A*. Our person has more *Y*, and the more he has of a good (the amounts of other goods being unchanged), the less its personal value. That steeper *slope* indicates a reduced personal value of a unit of *Y* relative to *X*: it takes more of an increment in *Y* to offset the unit change in *X*. Remember that the

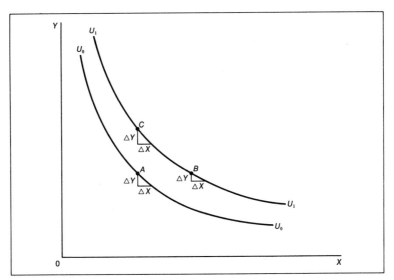

Figure 2–2
Convex Constant Utility Curves for Some Person

Any point on $U_1U_1$ is preferred to any point on $U_0U_0$. At each point, the slope
of the curve measures, by $\Delta Y$, this person's valuation of $\Delta X$, a uniform increment
of $X$. Slope at $B$ is less than at $A$; and at $A$ is less than at $C$. Also, slope of a curve
diminishes along curve as one moves from upper left to lower right. That is,
personal valuation of $X$ decreases as one moves from much $Y$ and little $X$ to less $Y$
and more $X$.

larger $\Delta Y$ is for a unit change in $X$, the *lower* the personal value of $Y$
(and the greater the personal value of $X$).

Line $U_1 U_1$ marks combinations of $X$ and $Y$, all of which are equally
preferred (i.e., equally desired, have the same utility) with point $C$ or $B$.
All combinations of $X$ and $Y$ through which $U_1 U_1$ goes are equally
desirable. In terms of our preference indicator, utility, all points on
$U_1 U_1$ have the same utility index.

Every point above and to the right of line $U_1 U_1$ is preferred to any
point on that line, since every point above it represents a bigger combination than any point directly below or to the left of it. Every point
below the line is less preferred than any point on the line. A curve,
$U_0 U_0$, drawn through $A$, shows all combinations indifferent to $A$. And,
of course, every point on $U_0 U_0$ is less preferred than any point on the
line $U_1 U_1$. (Be sure you see why!)

How does a convex sloped constant-utility line describe the postulates? First, it has two dimensions—two goods—not just one, which
reflects postulate number 1. Second, any basket with a larger amount
of either good (lying to the right or above) will be on a constant-
utility curve with a greater index of utility—which means that more of

$X$ (or of $Y$) is preferred. This is postulate number 2. Some goods (here, $X$ and $Y$) are scarce. Third, the $U_1 U_1$ line's constant-utility, or indifference, curves have *negative slopes*—which means that some increment of $X$ will make up for some loss of $Y$, and vice versa. That negative slope expresses our third substitutability postulate. Fourth, the slopes of the successive indifference curves that one crosses, from left to right, get flatter. At each point the slope, which is the personal valuation of $X$, decreases the more $X$ one has. This is postulate number 4. Also, as one moves up vertically—indicating more $Y$ for a *fixed* amount of $X$—slopes of successive indifference curves get steeper, which means his personal value of $X$ increases as $Y$ is increased. But this is the same thing as saying that his personal value of $Y$ decreases as $Y$ is increased.

For the shape and position of the $U_1 U_1$ curves to characterize these four postulates, the curves must be convex shaped, as shown in the diagram, and the indifference curves must show the preferred or higher-ranking utility index above or to the right of the lower-ranking utility line.

## Questions

1   Explain the difference between the statements "People act in accord with certain fundamental propositions" and "People consult or refer to such propositions for guidance in choosing their behavior." Does either interpretation assume "free will" or independence from other people's behavior or tastes?

2   "The college football team has a goal."
a. Is it the social goal of the "team," or is it the common individual goal of each member of the team?
b. Are you sure that each member has only that goal and not also one of playing more of the game himself?
c. Is it helpful to talk of one goal's being preferred over another?

3   In trying to understand some policy enforced at your college, why is it misleading to ask why the college adopts that policy?

4   "All goods or goals are incompatible. And at the same time they are compatible." Can you make sense of that?

5   "People want wealth, power, and prestige." What is wealth? Power? Prestige?

6   Are the words "scarcity" and "shortage" synonyms? If not, what is the difference?

7   If you don't smoke, is tobacco a good? Are purchase and sale necessary for an entity to be considered a "good"?

8    "A free good is an inconsistency of concepts, because no one wants what is free; otherwise it wouldn't be free. And if no one wants it, it can't be a good." Evaluate.

9    Explain or criticize the following statements and questions about the substitution postulate:
a. "Every student substitutes romance for grades when he dates rather than studies as much as he otherwise could have." Criticize.
b. "The substitution postulate says that a student does not seek the highest possible grades." Explain.
c. Does the substitution postulate deny that water, food, and clothing are more basic than music, art, and travel? Explain.
d. "There is no hierarchy of wants." What does that mean? Can you disprove it?
e. Is travel in Europe a substitute for formal academic education? For some food? For a bigger house or new clothes or medical care? For what would it not be a substitute?
f. "I'd like to play poker with you again tomorrow night, but I don't think my wife would like it." Is this consistent with the substitution postulate? Is the wife's utility being compared with the husband's? Explain.

10    In testing a person's preference between two known options, it has been suggested that if a person agrees to let some unknown second party choose between the two options for him, then he is indifferent between the two options. Do you think that is consistent with the postulates listed in the text?

11    Suppose that I am indifferent if given an option among the following three combinations of steaks and artichokes:

|         |   | Steaks |     | Artichokes |
|---------|---|--------|-----|------------|
|         |   | pounds per year | | |
|         | A | 100    | and | 30 |
| Options | B | 105    | and | 29 |
|         | C | 111    | and | 28 |

a. What is my personal value of steak (between $A$ and $B$)?
b. What has the greater utility to me, $A$ or $B$?
c. What is my personal value of artichokes (between options $B$ and $C$)?
d. If the amount of meat in $A$ were doubled to 200, what do you think might be the amount of meat required in $B$ to make it of equal utility to $A$?
e. Using your answer to (d), compute my personal valuations between the new $A$ and the new $B$. Is your result consistent with the fourth postulate?

12    The following are combinations of $X$ and $Y$, all of which are equally preferred by Mr. $A$.

| Equal Utility Combinations | X | Goods | Y |
|---|---|---|---|
| A | 9 | and | 50 |
| B | 10 | and | 40 |
| C | 11 | and | 34 |
| D | 12 | and | 30 |
| E | 14 | and | 26 |
| F | 17 | and | 21 |
| G | 21 | and | 17 |
| H | 26 | and | 13 |
| I | 33 | and | 10 |
| J | 40 | and | 9 |
| K | 47 | and | 8 |
| L | 57 | and | 7 |

a. Plot each of these combinations as points on graph paper ($Y$ on vertical axis and $X$ on horizontal). The Appendix discussion will make this question easier.

b. Connect the points with a smoothed line.

c. What postulate is expressed by the fact that there is more than one combination of the same utility to Mr. $A$?

d. Do these combinations conform to the postulates?

e. What postulate is expressed by the negative slope of the line connecting these combinations (the iso-utility line—sometimes also called an indifference curve, to connote that the person is indifferent among the combinations on this line)?

f. What postulate is reflected in the curvature (not the slope) of the iso-utility line?

13    If I regard each of the following combinations as equally preferable, do I conform to the postulates of economic theory? If not, which postulate is denied?

| | | X | Goods | Y |
|---|---|---|---|---|
| | A | 100 | and | 70 |
| Options | B | 105 | and | 69 |
| | C | 110 | and | 68 |
| | D | 115 | and | 67 |

14    Suppose that Mr. $A$ is indifferent between options $A$ and $C$ of the following combinations.

| | | X | | Y |
|---|---|---|---|---|
| | A | 100 | and | 200 |
| Options | B | 110 | and | 180 |
| | C | 120 | and | 160 |

If he is given a choice among the three options, prove that, according to the postulates, he will choose option $B$ over either $A$ or $C$. (The proof is easy—but it is *not* easy to discover that proof.)

15    What refutable proposition is revealed by the statement "$A$ has more utility than $B$ for me"?

16    Explain why the following statements are or are not consistent with the postulates.

**a.** Diminishing personal value means that the more a person has of something, the less satisfaction he gets.
**b.** Diminishing personal value means that, as a person consumes some good, he gradually gets less satisfaction.
**c.** Diminishing personal value means that as a person acquires more of a good, he begins to value other goods more than this one.

17    How could you show graphically, on the diagram you drew for question 12, the meaning of postulate 3?

18    Many, if not all, of the postulates do not apply to some people. What happens to those people? Why?

19    Four postulates were used to characterize some aspects of human nature and behavior.
**a.** Do you think any of them are also applicable to nonhuman animal life? For example, which of the postulates would give valid characterizations of behavior of monkeys, ants, bees, tigers, and birds?
**b.** Which postulates, if any, do you think serve to distinguish human from nonhuman behavior?
**c.** What evidence can you cite to support your answers?

20    Do you think the human race would survive if it lost the attribute described by postulate 3 while some animals retained it?

21    "Economic theory is rational and logical, but man is not necessarily that way." What is the difference between a rational man and a rational theory?

22    "Don't be selfish, Jane," said Mother. What did Mother mean?

23    Would man be better off if he weren't selfish? How do you know?

24    Why is it that economic theory—in using the principle of utility maximization—does not assume that man is maximizing some psychological entity?

25    Answer the following questions concerning applications of functional analysis.
**a.** "Air density diminishes as altitude increases." If this is true, is density a positive or a negative function of altitude?
**b.** Do you think one's rate of gasoline usage is a positive or a negative function of his wealth? Of his family's size? Of his age?

c. In the relationship between gasoline consumption and wealth, which is the explanatory, predicting, or independent variable; and which is the explained, predicted, or dependent variable? Can you suggest a situation for which the direction of explanation between these two variables is reversed?

d. In the functional relationship between the amount of a person's smoking and the state of his nervousness, which is the independent and which the dependent variable?

26    "Older people have more wealth than young people. Wealthier people eat more candy than poorer people. Therefore, older people eat more candy than younger people." What is the hidden assumption in that line of argument?

27    "Smoking shortens one's life." Does this mean that smoking is the only cause of death? That smoking is the only cause of a shorter life? That smoking is undesirable? That everyone who has ever smoked will surely die earlier than he otherwise would? That advertisements for tobacco should be prohibited?

28    A recently published book was entitled *Social Needs and Private Wants.* Would the title have suggested something different if it had been *Social Wants and Private Needs*? Why do you suppose the first title was chosen?

29    Suppose it were claimed that a denial of college facilities for the purpose of exercising free speech is a denial of the right of free speech. Show how that argument confuses free resources with free speech.

# 3

**Basis of Exchange**

An important implication of our postulates is their interpretation of *trade*, or *exchange*. To expose that implication easily and clearly, we shall at first use "toy" problems, devoid of unessential, cluttering details. Real-world applications will be made in succeeding chapters.

## Mutually Advantageous Trade and the Middleman

### Cuban and Hungarian Refugee Camp

Imagine a camp where Cuban and Hungarian refugees are temporarily housed. Weekly, each person receives a gift parcel of twenty bars of chocolate candy and twenty cigarettes. Into this camp a new refugee, for whom there are no gift parcels, arrives from an unknown country. He is clever and knowledgeable about human nature. To a Cuban he suggests the possibility of a favor— he could arrange for the Cuban to have thirty candy bars and thirteen cigarettes instead of twenty each. "Merely give me seven of your twenty cigarettes," he says, "and I will give you ten bars of candy." The Cuban considers and accepts; his acceptance reveals that to him ten extra candy bars are worth *more than* seven of his cigarettes. He thinks to himself that he is taking advantage of the newcomer, because, while he would have been willing to forsake as many as eight cigarettes for ten more bars of candy, he was asked to give only seven.

Table 3–1 gives the composition of three different consumption-combination "baskets": $A$, $B_1$, and $B_2$. The Cuban started with $A$ and voluntarily accepted a move to $B_2$. Now, consider basket $B_1$, which has the *same* utility as basket $A$; although it is different in composition from $A$, it is no better or worse. The reduction in cigarettes, eight, exactly offsets the increase of ten candy bars—which is another way of saying that ten more candy bars are as valuable to the Cuban as eight cigarettes, given his present circumstances. But in fact he is asked to forsake only seven, so since $B_1$ is equally as desired as $A$, and since $B_2$ is bigger than $B_1$ (more cigarettes and the same amount of candy), $B_2$ is a better basket than $B_1$ or $A$. He achieves a more desired combination with $B_2$.

Table 3–1
Equivalent and Preferred
Baskets for Cuban

|  |  | Candy | Cigarettes |
|---|---|---|---|
| Equivalent: | Basket A | 20 | 20 |
|  |  | (+10) | (−8) |
|  | Basket $B_1$ | 30 | 12 |
|  |  | (+10) | (−7) |
| Preferred: | Basket $B_2$ | 30 | 13 |

*Personal values.* The ratio between eight cigarettes and ten candy bars, 8/10, is our old friend the marginal consumption-substitution ratio between candy and cigarettes. It is the individual's *personal subjective value* of candy relative to cigarettes, his *indifference ratio* between candy and cigarettes. It is simply that ratio of exchange to which the person is indifferent, or which leaves him at the same level of utility.

*Choice: value and cost.*    What underlying concepts are involved here? One is *substitutability*, evidenced by his willingness to give up some of one good in order to have more of another. Another is *cost*. When the Cuban is faced with a choice between options (twenty each of candy and cigarettes versus thirty candy and thirteen cigarettes), whichever combination he chooses means that he will have sacrificed the other. *Choice*, by definition, involves *cost*. His personal valuation of the option selected is assumed to exceed his personal valuation of the best of all the other available options. The value of the selected option exceeds its cost—*cost* being the *highest-valued rejected option.*[1]

*Exchange and personal values.*    How do we know whether the opportunity rate of exchange presented to a person is in fact less or greater than his personal value? We rarely know; but by assumption, "A person chooses to accept an opportunity only if he feels it will put him in a preferred position—whatever may be the factors that he regards as relevant." We need not know his personal valuation at each possible situation. We need to know only that the person has accepted some of these opportunities and refused others. For the moment, we assume that we know the exchange rates at which he would and would not trade—simply to help expose the underlying concepts.

Where does the newcomer acquire candy for the Cuban? From some other refugee—say, a Hungarian. To the Hungarian he offers five cigarettes for ten candy bars. Faced with this trading opportunity, the Hungarian accepts. The Hungarian's *personal value* of cigarettes relative to candy is (as we can see in Table 3–2) 10/4 or 2.5, but he is offered cigarettes at a cost of only two candies. His personal value of cigarettes (in units of candy), 2.5 candy bars, exceeds the cost of getting more cigarettes.

The Hungarian in effect trades his basket $A$ for basket $B_2$. Basket $B_2$ is superior to $B_1$, for it contains more cigarettes and as much candy; and since basket $B_1$ is to the Hungarian exactly as desirable as basket $A$, the Hungarian has moved to a more preferred consumption basket, $B_2$, as shown in Table 3–2.

And so—by the newcomer's transferring some candy from a Hungarian to a Cuban and some cigarettes to the Hungarian from the Cuban—*both* the Cuban and the Hungarian have moved to improved situations. They both hope that

---

[1] All choice involves the concepts of substitutability, cost, and value. In most real circumstances, the estimation of cost is not so simple. In a later chapter we shall explain various measures in some detail.

the newcomer will repeat his offer next week, after the new gift parcels arrive.

Table 3–2
Equivalent and Preferred
Baskets for Hungarian

|  |  | Candy | Cigarettes |
|---|---|---|---|
| Equivalent: | Basket A | 20 | 20 |
|  |  | (−10) | (+4) |
|  | Basket B$_1$ | 10 | 24 |
|  |  | (−10) | (+5) |
| Preferred: | Basket B$_2$ | 10 | 25 |

*Gain from trade.*    We now have an amazing situation. The newcomer has two cigarettes left over for his own use. He has taken two cigarettes from the total stock of forty cigarettes previously divided between the Cuban and Hungarian. Yet—although they have less goods in total—both say they are better off. How can they be better off with a *smaller* stock of goods? Hasn't the newcomer exploited them, when all the time they thought they were being benefited? Suppose the Hungarian and Cuban get together and find they have, between them, lost two cigarettes? How can the newcomer explain or defend this odd result? Using our postulates, he could explain as follows:

"You have not been cheated. In fact, you both have been made better off. Although, of course, you both could use all the candy and cigarettes that you formerly had, each of you preferred a slightly different combination. I made it possible for you to shift to preferred combinations. The cigarettes can be considered a payment for my helpful services. To be sure, I did not do all this with the sole intention of helping you. I helped you revise your baskets because I was interested in myself. And—admit it—each of you thought you were outwitting me, because you were prepared to give up more (or receive less) than you did. Certainly you would have been even more benefited if I had kept fewer than two cigarettes, but there is no denying that you *are* now better off than initially because of the revised proportions of candy and cigarettes. None of us has been foolish."[2]

*Conditions for gains from trade.*    To isolate the essential condition in which people gain from (that is, prefer to) trade, even if they have to pay middlemen to facilitate trade, compare the initial personal valuations of the Cuban and the Hungarian. Table 3–3 shows the Cuban's personal value of candy is .8 (in cigarette units), while the Hungarian's personal value of candy is .4 (in cigarettes). To each, his personal value of candy indicates the price below which he would buy candy and above which he would sell candy. For example, the Cuban would buy more candy if the price of candy were lower

[2] For an alternative, more powerful explanation of the principles of exchange, see the Appendix to this chapter, where the Edgeworth Box is utilized.

than .8 cigarettes; but he would sell and hence consume less candy, if the price were over .8. The Hungarian, whose initial personal value of candy is .4 cigarettes, would buy more candy at any price below .4 cigarettes but would sell if the exchange rate were over .4. The direction of trade will always be such that *commodity X moves from the person with the lower personal value of X to the person with the higher personal value of X.* Candy, in our example, moves from the Hungarian to the Cuban. In summary, *in any situation in which personal values differ, an opportunity exists wherein appropriate exchange will result in a more preferred position for each person.*

Table 3-3
Results of Trade

| | | Cuban | | Hungarian | |
|---|---|---|---|---|---|
| | | Candy | Cigarettes | Candy | Cigarettes |
| Equivalent: | Basket A | 20 | 20 | 20 | 20 |
| | | (+10) | (−8) | (−10) | (+4) |
| Preferred: | Basket B₁ | 30 | 12 | 10 | 24 |
| | Basket after | | (−7) | | (+5) |
| | exchange | 30 | 13 | 10 | 25 |

This exchange proposition is one of the most important in economics. An *inequality of personal substitution rates (or values)* is a condition of "inefficient," and hence improvable, allocation. It will be applied again later in numerous different contexts: production, specialization of labor, bearing of risks, and interregional trade. Exactly the same kinds of numerical examples will illustrate the principle in these later applications.

Warning: Do not confuse efficiency with equity. The preceding proposition refers to efficiency in re-allocation of goods *given an initial allotment.* When no further revision would increase the utility of any pair engaging in further trade, we have an efficient exchange situation. But it may not be equitable, depending upon who is judging. The initial allotment from which each person started in our toy problem was "equal," at least in terms of amounts of each good. But that may or may not be equitable. "Equitable" is a matter of personal judgment. I may think it equitable for brown-eyed people to be born smarter, to inherit more, and to be taxed less, while someone else may think the opposite or whatever he likes. Economic analysis contributes nothing to the judgment of an "equitable" situation. All we have analyzed is efficiency of exchange, whatever the initial allotment was.

Obviously, this "toy" example abstracts from many details, but that is precisely its purpose: to reveal the crucial aspects of the explanation of trade in bold, uncluttered fashion. For example, we did not ask whether the Cuban likes candy more than the Hungarian likes candy. As explained in our discussion of postulate 5 in the preceding chapter, no interpersonal comparison of absolute psychological level of desire for each good is involved. The Cuban may regard candy and cigarettes as barely desirable goods, while the Hungarian drools and pants for both. As long as the Cuban has a combination in which he subjectively values candy *relative* to cigarettes at a rate *different* from that of the Hungarian, trade with the Hungarian (via a middleman, if need be) is to the benefit of each.

In this example, the middleman seems to serve only a trivial role that could just as well have been performed by the Cuban and Hungarian themselves. But we cannot ignore the costs of collecting, transporting, displaying, and searching out offers and bids of potential buyers and sellers. The service of the middleman in "making a market" is no trivial task, as anyone will discover who attempts to sell his own used car to some other car user directly rather than *via* a used-car dealer. It has even been argued that such examples show how capitalistic middlemen exploit the ignorance of the consumer. Indeed, that is true, in exactly the same way a teacher exploits the ignorance of students, doctors the ignorance of patients, and authors the ignorance of their readers. (Do not confuse ignorance with stupidity or carelessness.) A most economical way to behave is not to try to learn everything, but to specialize and exchange information for other information or goods. Of course, it is much more spectacular to call this "exploitation."

### Diminishing Personal Values

We have learned *why* trade will occur and in what *direction* it will occur. We have not yet discerned the *extent* to which people will revise their consumption patterns. How much will the Cuban, for example, revise his consumption pattern by trading cigarettes for more candy before he says, "Stop; I have reached a most preferred combination of candy and cigarettes"? The answer requires the application of our fourth postulate, which states how personal values of goods depend upon the combinations of the goods available.

Our newcomer (middleman) has just completed his first trade. Why not buy still more candy from the Hungarian to sell to the Cuban for an extra gain of .2 cigarettes per bar of candy sold per week? But when the trader tries to buy additional candy from the Hungarian, he discovers he cannot get more at the old price. Although the Hungarian happily gave up the first ten bars of candy for five cigarettes *when he had twenty of each*, he is not willing to give up another bar for the same old price of .5 cigarettes for a candy bar. As he puts it, "When I have less candy and more cigarettes than formerly, cigarettes become less valuable relative to candy. More than .5 cigarettes is now required to compensate me for having one less candy bar this week." In our economic terms, his subjective or personal value of candy has risen (relative to cigarettes). Therefore, only at a higher price of candy would he be willing to revise his consumption pattern toward even less consumption of candy.

The middleman is experiencing postulate 4. One's personal valuation of any good is higher the less he has of that good (with constant or greater amounts of other goods). Since the same postulate holds for the Cuban (with goods changing in the opposite direction), the middleman will now have to offer even more candy than before to the Cuban for the purchase of cigarettes. In sum, if the middleman wants to expand the amount of weekly exchange between the Cuban and the Hungarian, he will have to pay a higher price to buy candy from the Hungarian and accept a lower price for the candy he seeks to sell to the Cuban. The middleman must determine how much candy, in total, he should sell each week to the Cuban and buy from the Hungarian, and conversely for cigarettes—so as to yield for himself the maximum profits. That solution would be the equilibrium extent of exchange, *assuming that he is the only middleman.*

Competition between Middlemen

Before the first middleman discovers how much to revise prices and trade to increase profits, his wonderful world of profits is shattered by the appearance of another wily refugee. An old hand at the art of trading, this newly arrived dealer offers better terms to the Cuban: ten units of candy at a price of only six and a half, rather than seven, cigarettes—the old price of the first dealer. The Cuban accepts, happy to buy candy at a lower price, and (what is the same thing) to sell cigarettes at a higher price.

To the Hungarian, the new middleman offers five and a half, rather than only five, cigarettes for ten bars of candy. This, too, is a better offer than that of the first established middleman—who argues that the new middleman is an unreliable fly-by-night who will not deliver; or, if he does, will deliver stale candy or dry, wrinkled cigarettes, and will not give service with a smile, and in any event cannot possibly cover costs of good service with such prices. But the Hungarian takes his chances and buys from the new trader. Both the Cuban and Hungarian prefer the new prices. The price at which the Cuban can now buy one candy bar is down to .65 (from .70) cigarette. The selling price available to the Hungarian from the middleman is up to .55 (from .50) cigarette for each bar of candy. Buyers like lower prices, and sellers like higher prices.

If bigger baskets are better than smaller ones, the Cuban and the Hungarian are better off, since each has .5 cigarettes more than when trading via the first middleman, as shown in Table 3–4.

The old dealer, outbid by the new and spurned by the Cuban and the Hungarian, no longer gets any gain. Competition between middlemen has reduced the spread between buying and selling prices. The consumer now pays a lower price and receives a higher price for what he sells. The spread between the buying and selling price for candy is narrowed from .2 to .1 cigarette per candy, and the gain to the middleman is now one instead of two cigarettes.

Competition between middlemen reduces the buying-selling price spread until it just covers the "costs" of providing the service at the quality wanted by the consumers. If the spread were larger, more middlemen would be attracted; and they would shave the margin in order to get business. If the profits were negative, some middlemen would not survive as middlemen; and only those who could produce the middleman's service at lowest costs would be left in the business. The competition that reduces profits is the competi-

Table 3–4
Consumption Baskets before and after Competition
among Middlemen

CUBAN

|  |  | Candy | Cigarettes |
|---|---|---|---|
| Before Trade |  | 20 | 20 |
| After trade | via First middleman | 30 | 13 |
|  |  |  | (+.5) |
|  | via Second middleman | 30 | 13.5 |

HUNGARIAN

|  |  | Candy | Cigarettes |
|---|---|---|---|
| Before Trade |  | 20 | 20 |
| After trade | via First middleman | 10 | 25 |
|  |  |  | (+.5) |
|  | via Second middleman | 10 | 25.5 |

tion of middleman against middleman, *not* consumer (or seller) against the middlemen. Middlemen do not compete with consumers; they compete with other middlemen.

## Open Markets, Costs of Exchange, and Profit Elimination

The smaller spread between buying and selling prices is a consequence of free-entry market competition or, as we shall call it, *open markets. Open markets mean that access to markets is open to all people without legal or arbitrary barriers*—not that there are no costs involved in providing exchange-facilitating services.

When there are no artificial barriers to exchange, the price paid by the buyer will be lowered until it leaves just enough to cover the costs (the middleman's services). A difference between the price at which the middleman buys candy from the Hungarian and the price at which he sells it to the Cuban does not necessarily indicate "profits." There are costs of conducting exchange; these include rent for space in which transactions can be conducted and materials can be stored for inspection and immediate delivery; costs of record keeping; the cost of inventory, advertising, light, heat, and insurance. In part, lower-cost discount houses permit the consumer directly to bear part of the costs of exchange—for example, collecting information about the item, return privileges, credit buying, delivery service, convenience of shopping conditions and location, speed of service by salesmen. All of these can be substantial portions of the total cost. Exchange costs could be reduced to zero only if *everyone* knew (without incurring any costs) *all* the characteristics of what *everyone* else was willing to sell or buy, at what time, and at what price.

And in this extreme case, the personal values of every person for any good would be equated among everyone. Any spread between two people's personal values for any good would mean that a trade between the two people would be profitable. Trade would occur until everyone's personal value moved to equality with each other's, as the initially widely disparate personal values of the Cuban and Hungarian converged toward each other with the execution of trade and revision of the combinations of goods possessed by each party. If there are costs of negotiating and conducting trade, the buying and selling price spread will reflect those costs and prevent complete equality of everyone's personal value for the particular good. (Ignoring the values of those services. But if the values of such services are included, then there will be equality of values for "goods plus services of negotiating exchanges.")

### Constrained Markets

An open market is not a universal condition. Constraints *are* interposed— often at the urging of those already in the business, in order to protect or increase their wealth. A brief description of a possible episode in the refugee camp will illustrate some common types of constraints; in later chapters we shall analyze the constraints in more realistic settings.

### Threat of Violence

The original middleman thinks: "The gains to the Cuban and to the Hungarian (and my profit) were the result of *my* acuteness, and now someone has stolen my discovery." To protect his interest, he therefore warns the new trader that any poaching will cost him his teeth. But if the Cuban and the Hungarian promise to protect the new trader, the first trader must turn to other tactics.

### Control of Business Hours

The original trader notes that the refugees are trading with the new trader at unheard of hours of the day, at nights, and even on Sundays. Arguing that it is improper to work at night or on Sundays, he suggests that trading be permitted only from 8 to 5 on weekdays. The camp manager agrees, thinking that this will be conducive to order and genteel life in the camp. Unfortunately, the new trader is so busy during the hours of 8 to 5 that he is then unable to offer his services so cheaply as a middleman to all his former customers. Furthermore, for some refugees it is inconvenient to negotiate with middlemen during the designated hours. Thus, some who had formerly found it preferable to deal with the new trader after working hours are now restricted to dealing with the old trader, whose prices are less favorable. However, difficulties of enforcing this 8 to 5 restriction soon lead to its abandonment.

### Coalition by Merger or Collusion

Cunningly, the old trader approaches the new and offers to merge businesses. He points out that both have been forced to lower their selling prices and raise their buying prices to a very narrow spread. Through agreement, they might restore the buying–selling spread to two cigarettes per candy (with one going to the new trader and one to the old). This proposal appeals to the new trader, for it will give him a one-cigarette margin on *all* the candy trades at the new prices instead of one cigarette on only those exchanges that he himself would have conducted at the previous prices; the old trader will get the same benefit. The profitability of this coalition will attract new middlemen, who either have to be bought off or let in on the group profits. In either case the attempt to maintain high profits for the two middlemen will fail as profits are spread over more and more new middlemen, until the net gains per middleman over and above costs of exchanges are brought back to zero—a result achieved not by reducing prices to consumers but by raising costs of exchange because of the excess number of middlemen.

### Compulsory Licensing and Self-Regulation

A means of preserving the profitability of the collusive group is the prohibition of new entrants. To this end, the two original middlemen persuade the camp manager to permit only "approved" (that is, duly licensed, properly trained, ethical) traders. The camp manager naturally agrees that the best judges of "proper training, competence, and ethics" are those already in the business (who automatically get licenses). They, of course, determine when "public necessity and convenience" calls for additional licensed middlemen. This arrangement, called *self-regulation*, is supposed to protect the unwary, unsophisticated customers from unscrupulous, incompetent, quack middlemen. As expected, the "standards" are so high and their concern for consumer welfare is so great that they award no more licenses. So the price spread is maintained at a level sufficient for a *few* respectable, qualified middlemen to enjoy the standard of living they think they deserve.

To make life easier for the "self-regulating" middlemen, the cartel (which is the name of a group with the right to exclude newcomers from the market) permits trade only between the hours of 9 and 3, weekdays. The traders say longer hours would serve no purpose, since they can take care of everyone during that time. Customer convenience is somehow forgotten.

Yet, all is not tranquil. Every existing licensed member has an overwhelming temptation to get more customers by special services, gifts, and advertising. Thus, pains and costs must be incurred to prevent such mutually damaging competition. Costs must be incurred to hire spies and agents to detect secret price cutting by members of the cartel.

Franchise Fees

Not long after initiation of the self-regulating, licensing scheme, the camp manager realizes that he can capture part of the dealers' enhanced wealth by charging a "fee" for the right to be licensed. He calls it a license or franchise fee. This fee happens almost to equal the value of the anticipated future profits earned by the licensees in excess of what they would have earned if there were an open market. Or he could levy a special "tax" on them. In this way, the camp manager transfers to himself the present and future monopoly-protected profit.

### A Few Implications of Exchange Analysis

We can more fully appreciate the problems of maintaining constraints or recognize the forces that operate in their absence, if we investigate real markets, wherein millions of people are involved with uncounted numbers of goods and services and money. We shall start on that task in the next chapter, but before doing so, a few other implications should be elaborated.

#### Exchange Directed by Personal Values of Goods, Not by Importance of the Users

The feasibility of exchange arose because people had combinations of goods for which they had different personal, subjective values. Neither the Cuban nor the Hungarian had to tell what he was going to do with the goods or to determine who had the more important function to perform with his goods. Interpersonal comparison of importance was totally irrelevant . . . for exchange. But it is important for deciding how *large* a basket to give each person *initially*.

An excellent example of this is provided by the Army and the Navy. We might decide the Army should have twice the total budget or amount of goods that the Navy should. That would depend upon how much another batch of goods devoted to the Army would provide in the form of defense capability compared to the same batch, if given to the Navy. But once that decision was made and the Army and Navy were given a pile of resources, might both their defense potentials be increased if they could *exchange* some goods with each other? Perhaps the Army would trade *some* men for *more* nuclear material.

For that nothing whatsoever must be known about the ultimate importance or value of Army relative to Navy services. That is relevant *only* in deciding how *big* a batch of goods, or budget, to give each. All we have to know is the

Army's own subjective value of nuclear materials in terms of men and the Navy's own valuation of nuclear material in terms of men. Each service branch could compute its own valuation. The one that places a higher value on more nuclear material (in terms of men) will find it advantageous to trade some men for some more nuclear material, and the other branch will find it advantageous to give up some of its nuclear material for those men. To see why, go back to our preceding example and change the names of the two people from Cuban and Hungarian to Army and Navy, and the Cokes and cigarettes to men and nuclear material.

Yet until about 1960 such calculations and exchanges between the military services were not systematically performed. Subsequently, however, the services have begun to make intra-service valuations and negotiate exchanges. Simple economics can have enormous benefits.

### Marginal Values, Not Total Values

The *value* of a commodity is defined and measured only in terms of *one* unit more—that is, what a person will give up for one more unit or what he will insist on getting if he is to have one unit less. Prices do not measure the *total* value of the community's *total* stock of any good. Multiplying the price of a good by the total number in existence is sometimes treated as a measure of the value of the total stock of those goods. This can be very misleading; it certainly is not a legitimate extension of the meaning of a price, as we shall see later. And for the questions we are trying to answer here, there is no point in seeking a measure of the "total value of the total stock." Only the *marginal* values, or prices (the value of *one more* or *one less*), are involved in explaining trade and how mixes of goods are determined for each person.

There remain the questions "Why is a gram of diamonds more highly valued than a gram of wheat?" and "Why are prices what they are?" We will consider these later—not simply for the sake of seeing how prices are determined, but because social and individual behavior is better understood by learning what determines prices.

### Some Analytical and Ethical Aspects of Exchange

The preceding analysis is helpful in appreciating (1) assertions about the reasons for trade, (2) the productivity of middlemen, (3) ethical arguments for and against free trade in open markets, and (4) criticisms of economic analysis.

### Reasons for Trade

Trade between two people is sometimes said to rest on the fact that one has a "surplus" to dispose of. Even responsible social scientists have held this fallacious notion: "The development of cities rests ultimately on food surpluses of agricultural producers above their own requirements." But nowhere in the preceding was there any "surplus" of cigarettes or candy. Surplus has nothing whatever to do with the possibility of exchange.

### Productivity of Exchange

Our analysis implies also that trade is productive. Middlemen (retailers, salesmen, brokers, wholesalers, transporters, to name a few) are productive in the only sense in which the word "production" has economic meaning. *Production* means an act that increases utility. A productive act improves the shape, place, or even the time of availability of something. Profit-making middlemen are not "parasitical intermediaries." They enable the rest of us more easily to reach preferred mixtures of goods.

### Ethics and Free Trade

Economic analysis does not demonstrate that exchange makes people *better off* in some moral or objective sense. It does not even show they should have the right to trade. If you believe it is "good" for a person to get what he thinks he will prefer, then you can conclude that trade contributes to "goodness." However, the trader may find that his new chosen position is not as nice as he imagined it would be. Information before the exchange is sometimes inaccurate and inadequate; the assumption that the trader preferred to get what he actually did get is then open to doubt. Could someone else be so well informed about the consequences of various choices *and* about other persons' preference patterns that he could make a better choice for the individual than the individual could make for himself? As an answer to this vexing question, one may hear that individuals know "well enough" what the consequences are. Or that although other people may know more about consequences, their inferior knowledge of individual preferences more than offsets knowledge of consequences. Or that you can't trust other people to act in your interest. Or that people, as a moral duty, *ought* to make their own choices because this will produce in them the responsibility and self-reliance that *ought* to be characteristic of the "good" society. Some believe that whether or not people *ought to*, they *do* in fact want the right to make their own choices. It is wrong, they say, to restrict the actions that other people can mutually agree upon, even if what they do doesn't accord with what we think is "for their own good."

On the other hand, some humanitarian and thoughtful persons believe that some people are not capable of proper understanding and therefore should be influenced or controlled "for their own good," much as with children. In many instances—for example, for medical care, food, education—adults are prohibited from entering into mutually agreeable exchanges with whomever they please to exchange whatever they please.

The critics of free exchange in open markets probably attach more weight to the regrettable consequences for those who make unfortunate choices; they attach less weight to (1) the forsaken gains removed from those who would otherwise have made fortunate choices and (2) the desirability of individual choice *per se*. Those who favor enlarging the range of individual choice of exchanges and responsibility probably make exactly the opposite evaluation. Neither group is necessarily more humanitarian or socially conscious than the other.

Very different from these two groups—both of which profess to be helping the individual live more freely and expressively—are those who contend that other people's tastes and preferences are simply wrong or improper and that they should learn to have the right kinds of tastes and preferences. People *ought* to prefer classical music to jazz and modern music; realistic art to surrealistic and abstract art; clean, upright literature to immoral, decadent literature; wine to beer; opera and theater to TV and movies; compact, severe cars to chromium-splashed cars; adult education to bridge and poker; and study to football. These critics would rebuild the world to accord with their preferences. They would reduce the scope of the free-exchange market (because access to that market enables people to realize their "idiosyncratic, cruder" preferences and odd tastes, just as the Cuban chose more fatness and the Hungarian more cigarette cough); or they might try to change tastes and preferences by educating, informing, persuading, or propagandizing.

### Freedom: As You Like It

This evaluation of the right to voluntary exchange of goods in the open market is part of the clash between the capitalist and socialist cultures. We have advisedly not expressed the matter as "free versus unfree" or "democratic versus undemocratic." The socialist could say that people are freer in Russia, because they are free from the task or risk of making uninformed choices. They are freed from the danger of making certain kinds of later-regretted choices, just as you and I are "freed" (prevented) from the risk of hiring a quack to perform an operation or advise us about our illnesses, or from the possibility of buying whole milk with too low a cream content, or from all sorts of possibilities of acquiring inferior things—substandard food, substandard airplane flights, substandard houses. In all these instances, we are supposed to be protected from our own folly; we are "freed" from doing things that someone thinks we do not *really* want to do or ought not to do. This may seem an unusual meaning of "free," but it is a widely accepted meaning in Russian *and* American life. It is easy to allege that one's proposed restrictions on other people are those that give them "more freedom," promote "good" and prevent "bad" consequences. Restraint from doing what is "bad" is, we all like to think, no restraint on "true" freedom. But different individuals have different notions of what is good and what is bad. Thus, to use the term "freedom" is to beg the question.

Nor do we speak of democratic versus undemocratic economic rights. Democracy is a way of allocating political power, not a criterion of what is done with it. A dictatorship which is undemocratic could enforce economic and legal rules that are conducive to what some might call a desirable society. A democracy can, by majority revision of various economic and legal rules, produce an "undesirable" society. Indeed, it is *not* perfectly self-evident that democracy as such is more conducive than *any* other system to the emergence or continuance of a society that many, but not all, would call "free," "open," or "desirable."

### Criticisms of Methodology

A misconceived objection to the economic analysis of exchange contends it assumes an unwarranted degree of rationality or of calculating behavior. Economic postulates, as we pointed out earlier, are formulated only on the basis of *observed* behavior. Economics describes how people react in exchange situations. And people are not necessarily aware of the principles of economics when they exchange. Sticks and stones and birds behave according to the law of gravity, even though they do not know what it is; human beings obey this same law even before they have learned anything about it—and their behavior conforms to the economic postulates in the same way.

Of course, people *do* calculate, and habit itself is a form of purposeful behavior. People, in large part, resort to habitual patterns. If a person discovers that these habitual or conventional purchase patterns are less useful than other patterns, he forms a new habit or customary pattern. Habits are economic ways of avoiding unnecessary mental effort. Thinking, comparing, calculating, and deciding are difficult and costly activities. They take time away from other, more pleasant activities—as every college student knows.

A partially effective criticism of the preceding analysis of exchange is that one party to a potential exchange may dislike the other or fear his motives and refuse to trade because an improvement given to the second party may be turned against the first. Witness our restrictions on trading with communist countries: we fear their consequent gain in economic strength may ultimately be used against us; therefore, we forego immediate gains and refuse to trade. In our analysis, we assume that each person's utility is independent of what other people own. More generally, we assume that each person does not regard a more preferred position for the other person as undesirable in itself. If we were to consider motivations of envy or fear, then the analysis is even more complex. We would have to consider each person's attitude not only toward the effect of exchange on his own "basket" but also toward the relative effect on the other person's basket. With envy or interpersonal animosity, trade may still be implied.

Another criticism notes that some days a person eats candy, and on others he may smoke. He varies his daily consumption mixture. Hence, the preceding concentration on a particular mixture that is supposed to be preferred over some other mixture is "artificial." Not at all. We said only that a person can in the course of a week consume candy and cigarettes. He is at liberty to eat all the candy at once or spread it out over time, any way he wants.

Summary

1   As long as there is a *revealed* disparity between the *personal values* of goods for any two persons, the allocation of these goods can be revised by trade so that each person moves to a more preferred situation, *provided the costs of discovering the people whose values are unequal and negotiating the exchange contracts and transporting goods* are not prohibitory.

2   Every choice has a cost—the highest valued option forsaken.

3   Each party shifts toward *more* of the particular goods for which his personal value exceeds the market-exchange rate (price). Trade moves goods toward the higher personal values.

4   Each party will increase (reduce) his stock of a good, relative to other goods, until the personal value he places on it is reduced (increased) to equality with market price.

5   At equilibrium, each party has the same personal value of a good as every other party—a value that is also equaled by the market price at which exchange is available.

6   Every seller in the market has an incentive to try to keep out other sellers. In the absence of arbitrary obstacles or legal restrictions, the prospect of profits will entice new sellers into the market. Existing sellers have incentives to reach agreements to avoid cutting price. But these agreements are more difficult to enforce, the more the prospective gain from the collusion, because the enticement to violate the agreements also increases with the size of the gain from the collusion. The government will be appealed to as a means of keeping out new competitors—that is, restricting the open market in order to maintain a larger buying-selling price spread, under the guise of protecting the consumer from unscrupulous sellers, who would undermine the quality of the product. The legally protected "profits" often are taken by the government.

7   The importance of what a person does with his goods is not relevant for determining either the direction of trade or the final combination of goods held by that person.

8   Exchange rates do not measure a value of the *total amount* of some good; they measure only the value of an *increment*.

9   Trade is not a result of a "surplus" of some good to one party while another has an "insufficiency" of that good.

10  Economics does not imply that trade is a good thing, in any sense other than that people, if given the opportunity, will engage in trade. The right to trade may put some people in a regretted position—when they discover that the new combination was not as desirable as they anticipated.

### Appendix: The Edgeworth Exchange Box

The Edgeworth Exchange Box is such a powerful method for explaining the principles of trade in its various forms that this Appendix will give students a deeper grasp of economic theory than is ordinarily obtained in an elementary course. Furthermore, some instructors use this method of explanation, and their students will find this Appendix a convenient review of the classroom blackboard exposition.

The Edgeworth Box was named for Francis Ysidro Edgeworth, who first suggested it in his *Mathematical Physics* (1881). The box consists of a combination of two utility or preference maps (explained in the Appendix to the preceding chapter, on pages 29–32) for two people called Cuban and Hungarian, between whom there will be trade (without a middleman).

To construct an Edgeworth Box, the utility or preference map of the Cuban and the map of the Hungarian are superimposed as in Figure 3–1, *after* rotating one of them 180 degrees so that it appears upside down and with the conventional left-hand scale on the right side running from top to bottom. Here the Hungarian's map has been rotated so that *his* zero point, $0_h$, is in the *upper-right* corner. The length of each side of the box represents the *total* amount of $X$ and $Y$ available to these two people. The total amount of $X$ is measured on the horizontal axis and is allocated with $0_c X_c$ to the Cuban as his initial amount of $X$; $0_h X_h$ (shown at the top of the box) is the remainder and is the amount of $X$ initially held by the Hungarian. Note that the distance $0_c X_c$ plus the distance $0_h X_h$ exactly equals the width of the box, denoting the entire existing amount of $X$.

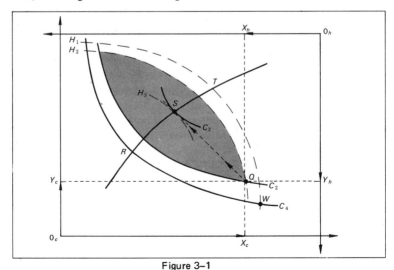

Figure 3–1

Edgeworth Exchange Box

Similarly the initial division of $Y$ shows that the Cuban has the amount $0_c Y_c$, measured vertically up from the lower-left origin, $0_c$, for the Cuban; and the Hungarian has $0_h Y_h$ of $Y$, measured down from the upper-right origin, $0_h$, for the Hungarian. The distance $0_c Y_c$ plus $0_h Y_h$ equals the vertical height of the box, and denotes the total amount of $Y$.

Point $Q$ in the box denotes these initial allocations of $X$ and $Y$ to the Cuban and Hungarian, with the horizontal distance of the point measuring the amounts of $X$ available to the Cuban (on the left) and to the Hungarian (measured from the right). The vertical height to the point $Q$ indicates the amount available initially to the Cuban, and the vertical distance down from the top side indicates the amount of $Y$ initially available to the Hungarian.

The curved solid lines are the utility isoquants, or indifference curves, of the Cuban. The dashed curved lines are the utility isoquants or indifference curves for the Hungarian; these may at first sight appear to be curved in the wrong direction, but remember that his map is turned upside down so that its origin is in the upper right, at $0_h$.

Point $Q$ is on the utility isoquant, $C_2$, for the Cuban. Line $C_1$ is another of his indifference curves, but with lower utility, while $C_3$ is a higher one of his indifference curves. Similarly point $Q$, measured with reference to the origin, $0_h$, is on an indifference curve, $H_2$, for the Hungarian. Turning the book around again, you will see that the curves $H_1$ and $H_3$ are lower and higher indifference curves, respectively.

The *slope* of the indifference curve, $C_2$, as explained in the Appendix to the preceding chapter, shows the Cuban's personal value of the commodities, or marginal rate of substitution between $X$ and $Y$ in consumption at point $Q$. If he could trade *some* $X$ for *some* $Y$, at a rate of exchange indicated by the slope of the *dotted* straight "trading" line emanating from point $Q$, he could move to higher utility on $C_3$, at point $S$. If at the same time the Hungarian were to get what the Cuban gave up—i.e., if the Hungarian and the Cuban were trading with each other—then the Hungarian would also be revising his combination of goods from $Q$ along the dotted line to $S$. He, too, would be moved to *higher* utility, say $H_3$. So long as they trade with each other along some dotted line that moves each to higher indifference curves, trade can be mutually agreeable. *And any dotted trading line that starts from a point like $Q$ and runs inward into a football-shaped shaded area, bounded by the two indifference curves through point $Q$, will move both the Cuban's and the Hungarian's resultant mixture of goods to preferred combinations, i.e., to higher utility lines for each person.*

In general, so long as the dotted straight trading line (whose *slope measures the price* for $X$, and $Y$, at which the Cuban and Hungarian might trade) *cuts* the utility curves of both the Cuban and the Hungarian at point $Q$, it will pay each to move on that trading line in the direction that moves both to higher utility curves. The dotted trade line at point $Q$ has a slope *between* that of (1) the Cuban's indifference curve slope through point $Q$ and (2) the Hungarian's indifference curve through the point $Q$ (with reference to the upper-right corner, since his map is upside down); this means that the proposed buying (and selling) prices of $X$ (in terms of $Y$ units) differ from the personal values placed on $X$ relative to $Y$. Such a trading price will enable both parties to reach combinations with higher utilities.

Through every point on the diagram there is an indifference curve for $C$, and there is also one for $H$. Wherever one man's curve cuts the other man's curve, some trade would improve each person's utility. Only for a special series of points do the utility curves of one person not intersect those of the other person. These special points form the "contract curve," indicated by the thick line, labeled $RST$. This "contract curve" line indicates *all* the combinations of goods $X$ and $Y$ for each person at which the indifference curve for the Cuban for that combination is *tangent* to the indifference curve for the Hungarian. To say the indifference curves are *tangent* is to say that at that point they have the same slopes. Inspection of the diagram will soon convince you that any initial allocation of $X$ and $Y$ between the Cuban and Hungarian (except those indicated by the line $RST$) can be improved by trade along a trading line toward $RST$. In our diagrammed example, the straight trading line from $Q$ to $S$ extends into the football-shaped enclosure bounded by the initial situation's two indifference curves. This is a line along which they could move by trading with each other, until they came to point $S$. If they moved along their trading line past $S$, they would each be moving to lower indifference curves (i.e., to less preferred positions). Once they have reached the $RST$ line, they have exhausted the possibilities of *mutual* gain from trade with each other, no matter from where they started. The line $RST$ is called the contract curve, because it is to some point on this curve that their contracts for trade will take them.

The point on the contract curve to which the two parties move by exchange depends on the starting point. At any *initial* position, two indifference curves (one for each person) pass through that starting point. If the two indifference curves intersect, they enclose a football-shaped space. Point $W$ might have been a starting point had the initial allocation of $X$ and $Y$ been different, and then trade would have taken them toward the interior of the enclosed area and to a point on the segment of the contract curve between the isoutility lines, $H_1 C_1$. To which point on this segment of the contract curve they will move depends upon the sequence of trial and error prices negotiated in the trading process. But as they converge to some point on that segment of the contract curve, the trading price between $X$ and $Y$ (shown by the slope of the trading line at that point) will match the personal values of each person (shown by the slope of the two indifference curves where they are tangent on the contract curve). This tangency of the two indifference curves and the trading price line means in economic terms that the price between $X$ and $Y$ equals the personal values placed on $X$ relative to $Y$ by both the two trading parties.

Once they have reached the contract curve, no further *mutually* acceptable revision of consumption patterns is possible. Going *past* the contract curve would "harm" both parties. Moving *along* the contract curve means that one party gives up some goods to the other. That would not be an act of exchange; it would be a transfer of wealth between the two parties.

If we accept the premise that each party should be the judge of his own interests, then any combination of goods $X$ and $Y$ between the two parties represented by a point off the contract curve is *inefficient* in the sense that things could be improved for everyone, in this case by trading and moving to a point on the contract curve at which no *jointly* beneficial revision is feasible. Hence any point on the contract curve is efficient in the sense that it is impossible to make a change that would improve the position of *both* parties. Efficient allocations of goods are those from which there is no possibility of improving the situation of someone without reducing the utility of someone else.

Questions

1    The left half of the table below shows three combinations of vegetables and meat among which Linus would have revealed indifference if he had been offered a choice; that is, all three are equally desirable to him. The right half shows three combinations among which Charlie would have revealed indifference.

| | Linus | | | | Charlie | | |
|---|---|---|---|---|---|---|---|
| Options | Vegetables | | Meat | Options | Vegetables | | Meat |
| A | 10 | and | 14 | A | 40 | and | 16 |
| B | 13 | and | 13 | B | 45 | and | 15 |
| C | 17 | and | 12 | C | 52 | and | 14 |

a. If Linus has combination $B$, between what limits is his consumption-substitution ratio between vegetables and meat?

b. If Charlie has combination $B$, approximately what is his personal value for vegetables?

c. In what sense is it impossible to say who likes vegetables more, Linus or Charlie? In what sense is it possible?

d. If Linus and Charlie each have their combinations designated $B$, does any possible trade exist whereby each could reach a preferred combination? If so, give an example.

e. State the necessary consumption-substitution exchange-rate conditions if exchange between two people is to move them to preferred positions, even though part of their goods might be lost in the process.

2      Suppose that Charlie and Linus have the following initial indifference consumption-substitution ratios:

Charlie:  7 meat = 1 fruit
Linus:     3 meat = 1 fruit

a. Compared to Linus, is Charlie more fond of fruit or meat?

b. If the government makes it illegal to trade fruit for meat, always assuming that the law is obeyed, who gains and who loses? Why?

c. Now, the government relents and allows trade, but makes it illegal for anyone to trade at any exchange ratio other than one meat for one fruit. Explain the likely consequences of this new ruling.

d. Next, suppose the government relents still more, but—in order to protect the "little people" who consume fruit—a price ceiling is put on fruit. The maximum price of one unit of fruit is set at four meats. Who is likely to gain, and who is likely to lose by this price control? Explain.

e. Finally, imagine that the government takes off all restrictions on the trade of meat and fruit. Introduce a middleman who conducts the trade between Charlie and Linus. What is the *maximum* cut the middleman can take in the form of meat? Or of fruit?

3      "The postulates of economics imply that to permit trade is better than to prohibit trade." Do they? Explain.

4      Your college allots some parking space for your car while a friend is alloted a desk in the library stacks. Suppose that you and he would each be better off if you were to trade your parking space for his desk space.

a. This kind of trading is almost invariably prohibited by the college authorities. Why?

b. If you were the college president, why would you prohibit it?

c. Would you consider solving the whole problem by simply selling parking space to one and all at the market-clearing price, like a downtown parking garage? Why?

5      "Trade between the Mediterranean and the Baltic developed when each area produced a surplus of some good."

a. What do you think this quotation, from a widely used history text, means?

b. Can you propose an alternative explanation?

6      A parent gives each of his two children some milk and meat. The two children then exchange with each other, one drinking most of the milk and the other eating most of the meat. If the parent does not permit them to make that exchange which of the postulates (if any) is he denying? Or does the explanation rest on some new postulate not made explicit in the text?

7      Can you explain how what is often called "impulse" buying is consistent with the postulates of choice? Can you explain why habitual buy-

ing is also consistent with the postulates of choice? Can you suggest some behavior that would not be consistent with the postulates?

8    "Economic theory is built on an idealization of man: that he has tremendous computational power, a detailed knowledge of his desires and needs, a thorough understanding of his environment and its causal relationships, a resistance to acting on impulse or by habit. It is difficult to bridge the gap between that model of economic man and the groping uncertain man of the real world." Does this statement correctly characterize the state of economic theory? Explain.

9    In 1966 Governor Brown of California asserted that the reduction of Mexican labor in California did no harm, because the total value of the crop harvested was larger than before. Evaluate the relevance of that criterion.

10   "Competition is never 'buyer against seller' but always seller against other sellers and buyers against other buyers."
a. Is this true for you when you buy food? Automobiles? Shoes? Sell your labor?
b. Can you cite a case in which it is not true?

11   According to economic principles of competition, which tactic would be more likely to get you a lower price on a new car: going to just one dealer and acting like a tough and aggressive bargainer; or going to several dealers and mildly asking for their selling price while letting it be known that you really intended to buy a car? Explain why. Can you cite any evidence?

12   It is estimated that 25 percent of the price a housewife pays for a head of lettuce goes to the farmer, while the remaining portion is for middlemen and distribution costs.
a. Would you, as a farmer, necessarily prefer to have your percentage raised? Explain why not.
b. Would you, as a consumer, prefer to see his percentage raised? Explain.

13   "Middlemen and the do-it-yourself principle are incompatible." Explain.

14   Some discount stores advertise that they can sell for less because they buy directly from the manufacturer and sell to the consumer, thus eliminating many middlemen. What is the flaw in this reasoning?

15   Which of the following are compatible with open (or free) markets:
a. A lawyer must get permission of present lawyers before he can engage in that trade.
b. Medical doctors must pass a state examination before being allowed to sell medical services.
c. Banks must first obtain a license from the state before being allowed to operate—and not everyone can get a license merely for the asking.

d. Selling is prohibited on Sunday.

e. Pure food and drug laws restrict the sale of "impure" foods and drugs.

f. Consumption, manufacture, or sale of alcoholic beverages is prohibited.

g. Dealers and agents must be certified by the U.S. Securities and Exchange Commission before they can act as middlemen in buying and selling stocks and bonds; that is, before they can be security dealers.

16    Suppose you succeed in leading an army of liberation to rid Cuba of Castro Communists. Upon taking office as new dictator, you abolish all existing monopoly rights.

a. Would you then grant new monopoly rights?

b. If you did, how could you benefit the government (you)?

c. If you didn't think of doing that, who would suggest it to you?

17    You are campaigning for mayor or councilman in your home town, in which the taxi service (or, for that matter, garbage service, milk delivery, electric power, water, gas, etc.) is provided by anyone who wants to operate a taxi business or drive his own cab. In other words, the taxi service is provided by an open market. You campaign for more government control of taxi drivers in order to ensure better quality of service.

a. If elected, would you initiate a system of giving just one company the right to perform the service? Why?

b. If so, how would you decide which company?

c. Do you think that company would be one of your campaign financiers?

d. In California the right to sell liquor is restricted by the state government to a number far below that which would prevail otherwise. Would you be surprised to learn that the liquor dealers are a strong political "lobby" and source of "power" in state politics? Why?

e. What generalization does this suggest about a source of political power?

18    "It is well to remind ourselves from time to time of the benefits we derive from a free-market system. The system rests on freedom of consumer choice, the profit motive, and vigorous competition for the buyer's dollar. By relying on these spontaneous economic forces, we secure these benefits: (a) Our system tends automatically to produce the kinds of goods that consumers want in the relative quantities in which people want them. (b) The system tends automatically to minimize waste. If one producer is making a product inefficiently, another will see an opportunity for profit by making the product at a lower cost. (c) The system encourages innovation and technological change .... I regard the preservation and strengthening of the free market as a cardinal objective of this or any Administration's policies." (President J. F. Kennedy, September 1962, speaking to business magazine and newspaper publishers.)

Is it not surprising and confusing that while espousing the virtues of an open competitive economic system, businessmen and politicians restrict markets—for example, by controlling allowable imports of sugar so as to maintain sugar prices in the United States at about twice the open-market level—in order to maintain larger wealth for incumbent businessmen and their employees? A confusion between freedom *of* competition and freedom *from* competition is suggested. What explains this espousal of the virtues of a system of private property and open markets with simultaneous attempts to suppress it?

# Demand and the Laws of Demand

The preceding chapters presented the principles of trade between only two people. Does trade in a large community operate consistently with those principles?

## Markets

Without a market place, trading would be difficult. When considering the possibility of securing more of one good in exchange for some of another, would you sample people at random, testing if he and you could agree on some barter? Imagine the required time and effort. But suppose there is a particular place where a person can compare his personal valuations with all other people. This is precisely the purpose of marketplaces. To facilitate market activity, people resort to advertising—publicly informing other people—to help find potential buyers or sellers. And that, despite all the criticism of advertising, is its major role: to call attention to the fact that one is prepared to exchange certain described items. This way of identifying sellers and buyers reduces the cost of searching for information of exchange opportunities. Another information-economizing activity is provided by re-tailers, brokers, or specialized trading agents who establish a meeting place for potential buyers and sellers and furnish cheap access to information about particular goods and prices. Because a pooling of information generally means cheaper information, buyers and sellers tend to go into one larger market rather than many dispersed exchange locations.

A market is a place or device enabling people to negotiate exchanges. Usu-ally markets are concentrated in well-defined geographical areas and times. A city or village is basically a market—a group of people living near each other to facilitate exchange of goods (as well as of productive services). So widely recognized are advantages of a market that "primitive" tribes have truces on market days. In the Bronx of New York City on a certain street at a certain day of the week there assemble people interested in buying and selling bak-eries. In medieval times, some political leaders amassed fortunes by fostering marketplaces (fairs) in their favorite cities and permitting foreigners to enter the market—for a modest fee. Today, cheap telephonic and other means of communication and transportation have made markets more efficient. Yet, at the same time, people have continued to restrict access of their competitors to the market, by devices and rationales mentioned in the last chapter and which we shall investigate later in more detail.

## Money

### Common Medium of Exchange

When we buy shoes, we pay money. When we sell labor services or a used car, we are paid money. We do not normally pay for shoes by giving up cigarettes, candy, or nails. Nor do we normally receive payment in such goods. We buy with money and sell for money, because it is more economical and convenient. Imagine the problem of carrying around a sample of various goods to be used in exchange for other goods. We would have to guess what goods various people with whom we might trade would want at the time we considered an exchange. We would tie up a larger portion of our wealth (and time and energy) in various goods destined for trading purposes than if there were a common medium of exchange. A common medium of exchange—money—is used because it makes search over the population for mutually advantageous exchange less costly and releases more wealth for other purposes. For now, it is not necessary to investigate the question of which good will serve as money. It suffices to understand that the existence of money, as a common medium of exchange, reduces the costs of engaging in exchange. The cost-reducing property of money is generally described as "lower transaction costs." Sometimes this attribute of money is called "liquidity."[1]

### The Common Measuring Unit of Values

Imagine the difficulty one would have in deciding upon his purchases if, when he went to the market, he found the price of shoes expressed in pounds of cotton, the price of shirts in pounds of iron, and the price of meat in pounds of wool. Imagine his even greater confusion if different sellers used different commodities as the basis for the price of meat—for example, if one seller used cotton as his basis, another used pounds of iron, and still another used gallons of gasoline. Money is a convenient common denominator for expressing exchange rates *and* facilitating comparisons of values of various commodities. The use of money makes comparisons so easy that when we contemplate the prices of various items—say, of milk, margarine, butter, jam, and bread—we scarcely realize that we have implicitly included ten pairwise comparisons in these five money prices (or personal values in money units). And in having some idea of the money prices of 100 different goods, we have summarized or dispensed with the necessity of 4,950 pairwise comparisons as a precondition to more effective trading.

---

[1] Though money is an excellent facilitator of exchange, it also is a buffer that prevents reduced demand for some goods from being offset by increased demand for other goods. For example, if investors should view future investment prospects more hesitantly and less profitably, they will reduce expenditures on investment goods; and instead of shifting to more purchases of consumer-type goods, which would induce increased production of such goods, they will seek to hold larger money stocks. As a result, depressions can be created. Also, rapid decreases in the stock of money available to the community can have depressing effects as people are forced to revise prices downward. Analyses of these events and corrective policies form the core of the other portion of an introductory economics course.

The Demand Function

When a person buys some good, he will in the first instance give up money—and ultimately, of course, some of other goods that he might otherwise have had. The *rate of consumption* of a good depends, among other things, upon its *price*; this dependence is expressed as a *demand function*, or, as it is sometimes called, a demand schedule—characterized by a schedule of potential prices and the amounts demanded at each price. Table 4–1 shows some possible prices and the amount demanded at each. If the price is $1 per unit, one dozen eggs is demanded per week; at 90 cents, the amount demanded would be two dozen per week. At lower possible prices, larger amounts are demanded.

Table 4–1
Demand Schedule

| Price | Dozen Demanded per Week |
|-------|-------------------------|
| $1.00 | 1 |
| .90 | 2 |
| .80 | 3 |
| .70 | 4 |
| .60 | 5 |
| .50 | 6 |
| .40 | 7 |
| .30 | 8 |
| .20 | 9 |
| .10 | 10 |

If three dozens are consumed at 80 cents, and only two at 90 cents, the third dozen per week is personally worth less than 90 cents but at least 80 cents. A buyer prefers a third dozen per week to the 80 cents (or whatever he could buy with 80 cents). So long as he can buy whatever amount he chooses, he will buy at that rate at which he values one more unit as equal to the price. To buy more would yield a lower personal value on the extra unit, so he would be willing to buy more per week only if the price were lower.

All this is expressed by the demand function or schedule, line $D_1D_1$ in Figure 4–1, which shows how the amount of any good demanded by a person, or community, depends on price. The amount demanded at any specified price depends upon many things in addition to the price, such as a person's wealth, age, sex, tastes, past experience, and collection of other goods he happens to have. Our purpose in setting up a demand relationship dependent only on price is to concentrate on how price affects the allocation of goods among people.

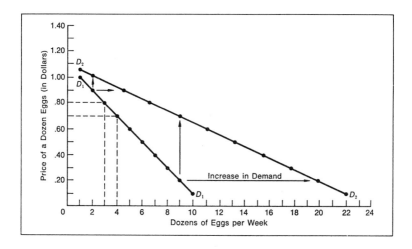

Figure 4–1
Demand Curves

Two different demand schedules, or demand curves, are shown (they are called curves even if they are actually straight lines, as in this illustration). If state of demand shown by $D_1D_1$ prevails, at price of 80 cents, three dozen eggs per week are purchased for consumption. If price falls to 70 cents, rate of consumption increases to four dozens. This is not an increase in demand; it is a change in *amount demanded*. Increase in demand curve (that is, a change in state of demand) is shown by a shift in the demand curve to the right, as to $D_2D_2$, where at price of 80 cents the consumption rate would increase to 6.4 dozens per week. We slide along a curve when the price of the good changes. We shift the curve when factors other than the price change the demand.

Changes in Amount Demanded
versus Shift in Demand

The changes in amount demanded are shown by moving up or down the columns in Table 4–1 or sliding along the unchanged demand line in Figure 4–1. Changes in the amount demanded because of changes in *price* of that good are called changes in the *amount demanded*; they are not called changes in "demand." A *change in demand* reflects the effect of factors *other* than price. For example, if a person's wealth or family should increase, and thereby increase his demand for eggs, the amounts of eggs demanded would increase for every specified price as illustrated in Table 4–2. At any price more is demanded than formerly. This increase in *demand* (in response to factors other than the price of this good) is indicated graphically by shifting the demand line to right, as in Figure 4–1. *An increase in demand does not refer to the effect of lowering the price.* It means that *at each price more is demanded than formerly.* A change in price of a good changes the *amount demanded,* but it does not change or shift the demand schedule—called "demand" for short. Only a change in factors other than the price of a good will change or shift the "demand." This distinction between changes in amount demanded by a movement *along* a demand schedule (as the price changes) and a *shift* in the whole demand schedule (as other factors change) is crucial to error-free economic analysis, as we shall see later.

Table 4–2
Increase in Demand

| Price | Old Demand | New Demand |
|-------|------------|------------|
| $1.00 | 1 | 2.0 |
| .90 | 2 | 4.2 |
| .80 | 3 | 6.4 |
| .70 | 4 | 8.6 |
| .60 | 5 | 10.8 |
| .50 | 6 | 13.0 |
| .40 | 7 | 15.2 |
| .30 | 8 | 17.4 |
| .20 | 9 | 19.6 |
| .10 | 10 | 21.8 |

Meaning of a Change in Price
and of a Change in Quantity

A change in price means a change in price of a good *relative* to prices of other goods. If the price of eggs falls from $1 a dozen to 90 cents, and if other prices are unchanged, the egg price has fallen relative to other prices. This is a fall in both the absolute (money terms) and the relative price of eggs (relative to prices of other goods). However, if the price of milk had also fallen from 20 cents a quart to 18 cents, then the price of eggs and the price of milk both are lower by the same percentage so that neither has fallen relative to the other. Hereafter, we shall always be referring to a *relative* change in the price of a good.

*The measure of the amount demanded.* In Table 4–1, the quantity column gives *rates* of consumption per week. It does not mean that a person buys or consumes that quantity at one instant. The fact that individuals do their shopping sporadically or at irregular intervals and do not consume goods at the moment of purchase causes no difficulty in the analysis, even if it makes a difference in shopping habits and creates inventory problems for retailers and manufacturers. "Durable" goods (automobiles, houses, pianos, appliances) do not create a problem in interpretation of the demand curve. Since most people have only one house, stove, and automobile, is there any sense in a demand schedule that indicates a person will consume more when the price is lower? How can a person consume more than one car if he owns only one at a time? The answer is that he can buy them more frequently, with a higher replacement rate; or he can buy a more awesome car, or he might buy two cars. In any event, whether we possess more units at one time, or replace them more frequently, or buy bigger ones, we have a schedule relating prices to amount demanded. Whether the quantity refers to amount owned, rate of consumption, rate of purchase, rate of replacement, or size of item owned, the principles of demand, to be presented shortly, still will hold true.

Consider one last point about the measuring unit of the quantity. The amount shown in Table 4–1 at 90 cents is two. This means he demands eggs at the *rate* of two dozen per week *or* at the *rate* of 104 dozen per year *or* at the *rate* of about eight dozen per month. All these measures of the rate are exactly the same.

As a test of our understanding of the demand schedule, let's try a few interpretations. A person faced with a price of $1 per dozen eggs will— according to our data in Table 4–1—purchase about a dozen per week. Suppose that he has just purchased a dozen; while going home, he notices the price at a neighboring store is 80 cents. According to his demand schedule— which we assume we miraculously know—at this price he will buy and consume about three dozen per week. Does he immediately go in and buy more? He might, but he need not. What he will probably do is keep the lower price in mind and consume the eggs he just bought at a faster rate (three dozen per week), knowing that he can replace them at the lower price of 80 cents. Bygones are bygones, and the price *now* is 80 cents; so he increases his consumption rate, in accordance with the new price, and consumes the dozen eggs in less than a week. *Assuming that his state of demand as characterized by his demand schedule remains unchanged,* his *rates of consumption* and purchase rise when he see that he can buy eggs at a lower price.

Similarly, if he discovers that the price is higher, will he try to sell back some of the eggs he has purchased? No. He will consume them at a slower rate, purchase at a slower rate, and keep a smaller stock on the average.

### The First Fundamental Law of Demand

A fundamental law of demand can now be restated: "The demand (schedule) for any good is a negative relationship between price and amount." Or: "The higher the price, the smaller the rate of consumption." More elaborately: "Whatever the quantity of any good consumed at any particular price, a sufficiently higher price will induce any person to consume less." Or: "Any person's consumption rate for any good will be increased (decreased) if the price is lowered (raised) sufficiently."

From whence comes this last? The mind of man. It is an invention to describe the observed behavior of people. This present proposition of demand is a law simply because it describes a universal, verified truth about peoples' consumption and market behavior.

### Elasticity of Demand and Total Expenditure

The responsiveness of the quantity demanded to a change in the price (*with the demand schedule unchanged*) is called the *elasticity* of demand. More precisely, the ratio of (1) the percentage change in quantity to (2) the percentage change in price is the elasticity of demand for any good. Usually, the price change is taken to be a small percentage change (because the *relative* response may vary with the size of the price change). The demand schedule is said to be "elastic" where the percentage change in quantity demanded is numerically greater (and "inelastic" where the percentage change in quantity is less) than the percentage change in price.[2]

As the price of a good is reduced, more is sold, but will the increase in the number sold offset the effect of the lower price on total expenditures? Table 4–3 presents, in addition to the same data as Table 4–1, the *total*

Table 4–3
Demand Schedule, Total Receipts,
and Elasticity

| Price | Amount Demanded | Total Receipts | |
|---|---|---|---|
| $1.00 | 1 | $1.00 | |
| .90 | 2 | 1.80 | Elastic demand in this range of price |
| .80 | 3 | 2.40 | |
| .70 | 4 | 2.80 | |
| .60 | 5 | 3.00 | |
| .50 | 6 | 3.00 | ← Unit elasticity between prices of $.60 and $.50 |
| .40 | 7 | 2.80 | |
| .30 | 8 | 2.40 | Inelastic demand in this range of price |
| .20 | 9 | 1.80 | |
| .10 | 10 | 1.00 | |

*receipts* (or expenditures) for this good at several prices. At all prices above 60 cents, the demand is elastic. This means that between any pair of prices above 60 cents, if we were to *reduce* the price, the total receipts would be *increased*. The total receipts increase with lower prices down to 60 cents. At any price below 60 cents, a reduction in price results in *smaller* receipts, for the percentage increase in amount purchased would be smaller than the percentage cut in price. We can summarize as follows:

1. "A price *reduction* leads to an increase (decrease) in total receipts" means that the demand is elastic (inelastic) at those prices.
2. "A price *increase* leads to a decrease (increase) in total receipts" means that the demand is elastic (inelastic) at those prices.
3. "A price *change*—fall or rise—leaves total receipts *unchanged*" means the demand has "unit" elasticity at those prices.

---

[2] In mathematical terms, point elasticity for continuous functions is defined as $dx/x \div dp/p$ of the demand function $x = f(p)$, and $\Delta x/x \div \Delta p/p$ is called arc elasticity. Note that point elasticity is the limit of arc elasticity as $\Delta p \to 0$.

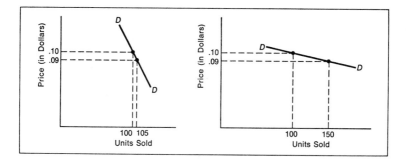

Figure 4-2
Inelastic and Elastic Demand

Left demand curve is inelastic between prices of 10 and 9 cents. Right curve is elastic at these prices. With left curve, total sales revenue falls from $10.00 to $9.45. On right curve, it increases to $13.50. Price cut on original 100 units reduces income $1.00 (1¢ X 100), but sales value of extra fifty units sold at 9 cents is $4.50. On left curve, the $1.00 loss of sales revenue on original 100 units is offset to extent of only $.45 from extra five units sold at 9 cents, giving a net loss of sales revenue. On right curve, amount demanded increases 50 percent with a price cut of 10 percent, whereas on left curve amount demanded increases only 5 percent, which is less than the 10 percent cut in price. (What is the quantity that must be demanded at price of 9 cents if curve is to have unitary elasticity between 10 and 9 cents?) Areas of rectangles at each price for each curve measure total revenue at each price. For right-hand demand curve, note larger area of rectangle at price of 9 cents compared with area of rectangle at price of 10 cents. And note reverse relationship with left demand curve.

Estimates of Demand Elasticity

Statistical studies show that cigarettes seem to have an inelastic demand in the area of current price. The total community demand for beer and wine appears to be elastic in the range of observed prices. However, classification of commodities by elasticities at various prices is difficult; furthermore, the classification would depend upon the particular prices at which the elasticity was being measured. There are no known general characteristics of goods from which economics can deduce the elasticity of any good in the real world. What is the elasticity of demand for salt at the current price? For ice cream? For chocolate ice cream? We can only conjecture. But all is not lost. In the first place, we know that the closer the substitutes available, the greater is the elasticity of the demand schedule for a good at any specified price. If practically the same good can be purchased around the corner, any change in price by one seller would have a big effect on his sales. Later we shall see how this important proposition can be used to analyze effects of attempts to raise wages or prices of inputs used in producing goods.

## The Second Fundamental Law of Demand

The second law of demand says something about elasticities: *"The longer any price change persists, the greater the elasticity."* Although a price change will have an immediate effect on the rate of consumption, the effect will be greater after a week and still greater after a month, until eventually the full adjustment will be effective. *Elasticity of demand is greater in the longer run than in the shorter run.* Why? In the first place, more and more people will learn about the price change. Second, the cost of revising consumption patterns or activities is less if done with less haste and with more economical side adjustments. For example, if the price of water were to be increased by 100 percent, the immediate rate of consumption would decrease—but it would decrease a great deal more within a few months, after people had made adjustments in associated activity and in water-using equipment.

Diagrammatically, the increase in elasticity with persistence of a new price is illustrated in Figure 4–3. Let the price change from $p_1$ to $p_2$. The different demand curves (1, 2, 3, etc.) show the greater amounts for the lower price at succeeding moments after the price change, with the ultimate rate indicated by the curve labeled $n$. After one "day" the rate is up to $X_1$, after two days it is $X_2$, etc., until at most it reaches $X_n$. The more time available, the flatter

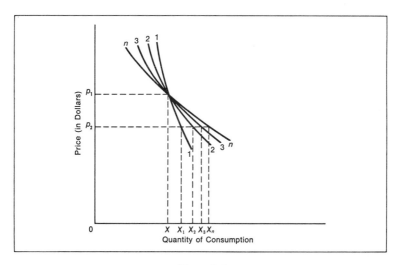

Figure 4–3
Effect of Time on Price-Elasticity of Demand

The longer the time after a price change, the greater the effect of that price change on the amount consumed—shown by the flatter curves for more elapsed time after a price change.

the curve (whether the price moves up or down from initial level)—up to some limiting demand curve when the full consumption adjustment to the new price will have occurred (or until price changes again, in which event the analysis starts over from the newly changed price).

"Demand," then, really refers to a host of demands, each applicable to a different lapse of time subsequent to any price change. If it were necessary to know all these curves and their exactly paired price-quantities, we would be lost. Fortunately, because we know that these curves, whatever their location, are (1) negatively sloped with respect to price and (2) even flatter for longer-persisting price changes, we can draw some important explanations or implications about economic activity.

### Some Illustrations of the Laws of Demand

#### Demand for Food

A higher price of meat will induce people to economize on it—to shift their pattern of expenditure, buying less meat and more of other things. Alternative sources of protein—eggs, fish, cheese, milk—are fairly obvious. Vegetables and even candy substitute for meat. So do some drinks. Even more distantly, since some of us eat for both nutrition and pleasure, we can reduce this source of pleasure and substitute more recreation, reading, or entertainment.

We should not speak of the "demand for food" as such, since no one buys "food." He buys particular commodities, each of which is a part of his "food." For each of these, his total consumption is affected (or limited) by its price. But even if one insists on talking of the "demand for food," the law of demand asserts that the amount of food consumed is affected by the price of food. To deny this is to assert that one is *completely unconcerned* about what he could have if he gave up a little food, or that all he wants in life is food and no amount of other goods and services, *no matter how large*, would induce him to consume a little less food. (Remember the postulates?)

#### Demand for Wood

The law of demand applies to wood, too. If its price rises, we will substitute more plaster, plastics, steel, aluminum, copper, glass, paper, coal, oil, and electricity; so, less wood will be demanded at the higher price. You and I may not respond very much, if at all, to a 10 percent rise in the price of wood. But since industrial engineers, product designers, and businessmen will shift in varying degrees to substitutes, the things we buy will have less wood in them and more of other things. Furthermore, since wooden furniture will rise in cost relative to metal or plastic furniture, some of us will shift in some degree to the latter. It is not necessary that every person revise his purchase habits. There are *some* people on the margin of choice between one and the other; and, as prices change, these marginal choices shift.

An especially instructive and powerful example is the demand for water. Surely, since people cannot live without it, no one will reduce his use of water just because its price goes up. As a matter of fact, however, water is not an exceptional commodity. The amount that people use depends upon its price. We could all use more water than we do now, and we could all use less. The reason that people in the arid regions use less water is not that they couldn't use more but that they don't *want* more, given the *high* price of getting more water (say, by pumping it thousands of miles). Because the price is high, they choose to consume less and to use for other, more desired, purposes the resources that would otherwise have been used in making more water available to that area.

In the United States the average per capita daily use of water varies among cities from, for example, 230 gallons in Chicago to 150 in New York and Los Angeles, to 120 in San Diego and 110 in Boston. The quantities reflect, for one thing, differences in industrial uses. Chicago has steel- and oil-refining industries, which use a great deal of water; New York City businesses—finance, retail, apparel—are light water users.

The law of demand says that *one* way to reduce consumption is to let the price of water rise to reflect its value in various uses. If water prices rise, water will be more worth saving. Reduction of waste is not costless and will be done more the higher the price of water. In New York City, 10 percent of the total water consumption is estimated to be from leakages in street mains. As costs of water rise, it will pay to spend more money to reduce that loss. For example, water meters, which make people pay according to use, are not universally used in New York City! If they were installed, people would have stronger incentives to waste less water (by repair and modification of faucets and water-using equipment). The New York water shortage could then be eliminated by raising the price of water consumed, assuming the cost of installing meters was not prohibitive.

Some waste-reducing activities are not so obvious and occur in an indirect way. With higher water prices, residential areas will have smaller gardens and lawns. Sprinkler systems will be used more because they waste less water. Gardeners will sweep, rather than wash off, lawns and sidewalks. Rock gardens, paved yard areas, and brick patios will become more common, relative to grass areas. Automobiles will be washed less often. Water will be softened to conserve it; already several cities partially soften the water to make it more effective. In sum, it has been estimated in studies of domestic water consumption that a doubling of water prices would within a year reduce domestic household water consumption by about 30 to 50 percent.

Still more ways of conserving water exist. Industrial users take about half the water in many cities. They are probably more responsive to price than are domestic users. As shown in Table 4–4, there are great differences in the use of water even within the same industry. The figures in the "maximum" column represent the amounts used in the most profligate plants in each industry, while the "minimum" column shows the least amount used per unit

Table 4–4
Variations among Firms and Products in Industrial
Consumption of Water, per Unit of Output

Draft (in gallons)

| Product or User and Unit | Maximum | Typical | Minimum |
|---|---|---|---|
| Steam-electric power (kw-h) | 170 | 80 | 1.3 |
| Petroleum refining (gallon of crude oil) | 44 | 18 | 1.7 |
| Steel (finished ton) | 65,000 | 40,000 | 1,400 |
| Soaps, edible oils (pounds) | 7 | . . . | 1.5 |
| Carbon black (pound) | 14 | 4 | 0.25 |
| Natural rubber (pound) | 6 | . . . | 2.5 |
| Butadiene (pound) | 305 | 160 | 13 |
| Glass containers (ton) | 670 | . . . | 120 |
| Automobiles (per car) | 16,000 | . . . | 12,000 |
| Trucks, buses (per unit) | 20,000 | . . . | 15,000 |

Source: H. E. Hudson and Janet Abu-Lughod, "Water Requirements," in Jack B. Graham and Meredith F. Burrill (eds.), *Water for Industry* (Washington, D.C.: American Association for the Advancement of Science, 1956), Publication No. 45, pp. 19-21.

of output produced. Note the tremendous range in the first three industries, which happen also to be the heaviest industrial water users. Many industrial firms use large amounts of water for cooling purposes on a once-through basis without recirculation through cooling units. Some steel mills use 65,000 gallons of water per ton produced, but the Kaiser steel mill (in the Los Angeles area) has reduced it to 1,600 gallons. One soap plant in the same area has installed recirculatory cooling towers to reduce water consumption from about six million to less than half a million gallons per day. At higher water prices, the value of the water saved, appearing as savings to the firm, would make the cost of recycling worthwhile. Clearly, the amount of water "needed" is a variable depending upon various factors, one of which is price.

There are still other ways to adjust the uses of water in response to price. The largest user of water in Southern California is agriculture, which accounts for approximately 80 percent of the water usage. Water is sold to farmers for irrigation at prices much lower than those at which it is sold to urban dwellers, even after allowance for distribution and purification costs. What would the farmers do if the price of water were allowed to rise to reflect its higher value in city uses? Some of them would go out of business—a blunt way of saying that the water used by farmers is *worth more in other uses* than in agriculture and is being transferred there. The community communicates this fact via the impersonal indicator—water prices. Higher prices for water would indicate that some water now used to grow watermelons, lettuce, and celery, for example, is more useful elsewhere. Less of these products would be grown in Southern California; they may be grown elsewhere, where production is cheaper, and shipped to Southern California, because that is cheaper than shipping in the water with which to grow them. Some areas or towns may decline as people find it preferable to move to places where water is cheaper or to tasks that use less water. That is, after all, the reason that the Western deserts are sparsely populated.

How do consumers discover how to use less when the price rises? Some people make a living by giving just such advice and information. Business is constantly sought by industrial engineers, architects, home-economics consultants, and commercial *salesmen* of water-recycling equipment, water softeners, automatic faucets, fertilizers, irrigation and sprinkling equipment, air-conditioning machinery, hard-top patios, chemicals that reduce evaporation, washing machines that use less water, steam generators, etc. Every rise in water costs provides them with more business prospects. Salesmen make it their business to detect situations in which their equipment is economical to use and to convey that information by advertising and personal solicitation. As students and teachers we may think that all worthwhile education and knowledge comes from schools, teachers, and books. But a very large amount of information and knowledge of practical matters is provided by salesmen—not because they are interested in us, but because it is to their personal interest to see that potential customers are educated to particular facts. We slurringly call this "advertising and propaganda," and indeed it is; but that does not change its educational value, assuming it is truthful. Even though no one can now precisely know how the use of water, rubber, wheat, sugar, steel, or gasoline would respond to a change in price, the users of those goods would soon be swamped with information about new uses or substitutes if the price changed.

We can classify these effects of price changes on quantity. Suppose that price falls. First, more of the item will be used in *current uses*. Second, *new uses* will be observed—uses that are valued too low to justify paying the former higher price. Third, *new users* will appear—people whose tastes were different or whose incomes were too low. And the reverse holds for higher prices. As long as we think only of the first possibility (that is, using more or using less in the same old customary ways), we will underrate demand elasticity.

Needs versus Demand

The law of demand is a denial of the idea of "needs." People often say that they need more water. What do they mean? That less than the "needed" amount would be absolutely intolerable? That even more would be useless? Of course not. Less water (not *none*) could be tolerated (although clearly less is not desirable). Statements that certain areas or people have water "requirements" suggest that they simply *must* have *that* amount of water. And to get that water it is often proposed that water committees or boards be set up to assure that there is no "unjustified" competition for water and that all areas have their "needs" satisfied—regardless of cost, presumably. But when they refer to "needs" in an absolute sense, people forget that the market price of water affects the amount used (the law of demand). They are talking nonsense.

It is said that we "need" more highways. Does this mean that we should have them regardless of the cost—that is, despite the forsaken alternatives? If someone says that we "need" more teachers, does he mean that, if *he* had to pay the costs of getting more teachers, he would hire more? When someone says there is a "need" for something, he should always be asked, "In order to achieve what, at what cost of other goods or 'needs,' and at whose cost?"

If he says, "We need something," for whom is he speaking? When my wife says, "We need a new car" or "We need a larger house," if I want to object, I "agree" by saying, "Of course we need it. What shall we give up to get it? What do we need less?"

We know of no more common denial of the law of demand than the repeated talk about "vital needs." At best, such talk is the result of ignorance that goods are scarce. At worst, it is a calculated attempt to confuse the reader or listener into paying the costs of what the speaker wants. Yet, do not conclude that you should never speak of *your* "critical, urgent, crying needs." As a matter of practical, good advice, you may find it worthwhile to speak that way in an attempt to con others into paying for what you want. But do not confuse yourself with your own language or be confused by others who talk of "critical needs."

### Alleged Exceptions to the Laws of Demand

Some people think that they know of counter-examples to the laws of demand. The first law of demand asserts that people buy *less* in response to the higher price. Someone might object to this assertion by pointing out that people *could* conceivably be insensitive to price or that they *could* buy more of some things when the price rises. Indeed, they *conceivably* could; but the law of demand says that *actually* they do not. Possibility or conceivability, therefore, cannot be regarded as an exception; for it is the *actuality* of such behavior that the law of demand denies. The pertinent question is "Does such denied, but conceivable, behavior actually occur?" Three cases bear examination.

An exception to the law of demand is alleged to occur when the price of, say, wheat falls and the buyers think to themselves, "Price is falling. It will fall further. If I wait, I can later buy more cheaply. Therefore, I will withdraw current orders to buy." This appears to mean that a lower price has resulted in less, not more, purchases. But has the price fallen? It is lower now than it was earlier. However, the relevant fact is that future prices are expected to be even lower. Therefore, relative to expected future prices, the present price has *increased*. People who have the alternatives of buying now or buying later transfer their purchases from relatively high-price times to relatively low-price times—exactly as implied by the law of demand. Remember, it is relative prices that count.

Another alleged case is that of "prestige" goods—like Mumms champagne, Cavanaugh hats, Rolls Royce cars, Orrefors crystal, Bristol Cream sherry, Countess Mara ties, Harvard degrees, or whatever you aspire to. The allegation is that the high price of these goods makes the demand higher than it otherwise would be. Presumably, people are motivated to buy high-priced goods because possession of such goods sheds prestige on the buyer. Undoubtedly the possession of such goods can enhance the "prestige" of the owner. But prestige goods do *not* produce a demand curve that is *positively* sloped with respect to price; they do *not* deny that the amount demanded will be smaller at higher prices and bigger at lower prices. Let the price of the "prestige" good be still higher, and less will be bought. Lower its price, and more people will be buying it. Otherwise, what would prevent the price from rising higher and higher without limit? Perhaps the advocates of the prestige-good case have in mind the so-called "fashion" goods—items that experience violent fashion swings. But again fashions mean simply that demand *schedules* increase violently in response to a general shift in tastes. The new, higher demand curve still will have a negative slope. Mink stoles would be even more common if the price were lower. Perhaps when everyone has one, prestige will be enhanced by some other distinctive items. The pursuit of discriminatory distinctiveness is not inconsistent with the laws of demand.

And there is the case in which a person offers to sell at a higher price to make the buyer believe the item is better. Similarly, anyone who proposes to sell something at far below its current market price will immediately stir doubts about the genuineness of the item being offered. But this attitude results from the fact that a higher price is an index of quality in open markets. If I offer to sell my new Plymouth for $1,000, a potential buyer will probably hesitate, suspecting that I don't really own the car or that it isn't in good condition. If he can satisfy himself that the lower price is not the result of lower quality, he will buy the car more readily than if I asked $3,000. Normally, an inferior-quality good is sold at a lower price because only then will anyone buy it; at the same prices, everyone would prefer the better item. Fundamentally, then, inferior goods sell at lower prices. The public's association of higher price with higher quality is a consequence, not a refutation, of the law of demand.

Showing the error in these alleged exceptions does not prove the laws correct (we call them "propositions" until the evidence is overwhelming). We shall very briefly hint at some of the evidence—both direct and indirect—for the validity of the laws of demand. (A possible *exception*, in principle at least, is the inferior-good income effect, already discussed on page 24.)

### Direct Evidence of Validity

Do merchants advertise by announcing that they are temporarily raising prices? Have you noticed that prices of fruits and vegetables are lower when the crop is in season? The greater amount can be sold only at a lower price. If prices did not change with seasons of perishable crops, the law of demand would not be true. If the law of demand were not true, there would be no limit to how high you could set prices, short of taking every bit of a person's wealth for one unit of whatever you sell to him. If poorer-quality goods sold for the same price as better-quality goods (in those cases where everyone agrees in ranking of quality), the first law of demand would not be true. Can you see why? Even more, there would be no point in charging prices so as to collect more from those who buy more, for that would have no effect on how much they buy, if amount demanded does not respond to price.

### Indirect Evidence of Validity

Usually, it is in the corroboration of less direct, hidden implications that the power and validity of a law are made strikingly evident. For example, how does one explain the larger *proportion* of *good* oranges or grapes sold in New York than in California? Why is a larger proportion of the good, rather than bad, shipped to New York? Is it because New York's population is richer or more discriminating? Possibly; but then why are the oranges and grapes sold even in the poor districts of New York better than those sold in California? The same question can be posed for other goods: Why do Asians import disproportionately more expensive American cars rather than cheaper models? Why are "luxuries" so disproportionately represented in international trade? Why do young parents with children go to expensive plays rather than movies *relatively* more often than do young couples without children? Why are "seconds" more heavily consumed near the place of manufacture than farther away? Why must a tourist be more careful in buying leather goods in Italy than in buying Italian leather goods in the United States? Why is most meat in Alaska "deboned"? The answers are implications of the law of demand. Let us see why.

Suppose that grapes are grown in California, that it costs 5 cents a pound to ship grapes to New York, whether the grapes are "choice" or "standard" (poorer), that the production of grapes is 50 percent "choice" and 50 percent "standard," and that in California the "choice" grapes sell for 10 cents a pound and the standard for 5 cents a pound (in California 2 pounds of "standard" and 1 pound of "choice" grapes sell for the same price). If grapes are shipped to New York, the shipping costs will raise the cost of "choice" grapes to 15 cents and of "standard" grapes to 10 cents. In New York, then, the price of "choice" grapes is lower, *relative* to "standard" grapes (1.5 to 1), than in California (2 to 1). To buy 1 pound of "choice" grapes in New York would mean a sacrifice of 1.5 pounds of "standard," whereas in California it would cost 2 pounds of "standard." According to our first law of demand, New Yorkers, faced with a lower price of "choice" relative to "standard," will consume *relatively* more "choice" grapes than Californians. In California, where "standard" grapes are cheaper relative to "choice" grapes, a larger fraction of "standard" grapes should be consumed. And it is so.

Try the same analysis on choice versus commercial grades of meat in Alaska and Texas, or French wines in New York and France. A transport cost is added—a cost that is almost the same for the two classes of items; the price of the better item, relative to the poorer item, is *relatively* lower after shipment than it is at the place of manufacture. Because the *relative* price of the higher-quality good is lower at the more distant places than at the place of origin, the more distant consumers will purchase a larger proportion of superior to second-grade items than will consumers nearer the place of manufacture. And, again, this is what indeed does happen. For instance, Italian producers export their better items; the lower-quality goods are left at home, so that tourists have a greater chance of finding inferior goods in Italian markets than in the countries to which Italy exports goods.

What about the parents of young children? If they hire baby sitters at, say, 75 cents an hour and are out for four hours, they will be paying $3 just to leave the house. Now, add the cost of two movie tickets at $1 each, and compare that total cost with the cost of going to the theater (at $4 per ticket). The theater costs a total of $11, and movies cost a total of $5. The theater, then, costs just slightly more than twice what a movie costs. But if a couple has no children and can avoid the baby-sitter fee, the movie will cost $2 and the theater $8—a ratio of 4 to 1: the theater now becomes relatively more expensive. In our original question, we did not assume that parents will go the the theater *more* than people who have no children; we said that, *when* baby-sitting parents go out, they will go to the theater a *larger fraction* of the time than will childless couples. Q.E.D.

Summary

1    Markets reduce the costs of obtaining information about exchange possibilities.

2    Money is the common medium of exchange and common denominator of value. It economizes on information costs about other people's demands for special goods and releases wealth for other purposes.

3    The demand function or schedule, often called "demand" for short, is a relationship between price and amount of a good demanded. Keep distinct the "demand" and the "amount demanded." The latter is the amount *at a specified price*.

4    A change in price means the price has changed relative to prices of other goods.

5    The first fundamental law of demand states, "The demand for any good is a negative relationship between price and amount demanded." Or:

"Whatever the quantity demanded at any price, there is a higher price that will induce a reduction in the amount demanded."
Examples of verified implications of the first fundamental law of demand are available in seasonal prices, sale prices, the fact that prices are used at all, relative quality of items sold near and far from the place of production, and effects of changing the price ratios between two goods. Alleged exceptions to the law of demand are not exceptions—for example, falling (as distinct from lower relative) prices, prestige goods, and "abnormal" price effects.

6    The elasticity of demand is a measure of the responsiveness of amount demanded to changes in price. In general the ratio of the relative (percentage) response in amount demanded to the relative (small percentage) change in price is the elasticity at that price. An elasticity greater than "one" implies that a reduction in price increases the total receipts, in the neighborhood of that price.

7    The second fundamental law of demand asserts the elasticity of demand is greater in the longer than in the shorter run.

8    At lower prices more of the item will be used in current uses, new uses will be observed as they become economical, and more people will use the good.

9    "Need" is a word often used to conceal the cost of what is desired.

Questions

1    If one pair of shoes can be exchanged for four shirts, and one shirt trades for two pairs of socks, and if one pair of shoes trades for six pairs of socks, what series of trades could you make to get steadily richer? (This is known as "arbitraging" among markets for different goods.)

2    What are prices? Can there be prices without money?

3    What properties of a good will enhance its chances of being used as money? To what extent are these properties attributes of gold, bricks, cigarettes, chewing gum, seashells, pearls, cattle, matches, diamonds, platinum?

4    To say that a person purchases and consumes water at a *rate* of 50 gallons per day, or 350 per week, is to say the same thing in two ways. What is the equivalent statement in terms of rate per year?

5    The following questions are intended to reveal clearly the difference between a *stock* and a *rate*. (Thus, they ignore the argument of the woman who told the traffic policeman that she couldn't have been driving 60 miles per hour, since she had been traveling only ten minutes.)

a. How many eggs does a person eat in one week at the *rate* of 365 per year?

b. How many miles does a person walk in seven hours at a *rate* of 24 miles per day? At the rate of 1 mile an hour?

6    Mr. *A* currently uses water at a rate of 3,650 gallons per year at the present price. Suppose that his demand doubles, so that his rate increases to 7,300 gallons per year. How many more *gallons* of water will he consume during the first week of higher demand?

7    If the price of candy rises from $1 to $1.25 a pound while the price of ice cream rises from 50 cents to 75 cents a gallon, in what sense is that a *fall* in the price of candy?

8    Can Table 4–1 be read as follows: "A person sees a price of $1 for one pound of candy, and he therefore buys one pound. The next day he sees that the price has fallen to 80 cents; so he dashes out and buys three pounds. A couple of days later, the price rises to 90 cents; so he buys two pounds." If it can't be interpreted that way, and it can't, then how is it to be interpreted?

9    a. Because we represent a demand curve with precise numbers, does that mean that people have these numerical schedules in their minds?

b. What essential property illustrated by the demand-schedule data does characterize their behavior?

10    "According to the law of demand, the lower the price of vacations, the more vacations I should take. Yet I take only one per year. Obviously the law of demand must be wrong." Is it?

11    Do you think the demand for children obeys the fundamental theorem of demand? The demand by immigrants for entry to the United States? The demand for divorces? The demand for pianos? The demand for beautiful women? The demand for a winning college football team? The demand for "*A*'s" in this course? The demand for appendectomies?

12    "Elasticity is a measure of the percentage increase in demand for a one-cent change in price." There are two errors in that statement. Rewrite it correctly.

13    Are the following statements correct or incorrect? Explain your answers.

a. "A 1 percent rise in price that induces a 3 percent decrease in amount taken indicates elasticity of less than one."

b. "A 1 percent fall in price and induces a 3 percent increase in amount purchased indicates an elasticity of greater than one."

c. What is wrong with asking whether a 1 percent rise in price induces a 3 percent decrease in demand?

14    An increase in demand is shown graphically by a demand cuve (to the right of) (above) (below) (to the left of) the old demand curve. Select correct options.

**15**    A person purchases and consumes eggs at a rate equivalent to seven per week if the price of eggs is 5 cents each. Another person purchases and consumes eggs at the rate of 365 per year when the price of eggs is 4 cents. Who reflects a greater demand?

**16**    Sometimes luxuries are defined as goods that have an elastic demand, while necessities are those with an inelastic demand. Evaluate the usefulness of those designations. How would you define a luxury and a necessity? For what problems is it useful to attempt the distinction?

**17**    "If the price of gasoline fell by 10 percent, the average person would not change his rate of consumption." Explain why this does not refute the law of demand.

**18**    The demand schedule of Table 4–1 shows that at a price of $1, the weekly consumption is 1 unit. At a price of 90 cents, the weekly consumption is 2 units.
a. Can it be said that this person wants *each* one of those 2 units more than he wants 90 cents' worth of weekly expenditures on any other goods?
b. Note that at the price of $1, he spent weekly $1.00 on this good; whereas, at a price of 90 cents, he spent $1.80 or 80 cents more than previously. Do you still say he values the extra unit at approximately 90 cents, even though he spends only 80 cents more?
c. Explain why. In doing so, explain clearly what is meant by "value."

**19**    Can you think of a good for which the demand is absolutely inelastic (the amount demanded will not change, no matter how high the price)? If you name one, what would happen if its price were raised by a factor of 100? If cut by a factor of 100?

**20**    a. If the price of gasoline were 30 percent lower, would automobile manufacturers be induced to make changes in the designs or operating characteristics of automobiles?
b. What effect would they have on gasoline consumption?
c. Would the effect be more extensive at the end of three months or at the end of three years?

**21**    Which of the following do you think would increase a woman's demand for wigs?
a. A raise in her husband's salary.
b. Higher price of hats.
c. Having a swimming pool.
d. Rise in cost of hair care.
e. Getting divorced.
f. Number of other women who wear wigs.
g. Lower price of wigs.

**22**    Which "needs" do you think are more important: urgent, critical, crying, vital, basic, minimum, social, or private needs?

**23**    Explain wherein each of these is a denial of the law of demand and the basic postulates of economics:
**a.** "The budget of the Department of Defense covers only our basic needs and nothing more."
**b.** "Our children need better schools."
**c.** "Nothing is too good when it comes to education."
**d.** "America needs the atomic bomb."

**24**    "Economics does not admit of the concept of a 'need' as a 'necessary amount' of any good." Explain.

**25**    Diagnose and evaluate the following news report from the *Los Angeles Times*: "Los Angeles needs 24 more golf courses, according to a report submitted to the City Recreation and Park Department by the National Golf Foundation. The survey discovered that there are 160,000 golfers in the Los Angeles area, and many of them do not play as often as they would like because of the lack of courses." How does this differ from the situation of filet mignon steaks, champagne, and autos?

**26**    Does a prestige good *give* prestige or *reflect* one's prestige?

**27**    Let $p_1$ and $p_2$ be the domestic prices of two goods. Let $T_1$ and $T_2$ be the transport costs of these goods to a "foreign" market. Show that if $T_1/T_2 < p_1/p_2$, then *relatively* more of good "1" will be shipped; if the inequality is reversed, relatively more of good "2" will be shipped. "Relative" to what? In your answer, what do you assume about demand conditions in domestic and in "foreign" markets?

**28**    Economics asserts that people prefer more goods to less. Yet there are waiting lists of people seeking small apartments in slum areas while bigger, better apartments do not have a list of applicants. How can people want smaller, less luxurious apartments rather than bigger apartments, without violating our postulates about people's preferring more economic goods?

**29**    A competitor to this text publishes a *Study Guide* as a supplement and asserts it is "invaluable." Does that sound consistent with economic analysis?

**30**    In the graph below, which of the three demand curves has the greatest elasticity at price $p_1$? At price $p_2$? Does the elasticity change as the price changes?

# 5

Market Demand, Allocation, and Equilibrium Price

In this chapter, we use the market-demand concept in an allocation problem to show how market pricing directs exchange.

### Demand in a Four-Person Society

We start with a society of four people, *A, B, C,* and *D,* each characterized by his demand for automobiles, as given in Table 5–1. Assume that all automobiles are alike. The schedules for each person and for the group conform to our first law of demand: greater amounts are demanded at lower prices and lesser amounts at higher prices.

Table 5–1
Car-Ownership Demands of *A, B, C,* and *D*

Quantity of Automobiles

| Price | A | B | C | D | Total |
|-------|---|---|---|---|-------|
| $1,000 | 2 | 0 | 1 | 1 | 4 |
| 900 | 2 | 0 | 1 | 1 | 4 |
| 800 | 2 | 0 | 1 | 2 | 5 |
| 700 | 2 | 0 | 1 | 2 | 5 |
| 600 | 3 | 0 | 1 | 2 | 6 |
| 500 | 3 | 1 | 1 | 2 | 7 |
| 400 | 3 | 1 | 2 | 2 | 8 |
| 300 | 3 | 1 | 2 | 3 | 9 |
| 200 | 3 | 1 | 2 | 4 | 10 |
| 100 | 4 | 2 | 2 | 4 | 12 |

At first glance, one might guess that *A* is richer than *B.* In fact, *B* might be a wealthy old man who rather regrets the invention of the internal-combustion engine; and *A* might be the head of a poor family, with everyone in the family commuting to work. We may reasonably suppose that a *given* individual's demand for automobiles will increase if his income increases, but the fact that *one* person's demand is greater than *another* person's demand is not proof that the first person is wealthier.

### Re-allocation of Cars

Suppose there are seven cars in this community, and three of them are owned by *A,* one by *B,* one by *C,* and two by *D.* It happens, as seen in Table 5–1, that this distribution of present ownership is the same as the pattern of amounts *demanded* at a price of $500. With the community holding seven cars and wanting seven cars, the *equilibrium price* is $500: no one would pay more than $500 to get another, and no one would be willing to sell a car for $500 or less. The market is cleared. This is called an *equilibrium distribution.*

But an initial distribution won't necessarily be an equilibrium distribution. Suppose that at first all seven cars are owned by $A$. (And suppose, for expository simplicity, that the demand schedules are not changed perceptibly by the particular sequence of trades in reaching an equilibrium.) The following is one possible scenario of exchanges leading to an equilibrium. $A$ would sell some even if he could get only $100 per car. (Query: How many?) $C$ and $D$ each offer to buy a car for $900. $A$ will sell. Then $B$ offers $400 for a car; again, $A$ sells. (We shall assume for simplicity that $100 is the minimum possible price change.) These exchanges leave $A$ four cars, and $B$, $C$, and $D$ one car each. $C$ buys another car from $A$ at $300; $A$ sold because he would rather have $300 than a fourth car. Though $D$ is prepared to offer up to $800 for a second car, he now offers $A$ only $300 for a second car, but $A$ says that he doesn't have any cars to "spare" now that he has only three. However, he has a car to spare if $D$ will pay at least $700. By this time, $B$, alert to the market, offers his car for $600, even though he just bought it. But $C$, who values his second car at only $400, will undercut $B$'s price by offering to sell at $500. At $500, neither $A$ nor $B$ would sell. Only $C$ is left as a seller, and $D$ is willing to pay that price. So $D$ pays $500 to $C$ for a car; thereafter everyone is content with his *pattern* of goods, given his preferences and *wealth*.

### An Equilibrium Allocation and Price

The cars are now distributed as follows: $A$ has three, $B$ has one, $C$ has one, and $D$ has two. And, during every stage of the exchange process, each buyer and seller moved to a position he preferred. Several alternative possible sequences of trade could be conjured from the illustrative data. All lead to the same equilibrium pattern of distribution of goods, and in each sequence the equilibrium price is $500.[1] The equilibrium price (1) makes the total amount demanded equal to the total available stock, *and* (2) it will also equate the number of cars that people wanted to buy (in addition to what they already had) with the number that other people wanted to sell from their holdings.

With this final equilibrium allocation, *no further exchange of cars would be mutually acceptable. This is a "market-clearing" situation.* In order to improve his situation further, a person would now have to take away some cars from someone else—that is, without mutually acceptable exchange. We

---

[1] Furthermore, depending upon the sequence of exchanges and interim prices, each person's wealth will change and affect his demand for cars. However, here we have ignored these wealth-change effects and have kept individual demands unchanged. Were we to take these into account, we would have to trace a sequence of prices gradually converging to some equilibrating price, slightly different from the one reached here. Our convergence to a unique equilibrium is permissible analytically in this kind of exchange problem, but for more advanced analyses concerning determination of *production* and *employment* as well as exchange of produced products, more general and complex considerations must be introduced. Then the convergence may be sufficiently slow to cause serious income and employment effects.

These matters are the subject of general employment and national income theory (usually called "macroeconomics"), which in conjunction with the material in this book form the conventional core of the elementary course.

have here simply shown *how* various goods are allocated. We have not judged whether this is the best possible distribution or whether there should be a more or less equal distribution.

The free play of demand and supply is important not simply because it sets a price but because, in the process, it reveals relative subjective values; it sets a price that enables people to exchange so that they achieve a preferred combination of goods. Although we imagined a four-person society, the principles are applicable to a million-person economy, with the addition of middlemen to economize on the costs of search for exchange opportunities.

### Demand Functions Need Not Be Known

It may be objected that no one knows demand schedules with the accuracy specified here. But we have *not* assumed that anyone knows the demand schedules. No one need know even his own demand schedule in the sense that he can write it out for you. All we require is that when faced with the opportunity to buy or sell a car at a price, *he can make a decision.* To this we add our first law of demand: At a higher price he will buy less than he will at a lower price. Precisely *what* that larger or smaller amount is for each and every price is not necessary information. Our explicit use of numbers merely makes it easier to follow the analysis.

Even without the data, we can see that when people are given the opportunity to engage in trade, each will revise his pattern of consumption to what he thinks is a preferred position, if such a possibility exists. Furthermore, we see that market-price bidding and negotiations reveal to each person whether there are any further possible exchanges that will bring him to what he regards as a preferred pattern of goods. The process of bidding higher or lower prices, in accordance with each person's attempts to improve his situation as he sees it, is the essence of the operation of the law of demand in the market.

### Markets as Economizers on Costs of Information

It is convenient that each person simply looked at a market price and then decided how many to buy or sell. That is how markets appear to operate for most of us for many goods. But if there were no formal marketplace or its location were unknown, we would have to incur greater costs scurrying around trying to discover at what prices all other people in the community were willing to buy or sell. Clearly, the less well that markets are organized, or the more difficult it is for people to communicate even in well organized markets, the more time that will be spent discovering and comparing offers of potential sellers and buyers to arrange the best possible exchanges. As we shall see later, "unemployment" is in no small part a result of the high cost of discovering the demands of all other people and of communicating with them to learn more about the particular attributes they might want to "sell" or "buy."

## Market Supply and Demand:  Graphic Interpretation

An analysis of pricing and allocation is easier with diagrams of demand and supply curves than with numerical tables.

In Figure 5–1 the individual's demand curves, *AA, BB, CC, DD*, indicating demand to own cars, are added *horizontally* to get the total demand, *TT*. The available supply, seven units, is shown by a supply curve, *SS*; it is vertical because, regardless of price, the stock of cars available is fixed at seven. The *total* demand and supply curves intersect at $500, and at that price the number of cars demanded by *A, B, C,* and *D* is three, one, one, and two, respectively, for a total of seven. Only the *final* equilibrium outcome is shown. The *process of adjustment* is not shown, but the net change from initial to final pattern for each person can be deduced.

Inspection of Figure 5–1 suggests that the community would want fewer cars than it actually has if the market price somehow were held at $800, which is greater than the equilibrium price. A law might stipulate that cars can be sold only for $800. There would then be a *surplus* of cars. At the legal price of $800, people would want to own only five, but they have seven. In particular, *A* and *B* would claim that they have a surplus of one car each. This means each would prefer $800 over the car.

On the other hand, the surplus would instantly become a *shortage* if the maximum price somehow were set at $200, below the equilibrium price. Everyone wants more cars at $200 than at $800. Everyone asserts there is a shortage of cars. *At the price* of $200, more cars are demanded than are available. *A* says that the car he "needs" would be used by his daughter in going to college. Currently she has no car and uses taxis and buses to come home. She "needs" a car. Of course, when the price of a car was $800, that "need" was less urgent than the "need" for what else one could get with the $800. Or, in more scientific language, "At $200, *A* finds a car preferable to $200 worth of other things." And the same goes for everyone else.

How could these "surpluses" or "shortages" be eliminated? A price of $500 would eliminate them. At that price, the amount that individuals want (or say they "need"), as reflected in the desired patterns of various goods, matches the total available. This is what the intersection of the demand and supply curves means. This equilibrium price is a *market-clearing price*. There remain no unexploited exchange possibilities.

### Adjustments to Changes in Supply

What happens if the total supply changes? Suppose a car belonging to *A* is destroyed by fire. Even if no one else knows of the loss, everyone will be

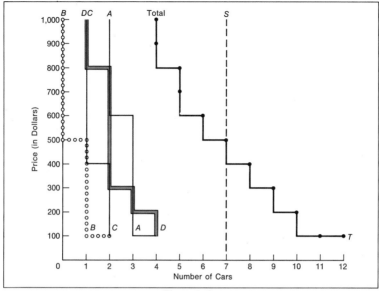

**Figure 5–1**

Individual and total community demand curves with existing stock of automobiles as the supply. The total demand curve is the sum of the horizontal distances of each of the individual demand curves at each price.

affected. The total supply has decreased to six, as can be shown by shifting the supply curve to the left to six on the horizontal line in Figure 5–2. The intersection of demand and supply is now at $600. This suggests that the price will rise. But how does a higher price come to pass? And what function does the higher price fulfill?

The reduced supply *is* an increased scarcity of cars. Who suffers? *A* has lost some wealth—his car. If that loss is not great enough to affect his demand for cars perceptibly (as we assume in this example), *A* will try to buy another car at the old price of $500. But no one wants to sell a car at $500. There is a "shortage of supply" or an "excessive demand" at that offered price. Everyone prefers his car to an additional $500. *A* prefers a third car even to $600; he will, if he finds *B*, get a car, because *B* would rather have $600 than a car. Initially, *A* was pushed to a less preferred position *by the burning of the car*, but he has now moved to a more preferred level, although not so high as before the fire. Inducing trade by offering a higher price enabled *A* to reach a position preferred to the one he was put in by the fire.

The fire brought a benefit to *B* as he judges his position. It may seem "unfair" that someone else gains because of *A*'s loss. But under the system of private property, this can happen.[2] However, don't overlook that the gain to

[2] Voluntary insurance is a method for distributing the loss over all co-insurers, rather than concentrating it on one person.

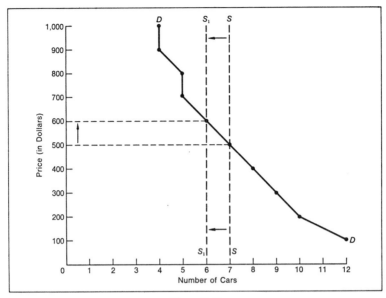

Figure 5–2

Reduction in supply is shown by a shift of the supply curve to the left. With a *fixed* number of cars available regardless of price, the supply curve is a vertical line. The rise in price from $500 to $600 facilitates a redistribution of cars from those who value a car less than $600 to those who value a car at least at $600. Without the option of bidding higher prices in response to a reduction in supply, cars would not be re-allocated according to relative personal valuations. The demand line is smoothed for ease of reading.

*B* occurred as he helped *A* to recoup part of his loss. By offering to improve *B*'s situation, *A* was also able to improve his own—as judged by *A* and *B* themselves.

Whether it was *A* or *B* or the reduced supply that raised the price is impossible to say and *irrelevant*. If price is not allowed to go up to reflect *A*'s and *B*'s demands for cars in the face of the reduced supply, *A* will remain at the lowest post-fire position.

One way to prevent this mutually agreeable change—*given* the disaster, about which nothing can be done now—is to limit the price at which cars may be sold to the pre-disaster price of $500. *B* is prevented from "gouging" *A* or, as it is sometime said, "profiteering from *A*'s misfortune." We might think we were doing *A* a favor by preventing him from buying cars at over $500. But he *cannot* get any cars at that price. A *shortage* has been created—not by the burning of a car, which *increased* the scarcity, but instead by the prohibition of higher prices. In *A*'s opinion, is he helped or hurt by a price ceiling at $500 if the price ceiling prohibits full exploitation of mutually preferred exchanges?

Adjustments to Changes in Demand

Suppose with the original situation of seven cars, a newcomer, $E$, joins the community. His demand schedule and the new market demand are shown in Table 5–2.

Table 5–2
Car-Ownership Demand Schedules of A, B, C, D, and E

Quantity Demanded

| Price | A,B,C,D | E | Total |
|-------|---------|---|-------|
| $1,000 | 4 | 0 | 4 |
| 900 | 4 | 1 | 5 |
| 800 | 5 | 1 | 6 |
| 700 | 5 | 1 | 6 |
| 600 | 6 | 1 | 7 |
| 500 | 7 | 1 | 8 |
| 400 | 8 | 1 | 9 |
| 300 | 9 | 2 | 11 |
| 200 | 10 | 2 | 12 |
| 100 | 12 | 3 | 15 |

$E$ prefers a car to $500 but is unable to get one at that price. Why? Because now the community's demand curve for cars, including his own demand, has moved to the right; the demand for cars has increased. This *increase in demand* means that at the *same* price more is wanted than formerly. In this instance, the demand has increased because a new member has joined the community.

What happens now? According to Figure 5–3 the equilibrium price is higher (in this case, $600) when demand increases—and lower when demand decreases. More pertinent is an understanding of what function is served when higher offers are permitted in the markets to push price to the new equilibrium. A *re-allocation of the pattern* of ownership of various goods occurs. Each member of the community can reach what *he* regards as a preferred pattern of consumption or combination of assets. $E$ prefers a car to any amount of money up to $900. An offer of $600 would attract a car from $B$, who prefers a pattern of wealth consisting of $600 more and one car less over the pattern he now has. Exploration and discovery of opportunities are possible if $E$ is allowed to offer whatever amount he chooses.

This equilibrium price is defined by the intersection of the new demand and supply. If price is pushed to that equilibrium value, the resulting distribution of goods will give each person the pattern he prefers at that price. No further revision of the individual's *pattern* of consumption of goods is acceptable to *any* two persons (it takes two to trade), given the distribution of the total stock of all goods and the wealth and income and the demand of each person. (However, still more wealth would be preferred.)

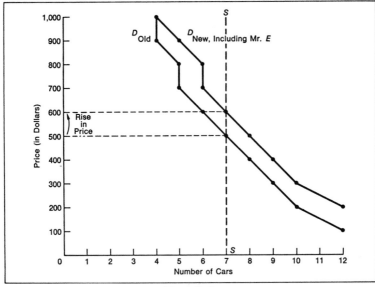

Figure 5–3

Higher-price effect of increased demand. Important conclusion is not merely that price is increased, but that the higher price permits a re-allocation of an automobile to *E* from *B*, who prefers $600 to an automobile.

### Role of Intermediaries

If the exchange of cars had been conducted with the aid of intermediaries (used-car dealers), the buyers of cars would probably complain that middlemen had unscrupulously hoisted prices. In truth, used-car dealers do raise prices scrupulously when demand increases—and they must raise prices to replenish their inventories. They must attract more cars from the rest of the public who prefer the greater amount of money to cars. And the reason the used-car dealers *can* offer more for cars (*and* still stay in business) is that the consumer-demanders of more cars are offering more to get cars rather than go without. It makes no difference whether the higher bids *first* come from the potential buyer or a used-car dealer. The willingness of some people to pay more to get a car, combined with unchanged willingness of the rest of the public to sell cars, will result in a higher price—even without the used-car dealers as intermediaries. One thing dealers do is make it cheaper for the buyers to communicate (indirectly) with other car owners and negotiate exchanges.

Used-car dealers are not responsible for the higher equilibrium price. They buy and sell only at prices between the "offer" and "asking" prices of the public. The price spread provides for their services in economizing on costs of communication between all potential buyers and sellers. As people's demands change, the dealers must move prices to stay in that range; otherwise, used-car lots will either overflow or empty.

To let changing demands be reflected by "bids" and "asks" (offers), even when the supply is fixed and non-increasable, is *not* a matter of tolerating higher or lower prices for their own sakes. Instead, it is a matter of facilitating revisions in people's consumption patterns to what they consider preferred patterns.

### Purpose of Demand and Supply Concepts

What is the point of all this demand and supply apparatus? It attempts (1) to explain how markets enable people more cheaply to revise their consumption patterns to suit their tastes; (2) to show how interpersonal competition for existing goods is resolved in the marketplace; (3) to explain how price adjustment or price negotiation aids re-allocation of goods; (4) to see how the market and market prices economize on the search activities that people would otherwise engage in at much greater cost and loss of time; and (5) to prepare ourselves for comparing this system of allocating goods with systems with restrictions against negotiated prices that would be mutually acceptable to both parties.

### Interdependent Demands and Prices

The amount of butter demanded depends on the price of butter and also on the prices of margarine, peanut butter, cheese, milk, and bread. The amount of gasoline demanded depends on the prices of tires, automobiles, bus fares, and taxi rates, in addition to its own price. For almost every good, prices of other goods also enter demand. Those prices and events that affect, but are largely unaffected by, prices and events in a particular market are called "exogenous" factors. Those that affect, and also are in turn affected by, prices and events in a particular market are called "endogenous."

A more explicit formulation is achieved by showing, for example, that the amount of butter demanded depends (1) on the price of butter, i.e., its own price, *and* (2) on the price of margarine, i.e. the price of other goods. This is done by *shifting* the demand curve for butter when the price of margarine changes—that is, for each price of margarine there is a different demand *curve* for butter. Figure 5–4 shows two demand curves for butter, the lower one for a margarine price of 30 cents per pound and the upper one for a price of 60 cents. This means that butter and margarine are *substitutes*.[3] If the price

---

[3] If a higher price of one good lowered the demand curve of another good, the two goods would be called *complements*. Examples are gasoline and tires, golf balls and golf clubs. (What about ham and eggs? Why can't you be sure?)

of margarine is increased, people will shift from margarine to butter, increasing the amount of butter demanded at each possible price of butter. If the supply of butter were $B$ in Figure 5–4, the price of butter would be $p_2$ when the margarine price is 60 cents and $p_1$, a lower price, when the price of margarine is 30 cents.

All other factors affecting the demand for butter are still taken as given or unchanged. For example, factors like wealth, age of the consumers, price of bread, population, and attitudes toward butter—which we presume to be essentially independent of the price of butter—are not explicitly specified in the analysis of the butter market. But after we recognize that the price of margarine is *dependent* on what happens to the price of butter, we must make a complete demand-and-supply analysis of the margarine market simultaneously with the butter market. As a result of the simultaneous, joint analysis, we derive the implied process of clearing the markets for both butter and margarine by interdependent changes in both prices rather than only one.

In brief, an increase in demand for butter will raise the price of butter, which will increase the demand schedule for margarine, thereby raising the price of margarine. Since the demand schedule for butter depends in part on the price of margarine, a higher price of margarine will increase the demand schedule for butter—pushing butter prices still higher, which will again raise margarine prices, and on and on. Where will the process end? The prices rise less and less and *converge* toward an equilibrium pair of prices. The analysis of that is beyond the elementary level. It is sufficient for present purposes to see that attempts to legally constrain one price will necessitate attempts to control other prices as well. Suppose, for example, that the price of butter were artificially raised by some law. The effect would be to increase the demand for margarine, and this would push up the price of margarine. The interrelationship among demands for commodities, and hence their prices, is so pervasive that attempts to control prices of some goods lead one into a much wider range of price controls.

The range can be appreciated by tracing some effects of a reduction in the supply of gasoline. The rise in price would restrict the amounts demanded to that available; a rise to double (say) the former price would induce people to walk a bit more on short errands, to travel more by group transportation. Motels would experience a reduced demand. Some motels, hotels, and service stations would lose employees to other jobs, some in public transportation and some in TV and entertainment serving as substitutes for "joy rides." Automobiles would be reduced in size as demand increased for lower horsepower engines. Trucks would be less widely utilized while railroads expanded. Farms closer to the city would be advantaged because transportation costs would be more effective in determining profitability. The demand for housing near places of work would increase. With a little imagination you can pursue the matter on your own as people adapt to the new circumstances and revise their demand patterns. If one tried to control the price of gasoline to prevent it from rising, he would soon find he had to extend the web of controls to a vast myriad of other "substitute" goods for which demand had also increased.

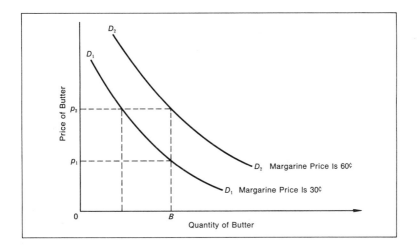

**Figure 5-4**
**Shift of Demand for Butter with Change**
**in Price of Margarine**

This shows how the demand for butter increases with higher price of margarine. Equilibrium price of butter is interdependent with price of margarine. This diagram does *not* give equilibrium price of butter or of margarine. Because prices are interdependent, price of $p_2$ for butter may not be consistent with margarine equilibrium price of 60 cents. The equilibrium pair of butter and margarine prices can be derived only with more complex, multidimensional analysis.

### Other Kinds of Demand and Supply Concepts

We can express demand in terms of either (1) the total amounts people want to *have* on hand or (2) the amounts they want to *acquire* (or dispose of) in order to adjust the stock they have to the desired level. The first concept is often called the *reservation* demand, indicating the amount, at each price, that a person wants to reserve for himself. The second indicates acquisition by *purchase* (or *sale*) to adjust the amount of the good possessed to the desired level.

Errors of analysis can result from failure to see the logical tie between the two interpretations of demand. Consider the demands-to-own for our initial four-person community (discussed on pages 85–86). And suppose the cars initially held are two by *A*, none by *B*, two by *C*, and three by *D*. The differences between the amount each person *has* and the amounts he *demands* to own at different prices (given in Table 5–1 on page 85) are the amounts *demanded* to *purchase* (or *supply for sale*) at each price. In the schedule for *D* in Table 5–1, at a price of $300 he wants three, which is what he has. At a higher price, say $500, he wants fewer and would offer to sell one (−1), while at a lower price, say $200, he wants one more and hence would demand to buy some (+1). The amounts each person would *demand to buy* (to increase his holdings) and *supply for sale* at each price (to reduce his holdings) are shown in Table 5–3.

Table 5–3
Purchase Demand and Sales Supply

|  | Individuals | | | | Aggregated | |
|---|---|---|---|---|---|---|
|  | A | B | C | D | $D_p$ | $S_p$* |
| $1,000 | 0 | 0 | −1 | −2 | 0 | 3 |
| 900 | 0 | 0 | −1 | −2 | 0 | 3 |
| 800 | 0 | 0 | −1 | −1 | 0 | 2 |
| 700 | 0 | 0 | −1 | −1 | 0 | 2 |
| 600 | 1 | 0 | −1 | −1 | 1 | 2 |
| 500 | 1 | 1 | −1 | −1 | 2 | 2 |
| 400 | 1 | 1 | 0 | −1 | 2 | 1 |
| 300 | 1 | 1 | 0 | 0 | 2 | 0 |
| 200 | 1 | 1 | 0 | 1 | 3 | 0 |
| 100 | 2 | 2 | 0 | 1 | 5 | 0 |
| Current holdings | 2 | 0 | 2 | 3 | | |

Price at which aggregated demand $D_p$ and supply $S_p$ are equal ($500) is the price that would permit all mutually advantageous exchange or re-allocation of cars. At a higher price a "surplus" of cars would exist, since some would prefer to sell cars for that higher amount than have so many cars. And at a lower price a "shortage" would exist, for those who prefer the money to cars are offering fewer cars than others are willing to buy. The "surplus" and the "shortage" indicate feasible mutually advantageous, but unexploited, exchange opportunities. (*Minus sign omitted.)

If *at each price* we add all the *positive* amounts, we obtain the *demand for purchase* by those who would like to buy more. Adding, *at each price*, negative quantities, we get the schedule of amounts offered as the *supply for sale* by those who have more than they want. These quantities in the last two columns constitute the schedule of quantities demanded for *purchase* ($D_p$) and the schedule of quantities supplied for *selling* ($S_p$). Figure 5–5 graphs these purchase-sell schedules, intersecting at $500, at a quantity of two. Two items will be sold (one each from C and D, to A and B). Then every person will have the amount demanded by him at that price.

The lines, $D_h$ and $S_h$, on the right side of the figure, depict the schedules of *demand to have* and *supply in existence*. These lines also intersect at $500.

*Both pairs of matched demand and supply curves give the same equilibrating price.* They must, because the two pairs of schedules are logically related. How? The difference between the amounts demanded for purchase and the

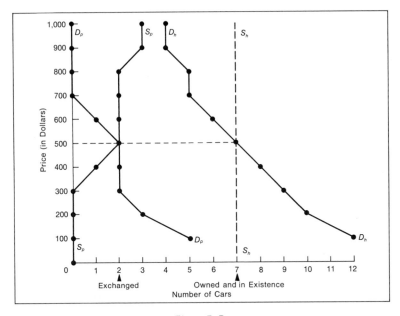

**Figure 5–5**

Demand-to-buy $(D_p)$ and supply-to-sell $(S_p)$ curves are shown with demand-to-own $(D_h)$ and supply-in-existence $(S_h)$ curves. The horizontal distance between one coordinated pair is, at a stipulated price, equal to the horizontal distance between the other coordinated pair. Either pair can be used to ascertain effects of changes in demand or supply on determination of price. Do not use demand curve from one pair with the supply of the other.

amounts offered for sale at any price (say, one unit at price $400) *is* the excess that people demand to own over the supply amount in existence. That is, $D_p - S_p = D_h - S_h$.

At the equilibrium price, people with excess amounts will sell to those with deficiencies. After the exchanges, everyone will have the quantity he wants at that price. Price will stay there until there is a subsequent shift in the state of demand or supply. If the good is durable, currently held in large stocks, and subject to resale (like cars, corporation common stocks and bonds, houses, paintings, land, buildings, etc.), the demand and supply are conveniently expressed in terms of demand to *hold* and the stock in *existence*. This is sometimes called a "stock" demand and supply approach.

If the good is neither durable nor commonly resold, but is instead usually bought once and for all by the ultimate consumer, *purchase* demand and *sales* supply concepts ("flow" concepts) are commonly used.

Summary

1    The demands of people can be aggregated into a total market demand by adding at each price the amount demanded by each person.

2    An equilibrium price in the market is one at which all possible mutually beneficial exchanges can occur. At that price, each person can have exactly the amount of each good that he would like, given his total wealth.

3    By looking at the one market price, each person is saved the trouble, cost, and time of inquiring of everyone else what their subjective, personal values are for a good; people can thereby more cheaply ascertain the exchanges they can make.

4    Suppressing access to the market or to freely negotiated prices raises the costs (and reduces the extent) of mutually preferred exchanges.

5    The amount demanded of a good depends on other prices, as well as its own prices. This makes prices interdependent.

6    The two concepts of the amount demanded—(a) to own some *total* amount (reservation demand) and (b) the *extra* amount desired to bring one's holding to the desired total amount (purchase demand)—can be paired only with the corresponding supply concepts.

Questions

**1**    The demand to own by $A$ and by $B$ for good $X$ are:

| Price | A's Demand | B's Demand | Market Demand |
|-------|------------|------------|---------------|
| 10 | 0 | 0 | ___ |
| 9 | 1 | 0 | ___ |
| 8 | 2 | 0 | ___ |
| 7 | 3 | 1 | ___ |
| 6 | 4 | 2 | ___ |
| 5 | 5 | 3 | ___ |
| 4 | 6 | 3 | ___ |
| 3 | 7 | 4 | ___ |
| 2 | 8 | 5 | ___ |
| 1 | 9 | 6 | ___ |

**a.** What is the market demand by $A$ and $B$?
**b.** If six units of $X$ are available, what allocation will there be between $A$ and $B$ if open-market exchange is used?

**c.** With six units available, if price were legally imposed at 4, would there be a shortage, a surplus, or an exchange equilibrium?
**d.** If the price were legally imposed at $9, would there be a shortage, a surplus, or exchange equilibrium?
**e.** How can there be a change from a shortage to a surplus without any change in supply or demand?

2    In problem 1 above, increase the amounts demanded by *B* uniformly by two more units at each price.
    **a.** What will be the new open-market price?
    **b.** What will be the allocation between *A* and *B*?
    **c.** If the price is held at the old level by law, will there be a surplus or a shortage?
    **d.** How can that surplus or shortage be eliminated?

3    The following is characteristic of Mr. *A*'s market demand for shoes. Each price is associated with the number of pairs of shoes he demands to own.

| Price | Quantity | Total Revenue |
|-------|----------|---------------|
| 10 | 1 | $10 |
| 9 | 2 | 18 |
| 8 | 3 | 24 |
| 7 | 4 | ___ |
| 6 | 5 | ___ |
| 5 | 6 | ___ |
| 4 | 7 | ___ |
| 3 | 8 | ___ |
| 2 | 9 | ___ |
| 1 | 10 | ___ |

    **a.** Compare the total revenue.
    **b.** At a price of $6 Mr. *A* would own five. At a price of $5 he would own six. At each of these two prices, he would have a total of $30 in shoes. Does this mean that he attaches no value to a sixth one? What value does he attach to a sixth one?

4    Using the demand-schedule data for Mr. *A* in problem 1, suppose that these refer to shares of common stock in a corporation and that he now owns four units of *X*.
    **a.** How many units of *X* would he buy or sell at each possible price?
    **b.** If the exchange-equilibrium price in the market turned out to be $3, how many would he want to buy or sell and how many would he then own?

5    "In analyzing the allocation of stocks of goods, such as houses, we can refer to demand for a finite amount of houses or to the demand to have *more* (or fewer) houses. The latter gives a flow of houses through the exchange market—sales or purchases—while the former does not. But neither of these has to be expressed in rates; both can be expressed as finite stocks or quantities." True or false?

6    Consumption is a rate concept, even though the good being consumed may be held as a stock or finite amount of goods. True or false?

7    For goods like shoes, a rise in price will reduce the number of pairs of shoes a person will want. Since the price at which he can sell used shoes is low relative to the new-shoe price, he will not sell some shoes in order to reduce his stock of shoes. How does he adjust his stock of shoes to the new, lasting, higher cost of shoes? (Hint: How does a person adjust his stock of clothes to his new demand after experiencing a reduction in demand consequent to a reduction of his income?)

8    There are *three measures* of the amount demanded: (1) The *rate* of consumption or purchase; (2) the quantity a person wants to buy in order to increase his current stock; (3) the quantity of the good held or used at one time. As an example of each: (1) a person may consume eggs at the rate of 6/7 per day (which does not necessarily mean he eats a fraction of an egg each day); (2) and on Saturday he buys a half-dozen eggs; (3) he may have an average of three eggs in his refrigerator. Normally, explicit distinctions between rates of purchase and rates of consumption are not necessary since they are so highly related. We can use whichever demand is convenient; for example, if one is analyzing a particular day's sales in the markets, the third is the relevant one to use. In each discussion the context will indicate whether it is the stock on hand, the rate of consumption, or a particular day's purchase that is the "quantity demanded." Which of these three measures must be expressed as a rate of activity and which as a "stock"?

9    The demands for tires and gasoline are interrelated, somewhat in the sense that butter and margarine were related.
a. Make a demand-and-supply graph to show the effects of a reduced supply of gasoline on the prices and quantities of tires and gasoline. (Hint: use two demand curves for tires: the demand before and after a gasoline-price increase.)
b. In what sense can one say butter and margarine are substitutes whereas tires and gasoline are "complements"? (Hint: see footnote on page 93.)

10    "With open-market pricing, housing units are scarce or expensive, whereas with rent control the housing market is characterized by shortages." Explain.

11    "If half the forests of the United States were destroyed, and if thereupon the price of lumber more than doubled, the value of the remaining forests would have increased. This shows how irrational economic value is: a smaller real stock of goods has a higher economic value than a larger stock! Something must be wrong with the measure of value." What is wrong?

12    If in Table 5–3, the first four columns (or the last two, with $S_p$ treated as negative amounts) are added, we get a schedule called the "*excess demand*" schedule. Compute the schedule. At what price is excess demand equal to zero? At what is it positive? Negative?

13    "The community's demand to own houses may remain unchanged; yet the demand to *purchase* houses may increase (or decrease) enormously." Explain why this is true. Give a numerical example of the demand to hold houses (in a two-person community) that stays constant, while the demand to purchase houses increases.

# 6

Applications of Demand Analysis to Market Pricing and Allocation

Having learned the laws of market demand and exchange, we now apply them to some real situations to see how open markets and prices ration existing supply by discriminating among claimants.

Demand-and-supply analysis can be applied to rentals as well as to purchases of goods. A person renting a house will feel the effect of increased demand by other people for more housing space when the price (rent) rises. At the higher price he will tend to rent a smaller house or one of poorer quality, which is to say that he has been induced to release some housing to those whose demands have increased. Since the renter does not own the house, he will not capture the gain in wealth from the higher value of the house.

This can be analyzed graphically. We shall use the "demand-to-have" curve plotted against the total stock in existence, because we want to compare holdings of housing space before and after the demand change. In Figure 6–1, curve $D_a + D_b$ represents the community's total demand for housing space *before* the increase in demand. $D_a$ represents the demand for space by those whose demand is unchanged, and $D_b$ is the initial demand by those whose demand later increases. Initially, rental price was $p_1$, and the space was rented, with $OX_a$ held by group $A$ and $OX_b$ by group $B$. After group $B$'s increase in demand, their demand curve is shown by $D'_b$. The total demand, formed by summing the demands $D_a$ and $D'_b$, is now $D_a + D'_b$. This demand intersects the existing housing supply at price $p_2$, greater than $p_1$.

If rents do not rise from $p_1$ to $p_2$, the amount of housing space demanded will exceed the amount available, shown by the distance between the supply line and new demand curve at all prices less than $p_2$. This excess demand is commonly called a shortage; rarely is it called excess demand. At prices below $p_2$ there simply is not enough to satisfy amounts of housing demanded or, as it is misleadingly called, "housing needs." With open-market bidding for the available housing, the price will be pushed up, toward $p_2$, as frustrated demanders make higher offers to get more housing. The market for housing will be called "tight" or "strong" or a "seller's" market. Vacancy rates that normally exist to facilitate the flow of movers, just as stores maintain inventories, will diminish.

When rents rise from $p_1$ to $p_2$, as group $B$ seeks more housing by trying to outbid other people, what happens to the housing allocation? Group $B$ obtains the larger amount $OX'_b$ instead of only $OX_b$. Members of group $A$ end up with $OX'_a$. The decrease, $X_a - X'_a$, to those whose demand did not increase is the increase to group $B$. (At the present stage of analysis, we are leaving the effect on production or supply for later; however, any increase in housing production as a result of a price increase would offset part of the decrease imposed on group $A$ and also reduce the price rise.)

As the price rises in response to the increased demand (represented by the shift to the right of the market-demand curve), claimants for housing space will reduce the amount demanded—the higher price moves them, figuratively, back up along their demand schedules to smaller amounts demanded. Their demands have not decreased. It is the increase in demand, the shift in the demand schedule, that produces a shortage *at the old price*. But when price rises, people are induced to reduce the amount demanded; they are pushed back *up along* their current demand curves.

House owners get more rent; their houses are worth more. The members of the *A* group, whose demand did not increase, pay higher prices and use less housing space. The members of group *B* present a more complex result. Those whose demands increased most get more space than they were getting at the lower price. Other members of group *B*, those whose demands increased by only a very little, may end up paying higher rents and getting very little more or even less space than originally. To the *A*'s and the *B*'s, the source of their trouble seems to be the higher rent for housing, so they blame the owners for raising rents. But what enabled the owners to get higher prices? The *increased demand* by tenants in group *B* pushed up the rent. Had their demand not increased and had they not offered to pay more, the owners would not have raised rents. The owners simply echoed the higher bids by the *B* people. The owners, in effect, told the *A* people to meet the competition of the *B*'s. Maybe the *B*'s and *A*'s are friends and neighbors who complain to each other about the higher "exorbitant" rentals that the landlords are charging—never thinking to blame their own competition for the higher price.

Objections to the higher prices are objections to the competitive superiority of other people in providing offers that are more favorable to the owners than formerly. If anyone wants to gain from the possibility of trade, he must be prepared to face the fact that the *terms* of trade and the realizable *gains* from trade will vary from day to day. To put it differently, trade can, under commonly found circumstances, enable each party to move to a situation preferred to *no* trade at all; but the gains from *today's* available trade may be larger or smaller than the gains from *yesterday's* trade. Economics does *not* say that with *every* change in demand *everyone* moves from one exchange equilibrium to still more preferred positions. It implies only that, with fully exploitable trade opportunities, any person can reach the most preferred of all the *possible* patterns, given other people's rights to compete in the same way.

### The Cost-Price Illusion

The avenue from increased demand to higher exchange-equilibrium prices often is concealed by *inventories* in the distribution chain from producer to consumer. As a result, many prices appear to be set by costs of production instead of competition among consumers. The cause of this widespread illusion is illustrated in the following example of an increased demand for meat. In following the analysis, you will find it convenient to use again Figure 6–1, replacing "housing" with "meat."

To start, for some reason people's desire for meat increases. Housewives express their increased desire for meat by increasing their market demand. Market demands reflect what people do in the marketplace, not simply something they dream about doing at some later time. Housewives reveal an increased demand by buying in the meat markets more than formerly. Retail butchers have inventories adequate for a day or two at usual rates of sale. As sales increase, the inventory is depleted more rapidly than expected. No single butcher knows that the demand has risen for the community as a whole. No single butcher knows that he could raise his price and still make no fewer sales than earlier. All he knows is that *he* has sold more meat at the existing price. But the increased demand takes its toll of inventories. Whether or not a butcher believes that the increased rate of sale is a temporary fluctuation, he will buy more meat than usual the next day in order to restore his inventory from its abnormally low level; and he will buy even more than that if he believes the increase in sales will persist. If the demand for meat does increase so that one butcher's increase is not merely some other butcher's loss, the purchases by the aggregate of butchers from the packers will increase.

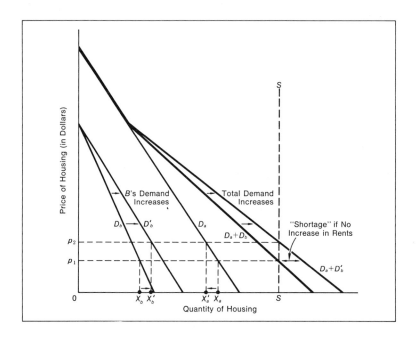

Figure 6–1

Price and amount of housing. Change in price of housing enables re-allocation of housing space among competing demanders, *A* and *B*.

Just as butchers use inventories, so their meat suppliers—packers—also rely on inventories as a buffer to their sales fluctuations. We assume that the first day's change in demand was within that inventory limit and therefore was met without a price increase.

Packers restore inventories by instructing their cattle buyers (who travel among the cattle raisers and fatteners and to the stockyards where cattlemen ship the steers for sale) to buy more cattle than usual. But with all the packers restoring their inventories in this manner, the cattle available for sale each day are inadequate to meet the increased amount demanded *at the old price*. There are not sufficient cattle in existence to take care of this increased demand. Either some buyers for packers must report that they cannot get the amount requested, or they must boost their offer prices in order to persuade cattlemen to sell the steers to them rather than to some other packers.

Rather than go without any increase in stocks, some buyers raise their price offers. This rise in offer prices may occur nearly simultaneously among the buyers, as if there were collusion among the cattlemen or buyers. The cattlemen simply let the buyers bid against each other until the price rises to a point where the packers will not want to buy more meat at the new high price than they did at the old lower price; that is, the packers are induced by the higher price not to buy more than is available from the cattlemen.

In terms of our demand-and-supply apparatus, the supply curve of cattle is vertical. An increased demand by packers for cattle (a demand *derived* from ultimate consumer demand for meat) implies an intersection at a higher price but at the same quantity. Each packer is therefore forced to move back up his new increased demand curve to a higher price, at which point he buys less than he had planned at the old price. The total amount purchased is no greater than before, but the price of cattle is higher. At this high price, the amount wanted on the new demand curve equals the constant amount supplied. Each packer must pay a higher price for cattle in order to avoid getting less than before. Competition among the packers has raised the price of cattle during the immediate period when cattle production cannot be increased.

Cattle raisers bask in the glow of higher receipts. But the packers, faced with higher prices, experience *a rise in costs*. Why did their cost rise? The costs of raising cattle did not increase. Nor did the costs of getting cattle to market, nor of slaughtering, nor of distributing meat. The price paid by wholesaler-slaughterers to cattlemen rose in response fundamentally to the increased demand by consumers—the housewives. Their demand, from retail meat stores through slaughterers, was first met by depleting inventories. But the cattlemen did not have inventories that they could deplete and then restore quickly. Therefore, they simply let the buyers bid for the available amount (rather than allocating the cattle among slaughterers on some other principle).

Whether or not anyone is aware of the law of demand and supply, which says that a *higher demand will permit higher prices*, and whether or not they are aware that demand has increased, the higher price of cattle (higher *costs* to the packers) will mean that the packers must charge a higher price to butchers *if* they are to continue as profitable meat packers. And they will be *able* to charge a higher price in response to higher costs without any loss in sales because demand had increased first. In sum, a higher price occurs because the demand for meat has increased. The retail butchers, in turn, post higher prices to the housewives. When housewives complain about the higher price, the butcher in all innocence, honesty, and correctness says that it isn't his fault. The cost of meat has gone up. Cost, to him, is the cost of getting meat. The butcher can say, "I never raise prices until my costs go up." And the packers can honestly say the same thing. And if the housewife wants to know who is to blame for the higher costs and hence higher prices of meat, she can look in the mirror behind the butcher's counter and see her face and those of all her neighbors. She might then turn to each of them and say, "If you didn't want more meat, I could have more." But that observation and tactless behavior is neither useful nor fostered by the competitive exchange system. The exchange system tends to conceal this facet of competition and makes it appear as if the higher price of meat were caused by butchers' or packers' or farmers' greedy behavior—not that of ourselves or our neighbors.

The consumers' increased demand for meat, then, brought about a rise in the price of meat to consumers. This rise *appeared* to be the result of a rise in costs because the first price effect of the increased demand occurred at the cattle raisers' end of the line. The demand increase pulled up the price in the first stages of the production and distribution channels. The first rise in price could have occurred in the butcher shops and then have been transmitted back step by step to the farmers. But butchers' inventories are usually adequate to cushion the changes in demand temporarily until the impact of increased sales goes all the way through the productive processes. This explains the common illusion that increases in costs are responsible for higher prices.

### Prices of Common Stock

Some 500,000,000 shares of American Telephone and Telegraph stock are owned by 2,500,000 people. Yet on any typical day only about 500,000 shares (1/10 of 1 percent of the total owned) are bought and sold by 1,000 people (less than 1/20 of 1 percent of the owners). From these figures, it is sometimes concluded that the remaining shares and their owners do not affect the price. It is said, "Clearly, this is a case of the tail wagging the dog and illustrates the power of active stock traders." Or, in another context, it is said, "Used-car prices are determined by the few people who daily buy cars from the even fewer used-car dealers. The rest of the people don't affect the value of used cars unless they enter into the market to buy or sell their cars."

To check the logic of these allegations, we apply demand-and-supply analysis. In doing so, we must keep the ownership and exchange schedules properly paired.

Shares of this stock are exchanged daily because people's personal situations are changing. While some decide to sell their A.T.&T. stock at its current price, in order to buy something else, others are saving or have just received an increase in wealth or wish to hold more of their wealth in the form of ownership in A.T.&T. Because of these varied events, *individual* demands to own shares change every day. The situation is shown in Figure 6–2 with *two* pairs of demand-and-supply lines. One pair is $D_pD_p$ and $S_pS_p$. These curves apply, say, to each morning. Curve $D_pD_p$ is the demand to *purchase more* shares by those who want more shares than they now have. The $S_pS_p$ curve is the schedule of offers to *sell* by those who have more shares than they would want to hold at alternative prices. Where the $D_pD_p$ curve touches the price axis no one would want to buy any more than he now has. Similarly, at a low enough price, no one would want to *sell* any shares.

On the other hand, $D_hD_h$ is the total demand to own, indicating for each possible price how many shares people want to *own* (not just buy more); and the $S_hS_h$ curve indicates the constant supply in *existence*.[1] At any price above the intersection of $D_hD_h$ and $S_hS_h$, the horizontal distance between them is the amount by which the *supply available* exceeds the amount people want to *hold*; and this amount is the *same* as the excess of the amount people want to *sell* over the amount other people want to *buy*. The distance between the $D_pD_p$ and $S_pS_p$ curves at each price must, by definition of the concepts, equal exactly the distance between the $D_hD_h$ and $S_hS_h$ curves.

During the day, as exchanges are completed and people adjust their holdings to amounts desired, the $D_pD_p$ and the $S_pS_p$ curves will jointly shift to the left, since one person's purchase is someone else's sale. The $D_pD_p$ and $S_pS_p$ curves will shift together to the left with each exchange, until all desired exchanges have occurred. Then, at that moment, the $D_pD_p$ and the $S_pS_p$ curves will intersect at $70 and on the left-hand vertical scale at zero further exchanges. None of the exchange transactions affects the position of the $D_hD_h$ and $S_hS_h$ curves.

Overnight, people's circumstances again change, so that the $D_pD_p$ and $S_pS_p$ curves will again have shifted to the right, and some now want to buy shares and others want to sell. If the demand to buy additional shares has increased more than the willingness to sell, the $D_pD_p$ curve will have moved farther to the right than the $S_pS_p$ curve so that the next morning's $D_pD_p$ and $S_pS_p$ curves will intersect at a higher price. (But so also will the new $D_hD_h$ and $S_hS_h$ curves intersect at that higher price, since the curve $D_hD_h$ must move if the curve $D_pD_p$ shifts to the right *more* than does the $S_pS_p$ curve.) Only if the shifts in the purchase demand and supply are exactly offsetting will there be no shift in the $D_hD_h$ curve and no change in the price—even though many exchanges occur.

The question now can be answered: "If only a few thousand shares are being sold, does this mean that the price is set by these few thousand shares and that the other millions have no effect? Does the tail wag the dog?" No. Given the aggregate supply, $S_hS_h$, the price will rise only if the demand to *hold* shares, $D_hD_h$, increases; and if $D_hD_h$ increases, the demand to *purchase more*

---

[1] Review the explanation of the two demand and supply functions on pages 96–98.

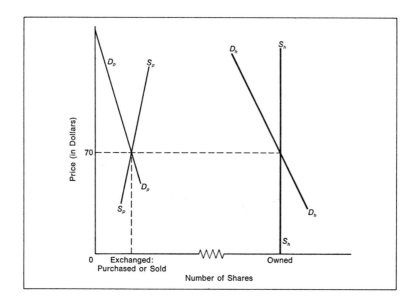

Figure 6-2

Effect of price on A.T.&T. via demand and supply schedules. The same price simultaneously equilibrates (1) the demand and supply to purchase and (2) the demand and supply to own common stock in American Telephone and Telegraph.

shares, $D_pD_p$, increases more than does the desire of other people to hold *fewer* shares (i.e., to sell some shares, shown by a *shift* to the right of the curve $S_pS_p$). And the price will fall if the opposite is true. Not all 500,000,000 shares in existence will be exchanged each day or even each decade. It suffices, insofar as the effect on price is concerned, that the owners want to continue to own their shares at the existing prices. Because shares are not offered for sale at prices of $70 or less, these millions of shares contribute toward keeping the price where it is. That is why the price doesn't go lower than $70. And price isn't higher because more shares would be offered by current owners than could be sold at a higher price.

This explains also why the price of stock can make a tremendous jump or drop with just one share being sold. If the current owners' individual demands to own should increase greatly, the price would have to rise a lot to get any of them to sell even one share.

We can summarize: The *price* will change if there is a disparity between the total "demand to own" of all people and the supply of the whole community at that price. *Sales* (purchases) occur whenever the demand of *any* individual to hold stock changes relative to the demand of any other individual. Exchanges will occur without a change in price only if the *total* demand to *own* does not change. And if *every* individual's demand increases proportionally, there can be a rise in price even though no shares are exchanged.

Pricing and Discrimination

These examples show how the pricing and open-market exchange process allocates the existing supply of a good among the competing claimants. It is an analysis of discrimination among competing claimants, in which some obtain more favorable treatment—get more goods—while others get less. The discrimination, or competitive, criterion is heavily weighted by the amount of money (that is, claims to other goods) offered in exchange for the particular good at issue. The pricing process is a distributive, discriminatory process. So is *every* allocative system. Our interest in pricing is not in whether prices are high or low, but instead in how they influence who gets what.

The analysis does not say that this system of competition or discrimination among claimants is good or bad. People bid for some goods by offering other goods in exchange (via the intermediary of money). Sometimes it is said that under this system the goods go where there are the "most votes" or dollars. It seems misleading to say that the private-property exchange (price) system puts goods where the *most* dollar votes are. Rather, it puts *more* goods where there are *more* dollar votes and less where there are fewer and none where there are none. It is not an all-or-none allocation in which the winner takes all while the loser gets nothing. It is more akin to proportional representation than to majority rule. The exchange system puts some goods *wherever* there are some dollar votes *per unit* of the good, rather than only where the *most* votes are. A poorer person can match the per unit *price* of a rich bidder, if he wishes, by bidding for a proportionally smaller amount: thereby he will get *some* of the goods. For example, no one has to be rich to have some services of a big expensive jet plane.

Sometimes it is said that the system permits rich people to feed dogs while poor children have too little milk. Two questions here easily get tangled. Does only this system *create* rich people? No. Then is this system unusual in that it *enables* rich people—however they got rich—to buy food for their dogs rather than provide milk to poor neighbors? If so, the system is permitting people to do what they want with their wealth. One might then object either to people's being rich or to being allowed to feed dogs while children still want milk. You may seek either a different distribution of wealth or a different pattern of tastes in utilizing wealth. But do not think it certain to find a feasible system or mechanism which will result in a wealth distribution *and* a taste pattern which conform to your ideas of a better world.

We are not saying that the price-exchange system for allocating goods is desirable or undesirable—only that we should not misinterpret its operation. This discussion, of course, suggests the desirability of investigating what determines how much wealth each person has, and we shall do that later. For the present, we are taking the distribution of wealth as simply given—but not ordained as "naturally proper."

Price Controls as a Restriction on Market Exchange

Because we never miss the water until the well runs dry, we can better understand how a free-market pricing system allocates goods if we try to get along without it for a while. Our analysis of the market pricing system suggests that everyone can buy all he chooses of any good, given his wealth, and can sell all he chooses at the going market price. According to our preceding analysis, there should not be queues or waiting lines or shortages. But at the going, current market prices, you may find there *is* a long waiting list for some goods. In other situations, sellers find that at the market price, there are *no* buyers. What has gone wrong with our analysis? (Do not ask, "What has gone wrong with the world?") One answer is that we failed to recognize legal or customary restrictions on permissible market prices. We assumed, not entirely correctly, that potential buyers and sellers could negotiate exchanges with each other at whatever prices they chose. If, as is sometimes the case, prices are restricted or controlled, we must modify our analysis. However, our laws of demand are not changed. We must not use them solely for open markets, which are markets in which everyone is allowed to buy and sell whatever they wish at mutually agreeable prices. In many parts of the world—and for many goods, the negotiable terms of trade are restricted by law or social custom enforced by ostracism. In New York, maximum rents you can pay for old apartments are set by law; in New York City, there is no price for a unit of water—there is just a flat fee for the right to use as much water as you can get out of your tap; in most cities taxi rates are set by law, and taxis cannot legally collect higher fares during rain or snow or rush hours. All these cases are characterized by "shortages," queues, or waiting lists.

To analyze what happens when price controls restrict exchange negotiations, suppose that demand for, say, housing space, increases and that rents or house prices are not allowed to rise.[2] The total amount demanded exceeds the supply available at the old, continuing, legal-limit price. People cannot get as much as they want at the controlled price.[3] A shortage, or, what is the same thing, an "excessive demand" develops.

This situation can be analyzed with the demand and supply graphs of Figure 6–3, a diagram basically the same as Figure 6–1. The demand lines of $A$ and $B$ are shown as they were before a demand increase by $B$ and also as they are after his increase in demand. At the old price, $p_1$, the total amount demanded is now in excess of amount supplied, $S$. As long as the price is held at $p_1$, $B$ will want more housing space than he initially had (or still continues

[2] In a later chapter, we shall investigate the effects of legally imposed *minimum* prices.
[3] Although the legal maximum price of housing is deemed "fair," some demands are not met at that price. Any person caught in that situation could ask, "What is the meaning of a price at which I *can't* buy?"

to rent). He complains of a shortage since he can't get as much housing space as he "demands" (or as he is likely to say, "as much as he needs"). If the price were kept by some law at not over $p_1$, the "shortage" would continue and along with it would occur two other effects: a wealth transfer and an increase in nonprice competitive discrimination.

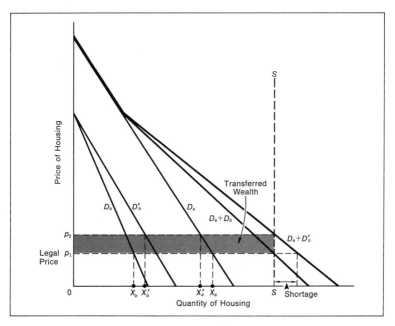

Figure 6–3

Effect of rent control. Shortages are created by rent controls, resulting in trans-feral of wealth.

### Wealth Transfer

The wealth transfer is easy to discern. Suppose a tenant were allowed to sublease to others at uncontrolled prices, while the rent paid to the landlord was restricted to $p_1$. With his new demand, $B$ values another unit of housing space higher than $p_1$. It would clearly pay him to rent more $(X_a - X_a')$ space from $A$ and pay a price of $p_2$ per unit of space to get that space, all of which will go to $B$ and appear as $X_b' - X_b$. $A$ prefers this because he would rather have the extra money income than the space, and $B$ prefers the extra space to the money. The greater market value of housing would all be retained by the tenants. The part of the value kept by $B$ would be $(p_2 - p_1)X_b'$, and the part to $A$ would be $(p_2 - p_1)X_a'$.

This wealth transfer occurs whether or not subleasing side-deals like those contemplated in the preceding paragraph are permitted. If permitted, they enable a re-allocation of housing space to help both $B$ and $A$ reach mutually preferred positions, but with no gain to the housing owner. If not permitted, the housing space is not re-allocated so effectively, but the higher value is still retained by the tenants.

In this subleasing case, the increased wealth that would belong to the owners is taken from the owners by the legal rent limit, and the original tenants get that wealth from the owners. Hardly anyone has proposed that under rent controls tenants really be allowed to sublease at market-clearing prices—despite the gains that would accrue to tenants. Is it because this would make the whole element of wealth redistribution too transparent to be acceptable politically? Or is it that subleasing is in some other respect "bad"?

The issue comes down to whether the apartment-house owners "deserve" the right to the value of their housing space or whether that wealth should, with rent controls, be transferred to the renters under the doctrine that wealth should be taken from the rich (apartment-house owners) and given to the poor (tenants). Under rent controls, without subleasing at market prices, the same amount of wealth is being taken from the house owners. Since there is no open-market exchange-equilibrium value being openly expressed, wealth is transferred to the tenants, but not so obviously and not so efficiently.

We say "not so efficiently" because when tenants cannot sublease at higher rents, they gain only insofar as they have the greater wealth *in the form of housing space*. It is a gift, given on the condition they use it for their personal living space instead of being allowed to exchange it for other, more preferred goods. Even if landlords were on the average richer than tenants, wealth would be transferred from *landlords* to *tenants* and not generally from rich to poor. In any event, the ethics of such a purposeful wealth transfer lies beyond the scope of economics, which can indicate only the circumstances under which the wealth transfer occurs and some of its effects.

### Nonmoney Competition

Suppression of open-market pricing and exchange means that (1) more of the good is wanted than is available at the suppressed, controlled price; (2) the extent of re-allocation is reduced; and (3) other criteria will be used for discriminating among claimants for the available good. As the authors discovered during World War II, when meat prices were controlled at below market-clearing prices, their wives' extraordinary beauty suddenly began to count more heavily in the butcher's eyes when he decided to which customers to give the amount of meat demanded and which to disappoint. The butchers favored our wives, while old, homely women were told there was no meat or only a little. Similarly, with controlled housing rentals, our beautiful wives were the ones we sent to apply for an apartment that was going to be vacant. As long as the landlord couldn't get a higher price as an inducement from the homely people, why should he ignore the virtues of delightful tenants? While rentals and meat prices were uncontrolled the money offers from the "less desirable" types made it more costly for the butchers and landlords to exercise their preferences for beautiful women as customers and tenants. When not allowed to offer higher prices, handicapped people, rich or poor, are less able to induce others to overlook their "undesirable" features. One can more probably overcome a handicap when he is free to use *all* his competitive powers, including price competition, for exchange opportunities.

A difference between personal-characteristic competition and wealth-bidding competition is that a dollar of resources bid for one good necessarily means the bidder then has a dollar less for other goods. The amount of his biddable claims is some fixed total at any moment—given by the monetary value of his wealth. But the competition of "personal-characteristic wealth" does not necessarily involve this degree of exclusivity among one's bids for various goods. More "beauty" as an advantage to get more meat does not mean that that much less beauty is available for vegetables. One can get more of "this" without having to take less of "that." Competition by personal characteristics has elements of an all-or-nothing system, whereas competition by money-exchange inducements is a sharing or pro rata division.

Since scarcity, competition, and discrimination are inseparable, the basic economic question "For whom?" is merely a polite way of asking, "What will be the criteria for discriminating among the competing claimants?" With open-market prices to restrict the amount demanded to the amount available, less (not necessarily *no*) weight will be given to nonmonetary characteristics of the competing customers. In either event, poorer people will get less. But whatever your pecuniary wealth, you will get still less if you are poorer in the nonmonetary desirable characteristics—for example, if you are a foreigner or a homely person. Price controls will reduce the ability to counteract these "undesirable" personal attributes by greater competition in pecuniary price offers—whatever your pecuniary wealth. Your nonmonetary, personal, disadvantageous traits are more important in determining what you get, because of your reduced ability to induce the seller to offer you more goods in return for the higher price. Of course, if you are beautiful but poor, you may prefer price controls for some goods, for then the homely rich will find they are restricted in their legal ability to offset homeliness with higher monetary offers.

This point should be kept in mind by "unpopular" people who believe that holding prices below the free-market, demand-and-supply-equating price will necessarily help them in comparison with people who are richer in money. These "unpopular" people forget that the *other* forms of competitive power are then more relevant in choosing among customers. The disadvantageous personal characteristics, which they could more effectively make up for by a willingness to pay a higher money price, are no longer so effectively overcome.

The connection between rent controls and manifestation of greater discrimination by personal characteristics is exemplified in New York City, almost the only American city still imposing rent controls. Perhaps no city is so beset with complaints of shortages and of racial discrimination in rent-controlled apartments and publicly subsidized housing—all involving rentals at less than exchange-equilibrium rates.

It is not clear which competitive systems give greater *equality* of distribution of all goods. If people's economic wealth were more disparate than their personal characteristics, it would not follow that the disparity of their share of goods would increase—because money bids help to offset the all-or-nothing feature of personal characteristics. The actual comparative outcome depends upon the degree to which people with inferior personal characteristics are also relatively inferior in other competitive characteristics, and upon their diversity of preference patterns and the society's attitudes toward personal characteristics. Little is known about this complex of factors. All we can conclude is that if you want to give more importance to race, creed, religion, and other personal characteristics in allocating goods, you should seek to reduce the effectiveness of the money offer in the market.

### Rationing

A perceptive student might ask, "Why not avoid nonmonetary personal discrimination by *rationing* the available stock—either giving equal portions to everyone or allocating to each the same amount he got before?" Either procedure will eliminate discrimination, nonmonetary and personal. But each recipient will still be seeking to obtain a more preferred *recombination* of goods by a further exchange re-allocation with other people, exactly as were the Cuban and Hungarian in our refugee camp. Rationing schemes restrict the realization of these more preferred combinations arrived at by exchanging the rationed goods: take your allotted share and no swapping.

### Popularity of Price Controls

Students persistently conjecture that the exchange restrictions should make price controls unpopular. The popularity of price controls, or of any other devices that keep prices below the exchange-equilibrium level, can be attributed to several factors. First, as we have seen, wealth is transferred from the owners of the price-controlled resource to the users (renters or buyers). Those who expect to receive sufficient amounts of the good at that price will be inclined to want price controls. However, price controls bring about *inefficient* transfers of wealth. Always, those who get the wealth taken from the owners of price-controlled goods could in fact have been as well off with a cash gain in wealth which is less than the loss of wealth imposed on the owners (as we shall see in detail in Chapter 8). Nevertheless, one feature of price controls probably contributes to their viability: they permit transfers that are not readily apparent to all people, under the rationale of keeping prices "reasonable"—and who can object to "reasonable" prices? Furthermore, price controls are imposed by a political process; if the tenants far outnumber the owners, rent controls are even more likely. And in New York City, where tenants enormously outnumber owners, rent controls have continued since 1941 (and in Paris since 1914).

Price controls occur for a second reason. Some people think others should be restricted in their choice of consumption patterns. If I wanted people to eat a specific amount of a certain kind of food or hear a certain amount of highbrow music, I would seek to keep the prices so low that everyone would want at least as much of that food or music as I thought proper. When the shortage developed, I would ration these goods. And then to keep people from re-exchanging rights to those goods among themselves, as they would if allowed to compare their different subjective values via open-market price offers, I would prohibit any sales or offers at prices other than those low prices at which the initial allocation was made. People would then have much less incentive to trade these goods among themselves and alter their consumption patterns. Private property—which implies the right to buy and sell at any mutually agreeable prices—makes it harder for third parties to restrict the consumption patterns of people who have private-property rights in goods. People who want to be paternalistic, dictatorial life-arrangers, and who want to impose their preferences on other people, will find that price controls or restrictions on trade will make their task less difficult.

Third, price controls are popular because they are an alleged antidote for inflation. However, the price controls will merely suppress trade, not the general increase in demand.[4]

Another reason sometimes given for *rationing* applies in special circumstances of disasters accompanied by a *temporary* loss of production or goods. If people somehow could be kept alive, ultimately they would be able to produce enough to maintain a viable economy. "But," it may be countered, "if these people will be productive in the future, they can borrow against future earnings to survive in the interim. Or they can find charity, relatives, or employers who will tide them over." In times of catastrophe, the legal structure is not likely to be so well organized and reliable, nor is the loan market likely to be as efficient as it normally is. Loans therefore will be hard or impossible to negotiate because of defects in the enforcement of contracts. And so rationing and price controls are proposed. Rationing, yes, but why price controls? Isn't rationing sufficient, for people could then exchange the rationed goods to reach higher utility levels? That would be more efficient than restricting each person to the rationed amount. Why then add price controls? Probably because high prices would make the suppliers of rationed goods and everyone else more keenly and fully aware of the wealth potentially available to them. When the prices of "food" are held down, suppliers do not appear to lose wealth; hence, the transfer of wealth is easier on the public's conscience. In effect, the survival of some people is being financed

[4] Resist mightily the temptation to reason erroneously as follows: "Increased demand is only *a* factor. Demand could remain at a constant level for two years, while labor unions in the steel industry successfully struck for higher wages. It is realistic to assume that other unions in other industries also would be spurred to successful efforts to get higher wages. So a number of industries are forced to grant wage increases, which when translated into higher costs and consumer prices means that in time there has been a general rise in prices. All this time demand has remained static, so that price controls help to restrain higher prices in other parts of the economy, thus restraining the inflationary spiral of costs." If this line of reasoning seems plausible to you, you can gain from a study of economics!

(which is a technical way to say that the resources are being provided) by producers of the rationed goods. Alternatively, to get food at free-market prices, the government might have taxed everyone and redistributed some of that wealth to the poorest. This is not done for at least two reasons: it is too obvious a redistribution of wealth, and it requires more time to initiate and bring to pass than do price controls and rationing. Whatever the facts, remember that this fourth reason is a reason essentially for rationing and applies only to those *particular* goods for which it is believed an open-market distribution would lead to starvation of some people who would subsequently become *productive* and who temporarily cannot obtain *loans*. As soon as any of these circumstances ends, this particular argument for rationing ends.[5]

From the preceding, we discern three results of effective restrictions on open-market pricing:

1. The distribution of goods and services depends more upon other utility-increasing (nonmoney), personal-characteristic preferences of the people whose supplies are being exchanged at less than the free-market exchange-equilibrium price.
2. The realized extent of mutually advantageous exchange is reduced.
3. Wealth is transferred from the owners of goods to those who get the goods.

### Economic Rent

A misconception often arises in situations in which the supply of a good is *not augmentable*. It is complained that an increased demand and higher price lead only to unjust enrichment of current owners without increased production. Therefore, it is argued, higher prices should be prevented, for they serve no useful function. Holding in abeyance the question of the "unjustness" of the enrichment of current owners of the good, it is not true that higher prices serve no function. As we have seen, bidding up prices in response to an increased demand serves as a discriminating device to allocate the existing stock among the competing claimants. The higher price, like it or not, does serve the function of deciding who will get how much. If the price were not allowed to rise, some other technique would have to serve this function.

To avoid confusion between these two functions of market pricing—the *allocation* of the existing supply and the control of *production* of goods—the concept of economic rent has been developed. Although "rent" connotes a payment for housing space, the term here has a different meaning. "Economic rent" of a good is the portion of the price that does not influence the

---

[5] This is not a complete analysis of price controls. *Production* effects have been ignored in order to concentrate the analysis on interpersonal allocation and exchange of existing goods.

amount of that good in existence. In our earlier automobile example, the number of cars was fixed and unchanging, regardless of price. Consequently, the entire price received for, or value of, each car would be "economic rent." There is a persuasive reason for calling this an economic rent rather than a "surplus." It is not a surplus because it is necessary for allocating the good to the highest-valued competing uses. Any lower valuation would fail to clear the market supply among all those who want some at its current price. Economists have long realized that prices, although not always affecting the amount in existence, did affect the *particular use* to which a good was allocated. From the point of view of the current *existence* of the good, the payment may be regarded as an ineffective surplus; but for another purpose— that of allocating among uses—it is effective. Hence, it is called a rent, rather than a surplus.

Economic rent serves a rationing function. From the point of view of any individual user, the payment made in order to get that resource is a cost. The willingness to pay at least that price to get some of the good is his competitive way of (1) asserting that the use he will make of the good yields greater value than other uses and (2) getting that good assigned to him for his use. The classic example of this kind of rent is the value of a piece of land. The value of the land (or the rent paid for it) is far in excess of the amount necessary to keep that land in *existence* or even to get it produced. Yet for the important decision of determining the *use* of that land, the rent value is crucial. Any renter or subsequent purchaser must pay that rent to bid the land away from other competing claimants.

### Quasi-Rent

Although "rent" does not affect the *present* amount in existence, it may affect the *future* amount. A tough-minded logician could push us into a corner by asking, "Even for those goods that are produced every day, the currently available supply *is now* in existence no matter what its current price may be. Even at a zero price, the existing stock of goods would still be in existence. Therefore, does it not follow that any payment for any existing good is an economic rent?" The answer is "Yes, but only momentarily."

But the existing price has an effect on future supplies, because expectations of future prices are not independent of current prices. Furthermore, very few goods are indestructible. To emphasize the impact on the *production* of goods, economics has developed the concept "quasi-rent." A quasi-rent is a payment that has no effect on the amount of the good in *existence now*, but which does affect the *current rate of production* and hence the amount that will exist in the *future*. Payments for goods that will wear out are quasi-rents, for the current rate of production and the current rate of maintenance will depend upon current price.

Some goods that people think indestructible are really not. Land, for example, is surprisingly perishable. What is land? Its attributes include level-ness, and absence of rocks, trees, and bushes if it is to be used for agricultural purposes. But any farmer can tell you that all these are extremely perishable; he labors to preserve his land against erosion, loss of fertility, and growth of unwanted bushes and trees. Truly indestructible economic goods that require no maintenance are rare indeed . . . so rare that we cannot think of one example.

### Land Rent—A Taxable Surplus?

Some people, noticing that the payments for some goods seem to be unnecessary to create either the existing or the future supply, have concluded that the price, or economic rent, should be taxed away from those who get it. Prominent among these are the "single-taxers"—followers of Henry George, a nineteenth-century novelist and reformer, who believed that land rent is an economic rent and should be taxed away. (Somehow they have overlooked an equally "pure" economic rent on another resource—beautiful women.)

Other doctrinaire advocates of taxing, or nationalizing, land rents are the socialists. The English Labour party theorists argue that landsite values reflect the actions of society as a whole and not the owners of a particular parcel of land. Therefore the site value of the land—its rent—should belong to all the people. This sounds plausible, if you are interested only in sounds. It fails to explain why every person in the society should have to bear the consequences of changes in value of every parcel of land—even those he will never see or have any effect on. Some people might not want to carry the risks of gains or losses to some particular parcels of land and instead might want to trade their share of public ownership to those goods in exchange for risks of value changes of other goods at a mutually acceptable price. We can then re-allocate and specialize in bearing the risks of value changes from various goods among ourselves just as we now re-allocate ordinary consumption goods among ourselves to conform more to our personal differences in tastes. Of course, to do this we would have to be permitted private-property rights. But the socialist cannot permit private-property rights in productive resources. The socialists imply it is better that everyone have the same pro-rata nontransferable share in the value consequences of certain goods—hence those goods are socialized.

It has been argued that even if the land ownership were socialized so that the land rent went to the government, the *use* of the land would be unaffected, since the government would rent the land to the highest-bidding user. This could be correct if it were not for the difference in incentives and costs of information about potential values in various uses of land. The incentive for a private owner to incur the expenses, risks, and trouble of discovering the highest-valued uses is different from that of a government employee in charge of the use of socialized land. Further, the penalties for failure to find the highest use value are different. The government employee is less likely to put the land to its highest market-valued use. Whether this be good or bad depends in part (and only in part) on whether you think the highest-valued use as judged by individuals competing in the market, and reflected by market prices, is a good or bad criterion. It is a little early to hazard judgments about that. Many other differences between socialized ownership and private property remain to be investigated; for example, effects on ability to be different in beliefs, ideas, and behavior; willingness to produce new, varied goods; cultural mores; attitudes about personal responsibility; distribution of wealth; ability to communicate ideas with other people; costs of disagreeing with wealthier, more powerful people; and discrimination by race, origin, or creed.

## Summary

1   Prices are demand determined, even though they appear to be changed with changes in costs.

2   Shortages of goods are implied by price controls. The resulting allocation of goods and services depends more heavily on nonpecuniary attributes of demanders and tastes of sellers—for example, preferences reflecting race, religion, family size, and personality. Some potential exchanges are prevented.

3   Price controls have a greater political viability if those who benefit constitute a stronger voter bloc.

4   Prices (payments) not required for the current supply of a good (that is, rents) are important in directing the use of the good.

## Questions

1   When prices on the stock market fall, the financial pages report a surge to sell stock; yet every share sold is bought by someone. Why don't they refer to a surge to buy?

2   "Higher prices cause higher costs." Explain why.

3   "Allowing the prices of goods to rise in periods when none of the good is being produced is immoral, because the higher prices do not induce a larger output. They merely give unwarranted profits to those who are lucky enough to own the goods. Either prices should be prevented from rising, or the government should take over ownership in order to prevent unjust enrichment." Do you agree with this analysis? If so, why? If not, why not?

4   "The rent for land in New York City is not a payment that is necessary to produce that land. It is a necessary payment to obtain use of the land. From the first point of view, it is an economic rent; from the latter point of view, it is a cost." Do you agree? If so, why? If not, why not?

5 Which of the following do you think contain some economic rent? Insofar as any of them contains rent, for what is that rent unnecessary? For what is it necessary?

a. The wealth of those who owned land in Palm Springs, California, from 1940 through 1960, when land values boomed.

b. Elizabeth Taylor's income.

c. The income of a genius.

d. The income of smart students.

e. The salary of the President of the United States.

6 "Demand and supply is not simply a classification that is applicable only to private-property market exchange. Demand and supply is a categorization that is applicable to any problem of allocating scarce resources among competing uses. In any given possible use, the usefulness of the resource in that use is what is meant by its demand, while its usefulness in all alternative uses (against which this particular use must compete) is the supply." Do you agree? Explain.

7 The Council of Economic Advisers (to the President of the United States) has argued that keeping down the price of cattle could keep down the price of meat to the consumer. Explain how the application of economic analysis given in this chapter rejects that argument.

8 When both are the same price, you choose a color television set over a black-and-white set; but when a black-and-white set costs half as much as a color set, you choose the black and white. In which case are you "discriminating"?

9 Which of the following choices involve discrimination? (a) Cadillac versus Chrysler, (b) Van Gogh versus Gauguin, (c) blondes versus brunettes, (d) beautiful versus homely women, (e) Negroes versus whites, (f) Japanese versus Koreans, (g) filet mignon versus hamburger.

10 "Under open-market, private-property pricing, a person is allowed to make any kind of appeal to a seller to get some of the good—even offering him money as a common medium of exchange for other goods. Under price controls, the buyer is told that there is one particular kind of appeal he cannot use—i.e., offer of a larger amount of other goods." True or false?

11 Do you think rent controls would be good or bad for each of the following: (a) Middle-aged couple who do not contemplate moving, (b) young married couple with two children moving to a new town, (c) Negro moving to a new town, (d) young person receiving a raise in salary, (e) old person in retirement, (f) person who likes to drink and smoke, (g) beautiful young woman, (h) homely immigrant, (i) Mormon in a Jewish community, (j) Jew in a Mormon community, (k) excellent handyman who likes to work around the house and care for gardens, (l) old couple who have saved wealth and invested in apartment house.

**12**    "Price controls are used in order to give adequate housing to those in the lower-income levels who would otherwise not be able to afford it." Subject this proposition to economic analysis.

13    In Figure 6–3 (page 112), showing the demand for $X$ by $A$ and by $B$ and the total demand, let price be held at $p_1$ by some legal authority. Suppose that one-half the supply is sold to $A$ and the other half to $B$ at the legal price. Show that $A$ would prefer to buy some more from $B$. How much would $A$ be prepared to pay, and would $B$ find this a desirable trade—if it weren't for the legal prohibition against sales at a price above $p_1$? What legal inducements do you think $A$ and $B$ could construct to consummate a sale at the legal price $p_1$?

14    The military draft of the U.S. government involves price control—in which the maximum price that can be paid by the military services is set by law. As a result, the number of personnel demanded exceeds the supply *at that price*; but the buyers, instead of letting the sellers provide the amount they are willing to provide at that proffered price, resort to a compulsory draft to satisfy their "excess" of demand. Graphically, in Figure 6–3 (page 112), the price, military wages, is limited to $p_1$, at which the excess demand is obtained by the draft. Who gains what by this system of price controls? (Before presuming that military personnel could not be obtained by a wage system, note that the permanent military officers, the leaders, are obtained by a voluntary open-market wage system. So are policemen and firemen.)

**15**    News item (July 15, 1963): "Seoul, Korea (AP). The city government ordered the capital's 1,500 restaurants not to sell any meal containing rice during lunch hours. The measure is designed to encourage the customers to take other food. South Korea is experiencing a serious food shortage because of a poor rice crop." Would open-market prices achieve the same result? How effective will this measure be?

**16**    A distinguished professor of law has said: "Some people believe that every resource which is scarce should be controlled by the market. And since, in their view, all resources except free goods are scarce, all resources—even rights to radiate radio signals—should be so controlled. But surely some resources are 'scarcer' than others, and thereby possibly merit different treatment. It doesn't advance the argument very much to place a label of 'scarcity' on everything." Do you think economics should be studied by professors of law? Why?

**17**    "In the capitalistic system, only money or market values count in allocating productive resources." Evaluate.

**18**    "In capitalism, commercialism dominates and suppresses social, artistic, and cultural values." Evaluate.

19    It has been argued that politicians tend to gain from price controls and hence they advocate them. What line of reasoning would support that argument?

# Price-Takers' and Price-Searchers' Markets

As we know from Chapter 5, there is a price at which every buyer can buy as much as he chooses and every seller can sell all he wishes. That price is reached by open-market competition among many buyers and sellers. It is represented by the price at the intersection of the demand and supply curves. At that price, there would be no shortages, no surpluses, no queues of waiting buyers or sellers. There would be no sellers' advertisements extolling the virtues of products; no seller would keep inventories awaiting customers. The facts of the world fly in the face of all these implications. What is wrong with our analysis? We can overcome these difficulties and generalize much further if we categorize markets according to demand conditions facing the individual seller.

### Price-Takers' Markets: Horizontal Demand Facing Individual Seller

A useful distinction we have ignored can be framed in terms of the demand conditions seen by an individual seller. We first consider the case in which each seller in the market provides so insignificant a part of the total market supply that he could not depress the price by offering to sell more. This is portrayed in Figure 7–1. His supply is not a significant portion of total market supply. If he reduced his amount offered, he would sell less, but the price would be unchanged. If he tried to sell above the price prevailing in the market, he would sell nothing. At the prevailing market price, he can sell as much as he has available. This kind of market situation is called a *price-takers'* or "atomistic" market.[1] It is for price-takers' markets that we can correctly say everyone can buy or sell all he demands at the market price—a price at the intersection of demand and supply.

#### Market-Equilibrium Price

If the total community demand for a good should fall (meaning that the total amount that people want to have at any price is less than before), the equilibrium price will fall—as indicated by the intersection of the new lower demand and same supply at a lower price. In Figure 7–2, the demand has fallen from $D_1 D_1$ to $D_2 D_2$; and at the price $p_1$, which prevailed with demand $D_1 D_1$, the

[1] In the literature of economics, this market situation—where each seller is faced with a horizontal demand curve for his output—has been given special names: "pure competition" and "perfect competition." These names are misleading, since this market situation is neither more nor less competitive than many others. We use the term "price-takers' markets" to describe a class of markets where every supplier (and also every demander) provides so small a portion of the supply (or demand) that his output (or demand) has no significant effect on price; hence, he "takes" the market price as if it were given by outside forces. The name "price-taker" apparently was first used by T. Scitovsky in his advanced textbook, *Welfare and Competition* (Homewood, Ill.: Richard D. Irwin, Inc., 1951). The name "atomistic" is, however, becoming more popular.

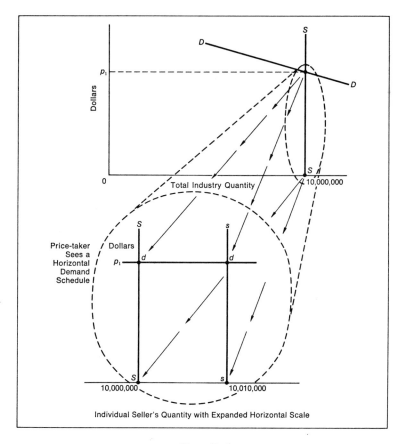

Figure 7–1
Price-Takers' View of Market Demand

Curves *DD* and *SS* are the market demand and supply totaled over *all* demanders and suppliers. Curve *SS* is a vertical line indicating an unchanging stock of the good regardless of current price. Each supplier accepts the market price given by the market demand and supply. The supply from any *one* supplier, shown by *ss* and measured from *SS*, not from the origin, is so small that even if it were withheld from the market the shift in the total supply along the total demand curve would be insignificant and hence would not affect price. Therefore, any one supplier can sell all he has at the market price—a condition portrayed by a *horizontal* demand curve, *dd* at the price $p_1$ for his product. This is the market demand for *his product*, not the demand by him for the product. The demand curve shown here is flat, at least until beyond the range of his supply. In saying that the demand line facing a price-taker seller is a *horizontal line at the existing market price*, we mean that the line is so close to being horizontal that a literally horizontal line captures all relevant features of the situation. The demand seen by the seller still conforms to the law of demand: raising the price sufficiently (and here the slightest rise is sufficient) will reduce (to zero) the amount demanded. The elasticity of demand facing him is "infinite," because the slightest increase in price will result in a loss of *all* his sales.

amount of goods $X_1 - X_2$ would be unsold. That unsold amount would be a *surplus*. Some suppliers have the choice of selling nothing at the old price or of lowering the offering price to $p_2$, where enough buyers can be induced to buy the existing supply, thus eliminating the surplus. Of course, those lucky sellers who formerly sold at the higher price would like to prevent would-be sellers from cutting the price. But the frustrated sellers prefer to cut price to whatever level is necessary for existing stocks to be sold. The price-cutters can be thought of superficially as setting the lower price. Basically, however, the *reduced demand* lowers the market price at which the entire supply can be sold. The frustrated sellers *reveal*, rather than determine, the new market-equilibrium price. Price will fall to the intersection of the new lower demand and supply curves, at which price every seller can sell all he wants and each buyer can buy all he wants. There is no pressure to lower price further.

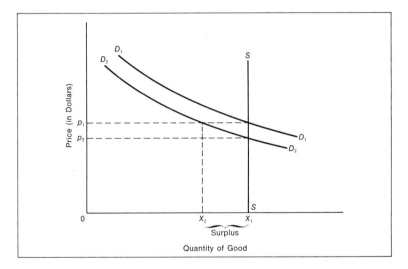

Figure 7–2
Equilibrium Pricing, with Market Demand and Supply for Price-Takers' Markets

We repeat an earlier warning. What is important is not merely that a change in demand indicates a changed intersection price in the demand and supply diagram, but that price will change *in order* to permit individuals to find and exploit mutually preferred exchange opportunities. If for some reason price were not allowed to change—because of legal or moral restraints on price changes—some buyers and sellers would be unable to discover feasible, mutually preferred exchanges. This does not mean that price *should* be allowed to change to permit those exchanges to occur. That depends upon whether or not one "likes" the consequences of an individual-choice, voluntary-exchange system. And many of these consequences still remain to be more fully revealed.

In open *price-takers'* markets, with price equating amounts demanded and supplied, the personal value between any two goods is made equal for all individuals. If anyone values cigarettes more, relative to Cokes, he purchases more cigarettes and fewer Cokes per week so that the increased stock of cigarettes relative to Cokes in his consumption pattern reduces his personal valuation of cigarettes relative to Cokes. At the market-equilibrium price, for all persons with access to the market, no unexploited opportunity of trade remains to enable any person to reach still more preferred situations by revision of the allocation of goods.

## Price-Searchers' Markets:  Sellers Face Negatively Sloped Demand

In many markets the sellers are each sufficiently large suppliers relative to total amount demanded that each can set his selling price higher (and sell less), or lower (and sell more). But fundamentally demand controls price even in these cases. We shall call these markets *price-searchers'* markets to emphasize that the sellers must constantly search for the best price at which to sell. By "best" we mean the price that maximizes the income, wealth, or profits of the seller.

Suppose you are a seller faced with the demand schedule of Table 7–1, and each day you have a total supply of ten units available *at no cost whatsoever*. What price would maximize your wealth? At a price of $6 per unit you will sell five, and at a price of $5 you will sell six. Either way your total daily revenue is $30. No other single price for each unit gives so much. The price that maximizes your wealth is either $5 or $6, your equilibrium prices. The reason for the name "price-searcher" is now apparent. He must search for the

Table 7–1
Illustrative Demand Schedule with Marginal-Revenue Data

| Price | Daily Quantity Demanded | Total Daily Revenue | Marginal Daily Revenue |
|---|---|---|---|
| $10 | 1 | $10 | $10 |
| 9 | 2 | 18 | +8 |
| 8 | 3 | 24 | +6 |
| 7 | 4 | 28 | +4 |
| 6 | 5 | 30 | +2 |
| 5 | 6 | 30 | 0 |
| 4 | 7 | 28 | -2 |
| 3 | 8 | 24 | -4 |
| 2 | 9 | 18 | -6 |
| 1 | 10 | 10 | -8 |

wealth-maximizing price. He provides so much of the total supply that he sees his demand as characterized by the law of demand. If he tries to sell more, he must lower the price in the market. If he sets a higher price, he will sell less.

The demand "curve" facing him is a negatively sloping demand "curve" with respect to price—not a horizontal curve. To show the full consequence of the negative slope, we use the concept of *marginal revenue*—the *addition to total revenue* when *price is reduced just enough to sell one more unit*. The simple data in Table 7–1 illustrate. A price of $10 per unit induces daily sales of one unit. Alternately, a price of $9 sells two units. Total daily revenue changes from $10 to $18, an increase of +$8, when two units instead of one are sold daily. The *increase* in total revenue is *not* the *price* of the extra unit sold. Selling *both* units at $9, rather than just one at $10, increases receipts by $8. The $9 of the second unit is in part offset by the $1 reduction of price on the other one sold.

The fourth column in Table 7–1 shows the difference in total revenue between prices that are just enough different to increase the daily sales rate *by one unit*. For example, the marginal revenue for a sales increase from five to six per day is zero. This is expressed as a zero marginal revenue for six units (not for *the sixth*). Marginal revenue is–$2 when sales are at a level of seven, even though the seventh unit itself sells for $4. The data of Table 7–1 are plotted in Figure 7–3.

The area within the marginal-revenue vertical rectangles from the vertical axis out to a stated rate of sales measures the total revenue. For example, at daily sales of six units, the total area of the marginal-revenue rectangles ($10 + $8 + $6 + $4 + $2) gives a total value of $30. This is also equal to the area of the dashed rectangle, one corner of which touches the demand curve at the five-unit, $6 price.

For the price-searcher, marginal revenue is *less* than average revenue (price). But for the price-taker, who can sell all he wants at the market price, the marginal revenue line is identical to the average revenue line—the demand line facing him. If the price-taker sells one more unit at the existing price, his total receipts increase exactly by the value of that increased unit of sale; there is no reduction in price on any of the units sold. Marginal revenue, which measures the change in total revenue, is equal to the price of the extra unit sold. This is summarized in Figure 7– 4.

The difference in demands facing a price-taker and a price-searcher can be expressed also by the elasticity of demand. The demand for the price-taker's goods is infinitely elastic. He can sell more without *any* reduction in price; but his sales would drop to zero with the slightest rise in price. On the other hand, the price-searcher faces a negatively sloped demand for his goods. The

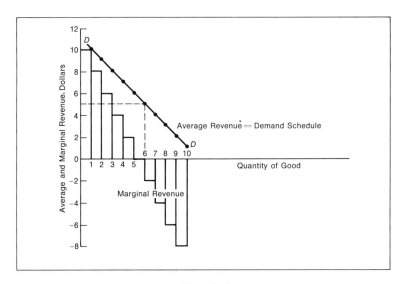

Figure 7–3
Average Revenue (Demand Schedule) and Marginal Revenue
Seen by Price-Searcher

At a given rate of sales (for example, 6), all units sell at the same price ($5); marginal revenue is less than average revenue. The *area* of the rectangle, based on the quantity sold and the price (the average revenue), depicts the total revenue. If the price were *lower* by just enough to sell one unit *more* per day, the new rectangle's area may be larger or smaller than the old rectangle. If it is larger, total revenue is larger and marginal revenue is positive: the *increase in units sold* at the lower price brought enough additional revenue to more than compensate for the *lower price* on all the units. For each rate of sales and associated price, marginal revenue shows the change in total revenue (as compared to total revenue at a sales rate of one unit less).

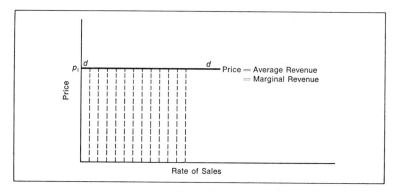

Figure 7–4
Demand Line as Seen by Price-Taker

Price-taker can sell all he has without affecting price, $p_1$. Hence each unit sold adds each unit's price to his revenue.

elasticity of demand for his goods is less than infinite and in some price ranges may be less than unity.[2]

The "price-searcher" has to search for the wealth-maximizing price. Of the many different prices he could set, which is it?[3] If he *knew* the demand schedule, he could answer very easily. But no seller knows that schedule with the required degree of accuracy. In Chapters 11 and 12, after analyzing production conditions, we shall explore actual price determination in such a market.

Effect of Difference between Marginal Revenue<br>and Price on Seller's Pricing Behavior

The difference between marginal revenue and price of each unit sold implies a difference between price-takers' and price-searchers' pricing tactics. Suppose the existing supply of some fine drinking water comes from ten wells owned by ten different owners, each of whom gets one gallon a day, with no costs of producing or bottling the water. A total of ten gallons is available every day. What will be the equilibrium price of water? If we knew the market demand we could tell what the price would be in a price-takers' market. Assume that the schedule in Table 7–1 is the demand for this water. With ten different sellers competing for buyers and if no one of them were able significantly to affect the price by reducing the amount of water he offers for sale, the price will be $1 a gallon. At that price the amount demanded equals the amount supplied. Total receipts of the group of ten owners are $10 per day. Each seller sells all he has available, and each buyer gets all he wants at that price. Price is at the intersection of the demand and the supply schedule (ten units).

To contrast this with a price-searchers' market, let all the wells be controlled by a single agency representing all the owners (leaving for later a discussion of how this might be accomplished). By holding part of the water from the market, the single controlling agency could obtain a total daily revenue of $30 a day by raising the price to $5 (or $6) and selling only six (or five) gallons a day. Each owner would get $3 a day, even though only half the water were sold. Any other price would bring in smaller net receipts for the *group as a whole* (remembering that costs are zero). The agency would be delighted to sell more water *at the set price*, but no more is demanded. Rather than cut price to sell more water and thereby reduce net revenue to the group, the unsold water is wasted. A lower price would indeed sell more water, but the receipts from the extra water sold would be more than offset by the reduced receipts from the initial amount of water sold each day.

This example shows the potential wealth gain available *if* one could convert a price-takers' market into a price-searchers' market by coordinating or organizing all the price-takers into one agency or firm. (But beware of jumping to conclusions. It does not follow that price-searchers' markets are neces-

---

[2] Review the meaning and measure of elasticity given in Chapter 4.

[3] Warning: only with *zero* costs of production will he seek to maximize total *receipts*—for only with no costs are receipts and profits the same.

sarily more profitable than price-takers' markets.) The difference between price-takers' and price-searchers' markets is fundamentally a difference in the wealth-maximizing *output and price program*, not in the *amount of profit*. (It is true that in the present example there is a difference in profits also, but we shall see later how the present example belies several pertinent facts of life. For the moment we continue with attention on the pricing process as a facilitator of exchange.)

In a price-searchers' market, less water is sold than in a price-takers' market—if the basic conditions of supply are the same. The equilibrium price is higher, and *the equilibrium extent of exchange is less*. If we define as inefficient any situation in which resource use could be revised to increase the utility of some people without reducing that of anyone else, then price-searchers' markets can result in inefficient exchange. Here the inefficiency is the nonexchange (nonuse) of half the water.

One warning: Although a price-takers' market was changed to a price-seachers' market by concentrating ownership of supply (which made the one gross supplier so large, relative to the market, that he operated along a significantly large range of the demand curve for his product to have an effect on price), it does not follow that the only, or even the most important, source of price-searchers' markets is concentration of ownership. Even if it were, one could not justifiably recommend, on the basis of anything investigated so far, a policy of enforced dispersal of ownership in order to create price-takers' markets as a means of achieving market-exchange efficiency. In the first place, the recommendation would presume that efficiency is *better* than inefficiency. That is an ethical decision; and though many readers might be surprised, many people advocate laws to prevent exchange "efficiency." For example, compulsory licensing of doctors, required prescription of drugs, prohibition of alcoholic beverages, non-enforcement of contracts by minors, control of hours of business—all are examples of laws that restrict the extent to which exchange potentialities, and hence efficiency, are achieved. Perhaps, after all, exchange efficiency is not "good," especially if it means that people will be more able to trade and consume some goods or services (marijuana, tobacco, alcohol) which you think, for their own good, they should not.

The second reason we cannot yet conclude that dispersal of ownership should be forcefully introduced is that even if efficiency were clearly good, the means of enforcing dispersal involves a change of private-property rights, and we should examine the ancillary effects before concluding that dispersal to achieve efficiency is worth the costs. We are not yet in a position to do that.

### How Price-Takers' and Price-Searchers' Market Behavior Differs

We have accomplished our first objective of this chapter—to explain behavior inconsistent with price-takers' markets where price is at the intersection of demand and supply schedules. (1) Not every seller can sell all he would choose to sell at the current market price. And he refuses to lower price to sell more. (The price-taker seller could sell all his supplies at the price at which he could sell any.) (2) Unsold water is kept as an inventory he will happily sell if the amount demanded *at the current price* should increase. (The price-taker had no inventory for potential sales at the existing price.) (3) It will occur to the price-searcher that some advertising might increase demand for his product so he could sell more of the available water. (The price-taker, who could sell all at the existing market price, would not gain sales by advertising or get a higher price.) (4) Finally, the price to the price-searcher is not determined for him as if by some impersonal market mechanism. Instead he must search out the optimal (wealth-maximizing) price. And, not knowing the demand schedule exactly, he will have to resort to trial-and-error search processes. No demand-and-supply intersection principle determines his price, although the demand (and, as we shall see later, the costs of production) plays a crucial role in determining his prices.

### Multipart Pricing

The analysis of price-searchers' markets does more than explain behavior not observed in simple price-takers' markets. It helps to explain the rationale of some relatively unusual pricing and selling tactics. Our price-searcher water-selling agency will not necessarily let part of the water be unused. There *are* tactics for selling that water and avoiding waste, even short of converting the price-searcher to a price-taker.

Sellers do not always permit the buyer to buy *whatever amount* he wants at a particular price; yet that was the only kind of offer considered in the preceding discussion. The seller might set up a *sliding scale* of prices, with prices depending upon the amount taken. This procedure can give an even greater income to the seller (while also increasing the amount of water sold). Imagine him to be faced with the simple demand schedule characterized by the data in Table 7–1. The seller has ten units available for sale each day, and it costs him nothing to produce them. (This last assumption enables us again to isolate selling policy from production problems.) How can he maximize his daily income? We know a flat price of $5 (or $6) will bring in total receipts of $30 daily, with sales of six (or five) units. And the remaining unsold units are wasted (unexploited exchange opportunities).

Our clever seller might, instead, tell the buyer that the price is $5 a unit only *for the first six units*. After purchasing the first six units, the buyer may, as a quantity discount, buy more at $3 each. The buyer will buy six at $5 each (paying $30) and then buy two more at $3 each. How do we know? According to his demand schedule, he would have bought eight per day if the price had been a flat $3 for every unit. From this it can be deduced that he will buy *some* additional units at $3 after buying six at $5; that indeed he will demand about two more units; and that, for present purposes, he will demand exactly two more.[4] The buyer prefers buying the first six units at $5 and two more at $3 to the former situation, in which he acquired a total of only six; and the seller, too, prefers the new pricing arrangement, which gives him greater income. And note that only two units are now left unsold—that is, the extent of exchange is increased, and waste is reduced.

An even more clever seller can set up a more detailed schedule of discount prices and get still greater daily income from the sale of the water. Knowing the demand schedule for his water, the seller knows that the buyer regards having one unit per day as worth $10 more than having none. You know this because he prefers to pay $10 for one rather than to have none. Furthermore, if we continue to assume a negligible effect on wealth, he would rather pay $9 more to get a second one daily than be confined to only one daily at $10. How do we know? The schedule shows he would buy two at $9 each rather than just one; therefore, a second one daily must be worth to him at least $9, given his current total wealth and state of preferences. This means we could induce him to buy two units daily in either of two different ways: (1) offer him all he wants at $9 each, or (2) offer him one for $10 and then a second one for $9.[5]

As a seller, you could offer the great bargain of "$10 for one or two for $19"—which is precisely the same thing as $10 for the first one and $9 for the second one. The buyer may think you are doing him a favor, and you are—compared to charging a flat price of $10. As a seller, you are interested in doing favors for other people insofar as the favor also improves your situation.

Why not offer the buyer three for $27? Then he can buy three at a cost of only $8 more than for two. According to the demand schedule, he will prefer to buy three for $27 rather than only two for $19. There are two ways of expressing your sale offer: (1) "One for $10, or 2 for $19, or 3 for $27." (2) "Ten dollars for the first one, $9 for the second, and $8 for the third one." Either way, you will sell three and get $27 daily.

---

[4]We are comparing two alternative cases: (a) buy eight units at $3 each—which is indicated in the demand schedule; and (b) buy eight units, six of them at $5 and two at $3. Certainly, the alternatives are not identical: total expenditure in the first case is $24, and it is $36 in the second. In the first case, in which all units sell at the same price of $3, the eighth unit is worth $3 to the buyer; but in the second case, in which he is $12 poorer, the eighth unit may be worth slightly less than $3. And the reason for this possible modification of demand may be labeled the "income (or wealth) effect." We shall discuss it further in the following paragraphs of the text and the next footnote.

[5]What he pays for the first one is *almost* irrelevant in his demand for a second one. If he pays $10 instead of $9 for the first one, that would not reduce the value of the second one to him by $1, even though the effect of the $10 price for the first unit is to reduce by $1 his income available for *all* other things. This reduced-wealth effect will be spread over *all* his purchases. In fact, there *will* be a small effect on his demand for this article; and the amount he would be willing to pay for a second one, if he paid $10 for the first one, would be not $9 but, say, $8.90. A price of $10 for the first item and a price of $8.90 for the second would get two items sold for a total daily income of $18.90, compared with $18 for two units at a flat price of $9 each. As before, in order to avoid these minor adjustments, we continue as if the demand schedule stays unchanged, so that the seller can sell the first one for $10 and a second for $9.

If you now offer the buyer a fourth one for $7 ("or four for $34"), he'll accept, because he would rather have a fourth one than $7. You now have total daily receipts of $34. Continue the process. Offer the buyer a fifth one daily for $6 (after he buys the first four on the preceding terms) or offer him a package of "five for $40." He'll take the offers. So extending the logic, offer him a sixth for $5 (or a package of six for $45); a seventh for $4 (or a package of seven for $49); an eighth for $3 (or eight for $52); a ninth for $2 (or nine for $54); and ultimately a tenth for $1 (or a package of ten for $55); at most, he would buy ten per day for a total outlay of $55.

You have made offers to the buyer that are just sufficient to squeeze from him approximately all they are worth to him.

Before seeing where this kind of pricing is actually used, notice that it is equivalent, in extreme form, to what appears to be a still different pricing system. Suppose that, as the seller, you announce a fat daily *fee* of slightly less than $55, which entitles the buyer to have all he wants each day. He will take ten. (An eleventh is worth zero, so he is indifferent about whether or not he gets it.) The buyer pays almost $55 each day as a fee and then gets all the daily service he wants free (at no subsequent cost). This is precisely the same kind of offer as the earlier graduated sliding scale of prices and requires the demand curve to be known with extraordinary precision.

In point of fact, no seller ever knows a demand curve exactly. We have used an extreme case of complete information to the seller (and we have ignored other sellers who might underprice him). This extreme example is designed merely to expose the basis for multipart, or fixed-fee, pricing. If this theory is realistic, we should observe this kind of pricing in the real world. And it does occur, though usually in much cruder form.

### Examples of Multipart Pricing

At the grocery store, some goods are marked "15 cents, two for 25 cents." You may take the cynical view that quantity discounts make the price higher to those who buy only a few, or you may view them as a special favor to the customer who buys more. Whichever interpretation you choose, quantity discounts are used because the seller wants to increase his income. But this does not mean the seller must think of the device; actually, the *buyer* can suggest it. Reconsider our water seller faced with the demand data of Table 7–1. The buyer, seeing unsold units, may suggest that the seller accept, say, $2 for each one the buyer takes in excess of six per day. Certainly the seller will accept that proposition rather than continue to sell only six at $5 each. Both buyer and seller prefer the new arrangement. Notice that the new arrangement can be viewed as a scheme whereby the seller squeezes most of the exchange advantage from the buyer, or a scheme whereby the buyer gains over the one-price system that the price-searcher might otherwise use. In either event, the amount sold can, by multipart prices, be extended to the full amount available, so that none is left unused.

Electric power, water, and gas prices from public utilities are almost always sold on multipart-pricing schedules, where the unit price depends upon how much customers buy. Telephone service and sometimes water are sold for a fixed total fee of so much per month, with the buyer taking all he wants. Social, recreation, and golf club membership fees are often flat "dues" per month. Is the motive to reach a more extensive use of the available goods, or is it to induce buyers to take more of the product for the benefit of the sellers? As we have seen, the motives are hard to isolate; several can operate to the same effect. This kind of pricing will be viable to all parties concerned when the seller is a price-searcher provided certain conditions are satisfied, as we shall see in the next section.

### Obstacles to Multipart Pricing

Multipart pricing, although simple in concept, is difficult to achieve in *open* markets. *Buyers must be prevented from reselling to each other*; otherwise, one buyer will buy large amounts at lower prices and resell to other buyers. If I can buy two items for 25 cents and resell to other people for 14 cents each to beat the 15 cents price they must pay for just one (assuming they would have bought only one themselves), I can undersell the original seller.

Effective in restricting resale is the cost of finding other buyers and convincing them of product quality. If I, a stranger, offered to sell you a diamond, a tire, a car, or a fur coat, would you have confidence that what I offer is really the same as the item purchased in an established retail store? Certainly not for items that you cannot easily test prior to purchase. Even if you ignore the issue of whether the seller has proper legal title, you would buy little from a stranger, after brief inspection, because the quality of few items could be discovered in a five-minute inspection. Some people have succeeded in spreading knowledge of the attributes of *their* products or services. These persisting retailers or manufacturers are not merely people from whom we can buy a known type of product, but they also are people prepared to provide information and assurance of supplies. A stable location offers a greater incentive to sell items that are more likely to be what they purport to be, because of the prospect of obtaining "repeat purchases" if the seller is more honest. Knowledge that the local supermarket exists at a certain location and is available when you want to shop is no inconsequential matter. The casual, itinerant seller provides less service; and if sometimes he is able to sell for less, it is in part because he chooses not to incur the costs of maintaining the conventional retailer's greater service. Price differences among sellers often reflect differences in their services. Therefore, one should not expect to find every buyer from lower-priced retailers reselling to customers of higher-priced retailers.

Sometimes the original seller can get laws passed prohibiting his customers from reselling to other consumers. For example, in many states milk cannot legally be resold by a customer to other people. The ostensible reason is to protect the purchasers from buying "impure" milk from those intermediate customers (who, it is alleged, will "water" the milk to make an even greater gain). Power and gas are sold more cheaply to larger users, who by law cannot resell the power or gas to smaller users at prices under the higher prices charged by the power company to the smaller customers. Nor can one family purchase telephone service and then resell some service to a neighbor—say, by running an extension over to his house. In Chapter 18 we shall investigate some of the reasons advanced for these legally enforced restrictions on resale.

## Kinds of Market Pricing

We have distinguished between price-takers' and price-searchers' markets; also we have distinguished between single-price offers and multipart-price offers. Although we did not explicitly say so earlier, the two kinds of price offers can be found only in price-searchers' markets.

We now can summarize three kinds of market pricing, all with free-access, *open markets*: (1) price-takers' markets; (2a) price-searchers' markets with single price; and (2b) price-searchers' markets with multipart pricing. Case 1 yields efficient exploitation of exchange opportunities. Case 2a does not. In Case 2b, exchange opportunities are more fully exploited than in 2a, so that goods are directed to their higher-valued uses. Case 2b also gives the *seller* a bigger income and a greater efficiency of exchange. Case 2b differs from Case 1 less in the extent to which full exchange or use of goods is achieved, and more in the resultant distribution of income. In Case 2b the seller gets more wealth than in Case 1. You may have an opinion about which is preferable, but you can't derive it from any principles of economics.

## Why Price-Searchers?

Having analyzed some elementary differences in pricing and exchange activities between price-taker and price-searcher markets, we can now add a few remarks about the *sources* of these different kinds of markets. This discussion will be incomplete, however, because some of the conditions are results of costs and production conditions, yet to be analyzed.

General Motors, a giant assembling almost half the cars in the United States, is a price searcher. So are U.S.Steel, Du Pont, Alcoa, and Boeing. And so is the tiny drugstore catering to its small neighborhood, as is every retail store. What attribute makes them each a price-searcher? His supply must constitute a significant portion of the total supply of the product in the market in which he is selling. The local grocer is a larger seller *relative* to the demand in his neighborhood. He can raise the price of his beans above that of neighborhood rivals and still sell some beans, although not as much as at a lower price. The local gas station can charge a higher price than its nearby rivals, and still sell some gasoline. Distinctiveness of product or seller's services means that there are separate demands for each seller. He can charge a slightly

higher price than for similar, but different, products. These close, but differentiated, substitutes—such as brands of cigarettes, soap, gasoline, oil, cars,
shirts, stockings—are not exactly alike in every respect. Customers discriminate among the myriad major and minor details of the product or associated
service.

Some people think that most product differentiation is silly. Are Chester-
fields not the same as Lucky Strikes, Cokes the same as Pepsis, and Palmolive
the same as Lux? Although the physical differences may be trivial, in the
minds of some customers they are significant. All men are created equal; yet
women are disconcertingly choosy about them. The difference between mink
and rabbit fur is "slight," except perhaps to minks and rabbits. Yet the
public's preference between them is enormous, even if it is all a matter of
looks and feel. The difference between two gasoline stations may be merely
in their location, some hundred feet apart. Yet that is enough to give one a
preference. Ridiculous? Not in the eyes of the customer. The attendant may
be more pleasant and cordial. Irrelevant? Not in the opinion of real people.
How many marital mates are chosen on more substantial grounds? Differences that do not matter to us will matter to others—and *they* may think that
what matters to *us* is of no matter. You may think it really is of no matter
whether you eat pork rather than beef, or meat rather than vegetables, or
worship this deity rather than that one, or rest or work on Sunday; but many
people do and have killed over such "trivial" issues. You could declare them
prejudiced, ignorant, or discriminatory, but all you mean is that their tastes
or preferences differ from yours. And this should give us reason to pause
before confidently asserting that buyers who discriminate among brands of
cigarettes, aspirin, paper tissues, soap, corn flakes, or canned milk do so only
because they are irrational or uninformed.

The difference between two cola drinks, Coke and Pepsi, is minor, but real,
in my opinion; at the same price I would always choose Cokes. If the former
were priced 25 percent higher, I would still take Coke. But at a 100 percent
difference in price, Pepsi would capture a dominant if not entire portion of
my cola purchase. The smaller the difference between prices of goods, the
greater is the influence of any other difference on the purchase decision. This
is, of course, merely an application of our old friend, the law of demand.

Much product differentiation is "natural," and no one else, try as hard as he
can, can duplicate the product or service. Bing Crosby, Elizabeth Taylor, Bob
Hope, and Arnold Palmer have attributes that no other person can duplicate.
Each is a price-searcher for the service he renders. Crosby can raise his fees
and still perform, even if less frequently. There is no legal restriction against
anyone else's trying to sing like Bing Crosby, but the consumer can tell the
differences even without trademarks or copyrights.

Some preferences may result from ignorance (not stupidity). Sears portable
electric typewriter is the Smith-Corona typewriter, except for the exterior

shell. The prices for the two are different, if you don't shop around for special sales or discounts. Some people do not know this, and hence they pay a higher price for the "identical" item (assuming that the value of the superficial design difference is less than the price difference). However, to point out that such behavior reflects ignorance is to say nothing useful, since everything we do reflects a lack of perfect knowledge. To say that buying behavior is based on ignorance would be more meaningful if one meant that it is based on the high cost of acquiring more information—because usually the extra cost is expected to exceed the value of the extra information. Why do I buy gasoline from the local distributor when it happens to be selling today at a lower price three blocks farther down the street? Simply because I didn't know it was cheaper there. You may know it, but how am I supposed to know that if I drive around those three blocks I'll find a station selling gasoline at a cheaper price—ignoring considerations of convenience and quality of service.

But elimination of ignorance, if you knew how to do it, would not eliminate preferences. People would still not think that all goods of all sellers are identical; a seller of a preferred product would be able to raise his price relative to that of any other seller without losing *all* his sales. If every person evaluated all the various goods precisely in the same way as everyone else *and* if there were enough sellers so that no one supplied enough to shift the supply up or down along the community's demand, then, and only then, could price-searchers' markets be avoided. But such a revision of the world is simply impossible.

### Oligopoly

The number of sellers of some *un*differentiated, homogeneous product may be so small that any action by one will induce the others to react in a way that the first seller must take into account. This is presumably true for steel, coal, aluminum, and possibly bread retail stores. If U.S. Steel reduced its output or raised its price, the impact on sales of other firms (by shifting the demand curve facing those firms) would be sufficient to induce them to respond with a price change, which the first party would have anticipated. U.S. Steel would be aware of this response of other steel producers while considering its initial possible action.

Price-searchers, then, can be comprised of sellers of slightly differentiated products but also of the *few sellers* of *one product*. In this latter case, the sellers (1) are faced with negatively sloped demand curves and also (2) give heed to potential responses of other sellers. Economics has a name for this situation: oligopoly, meaning a few sellers (from Greek *oligi* for "few" and *polein* for "sell"). "Few" means sufficiently few that one has an effect on prices of *other* sellers and not merely its own prices.

Thus, although steel is produced by over one hundred companies in the United States, many are big enough so that if any cut production in half, the output of the industry would be reduced enough to cause a rise in price to its competitors—even though all firms produced identical steel and sold it under identical sales conditions. U.S. Steel Corporation certainly has the power to raise the price of steel for all steel producers if it is willing to reduce its output and suffer the consequences.

A question we *cannot* answer is "Why are some goods produced under conditions of oligopoly?" Except for monopoly laws that prohibit entry of new firms, we can give no satisfactory explanation other than the question-begging remark that it depends upon the technological characteristics of the product or the production process.

## Monopoly

Reducing the number of sellers down to one gives us "monopoly." A monopolist is sometimes said to be the only seller of a good, as if he faced no competition from close or distant substitutes. But the telephone company faces the mails, telegraph, microwave radio, or even personal travel. The electric company faces the competition of gas and oil and diesel generators for power and heat. The bus company faces taxis, private autos, rented autos, and walking. No one is an absolute monopolist since all goods are substitutable to some degree. But degrees are important. We shall therefore refer to the "monopolist" as the extreme *limiting* case in which a seller faces a negatively sloped demand curve but has no significant *reaction* from any other sellers in response to his pricing or output programs. Unlike other price-searchers, who also have negatively sloping demand curves, he is free of other seller reaction effects—as is a price-taker. But unlike the price-*taker*, who is free of reactions of other sellers, he does not face a horizontal demand at a going market price.

The distinction we have used between price-takers and price-searchers has hinged upon the slope of the demand conditions facing the seller. We have given relatively little attention to the reaction of other sellers, because for the moment we are interested in explaining why the behavior of market price cannot be typically categorized as one in which price is set at the intersection of a demand and supply curve—with no shortages, surpluses, queues, advertising, inventories, and conscious price administration by sellers. The negatively sloped demand facing each seller is sufficient to explain all these. The interdependence effect explains still more activities, but we shall postpone our consideration of that.

In using the word "monopoly," we have opened the door to confusions. To bar that door, we note that "monopoly" is often used in two different ways. (1) Historically, it means a grant of exclusive right to sell some good. The state or society would prohibit other sellers from access to the market. The market was closed to all except those given the monopoly franchise or license. Elizabeth I granted to Essex a monopoly on the importation and sale of French white wines, and to Raleigh the monopoly for sale of playing cards. These grants were rewards for special service to the Crown. The French state retained the monopoly of salt sales. Today, many governments retain monopolies in television, radio, telephone, and railroads. In most large cities, taxi

Table 7–2
Classification of Sellers and Markets

| | Degree of Legal Restraint or Closure of Access to Market for Sellers | |
| --- | --- | --- |
| | No restriction | Closed |
| Price-takers<br><br>Horizontal demand curves | Open-market price-takers | Closed-monopoly price-takers<br>(Cartel) |
| Price-searchers<br><br>Negatively sloped demand curves | Open-market price-searchers or Open monopolists (Oligopolists, differentiated product sellers, monopolistic competitors, imperfect competition) | Closed-market Price-searchers or Closed monopolists<br><br>(Cartel) |

Our two criteria of classification, (1) price-searcher or price-taker and (2) closed or open markets, are summarized. In each cell is the name for markets or sellers categorized in that cell, with other commonly used names in parentheses.

Table 7–3
Market Seller Classification Criteria

| | | | Entry Condition | |
| --- | --- | --- | --- | --- |
| | | | Open | Closed |
| Elasticity of Demand Facing Seller | Infinite | Price-takers | Cattle growers, truck farmers, common laborers | Producers of wheat, oranges, cotton, tobacco, oats, lemons, milk |
| | Near Unity | Price-searchers | Retailers, movie stars, artists, most manufactured goods | Patented goods, taxis, airlines, public utilities, musicians, physicians, lawyers, longshoremen |

We have emphasized in this chapter the classification criterion on the left-hand side, comparing price-takers and price-searchers. Later we shall examine in more detail the horizontal scale criterion—market closure.

owners constitute a legal monopoly in that no other people are allowed to enter the taxi business. The market is closed. This kind of monopoly we shall call *closed monopoly*, a shorter expression than "closed-market monopoly."

Closure may not be absolute but only severely restricted. (We shall discuss that in more detail in Chapter 18.) (2) "Monopoly," in modern technical economics, means a seller faced with a negatively sloping demand line for his product, *whether or not* the market is open or closed to other sellers. Both kinds of monopolists are called price-searchers, because the term describes pricing activity of sellers faced with a negatively sloped demand (whether or not in closed or open markets). But price-searchers in closed markets can and do behave differently from those in open markets. Possibly it would be better to refer to "open monopolies" (open-market price-searchers) and "closed monopolies" (price-searchers in closed markets).

### Wealth versus Utility Maximization

Have we been a little careless? How did *wealth*, or income, slip in to replace utility maximization? The explanation is simple. One way to increase your utility is by increasing your wealth. You could work sixteen hours a day and get more money wealth than if you worked ten hours a day. But you would be sacrificing other sources of utility such as health, leisure, and recreation—losing more utility than the utility gained from money wealth.

In some situations these effects on other sources of utility are trivial. Suppose we are analyzing a businessman's pricing policy. If we assume that his decision to set a high or a low price involves no other factors affecting his utility, then we can concentrate solely on the wealth-maximizing effect of his pricing decision. Whether he sets a high or a low price, he will have to go through the same analysis and take just as much time and trouble. Therefore, he will pick the price that maximizes his wealth. In such cases we can simply assume he is a wealth maximizer—for that is now a special subcase of a utility maximizer. In other problems we shall not want to be so limited in our perspective, and we will then treat wealth as only one of the components that affect his decisions.

Some people honestly say they run a business for the fun of it, as sometimes contended by owners of racing stables and professional athletic teams. Still, the higher the costs of that activity in terms of losses of wealth, the less likely will that hobby be sustained. Ultimately, utility maximization is the objective, but, as we have said, if some of its component sources, such as marketable wealth, can be increased without any decrease in other component sources, we can use wealth maximization as the proximate criterion.

### Consumer Sovereignty

"Consumer sovereignty" is often called a characteristic of the capitalistic open market, because ultimately the salability to a consumer determines a product's market value and hence profitability of continued production. Producers may decide what goods to proffer, but consumers decide which to prefer. Producers won't continue to produce goods salable at prices below costs—unless they do not care to maintain their wealth or are supported with funds from sources other than market sales receipts, such as tax-financed subsidies. To the extent the producer's wealth is less dependent on his production (e.g., absence of private-property rights in producers' equipment or closure of markets to other potential producers)—to that extent he is able to escape the force of "consumer sovereignty." So long as private-property rights exist in consumers' *and* in producers' goods, the consumers' market-revealed demand will control the viable, profitable output.

As we shall see in the next chapter, there are many situations in which a producer's personal wealth situation is less affected by the forces of the market in which he sells goods—e.g., as in firms that are not privately owned or are "not-for-profit." It should come as no surprise that, in controlling production and rationing output, market prices and consumers' preferences then play a reduced role. Whether that reduction is "good" or "bad" is a subject of much moral, philosophical, and ethical debate.

## Summary

1    Price-takers face a horizontal demand for their goods at the market price. Their marginal revenue equals price. For price-takers' markets, buyers and sellers can buy and sell all they wish at the prevailing price. Price is accepted and not subject to change by an individual seller's supply situation.

2    Price-searchers face a negatively sloped demand for their goods. They would like to sell more at the wealth-maximizing (equilibrium) price. Marginal revenue is less than price. Price-searchers must search out and test the market demand to try to find the equilibrating (wealth-maximizing) price. With uncertainty and incomplete knowledge about the demand facing him, no seller can be positive he has found the wealth-maximizing price.

3    In price-searchers' markets, the disparity between price and marginal revenue can lead to an underexploitation of exchange opportunities. Pricing and selling tactics that increase the fulfillment of exchange opportunities include multipart pricing. Multipart pricing involves a sliding scale of prices rather than unit prices. For multipart pricing to be successful, subsequent exchanges by buyers must be prevented.

4    Markets can be distinguished by the degree of restraint on them. Sellers can be distinguished by the elasticity of demand facing them. A monopoly exists where there is a legal restriction against new sellers who might enter the market, or where sellers have negatively sloped demand curves for their goods. Pure "competition" denotes open, price-takers'

markets. Pure "monopoly" usually denotes closed, price-searchers' markets. Price-searchers in open markets are often called monopolistic competitors, imperfect competitors, or, if there are only a few sellers, oligopolists.

## Questions

**1**  This question is designed to illustrate the demand situation facing an individual seller in atomistic, price-takers' markets. The community demand for wheat is shown below, in the vicinity of the market price, $2 per bushel. (Conventionally, wheat prices are expressed to the nearest eighth of a cent per bushel.)

### Demand Function

| Price | Quantity |
|-------|----------|
| $2.01 | 9,986,000 |
| 2.00-7/8 | 9,987,000 |
| 2.00-6/8 | 9,988,000 |
| 2.00-5/8 | 9,990,000 |
| 2.00-4/8 | 9,992,000 |
| 2.00-3/8 | 9,994,000 |
| 2.00-2/8 | 9,996,000 |
| 2.00-1/8 | 9,998,000 |
| 2.00 | 10,000,000 |
| 1.99-7/8 | 10,002,000 |

**a.** You have 1,000 bushels. Could you detectably affect the market price by withholding all or any of your supply from the market?
**b.** The rest of the suppliers provide the remaining 9,999,000 bushels. If you tried to sell at $2.00 1/8 while the market price was $2, would anyone buy wheat from you?
**c.** What does the demand curve for your wheat look like?

**2**  Suppose you had 6,000 of the 10,000,000 bushels provided by all farmers.
**a.** Could you sell *any* wheat at a higher price than the market price of $2? How much would you sell if you asked $2.00 1/8? If you asked $2.00 2/8? $2.00 3/8?
**b.** What does the demand curve facing you look like? Draw one on graph paper. Would you agree that it is, for all practical purposes, essentially regarded as a horizontal line at the market price?
**c.** Would it pay you to ask for a price above the market price of $2 in view of the effect on the sales revenue?
**d.** Suppose you owned 1,000,000 bushels of the 10,000,000 bushels of wheat. Could you now affect the market price to a significant extent?

3 A sugar-beet farmer produces and sells 300 tons of sugar beets at $80 per ton for total revenue of $24,000, in a price-takers' market; he cannot affect the price he gets by changing the amount he offers to sell. The demand for *his* product can, therefore, be described by the following table, in which you are to compute the data for the marginal-revenue column. (Remember, marginal revenue is associated with a *unit* increment in sales.)

| Price | Quantity | Marginal Revenue |
|-------|----------|------------------|
| $81 | 0 | ———— |
| 80 | 1 | ———— |
| 80 | 2 | ———— |
| 80 | 3 | ———— |
| 80 | 4 | ———— |
| . | . | |
| . | . | |
| . | . | |
| 80 | 100 | ———— |
| 80 | 200 | ———— |
| 80 | 300 | ———— |
| 80 | 400 | ———— |

4 In a price-takers' market, does the marginal revenue of each seller equal the average revenue (price)? Why?

5 In a price-takers' market, is each seller's marginal revenue constant, or is it a decreasing function of the amount he sells? What about a price-searcher?

6 You own 1,000 shares of General Electric common stock. If you try to sell some, you find you can get a price of $61 1/2 per share for all 1,000 shares. If you offer only 500 shares, you can get a price of $61 5/8—12 1/2 cents more per share. By reducing your amount sold by a half, you can get a price that is higher by about 1/500. And if you sought a price of $61 3/4, you would sell nothing. This is an insignificant rise in price for you, but effective in reducing amount demanded as a result of withholding one's supply. Is this a price-takers' market? Compute your marginal revenues as best you can with the given data.

7 If price is set by demand and supply in an open market, then which of the following will not be observed in price-takers' markets? (a) Rationing by waiting lists, (b) sellers who would like to sell more of their available supply at current prices, (c) buyers who want more at current prices but find no more available, (d) queues, (e) buyers forced to buy at least a certain quantity to get any at all, (f) tie-in sales, wherein to get one good you must buy some of another, (g) advertising, (h) inventories.

8 At a price-takers' market-equilibrium price, every buyer can get all he wants at the price; and every seller can sell all he wants to at that price.

a. Do you know of any firms that do sell in price-takers' markets?
b. Try tentatively to classify the following as price-takers or as price-searchers: (1) egg producers, (2) chicken farmers, (3) tomato growers, (4) crude-oil producers, (5) corner drug store, (6) local service station, (7) medical doctors, (8) music teachers.

9    Answer the following questions concerning the demand schedule below.
a. Complete the total-revenue, marginal-revenue, and average-revenue data.

| Price | Quantity | Revenue | | |
|---|---|---|---|---|
| | | Total | Marginal | Average |
| 20 | 2 | 40 | +17 | 20 |
| 19 | 3 | 57 | +15 | 19 |
| 18 | 4 | 72 | ____ | 18 |
| 17 | 5 | ____ | ____ | ____ |
| 16 | 6 | ____ | ____ | ____ |
| 15 | 7 | ____ | ____ | ____ |
| 14 | 8 | ____ | ____ | ____ |
| 13 | 9 | ____ | ____ | ____ |
| 12 | 10 | ____ | ____ | ____ |
| 11 | 11 | ____ | ____ | ____ |
| 10 | 12 | ____ | ____ | ____ |
| 9 | 13 | ____ | ____ | ____ |

b. What happens to the difference between selling price and marginal revenue?
c. How many units would you want to produce and sell if you could produce as many as you wanted at an average cost of $8 per unit and if you want to maximize your net receipts (revenue minus costs)?
d. What price would you charge?
e. Could you charge $18 if you wanted to? What would be the consequences?
f. What are the consequences of charging $14?

10    a. How can a price-searcher be searching for a price, when in fact there is available a wide range of prices—any of which he can charge?
b. What happens if he is not good at finding what he is searching for?

11    Most elementary arithmetic books contain the following type of question: "Mr. Black, the grocer, can buy bread for 15 cents. What price should he charge to make a profit of 50 percent?" Without worrying why Mr. Black should be content with 50 instead of 500 percent profit, wherein does this question ignore a basic economic fact of life? Suggest a formulation of the problem that will enable students to learn how to manipulate percentage calculations without being taught erroneous economics.

12    Let the demand schedule of Table 7–1 (page 128) represent the characteristics of the demand for your services as a gardener, and suppose you sell in a price-searchers' market.

**a.** What price should you charge per garden to maximize your daily net receipts if the "cost" of caring for a garden is zero?
**b.** If your time is worth the equivalent of $3 per garden maintained, what price would you charge?
**c.** Is this the "highest" price the traffic will bear, the highest price possible, the lowest price possible, or a "reasonable" price?

13 "A price-searcher does not have a supply curve, i.e., there is no schedule of amounts that he would offer at alternative possible prices, and which can be juxtaposed on a demand schedule." Explain why this is a correct statement.

**14** You are buying trees to landscape your new home. The following demand schedule characterizes your behavior as a buyer:

| Price of Trees | Quantity Demanded |
|---|---|
| $10 | 1 |
| 9 | 2 |
| 8 | 3 |
| 7 | 4 |
| 6 | 5 |
| 5 | 6 |
| 4 | 7 |
| 3 | 8 |
| 2 | 9 |
| 1 | 10 |

The price is quoted at $6. Accordingly, you buy five trees. Then *after* you buy the five trees, the seller offers to sell you one more for only $5.
**a.** Do you take it?
**b.** Suppose, strange as it may seem, he then offers you an opportunity to buy more trees (*after* you have already agreed to purchase five at $6 each and one more for $5) at the price of $3. How many more do you buy?
**c.** If the price had been $3 initially, would you have bought more than eight trees?
**d.** Suppose you had to pay a membership fee of $5 to buy at this nursery, after which you could buy all the trees you wanted for your own garden at $3 each. How many would you buy? (Assume price at other nurseries is $4, with no membership fee.)
**e.** If you could buy trees at $3 each from some other store without a membership fee, would you still buy only eight trees—saving the $5 for use on *all* your consumption activities?
**f.** Now explain why, according to the demand schedule, your purchase of eight trees at $3 each, at a total cost of $24, is a consistent alternative to your purchase of eight trees under the former sequential offers, in which you pay a total of $41 (five at $6, one at $5, and two at $3). (In this example we assume we can slide down an *unmodified* demand

curve, because the required modification by the change in wealth is slight.)

15    In the text, two kinds of pricing by a price-searcher were discussed: (1) uniform prices to all buyers, at which each *buyer* can buy all he wants; (2) multipart pricing, in which a buyer cannot buy all he wants at one price; instead the prices depend upon how many he buys. We now consider briefly a third type of pricing policy by a price-searcher: he charges *different* prices to *different* customers—called "price discrimination." Within this third category there are two subcases: (a) "simple discrimination," where the price at which a buyer can buy all he wants is systematically different from the price to other buyers; (b) "multipart price discrimination," where multipart pricing is applied to *each* customer, with different sets of prices to each buyer. We shall now by means of a series of questions explore these possibilities.

a. First, we see how simple price discrimination among different customers can give greater revenue to the seller than uniform prices. Suppose you are a gardener and are faced with the following demand for your services from garden owners:

| Price per Garden | Hours of Services |
|---|---|
| $10 | 1 |
| 9 | 2 |
| 8 | 3 |
| 7 | 4 |
| 6 | 5 |
| 5 | 6 |
| 4 | 7 |
| 3 | 8 |

If one customer cannot sell your gardening services to another customer, can you think of some pricing technique that would maximize your daily income without increasing your work, assuming that it always costs you $3 in time and effort to care for a garden? What prices are involved and what would be your income?

b. An obstacle to *discriminatory* pricing is that other gardeners will find it profitable to underbid your higher prices. They would offer to sell to your customers at a slightly lower price than you charge. In this way several gardeners would, by competing for the higher prices, be led to a single price. You must prevent other gardeners from undercutting your higher-priced sales. But with open access to the market, there is no way to prevent them. For this reason, discriminatory pricing is difficult to achieve in open markets where entry is economically cheap. (We shall later investigate some cases where markets are "closed" by government action to all except a particular class of sellers.)

c. To discriminate successfully, sellers must prevent customers from reselling the good among themselves. The advantage of keeping your customers separate (which is hard to do if they can buy from your competitors or if they easily buy and sell to each other) is illustrated by the following two demand schedules of two different customers.

| | Demand of | | Marginal Revenue | |
|---|---|---|---|---|
| Price | A | B | A | B |
| $10 | 1 | 0 | 8 | 0 |
| 9 | 2 | 0 | 6 | 8 |
| 8 | 3 | 1 | 4 | 6 |
| 7 | 4 | 2 | 2 | 4 |
| 6 | 5 | 3 | 0 | 2 |
| 5 | 6 | 4 | -2 | 0 |
| 4 | 7 | 5 | -4 | -2 |
| 3 | 8 | 6 | -6 | -4 |
| 2 | 9 | 7 | -8 | -6 |
| 1 | 10 | 8 | | |

Suppose you have seven units of this good available, the demands for which are shown in the table in this question. At the price you ask of A you must let him buy all he wants, and you must permit B to have all he wants at the price you charge B; but the price charged A and B can be different.

(1) What price should you charge A and what should you charge B, given the demand schedules, if you want to maximize your revenue?

(2) If you charge the same price to both buyers, what is your best price and revenue?

(3) Suppose you can produce this good at a cost of $4 for each unit you make. How many should you make, and what price should you charge to A and what to B? How many will A buy, and how many will B buy? What will be your net revenue?

d. Assume that you are the seller with the data just given; construct an example of *multipart pricing* with *different sets* of prices to each buyer, so as to get still more revenue than in the preceding example. Why do you think this kind of multipart plus discriminatory pricing is relatively uncommon? Can you give some examples of it? (Hint: Check the water, telephone, gas, and electric rates charged in your community; what prevents new sellers or customers from reselling to each other in all these cases?)

16    Consider another ingenious pricing policy: a seller makes two different products and sells them to different customers. In particular, suppose that you are a movie producer and have made two movies: A, a social-problem-oriented drama, and B, a horror movie. You rent your pictures to various exhibitors, two of whom are "Roxy" and "Drivein." You know the amounts that Roxy and Drivein would pay for each movie rather than not get them.

|          | Movie |      |
|----------|-------|------|
|          | *A*   | *B*  |
| Roxy     | $100  | $70  |
| Drivein  | 60    | 80   |

We now investigate three alternative price schedules you could set.

a. Set a price on *A*, with Roxy and Drivein each being allowed to rent at that same price; and set another price on *B*, with each being allowed to rent *B* at that price. Under this arrangement the revenue-maximizing prices are $60 for *A* and $70 for *B*. Your revenue is $260.

b. Set a price on *A* for Roxy and a different price on *A* for Drivein. Also set different prices on *B* for Roxy and Drivein. You may have four prices. What is the revenue-maximizing set of prices, and what is that revenue? ($310 is the total revenue.)

c. We come to the third alternative and the purpose of this problem. Suppose that you are *not* allowed to charge different prices to Roxy and Drivein. However, you do discover that you can engage in "block booking," whereby an exhibitor must take both pictures if he is to take any from you. What price (*same to both exhibitors*) would you set for the *pair* of pictures as one "block book," if you wish to maximize your revenue? What is the maximum revenue you can get this way? (Answer: $280.)

Explain how you determined the best block-booking prices. (Answer: For each exhibitor compute the sum of the highest amounts that would be offered by each exhibitor for each picture. Charge the lowest of these two sums as the price of the "block." As a seller, it pays to engage in block booking only if your customers assign different relative values to the various products in the block. To show this, try to get a gain—over uniform prices for separate pictures—by block booking when both exhibitors value the various pictures in the same relative way. Remember, in block booking you charge the *same package price* to all exhibitors. You will see that block booking gives no advantage to the seller in this case—and no disadvantage either relative to the pricing tactic explained in b.)

d. The exhibitors Roxy and Drivein, who would prefer to prohibit block booking and discriminatory pricing, force you to sell the pictures at the same price to Roxy and Drivein, although permitting a different price for *A* than for *B*. (In this case, as we have seen in part a, the most you could get is $260.) In an effort to keep down their costs, Roxy and Drivein complain to the government that under block booking you, the producer, really are "tying" *B*, the poor picture, to *A*, the better picture, in order to get rid of your inferior picture. They complain they do not have freedom to buy what they want and that you are an unfair monopolist. Explain why the complaint is in error. Is the producer forcing the exhibitors to buy goods they do not want? Explain why or why not.

e. What open-market forces reduce your power to engage in block booking? (Block-booking is used by TV networks.)

17    The market for professors in most colleges is completely open. No requirements about training or prior experience exist as a condition of teaching. A majority of the profession has opposed certification—under which a certification board, consisting of professors, would administer standards of competence. Consider the following:

a. If all present college professors were automatically certified (under a kind of exception called a "grandfather clause"), but all new entrants had to obtain certification by passing certain tests, would the market be open or restricted?

b. If the number of professors admitted were controlled by the board of college professors, which is what would happen, do you think they would restrict entry to the "needed" numbers and would keep out inadequately trained people in order to protect students? Would this have any effect on wages of college professors? What would be the effect on the number of professors?

c. Similar systems of certification (or admission or licensing or self-policing) are used by doctors, lawyers, pharmacists, architects, dentists, morticians, butchers, longshoremen, psychiatrists, barbers, and realtors, to name a few. What do you think it implies about the wages in these professions relative to wages in an open market? What does it imply about the quality of those who actually practice the professions? About the quality and quantity of services provided the community? Is there a difference between quality of competence of those certified and the quantity of service obtained by the public as a whole?

18    "Retail grocery stores are monopolies." In what sense is that correct and in what sense is it false? "The medical profession is a monopoly." In what sense is that true and in what sense false? Which kind of monopoly implies a higher price?

# Nonclearing Market Prices

At an instantly established market-clearing price, consumers can always buy all they want, given their incomes and tastes. No queues, waiting lists, or shortages exist. Sellers can sell all they want to sell at the market-clearing price, if they are in a price-takers' market. But price-searchers would like to have greater sales at the equilibrium price; lowering the price would not enhance their wealth, nor would raising it. However, even a casual look at the world will reveal queues, shortages, surpluses, unemployment, and inventories of goods awaiting buyers. Not all of these are explicable by statutory maximum or minimum price controls or even by price-searchers' markets. Clearly we must relax some more simplifying assumptions in our preceding analysis.

So far we have assumed that costs were zero (1) for obtaining information about potential bids and offers in the process of negotiating exchanges, (2) for using a money price system, and (3) for negotiating and enforcing contracts and property rights. (4) We assumed private-property rights in all goods and firms. We assumed (5) no public goods and (6) no philanthropic activity. We now relax all these assumptions, one by one.

### (1) Costs of Information about Exchange Opportunities

Some observers of the economic scene forget that information about potential bids and offers and attributes of various goods is not *instantly* available at *zero* cost to everyone. They regard markets as "imperfect." But we must accept that information is costly, just as the production of steel and wheat is costly. If markets operate in ways not accounted for by our theory, it is the theory which is imperfect.

If information about everyone else's offer and asking prices, their current interests, and their potential buying and selling plans were instantly and costlessly available to everyone, then indeed we would be hard put to explain the phenomena of slowly responding prices, "unemployment," and "idle" resources. Furthermore, the marketplace would be simply a place for exchange of goods and services. But actually it is also a device whereby people can collect and compare information about various goods and potential sellers.

Recognizing that information is costly and obtainable only with effort and expenditure of time, we should expect to see substantial resources devoted to collecting information about exchange possibilities. And we do. Real-estate agents, retailers, salesmen, brokers, and wholesalers act not only as sellers of goods but also as providers of information about various goods and services and potential buyers and sellers. Housewives devote substantial time to comparison shopping and inspection of goods—that is, to collecting information about purchase possibilities. That a retail store provides information about goods as well as the goods themselves is made painfully obvious to those who try to buy only by mail order.

The student just completing his formal education quickly discovers the cost of collecting information about the details of working conditions and wages of various potential employers. He spends hours and money in learning about and comparing different employers. Information about more distant employers is so costly that often he doesn't try to get it. Similarly, employers devote large sums of money to telling students about working conditions and to discovering the attributes of various potential employees. Look, for example, at the advertisements of employers seeking employees.

If complete information about all job possibilities and all workers and all goods were free and instantly available, there would be no point to shopping or waiting for better offers. One would instead instantly take the best one. But information is neither free nor complete, despite the existence of markets which certainly do help to lower the costs. Consequently, people will devote resources to collecting more information so as to make better purchase and sale decisions. A failure to grasp this has led to much confusion and misinterpretation of the role of certain kinds of economic activity—especially much of that which is called "idleness" or "unemployment."

Before investigating some of the actions consequent to the recognition of the cost of information collecting, we state four central propositions.

(1) *Information is not free.* (2) *The more rapidly it is obtained, the greater the cost of information.* Making the search less hastily is less costly per unit of new information obtained. Production and acquisition of information, as with any other good, conform to the general laws of production. More rapid acquisition may or may not be worth the extra cost, as we shall see. (3) *Adjustment of resources to new uses or customers is costly, and the more rapidly a move is made the more costly it is.* Again, moving from one place to another or from one job to another uses up productive effort and resources. As with other production, "moves" are not free goods. They involve costs. (4) *Information about attributes of goods and about potential offers is sometimes cheaper to obtain with inventories of "unemployed" goods.* Inspection of goods is easier and cheaper if inventories are on display. It would be costlier to have to inspect items already being used by consumers and then order similar items to be manufactured.

Given these facts about the costs of information, about potential buyers and attributes of goods, and about transfers of resources, how do people react to changes in demand for their goods and services? How do they collect information about the change? What use of resources is economical in the face of the costs of getting information? The behavior implied by the answers often gives rise to what are called "unemployment" and "idle" resources—with a consequent misinterpretation of the purpose being served by this apparently undesirable state of affairs. *This does not mean that all forms of behavior that are called unemployment are merely economic adjustments to the higher costs of acquiring information more rapidly; nevertheless we will see that many forms of it are.* Even in mass unemployment during depression, uncertainty and the cost of acquiring information play a vital role. But before we can conveniently apply economic analysis to mass unemployment during depressions, we must see how people react to these costs.

Actions That Economize Information and
Adjustment Costs and Reduce Price Fluctuations

Buffer Stocks: Inventories

In the presence of uncertainty of foresight and recognition of information-collecting costs, stocks of goods are held in inventory, even though these may appear to be "idle" or "unemployed." What may appear to be wasted or unemployed is more accurately identified as economical "information-collecting" uses of resources. Consider, as a simple example, the problem facing a newsboy who expects to sell at a stated price an average of one hundred copies of each edition of a local paper—but not exactly one hundred each day. He has several options. He could spend money to find out who was going to buy copies each day. He could stock less than one hundred and rarely have any unsold copies. He could stock more and have copies left over. He could stock one copy, and each time he sold one he could order another one, getting special-delivery service. The first and last options are very costly. The more accurately he tries to predict or the more quickly he tries to adjust to demand fluctuations, the more expensive the process. Customers prefer to have him stock an excessive number on the average in order to have instant availability out of inventories, despite a slightly higher cost of the newspaper (implied by each seller's ending up with extra copies). The higher cost to customers need not appear as a higher money price; it may appear as a smaller newspaper or as fewer retailers. But this cost of extra copies will be less than if the newspaper sellers attempted to obtain *complete* information or make *instantaneous* adjustments in the number of papers.

An apartment owner will build more apartments than he expects on the average to have occupied. It will pay him to build more apartments in order to satisfy the unpredictable vagaries of demand rather than relying on instant fluctuations in rents to clear the market. The apartment-house owner can keep the apartments fully rented at a lower rental; or at a higher rental he can have some vacancies part of the time. In providing some occasional vacancies, he is catering to renters' desires to move when they want rather than making plans and reservations far in advance. The situation is exactly analogous to a person's building a home with enough bathrooms and dining space to seat more visitors than he will ordinarily have. To say that he has "wasted or "idle" or "unemployed" bathroom or dining-room capacity is to consider only the cost of that extra capacity and to misunderstand its value and to overlook the higher costs of alternative ways of obtaining equally high convenience or utility.

Empty apartments *per se* are not waste. They are a method of production to economize on the high costs of predicting the future and also of the high costs of *immediately* producing whatever a person wants. By producing in advance at a less hasty, more economical rate and holding resources available for contingent demands, we economize in having more housing services at a cost that is worth paying, taking into account the value of being able to move without long, advance, "reservation-type" planning. We could reduce implicit costs of housing by more advance planning of people's activities and refusals to allow them to change their minds, but this would also reduce housing services and convenience.

In a given community, there will be more houses or apartments than people want at any given moment to occupy. There will also be an "extra supply" of service stations, barber shops, dress shops, real-estate agencies, insurance salesmen, and car dealers. The extra supply is really an inspection supply or a convenience supply. Imagine what it would be like trying to move in a community that had as many apartments as families and every apartment was now rented. "Costs" would be imposed on tenants who wanted to move. Vacant apartments are "waste" only in an imaginary world of perfect predictability at zero cost or in a world where instant production to every moment's demand is no more costly or troublesome than is advance preparation.

Moreover, buildings will be provided with fire escapes and residential areas with fire hydrants; first-aid kits will be located in homes and fire extinguishers in strategic places in buildings. Such provisions would not be necessary if information about the future were free and available immediately. Everyone could know early enough how to avoid catastrophes. Or if information were not free, but it were just as cheap to make instant physical adjustments as slow ones, then upon word of fire the building could immediately be altered to have fire escapes. Water lines could be laid to the site of the fire. This suggestion is absurd; it denies higher costs for more rapid acquisition of information and more rapid subsequent physical adjustments. If "instant production" could be achieved at no more cost than less hasty production, if instant information were as cheap as less rapidly obtained answers, there would be no "idle," "excess," "unemployed" resources. But instant adjustments *do* cost more than less hasty adjustments. We therefore expect to observe what might carelessly be called "idle" resources.

Effects of higher costs of acquiring information and making more rapid adjustments are evident not only in the production of new goods but also in the re-allocation of existing goods. Earlier chapters indicated that prices serve to re-allocate goods among competing claimants. How rapidly do they re-allocate in response to changes in demands? How rapidly and accurately are new alternatives revealed? Information about changing purchase demands and supplies is not free. An essential function of the market is to make that information more readily (cheaply) accessible. But it does not become "free."

### Price Stability in Face of Transient, Unpredicted Demand Fluctuations

Higher search costs imply more price stability in the face of transient, temporary, unpredictable fluctuations in purchase demand. A seller might instantly and temporarily vary the price upward or downward as inventories fell or rose so as always to clear the market to customers without their waiting in line. But imagine a restaurant in which the price of food varied instantly to newcomers to avoid their waiting in line. The greater the possibility of surprising price fluctuations, the more customers would devote resources ahead of time to looking for sellers with lower prices at that moment. But persistently looking for places with lower prices is more costly, and people will prefer to stand in line a bit, the higher are the costs of search. Some seller could charge even a slightly higher, predictable, stable price (to cover inventory buffer costs), and customers would still prefer to patronize him because of their cheaper knowledge of the price he will charge. Given these considerations it will pay some sellers to provide inventories as a buffer to shorten queues and to reduce customers' search costs, especially where search costs are relatively high. For example, in the stock market, where costs of finding other sellers of a common stock like American Telephone and Telegraph are very low, prices will fluctuate more transiently and sensitively to transient purchase demands than in most other markets.

## (2) Costs of Negotiating Exchanges and (3) Enforcing Property Rights

For market prices to guide allocation of goods, there must be an incentive for people to express and to respond to offers. If it is costly to reveal bids and offers and to negotiate and make exchanges, the gains from exchange might be offset. If each person speaks a different language, if thievery is rampant, or if contracts are likely to be dishonored, then negotiation, transaction, and policing costs will be so high that fewer market exchanges will occur. If *property rights* in goods are weak, ill defined, or vague, the re-allocation of goods is likely to be guided by "biased" offers and bids that understate the personal values of various goods. Who would offer as much for a coat, if he thought it was very likely to be stolen?

In all our preceding analysis we assumed strong private-property rights and low exchange and information costs. But a significant portion of the goods in our present economy is not controlled by private-property rights, and transaction costs (negotiation, contracting, and policing) are not always sufficiently low relative to the value of the goods.

Most of us are so accustomed to private property that we do not realize its rarity. Yet few places outside of Western Europe and the former English dominions have private-property rights as we know them in the United States. The higher market value attaching to goods with strong ownership rights spurs individuals to seek laws that would strengthen private-property rights. However, not all jurists and politicians have viewed with uniform sympathy the tendency to secure private-property rights. To the extent that private-property rights exist, the power of government officials to control uses of goods decreases; the major alternative to private property is government property. History is a long story of fluctuations and variations in this development. At times, private-property rights have dominated; at others they have been weakened and replaced by socialism, government ownership, or communal tribal ownership.

Property rights are the expectations a person has that his decision about the uses of certain resources will be effective. The stronger those expectations are upheld, in one way or another (custom, social ostracism, or government punishment of violators) the stronger are the property rights. Private-property rights in goods constitute the exclusive rights of the owners to use their goods, *and only their goods*, in any way they see fit, including the right to transfer these rights to other people. I cannot throw my hammer through your window without violating your right to use your window as you decide. If, in using my goods, I affect your goods, then I am violating your rights to the use of your property. However, I can legally throw a rock through your window or tear down your house and occupy your land, if, and only if, I obtain your permission or buy the rights from you. Exclusivity of control constitutes a basic component of the private-property economic system. We emphasize that property rights are *not* rights *of property*; they are rights *of people* to use of property. In sum, two basic elements of private property are *exclusivity* of right of use and *voluntary transferability* or exchangeability of that right.

Transferability is the right to exchange property rights with other people at mutually agreeable terms. In the strong sense, transferability means exchangeability at terms that only the buyer and seller need approve. No third party can impose the terms. In a weaker sense, transferability could exist even if exchanges were permitted only at prices set by a third party.

A series of United States Supreme Court decisions vacillates as to whether private property is to mean strong or weak transferability. Early in the nineteenth century imposition of legal limits on market prices was declared not to be a denial of private-property rights; but about fifty years later the decision was reversed, and a legally imposed price was declared an invasion of private-property rights. Subsequently, the Supreme Court again reversed itself and declared that price controls are not invasions of private-property rights as defined in the Constitution.

A person has private-property rights to uses of goods if decisions about those physical uses are not made by other people. The person who controls decisions about *all* physical attributes or uses of goods is called the owner. If I own a house, you cannot paint it, burn it, or otherwise affect its technological or physical characteristics without my permission, under the laws characterizing a private-property economy.

If all the costs of use of a good are borne solely by the owner, there is said to be an identity of private and social costs; the owner does not inflict some of the cost on the rest of society. However, rights to control every physical attribute of goods are not always clearly assigned to particular people or owners. If I burn refuse or operate a factory so as to emit smoke, ashes, smells, soot, and airborne acids on and over your land, I am using my goods in ways that harmfully change "your" goods without your permission. When a neighbor walks his dog for its nightly relief, my property is damaged. When I drive my scooter with a blaring exhaust that sends sound vibrations across his property, I momentarily change its physical attributes for the worse. These are examples of actions that change the characteristics of the goods other people are said to own—except that here the owner does not so effectively "own" rights to those affected attributes.

Think of private-property rights as a person's rights to decide on the use of his and only his goods and services (that is, without violating the same rights of other people) and to sell or exchange those rights. We do not exchange goods *per se*; we exchange *rights* over goods. Physical possession is not the essence of property rights; at best, physical possession is a means of asserting or giving evidence of rights. If I have no recognized rights to some automobile, I do not have much to sell you. And when a car's ownership is less secure or is disputed, the market price will be lower than if title is clear.[1]

The costs of market exchange comprise the costs of finding other people to buy the rights, to transport the goods to the market, to write up a bill of sale, to make the cash payment, and to assure the new possessor protection of the transferred rights. Millenniums ago man learned geometry and trigonometry and how to demarcate specific plots of land. Identification and, hence, sale and resale of land became cheaper and more prevalent. Today we are learning how to exchange and police rights over radio "waves," just as we do land rights. Airlines are learning how to keep track of planes with sufficient accuracy to measure, police, and exchange rights to moving cocoons of airspace. Water is still a relatively expensive item to control in its natural state, though not after it has been captured in reservoirs, canals, or pipes. Water meters are cheap enough to be used extensively in almost all cities (though not New York). Therefore, pricing of water is used to ration and allocate water among most residential and industrial users, though not so commonly to agricultural users. "Shortages" of water are less likely to occur where meters are used since the price of the water can make the amount demanded equal to the amount supplied.

Undoubtedly the future will bring new, more economical metering, policing, or contracting devices for the control of water, streets, airspace, radio-TV, and the ocean floor. As radar ranges increase and boats become faster and use longer-range guns, greater distances from the shore can be policed and will therefore be worth claiming by the nearest country—as has already been done for oil rights hundreds of miles into the North Sea. Peru is selling rights to

---

[1] This discussion reveals how silly it is to speak of a contrast or conflict between human rights and property rights. Property rights *are* human rights to the use of economic goods. Furthermore, a presumed conflict between human rights to use property and civil rights is equally vacuous. However civil rights may be specified, they do not conflict with human rights to use goods. The dispute is one of what the structure of human rights to use of economic goods should be.

fish "her" ocean 200 miles out from the shore; this gives Peru an incentive to conserve the ocean resources rather than wastefully exploit them.

We now investigate some examples of the effects of negotiation and property-enforcement costs on the use of queues, waiting lists, and other (nonmarket-clearing price) means of allocating use of goods. A practical example is provided by a parking lot. If it costs a landowner more to collect the price and police the transactions for a parking space than the value of the parking space, he has no incentive to rent the space for parking. He either gives away parking rights "free" or lets no one park, depending upon the side effects. Formal market exchange and prices will be used only if devices are invented (for example, parking meters with police enforcement) to lower the costs of exchange (or if the demand rises sufficiently to raise the value above the costs of policing contracts). In European countries where labor is cheaper relative to land values than in the United States, the costs of using parking attendants to collect fees and police the space is lower relative to the value of the space. Therefore, we observe a greater use of such attendants than in the United States.

The variety of prices of theater seats is affected by the cost of ushers to enforce multiple-sectioned seating. If ushers' wages are high relative to admission prices, fewer ushers will be used; this will make it more difficult to ensure that those who pay premium prices are the only ones in the premium seats. In Europe, because of the lower wage rates *relative* to values of theater seats, there will be a greater variety of price classes than in the United States. Various seats within the theater will be priced more closely to the price that equilibrates demand with supply.

If theater seats are sold at various prices according to location in the theater, there will be less incentive to come early to stand in line to get a "good" seat; good seats are not then allocated on a first-come, first-served basis. Otherwise, the better space is rationed by the cost of standing in line—which is a cost to be borne by the standees. This means it cannot be asserted that a lower than market-clearing price lets people get goods at a lower *cost*. The cost to a buyer is not always as low as it seems; if the buyer must wait in line, he must include the waiting as part of the cost. The longer the line, the greater the "standing" costs. It is "time and standing" that now clear the market.

Parking meters permit cheaper metering of street parking, so more of the spaces can be allocated by a formalized market price system. Why doesn't the market control the allocation of *traffic lanes*? As yet no one has devised an economical way for drivers who want to use the parking lane as a traveling lane to bid away that space from those who want to park. Since each driver would use the lane for only a short time, one can imagine the task of trying to buy up the right to a cleared traffic lane from people who want to park. The cost of negotiating these exchanges far exceeds the value to one buyer.

Similarly—partly because of the high costs of negotiating exchanges—the market exchange system has not been used for allocating radio and television programs to listeners. In the past, it was simply too costly to provide an electronic device whereby a receiver could pick up a program only if he had paid for it. Economical devices for scrambling and then descrambling programs and collecting payments have now been developed, but so far the U.S. government has prohibited their use, unless the programs are carried directly by cable from station to home.

Another example of economical market-exchange operations is the coin vending machine. Telescopes at viewpoints operate with coin-controlled machines; some airport waiting rooms have coin-operated turnstiles to allocate seats in which patrons can view airport operations; coin-operated devices control access to dormitory rooms and restrooms for travelers between flights. We have coin-operated rental typewriters at libraries and pay telephones. (Why not "pay" drinking fountains?)

A capitalist system is aided by cheap transferability and exclusivity of rights to physical use of human and nonhuman goods. When these rights do not prevail, or are "expensive" to define or exchange, the market exchange system fails. Other forms of competition for determining uses of goods dominate. Examples are plentiful. (1) The western states fight each other in the courts over use of water from various watersheds, but they don't fight about the use of forest timber, oil, iron ore, coal, or other "natural" resources—because rights to water are not transferable as are those for oil and lumber. Government agencies allocate water, whereas no agencies are required for wood or oil. (2) Traffic conditions on the public highways and behavior on public beaches are examples of rights-claiming competitive behavior with "fleeting, insecure, undefined, nonexchangeable" rights to road space. (3) Sewage provides another example of unusual competition: cities upstream dump sewage, and cities downstream bear the consequences; so each city is tempted to build a pipeline farther upstream nearer the source to catch purer water.[2]

### (4) Allocation under Rights Other Than "Private Property": Nonprofit Institutions

The preceding analysis of pricing and exchange was all based on systems of private property. Let us now examine allocative behavior under forms of property rights that are not what we ordinarily call private-property rights. We shall consider nonprofit institutions and state- and city-owned property.

In a *nonprofit* corporation, there is no group of trustees or directors or "owners" who can decide to distribute the net gains to themselves as their own wealth, as can be done in a for-profit corporation. Funds must be spent in the enterprise to further the purposes of that enterprise. Most private academic colleges are nonprofit institutions, and money must be devoted to

[2] A more complete investigation of the effects of costs of enforcing private-property rights on production is given in Chapter 11.

the educational aims of the institution, although precious few colleges cover their costs by tuitions. Most charitable foundations—for example, the Ford and Carnegie Foundations—are nonprofit organizations; all the profits of their investments are to be used not for the benefit of the trustees but to further the stated aims of the foundation. The Rose Festival Association, the Metropolitan Opera Association, and almost all religious and fraternal organizations are nonprofit institutions. Look at a sample case, the Rose Festival Association, to see why queues, shortages, and "low" prices are likely to occur.

### Rose Festival Association

Each New Year's Day, the Rose Bowl football game is held in Pasadena, California. Every time, sure as fate, more tickets are wanted than are available at the price set by the association. Some buyers are prepared to offer higher prices to get seats; and yet the Rose Festival Association and the associated colleges refuse to accept those offers and persist in selling at a lower price to students, alumni, and Rose Festival Association affiliates (and to 2,000 winners of a race to get to the Rose Bowl box office for a special "public" sale). Furthermore, the association and the universities declare it illegal for anyone to resell his ticket to some other person at a price higher than he originally paid for it. (The authors, from personal experience, know that many tickets *are* resold at $40 over the authorized sale price.)

Why does the Rose Bowl association refuse to accept higher offers from frustrated buyers. Why does it refuse greater wealth? The Rose Festival Association is not *privately owned* in the conventional sense. One third of the gate receipts are used to finance its activities, such as providing the game, the Rose Parade, and other civic affairs. One third of the receipts goes to each of the participating universities and their athletic conferences. But no person can claim any *pro rata* part of the proceeds as being "his"; no one can spend the net proceeds in the way he could spend his privately owned wealth. In these circumstances, will the operator-members of this association—those who set its policies and determine the specific activities—behave as they would if they owned the association?

Forget that there is a large association, and assume that only one person (call him the manager) makes the decisions. At what price shall tickets to the football game be sold? The answer, in accordance with our familiar principle, will be "at the price that maximizes the decider's utility." He could set too low a price, so that more seats are demanded than are available. He might then, by virtue of his position, secure tickets and resell some of them at market-clearing prices, thereby unethically diverting wealth to himself. But, being a moral person, he eschews *this unethical* line of "gain." He can still gain utility by this "too low" price policy. First, by underpricing the tickets, he can buy tickets for himself more cheaply, thus releasing a bit of his own private wealth for other uses. Second, the excess demand for tickets enables him to grant favors to certain selected applicants for tickets. This priority means that the "right" people can get tickets at a price less than they *and others* are willing to pay. Favorable treatment for certain people will enhance his utility. His prestige is increased: he is invited to the best places, clubs, and circles; and even when he buys a car or furniture, past favors are fondly and effectively recalled. This price policy will cost the association some of the wealth it might have earned. Although smaller receipts for the association reduce the manager's own utility, he must weigh this reduction against his utility increase from being able to distribute tickets cheaply and to favor certain individuals.

But what if the association were a privately owned corporation with private-property rights residing in the stockholders? Would the manager still prefer a low pricing policy? If so, the *owners* (stockholders) will have a stronger incentive to fire him or place him on a commission basis, to reduce the discrepancy between their gains and his.

Let's strain the analysis a bit further. If there are several kinds of seats, which seats will be underpriced? Primarily the kind that the manager and the association members would want. These are the best seats. Market-clearing prices will more likely be charged for the inferior seats that go to people who are neither students nor alumni.

There is still more to the situation, for the universities surely should want maximum receipts and therefore should oppose underpriced tickets. But the "universities" also are nonprofit, nonprivate-property institutions, and so the *individuals* who make the decisions on this matter are also acting in the absence of private-property rights. The university administrators of athletic affairs are like the Rose Bowl administrator. Thus, the same story is repeated.

### Other Nonprofit Associations

Nonprofit corporations under research contracts to the federal government (for example, RAND Corporation, Aerospace, Franklin Institute) will allocate their available resources with a weaker incentive to maximize wealth. This does not mean they will provide poor services or underprice the services. Rather, they will have incentive to provide services in a more expensive manner, with smaller profits. Why? Because no one could claim the sacrificed potential savings in the same sense that a privately owned for-profit organization's owners could. Costs to the managers of exercising their idiosyncratic tastes are lower. The managers like pretty women, so they will have prettier secretaries, even if they ask higher wages than unattractive secretaries might. If the managers prefer whites to equally productive but lower-priced Negroes, the managers will hire fewer Negroes and more whites. Furniture and equipment will be more luxurious than for employees doing the same quality of work in private for-profit businesses. Such are the implications of economic analysis. And data being collected are slowly providing corroboration.

The foregoing considerations may be interpreted as favorable or unfavorable to the private-property system, depending upon whether one prefers that resource use and allocation respond to the wealth influence of other people via the marketplace. The analysis is simply an indirect application of the law of demand in alternative property-rights contexts: "The lower the cost, the more of a good that is demanded." The cost to the manager of a nonprofit association of engaging in activities costly to the organization is lower than for the manager of a privately owned organization. Why? In the latter, the cost (forsaken wealth) to the organization is more fully imposed on people who could have had that forsaken wealth: The forsaken wealth is more effectively impressed on the manager as a cost that he must bear in a lower salary or a higher probability of losing his job. In strict logic, the analysis implies that only with private property will market prices behave as equilibrium prices. However, notice that the *law of demand* holds, no matter what the form of property right and regardless of the extent to which formal market exchange is used.

## (5) Public Goods

So far we have dealt only with goods for which (1) the utility a person gets depends upon how much of that good he has *and* (2) the more he has of that good the less someone else *must* have. For hot dogs, the one I eat is one no one else will eat. My utility from hot dogs depends upon the amount that *I* get, not the total amount produced. However, for some kinds of goods, the amount I consume does not reduce the amount you can consume. I can view a television program *and* you can too. My viewing is not at the cost of your viewing (*once the program is put on*). The same holds for some forms of national defense. Increased defense means more for me with as much for you, unless it is a kind of local antimissile defense for your town rather than mine. "Public" (or "collective") goods are those for which *the extent of consumption or use by one person does not diminish the amount available for other people (once the goods are produced)*. For "private" goods, more for one person means less for someone else. Some goods have mixtures of private- and public-good attributes. A band concert has both attributes. The space around the band is limited, and a better space for some of us means a poorer space for others.

Some examples of pure public goods or goods almost exclusively composed of public-goods attributes are mathematical theorems, TV and radio programs, songs, poems, technology, ideas, and knowledge. One person's use of an idea does not prevent anyone else from using it. One viewer of a TV program does not displace another. For pure public goods there seems no point in requiring someone to give up some other goods in exchange since (once the pure public good is created) any person can have as large a part of the available amount as he chooses without anyone else having less. No price is necessary, for *there is no rationing problem for the existing amount of the pure public good*. There is no apparent reason to have the existing public-good service moved toward users with the higher personal valuation for the good, as for hot dogs in a private-goods system. Everyone can simultaneously use all that exists.

Although pure public goods pose no *rationing* problem, there is the problem of determining how much and which public goods to *produce*. Production is not costless. If no price is charged, how can its value to society be determined relative to other goods? Potential users of new public goods are tempted to conceal their valuations of the good for fear they might be asked to pay for its production. If someone else can be inveigled into paying, then those who do not pay can, *once the good is produced*, use all that is available without having borne its production costs. But given the costs of production, how much should or would be produced and at whose expense?

Some services with public-goods attributes are produced outside the normal market-exchange system. Often they are produced by government and financed by taxes or fees for the services, as in England where radio and some television are provided by the government and financed by a tax on every receiver. In the United States, national defense is provided by government and financed by taxes. In cities and towns, police protection is financed by taxes, although in some cities private police forces are financed by revenue from those desiring extra patrol service.

Be careful of jumping to incorrect conclusions. Some have concluded that it is wrong to permit pay-television, because the price charged for looking at a program would dissuade some viewers without making more available to others. The dissuaded viewers, therefore, will wastefully be prevented from seeing existing programs. This is correct *so far as it goes*, but it doesn't meet all the inescapable issues. Allocation or utilization of the service *once it is created* is only part of the problem. Producing TV programs or public goods is costly, and the cost must be borne by someone. The decision of how much and what kind of public goods to produce also must be faced in a world of scarcity. Public goods are not "free" goods; they are scarce. Those who advocate pay-TV are concentrating their attention on bringing to bear viewer's direct influence on what and how much shall be *produced* and who should bear the costs. But pay-TV advocates, in turn, must not ignore the absence of the rationing problem of the program *once it is created*.

A few more remarks are appropriate here. If there are two potential users of a public good, one valuing it at $10 and the other at $20, and since *both* can enjoy its services, one more unit of that service would be worth $30, not merely the $20 of the single highest-valuing user. The value of another unit of such services is the public's *summed* value of $30 since *both* people get their individual values. Another unit of the public good would be produced if it cost up to $30 and if the *sum* of the individual private valuations were *brought to bear as an inducement to production*. If the users do not or cannot express the *sum* of their values, there would be too little produced, according to users' valuations.

It is not demonstrable that the solution to the problem of determining how much of which public goods to produce can best be solved by government or socialist methods. Similarly, it is no solution to say, without recognition of differentiating attributes, that public goods should be produced and distributed just like private goods. Each method involves "undesirable features." To analyze this further, we must know some principles of production and its control. Then later, in Chapter 12, we will return to study some techniques of distributing, producing, and financing public goods.

(6) Philanthropy

Charity or philanthropy is a deliberate allocation outside the market; it totals to billions of dollars annually. Charitable foundations and colleges are two prime examples—not to mention religious groups and individual gifts. Musical concerts, museums, libraries, and art galleries are open to the public at prices far below those that would clear the market, precisely because the sponsor wants to be charitable. The Ford and Rockefeller Foundations, to name but two of the largest, are supposed to give away wealth—not sell it. Almost every college provides services at less than market-equilibrium prices, because they are supported by people who want to give educational opportunities to (*smart*) young people. In all of these cases, because the price is below the market-clearing or equilibrium level, a long list of applicants must be screened on some other competitive, discriminatory basis. How do the results differ from those of market-price competition? Economic analysis will shed light on that question—perhaps with some surprises.

The *economics* of philanthropy, charity, or gifts may seem contradictory. If, according to economic theory, people seek to increase their own utility, how then can they give gifts? Are these acts to be set aside from economics as unexplainable behavior? Not at all. The postulates of economic theory do not say that man is concerned only about his own situation. He can be concerned about other people's situations also. If other people are miserable, he may himself feel a lower level of utility. Other people's situations as well as his own can affect *his* utility—which means that *his choices* of what he does with resources at his command can depend, in part at least, upon the effects upon other people.

From my point of view, increased wealth for you is preferred (a source of increase of utility to me). It is even possible that a $1 decrease in my wealth could reduce my utility by *less* than a $1 increase in *your* wealth would increase *my* utility. Then I would contribute wealth to you. That is irrefutable, by definition. But the likelihood of this happening is greater if my wealth is large and yours is small. And that is a refutable proposition. As my wealth decreases relative to yours, my willingness to contribute to you will decrease, just as a decreasing amount of candy decreases my willingness to give up additional candy for Cokes. (This is postulate 4.) Furthermore, a *matching grant* would induce me to give still more, because now I know that each dollar I give up gets you more than $1. This implies that matching grants should be commonly observed in charity. And they are.[3]

---

[3]Income-tax reductions for gifts are another way to reduce the donor's costs of giving money to other people—by making other taxpayers pay more to offset my reduced tax payments.

A gift can be defined as an allocation at a price set *intentionally* below the open-market price by those "giving away" the goods. Suppose I own a house that would rent for $100 at the open-market price; however, I offer it to you for only $40 as a favor. Suppose that you would not have paid the open-market price of $100 for this particular house, but would have been prepared to pay $80 for it. We now have three valuations: $A$—the market rent of the house ($100), $B$—the price at which you *would* have been willing to rent the house ($80), and $D$—the actual price of the house to you ($40). We want one more item of information: How much would you have spent for housing if I hadn't made you this special offer? Your answer we shall suppose to be $65, denoted by $C$; that is, you would have chosen a smaller or more inferior house than the $100 one I offered you for $40 per month. The following relationships can now be specified. The difference between $A$ and $D$ (*i.e.*, $A - D$) is the total wealth transferred *from* me. The house is worth $100, and I get only $40 for it. In this transfer of $60 of wealth from me, what did you get?

First, compare what you did pay, $40, with what you would have paid for some house ($65) had I not provided you with this unusual opportunity. This difference $(C - D)$ is $65 -$40, or $25, a measure of how much money you have had released every month from housing purchases and which you may now use in any way you like. We call this an increase in your "money" wealth, a gift of $25 to you. The quantity $(C - D)$ *could* be negative, indicating that the recipient would have spent less on this kind of good than if the subsidy had not been offered.

Second, compare the cost of whatever housing you would have bought had this special offer not been made with what you would have paid for the house that I made available to you. This difference $(B - C)$ is, in our example, $80 - $65 = $15. You now have $15 more of wealth in the *specific* form of housing than you otherwise would have had.

Of the $60 wealth transfer, we have accounted for $25 $(C - D)$ as a *general* (money) wealth increase to you and $15 $(B-C)$ more of a *specific* resource, housing; that leaves $20 $(A - B)$ unaccounted for. As far as *you* are concerned, that extra $20 is simply wasted: you have acquired for $40 a house that you value not at $100 but at only $80. Although I have borne a cost of $60, the gift is worth only $40 to you. From your point of view, if I had given you $60 in money and let you spend it as you wished, you would have been better off by $20. This "waste" (from your point of view) of $20 is the third component of the $60 gift.

Don't forget *my* (the donor's) point of view. Is there a waste of $20? If I am fully aware of these implications, and nevertheless choose to make the particular gift that I do, then from my point of view it is worth $60 to give you the gain of $25 in cash and $15 in superior housing. It is worth more than $20 to *me* to induce you to live in a house that costs $100 (but which you think is worth only $80). I put you in an environment that I prefer for you.

For *every* instance in which goods are transferred (from me to you) at less than the free-market exchange-equilibrium price, we can summarize the analysis succinctly if we let

A  be the market value of the transferred goods.

B  be the hypothetical price which, if existing, would have induced you to buy the good.

C  be the money you would have paid for whatever amount of the transferred good you otherwise would have purchased.

D  be the amount actually paid by you.

Then,

*(A − D)* is the net total cost to me of the resources transferred to you which can be subdivided into the following three components:

*(A − B)* is the waste, from your (the receiver's point of view, but not necessarily from mine (the giver's);

*(B − C)* is the value to *you* of the extra specific resources made available to you;

*(C − D)* is the general-purchasing-power wealth transfer to you.

We have ignored the impact that opportunities to capture subsidies or gifts will have on the behavior of potential receivers in their attempts to get the subsidies. Prospects of competitive applicants can be improved if they spend money or direct their activities so as to reach a more advantageous position, as judged by the allocative criteria used by the donor. Each applicant will be induced to spend an amount, at the most, equal to the value of the subsidy as valued by the potential recipient.

### Business Dinner Dance for Employees

To illustrate the consequences of a gift, let us apply the analysis to an employees' dinner dance sponsored by a business firm. Suppose the cost of the dinner is $14 per person, but the company sells tickets to employees for only $6. Question: Who gets what by this company gift? The quantity $A$ is $14, the market value of the service being sold for $6, which is denoted by $D$ (using the letters in the earlier example). We now consider employee I, who we ascertain would have spent $14 on a dinner dance anyway, even without this subsidy. His $C$ is $14. We also learn that he would have been willing to buy this particular dinner-dance ticket even if the price had been the full $14. His $B$ is also $14. Now we can carry through the computations. The company is spending $8 per ticket as a subsidy $(A − D) = ($14 − $6) = $8$. Employee I gets a cash gain of $8, $(C − D) = ($14 − $6) = $8$. His gain in *specific kind* of goods is zero, for $(B − C) = $14 − $14 = 0$. From his point of view there is no waste, for $(A − C) = $14 − $14 = 0$. The subsidy has given him simply a cash release of the full amount of the $8 subsidy, to spend however he wishes.

Consider employee II, who does not engage in so much dinner dancing and who would have spent only $7 for dinner dancing in the absence of this particular party. His $C$ is $7. Suppose further that he would have been willing to pay $9 for this particularly elaborate party if the price had been that high, but he would have refused this particular party if the price had been higher. His $B$ is $9. For him, $C - D = (\$7 - \$6) = \$1$; he gets $1 cash gain. His $(B - C) = (\$9 - \$7) = \$2$, which means he gets $2 (as he values it) more of dinner. dancing than he otherwise would. And the third component $(A - B) = \$14 - \$9 = \$5$ is a measure of the waste of company money. The company spent $14 for something worth only $9 to *him*. Of the total $8 net cost to the company, $5 was a waste and $2 went to give employee II more dinner dancing than he otherwise would have had, and $1 was his cash gain.

And then there is employee III, who doesn't think the dinner dance is worth even $6. He buys no ticket and gets no gain of any kind.

Question: If you were the owner of the company, what would you think of partially subsidized dinner dances as a scheme to aid the employees to have a good time? Which employees?

Reconsider employee II, who would have paid $9 for a dinner-dance ticket. Why doesn't he play it smart? Why doesn't he buy a ticket for $6 and sell it to some outsider for $14, thereby gaining $8? This is better for him than the alternative gain of $1 in money and $2 more of dinner-dance activity. But the company prohibits him from doing so, probably because the managers don't want outsiders at the dance. Then why doesn't he resell the ticket to some other employee? There are two cases to consider. On the one hand, the supply of tickets at $6 may be large enough to provide all that the employees want at that price. But if the supply of tickets is not large enough at $6, the lucky employees who first get tickets could resell them at a higher price and take their gift entirely as generalized money gains, rather than as less-valued dinner-dance activity.

Would reselling to a fellow employee thwart the intent of the company managers? Did they want to encourage dinner dancing by employees? If so, allowing employees to resell will not reduce the number who attend. If the management wants more dinner dancing, it has to subsidize more tickets. The effect of permitting resale is to break the connection between dinner dancing and gifts, allowing some gift to those who don't dinner dance.

To make this analysis strike home, inquire if on your campus the faculty have special parking rights not granted to students. If so, apply the above analysis to discern what gains the faculty get and what would be the gains if they could sell the parking rights to students.

### Foreign Aid

The United States government grants aid (gifts) to some foreign governments, ostensibly for specific purposes. If the U.S. government gives $10,000,000 to the Egyptian government to build a dam, what has Egypt gained? What would the Egyptians have done without the gift of aid? Suppose they intended to build the dam anyway, financing it by domestic saving. To that extent, a gift for the dam releases wealth of the Egyptian government for other things. The gift purportedly "for a dam" is actually for general purposes—the Egyptian government now simply has $10,000,000 more than it otherwise would have. Conceivably it could lower taxes—thus giving the Egyptians that much more income for general consumption—or the government itself will spend the extra funds.

Why, then, do we give the money "for a dam"? One possible answer is that otherwise they would not have built the dam, so that the gift does provide one more dam. The embarrassing implication of this answer is that this particular use of the money for the dam is so unproductive that the Egyptian government itself wouldn't have paid for the dam. Or, if they were too poor to have done so, then a simple gift of $10,000,000 to the Egyptians with no strings attached for its use would have enabled the Egyptians themselves to decide what were the most valuable uses of the extra $10,000,000 of wealth made available. Of course, government officials of both the United States and Egypt understand all this, and the "conditional" form of the grant is employed primarily to try to induce the Egyptian government to behave more in accord with the interest of the U.S. government.

### Free School Transportation

Children in some public-school districts are given free bus rides to school. From this gift (subsidy) of bus rides to school children, who gains what? The answer should now be easy. The parents of the children must be classed according to those who would have provided transportation for their children and those who would have made their children walk. The first group receive all the subsidy as a general increase in their wealth. They can buy more of all things with the wealth which otherwise would have paid for their children's transportation. The other parents get no gain in general wealth, but take it all in the specific form of better transportation for the children. "Free bus rides" for school children turn out then to be composites of gifts of wealth to parents and of better transportation for children, with some families getting all of it in general wealth, some in mixtures, and some exclusively in transportation.

The corollary of our general proposition says that gifts might as well be resalable or given as money by the donors to the extent that the recipients already possess or use the services or resources given to them. If I am given a case of Coca-Cola each month by some kind-hearted person who thinks he is inducing me to drink more Cokes, he should note that already my family consumes a case a month. Therefore, I shall temporarily stop buying Cokes from the store and use the released wealth for other purposes. Whether he gives Cokes (whether or not he lets me sell them) or money is essentially irrelevant.

Unintentional Charity

Intentional and unintentional gifts cannot always be distinguished. Nor, as we shall see, can we conclude that every allocation of resources made at less than a market-clearing price, even at a price as low as zero, involves a gain to the recipient. Fortunately, intent is not necessarily to discern what happens.

Currently, anyone wanting to operate a new television station must first obtain permission of the Federal Communications Commission (FCC). Rights to operate a station are valuable, and many applicants appeal to the FCC for authorization.[4] Each will try to show why he is the proper person. How? In sales of government-owned forests and oil lands, the "right" person is the one who will bid the most, with the proceeds going to the public treasuries. But the law creating the FCC forbids it to allocate channels on the basis of competitive money bids. Nor is "first come, first served" the rule (although it was for radio in the early 1920s). Instead, the commission in some unspecified manner chooses among applicants.

The applicant is asked to show why the community "needs" another station—over protestations of the existing station owner, whose television station's value would fall. Because there is no money-price competition of the open-marketplace variety, other competition in terms of applicants' attributes takes on more significance. Money that would have been paid to the government under price competition for that right or "property" will instead be devoted, at least in part, to competition for the commissioners' support. Since something worth millions is at stake, duplicative millions are spent seeking the license.

On what criteria do commissioners select the winner? That, of course, is what the various applicants would like to know. They do know that the applicant should be a man of respectability, good moral standing, public service, and high education. If he is a newspaper publisher or a radio-station operator, he has an advantage, for he is experienced in news collecting and dissemination. If he doesn't put on religious programs, if he plays only jazz and Western shows and intends to present few if any "cultural" programs, he will lose competitive rank. He must detect the preferences, tastes, and kinds of shows that commissioners think the public ought to be shown; then he must suggest that he will present those programs. He must be careful not to offer explicit, detectable bribes to the commissioners. On the other hand, if in the past he hired some of the FCC technical staff to operate his other radio or television stations, or if he is an ex-congressman, or if he employs an ex-congressman as a legal counsel to advocate his case to the FCC, this indicates that he recognizes able people, and he therefore is a person who could

---

[4] The number of channels that could be used at one time is not a technologically fixed constant. It depends upon the kind of receiving and transmitting equipment. With more expensive and sensitive receivers and transmitters, the number of available channels could be greatly increased. And the increase with cable is enormous.

successfully operate a television station. All the value of the rights to broadcast accrues neither to the federal taxpayers nor to the winning applicant; instead, part is consumed in legal fees, costs of publicity, and other expenses incurred to win the competition for the license. Thus, even though the nominal price of the license is zero, the costs of getting it are substantial—not to mention the costs of the losers' efforts.

The magnitude of the gift is revealed by the amount that the stock prices of companies jump when they receive a license to operate a station or when an existing station is sold. Fortunately for the station owners, this wealth gain *is* transferable; they can sell that station to other people so they need not keep their gift in the form of ownership and operation of a television station. That value of the station is in part a measure of the wealth given away. Was it the intention of the government to make a gift? Presumably it is recognized that a gift (in some form to someone) is involved, but evidently the *motivation* of this rationing procedure is to "safeguard" the public (TV viewers) and help to provide to the public what is "good" for it. The preceding illustration does not imply that the Federal Communications Commission acts irresponsibly. The commissioners act just as anyone else would in the same situation.

More examples could be presented. Competitive prices are not used initially to allocate licenses to operate (a) passenger airplanes between cities in scheduled passenger service, (b) liquor stores (in many states), (c) taxis (most cities), (d) banks (most states), and (e) sugar beet and tobacco farms in the United States. But these rights are salable once they have been initially allocated. For example, the right to operate one taxi in New York City sells for about $25,000. The preceding analysis is applicable to all these cases and many, many more. The student is advised to apply the analysis to each case to see whether he can detect who gets what gain under what conditions.

### Nontransferable Gifts

There is a class of possibly unintended gifts where the allocated goods *cannot* be re-allocated or resold after they are initially allocated. Rights to enter college, obtain a medical training, enter the United States, join some unions, adopt a child, play golf on a publicly owned golf course, camp in a national park—these rights often are allocated at zero prices or at prices below those that would clear the market. (Consequently, there are "shortages" and allocation by methods discussed in the earlier examples.) Whether or not the allocated item is subsequently resalable does not destroy the fact of gift. However, that affects the extent to which the gift can be realized as an increase in the recipient's general wealth, instead of only as a gain in a particular kind of good. For example, when a municipally owned golf course underprices its services and has a waiting list and "shortage" of playing space, those "lucky" enough to get access receive a particularized gain—if they haven't had to pay other costs to get on the reservation list.

Nothing in economic analysis warrants a judgment about which allocative procedures are good or bad. That judgment must be based on criteria derived from other sources.

Conclusion

With this chapter we have completed our analytical survey of various modes of allocating existing goods among competing consumers. That analysis helps to discern effects of various modes of allocation, but it does not provide a *criterion* for evaluating them. Evaluation is a matter of personal ethics. Probably it is safe to say that no one believes that fully utilized exchange opportunities for all goods for all people are desirable (children, slavery, opium?) or, on the other hand, that no exchange should be allowed. We conjecture that most disputes about the desirability of various allocation methods reflect (1) degrees of difference in attitudes toward individual responsibility, etc., and (2) differences in understanding the ways different allocative markets and systems operate. This second source of dispute, we hope, has been reduced by the preceding analysis, which attempted to clarify how things do operate, not how the world ought to be.

Summary

1    The extent of mutually preferred revision of goods among consumers is affected by the costs of obtaining information about bids and offers for goods or their uses, by the costs of negotiating a binding exchange, by the costs of policing the contract, and by the kinds of property rights people have to the goods. The higher those costs or the more weakened are private-property rights, the less will mutually preferred re-allocation of goods occur. One person may be prepared to offer a second party more for goods or services than the second party is now getting from those goods and services, but with sufficiently high exchange-negotiation costs the mutually preferred revision or exchange will not occur.

2    High market-exchange costs or weak private-property rights will induce both greater use of nonmarket exchange and prices below the highest personal valuation of the goods. Nonmonetary attributes will have an enhanced weight in determining allocation. Nonprofit (that is, nonprivate-property) institutions provide weaker incentives to decision makers to utilize market-clearing prices.

3    For private goods, the amount of service a person gets from the good affects how much others can have; in particular, the more one person has, the less others can have. For public goods, the amount of service one person can have from a good does not reduce the amount others can have, once the good is created.

4    A positive (greater than zero) price for a public good is not necessary for rationing purposes, since anyone can have as much as is available,

without reducing the amount available to others. Prices could be charged for a public good, so long as the price did not reduce the amount any one person wanted below the amount available; any price in excess of that would unnecessarily reduce his consumption. Prices for a public good would have to be different for each consumer if no one is to be restricted to less than total amount available. Charging a price, while not necessary for the rationing task (since there is no rationing problem), would serve as a guide to the valuation of production of more or less of the public good. The price relevant for this valuation is the *sum* of the individual prices charged various users.

5   Intentional and unintentional philanthropic and charitable behavior is consistent with the economic laws of demand and supply.

6   Charity involves some combination of (a) gifts in kinds, (b) gifts of general purchasing power, and (c) waste from the recipient's point of view, though not necessarily waste from the donor's point of view. The recipient does not necessarily get net gain over market-clearing prices, since he may pay in equally costly activity to obtain priority for the nonmarket-allocated goods.

7   To the extent to which gifts are marketable by the recipient, he can convert his gains, if any, into monetary equivalents, rather than necessarily taking them in the particular "kind" of good in which the gift was granted.

Questions

1   Distinguish between the law of demand and the law of price that says price equates the amount supplied to the amount demanded. Which holds more generally?

2   It has been estimated that carrying a spare tire on automobiles costs the public about $150,000,000 or about $5 per year per car. Is this a wasted, idle resource? What do you think it would cost if that figure were cut to zero by not carrying spare tires at all? Do you think it would be cheaper to make tires more durable and to devote more resources to handling emergency "flats"? What evidence can you cite?

3   You are planning to build an apartment with eight units. You are told you can add a ninth unit for an extra cost of $10,000; and, if the extra unit is occupied all the time, it will be worth $15,000. If occupied three-fourths of the time, it will be a breakeven proposition.
a. Would you then consider building more apartments than you could expect to keep always rented?
b. Would you consider that apartment to be unemployed when not occupied?

c. Would you consider every unemployed person as a "waste"?
d. Why?
e. Is there any distinction between unfortunate and wasteful?

4   a. Can you make an estimate of the fraction of your wealth tied up in resources designed to ease the consequences of your own unforeseeable changing demands or circumstances?
b. How about the amount of money you hold; items in the medicine cabinet; waiting time for a haircut in the barber shop; food kept at home in the refrigerator, freezer, and in canned goods? Are these idle, unemployed resources?

5   If a cheap enough method could be invented for metering the extent to which each motorist uses a street, would use of streets be rationed more with a price system? Do you know of any such cases now in use? Name two.

6   Churches are typically nonprofit institutions. Can you think of a problem in allocation of church facilities that is solved without use of the price system?

7   The college you now attend is almost certainly a not-for-profit institution. Are any of its resources allocated at less than market-clearing prices? (Hint: Library facilities? Athletic facilities? Counseling? Course admission? Campus space?)

8   "To the extent that nonprofit private institutions do not use the price-exchange system to allocate resources, they are operated inefficiently." True or false? Explain.

9   Camping fees in almost all state and national parks are so low that people want more space than is available:
a. Why is the market price not at a market-clearing level?
b. How much space would people want at a market-clearing price?

10   In Los Angeles two closely situated golf courses, one privately owned and one publicly owned, are both open to the public.
a. Which do you think charges the higher price, and which do you think requires less or no advance reservation? Give your reasons.
b. Who is benefited in what respects by each course's policy?
c. As land values rise around the course, which one do you think will be converted to housing or business first? Why?

11   There are reputed to be over 100,000 voluntary health and welfare organizations soliciting contributions from the general public, in addition to hundreds of individual hospital-support groups, as well as about 100,000 fraternal, civic, and veteran's organizations and 300,000 churches which sponsor a variety of charitable activities, not to mention individual charities or gifts. A professor of public-health administration says, "It should not take over 100,000 voluntary agencies to provide private health and welfare services in the U.S." How many do you think it should take? Why?

**12**    The *New York Times* sponsors a charity appeal each Christmas and gives cash to selected poor families. The *Los Angeles Times* sponsors a charity appeal each summer to send children of poor families to summer camp. Given your choice, to which of these forms of charity would you contribute more? Why? Do you think people who choose the other way are mistaken?

**13**    In 1950 many public-welfare and charitable aid organizations refused to help families that owned a television set—no matter how poor the family might be. The welfare workers claimed they were not supposed to finance luxury. What would have been your policy if you were dispensing the aid?

**14**    Suppose you are running a university and the faculty is asking for higher salaries, some of which you will have to grant at the sacrifice of buildings and activities. Now, the Ford Foundation gives you $1,000,000, the income of which is to be allocated exclusively to faculty salaries. Who gains what?

**15**    Let your current college education involve a true annual cost of $2,000, of which you are required to pay $300, and for which you would have been willing to pay $1,200. If you had to pay the full costs of $2,000, you would not have purchased your present level of education; instead, you would have purchased a lower level of training costing $800.
**a.** What do you gain by being able to get the $2,000 education for $200?
**b.** If the above quantities ($300 or $200) refer to the amount your parents are willing to spend for your tuition, who gains what?

16    A parent spends 50 cents for his child's school lunch. Subsequently, the school initiates a low-cost subsidized school lunch program, so that now the parent spends only 40 cents for the same lunch.
a. Who gains what?
b. Suppose the new lunch is a better one that costs 60 cents but is provided at a subsidized price of 40 cents. Who gains what?
c. Suppose the school lunch is still better and costs 75 cents and is sold to students for 55 cents, so that the parent who formerly spent 50 cents now gives his child 55 cents to buy the bigger lunch. Who gains what?

17    Some colleges charge high tuitions, but at the same time they give a large number of tuition fellowships ranging from full tuition payment down to practically nothing. If you apply the principles of discriminatory-pricing techniques of an earlier chapter, can you show that tuition grants are a form of discriminatory pricing of education? Does that make them undesirable?

18    The faculty of many colleges are given free parking space even in areas where parking space is not a "free good."
a. Who gains what?

b. What would be the effect if the faculty could sell their space to students?

19    The state of Washington permits a person to collect twenty-four razor clams a day from its beaches.
a. Why is the right to collect clams given free, and why does the state limit the number to twenty-four instead of permitting more if a higher fee is paid?
b. Who gains what under the present system?

20    Immigration-quota rights to the United States are priced at "zero" instead of being sold at a market-clearing price to "acceptable" types of people. Who gains what? Why are these rights not sold at the highest price to acceptable people?

21    In 1963 the right of Northeast Airlines to offer commercial air service between New York City and Miami was rescinded by decision of the Civil Aeronautics Board, the U.S. government agency that allocates such rights.
a. What do you think happened to the value of the stock of Northeast Airlines upon news of that decision?
b. At the same time, the price of the common stock of two other airlines remaining in service on that route, Eastern and National Airlines, jumped about 25 percent. Why was Northeast Airlines not allowed to sell its right to that route to National and to Eastern instead of having the right taken away from it?
c. Who gained what by the decision to take that right away from Northeast Airlines and let National and Eastern remain as the two carriers?
d. As a final twist, after losing that right, Northeast Airlines reverted to the status of a "local-regional" airline, serving only the New England area. As such, it is entitled to federal subsidies. Who lost what by the transfer of flight rights by authority rather than by sale to other airlines?

22    Some state governments, when disposing of property, sell at auction to the highest bidder. The right to form and operate a bank, a liquor store, a race track, or a savings and loan bank is not sold at auction to the highest bidder among a set of "acceptable" businessmen. Instead, the "winner" is selected by a board, much as judges choose the winner in a beauty contest.
a. What is your explanation for not letting the highest bidder win?
b. Who gains what?
c. Which system do you think increases the wealth of lawyers? Of politicians?
d. Explain why a system of controlled entry is conducive to strong political lobbying groups.

23    "Californians are crazy. Near a beautiful California beach, there is a luxurious motel and a state-owned camping area. Despite the greater

luxury of the motel facilities, scores of cars are lined up for hours each morning seeking camping sites, whereas at the motel there is hardly a day that rooms are all taken. This shows that Californians prefer outdoor, dusty camps to the luxuries of a motel with pool, TV, room service, and private bath." Do you agree? Explain.

24    "Economic theory is applicable only to a capitalist society." Evaluate.

25    Public goods are those for which (choose the correct statement): (a) several people can simultaneously enjoy the good; (b) it is impossible to exclude some consumers; (c) no consumer reduces the amount of the good available to others by his act of consuming the good; (d) prices should not be charged; (e) the government should provide the goods.

26    A theater performance with several simultaneous viewers is not a public good. Why?

27    A melody is a public good. Why? What is the best way to induce people to produce melodies?

28    "More of a public good can be produced without the production of other goods being curtailed." Evaluate.

29    "Even if it were costless to exclude nonpayers from enjoying a public good, it does not follow that nonpayers should be excluded." Explain why.

30    "When a pretty girl wears beautiful clothes, the people who see her get a public good—for which they do not pay. Therefore the standards of dress for pretty girls should be regulated by law in order to induce sufficient amounts of well-dressed girls." Evaluate.

31    "Financing public goods by taxes is a means of excluding nonpayers, for nontaxpayers will be put in jail." True or false?

32    Name three goods that are partly public and private.

33    Shopping centers often provide free parking spaces. In effect, the shopping-center merchants provide free parking for some nonshoppers so that their customers will find adequate space. Some allege that the number of parking spaces is excessive (that is, more resources go into the provision of parking space than should) where the space that "should" be available is the amount that would clear the market when a charge is levied to cover the construction and maintenance cost of the parking space. However, policing "pay" parking spaces involves a cost of estimating charges, collecting fees, and prosecuting violators. Does the fact of that cost mean that it might be "better" to provide "too much" parking space than to provide the "right" amount with a price rationing system? Explain.

34      The U.S. Congress has agreed with governments of foreign countries producing coffee to prohibit the import into the United States of more than a specified amount of coffee, thereby raising the price in the United States and increasing the total proceeds to foreign countries. (What is the elasticity of demand for coffee in the United States assumed to be?) Why would Congress agree to a law that raised costs of coffee to American consumers? Explain how this could be considered a form of foreign aid that does not appear in the federal government's budget record of taxes and expenditures.

# 9

Allocation of Consumable Goods over Time: Speculation

What we eat today, we cannot eat tomorrow. We must allocate between *today* and *tomorrow*. After the summer's harvest of wheat, how much should we eat in the fall, winter, and next spring? Must a central planning agency set consumption quotas for each month until the next harvest? If not, how do we avoid famine in midwinter? In the United States no agency is responsible for seeing that we don't consume too much now. But some people, without delegated responsibility, devote their major activity to this task. In a capitalist system these individuals are acting in the interests of their own wealth; yet, in some mysterious way, their decisions influence the allocation of consumable goods over the year. In this chapter we shall study the way these actions affect that allocation. The example of the conservation of wheat between harvests will bring out the essential details. Although we discuss only harvests, the principles here apply to *all* goods, whether agricultural or manufactured.

### The Risk-Taker in Commodity Markets

The wheat crop (assuming only one type of wheat) is to be harvested. What will farmers do with the wheat? They *could* store it, gradually selling a bit each month until the next harvest. But, sensibly, farmers do not want to keep so much of their wealth in the form of wheat. They can sell the wheat when harvested, letting someone else store it and bear the risks of changes in value of the wheat stock and decide how much to sell to consumers each month. Who buys the harvested wheat? The millers, who grind the wheat grain into flour, don't want to store a year's supply of wheat in advance. Even the housewives refuse to take on this duty, because they do not want to make commitments so far ahead. But there is a very simple device to induce someone to store the wheat. If all these people refuse to store all the harvested wheat, the price of wheat falls. There is an increased prospect of profit in buying wheat at the lower price, storing it, and selling it later at a higher price after some of the wheat is consumed. In a capitalist open-market system, anyone may buy wheat at harvest time in a "self-centered" endeavor to make profit by selling it later at a higher price. This is known as speculation.

Except for these *speculators* who buy the wheat, the price would fall still lower until the less venturesome, less perceptive people were induced to buy the wheat. After all, at a *sufficiently* low price of wheat, millers (and even housewives) could be induced to buy a year's stock of wheat, because prospects for profits before the next harvest would then look so good. Differences among people in the willingness to bear risk, in their talents and facilities for storing wheat, in the profit prospects that will induce them to risk buying wheat—all determine how low the price of wheat will be after the harvest.

Permitting *any* or all persons to buy stocks of wheat for speculative purposes keeps the price from falling so far, thereby giving farmers a higher price for their crop than if some of these buyers were not allowed to buy the harvested wheat for speculation. And speculators' actually realized profits will be smaller. In the United States, anyone can buy and store wheat by telephoning a commodity-market broker who will arrange to have wheat purchased, stored in rented facilities, and insured against theft or spoilage.

The market for these transactions is the *futures* market. That market is characterized in folklore as a place where antisocial, money-mad speculators gamble on the price of wheat, corn, etc., causing prices to fluctuate even more as they are pushed down when farmers sell and pushed up when consumers buy.

We conjecture that this confusion about futures markets reflects the fact that many people do not understand the special character of a "futures" contract. An illustration will reveal the crux. You are a flour miller converting wheat grain to flour. You want your income to depend on efficient milling operations, not on a changing price of unmilled wheat grain. A drop in the price of wheat grain, after you have bought the grain, could ruin you. You therefore want to isolate your business income from that risk. You can do this in three ways.

1. Don't buy any wheat in advance of your milling operation. Buy it only after you have an order to mill some grain into flour. But this is expensive and does not allow a smooth flow of production. You won't survive with this system.

2. Find someone else to own the wheat and store it in your place of business while you buy it from him as you mill the wheat. In this way any fluctuations in the value of the stock of wheat are borne by the other person. This is expensive to do, as you will see if you try to find someone to do it.

3. You can buy the wheat yourself before receiving any orders for the flour you will make from the wheat, at the same time placing a side contract with someone else, so that if the price of the wheat goes *up* (giving you a gain in wealth) you will give the gain to *him*, but he will compensate *you* for a *drop* in value of the wheat you are holding. You are *hedging* by "betting" with him on the value of wheat. This is one thing the futures contract does. It enables separation of ownership of wheat from the fluctuation in its value. It is the cheapest known way of separating use of the wheat by the miller from his bearing the risk of fluctuations in wheat value. It also enables wheat millers to conduct their purchases of wheat more efficiently—but we shall not here elaborate on this feature.

All three methods involve risk bearing. They differ in who bears it and in how that is arranged. They do not eliminate gambling or speculation or risk of loss or gain in value from holding wheat. That risk is inevitable when the wheat is kept unconsumed. Perhaps the reason futures contracts are so widely regarded as sheer gambling is that they separate the risk-bearing element so cleanly, efficiently, and *openly* from the *use* of the wheat, and therefore appear to be only devices to satisfy hungry speculators, bent on profiting from changing supplies or demands.

Control of the Rate of
Consumption out of Stocks

What determines the *rate* at which the harvested stock of wheat is allocated to consumption? Who tells speculators how much wheat to sell each month for consumption? No one. Some *thing* does, and that thing also induces them to hold wheat: current price of wheat relative to expected future prices.

*Past experience*, that prime source of knowledge, provides the basis for *expectations* of what the price of wheat will do between harvests. And the closer the current price is to future price expectations, the more will sellers be willing to sell currently, because profit prospects of continuing to hold wheat are diminished.

The present (*spot*) price of wheat is affected by the consumption demand and the supply of wheat coming into consumption channels from storage. If current consumption demands should increase, the *current* spot price of wheat will rise and reduce prospects of profits from storing wheat, thus inducing storers of wheat to sell more wheat to consumption channels. *The relationship between the current "spot" price for wheat and the price that is expected in the future affects the rate at which wheat will be released from storage into consumption.* People now make contracts to deliver or to accept delivery in the *future* and to pay in the future at *presently* agreed-upon prices. This means that the prices now agreed upon for future delivery are predictions of what the price will be in the future; no one would purchase and store wheat today at a price higher than he thought the price would be in six months. Nor would anyone sell wheat *forward* (that is, contract to make future delivery) if the price were less than he thought it would be in the future. And the prices (*futures* prices) of current contracts for future deliveries of wheat reflect beliefs and predictions about the future price.

"Futures" Prices and "Spot" Prices

Suppose that it is now September, and you can buy wheat (in 5,000-bushel lots) for $2 a bushel for delivery immediately—on the "spot." Today's *spot* price of wheat is $2. Today, you also can make a *futures* contract for delivery of wheat and payment of $2.10 per bushel *next May*. The price of $2.10 agreed to now, but to be paid in May, is called the *May futures price* (formed in September of the prior year). The difference between the two prices (spot and futures) usually narrows to a spread just covering storage, insurance, and interest costs of holding wheat in the interim, because of competition among speculators.

Markets for Futures Prices

Prices in the commodity *futures* markets are reported in the financial sections of major newspapers. You will find (in September of 1968) something like the following for the wheat futures market (Chicago is the location of the market).

Wheat Futures Prices

| | |
|---|---|
| September 1968 (harvest) | $2.00 |
| December 1968 | 2.04 |
| March 1969 | 2.07 |
| May 1969 | 2.10 |
| September 1969 (harvest) | 2.02 |
| December 1969 | 2.06 |

The interval covered extends from one harvest into the next. Unless next year's harvest is anticipated to be unusually small, the September (after harvest) 1969 futures price presumably will be lower than the May 1969 (pre-harvest) price. May is the last month before the new crop harvesting begins. The September harvest cannot be used in the *preceding* May to increase the amount available for consumption; if it could, the May price would be pushed down and the September price raised.[1]

These *futures prices* in today's futures markets provide predictions of what the spot price will be in the future. If anyone can make a better prediction of next May's spot price of wheat (that is, one that in fact turns out to be a more accurate prediction), he can quickly reap a fortune. For example, suppose the present (in September 1968) futures price for May 1969 is $2.10, a price lower than he believes will actually exist in May of 1969. He could place a bet in this futures market that the presently quoted *May futures* prices is too low and that next May's spot prices will be higher. The process for placing this bet is to buy now a *futures contract* for, say, 5,000 bushels of May 1969 wheat at $2.10 a bushel—to be delivered to him and paid for next May. He agrees to this contract now in September at the presently quoted *May futures price* of $2.10 per bushel. Then he nervously waits until May; *if* the spot price next May is in fact higher than $2.10, he can take delivery of the wheat and resell at the then higher price, reaping the difference as a profit. If the price is lower, he suffers a loss.

An important consequence of this activity is that increased current demand for wheat for delivery in the future pushes up the current "futures price" of future (that is, May) wheat from $2.10 toward that predicted May price. In this way beliefs that the current "futures" price of future wheat is too low will increase the current "futures" price and *reveal to the world* the new expectations of future spot prices.

Of course, for every buyer of a contract for future wheat, there must be a seller who promises to deliver wheat in the future. That other person may believe the spot price in the future will be lower than the current futures price, and, if *he* is correct, *later* he can buy wheat at the lower spot price in the future and deliver it to the buyer for the currently agreed-to higher futures price. Or that other person may be a *hedger.*.

If the demand for current consumption increases so that the present price of

[1] There is some downward pressure on May prices, for consumers will reduce current consumption in the expectation of buying and consuming more wheat at a lower price after the new crop is harvested.

wheat rises, continued storage will be less profitable unless it is also expected that the price in the future will be correspondingly higher. A faster rate of consumption will leave smaller stocks and higher prices in the future. Currently, therefore, *futures* prices in the futures markets will be pushed up. What will push them up? First, the knowledge of the faster rate of consumption of current stocks of wheat will induce speculators to anticipate higher prices in the future, and they will act accordingly by demanding more futures contracts. Second, there is a sort of automatic force in the sense that this force does not require any general knowledge of a faster rate of reduction of the stock of wheat. This second force is the result of *hedging*.

The larger the inventories of wheat, the more wheat that is hedged by selling "futures contracts." The increased supply of futures contracts (reflecting large stocks) lowers the futures prices. In other words, the greater the inventory of wheat, the greater the supply of futures contracts—and the lower their price.

We are now in a position to see how a higher demand, higher spot price, and consequent faster rate of consumption out of inventories has an effect on futures prices. As the hedging inventory holders sell their wheat for the current consumption at a more rapid rate, they have less wheat to hedge, so that they want to cancel (buy back) their commitments to deliver wheat in the future. The increased demand to buy back futures contracts, as hedgers reduce their inventories, raises futures prices, which restrains their willingness to sell so much current wheat.

We have an answer to our question of who holds the wheat between harvests. Under the incentive of increased wealth (buying low and selling later at a higher price) anyone can shoulder this task—not because he *intends* to perform some socially useful function (storing and rationing wheat from harvest to harvest). Private interest motivates this method—a method not consciously designed or motivated by the social storage purpose but one discovered by a trial-and-error selective process and not widely understood by the members of society, not even by many of the speculators and farmers.

### Illustrative Application: Coffee Futures Markets

To illustrate the interrelationships of prices, stocks, and speculative decisions, we shall use a "scenario" of public reaction to price movements of coffee futures. The scenario is only semi-imaginary, being based on recent actual events.[2]

The news spreads that the next coffee crop now blossoming in Brazil has been nipped by unseasonably cold weather. During these snaps, no one really knows how much the buds are affected, but there is an increased probability

---

[2] In addition to the coffee market, today there are organized open futures markets for at least the following goods: wheat, soybeans, oats, corn, cotton, barley, sorghum, sugar, cottonseed oil, soybean oil, hides, lard, eggs (frozen, powdered, and shell), potatoes, frozen chickens and turkeys, silver, tin, rubber, cocoa, platinum, pepper, flaxseed, copper, lead, zinc, wool, and pork-bellies. One for Scotch whisky may open soon. One for onions was outlawed!

that next year's yield will be reduced. This implies greater (or surer prospects of) profits for those who own coffee today and who store it for next year's prospective higher prices. Immediately, the flow of coffee out of current stocks to consumption is reduced. Therefore, the current price of coffee to consumers will rise as less coffee is released for current consumption.

There is, of course, just as much coffee as there was before the news about a potential shorter crop. And yet the present (spot) price has risen. With the rise in price, congressmen, responding to housewives' protests, begin publicly to demand investigations. Sure enough, there is just as much coffee in existence *now* as before the rise, and greedy, antisocial speculators have driven up the price.

If you were a speculator—and they're people of all types: dentists, carpenters, students, salesmen—what would you tell complaining congressmen? What, according to economic analysis, were the source and the effects of the current price rise? Could you defend yourself by saying that you deserve not censure but a medal for having benefited *all* mankind; or were you working against the interest of other people? Your defense might run something like this:

"It is true that news of the cold weather suggested the coffee buds would be nipped and the coffee harvest reduced. This would mean higher prices *next* year. I believed that if I bought some of this year's currently stored crop at present spot prices, I could later sell it at next year's higher prices, thereby making a tidy profit. Fortunately, I was one of the first who believed the crop damage was severe and was able to buy coffee from some holders of current stocks who did not believe the future supply looked smaller. I was not alone; many people were competing for current stocks of coffee. Soon, those who had coffee were not willing to sell at the former prices. They, too, looked forward to selling the coffee next year rather than this year. Less coffee was released from stocks for consumption. No one would sell existing stocks at a price less than he could get by holding until next year (allowing for the costs of storage, insurance, and interest). The current price, therefore, rose almost to the expected future prices as reflected in 'futures prices' of coffee. This higher current price was necessary to attract coffee out of storage and to induce consumers to decrease consumption to match the smaller flow of coffee. All this is summarized in the first fundamental law of demand, which states that less will be consumed as price increases.

"I bought coffee as a speculator. However, quite incidentally and unintentionally, my action—like those of the many other similarly motivated, foresighted, more informed persons—augmented the supply of coffee for next year, by adding part of this year's stored stocks to next year's reduced harvest. The consumer next year will have more coffee to consume and at prices lower than if we speculators had not carried more coffee from this year over to next year. For that, the consumers should thank us—not condemn us!

"We speculators did not cause the reduced supply of coffee next year. Nature did that. There simply *is* going to be *less* coffee next year. The choice facing people therefore is: 'Shall we continue to consume coffee today *as if* there were not going to be less next year, and then reduce consumption next year by the full reduction in the harvest? Or, shall we reduce consumption this year in order not to have to reduce it so much next year?' The choice is *not* more coffee rather than less, nor is it lower prices rather than higher prices. It is 'when shall the available coffee be consumed?'

"If I must *defend* my actions rather than merely *explain* them, I would say that, like the middlemen in the refugee camp, we speculators enabled people to obtain greater levels of utility than they otherwise would have obtained, despite their protestations about the currently higher price of coffee. From the fact that prices are predicted to be higher next year than now, I know that people *prefer* to give up a pound now in order to have one more next year. This is precisely what the higher futures price for next year's coffee means, relative to the present price this year. And if we are right in that forecast, we will make a profit; if wrong, a loss. The profitability of our activity is an acid test that people did want coffee shifted to the future.

"As speculators, we have immediately relayed to people our prediction of less coffee relative to other goods next year. We are not responsible for that *bad event*, but we are responsible for anticipating the effects of impending unfavorable events so that people can more cheaply adjust to them—so as to keep their utility greater than if the news of the coming crop failure were hidden until even more of the current crop was eaten up. We speculators are blamed for bad events because people either confuse *news* of the event with the *event*, or because they sometimes think that news of bad future events is worse than not knowing about it.

"You say, 'But what if your predictions were wrong? Suppose only a few buds on each tree were damaged, while the hardier undamaged buds produced even bigger coffee beans—more than enough to compensate for the reduced number, so that the crop next year was going to be even larger! Or suppose the cold snap did no damage at all. Or maybe the news about cold weather was simply false. After all, South American governments have been known to issue false bad news about an impending coffee crop precisely to drive up the price of coffee now, so that they could sell some of their existing stock at higher prices. What then?'

"The answer is simple. If speculators are wrong and if anyone else thinks he can predict better, all he has to do is out-predict the present speculators, and his fortune is made. Moreover, if speculators or people who store coffee make *perverse* mistakes in foresight, they will lose wealth, which, in part, pays the rest of the community for the error. Speculators will have paid more for the coffee than they will get when they sell it.

"I will not go so far as to say that any damage done to other people by our *erroneous* forecasts is made up to them by the losses we incur—a transfer of some of our wealth to the rest of society. In part this is correct, but our perverse forecasts do more damage than our loss of wealth to the rest of society can offset. They do damage in the sense that if our forecasts had been more correct, everyone could have achieved a more desirable adjustment in his consumption patterns over time than he did achieve. Obviously, the more accurate our forecasts, the better for us and for everyone else. The less accurate they are, the worse for us, and the worse for everyone else. However, and this is crucially important, the results are not as bad for everyone else as they would be if everyone had to do his own forecasting and storing of stocks for his own consumption, thereby bearing the full consequences of his own forecasts—right or wrong.

"Clearly, then, the issue is not whether the forecasts of speculators are correct or incorrect. The issues are instead: (a) What systems exist for making and acting on better forecasts? (b) What systems exist for allocating coffee among people over time *and* for allocating the risks and consequences of the erroneous forecasts? Any system will have erroneous forecasts. Which one will have fewer erroneous forecasts? Who will bear the major burden of the consequences of erroneous forecasts?"

And so our scenario ends. While it answered one question, it ended up by posing two new ones, to which we turn.

### Allocation of Risks in Futures Markets

Do the speculative markets to which everyone has access predict future prices more accurately than some other possible scheme? The organized futures market in onions was abolished by federal law in 1959. Among those who wanted the markets closed were firms that specialize in assembling, storing, sorting, and distributing onions to retailers. Without an open futures market, information about onion conditions is less widely dispersed; insiders, such as these processors, can benefit by their more exclusive access to information and opportunity to buy and sell onions. How they managed to induce enough congressmen to vote for that legislation is a question for your professor of political science. However, as it happens, this prohibition provided a fine opportunity to compare the behavior of prices of onions—with and without futures markets. The record is clear. With the organized futures markets for onions, the forecasts were more accurate than when they were closed. In particular, spot consumers' prices varied less during the interval between crops with open speculative markets than without them. In other words, the forecasts of future prices—the futures prices—influenced spot prices more accurately toward what was going to happen, avoiding large fluctuations when spot price responds to unforeseen events.

How should consequences of forecasting errors be borne? It has been contended that only experts should be allowed to make speculative decisions; this would avoid the errors made by less-informed people. To this there are several comments. First, if experts are now better informed than the consensus of the markets, they could easily get wealthy very rapidly by speculating. Furthermore, experts' superior information would help move the present spot and futures prices in the "correct" directions. Second, there is the problem of finding experts. When the government employs a group of specialists in this matter, the specialists are not automatically superior forecasters. The predictions of "experts" differ. If, despite these inherent difficulties, a group of experts were responsible for making forecasts and controlling the storage rates, who is to finance that activity? Who bears the losses when the forecasts are erroneous? In other words, how are the consequences of ignorance about future events to be allocated among people? Shall we require that all people, whether they individually want to or not, shall bear, in proportion to their taxes, the changing wealth values of the stocks of stored commodities? If the speculative activity were a voluntary arrangement with open futures markets, those who want to bear more of the risk can hold more of their wealth in the form of goods to be stored, and those who want to be relieved of those risks can own other forms of wealth. This points up one fundamental attribute of a capitalist system: It permits individuals to adjust their patterns of risk bearing, as well as their pattern of consumption goods. If you wish to avoid the wealth changes of certain goods, you can choose to own some other goods. You can concentrate your risks on a few particular goods or on a large class of goods, by appropriate patterns of ownership of goods. Complete avoidance of risks is not possible, but selectivity and choice of types of risks are possible with open markets and private-property rights. But whether that is desirable, economics cannot say.

Speculative holding of goods is inevitable. People differ in attitudes or willingness to bear the risks of losses of wealth consequent to emerging prices. Given these differences, each individual can move to a preferred position, as he sees it, if he will let the risks be borne by those who are more confident about a price rise, or more willing to bear risks inherent in the uncertainty of futures prices. Of course, he will have to pay them to bear those risks, but if they regard carrying such risks as less burdensome than he does, the cost will be less than if he bore the risks. Abolishing futures markets raises the costs of performing the storage function, because it prevents those who are more willing to bear these risks from doing so, and forces the less willing persons to bear these risks.

Having chosen not to bear the risk of wealth changes of a certain good, a person "should not" complain later if its price rises. His complaints would amount to the assertion that "hindsight is wonderful" and that insurance is wasted if the insured-against disaster doesn't happen! (In this case, by not holding stocks in advance of use, he has insured against decreases in their value.)

Sometimes it is mistakenly believed that speculation can be avoided by legally imposing fixed prices on commodities. This is identical to painting the thermometer to avoid a fever. Price controls do not prevent shifts in demand or supply. They reduce the opportunity of people to adjust by exchange to differences in interpersonal values among goods as well as among risks.

Speculative Markets under
Different Economic Systems

Who will bear the profits and who the losses is an issue in all societies, and it cannot be avoided by abandoning a capitalist system. Only the method of allocation changes. In a capitalist system, individuals can negotiate among themselves, offering to exchange "this" risk of loss or gain for "that" risk. Just as people negotiate for the particular pattern of consumption goods they shall have, so they can negotiate about the pattern of risks they shall bear. Although the option of bearing no risk at all is open to *no* man, in a capitalist society risks may be exchanged for other risks or kinds of wealth. In a socialist system, the risks of value changes, for state-owned goods—or those owned by the people as a whole—are borne by everyone in accord with tax liabilities and access to state services. The risk patterns are not individually negotiable with other people.

If you believe that people individually should have less choice of risk patterns and if you think that risks should be separated from the people who control the use of goods, you will prefer to reduce the scope of private property. But if you prefer a wider choice of risk patterns and a closer correlation between risk bearing and control of use, you will prefer a greater range of private property.

Summary

1    Allocation of goods between harvests and over time is affected by present prices relative to prices expected to prevail in the future. A drop of spot prices immediately upon harvest induces some people to buy the crop and hold some of it in the expectation of a profit.

2    Futures markets are markets in which contracts are made in terms of future prices of future goods. Current "futures" prices negotiated in a futures contract—which is essentially a contractual agreement to compensate or be compensated for a price change—are predictions of what price will be in the future of the good.

3    Not everyone has to carry his own consumption supply through the interharvest period. People who are more willing to bear the risks of wealth fluctuations in the good will be the formal "speculators." People who use large stocks of the good in their business can shift the major portion of risks of price changes to speculators by futures contracts. Without hedgers seeking to have speculators bear the risks of price changes, the futures markets would not survive.

4    Concurrent increases in the "futures" prices and in the present (spot) price of a good may reflect, not a smaller current stock on hand, but an anticipated smaller future stock or larger future demand. More of the current stock will be carried over to the future, by releasing less for current consumption, which raises current prices.

5    Just as exchange occurs between two people now, so exchange occurs between people now and people later. Higher predicted (futures prices)

values for the future will attract goods from the present (by reducing present consumption), whereas lower expected future values will increase present rates of consumption of existing stocks, leaving less for the future. (Future goods *cannot* shift to the present; instead *less* of presently available goods are shifted to the future.)

6   All risk bearing cannot be eliminated, although it can in part be pooled and in part shifted to the more willing holders. The futures markets facilitate that specializing and pooling, as well as guiding people's opinions about future values of currently available goods or ripening goods.

7   Economic systems differ in the determination of who will bear which risks of the changing values of existing goods. In capitalism, they are individually negotiable or pooled. In socialism, they are pooled and borne by people more in accord with their tax liabilities and access to state services.

Questions

1   The following was reported in the *New York Times* on July 28, 1966:

Prices of Wheat Futures (Chicago)

| July | 1966 | $1.81 |
|------|------|-------|
| September | 1966 | 1.85 |
| December | 1966 | 1.91-7/8 |
| March | 1967 | 1.95-3/4 |
| May | 1967 | 1.92-7/8 |
| July | 1967 | 1.82-1/8 |
| September | 1967 | 1.84 |

a. In what months does it appear that the new crop is harvested?
b. Explain the basis of your answer.
c. Approximately how much does it cost to store a bushel of wheat for one month?

2   Does storage from one crop season to the next season occur because people are far-sighted and contemplate their own future demands, or is it done because people think they can make a profit?

3   Which good will have a greater fall in its price as the crop is more fully harvested: one that will store readily or one that is more perishable? Why?

4   What is the difference between a "futures" price and a "future" price?

5   Today you can buy 100 bushels of wheat to be delivered today and paid for today. Does this involve a spot or a futures price?

6    In May, what is the September futures price an estimate of?

7    I own wealth of $1,000, while your wealth is $500. Who bears the greater risk?

8    I own $1,000, and tomorrow I will own either $2,000 or nothing depending upon whether an oil well I am drilling strikes oil. You own $1,000 in wealth, and it is all in cash. Who bears the greater risk for the next twenty-four hours?

9    Explain how markets in which people can bet with each other can result in (a) exchanges of risk, (b) reductions in risk, or (3) increases in risk. If such a market increases risk, is it bad? Why or why not?

10    The Los Angeles Dodgers and New York Mets are tied for the National League baseball title. They are to have a play-off game in a neutral stadium. The winning team will then be host for the World Series, with consequent receipts to the owners of neighboring parking lots. I own a parking lot near the Dodgers' stadium, and you own one near the Mets' stadium. If the Mets win the play-off, you gain; if the Dodgers win, I gain.
a. Into what kind of contract can we enter to reduce the risk each of us bears?
b. Have we exchanged or reduced risk? Can you construct a kind of "futures contract" that would accomplish the same effect?

11    "That speculators push up the price of a good is evidenced by the fact that the price often rises before there is any change either in the rate of consumption or the existing supply." Do you agree? If so, why? If not, why not?

12    A soybean processor buys in March 50,000 pounds of soybeans at $2.35 per 100 pounds. He expects to crush the beans and sell the soybean oil in about two months. He sells "futures" in soybeans at the same time he buys soybeans, hoping to obtain some protection from wealth changes resulting from changes in the price of soybeans and soybean oil. He sells futures in soybeans—say, May futures—to the extent of 50,000 pounds. Suppose the price of soybeans falls to $2 per 100 pounds in the interim, and therefore the price of soybean oil also falls. How will this enable the processor partially to avoid wealth changes caused by fluctuations in soybean prices?

13    In what sense is insurance a one-sided hedge?

14    "If forecasts are correct, some speculators will reap a profit. Also, they will have pushed up present prices, which will reduce current consumption and give a larger carryover to next season, so that prices in the future will be lower than they otherwise would be; but current prices are higher than they would have been had foresight been less perfect." In what sense can it be argued that this is "preferable" to a higher price later and lower price now?

15    "When speculators' foresight is good, they make a profit and perform a service to society. When it is bad, they incur losses and thus compensate the rest of society for the maldistribution of goods they induced." Do you agree? If so, why? If not, why not?

**16**   There are no speculative futures markets in some countries. Does that mean there is no speculation? Explain.

**17**   "If the speculative commodity markets were closed, there would be less speculation and smaller fluctuations in the prices of goods. Farmers could more reliably know what their crop would be worth, and consumers would be spared the price swings that are initiated in the speculative futures markets." Do you agree? If so, why? If not, why not? Can you cite any evidence?

18    In 1963 a U.S. Senate Agriculture Committee recommended the prohibition of futures trading in potatoes in formal speculative markets.
a. Would such a prohibition stop speculation in potatoes?
b. What would be its effect?
c. Why do you think congressmen were induced to advocate the prohibition of futures markets in potatoes?

19    News item dated August 5, 1963: "The New York Sugar Exchange, where sugar futures prices soared and then dived in May 1963, will have to be placed under government supervision according to Rep. Leonor K. Sullivan (Democrat, Missouri), chairman of the Consumer Affairs subcommittee of the House of Representatives. Her report said in part, 'It was excessive speculation in futures, rather than manipulation, that stimulated the price advance and the subsequent price break. The investigation did not show indications of price manipulation on the part of any individual or groups of traders.' Mrs. Sullivan said the interest of consumers—'who are still paying higher prices for sugar and products containing sugar because of the market behavior'— requires some measures to dampen speculation. What do you think of Representative Sullivan's economic analysis? Explain.

**20**   "Short selling" consists of selling promises to deliver at a specified date in the future some goods that the seller does not now own. Newspapers sell short when they take subscriptions with advance payment. A house buyer sells short when he borrows money, for he is promising to pay money in the future—money that he does not now have. A college that charges tuition and room and board in advance is engaged in short selling; it sells something it has yet to produce. I sell short if I sell a promise to deliver 1,000 bushels of wheat to you next year for a price currently agreed upon and in receipt for payment now from you. Why is short selling often regarded as immoral, improper, or bad?

**21**   The Chairman of the U.S. Securities and Exchange Commission proposed to prohibit or restrict short selling at times when the market prices are under "temporary pressure or distress." The presumption is that short selling destabilizes the market and induces larger downward swings than are justifiable in times of temporary distress. Suppose you were appointed by the President to decide when to restrict short selling in order to prevent it from pushing prices down lower.

a. How would you decide when a drop in prices was temporary and unjustified?

b. Who would decide when a drop in prices was "justified"?

22  Futures markets exist for stocks and bonds. These are known as the markets for "Puts" and "Calls." A "Call" is a right to purchase a stock within the next six months at a prespecified price, regardless of how high the price of that stock may rise in the next six months. A Call is guaranteed or sold by a party who, in effect, has sold "short." He is betting that the stock price will fall in the interim. If it does, he will not have to fulfill his promise to sell at the higher specified price, since the buyer of the Call can buy more cheaply on the market. If the stock rises, the guarantor of the Call will have to buy the stock on the market at the higher price and deliver it to the holder of the Call for the lower contract price in the "Call" contract.

The buyer of a "Put" buys the right to sell a stock at a prespecified price within some agreed-upon period of time regardless of how low the price may have fallen in that interval. The other party to the agreement (the seller of the Put) enters into the agreement in consideration of a payment inducing him to undertake the commitment to buy later at the specified price. Thus, a person owning A.T.&T. common stock can guarantee himself against a serious decline in the value by purchasing a Put. If it falls, he exercises his right to sell to the seller of the Put.

On August 1, 1966 you could have purchased a Call for Uniroyal stock giving you a guaranteed price of $44 per share, at which price the seller of the Call would have sold 100 shares of Uniroyal stock to you at any time during the following ten months. That Call would have cost you $600. How far would Uniroyal stock have to rise for you to have made money by purchasing that Call? If the price rose $1 per share, would you have exercised your option? Or if the price fell $1?

23  The following was the set of futures prices of wool on August 1, 1966:

| October 1966 | 136.9 |
| December 1966 | 136.4 |
| March 1967 | 135.7 |
| May 1967 | 134.0 |
| July 1967 | 133.5 |
| October 1967 | 133.4 |
| December 1967 | 133.3 |

What explanation consistent with economic analysis can you give for this "reverse" sequence of future prices?

24    "Open speculative markets are defended on the premise that it is better to be aware of impending events than to be unaware of them. But for events like impending crop disasters, earlier news merely shifts forward the effects and thereby spreads them over a longer interval, to no one's benefit. People might prefer to experience a short, intense period of less coffee in the future rather than have an earlier, longer-lasting though less intense reduction in consumption." What does economic theory say about this?

25    There are no organized speculative exchanges or futures markets for orange juice, wine, raisins, dried peaches, coal, oil, gasoline, whiskey, or olive oil.
a. Does that mean there is no speculating in these commodities?
b. Who does the speculating?

# 10

Production, Exchange, Specialization, and Efficiency

Until this chapter, production of goods has been ignored. What is the system for determining which goods are to be produced, how they are to be produced, and who will produce them?

As with the task of rationing existing goods, there are many ways to resolve these questions: a dictator can direct slaves; people can work cooperatively in a communal-ownership society; they can act within a private-property market system—to mention a few.

We have concentrated on a system characterized by private property in goods and services, in which the owner has the right to decide how those goods shall be used or to whom he will pass the title (right to use). A person's right to his labor services were included in his own private property. To the extent that a person's rights to goods are restricted by threats of violence, anarchy intrudes. To the extent that the government enforces legal restrictions on the choice by individuals of use or of exchange of goods, socialism replaces private-property systems (capitalism). Socialism is a system in which decisions about the use of economic goods and services are exercised via governmental political processes. Every society is a mixture of capitalism and socialism; furthermore, the composition of the mixture varies over time, partly in response to changing attitudes toward risk, degrees of tolerance for idiosyncratic behavior, and ease with which competing groups can acquire government power.

Regardless of the system used, certain tasks are involved, and certain concepts are essential to analysis—for example, *production, efficiency*, and *specialization*. After defining and relating these concepts, we shall apply economic theory to see how production is controlled in a capitalist society; that is, the "production logic" of that system will be derived. We concentrate on that system because it is the dominant system for controlling production in the United States—not because it can be shown to be the "best" system. If one feels he must make judgments, the analysis provides a better understanding of the operation of that and other systems and thus permits a more informed judgment.

## Production and Exchange

In the broadest sense, production is the act of increasing one's utility. *Exchange* of existing goods is *productive* because, as we have seen, it increases one's utility. Production also can occur when the physical attributes of resources—including their time of availability, place, or form—are changed. Moving water from a well into a house is productive; carrying coal from the mine to the furnace is productive; tilling the soil, planting seeds, or caring for the crop is productive; so is harvesting, cleaning, grading, transporting, preserving, and distributing the crop to retail stores; so is advertising, wrapping, and delivery to the consumer's home. Production consists also of play and of entertainment. Any activity that I offer to pay a person to do (to increase my utility) is productive from *my* point of view. If he accepts my offer, the activity is productive from *his* point of view.

Economic theory analyzes ways in which given amounts of technical knowledge, effort, and resources can be organized or coordinated so that production can be achieved. Economic theory implies that people can increase their utility through exchanges of existing stocks of consumer goods; theory implies also that production of goods will increase when people appropriately "exchange" their productive activity. Adam Smith, in his famous book *An Inquiry into the Nature and Causes of the Wealth of Nations*, called this last principle "division of labor" or "specialization"; it is now generally labeled "comparative advantage."[1] In Smith's words:

> This division of labor, from which so many advantages are derived, is not originally the effect of any human wisdom which foresees and intends that general opulence to which it gives occasion. It is the necessary, though very slow and gradual consequence of a certain propensity in human nature which has in view no such extensive utility: the propensity to truck, barter, and exchange one thing for another.
>
> Whether this propensity be one of those original principles in human nature, of which no further account can be given; or whether, as seems more probable, it be the necessary consequence of the faculties of reason and speech, it belongs not to our present subject to enquire.

In the same way that *exchange for consumption* was numerically illustrated earlier, we will show how *specialization and exchange in production* can yield a greater physical output with higher utility to each person than if no exchange in production were permitted. Then we shall investigate some methods for inducing that specialization—one method relying on the free marketplace with individual incentives and private-property rights.

The existence of corporations, labor unions, credit buying, suburban shopping centers, trading stamps, discount houses, factories, and all the other institutions through which economic activity is conducted obscures the basic principles that underlie the organization of production in a capitalist society. A television set is a complicated mechanism; yet it is built up with a chain of relatively simple principles. Once these principles are grasped, the method by which a set operates is said to be understood. Even though one doesn't know how to make a television tube, resistor, capacitor, or transformer, he can understand the function of each and even assemble them into a working system. From the surface, the system looks enormously complicated and confusing. And, without a theory, it is. But if one has a valid theory, bewil-

---

[1] Had Smith lived today, he might have called it the *"Don't-*do-it-yourself" principle. It is interesting that Smith's book did not contain a logically-correct exposition; instead it contained a masterfully persuasive statement of the results of free exchange. It was Robert Torrens, who some forty years after the idea had been "sold," demonstrated its logical validity. Possibly, had Smith tried to give a logically air-tight demonstration, instead of a suggestive plausible interpretation, he would never have made his "point" popular.

derment is replaced by confidence, complexity by sequences of simplicity, and confusion by order.

What assurance do you have that the economic theory to be presented is valid? At the present moment, you have none—just as you have none when you take a physics or chemistry course. Experiments in a physics course *illustrate* the principles in special experimental circumstances. In precisely the same way, the principles stated in economics can *here* be illustrated. How does one know that these principles will apply to the rest of the world, which the student cannot yet observe? He doesn't know; and he doesn't know that the principles of physics will always work, either. He simply has to wait until he has had time to observe real events; in that way he tests, observes, and decides for himself whether to continue to believe in these principles and act accordingly. At present, we do tell the reader that overwhelming evidence supports the validity of the economic principles. With this prologue, we present in this chapter the principles of specialization in production, in the context of a simple two-man society with two alternative producible goods. Then in Chapter 11 we shall investigate the effects of enlarging the society; we also expand a bit to consider the effects of price-takers' and price-searchers' markets on the response of production to consumer demands. In Chapter 12 we go into further institutional features: (a) closed or restricted access to markets, (b) how private-property rights make one heed effects of his actions and thus influence his productive behavior, (c) the effects of costs of information about potential transactions, and (d) the problem of production of goods heavily loaded with "public-goods attributes." This will prepare us for analysis (Chapters 13–17) of further principles of production that are dependent upon still other institutional idiosyncratic features—large business corporations, labor unions, extensive durable goods, credit buying, advertising—that modify in one way or another some of these basic propositions about production.

## Specialization and Enlarged Output

Upon entering our two-person society, we first meet Mr. $A$, whose currently relevant distinguishing attribute is not his sex, color, age, religion, height, weight, marital status, eye color, blood type, political affiliation, or personality, but is instead his *production-possibility set* for two goods, here called $X$ and $Y$.

*The production-possibility boundary.* Suppose Mr. $A$ can, with a given amount of time and energy, produce daily six units of $X$, *or* three units of $Y$, *or* any linearly interpolated combination of $X$ and $Y$. If he devoted half a day to $X$ and the other half to $Y$, he could produce daily three units of $X$ and one and a half units of $Y$. Or he could produce three $Y$ and no $X$. Table 10–1 shows part of the set of possible daily output combinations of $X$ and $Y$. For each unit increment of $X$, he must forsake production of $.5Y$ (or, conversely, for each extra $Y$ he must forsake $2X$). His ratio of the *change* in output of $X$ consequent to a unit *change* in output of $Y$ is always $2X = 1Y$, or $.5Y = 1X$. This ratio is his *production marginal rate of transformation* between $X$ and $Y$. This can be expressed also by the statement that his marginal cost of producing $Y$ is $2X$. "Marginal cost" of $Y$ is the amount of the other goods that must be forsaken to get a unit increment in the production of $Y$.

Mr. $A$'s production-possibility set can be easily graphed. In Figure 10–1, all his possible output combinations are represented by all the points on the straight line; if he produces less than is possible, his production is represented by a point inside the triangular area bounded by that line and the axes. The daily rate of production of $X$ is measured along the horizontal axis and the daily rate of $Y$ along the vertical axis. The extreme upper-left point on the production-possibility boundary denotes an output of all $Y$ (3) and no $X$, while the lower-right-hand extreme point denotes the maximum possible output of $6X$. Point I denotes an output combination of $2X$ and $2Y$. Point II denotes $4X$ and $1Y$. Mr. $A$'s production technique will be called *efficient* if he is producing outputs *on* the production-possibility boundary at points like I or II, but not III *inside* the boundary. A production technique is "efficient," by definition, as long as the output of *both* $X$ and $Y$ cannot be increased. To be efficient means that the only way he can increase the output of any product, $X$, is by giving up some output, $Y$ (or conversely). Every point on his production-possibility boundary is an efficient *production* combination.

An impossible output of 2.25 of $X$ and 2.25 of $Y$ is portrayed by Point IV *outside* his production frontier. If he produces the same number of $X$'s as $Y$'s,

Table 10–1
Some Daily Combinations from Mr. $A$'s Production-Possibility Set

$X$ and $Y$

| 6 | and | 0 |
|---|-----|-----|
| 5 | " | 0.5 |
| 4 | " | 1.0 |
| 3 | " | 1.5 |
| 2 | " | 2.0 |
| 1 | " | 2.5 |
| 0 | " | 3.0 |

In one day Mr. $A$ can produce any of the listed combinations of output of $X$ and $Y$. He could produce $6X$ and zero $Y$, *or* he could produce $5X$ *and* $.5Y$, and so on. To increase his daily output rate of $Y$ by 1 unit costs him $2X$ per day. Thus his marginal cost of a $Y$ is $2X$. To produce, on the other hand, one more $X$ costs him the sacrifice of $.5Y$; hence, his marginal cost of $X$ is $.5Y$.

the best he can do is 2 of *X* and of *Y*. Unless Mr. *A* sacrifices leisure, gets extra productive resources, or learns better methods of production, he cannot be outside his production-possibility boundary, *AA*.

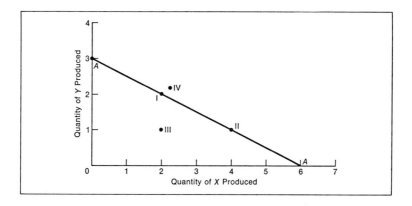

Figure 10–1
Mr. *A*'s Efficient Production-Possibility Boundary

Mr. *A* can produce any combination of *X* and *Y* indicated by any point on or inside the area bounded by the line *AA* and the two axes. To produce the combination denoted by III would be inefficient, because with no greater available resources he could produce more of *X and Y* (any point on the line between I and II). The combination denoted by point IV is not producible by Mr. *A*. It lies outside his possibility. All points on the line *AA* denote efficient outputs because at any point on that line, Mr. *A* cannot produce more *Y* without having to produce less *X* (or more *X* without having to give up some output of *Y*). The *slope* of the line measures marginal cost.

The *best* of all the efficient points (that is, the one that gives him the greatest utility) cannot be detected from just these data. That depends upon his demand conditions.

For the moment, we will arbitrarily suppose that for Mr. *A* the best is two units of *X* and two units of *Y* per day. He is self-sufficiently producing and consuming that output.

Mr. *B* is a second person in our community; his production-possibility set is indicated in Table 10–2 and Figure 10–2. Mr. *B* can produce any of these combinations he wishes. If he wants an *equal* number of *X* and *Y*, he can produce 1.5 of each. He could produce 2*X* and 1*Y*, giving up .5*Y* in order to get .5 more *X*. His marginal cost of producing *Y* is 1*X*, which differs from Mr. *A*'s marginal cost of *Y*, which is 2*X*. We shall see that this difference in marginal costs—portrayed by the differences in the *slopes* of the two production boundary lines, *AA* and *BB*—is a crucially important feature. Mr. *B*'s line, *BB*, has a slope of "minus one": with every increase of one unit in output of *X*, he has a decrease of one unit in *Y*. Mr. *A*'s slope is minus 1/2, because for

Table 10-2
Some Daily Combinations from Mr. *B*'s Production-Possibility Set

*X* and *Y*

| | | |
|---|---|---|
| 3 | and | 0 |
| 2.5 | " | 0.5 |
| 2.0 | " | 1.0 |
| 1.5 | " | 1.5 |
| 1.0 | " | 2.0 |
| 0.5 | " | 2.5 |
| 0 | " | 3.0 |

Mr. *B* can produce any of these combinations in one day. To produce one more *Y* costs him 1*X*; hence, his marginal cost of *Y* is 1*X*.

every increase of one unit in $X$, he incurs a decrease of a half unit of $Y$. The steeper the slope of the production-possibility boundary, the greater the marginal cost of $X$, because the greater is the amount of $Y$ that must be sacrificed to get an increase of one unit in $X$. Mr. $B$ has the steeper slope; i.e., he has higher marginal costs for producing $X$. Conversely, he must be the lower marginal-cost producer of $Y$.

A *straight-line* production-possibility boundary for each person means the marginal cost of production for each person is *constant* regardless of the rates of production of $X$ and $Y$. (Later we shall investigate a less special case.)

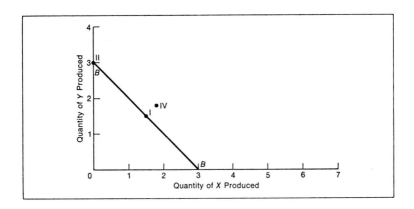

Figure 10-2
Mr. *B*'s Efficient Production-Possibility Boundary

Mr. *B* can produce any output on the line *BB* (or any output beneath it—but all beneath it are inefficient). Point IV is beyond his production capabilities. The slope of the line, "minus 1," tells us that the marginal cost to Mr. *B* of producing one more *X* is the loss (minus) of 1 unit of *Y*. His marginal cost of *X* is one *Y*. Contrast this with the slope of Mr. *A*'s line in the preceding diagram, where the marginal cost of an *X* to Mr. *A* is .5*Y*.

*Production and exchange.* Temporarily, suppose that Mr. *A* prefers a consumption mix such that for each *X* he has one *Y*. Also assume Mr. *B* wants the same ratio of *X* to *Y*. In this event, Mr. *A* would be producing and consuming 2*X* and 2*Y*, while Mr. *B* would be producing and consuming 1.5 of each—each combination being portrayed by points "I" on the respective graphs of the production possibilities. Both persons are self-sufficient.

The top half of Table 10–3 shows that the *total* "national" output of *X* is 3.5, and the total "national" output of *Y* is also 3.5. At best, *A* can have 2*X* and 2*Y*; Mr. *B* can have 1.5 of each—*if we prohibit production specialization.* But if specialization (and exchange) is allowed, then—*while still staying on each person's production-possibility boundary*—it *is* possible to get an output of *more* than 3.5*X* and 3.5*Y* to be allocated between Mr. *A* and Mr. *B*. This means each person can consume an amount *above* his production-possibility boundary. How can this "magical" increase in total output be achieved? Answer: By use of the principle of *specialization*, which rests on the fact of *comparative advantage*—a name for differences in marginal costs of production. To show how this principle of production leads to a *larger* output of *both X* and *Y*, we shall resort to a parable.

Table 10–3
Before Specialization: Production (and Consumption)

|         | X         | Y         |
|---------|-----------|-----------|
| Mr. *A* | 2  (2)    | 2  (2)    |
| Mr. *B* | 1.5 (1.5) | 1.5 (1.5) |
|         | 3.5 (3.5) | 3.5 (3.5) |

After Specialization and Exchange: Production (and Consumption)

|         | X         | Y        |
|---------|-----------|----------|
| Mr. *A* | 4 (2.25)  | 1 (2.25) |
| Mr. *B* | 0 (1.75)  | 3 (1.75) |
|         | 4 (4.0)   | 4 (4.0)  |

Mr. *A* can without specialization produce 2*X* and 2*Y* and he can consume those 2*X* and 2*Y* each day. With specialization he can produce 4*X* and 1*Y*, and then by exchange with *B* be able to consume 2.25 of *X* and of *Y* each, exactly .25 more of each than without exchange. Similarly, Mr. *B* can obtain an increase in his consumption potential from 1.5*X* to 1.75*X*, and a similar increase for *Y*. The increased output and the increased consumption with only the added work of engaging in exchange is the gain from trade (specialization).

In the community we are visiting, a dictator is responsible for all production control. At present Mr. *A* is producing 2 each of *X* and *Y*, while Mr. *B* is producing 1.5*X* and 1.5*Y*. By a clever reassignment of tasks, the dictator can get a bigger total output. The dictator tells Mr. *A* to reduce his output of *Y* by one unit and increase his output of *X* by two units. His output mix changes from 2*X* and 2*Y* to 1*Y* and 4*X* (represented by point II *on his* production-feasibility frontier of Figure 10–1). At the same time, the dictator orders Mr. *B* to reduce his output of *X* by 1.5 units, down to zero, and to increase his production of *Y* by 1.5 units to three units. This moves him from point I to point II *on* his production-feasibility frontier (Figure 10–2).

The "national" output is four units of *X* (4*X* from Mr. *A*) and four units of *Y* (1*Y* from Mr. *A* and 3*Y* from Mr. *B*). The national output has "miraculously" increased from 3.5 units to four units for both *X* and *Y*! Before "explaining" how this miracle occurred, we note from the bottom half of Table 10–3 that for Mr. *A* and Mr. *B each* to have *more X* and *Y* than before, the dictator may take 1.75 units of *X* (or anything less than two units and more than 1.5) from Mr. *A* and give them to Mr. *B* in return for 1.25 units of *Y* (or any amount less than 1.5 units and more than one) which he transfers from Mr. *B* to Mr. *A*. This will leave Mr. *A* with 2.25 units of *X and* also 2.25 of *Y*, which is exactly .25 units more of *X* and of *Y* than he was able to produce alone without the dictator's instructions. On the other side, Mr. *B* will have 1.75 units of *X* and of *Y*, or .25 more of each than he is able to produce. Several other combinations of total output and of its division could be selected, but we have chosen the one that makes the increase in output stand out in boldest, simplest numbers.

*Efficient specialization.* What has happened can be summarized by saying that Mr. *A specializes* in the production of *X*, while Mr. *B specializes* in the production of *Y*. To specialize means that a person *produces more of some commodity than he consumes.* It does *not* mean he produces only *one* thing; rather, he produces *more* of some things, and less of others, than *he* consumes. It most certainly does *not* imply "surplus" production of *X* by Mr. *A*, nor of *Y* by Mr. *B*. Except for the work involved in the dictator's instructions and actions, neither *A* nor *B* works any harder than before. Both were working on their production possibility before the revision; they were *individually* efficient. Now neither person has violated his production-possibility boundary—yet the total output has increased. Although each was *individually* efficient in his production, there was "inefficient" *social* production.

As long as the marginal costs of production of *X* and *Y* for Mr. *A* are different from those for Mr. *B*, it will always pay them to specialize. Mr. *A* can produce one more *X* at a cost of .5*Y*, while Mr. *B* produces one more *X* at a cost of 1*Y*. If Mr. *A* reduces his output of *Y* by one unit, his output of *X* could be increased by two. To offset this loss of *Y*, Mr. *B* could be instructed to produce one more *Y* at a marginal cost of only 1*X*. This gives a *net* gain of 1*X* (and no decrease in *Y*). Mr. *A* can produce one more *X* at a "cost" of only .5*Y*, but Mr. *B* can produce one more *X* only at a higher cost of 1*Y*. Mr. *A* is the lower-cost producer of *X*. Who is the lower-cost producer of *Y*? Mr. *B*. He can produce another *Y* at a cost of only 1*X*, whereas Mr. *A* has to sacrifice 2*X*. Table 10–4 shows the new production possibilities. This represents the output potential from the most efficient production assignments of Mr. *A* and Mr. *B*. It is impossible to get more *X* (or more *Y*), with each indicated amount of *Y* (or *X*), than given in this table. Try to beat it. (We safely offer $1,000 to every person who can.)

Table 10–4
Total Daily Production Possibility of X and Y by Mr. A and B

Output
X and Y

9 and 0
8  "  1
7  "  2
6  "  3
5  "  3.5
4  "  4
3  "  4.5
2  "  5
1  "  5.5
0  "  6

The production potentials of Mr. A and Mr. B can with efficient coordination
result in any of the listed output combinations. At the output combination of 8X
and 1Y, who will be producing how much of X and of Y? (Do you agree that
Mr. B will be producing 1Y with none from Mr. A? Check it.) Who will be producing how much of X and of Y at the combination of 2X and 5Y? Be sure you
can answer this question.

The principle for efficient production is simple. Efficient production of X is
obtained if it is produced by those with the lower marginal cost in production
of X, while resources with higher marginal costs in production of X should be
used in production of non-X.[2]

Other Rules of Production Control

Results of some other production assignments of Mr. A and Mr. B can be
illustrated by Figure 10–3. In that figure are plotted the production-
possibility boundaries of Mr. A and Mr. B individually, and the *total*
national-output boundaries for three different rules of production control.

I. Let both Mr. A and Mr. B produce Y, and then if any X is wanted, first
have Mr. B, the *higher*-marginal-cost producer of X, divert some resources
toward producing the desired amount of X. If even more X is wanted than
Mr. B can produce, let the next highest marginal cost producer of X then
produce X. Line I gives the total set of production possibilities yielded when
Mr. A and Mr. B are assigned to production of X and Y according to this
pattern.

[2] A proof of the logical validity of this proposition requires a bit more complicated
mathematics than our simple arithmetic example. For those who have had at least a year
of calculus, this proposition is a verbal translation of some of the conditions (marginal
equalities or inequalities) for a constrained maximum—that is, for a specified output of
Y, maximize the output of X, subject to the constraints of all the individual production-
possibility conditions.

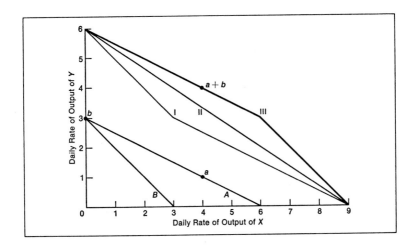

Figure 10–3
Production Possibilities for Different Production Rules

Line III denotes achievable combinations of $X$ and $Y$ that can be produced by $A$ and $B$ together. For example, if $A$ produces at point $a$ on his line, $AA$, and $B$ produces at point $b$ on his line, $BB$, the sum of the outputs of $X$ and $Y$ from $A$ and $B$ is given by the point $a + b$ on line III. It is impossible to get more $X$ and $Y$ from $A$ and $B$ than that indicated by point $a + b$. They could get more $X$, but only with less $Y$; this would slide them down the line III. If $A$ and $B$ do not coordinate their outputs in an efficient way, they will end up with amounts of $X$ and $Y$ less than those on line III—the efficient production-mix boundary. Lines II and I denote two *in*efficient output boundaries which would be achieved if inefficient rules for coordinating production were followed. Line II results from $A$ and $B$'s devoting *equal proportions* of resources to $X$ and $Y$. Line I results from reversing the lowest-marginal-cost rule for controlling production (the rule that gives boundary III). Which of the lines—I, II, or III—plots the outputs given in Table 10–4?

II. Line II is obtained by telling Mr. $A$ and Mr. $B$ always to produce $X$ and $Y$ in the same proportion as each other. If more $X$ is wanted, everyone is told to increase his output of $X$ by that desired percentage, and decrease $Y$.

III. Line III is the achievable set of outputs if the rule for line I is reversed. Let both Mr. $A$ and Mr. $B$ produce $Y$ if only $Y$ is wanted; but if some $X$ is wanted, assign first to its production the lower-marginal-cost producer. If even more $X$ is wanted than he can produce, assign the next higher-marginal-cost producer, Mr. $B$. The resulting set of production possibilities is indicated by line III, the outermost, and hence the most efficient, boundary. This is a graph of the unbeatable data in Table 10–4.

In effect, we first move down along Mr. $A$'s production-possibility boundary from all $Y$ toward more $X$, while keeping $B$ fixed at all $Y$ and no $X$; and we move down $B$'s boundary only after $A$ has moved to the point of all $X$ and no $Y$. Illustrating the earlier numerical example: Point $a + b$ on boundary III is obtained by assigning Mr. $B$ to production of $Y$ only (represented by his being at the upper-left-hand point, $b$, where his production line cuts the $Y$ axis) and by assigning Mr. $A$ to the point $a$ on his boundary. The sum of the outputs of $Y$ from Mr. $A$ and Mr. $B$ is represented by the height of the point $a + b$, while the sum of these outputs of $X$ gives the horizontal position of the point $a + b$.

## Achievement of Efficient Production
## by Market Exchanges

If the output decisions are made by an all-wise dictator who knows all the production possibilities of each person, presumably efficiency can be achieved—ignoring questions of how the dictator will get his orders enforced and how he will distribute the resulting product.

But in the event of a successful revolt against the dictator, is efficient allocation of productive resources possible? How can people know what to produce? What induces them to do so? What signals and incentives will be effective? One possibility is that after the revolt a system of private property is instituted in each person's rights to his labor services. He is a "free man"; he can work where and at what he wishes. He can sell his goods or services to others if both parties can find a mutually acceptable price (wage). In such a private-property capitalist system, the new "dictator" is the rule of law of private property if the government enforces that rule against all people, even those who do not like private-property systems.

What will each person do? Suppose, at first, each subsists off his own production; that is, each is self-sufficient. He will produce whatever mixture of $X$ and $Y$ he most prefers of those he can produce. If Mr. $A$ is producing a mixture such that he personally (subjectively) values one more $X$ as equal to $1Y$, he will note that he *can* produce one more $X$ if he forsakes only $.5Y$. Therefore, he will shift production toward more $X$ and away from $Y$, for he is *willing* to forego (in consumption) as much as $1Y$ to obtain one more $X$, whereas he *must* (in production) sacrifice only $.5Y$. He will continue to shift toward more $X$ until he values one more $X$ as equivalent to only $.5Y$. In this way he is led to a consumption pattern at which he personally values $1Y$ at $.5Y$, the same as his marginal cost of producing $1X$. His personal valuation of another $X$ is equated to his marginal cost of producing (getting) an $X$. Let us arbitrarily suppose this situation is reached when he produces $2X$ and $2Y$ per day.

Compare this with Mr. $B$. His marginal cost of $X$ is $1Y$ (instead of $.5Y$ as it is for Mr. $A$). Mr. $B$ adjusts his production output until he has a consumption mixture such that he personally values one more $X$ at $1Y$. Now his personal valuation of another $X$ is equated to his marginal cost of producing (getting) $X$. Suppose that this occurs at the output mixture of $1.5X$ and $1.5Y$.

Each person is a subsistence producer. He subsists on what *he* produces. He does not specialize, he engages in no exchange, he is independent, he is his own boss. We know, however, that if two people have different personal values of a good, exchange between them will put them in preferred situations—a principle developed in Chapter 3. Furthermore, we have just learned that production is efficiently organized if those who produce $X$ have lower marginal costs of $X$ than those who do not produce $X$. But here we have Mr. $B$ producing $X$ when his marginal cost of $X$ ($1Y$) is *greater* than Mr. $A$'s (.5$Y$), and Mr. $A$ is producing $Y$ when his marginal cost of $1Y$ ($2X$) is *greater* than Mr. $B$'s ($1X$). (If at this point you feel a bit swamped with comparisons, carefully recheck the numbers in Table 10–1 and 10–2 once more, because the hard part is over.)

We shall now see how exchange between these two people, each seeking to improve his own situation as he sees it, will lead to an efficient reorganization of production, just as under an all-wise dictator. The end results will be exactly the same as those shown in Table 10–3 (page 203) and reference to that table will help you follow the discussion. Since we have already investigated how a middleman facilitates exchange, we shall omit him and let Mr. $A$ and Mr. $B$ deal directly with each other—and be their own (unrealistically costless) middlemen.

We know that Mr. $B$ would be willing to buy $X$ at a price less than $1Y$ since it costs him that much to make $X$'s for himself. (See Table 10–2 on page 202.) Mr. $A$ can produce them at a marginal cost of .5$Y$. (Table 10–1, page 200.) Therefore Mr. $A$ would be willing to produce more $X$ to sell to Mr. $B$ for any price over .5$Y$. We shall *arbitrarily* assume he gets a price of .71$Y$ from Mr. $B$.[3] Each $X$ sold to Mr. $B$ gives Mr. $A$ a net gain of .21$Y$. From Mr. $B$'s point of view, he gets a net gain of .29$Y$ on each $X$ he buys at .71$Y$.

The next question is how many $X$'s Mr. $B$ buys from Mr. $A$. To answer would require knowing each person's relative demands for $X$ and $Y$. To avoid having to bring in, at this time, that extra analysis, we assume that the equilibrium amount of trade is such that Mr. $A$ sells 1.75$X$ to Mr. $B$ at a price of .71$Y$ for each $X$. This means that Mr. $A$ receives 1.25$Y$ from Mr. $B$. Each day they exchange those amounts of $X$ and $Y$.

How much does each person consume each day? If you check, you will see that Mr. $A$ produces 4$X$ and 1$Y$; he sells 1.75$X$ and gets 1.25$Y$, which leaves him with 2.25$X$ and 2.25$Y$, exactly .25 more of each $X$ and $Y$ than he had before trade and specialization (as in Table 10–3).

Mr. $B$ is producing no $X$ and 3$Y$, buying 1.75$X$ in exchange for 1.25 of his 3$Y$, which leaves him with 1.75 of $X$ and $Y$. The situation is precisely as it was before, under the all-wise, benevolent dictator, shown in Table 10–3. The national output is 4$X$ and 4$Y$, instead of 3.5 of each as it was before exchange and specialization. And each person, after exchange, gets more of both $X$ and $Y$ than before exchange. What is more, it is impossible to rearrange the assignments of production and trade to give each person a still bigger consumption.

---

[3]With this assumption we are *implicitly* specifying the demand conditions which are buried in this solution.

Each is specializing on his product of comparative advantage, *without a dictator*. Such specialization was induced by the compulsion, desire, or drive of each person to benefit himself by getting more goods, and a chance to negotiate acceptable exchange with other people. Even though this driving force is not imposed by other people, it is pervasive, persistent, and powerful. It is a response to the compulsive desire for more.

### Profits and Lower Cost of Living

The increased output of .5 units of $X$ and of $Y$ is distributed in the form of (1) profits and (2) reduced consumers' prices. Mr. $A$ produced more $X$'s and sold them at a price (.71$Y$) above his costs (.50$Y$). And in turn Mr. $B$ bought $X$'s more cheaply (for only .71$Y$, instead of 1$Y$). Reducing the cost of $X$ to the consumer and increasing the producer's profits are ways of distributing the increased output of $X$ to $A$ and $B$. (A similar division can be made for product $Y$.) Profits are part of the increases in product, *not* a result of exploitation of consumers.

### The Unseen Hand and Laissez-Faire

Production resources (human or physical) are guided toward an efficient allocation as if by an "Unseen Hand." The "Hand" is (1) the desire of each person to achieve a more preferred situation, in this case via increased profits and lower costs of getting goods; (2) open access to the right to exchanges; and (3) private-property rights in goods and services. This is often called a capitalist, *laissez-faire* ("let-it-do" by itself) system, because no one has to intervene to guide people, *assuming* in the first place a system of private-property enforcement and a marketplace where exchanges can be negotiated at mutually agreed upon prices. Compared to a subsistence or self-sufficiency system, appropriate specialization yields a larger aggregate output. Restrictions that prevent Mr. $A$ or Mr. $B$ from producing and exchanging goods will reduce the force toward efficient production by specialization. In our current example, if Mr. $A$ could not produce any of product $X$—because production and sale of $X$ is reserved exclusively for Mr. $B$ as a legal monopoly—then the aggregate feasible output in our example could *not* be achieved. The smaller output is a result of "monopoly restraints," restrictions on "open markets" or "free enterprise." This is why it is said that "legal monopoly" or "closed" markets or "entry restrictions" are bad. They are not bad for those who are protected by the restrictions; they have a larger wealth as a result, but a smaller gain than the loss imposed on the rest of society.

Although this toy example speaks of Mr. $A$ and Mr. $B$, it applies to America and Britain—and thus provides an explanation of international trade; or Albany and Buffalo, implying interregional trade; or Aluminum Company of America and Bulova, implying specialization by business firms. The essence of all exchange among producers is captured by this simple "two person" example.

Gains from Trade and the Size of the Market

A proposition of major importance can now be presented. *In general, addi-tion of another person with different talents will provide the rest of the community with increased total consumption potential.* Into the community of *A* and *B* comes another person, *C*, with talents different from those of *A* and *B*, say with the ability to produce 1*Y or* 2*X* daily (or linearly interpo-lated combinations of *Y* and *X*). If *C* specializes and trades with *A* and *B*, he will be able to realize consumption above his own production possibility. *A* and *B* will also be able *jointly* to realize a still higher consumption than without *C*'s presence. Before we illustrate this, a few preliminary remarks orient the analysis.

Not necessarily every person in the rest of the community prior to the newcomer will in fact benefit, nor will anyone necessarily lose. It depends upon how the increased product is distributed, and that depends upon who is producing how much of what. The increased consumption goes primarily to members of the community who do not compete in production with the newcomer. For example, if *C* enters the community he will be a competitor primarily of *B* in the production of *Y*. If you refer back to pages 201–202, you will see that *C* can produce *Y* at a lower marginal cost (.5*X*) than can *B*, whose marginal cost of producing *Y* is 1*X*. The resulting increased output of *Y* by *C* and lower price of *Y* will benefit *A* and hurt *B*. Former producers of *Y* will suffer from the lower price of *Y* while consumers will gain. The results can be illustrated with the data in Table 10–5, which is based on the data presented earlier in Table 10–3 (page 203). The amount produced and consumed by each person is shown in the top third of Table 10–5, where *A* and *B* trade with each other while self-sufficient *C* produces solely for him-self, prior to his entering the community. The total output is 4.67 of each *X* and *Y*.

If now *C* trades with *A* and *B*, *C* will find it best to shift production to *Y*, while *A* will find it best (in the sense of getting the highest income) to shift completely out of *Y* to all *X* (5*X* and no *Y*). *C*, the lowest-cost producer, is displacing some production of *Y* by *A*. *B* will still find it best to continue to produce *Y* even though he is now poorer (with the lower selling price of *Y*). The output for each person is shown in the second portion of the table; the total output of *X* and *Y* is 5 units of each (instead of 4.67). The resulting consumption distribution is shown in parentheses for each person. *A* con-sumes more of *Y* and *X*; *C* consumes more of each than when he was self-sufficient; *B*, the former major producer of *Y*, is poorer and consumes less. He has lost income to *A* and *C*. The legend in Table 10–5 explains with numerical detail just how this happens.

The entry of *C* as a competitor primarily of *B* has lowered the price of *Y* and hence *B*'s income. *A* and *C* benefit. The gains to *A* are in part the result of the lost buying power of *B*, now partially transferred to *A* via lower prices for buying *Y*. The other source of gain to *A* is the increased total output. Also part of *B*'s former income is transferred away to *C*.

It is true that the increased output potential to the community consequent to $C$'s entry is large enough so that even if $B$ were more than compensated for his lost income, everyone else would still have a gain from $C$'s entry. See the bottom of Table 10–5 for an illustration of a tax on $C$ that accomplishes this. (Part of the tax could have been on $A$ also.) Actually, such compensation by taxes and payments to those who lose from new entrants is extremely rare. More common is a law preventing entry of $C$!

This analysis of distribution of income effects sheds light on a related phenomenon. A person newly graduated from school enters the community with specialized talents. His entry and greater productivity contribute gains to many people in the rest of the community. These are a mixture of net productive gains and income transfers as in the former illustration. Some

Table 10–5
Production and Consumption before and after $C$ Enters the
Community of $A$ and $B$

Before Trade with $C$

|        | X           | Y           |
|--------|-------------|-------------|
| Mr. $A$ | 4 (2.25)    | 1 (2.25)    |
| Mr. $B$ | 0 (1.75)    | 3 (1.75)    |
| Mr. $C$ | .67 ( .67)  | .67 ( .67)  |
|        | 4.67 (4.67) | 4.67 (4.67) |

After $C$ Enters and Trades

|        | X        | Y        |
|--------|----------|----------|
| Mr. $A$ | 5 (2.3)  | 0 (2.45) |
| Mr. $B$ | 0 (1.6)  | 3 (1.55) |
| Mr. $C$ | 0 (1.1)  | 2 (1.0)  |
|        | 5 (5)    | 5 (5)    |

By entering the community, $C$ increases the consumption potential for $A$ and $B$ and for himself. With specialization he can produce no $X$ and $2Y$; with exchange at a rate of 1.1$X$ for 1$Y$, for example, he can sell 1$Y$ for 1.1$X$, giving him more than if he did not specialize. Similarly $A$ can buy 2.45$Y$ by paying 2.7$X$. $A$ can buy 1$Y$ from $C$ and 1.45$Y$ from $B$, giving $C$ 1.1$X$ and $B$ 1.6$X$. This, however, leaves $B$ worse off than formerly.

If we place a tax on $C$ of .25$X$ and .25$Y$ and give the total proceeds to $B$, we achieve the results shown below. Everyone then has more than prior to entry of $C$.

After Tax Compensation to $B$ from $C$

|        | X               | Y               |
|--------|-----------------|-----------------|
| Mr. $A$ | 2.3             | 2.45            |
| Mr. $B$ | 1.85 (1.6 + .25) | 1.80 (1.55 + .25) |
| Mr. $C$ | .85 (1.1 – .25)  | .75 (1 – .25)   |
|        | 5.0             | 5.0             |

people mistakenly leap to the conclusion that since education contributes to everyone else's welfare, everyone else ought to pay for a student's education. Such reasoning would suggest that everyone else ought to pay for every new investment or productive equipment or subsidize every new immigrant. The error is in failing to distinguish between (a) the gains from *increased productivity* and (b) *income transfers* to those who buy products at lower prices from those who are competed against by the newly trained entrants. That is why it is not possible to deduce who should pay for whose education—even when there are net gains to the rest of society. The joint presence of productive gains and transfers explains the conflict about immigration policies.

### Are Specialization and Efficient Production Good?

The more cheaply people can communicate, negotiate, and exchange, and the greater the possibilities of discerning and exploiting differences among their productive abilities and tastes, the greater will be the specialization and wealth in the society. In the words of Adam Smith, the gains from specialization depend upon the "extent of the market" and so does the degree of specialization. In small markets, you will find less specialization in medical services, and in types of auto, or TV, or watch repair services. Even bakeries will be less specialized.

#### Disadvantages of Specialization

Monotony and tedium are more likely—though rewarded by a greater wealth—for those who specialize. Apparently the monotony and tedium are worth bearing, for anyone who wants to forsake wealth can be more self-sufficient and poorer. It would be nice if there were some way to get all that increased output without specialization and exchange. But it hasn't yet been discovered.

Specialists are more dependent on each other; one's wealth depends heavily upon other people's tastes and activities. To specialize more effectively involves making advance investments in specific goods and kinds of training. Specialization seems to increase risks, because if other people's demands or willingness to work in certain tasks should change, some specialists will lose much of the value of their investment in goods and training. They will end up poorer than if they had specialized in something else, or possibly with even less than if they had been more self-sufficient like olden-day farmers. But do not make too much of this point, for the losses of overinvestment in certain goods and skill are not the consequence of specialization. They are the consequence of imperfect foresight. People know that their forecasts are fallible, and they correspondingly make smaller long-term investments in riskier trades. In part this reduces the possible losses and the extent of specialization. But even a self-sufficient nonspecialist will make long-term investments to get products for his own use. And does he know his own future demands any better?

Is Efficient Production Good?

"Efficiency in production" is desirable in the sense that more economic goods are preferred to less. But are you sure that the produced economic good is a "good" economic good? For example, the authors do not allow their minor children unrestricted access to the market, because the children would probably buy economic goods we believe they should not. We don't accept their judgment of what is a "good." If someone believes other people do not know what is good for themselves—as evidenced by differences of opinion about the use of tobacco, alcohol, opium, heroin, gambling, low-brow television programs, comic books, lewd literature—he may seek to prohibit their production. Many highly educated, socially conscious people do so. To them, the standard of efficiency is useful only insofar as the "right" goods are wanted by others. Doing the "wrong" thing efficiently is not desirable. Are they justified in their opinion? That depends upon whom you set up as the ultimate judge. Economics is neutral or amoral; it does not say what motivation or result is "good" or "bad." It develops merely the implications of whatever people regard as good. "Efficiency in production" is "good" in your opinion only insofar as you admit it is "good" that individuals should make and bear more of the consequences of their choices. And not all of us are willing to accept that.

## Socialism, Specialization, and Marxist Alienation

Karl Marx asserted that specialization of production with exchange "alienated" producers from understanding their social role and interrelationships with other people. Each producer was said to feel he was producing solely for some impersonal marketplace in response to impersonal market prices, rather than to human wants and values (as if the prices were unrelated to such human desires or as if the producers thought the prices had no relationship to human values). Marx said that since it is primarily through exchange of their products that producers come into social contact with one another, "The persons exist for one another merely as representatives of, and therefore as owners of, commodities." (*Capital*, Vol. I, Modern Library Edition, Random House, 1906, p. 97.) Social relations are said to be transformed into relationships among commodities and money. Marx went on to assert "the process of production has the mastery over man instead of being controlled by him." (*Capital*, p. 93.) To eliminate that alleged "mastery of production processes over man," he proposed that men should consciously control production by centralized production directives in accord with a preconceived settled plan, as if the workers of the society were in a single, huge factory. Hence, Marx called for socialism, i.e., government ownership of all the productive resources, believing this would eliminate "alienation."

Other interpretations of the roots of socialism in Marxist thought suggest that socialized production and centralized control would facilitate the ability of politicians in the government to control society and retain office. A still more recent interpretation is that centralized government control of productive resources and production according to a conscious plan is more efficient and gives a more rapid growth of output. The first of these is a well founded interpretation of the Marxist precepts. The second may be a convenient fact of life for the ruling political group. The third is completely unsubstantiated, and the authors believe it is falsified by historical evidence; you may believe what you wish.

Summary

1    Specialization is the production of more of some and less of other goods than a person consumes himself. Production is efficiently organized if for specified rates of production of all goods except one, that one is maximized; or, if it is impossible to increase the output rate of any good without reducing that of some other.

2    Specialization in a market leads toward efficiently organized production. A central planning and directive agency is not necessary to achieve efficient organization of production and consumption.

3    The production marginal rate of transformation (substitution among goods by production) between $X$ and $Y$ is the minimum change of output of $Y$ that must occur if the output rate of $X$ is to be enlarged by one unit. This is also called the marginal cost of production of $X$ (in units of $Y$ sacrificed). The principle of efficient organization of production requires that each good be produced by the lower marginal-cost producers of that good.

4    The gains from specialization are distributed as lower buying prices to consumers and profits to producers. The latter are competed away via lower prices to consumers and larger payments to the productive resources.

5    Specialization has undesirable features—for example, tedium and interdependence. Efficiency is neither morally good nor bad. It depends upon whether you think the goods produced more cheaply and in larger amounts are "good."

6    The larger the market in numbers of people with diverse talents, the greater the gains to its members from specialization and trade.

7    The gains from exchange that result from a larger market are mixed with income transfers among the members of the community. Gains that are income transfers *within* the group should not, in principle, be

confused with gains that are increases in real output. In principle the gains from new entrants are large enough to compensate fully any who might have lost income and still leave a net gain for the rest of the group. But the feasibility of determining the mix of such gains and transfers is another matter. Yet it may be preferable to engage in such attempted compensatory transfers with its resulting mix of gains and losses than to accept the unmodified one. This is an issue on which nothing constructive can be said with present knowledge.

Questions

1    *A* steals from *B* successfully.
    **a.** Is that "production"? Why?
    **b.** If you say "No, because someone is hurt," what would you say about the case in which a new invention displaces some other producers?
    **c.** Are there some kinds of production which you think should not be allowed?

2    Smith's production possibilities are indicated by the following table:

Alternative Daily Production Possibilities
by Smith

| Oats | | Soybeans |
|---|---|---|
| 10 | and | 0 |
| 9 | and | .2 |
| 8 | and | .4 |
| 7 | and | _____ |
| 6 | " | _____ |
| 5 | " | _____ |
| 4 | " | _____ |
| 3 | " | _____ |
| 2 | " | _____ |
| 1 | " | _____ |
| 0 | " | 2 |

**a.** Compute the missing data, assuming linear interpolation gives his production possibilities.
**b.** For each increment of oats, he incurs a uniform sacrifice of an amount of soybeans. The ratio between these two changes is called the marginal rate of transformation between oats and soybeans. This rate also yields his marginal cost of oats (in terms of soybeans). What is the marginal cost of a bushel of oats?
**c.** Of a bushel of soybeans?
**d.** If that marginal cost is constant for all combinations, then production is said to involve constant costs. Does this example reveal constant costs?

e. Graph Smith's production possibility, with oats on the horizontal scale.

f. On the graph, label, as point $I$, the output that has an equal number of bushels of oats and of soybeans.

g. What is the number of bushels of each?

h. Which is the larger output—1.67 bushels of each, or 5 bushels of oats and 1 of soybeans?

3    On the graph of the preceding question, plot the production possibility of Mr. $B$ (call him Black) taken from Table 10–2. Let $X$ denote oats and $Y$ denote soybeans.

a. Label this line $BB$ and mark the point of equal numbers of bushels of oats and soybeans (that is, 1.5 of each).

b. What is the maximum amount of oats that Mr. Smith and Mr. Black jointly can produce if they produce only oats?

c. Only soybeans?

d. What is the maximum amount of soybeans and oats they can produce if each person produces as many bushels of oats as he does of soybeans?

e. What is the total output of each if they divide their time and resources equally between oats and soybeans?

f. Which output is larger—the one where (i) each divides his time equally among the two products or (ii) where each produces as many bushels of oats as of soybeans?

g. Which output is better?

h. Would it be efficient for them to produce either of these two combinations?

4    On the graph for question 2, plot the outputs of soybeans and oats that represent the "efficient" total production-possibility set for Smith and Black.

a. Plot also the set of possible outputs obtained if Smith and Black use identical ratios when dividing their time between oats and soybeans.

b. Does this give the same production-possibility set as the preceding question?

5    a. If the price of a bushel of soybeans is $1 and the price of a bushel of oats is 50 cents, which good should Smith produce if he wants to maximize his wealth? Which should Black produce?

b. If the price of a bushel of oats rises above $1 while soybeans stay at $1, what should Black do if he wants to maximize his wealth?

c. At what ratio of prices would Smith be induced to produce soybeans?

6    What is meant by efficient production? Give two different versions of the definition.

7    What is meant by a subsistence, self-sufficient economy as contrasted to a specialized, interdependent economy?

8    Increased output resulting from more efficient specialization is distributed via what two means in a capitalist open-market system?

9    An open-market system presumes enforcement of certain institutions or
rules. What are they?

10    a. Do you think specialization will be carried to greater extent in a
large city or a small one?
b. Why?
c. Give examples of what you mean by greater specialization.

11    "It's wrong to profit from someone else's misfortune."
a. Explain why, if that were taken literally, we would *all* be poorer.
b. Does the doctor profit from your illness? The farmer from your
hunger? The shoemaker from your tender feet? The teacher from your
ignorance? The preacher from your sinfulness?
c. How are their earnings different from those of the liquor producer,
the race-track owner, the burlesque strip-teaser, and the dope peddler?

12    The following remark is commonly made about some rich people: "He
is an independently wealthy man." From what is he independent? Does
his wealth not depend upon other people's demands?

13    A premier or prime minister of a new "emerging" country bragged that
he was going to make his country self-sufficient and independent of
foreigners. Do the principles of this chapter suggest anything about how
you as a native of that country might be affected? Explain.

14    "Laissez-faire means the government should do nothing." Evaluate.

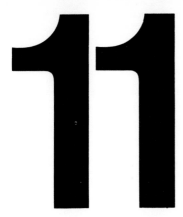

# Production in Various Market Conditions

Analysis of a many-person, many-good economy is basically the same as for a two-person economy. The necessary exchange information is contained in a *few* understandable, pervasive measures—money prices and costs. As we saw in the earlier analysis of exchange, each person with access to the market adjusts his mixture of consumption until market prices and personal values of various goods are equal. Market prices, therefore, depend upon the amounts of each good in existence, the preference patterns of individuals, and the distribution of wealth.

Inherent in the *allocation* of resources among competing uses is the concept of *costs*. Costs are values of alternative forsaken uses. In choosing between *A* and anything else, we ask what is the value of *A* and what is the value of the highest valued of the alternative possibilities that would otherwise have been realized; the highest valued forsaken opportunity is called the cost of *A*. And it follows that *A* should be chosen if and only if its value exceeds its cost.

None of the preceding makes reference to "labor, toil, trouble, and pain" as costs. Costs are *not* defined as the *undesirable*, or *painful*, consequences of some act, even though it may engender "undesirable consequences" that are weighed when one evaluates that act. For example, a swimming pool yields the pleasures of swimming and keeping cool, but it also involves the undesirable consequences of neighbors' children splashing up the yard. The desirable and undesirable are taken into account in assigning a *personal valuation*, but not the *costs*, of having a pool. Exactly how labor, toil, and trouble do enter into valuation is something we shall take up later, after hinting here only that they have some effect on the amounts of goods produced.

### Production-Possibility Boundary as Supply Schedule

Table 11–1 gives the production possibilities of five people, Messrs. *A, B, C, D,* and *E. A, B,* and *C* are the same people of the preceding chapter.

Mr. *C* is the least productive person of all, on an *absolute* scale. Maybe he is lazy, slow-witted, physically weak, poor in productive resources, very young or very old, or just doesn't want to work much. Mr. *D* and Mr. *E* are more productive. Mr. *D* can produce more *X* daily than anyone else, while nobody can outproduce Mr. *E* at *Y*.

Who will (not necessarily "should") produce what? At what rates? How are they induced to do so? One possible set of answers to these questions is the following. Let each person's production possibilities be reported to a dictator. If only *X* is desired, *A, B, C, D,* and *E* are told to produce only *X*, for a total of $25 worth of *X*. On the other hand, if only *Y* is wanted, then all will produce *Y*, for a total of 24 units.

Table 11-1
Daily Production-Possibility Functions and Marginal
Transformation Rates in Production

| | Goods | | | | Marginal Transformation Rates by Production | Marginal Cost of $Y$ in $\$X$ |
|---|---|---|---|---|---|---|
| Person | $\$X$ | or | $Y$ | | | |
| A | 6 | or | 3 | or all linear combinations | $2X = 1Y$ | $2.0 |
| B | 3 | " | 3 | " " " " | $1X = 1Y$ | 1.0 |
| C | 1 | " | 2 | " " " " | $.5X = 1Y$ | .5 |
| D | 9 | " | 6 | " " " " | $1.5X = 1Y$ | 1.5 |
| E | 6 | " | 10 | " " " " | $.6X = 1Y$ | .6 |

Mr. $A$ can produce $6 of $X$ or 3 units of $Y$ in one day. Or he can produce other combinations of $X$ and $Y$, but for each extra $Y$, he must forsake output of $2X$, as indicated by his marginal transformation rates. This means that his marginal cost of a $Y$ is $2X$ or $2 (valuing, as we shall, each $X$ as worth $1). Mr. $E$ has a marginal cost of 60 cents for production of $Y$. (Do you agree that Mr. $E$ could produce $3X$ and $5Y$ in one day? He can. Or that he could produce $9Y$ *and* $.6X$?)

Now make the dictator's task a little harder. If he wants precisely one of $Y$ and as many $X$'s as possible, whom should he order to produce the $Y$? At first sight, it appears that $E$ is the man. He can produce daily more $Y$ than can anyone else. In just one tenth of a day, he can produce $1Y$, whereas poor $C$ requires half a day. $E$ is "absolutely" the most productive producer of $Y$, while $C$ is "absolutely" the poorest producer of $Y$. Yet the truth is that the dictator should reverse the assignments! Absolute productivity is completely irrelevant for determining efficient production allocations.

Poor little $C$ is the person to assign first to the production of $Y$! $E$ is the *second* person to put to work on $Y$. And the reason is simply that $C$ is the *lowest-marginal-cost* producer of $Y$. Cost is not the amount of labor or time it takes to produce a $Y$; cost, as we have seen, is what is sacrificed when labor or time is used to produce a $Y$. No one can "save" time; it is used, like marriage, for better or for worse. What *can* be saved is sacrificed output. $C$ sacrifices only $.5X$ when he devotes half a day to producing a $Y$. $C$'s marginal cost is $.5X$ for $1Y$, while $E$'s is $.6X$ for $1Y$. With $C$ producing $1Y$, and the rest of the people producing $X$'s, total output is $1Y$ and $24.5X$. But if $E$ had produced the $1Y$, total output would be $1Y$ and only $24.4X$. (Which person would have been the worst to assign to $Y$? Had he been assigned, the total output would have been $1Y$ and only $23X$.)

If the dictator desires more than two units of $Y$, $E$ is the next worker, after $C$, to assign to $Y$. If the dictator wants more than twelve units of $Y$ (two from $C$ and ten from $E$), he will assign $B$, whose marginal cost of $Y$ is $1X$. If $C$, $E$, and $B$ produce $Y$, and $D$ and $A$ produce $X$, the total output will be $15Y$ and $15X$. No other assignment can produce more than $15X$ on days that $15Y$ are produced; other assignments will result in *less* than $15X$ being produced. (We again offer $1,000 to any student who can get more than 15 of each.)

We can summarize the principle of efficient allocation. Workers, or productive resources, should be ranked according to their *marginal* costs. Assign first those workers who have the lowest *marginal* cost for the particular good and then, as a larger output rate is desired, gradually divert to that task those with successively higher *marginal* costs. This principle holds for *all* economic systems, be they capitalist, socialist, communal, or "what-have-you."

The community's efficient total production-possibility frontier is listed in Table 11–2. When a man's name appears as a producer of both $X$ and $Y$, he is producing some of each. It is impossible to get more $Y$ for any stated $X$ or more $X$ with a stipulated $Y$. Any other assignments would eliminate efficiency.

Table 11–2
Community's Total Production Possibility

| Producers of X | Feasible Production | | Producers of Y | Marginal Cost of Y in Terms of X |
|---|---|---|---|---|
| | X | and Y | | |
| ABCDE | 25.0 | 0 | — | .5 |
| ABCDE | 24.5 | 1 | C | .5 |
| AB DE | 24.0 | 2 | C | .5 |
| AB DE | 23.4 | 3 | C E | .6 |
| AB DE | 22.8 | 4 | C E | .6 |
| AB DE | 22.2 | 5 | C E | .6 |
| AB DE | 21.6 | 6 | C E | .6 |
| AB DE | 21.0 | 7 | C E | .6 |
| AB DE | 20.4 | 8 | C E | .6 |
| AB DE | 19.8 | 9 | C E | .6 |
| AB DE | 19.2 | 10 | C E | .6 |
| AB DE | 18.6 | 11 | C E | .6 |
| AB D | 18.0 | 12 | C E | .6 |
| AB D | 17.0 | 13 | BC E | 1.0 |
| AB D | 16.0 | 14 | BC E | 1.0 |
| A D | 15.0 | 15 | BC E | 1.0 |
| A D | 13.5 | 16 | BCDE | 1.5 |
| A D | 12.0 | 17 | BCDE | 1.5 |
| A D | 10.5 | 18 | BCDE | 1.5 |
| A D | 9.0 | 19 | BCDE | 1.5 |
| A D | 7.5 | 20 | BCDE | 1.5 |
| A | 6.0 | 21 | BCDE | 1.5 |
| A | 4.0 | 22 | ABCDE | 2.0 |
| A | 2.0 | 23 | ABCDE | 2.0 |
| — | 0 | 24 | ABCDE | 2.0 |

This table shows the feasible daily combinations of $X$ and $Y$ producible by all five people. At the output of 22.8$X$ and 4$Y$, $X$ is being produced by $A$, $B$, $D$, and $E$ (part time), and $Y$ by $C$ and $E$ (part time).

Graphs of every person's production-possibility boundary are superimposed in Figure 11–1. Lying beyond all these lines, as a summation of them, is the community's total or aggregate production-possibility boundary. An inefficient assignment of producers will result in an output inside the boundary. Note that the community's production-possibility boundary starts at the lower right with the steepest slope (the same as that of *C*'s boundary line) and then moves upward to the left along lines that are successively flatter and flatter. The slope of that boundary with respect to the vertical axis is a measure of the marginal cost of producing *Y* (and the slope with respect to the horizontal axis is the marginal cost of *X*). Failure to follow the principle of assignment according to increasing marginal cost will give a boundary that lies inside the portrayed "efficient" boundary. The steepest boundary line (least loss of *X* for producing *Y*) is *C*'s; the next is *E*'s; and so on, until at last there is brought into the production of *Y* the producer with the least relative productivity of *Y* (in terms of *X*)—namely *A*.

On each straight-line segment is the name of a person. When the point of production (showing the combination of *X* and *Y* produced by the whole economy) is on a given segment—say, *E*'s segment—each of the other workers is producing a single good; *C* is producing 2*Y*; and *A*, *B*, and *D* are producing

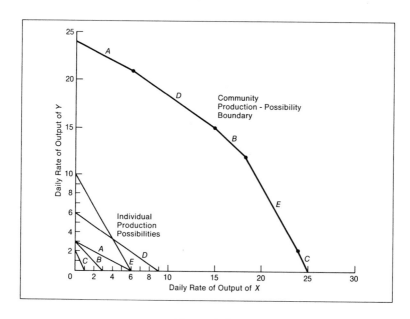

Figure 11–1
Total Production Possibility of Community
and of Each Person Alone

On the community production-possibility boundary, each segment is identified with the name of the person who in that interval switches from one product to some of the other. Reading from lower right to upper left, the sequence of letters indicates sequence with which people enter into production of *Y* if more *Y* is to be produced.

only *X*. *E* also produces solely one good if the production point is at one end or the other of his segment; he is producing *X* if the point is at the lower end and *Y* if it is at the upper end. If the point of production is at some intermediate position of *E's* segment, he is producing both commodities.

In the far right column of Table 11–2 are the marginal costs of producing *Y*, starting at *.5X* and increasing to *2X* at higher production rates. These are the marginal costs of the last person reassigned. Implied by this efficient allocation is the principle of *increasing* marginal costs. As the daily-output rate of any good is increased, marginal costs for producing it are also increased—if production is efficient. If we can interpret *X as the dollar value of all sacrificed outputs* necessary to produce *Y*, the marginal costs of producing *Y* increase from 50 cents at an output rate of 1*Y* per day, up to $2 at at output rate of 24*Y* per day. Figure 11–2 shows marginal costs for each output rate. This is the supply schedule of *Y* for the community if each producer acts like a price-taker, which we shall elaborate later.

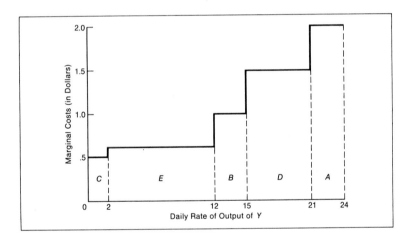

Figure 11–2
Daily Marginal Costs as Function of Rate of Daily Output of *Y*, with
Efficient Production

As output of *Y* per day is increased, marginal costs increase as individuals with successively higher marginal costs are brought into production of *Y*. As a result of efficient allocation of resources, *marginal* cost rises while daily rate of output of *Y* is increased.

### Production Controls under Private-Property, Open-Market System

Here we trace out the production assignments for *X* and *Y* from a slightly different viewpoint. We shall assume that the people feel that working at *X* is just as unpleasant as working at $Y$. (Later we shall see that differences in attitudes and willingness to work at different tasks can be taken into account.)

When everyone is producing $X$ and no $Y$, let Mr. $B$ decide that he would like some $Y$, even if it does cost as much as $1X$ to produce it himself. If he reveals that $1Y$ is worth up to $1X$ to him, as he can by expressing a willingness to pay $1 for $1Y$, some people will be induced to switch to production of $Y$. One of these is Mr. $E$, who can produce a $Y$ for only $.6X$ (60 cents) and sell the $Y$ to Mr. $B$ for, say, $.9X$ (90 cents). This transaction leaves Mr. $B$ with $2.10 of $X$ for the day and $1Y$, which is a bigger basket than if Mr. $B$ produced the $1Y$ himself. ($B$ would have had $2 of $X$ and $1Y$.) Mr. $E$ ends the day with $6.30 instead of the $6 of $X$ he had formerly, for he produced the $Y$ at a cost of 60 cents and sold it for 90 cents.

Other people are allowed access to the marketplace. If Mr. $C$ discovers that Mr. $B$ is paying 90 cents for a $Y$, it may occur to him that he can produce a $Y$ and sell it for, say, 80 cents (taking business away from Mr. $E$) and earn a net gain of 30 cents.

Only Mr. $E$ and Mr. $C$ can produce a $Y$, sell it for as little as 80 cents ($.8X$), and make a gain. If Mr. $A$ and Mr. $D$ think *they* are lower-cost producers than $C$ and $E$ in the production of $Y$ and test their belief, they will incur losses.

The issue is now between Mr. $E$ and Mr. $C$. Rather than lose all the business to Mr. $C$, Mr. $E$ can cut his price below 80 cents, even as far as 61 cents if necessary. And it is necessary, because Mr. $C$ can gain by producing some $Y$ as long as he can get anything over 50 cents for $1Y$. The result is clear. Mr. $C$ will drive Mr. $E$ out of the business of producing $Y$. Only Mr. $C$, lowest marginal-cost producer of $1Y$, will specialize in $Y$ if the community wants just $1Y$ or $2Y$. And the price that Mr. $C$ gets is at most 60 cents.

In our illustration, just what is the increase in product? And how is it distributed? Mr. $B$ wanted a unit of $Y$; producing it himself would have cost $1. But it is produced by Mr. $C$ at a cost of 50 cents, and sold to Mr. $B$ for, say, 60 cents. Mr. $B$ enjoys a 40-cent lower price, and Mr. $C$ obtains a gain of 10 cents; the total gain of 50 cents is the gain of specialization over no specialization. The right to buy and sell in a market provides this result.

Free competition (that is, open markets) for Mr. $B$'s business has resulted in only Mr. $C$'s specializing in the production of $Y$. "Greed," which induced Mr. $C$ and Mr. $E$ to make competitive offers in the marketplace, resulted in an increase of utility for Mr. $B$—although neither Mr. $C$ nor Mr. $E$ entered the market with that motivation. With Mr. $C$'s survival in production of $Y$, the total output is $1Y$ and $24.50 ($24.50X$)—precisely as large as under an all-wise planner. Apparently, central planning can be replaced by the capitalist private-property, open-market system.

If anyone wants more $Y$, he will have to offer the independent, private-resource owners a price at least equal to what they could get from producing other things. And that, of course, is measured by the marginal costs of producing more $Y$. The marginal costs of $Y$ rise as the daily-output *rate* of $Y$ is increased by efficient production assignments; this phenomenon is the *law of increasing marginal costs with higher or faster output rates*. Not only does the *total* cost of $Y$ increase as the output rate increases, but the total daily cost increases by *larger increments*: the larger the output rate of $Y$, the greater the marginal cost. This is a reflection of efficient resource allocation.

### Control of Production Rate with Price-Takers

At what rate will $Y$ be produced and sold in the market? To get a numerical answer, let us use the arbitrarily assumed demand schedule for $Y$ given in Table 11–3. According to this table, the daily sale of $Y$ is one if the price is set at \$2.00; it is two per day at a price of \$1.50; and so on. It will be profitable for Mr. $C$ to produce all the $Y$ he can $(2Y)$ and for Mr. $E$ to produce $3Y$ daily. This total of five per day can be sold at 70 cents each, and it would not be more profitable for Mr. $E$ to produce a fourth one each day (because that would cost him 60 cents, but he could sell it only if the price were dropped to 50 cents). Our equilibrium result is that, with this demand, five units of $Y$ (2 by Mr. $C$ and 3 by Mr. $E$) will be produced and sold daily at an open-market price of 70 cents.

Notice that we are assuming each person acts like a price-taker. He acts as though his output would have no effect on price. This may seem absurd given the small quantities we have assumed. However, we could imagine that these five people were just five of 500 producers, 100 each like $A$, $B$, etc. And we could have imagined the demand to be so large that the few items produced by each person had no noticeable effect on the selling price. Then the solution would be $2Y$ by each of 100 producers like Mr. $C$ and $3Y$ by each of 100 producers like Mr. $E$. In any event, we shall assume for the moment that the situation is a price-takers' market; then the equilibrium is $5Y$ (2 by Mr. $C$ and 3 by Mr. $E$) at an open-market price of 70 cents. Incidentally, we are keeping

Table 11–3
Daily Community Demand for Y

| Price in \$ | Y |
|---|---|
| \$2.00 | 1 |
| 1.50 | 2 |
| 1.10 | 3 |
| .90 | 4 |
| .70 | 5 |
| .50 | 6 |
| .40 | 7 |
| .30 | 8 |

This is an arbitrarily assumed demand schedule for $Y$ by the five-man community. Is the elasticity less, or more, than 1 at a price of \$1.50? As a further review, what is the marginal revenue when the quantity sold is $4Y$? $7Y$?

the price of $X$ fixed at $1.00 regardless of its rate of production, an assumption made solely for computational convenience. Ideally that price should change too; however, the *principles* would not change, and the arithmetic would become unbearably complicated and tedious.

Figure 11–3 shows the results. It is obtained by adding the demand curve to the graph of the marginal costs for the community of producing $Y$ (Figure 11–2). The curves in the two graphs would intersect at an output of five units of $Y$ per day, with an open-market price of 70 cents. Our community's *supply* schedule has turned out to be the *marginal-costs* schedule of $Y$ for all the members of the community added together where all act as price-takers. We have a demand-and-supply-curve intersection like that used in the first chapters—except that the supply curve, instead of being vertical, slopes from lower left (low prices and low daily rate of output) to the upper right (higher prices and higher daily rates of output). Higher prices on the market will elicit a higher daily rate of output, while lower market prices will reduce the daily rate.

Check our statements and calculations as we go along to be sure you understand our procedures. The arithmetic is easy, though a bit tedious. The principles explained are important, so work carefully and slowly. If you do, one of the things you might see is that a different equilibrium output is possible. The one we just arrived at with $5Y$ being produced and sold at a price of

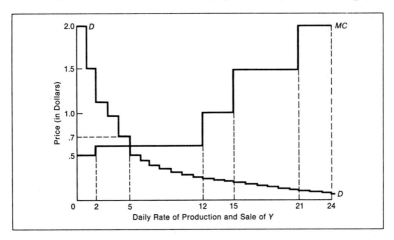

Figure 11–3
Community Demand and Supply for $Y$

If we assume each seller acts as if he were a price-taker and has no power to alter the price by his offerings of $Y$, the marginal-cost schedule for various daily output rates of $Y$ by the community is called the supply schedule of $Y$ for the community. The price that would clear the market is at the intersection of the demand and supply schedules—a price of about 70 cents. Actually, if Mr. $E$ produced one more than the three he is producing, price would fall to 50 cents (and would rise to 90 cents if he produced only two (which with Mr. $C$'s two units would give a total of four). We temporarily assume that Mr. $E$ is unaware of this.

70 cents assumed that each seller acted as a price-taker. Each seller of $Y$ acted as though the amount he offered for sale had no effect on the price of $Y$. Everyone took the market price as given by forces beyond his control. The result is that the group output mix is $5Y$ and $22.2X$.

### Output Control with Price-Searchers

Suppose Mr. $E$ realizes his production is sufficiently large to affect the market price of $Y$. It would be in his interest to act as a *price-searcher*. How much $Y$ should he produce to maximize his wealth? In Table 11–4 we list the revenue and costs for the different possible outputs he can produce. If he produces no $Y$, and all $X$, the market price of $Y$ will be $1.50; we know this because the demand for $Y$, given in Table 11–3, shows a price of $1.50 if two are produced in the community (and Mr. $C$ is producing $2Y$). If Mr. $E$ produces $1Y$, the total community rate will be three and the market price will have to be $1.10. His earnings are $1.10 from $Y$ and $5.40 from the $5.4X$, a total of $6.50. If Mr. $E$ produces $2Y$, the community total will be $4Y$ with a price of 90 cents. Mr. $E$'s revenue from the $2Y$ would be $1.80. This 70-cent increase of earnings from $Y$ is called his marginal revenue of producing $2Y$ daily.

By producing that second $Y$ each day, Mr. $E$ incurs a cost increase of 60 cents, the marginal cost, because his output of $X$ falls from $5.40 to $4.80. His income would increase by the difference between the marginal revenue and the marginal cost at $2Y$, a gain of 10 cents. His total income is $6.60. If he produces and sells $3Y$ daily at the lower price of 70 cents, his

Table 11–4
Revenue and Costs for Mr. $E$ as a Price-Searcher in Sale of $Y$

| Production of $Y$ by $E$ | Price of $Y$ | Total Revenue from $Y$ | Marginal Revenue from $Y$ | Production Value of $X$ | Marginal Cost of Producing $Y$ | Total Income |
|---|---|---|---|---|---|---|
| 0 | $1.50 | $0.00 | – | $6.00 | – | $6.00 |
| 1 | 1.10 | 1.10 | $1.10 | 5.40 | $.60 | 6.50 |
| 2 | .90 | 1.80 | .70 | 4.80 | .60 | 6.60* |
| 3 | .70 | 2.10 | .30 | 4.20 | .60 | 6.30 |
| 4 | .50 | 2.00 | –.10 | 3.60 | .60 | 5.60 |
| 5 | .40 | 2.00 | .00 | 3.00 | .60 | 5.00 |
| 6 | .30 | 1.80 | –.20 | 2.40 | .60 | 4.20 |

As a price-searcher, Mr. $E$ is now assumed to recognize that his production and sale of $Y$ have an effect on the market price. Assuming the same demand schedule as given in Table 11–3, with Mr. $C$ producing and selling the first two units of $Y$, Mr. $E$'s demand schedule is given by the first two columns. The output rate that maximizes Mr. $E$'s wealth is $2Y$ per day (in addition to the $2Y$ produced by Mr. $C$), at a selling price of 90 cents per unit. The consequence of price-searcher behavior is to reduce the quantity of $Y$ sold from five to four, and to increase the quantity of $X$ sold from 22.2 to 22.8. The total community output remains on the community production-possibility boundary (of Figure 11–1)—only a different combination of $Y$ and $X$ is selected. (*Maximum income production combination for Mr. $E$ is $2Y$ and $4.8X$.)

receipts from $Y$ will be \$2.10, instead of \$1.80, giving him a marginal revenue of 30 cents for $3Y$. The marginal cost of $3Y$ is 60 cents. The negative difference between marginal revenue and marginal cost means he would incur a reduced net income of 30 cents. His total income would be \$6.30 (= \$2.10 + \$4.20). To maximize his wealth as a price-searcher he would produce and sell just $2Y$, rather than the $3Y$ he would have produced in a *price-takers'* market (as we saw in the preceding section). The total community output in a price-searchers' market for $Y$ is $4Y$ and $22.8X$, which is less $Y$ and more $X$ than a price-takers' market.

Although the output combination for the community is different with a price-searchers' market, the assignment or allocation of producers to various outputs is still efficient. It is impossible to produce more than $22.8X$ with an output of $4Y$. Productive efficiency remains. What has changed is the particular output combination. See Table 11–5 and Figure 11–4 for a summary of results.

Table 11–5
Effect of Price-Searchers' Open Market on Output Combination

| Open-Market Situation | Production of $X$ and $Y$ |
|---|---|
| Price-takers | 22.2  and  5 |
| Achievable | (22.2  and  5) |
| Price-searchers | 22.8  and  4 |
| Achievable | (22.8  and  4) |

In price-searchers' markets, output combination is shifted, in this example from $22.2X$ to $22.8X$ and from $5Y$ to $4Y$. Less of $Y$ and more of $X$ is produced. $Y$ was assumed to be sold in a price-searchers' market. Effect is to shift output from price-searchers' markets to more of good sold in price-takers' markets. Nevertheless, while output mixture is changed, no potential output is lost for no productive inefficiency occurs; it is impossible to produce more than $22.8X$ given that $4Y$ is to be produced.

In Figure 11–4, the output mixture with price-takers' markets is shown as point $T$. With price-searchers' open markets the output (still on the production-possibility boundary)[1] is at point $S$, which is not an efficient combination in the sense of *utility* efficiency.[2] In Figure 11–4 utility inefficiency (as

[1] $P_{om}$ indicates all combinations of production efficiency in a *technological* productive sense in open markets.

[2] Everyone could be better off if the following were done. Everyone could agree to contribute toward paying Mr. $E$ a total of 65 cents for producing a third $Y$ which is worth 70 cents to them. They would agree also to continue to buy the first four units in the market at 90 cents (from Mr. $C$ and Mr. $E$). Mr. $E$ would accept since he would collect 65 cents more for producing the third $Y$ (and no less on the first two) at a marginal cost of only 60 cents.

This would make everyone better off (than staying at $4Y$ and $22.8X$) as each individually judges his situation. With output back at $5Y$ and $22.2X$, the distortion is gone. The trouble is in getting people together to make this agreement. There are other possibilities, too, which we shall discuss much later.

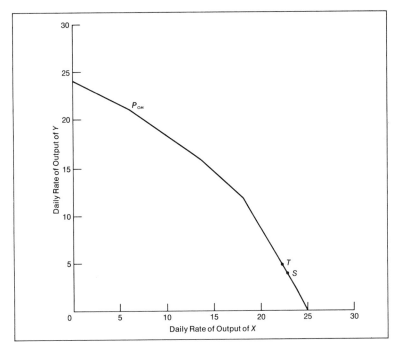

Figure 11-4
Socially Determined Combinations of Output in Price-Takers' and in
Price-Searchers' Markets

On the community production-possibility boundary, the output choice is $T$ if
price-takers' open markets prevail and $S$ in price-searchers' open markets. $S$ does
not achieve efficiency in the utility sense—in that some people could be better off
(and no one worse off) by moving production from $S$ to $T$ with appropriate side
payments. Price-searchers cannot be eliminated by law; they result from technological facts. Only a system of wealth transfers or subsidies could in principle be
effective. But what is possible in principle is not necessarily possible in fact,
because of political and institutional factors.

we shall explain on page 231) exists at any point $S$ if at that point the *slope*
of the production-possibility boundary, a measure of the marginal costs of
producing $Y$ and $X$, is not equal to the ratio of the selling prices of $Y$ and $X$.
In the present instance, we know $Y$'s are valued more highly relative to $X$
than the cost of producing another $Y$. Though this inequality is not revealed
in the figure, the figure shows the difference in the two outputs.[3]

[3] The Edgeworth Box presented earlier (pages 54–57) could be utilized in conjunction
with the production-possibility frontier to show this utility inefficiency graphically.

Productive Efficiency and Wealth Maximizing

Wealth or income maximizing gives an efficient *production* assignment of producers to various outputs. This holds true in both a price-takers' and a price-searchers' open market (whether or not the *output* mixture is *utility* efficient in consumption). The price-takers' market for $Y$ yielded an output mixture of $5Y$ and $22.2X$.

A check of each person's wealth situation in Table 11–2 will show that no other production pattern will earn him a larger wealth, given the prices of $Y$ and $X$ that prevail at the mixture of $5Y$ and $22.2X$. The price of $X$ is \$1.00, and the price of $Y$ is 70 cents. By referring to Table 11–1, we see that in one day Mr. $A$ can earn \$6 if he produces $6X$, or \$2.10 if he produces only $Y$. His maximum-valued output is obtained by specializing entirely in $X$. And that matches the efficient assignment of his productive resources for an output of $5Y$ and $22.2X$ (see Table 11–2). Similarly, $B$ will maximize his wealth if he produces only $X$—which gives him \$3. (Check our calculations.) Mr. $C$ earns \$1.40 if he produces $Y$, whereas he earns only \$1 if he concentrates on $X$. Thus, Mr. $C$ produces 2 of the $5Y$. Mr. $D$—who earns \$9 from producing $X$, compared to \$4.20 if he produces $Y$—will maximize his earnings by concentrating on $X$. Mr. $E$ can earn \$6 if he produces only $X$, whereas he can earn \$7 if he produces and sells only $Y$. But the most $Y$ he can sell at the market price of 70 cents, according to our demand schedule, is three; therefore (assuming he acts like a price-taker) he will produce that many and devote the rest of his resources to producing $X$. His daily earnings would be the value of the $3Y$ at 70 cents each, plus $4.2X$ at \$1 each—a total value of \$6.30.

If the demand for $Y$ increases and its price rises relative to that of other goods, some producers will be induced to revise output to maximize their wealth. Resources will be directed toward a new efficient allocation with production of more $Y$ and, therefore, less $X$. For example, if the demand for $Y$ increases so that it will support a sales rate of $14Y$ per day at a price of \$1.10 (with $1X$ equaling \$1), you should be able to show that individual wealths will be maximized if Messrs. $A$ and $D$ concentrate on $X$, with Messrs. $C$, $B$, and $E$ concentrating on $Y$. Also note that this allocation is efficient, in addition to being the result of each person's efforts to maximize his wealth. Thus, a private-property, open-market system is conducive to efficient production and resource allocation in a price-takers' open market.

The equilibrium price is 90 cents in the *price searchers'* market. Why? Again it will turn out that each person is maximizing his wealth under efficient production allocation. (Work out the calculations. For example, Mr. $A$'s income will be maximized at \$6 if he produces only $X$. Any output of $Y$ by him will yield him a smaller income.) Both in a price-searchers' and a price-takers' market the outputs are produced efficiently. The difference is in the equilibrium output *combination* of goods.

Productive and Utility Efficiency

Although production organization is efficient in both kinds of markets, in the sense that for any specified amount of $Y$ produced the largest possible amount of $X$ is being produced, is the particular output combination a most *preferred* one? (Most preferred by whom?) Is this economy producing the "wrong" output mixture efficiently—is it the "right" output mixture? To be specific, under a price-takers' market, the output mixture is $5Y$ and $22.2X$, while under the price-searchers' market it is $4Y$ and $22.8X$. Are these two alternative combinations equally "good"? That depends upon whether *you* think it is better for society to have more $X$ or more $Y$. But since no one is in a position to establish right and wrong for society, we can ask only whether it is good from each individual's point of view. And we can show that from the point of view of all, the price-searchers' market "distorts" the output mixture.

We know that the *price* a demander pays for a unit of $Y$ shows his personal valuation of the last unit of $Y$. If $4Y$ are being produced and sold at a price of 90 cents, we know each buyer personally values a unit of $Y$ at 90 cents. (See Table 11–3 or Figure 11–3.) If $5Y$ were produced, the price would be 70 cents, which tells us that the buyers personally value a fifth $Y$ as worth 70 cents.

If Mr. $E$ produces a third $Y$ (for a total on the market of five), he will sell each at 70 cents, for a total of $2.10 instead of $1.80. (See Table 11–4.) His marginal revenue would be 30 cents, although the price is 70 cents. *He has his eye on his marginal revenue, not the price of $Y$.* Since his marginal cost is 60 cents, he refuses to produce a third $Y$, even though everyone else values one more $Y$ at 70 cents. They prefer one more $Y$ (worth 70 cents) to the extra $.6X$ (worth 60 cents) now being produced. In other words, they prefer a mix of $5Y$ and $22.2X$ to a mix of $4Y$ and $22.8X$. Although each mix is efficiently produced, the price-searchers' mixture is the less preferred. It is not efficient in the *utility* sense.

The utility of *everyone* (including $E$) could be increased if the output were $5Y$ and $22.2X$. Distortion is caused by producers of $Y$ being guided by a marginal revenue that is less than the price of $Y$. It is sometimes called "inefficiency (in output mix) of price-searchers' or monopoly markets."

Table 11–5 summarizes, in the two top lines, the outputs in price-takers' open markets and in open markets with price-searchers for product $Y$. We have just seen in what sense the second is less preferred. The bottom two lines examine the effects of closing the market for $Y$ to all except Mr. $E$, which we shall examine in the next chapter.

The principle of having output at that rate at which marginal cost just equals *price* rather than marginal revenue is a necessary condition for utility efficiency in all economic systems—capitalist, socialist, or whatever—but the systems differ in the probability with which this condition may be achieved. As we have seen, price-takers' markets are more conducive to it than monopoly markets. And nonmarket-controlled production in socialist economies seems even less likely to approach it, if we judge by their system of incentives and their attempts to introduce free-market pricing.

Actual Attainment of Productive
and Utility Efficiency?

Nothing *guarantees* that the lowest-marginal-cost producer of *Y* will actually produce *Y* let alone doing so at the rate at which marginal cost equals price. If any of a host of things sufficiently interferes with his opportunity or willingness to risk wealth in the hope of greater wealth by producing *Y*, inefficient organization of production will continue. Efficient (that is, cheaper) producers will be discovered more easily if access to the market is not restricted, if more people desire wealth, and if the people are willing to take a chance for wealth. But the trial-and-error costs incurred by hopeful but overconfident people are great.

Which feature dominates? Over-entry into activities in which people lose wealth or under-entry into activities in which they would have increased their wealth? The answer is not known. For example, I *believe* that my costs would far exceed my market value as a professional in the following capacities: professional football player, musician, steel welder, farmer, doctor, lawyer, architect, electronic technician, stonecutter, watchmaker, shoemaker, coal miner, lumberjack, and so on. I may be wrong in this belief. Suppose I *could* operate a wine-grape farm at a cost less than the market price of grapes. My productivity as a grape farmer might really exceed the wages I get for teaching. But rather than run the risks and costs of an experiment to find out whether my relative productivity is higher in grape farming than in teaching, I prefer to continue as a teacher—simply because the "discovery" costs are too high to induce me to try the experiment. Therefore, as a teacher my utility (and wealth) is lower than it otherwise might have been. The allocation of my productive efforts is inefficient and my wealth smaller than if I were a grape farmer. That smaller wealth is said to reflect the reduction in total output resulting from my misallocation of productive resources. Too many resources (mine) are in teaching instead of in grape growing. Despite my unwillingness to switch to grape farming, the laws of production still hold. If the price of grapes should rise high enough relative to the wages of teaching, I shall switch. But I doubt that I shall see that ratio in the real market.

The pertinent questions are: (1) Is the dispersed knowledge utilized efficiently? (2) Is there incentive for a person to increase his knowledge of what he can do? To both, the answer is: Wider access to the market increases the likelihood of a "yes" answer. The market-exchange system, with its prices, provides more than a place to exchange goods. It is a place where information is collated and compared. A restriction on price and exchange information among interested parties would restrict not only the exchange of existing goods but also the transfer of productive resources from lower-value to higher-value uses.

It is easy to see why. First, market prices reflect consumers' demands, or values, of goods and services. They also reflect producers' costs of production. Each potential and actual producer, by looking at the selling prices, indirectly compares his estimated and realized costs with those of other producers, and with the values that consumers place on his product. If his (marginal) costs exceed prices, he will reduce or eliminate his production and move to something else unless he is willing to sustain a continuously falling wealth. The fact that his marginal costs are greater than prices indicates that other people can produce this good more cheaply than he can, and that consumers value his product less than other things he could do.

Second, specialization in production is in large part specialization and coordination of dispersed knowledge. Specialization of production does not mean simply that one person produces a pencil while someone else produces paper. It means also that different people produce the various component parts of goods and that different people perform the various special tasks that have evolved in making goods. In fact, in a modern society *no one* knows how to produce all of any one thing. Take the simple common pencil, which represents the culmination of the joint efforts and knowledge of millions of people. One person knows something about the paint; another about the graphite—how it is mined, transported, processed, shaped, and inserted in a pencil; others are knowledgeable in growing timber, cutting it, shaping the wood, and painting it; others make the steel holder for the eraser; and still others are involved in making the rubber eraser. Activities of thousands or possibly millions of people are coordinated to produce pencils at lower rather than at higher costs. Exchange prices among people in the market guide coordination, and each person strives to increase his wealth while being constrained by competitive suppliers and consumers' desires.

## Summary

1   Specialization brings about greater output and enables individuals to attain more preferred situations than under "do-it-yourself" or "self-sufficiency" systems of individual production. Specialization yields more efficient production if increases in the output rate of any good are provided by the lowest-cost producers. The principle of specialization relies on relative, not absolute, productivity. A person does not need to understand the principle of specialization in order to specialize in accord with that principle.

2   Unless all people are identical in productive ability, *every* person will *always* find some goods or services for which his marginal costs are less

than or equal to the market price; he can therefore produce these goods or services as a means of increasing his wealth (and utility) above what it would have been had he acted self-sufficiently—unless his access to the market is prohibited.

3    The cheaper the cost of access to the market, the greater the extent of specialization. Cost of a specified output is defined as the *highest* valued of the alternative forsaken opportunities. The measure of that cost is the market-exchange value of the forsaken output.

4    Human rights to property and access to a market in which mutually acceptable opportunities can be exploited provide incentives and means to produce efficiently.

5    The increase of output brought by increased efficiency is distributed via (a) profits to the owners of the productive resources and (b) lower prices to consumers.

6    As market demand for any good increases, and as the market price of that good rises, higher-cost producers will switch to that product.

7    Individual wealth-maximizing behavior in the face of market-equilibrating prices is conducive to productive efficiency.

8    Productive efficiency is not disrupted by price-searchers, but the output mixture is affected. Insofar as marginal revenue is less than price for price-searchers, the output mixture tends to be underweighted with products from price-searchers and is not utility efficient.

9    No economic system can guarantee continuous realization of productive efficiency.

## Questions

1    "Costs are an opportunity concept." Explain.

2    Are costs the same thing as the undesirable consequences of some action? Explain why not.

3    a. If there is more than one opportunity to be forsaken, which forsaken opportunity is the cost?
b. How are opportunities made comparable so that one can determine which one is the cost?
c. Can there be production without costs?

4    A lower-cost producer can produce more than a higher-cost producer. Do you agree? If so, why? If not, why not?

5    "The slope of the production-possibility curve is a measure of costs." Explain.

6    "An implication of efficient production is that marginal costs increase as the rate of output becomes larger." Explain.

7    Why are costs not measured in terms of labor hours?

8    *A* and *B* can produce according to the following:

Daily Rate of Output of
X   or   Y

| Mr. A | 10 or 15 | (or any linearly interpolated combination) |
| Mr. B | 5 or 10 | (or any linearly interpolated combination) |

a. Who can profitably produce $Y$ at the lowest cost and price of $Y$?
b. Who can profitably produce $X$ at the lowest cost and price of $X$?
c. If Mr. $C$ is allowed to trade with Mr. $A$ and $B$ and if $C$'s production possibilities are $4X$ or $4Y$ (or any linearly interpolated combination), who now is the lowest-cost producer of $X$? Of $Y$?
d. Who is not the lowest-cost producer of either $X$ or $Y$? Does this mean he will have nothing to gain by specializing and trade? Explain.

9    The following questions involve the production data of the five people given in Tables 11–1 and 11–2.
a. If the selling price of an $X$ were $1 and the selling price of a $Y$ were also $1, what should each person produce in order to maximize his wealth?
b. Would the resulting assignment of tasks be an efficient one?
c. What should each person produce in order to maximize his wealth if the selling price of an $X$ is $1 and the selling price of a $Y$ is $1.60?
d. Is the resulting job allocation an efficient one?
e. If the price of an $X$ is $3 and the price of a $Y$ is $3.20, what should each produce in order to maximize his wealth?
f. If the price of an $X$ falls to $2 and the price of a $Y$ is still $3.20, what should each produce to maximize his wealth?
g. Is the allocation of labor efficient?
h. Is it absolute prices or relative prices of $X$ and $Y$ that guide allocation?

10    The following questions are based on data in Table 11–3.
a. If all the prices in the table were to be doubled (while the price of an $X$ stayed fixed at $1), what would happen to output?
b. Is this the result of an increased demand for $Y$ or of a reduced demand for $X$?
c. Suppose a tax were to be collected from each producer of $Y$–a tax of 50 cents for each unit of $Y$ produced. If, before the tax, the prices of an $X$ and of a $Y$ were both $1, what effect would this tax have on job allocation and output?

**11**    The following questions are based on data in Tables 11–1 and 11–2.
a. What are the dimensions of the output of $X$ and $Y$? That is, are they measured in units of total output or in rate (speed) of output?
b. If the output is 15 per day, does this mean that 15 will be produced? (Hint: What if price changes at midday?)
c. What would be the total volume of output of $X$ in five days if $C$ and $E$ produced $Y$ exclusively and the other three specialized in $X$?
d. What would be the rate of output per hour for a ten-hour day?

**12**    "The increased output of increased specialization is distributed as profits and as a lower price to consumers." What determines the portion of each?

**13**    "Every profit represents the gain from moving resources to higher-valued uses." Do you agree? If so, why? If not, why not?

**14**    In the discussion on pages 224–225, let Mr. $C$ be a resident of Japan, while the others are residents of the United States. Mr. $E$ is a tuna-boat owner and fisherman; $A$, $B$, and $D$ are American workers in other American industries. Let $Y$ be "tuna" and $X$ be "other products." Mr. $E$ persuades his congressman to induce other congressmen to pass a law prohibiting the importing of Japanese tuna—product $Y$ produced by Mr. $C$. Who gains and who loses by a tariff or embargo on Japanese tuna? (This example captures the essence of the purposes and effects of tariffs and embargoes.)

**15**    The five-person problem in this chapter can also be interpreted as a case in which all producers of $Y$ must be members of an organization, and Mr. $C$ is denied membership in this organization. Who gains and who loses? Can you give some actual examples of this situation in the real world?

**16**    The five-person problem can also be interpreted as a case in which admission to the market for sale of one's production of $Y$ requires a license from the state, and this license is given only if the current output from those now in the production of $Y$ is deemed "inadequate to meet current demands." Who gains and who loses? Can you give some real examples of this situation?

**17**    Would the problem also serve as an example of the effect of apprenticeship laws that prohibit a person from acting as a "qualified" carpenter, meat cutter, etc., until he has served a specified number of years as an apprentice? Explain.

**18**    Does efficient production assume that perfect knowledge exists? Explain.

**19**    "Someone always has a comparative advantage in the production of some good." Explain.

**20**    The production-possibility schedules are:

| Mr. A | | | Mr. B | |
|---|---|---|---|---|
| X and | Y | | X and | Y |
| 5 | 0 | | 3 | 0 |
| 4 | 1.5 | | 2 | 1 |
| 3 | 2.9 | | 1 | 2 |
| 2 | 3.8 | | 0 | 3 |
| 1 | 4.5 | | | |
| 0 | 5 | | | |

**a.** Add these two production possibilities together for the efficient, combined production possibility. (Hint: Notice that Mr. A's production possibilities involve *increasing*, rather than constant, marginal cost of X. Use the condition that must hold between each person's marginal cost at an efficient allocation of productive inputs.)

**b.** Who would be first to produce profitably some X at a low price of X? Who would be last?

**c.** Who would be first to produce profitably some Y at a low price of Y?

**d.** Why is the answer to (b) and (c) the same?

**e.** At what ratio of the price of X to price of Y would Mr. B switch from production of X to production of Y?

**21**    Think of the five men A, B, C, D, E as being the five employees in a manufacturing company.

**a.** Can you think of any reason why the output data could be different if the five men were to work together rather than specialize separately with exchange of individual products? Do you think the output would be larger or smaller?

**b.** Why?

**22**    Open markets with price-searchers (or open monopolies) change the output pattern from that of open markets with price-takers. In what direction is the output pattern changed?

**23**    Evidence of the very extent of specialization of knowledge is provided by Albert Einstein's assertion just prior to his death (*Socialist International Information*): "The economic anarchy of capitalist society as it exists today is in my view the main cause of our evils. Production is carried on for profit, not for use." Give evidence of your superiority over Einstein by exposing his error in economic analysis.

# 12

Production with Market Restrictions, Exchange and Property
Enforcement Costs, and Public Goods

The principles of production, specialization, and exchange have been explained in a private-property, open-market context. Also, we have assumed implicitly that private property is enforced at essentially zero cost. However, markets are not open to all people and goods, nor are private-property rights costless to establish and enforce, nor are these the only kinds of rights that exist.[1] It is necessary for accurate analysis and valid results to consider the effects of market closure and significant costs of establishing and enforcing private-property rights.

The propositions can be demonstrated in Figure 12–1. Two production-possibility boundaries are shown, $P_{om}$ and $P_{cm}$. The one slightly inside is

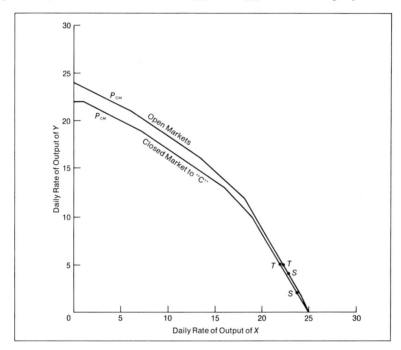

Figure 12–1
Production-Possibility Boundary Made Inferior by Market Closures
and Restrictions

The interior boundary, labeled $P_{cm}$, is for economies with market closures to some potential producers. In the present instance, it shows effect of closing market for $Y$ to Mr. $C$. Also shown are selected output mixtures with price-takers' and price-searchers' markets, $T$ and $S$, respectively. In each case, $T$ is the utility-efficient mixture for each boundary of production. It is possible to move from interior to exterior line by abandoning market restrictions, but it is not feasible to move from point $S$ to $T$, for reasons given in explanation of Figure 11–4.

[1] Read pages 157–164.

labeled $P_{cm}$ and results from closing the market for $Y$ to, say, Mr. $C$. The next section will explain why the $P_{cm}$ boundary is inside (inferior to) the open-market production-possibility boundary, $P_{om}$. In other words, it will show why productive inefficiency is associated with closed markets. Then we will explain, as in the prior chapter, how the price-searchers' market again alters the selected output mixture, even on an inferior boundary $P_{cm}$ associated with closed markets. The loss of production possibilities, shown by the line $P_{cm}$ being inside the other, is a result of inefficient selection of production techniques (wrong producers), in this case caused by market closure to some of the members of the community. But the difference between the selected mixtures of output $T$ and $S$ depends upon another factor—the presence of price-takers' or price-searchers' markets, as we saw in the last chapter.

Restricted Market Access: A Source
of Production Inefficiency

Not every activity designed to increase one's wealth will lead to efficiency. Thievery, violence, and restricted market access for one's competitors will obstruct efficiency. Although few capitalists would encourage theft and violence, many people who have benefited from capitalism advocate socialism and mercantilist restrictions on access to the market—not necessarily because they like socialism or mercantilism and dislike capitalism, but simply because their own wealth will be increased.[2] A common example is the legally instituted and enforced restriction on rights of access to the market. Such restrictions are mercantilistic. Mercantilism refers to an economy in which, though there is private ownership of goods, the right to buy and sell them or their services in the marketplace is reserved by law to a restricted set of people. The privileged groups are denoted by franchises, licenses, monopolies, or guilds—all enforced by law.

Examples of mercantilistic restrictions include laws controlling hours of business, Sunday closing, quality standards, apprenticeship, prices, interest rates, minimum wages, and professional licensing, to name but a very few. Support for such restrictions can be found among many successful business-men; it is not confined to so-called callous, unscrupulous people. Some of our most thoughtful humanitarians advocate them. Some justices of the Supreme Court of the United States deem them not only constitutional but desirable. The medical profession and many labor unions regard them as essential. Obviously, their support does not reflect an anticapitalist bias *per se*, but something else.

---

[2]In our own time, this has been increasingly associated with the euphemism "self-regulation" (by *existing* sellers).

We shall suppose that Mr. *E* is able to get a law passed preventing other people (for example Mr. *C*) from producing and selling *Y*. The results are shown in Table 12–1. In a price-takers' market Mr. *E* would then produce and sell all 5*Y* at the market price of 70 cents per *Y*. He gets $3.50 from sale of the *Y* and $3.00 from the *X* he makes with the rest of his time, for a total of $6.50 (20 cents more per day than with open markets as can be seen by reviewing page 224, lines 8–14). If this happens, the total community output is 5*Y* and 22*X* instead of 5*Y* and 22.2*X* as it was with open markets and price-takers (check it!). Because of restricted rights to the market, the total social loss is .2*X* or 20 cents per day. Productive resources are not efficiently organized—even aside from considerations of the particular output mixture of *X* and *Y*. (Check the data in Table 11–2 to see that with 5*Y*, more than 22*X* is possible.) This loss is a direct result of excluding Mr. *C* from production and sale of *Y*. Excluded producers, therefore, must use their resources in less valuable and less productive ways than if they could sell in the market.

The "national" income has fallen from $25.70 ($22.20 of *X* and $3.50 of *Y*) to $25.50 ($22.00 of *X* and $3.50 of *Y*). But Mr. *E*'s share is up to $6.50, from $6.30, while the rest of the population has $19 instead of $19.40 (check it). The upshot is that for Mr. *E* to gain 20 cents, the rest of the total population has to suffer a loss of 40 cents. The net social loss of 20 cents is the reduction in the output of *X*, caused by inefficiency. Clearly it would have paid everyone else to prevent such a market-restriction law from being passed. Why didn't they?

Table 12–1
Production of *X* and *Y* in Open or Closed and in Price-Takers' or
Price-Searchers' Markets

| Marketing Situation | Production of *X* and *Y* |
|---|---|
| Open: | |
| Price-takers | 22.2 and 5 |
| Achievable | (22.2 and 5) |
| Price-searchers for *Y* | 22.8 and 4 |
| Achievable | (22.8 and 4) |
| Closed: | |
| Price-takers for *Y* | 22.0 and 5 |
| Achievable | (22.2 and 5) |
| Price-searchers for *Y* | 23.8 and 2 |
| Achievable | (24  and 2) |

In closed markets, achieved production is less than achievable production. Achieved output is now on the inside community production-possibility boundary (of Figure 12–1), not because of any idle resource, but rather because of inefficiency ("misdirected" producers) resulting from restriction against resources entering markets where their uses are of highest value.

We can get a clue from some simple calculations. Suppose, as in our case, Mr. $E$ gets 20 cents more daily. Mr. $C$ would find it economical to try to prevent closure of the market. Being excluded costs Mr. $C$ 40 cents, for he could have earned $1.40 by selling $2Y$ at 70 cents, instead of earning just $1.00 of $X$ each day. Mr. $C$ could, therefore, spend up to 40 cents daily to protect freedom of the market—and his own wealth.

Every time someone manages to close out competitors, he gets a gain, but only at a greater loss to society. That loss will be borne by all buyers of this product—even those who are protected in sales of their products. As more people achieve protection for their own sales, the losses to society as a whole increase. It will alway pay any *one* person (for the moment) to get *more* protection for *himself*, but it would everyone else to prevent that if they could overcome costs of getting together to exert offsetting political pressure.

Ideal policy for a person interested in his wealth is to get the government to close his market to present and potential competitors, and at the same time to espouse the cause of free-enterprise, open-market capitalism when *others* seek to restrict open markets in which he buys.

Do laws restricting entry of competitors to the market involve political chicanery and immorality or bribery, considering that the protected parties pay part of their monopoly gains to the powers that be? No. The most noble monarchs of England have accepted these "taxes." Most of our states and cities in the United States do, too. The modern way is not to reward a particular official by paying him personally, but rather to be willing to "accept" a larger tax burden or pay a larger license fee for the privilege of being a monopolist or, as it is euphemistically put, a public utility—for example, water, light, power, gas, or taxi companies that have obtained operating franchises that eliminate competitors or raise the costs of getting into the market.

Various techniques for passing laws that restrict entry are moral, politically encouraged, and openly utilized. Later we shall examine some. For the moment, it suffices to indicate that laws can deny free access as well as protect it. For example, the government can help to *ensure* access by protecting entrants from private threats of violence and physical harm; it can *restrict* access by failing to grant such protection and by enforcing laws that keep "outsiders" from the market.

### Closed Markets with Price-Searchers

In the closed market situation just discussed, we assumed sellers were price-takers. We now suppose that Mr. $E$ is a price-searcher; he acts in awareness that his output affects price. Since he is the sole, privileged seller of $Y$, the demand schedule in Table 11–3 (page 225) faces him. He sees that the marginal revenue of selling $1Y$ at $2.00 is $2.00; the marginal revenue of selling $2Y$ is $1.00 (the difference between selling $1Y$ at $2.00 and $2Y$ at $1.50 each); and the marginal revenue of 3 is 30 cents. However, the marginal cost of a third $Y$ is 60 cents; so producing and selling $3Y$ would reduce his net income by 30 cents, the difference between the marginal revenue and marginal cost at $3Y$. It is not the selling price with which he compares marginal cost, but the marginal revenue. Since marginal revenue to a price-searcher is less than price—the value of another $Y$ to buyers—he will produce only $2Y$, and he devotes the rest of his resources to making $4.80 worth of $X$ per day.

The national output is $2Y$ and $23.8X$. The results of the different cases (1) with and without open markets and (2) with price-takers' or price-searchers' markets can be readily compared in Table 12–1. *Closing other sellers'* (except Mr. *E's*) *access* to the market for $Y$ resulted in smaller output. This loss reflects an inefficient organization of productive resources. A bigger output of *both* $X$ and $Y$ is possible by a different allocation of productive resources. The community output without closed markets could have been $22.2X$ (instead of $22X$) and $5Y$ for price-takers' markets; it could have been $24X$ (instead of $23.8X$) and $2Y$ for price-searchers' markets. These losses reveal the inefficiency of closed markets. The extent of the loss depends upon who is excluded and who is allowed to produce and sell in the market. If Messrs. $C$ and $E$ were excluded, and only $B$ were allowed, the loss would be even greater. (You can check this as an excercise.)

The effect of the *price-searchers'* market (explained in pages 227–232)is to *shift* the output *mixture* toward $X$ from $Y$ as can be seen in Table 12–1. Three less $Y$ (2 instead of 5) are being produced, each worth *at least* 70 cents; 1.8 more $X$ are produced (23.8 instead of 22), each worth *at most* $1.00. The negative difference of 30 cents ($=-\$2.10 + \$1.80$) indicates a loss to the members of society (aside from $E$ who gains, though less than the rest lose). This "loss" of utility between lines 3 and 4 is a result not of closing the market but of the difference in output decisions between price-taker and price-searcher. It is a "loss" from the less preferred output mixture, not from a smaller output of both $X$ and $Y$ that occurs when the market is closed. Closing the market prevents production efficiency, in addition. Price-searchers lead to a less preferred mixture of output, a "consumption-mixture" utility inefficiency. (If closing the market also makes the protected sellers price-searchers, then the market closure can be said to be a "cause" of the "distortion" in output mixture also.) But again a reminder: This concept of *utility* inefficiency rests on the premise that *individualistic personal* judgments about relative values of goods as measured by prices in price-takers' markets *should* be followed in deciding what goods to produce.

Property Costs

Costs of Safeguarding Property Rights

The more expensive it is to enforce the law against theft, the more common thievery would be. Suppose that thievery of coats were relatively easy (expensive to prohibit effectively); people would be willing to pay only a lower price for coats because they do not expect to have control over all use of the coat and because more people will steal a coat rather than purchase one. The lower market price of coats will understate the true value of coats to people; for it will not include the value to the thief when he uses a stolen coat. If the thief were induced to rent or purchase someone else's coat, the price of coats would more correctly represent their value to society. It follows that the cheaper the policing costs, the greater the efficiency with which values of various uses of resources are revealed. The more likely something is to be stolen, the less of it that will be produced. People seldom plant apple trees where passers-by can easily take apples even if the value of the apples to society would exceed the costs. It is necessary that payment of a value more than his costs be offered to the producer to induce production. And it will not be offered if the purchaser acquires "weak" rights.

### Costs of Defining and Exchanging Property Rights

Defining and sanctioning private-property rights for some goods may be more costly than it is worth. The cost of protecting a person's rights to property from *all* noise produced by other people may exceed the costs imposed on the people whose "rights" are attenuated by the noise. Similarly, the costs of disposing of old leaves by other than burning may be so high that people may prefer to burn them even though there is mutual contamination of each other's property. The costs of subduing some "torts" or "nuisances," as the law calls these denials of rights to exclusivity of use, may be greater than the damage done. For example, the costs of eliminating all smog-creating exhausts have been greater than the costs imposed by smog itself, but new inventions are changing the situation.

However, if property rights are cheap enough to define and enforce, we could compensate other people for any invasion of their property. The payment must, of course, be lower than the cost of other alternatives. I would rather pay a neighbor $50 for the right to dump refuse on his property than pay $200 to cart it elsewhere. If I build a shopping center near your house and change the physical attributes (via noise and bright lights) of your property so that you cannot enjoy it as formerly, I could pay you $100 a year for the right to do so, if you prefer $100 to no such "nuisance." But if the courts are sufficiently inept in defining private-property rights, I can create the "nuisance" without paying you anything.

Land-use rights are enforced because we can survey the land, detect trespassers, or "squatters," and apprehend and punish them at a sufficiently small cost to make that worthwhile. On the other hand, it is claimed, we cannot, when property is despoiled, detect dogs and identify their owners at a sufficiently low cost to make it worthwhile.

### Effect upon Maximum-Value Use of Resources

The great significance of the costs of negotiating contracts and policing property rights—called *transactions* costs—can be seen by imagining a world in which these costs were absent. In such a world, there would be no difficulties in knowing everyone else's preferences and values for all goods and activities. Everyone would know, or could find out at no cost of time or resources, what everyone else wants. (A major function of the market is to provide such information.) There would be no costs of policing contracts and enforcing agreements and property rights. In the fanciful absence of all these costs, (1) all the harmful and beneficial effects of any action would be brought to bear on the person authorizing that action, the property owner; (2) property (resources) would be used efficiently, in the sense that all exchange opportunities of mutual benefit would be realized and all production would be efficiently performed; (3) the uses of resources and the output produced with various goods would depend only upon the demand patterns and *not* upon who owns what rights to what goods.

All this can be made evident with an example. A new product is contemplated. If produced, it will attract customers from other goods. The producers of old goods will lose wealth. In this context, consider two alternative initial assignments of property rights: (A) Producers have the right to sell new products without compensating competitors for their loss of sales. (B) The existing producers are assigned a right to retain their customers, who cannot shift to a new product without the permission of the old producers. What difference would assumption of one alternative instead of the other make to the production of goods (use of resources)? None!

Under either alternative existing producers would bear losses, but under A, they can try to reduce their losses by paying the new producer to abstain from production, offering an amount up to that of the loss they would have suffered, *or* they could cut the prices on their product to retain customers. If the cost imposed on the old producers exceeds the gains proffered to customers by the new product, the old producers will be able to buy off production of the new good. But if the gain to the customers exceeds the loss to the old producers, the new producers could not be bought off.

Now consider alternative B in which the new producer would have to buy from old producers the rights to sell to customers. He would have to pay the old producers at least the loss of wealth they would suffer by loss of their sales (the same as the maximum the old producers would give up in the first alternative). Again, if the gains of the new producers would exceed the losses to the old, the new product would be produced; otherwise, the product would not be produced.

The important proposition is that *if transactions costs are absent*, then under either assignment of *clearly specified rights*, the same production outcome is obtained: resources are put to their highest values. In sum, it makes no difference who has what rights, so long as the rights are *specified and enforced and exchangeable at zero transactions costs*. Subsequent exchanges will shift the rights to uses of various goods to those who will put them to the highest valued uses.

In the real world, however, transactions costs do exist. They range from the trivial to the prohibitive. If the costs to the houseowner of detecting the driver of a noisy scooter and persuading him by a contract to stop are excessively large relative to the loss of value imposed by the noise or the value of being able to drive in noisy fashion, then noise will be made even though it inflicts a greater loss on one houseowner than the value to the scooter rider. And remember, there may be a hundred houseowners who suffer from the noise.

In Chapter 8 we analyzed the effects of "high" transactions costs on the allocation of produced goods. We saw that the higher the contracting costs, the more the market-exchange process was displaced by other rationing criteria. But there is more than a rationing problem; there is also the problem of producing the *appropriate* amounts of goods—the amounts that would be most desired *if* the costs of revealing demands were zero. If these demands cannot be cheaply revealed, an important incentive to producers is lacking. Too few of these goods are produced—because of the excessively high costs of discovering demand and negotiating a contract that can be effectively enforced. As in the case of the noisy scooter, *privately perceived* gains and costs do not reflect accurately the total gains and costs.

When transactions costs are excessive, resources are used in a way so strikingly at variance with what would be done if social benefits and costs were accurately recognized that people demand some kind of correction. Their first temptation is to ask for government action to either prohibit or require specified actions.

### Indefinite Property Rights

Even when transactions costs are not excessive, the assignment of rights may be so ambiguous that no one knows who has what rights. If the case is taken to higher authority, the courts or the legislature may decide the rights belong to the government and not to any individuals. If an unambiguous specification of private-property rights is made, the disputing parties can work out an exchange. No doubt, the initial assignment will determine that one party will be *richer*, but once that is settled, subsequent negotiation and contracting will reshuffle those rights in conformity with the principles of maximum-value use of resources.

#### Examples of Allocative Effects of Indefinite Property Rights

*Radio and TV.*    As a first example of what happens in the absence of clearly specified rights, we cite our use of radio and TV frequencies. In the 1920s, anyone could set up a radio transmitter and broadcast on any frequency he chose, regardless of who else might be broadcasting on the same or adjacent frequencies. Chaos resulted. The courts began to specify that the first broadcaster on a frequency owned the right, and new, subsequent parties would have to buy it from him. This would have stopped the chaos. Before this system of rights assignment could be developed, Congress, at the urging of the Navy (which wanted *sole* rights) and the Secretary of Commerce, decreed that the rights belonged to no one; therefore, the government should decide who could broadcast on what frequency. In essence, the government took the rights much as other governments have appropriated land rights. The higher valued uses of radio and TV cannot be achieved, because direct sale of programs to viewers (the consumers of the radio spectrum) is not generally permitted.

In contrast, land can be rented by private individuals and put to highest valued uses by offering present owners sufficient payment for the rights to the land. For radio and TV, private exchangeable rights are not allowed—that is, pay-TV by wireless transmission is prohibited. In other words, transaction costs are made "prohibitive" simply by declaring any such payment or exchange to be illegal. Consequently, the social benefits and social costs do not impinge on any persons as private benefits and costs; and, consequently, more valuable programs are not produced. This is an example of the disparity between social and private benefits and costs (of non-inducing externalities, or of prohibitive transactions costs). This disparity *in radio and TV* occurs only partly because of some naturally present transaction costs, but they are made prohibitively expensive *by law*.

The problem of "unsatisfactory" performance by radio and TV is partly a result of our legal structure which denies both exchangeable and specified rights to the use of radio frequencies. The Federal Communications Commission, appointed to *define and police* radio-frequency rights, has become a *control* agency determining acceptable programming and for what radio can be used—much as if we had no private exchangeable rights to land and therefore created a Federal Land Commission to decide how and for what land could be used.

*Water.* Property rights in water also are weakly defined, probably because of the problems of surveying and monitoring the water (underground reservoirs, for example). More extensive property rights in the more valuable commodity oil, however, have been defined.

*Airport noise.* If an airport were to be used by noisy jet planes, the planes' owners, or the airport owner, could compensate the nearby landowners for the noise nuisance, or, in effect, buy rights to particular uses of the land. However, this procedure is rarely followed. Instead, one of the following extremes is taken: (1) There is no compensation for the noise damage. (2) The planes are prohibited. (3) The neighboring land is bought and left *empty* as people are prohibited from living there—even though many would prefer to live there despite the noise, *if* they could buy the land at a low enough price, and thereby be compensated for the noise. These extreme policies are based on an assumption that it is impossible to buy the rights to "dump" noise on land.

*Smog.* A much more difficult problem arises from smog-producing processes. To eliminate smog completely would require prohibition of gasoline engines; and *that* now costs more than the gain from smog elimination. The other extreme is to permit unrestricted smog pollution. In between is some degree of legal restriction or incurring of costs to reduce smog. As yet, however, no one knows of an enforceable system of exchangeable private-property rights in clean air that would protect people from "excessive" air pollution.

*Creation versus operation of private property.* One confusion about the meaning of a private-property system has arisen from the various ways in which private-property rights are created. The way in which private-property rights are *created* and initially allocated is different from the way that system *operates* once it is in existence. An excellent example is provided by the Enclosure Movement in England about 500 years ago. Farmers had rights to *use* particular portions of land in common with other people but could not sell this right. If the rights had been legally salable, it would have paid a person to sell his use rights to the person who could make the most valuable use of the land. One would think that the law would have been modified, so that each holder of a right to use could be identified and allowed to sell his right to someone. If transferability by sale were authorized, all the use-right holders would have been compensated for transferring their rights. However, the common-use-right holders were not allowed to sell their rights; they simply had their rights expropriated, and some lucky (politically powerful) person was declared to be in control of the sole right. This method of *creating* private property has no bearing on how the system will operate thereafter, but to the people of the time, the *operation* of a system of private property (capitalism) was identified with this particular method of *creation* of a system of property rights—expropriation of common-use rights. Tenants who lost their rights regarded private property as theft.

Imagine how you as a student would feel if your rights to attend your present college were revoked and given to new students, who in turn could resell those rights. You would feel cheated. But if your current "rights" to attend were converted to a "private-property" right that *you* could sell to other people, you would not lose anything. (Of course, the university administration, including the faculty, would lose part of its cherished rights to decide who was admitted to college.)

### External Consequences

The term *private* property suggests that *private consequences to the owner* of a good dominate his decisions about the use of privately owned goods. Yet, the way we use our resources very generally has consequences for others, too. When you wear clean, good-looking clothes, or cultivate a pretty garden, or even read the kinds of books that I think you ought to read, my utility is increased. This kind of interdependence or external benefit was not ruled out in the preceding chapters; nor is it inconsistent with that analysis. Exchange, which is a use of goods, provides, as we saw, benefits to the other person, too. Still, there are actions you can take that would benefit other people, but which you do not take because you are not offered adequate inducements to take those actions.

Beneficial effects for other people that are *induced* by those who benefit are called *induced* external benefits. The gains from exchange and specialization analyzed in earlier chapters are "external" effects that have been induced by the reward of the *quid-pro-quo* exchange—a reward that reflects the value of the external service provided. The ability to sell or transfer goods or their services means that other people can influence the use of goods, no matter who owns them. Potential external effects are not all left without influence on the decision about how goods shall be used. Every home owner takes into account the effect of his uses of his house on the sale value of the house. The use everyone makes of his own marketable goods depends on the preferences and desires of other people. When one uses goods, he must reckon with the gains he otherwise could have. Sometimes this inducement feedback is called "internalizing the external effect." In essence, much of economic theory concerns the allocation of the uses of economic goods by *internalizing* external effects.

However, it is difficult to make the use of some goods respond to external effects. A public fireworks display at a Fourth of July celebration would benefit many viewers. An extra dollar's cost of display provides possibly 90 cents more utility to one person, 80 cents more to another, and 40 cents more to another. The extra cost is $1; yet the sum of the independent marginal values is $2.10. The extra dollar of use is not worth that much to any one person; yet, because it provides utility to several people simultaneously the sum of the marginal values over all the beneficiaries exceeds the extra $1 of cost. Still, no one, unless he could be excluded, will offer to pay the $1, if the service is provided.

### Costs and Incentives for Excluding Nonpayers

We must, however, be careful. The single fact that several people benefit jointly is not crucial. At a theater, everyone pays; his contribution is only a small part of the total cost of the performance. Jointness of beneficiaries does not upset the ability of market exchange to get desired services performed. Flood-control projects, national defense, sanitary campaigns—all are identical with theatrical presentations and football games insofar as *commonality and simultaneity* of benefit are concerned. A crucial element is in the *costs of exclusion of nonpayers*, i.e., of "free riders." For some goods and services, nonpayers are "naturally" excluded; consumption of food by one person naturally excludes other people. For other goods the cost of excluding nonpayers is prohibitive.

If there were a cheap way to exclude nonpayers from enjoyment of the service, the external effects would be "internalized." As we have noted, it may not be desirable to internalize the benefits if the costs of doing so exceed the value of service. But there are some techniques for internalizing the effects without excessive costs.

For example, a golf course provides benefits to the neighboring property owners, who benefit without paying. A golf-course builder could buy enough land to build a course and the surrounding houses. Then when he sells the surrounding property, he captures the higher value stemming from proximity to the golf course. Those external benefits have been "internalized" as inducements to build the golf course.

Another example is provided by the apartment-house owner who includes maintenance of the gardens and exterior appearance of each apartment in the rental price, rather than having the tenant provide it. Similarly, the purchase price of a cemetery plot usually includes the costs of maintaining the cemetery rather than permitting each owner to choose the degree of mainte-nance—again, because of the neighborhood external effect.

A most important institution to internalize external benefits is the partner-ship or corporation. These enable larger ventures to be undertaken so that more of the benefited resources can be owned by those who produce the benefits. If all the land of a suburban shopping center is owned by one enterprise, there can be a more complete response to the total effect of the shopping center on neighboring land values. A department store with all the departments in one building owned by one firm is another example of how the neighborhood effects of each department are "internalized" upon the others.

Another adaptation can be cited. A business firm that locates in a new area knows that it will provide a benefit to other firms that spring up in its neighborhood. Presumably, the initial firm would have to expect to capture the value of external benefits to other people in order for its decision to be influenced by those external effects. Yet the owner may instead "bet" that while his action provides external benefits to other firms that locate near him, he will get reciprocal external effects from other new firms that spring up. An anticipated exchange of external effects is an inducement, even though a formal contractual exchange agreement is not involved. Shopping districts spring up without formal advance contractual agreements among all who eventually open a business. Each businessman gambles on the mutual-benefit effect. A factory owner, when relocating his factory, "bets" that others will open nearby restaurants, apartments, housing tracts, and appurtenant services. House owners who cultivate gardens to beautify their homes "bet" that others will also do so with mutual external benefits. "Keeping up with the Joneses" is not always a silly social code.

One of the principal means for internalizing externalities and handling some public-goods cases is by ownership of a large piece of land on which a shopping center or entire residential community exists.[3] The landowner,

---

[3]Trailer courts, apartments, condominiums, hotels, shopping centers, large business buildings, department stores—all are examples of groups of people living in conditions where the external effects of their actions and the "public goods" provided by the complex are responsive to values totaled over all members.

heedful of the effects of each person's action on the willingness of others to continue as tenants, will restrict undesirable external effects and increase the extent of desirable ones—to enhance the rental value of the land in the entire complex.

We can see that the extent of so-called "non-influential" external benefits is not determined by "technological" conditions alone. The scope of uncaptured or non-inducing benefits is affected by the ownership arrangements, which are often adapted and modified so as to capture previously uncaptured benefits. People are ingenious. They scramble television signals so that only those who pay will get a picture. Fences are built around athletic arenas and high walls around theaters. Colleges keep out students by instructing professors to exclude *nonpaying students*.

### Public Goods Production

Even if it were costless to exclude nonpayers, it does not follow that nonpayers should always be excluded! There is a class of goods known as "public goods," wherein the amount of use of the good or service by one person does not reduce the amount available to others *if* the good has been produced.[4] Classic examples are melodies, poems, ideas, and theories. Anyone can use them without in any way reducing someone else's supply. If I hum a new tune, you can hum it too. *Once the good is produced*, any restriction on its use by some person, say by charging a price for each use, would be "inefficient"—in the sense that the restriction reduces the total utility of the members of the community. Someone has less utility and *no one* else thereby gets more. (It is not a *free* good once it is produced, for even more of it might be desired; but, it is a public good in the sense that no actual or potential user supplants some other possible user.)

Exclusion of any potential user would be undesirable if we accept the simplest ethical criterion that more for some people, if it does not mean less for anyone else, is certainly desirable. However, accepting this criterion creates a conflict of goals. We want to encourage the invention of new ideas, melodies, and literature, and we want them fully used. But to charge for their use in order to provide incentive for development and invention will restrict their use. How can we induce people to create public goods if we prohibit charging for their use?

Examine the example of a lighthouse. All shipowners benefit, and they would like more light. If the lighthouse builder were able to control the light rays so that any nonpaying shipowner could not see the light, beneficiaries could induce him to provide as much more of the service as it was worth. Barring this possibility, some shipowners will not voluntarily pay for their

---

[4] Review the earlier discussion of "public good" attributes on pages 164–165.

value of service received—pro-rated share (say, $100) of the light they other-wise would get free, plus an amount (say, $10) to cover the cost of a larger light that they each might prefer. They would have to share payment for all the light ($110), but the worth of the additional light they get by cooperating is only the marginal increment ($10). As far as any one user is concerned, the choice is between paying the pro-rata share of the total cost of $110 to get a $10 gain in value of light, or paying nothing and still getting some (or hoping others will provide) lighthouse service. Obviously, it will benefit him not to pay at all. And almost everyone will hope to get a "free ride." Too few lighthouses would be built too late. The consequence arises from the "unwill-ingness" of the nonexcludable beneficiaries to induce the provider of the service to provide more. Yet, *once the lighthouse is built*, exclusion of anyone could be wasteful (except that it is a very reliable means of ascertaining the value of the service for guiding production).

The landlubber counterpart is television. If all who wanted the program were to pay, the program would be available, but no one person is willing to bear the full cost of an "optimum" amount of service if he can view for nothing. Each person holds back in the hope that someone else will act.

If, fancifully, there were a way to measure the benefit obtained by each user and then have each pay not more than that amount to the producer, the problem would be solved. The user would pay a nonrestrictive lump-sum, and all who paid could use as much of the public good as was available. The lump-sum payment is not restrictive, because it is not a price for more use of the public good. It is an entry fee that one pays, once and for all, and thereby does not restrict the extent to which he makes use of the public good.

How to determine for each person what the appropriate lump-sum payment is and how to collect it? Everyone would want to conceal the real value to him while someone else paid to get the good produced. An excellent current example is the community television antenna for relatively isolated towns. Once the antenna is installed everyone can tap it with no loss of signal to anyone else. So why should anyone pay? And to prohibit its use by non-payers is to restrict needlessly the extent of viewing—needlessly, in the sense of maximizing total utility *once the antenna is installed*. But if, in the absence of pricing and restricting, the antenna were not constructed (not enough volunteer to cover the costs), then pricing may be desirable to *get* the antenna *constructed*. Is it better not to restrict (and have no antenna) or to restrict and have an antenna? Clearly, the latter is superior.

But there is another alternative. Let the government tax everyone on a lump-sum basis and, with the proceeds, build the antenna. Then do not restrict the number who use it. But this solution also has flaws. (1) The tax is compulsory even on those who do not want an antenna. (2) It, too, is exclu-sionary, for failure to pay taxes will "exclude" you. (3) Who decides what ideas and programs shall be produced by the tax proceeds? Without a price per unit of use, viewers have no means of directly rewarding producers of more desirable programs. The control of production passes to the political arena and is more controlled by group political competition than decen-tralized, market competition. For those who are strong in political competitive power, this may seem desirable. The choice is not determinable by some simple or even any known ethical criterion.

Another alternative to government is voluntary group action. The church is a prime example. In the United States, churches are not supported by taxes paid for support of the church, although they are in some other countries (Scandinavia). In Scandinavian countries, the number of churches per person is lower than in areas with voluntary contributions to church support. Are there too many in one system or too few in the other? We cannot tell.

The problem of public goods is a relatively new one in economic analysis. Perhaps in a few more decades, more definitive analyses can be accomplished and rigorous implications perceived. The problem is covered here to warn against blind carryover of principles from private goods to public goods as if there were no difference.

We can summarize the problem of "external effects." Some potential uses of resources also benefit people other than the current owners. Those "external" benefits can be made influential by paying the resource controller to adjust his use of the good. "External effects are thus internalized, or social effects are made private." For some goods this is prohibitively expensive; there then exists a disparity between social and private benefits and costs. For any good heavily loaded with the "public goods" characteristic, *once the good is produced*, there is no allocating or rationing problem, since no one user will deprive any other user. Hence, charging a price for its use would restrict use unnecessarily. But a means of defraying the costs of production and of discovering how much to produce is necessary. The conflicting objectives for "public" goods are (1) to induce beneficiaries to reveal their values of services and to pay for the production of the service and (2) the "unnecessary" restriction on use if any fee restricts use. Various devices were mentioned that have been adopted to meet partially both objectives of inducing appropriate production and of not restricting use once production has occurred. Some involve group action via private markets and some via government taxing or production.

### Summary

1    Productive efficiency is disrupted if markets are closed or restricted to potential entrants.

2    The private-property system specifies exclusive decision over use and transferability of specified resources.

3    For a large class of goods the private consequences of use to the owner are the entire set of consequences; the uses of many other goods have external effects. When the external effects are not taken into account by the decision maker, more harmful effects and less beneficial effects will be provided. Obstacles to making externalities influential are

reduced (a) the more explicitly property rights are known, (b) the more economically and surely they are enforced, and (c) the lower are the costs of negotiating rearrangement of rights.

4    If costs of negotiating contractual exchanges were zero, and if enforcement and policing of rights were costless, it would make no difference (so far as how goods are used) who initially had what rights to what goods. The contractual rearrangement of rights to use various goods would automatically put the goods in the hands of those who would put them to the highest market-valued uses. Radio, television, water, and roads are resources for which use rights have not been specified and made transferable; as a result, their uses do not approach the highest market-valued uses.

5    Public goods are those for which each person's consumption does not reduce any other person's consumption of that good. Beneficiaries of public goods prefer not to reveal the value of the goods to them, because they can realize the benefits without paying. To exclude those who benefit without paying is to reduce social total of benefit; there would be no offsetting gain to anyone else.

6    "Externality" inducement is partially provided by ownership of enough land to capture benefits of such services via higher rental.

7    If externalities are not sufficiently internalized and if goods have heavily public aspects, the government will probably provide or control such services. Closure of the market is also dominantly achieved by governmental legislation or governmentally policed licensing.

Questions

1    Closed markets (with either price-takers or price-searchers) imply a reduced output compared to open markets. Yet no increase in unemployment or idle resources is involved. Explain why the output is smaller and why there are no idle resources.

2    What is meant by an equality between private and social costs?

3    "Privately owned goods are those which a person has the right to use however he wishes." Explain why it is not necessary to add the clause "subject to not destroying other people's property." Explain why that first statement does not give an owner the right to hit you on the head with his hammer or to dump his garbage on your property.

4    The City of Palm Springs prohibits construction of any building whose shadow will fall on some other person's land between 9 A.M. and 3 P.M. Is that a restriction of private property or a strengthening of it? Explain.

5    A city passed a zoning ordinance prohibiting the owner of a large parcel of land from constructing homes on it because of a fear that the noise of a nearby airport owned by the city would be so disturbing to the new tenants that airport operations would have to be curtailed.
a. Whose rights were being curtailed by the zoning ordinance?
b. Under the definition of private-property rights, were the landowner's rights being taken from him?
c. Can you suggest some other solution to the problem?
d. If you were a taxpayer in that town and did not live near the airport, what solution would you have voted for?
e. If you owned vacant land near the airport, what solution would you advocate? If your vote is different in each case, do you think you are denying the morality of decisions by voting? Why?

6    "When property rights interfere with human rights, property rights have to give in." This statement is reported to have been made by a lieutenant governor of California. What do you think it means?

7    "National defense is shared by everyone. More of it for one person does not mean less for someone else. Therefore, it is a public good and should be provided via government taxes and operation."
a. Does greater anti-missile defense for New York City mean greater defense for Houston, Texas?
b. Do more public concerts on the west side of town mean more on the east side?
c. Does it follow that public goods—those that give benefits to several people without less to anyone else—really do not exist?
d. Do external benefits mean that more than one person benefits, or that a nonowner benefits, or that those who benefit do so without any less of the service to someone else?

8    If I don't reciprocate in social invitations with my friends, I find they stop inviting me to their social functions. If I am impolite to other people, they are impolite to me. Much of our social etiquette is a matter of formal, though nonmarket, exchange, with the exception that when I host a party I do not obtain a contract from my guests promising to invite me as a guest to one of their parties. Would it thereby follow that there are too few parties and too few guests invited? Why?

9    a. "Police activity must be provided only by the government." Do you agree? If so, how do you explain the fact that there are thousands of private policemen in London, and that many U.S. residential areas have private police service?
b. "Judicial activity is one kind of activity that must be handled by the government." Do you agree? If so, how do you explain the existence of private arbitration for adjudicating contract-term disputes between employees and employers?
c. "Lawmaking activity is one that must be handled by the government." Do you agree? If so, how do you explain the creation of

labor-employee relations law by contract negotiation, custom and common-law development from precedents of arbitration, and social custom and its enforcement via ostracism?

d. "Defense of the community is one activity that must be handled by the government." Do you agree? If so, how do you explain the existence of private armies in past history—armies to defend cities, paid by private citizens? How do you explain the papal army prior to the time of the papal state?

e. "There is no function that must be exclusively reserved to the government." Do you agree? If so, why? If not, which function refutes the assertion?

10    "The imbalance between governmentally and privately provided services is evidenced by the fact that the family that vacations in its air-conditioned, power-braked, power-steered car passes through cities over dirty, badly paved, congested streets, not to mention the billboards obstructing the beauties of the countryside. When the family picnics with excellent food provided by private business, they must sit by a polluted stream and then spend the night in a public park that is a menace to health and morals and littered with decaying refuse. Private abundance and public poverty are facts that assail every observant person. A plentiful supply of privately produced goods and a shortage of publicly provided services is inescapable testimony to the lack of a social balance between private and governmentally provided services."

Without trying to prove that there ought to be less or ought to be more governmentally provided services, tell why the arguments, taken from a popular book advocating more governmentally provided services, are faulty and do not indicate anything at all about whether there is too little of governmentally provided services. (Hint: Note the use of the term "shortage"; what does it suggest? How are governmentally provided services rationed?)

11    "The fact that some airplanes collide is evidence that there is too little air traffic control." Evaluate. (Hint: What would it cost to avoid all risk of air collision?)

12    a. Non-inducible externalities are one reason for government economic activity. Free libraries are often justified on that ground. Look up the history of free libraries to see how they were started.

b. Subsidized education is also justified on that ground. Look up the early stages of subsidized or free education to see how it started.

c. Religion is not financed by government activity. Is that because it has no non-inducible external effects? Is there too little wealth devoted to religion? What evidence can you cite?

d. Name the ten best universities or colleges. How many of them are "private"? How do you explain that?

e. Do the preceding four problems imply that government does either too much or too little in these areas?

13    "Social ostracism is a form of social control and is often a substitute for some government action." Evaluate.

**14**    If you use the proportion of government expenditures as a guide to the significance of government economic activity, you can be seriously misled. What types of government services or activity have a greater impact than indicated by the costs?

**15**    A restaurant opens near an apartment. The cooking smells annoy the apartment tenants. The apartment owner sues for invasion of property rights.
a. You are on the jury. Would you find in favor of the restaurant or the apartment owner?
b. Would your decision depend upon whether or not the apartment owner lived in the affected apartments?
c. Do you know what decisions have actually been rendered in similar cases?

16    *A* owns a hillside lot with a beautiful view. *B*, owner of the lot just below, plants trees that grow up to 50 feet in height and block *A*'s view. *A* asks him to trim the tops. *B* refuses. *A* offers to pay for the trimming. *B* refuses. *A* offers $300 in addition. *B* refuses; *B* asks for $2,000. *A* sues for $5,000 damages to the marketable value of his property.
a. As the judge, how would you rule?
b. If, earlier, *A* had sued to force the person to trim the trees, how would you have ruled?
c. What will our courts really decide today in such suits?

**17**    *A* owns and lives in a home near an area in which it is announced a series of twenty-story apartments will be built. This will have only trivial effect on a view, since the land is all flat. *A* sues to prevent the construction on the contention that it will create extra traffic hazards and congestion. In court, *A* proves to the judge's satisfaction that his allegation is correct. As the judge, how would you rule? Why?

18    In Mexico, landless people are invading large farms and settling on the land as "squatters." The government has not acted to maintain the property rights of existing owners. The new occupants are not claiming the right to sell the land to others. They claim only the right to the use and fruits of the land, called usufruct rights, which at law is the right to enjoy all the benefits of a thing without the right to sell it. Rights of usufruct often pass by inheritance or by occupancy.
a. What effect will this development have on the sale value of the land?
b. How will it affect the willingness of the owner to invest in the land?
c. If the usufruct rights and sale rights were assigned (owned) by the land owner, would that increase or decrease the incentive to invest in the land? Explain why.

19    You are asked by the government officials of a new "emerging" nation

whether occupants should have private-property rights in land or whether only usufruct rights should be allowed.

a. What would you recommend? Why?

b. You are then asked whether occupants should have the right to mortgage the land; some concern is expressed that the occupants might borrow against the land and then simply let the creditor have it. What do you recommend and why?

c. Would you permit tenant farming—whereby the land is rented from the owner by a farmer? (If so, you are permitting absentee ownership, which is widely held in disrepute.)

20 The following is orthodox Chinese Communist (Marxist) economic doctrine: "The goal of socialist production is not profit but the satisfaction of social needs. Goods must be produced as long as they are needed by society, even if a loss is incurred. Not profits, but the calculation of assigned target goals and their fulfillment is the most important consideration. This follows from the Marxist-Leninist tenet that, contrary to capitalism which seeks maximum profits, the objective of socialism is the maximum satisfaction of the material and cultural requirements of society. This fact gives the Communist Party, as representative of society, the right to determine society's requirements and what the economy should produce." However, in 1962 the Chinese Communists permitted some Chinese economists to publish the following ideas: "Profits should not be set against the goal satisfying social needs. The profit level is the best measure of the effectiveness of management. This would mean that no enterprise would operate at a loss because the output would be curtailed unless the state valued its product sufficiently to raise its prices, and no enterprise would try to exceed the output plan at the expense of profits. There would be less need for political participation in enterprise management decisions, if prices were more realistic, in reflecting either market values or costs. The capitalist evil connotations of profits are not present in socialism, because under socialism profit takes on an entirely different character, where it is a good thing."

But still later in 1962, the Communist Party authorities reaffirmed their orthodox doctrine and did so both directly and by indirection with an attack on "revisionist" ideas as exemplified by Yugoslavia, which engaged in what the Chinese Communists regard as backsliding policies—like adopting price reforms (permitting more prices to be set in the open market, decentralizing state enterprises and permitting more private property in farming and handicraft activities). In reaffirming their orthodox Marxist tenets, the Chinese Communists directed factory managers to adopt political and economic means to raise labor productivity and to overfulfill specified targets of gross value of outputs whenever possible.

In order to understand why the issues of "proper" pricing, the use of the market, and kinds of incentives are so crucial to the Communists, it is pertinent to understand the effects on the power position of the Communist Party politicians if the economists' 1962 proposal were adopted. What would those effects be? Explain why.

# 13

Capital Values, Interest Rates, and Wealth

Many goods are durable; they provide future services. All those present and future services have values summed into the present price of the durable good, called its capital value. Since durable goods are such an important portion of all economic goods, we must understand how these present prices or capital values are determined. To do that we must understand the "rate of interest."

People are interested in the future as well as the present. In our terminology and postulates, both present and future consumption are *goods*, and, as with all goods, a person is willing to substitute among them. He is willing to consider giving up *some* present consumption for *more* wealth or more future income. This kind of trade is called "saving." The reverse direction of substitution is known as "dissaving." It involves "borrowing" or consumption of wealth so that a person consumes more today and less tomorrow.

All this is extremely simple; yet adequate analysis of its implications requires careful use of some new concepts. Just as we have analyzed exchange of present goods between people, we can analyze exchange of peoples' rights to present and future income. In the earlier discussed exchange of goods, each person had a subjective value (rate of substitution in consumption) of one current good for another. Now we have a subjective value (acceptable rate of substitution) between present consumption and future consumption. Instead of asking how much candy a person would give up *now* for one more cigarette *now*, we ask how much candy a person would give up now in order to get one candy, say, a month *later*.

At first one might think, "Candy is candy; therefore, I would give up one candy now for the right to one candy a month from now." But second thoughts suggest if you give up candy now, you also will have given up the right to eat or otherwise use the candy any time during the next month. The candy you will get at the *end* of the month will not give back the right to use or eat candy *during* the month. You will have accepted a reduced range of possible actions—and you will have obtained nothing in return. On the principle that more is preferred to less, you are not willing to accept such an exchange. Candy now is preferred to candy available only at a later date: candy now and candy available a month from now are simply not the same commodity. The former, in our jargon, has more "utility." Therefore, *less*—even if not much less—than one candy now will be traded for one candy a month from now.

## Rate of Interest

Suppose you were willing to give up at most 0.9 candy today for the right to one a year from now (with no uncertainty or doubt about the payment). The *present* price of one candy *now* is, of course, one candy, while the *present* price of one candy available in a *year* is 0.9 candy. The relative price or exchange rate between present and future candy can be expressed as a ratio

1/.9, which equals 1.11. A current candy sells for a price premium, or higher price, of 11 percent over the present price of a right to one candy deferred a year. In other words, one year's delay in availability reduces the *present* value of something, by 11 percent in our numerical example. The value of earlier availability is 11 percent for one year; in technical jargon, the *rate of interest* is 11 percent per year.

Express this generally in money. If you were to ask me, "How much money would you give up today for the right to get $1 a year from now?" my reply would be, "I would today pay 90 cents." I would give up 90 cents now for the right to $1 a year later; I regard the loss of one year's availability of opportunity to use goods as equal to 11 percent of the present value of current goods. For every good I can buy with money, earlier availability of that (and all) goods is worth 11 percent per year.

Because money is the commonly used medium of exchange, it is customary to speak of the rate of interest on current and future *money* rather than commodities.

Although interest rates are expressed almost exclusively in terms of money loans, they represent the value (price) of earlier rather than later availability of nonmoney commodities, just as *money prices* for ordinary exchanges reveal the value of alternative commodities that must be forsaken. Nor does the fact that interest rates usually apply to *money* loans mean that interest is a monetary, financial distortion or exaction that financiers and bankers impose on ordinary people. Engineers often believe that the rate of interest on loans for financing building projects should be ignored in order to get at the "real" costs. That error amounts to saying there is no preference for earlier over later availability—a proposition that no one would defend once he realized what he was saying.

Economics does not say that people prefer to have something now rather than later because they are impatient or shortsighted. They may or may not be. It makes no difference for deducing a lower present value for deferred relative to nondeferred goods. Nor does a positive rate of interest exist simply to anticipate inflation.

Some other considerations also imply a lower present value of deferred goods. The certainty of death—the certainty that we shall some day *not* be able to enjoy some postponed goods may make us unwilling to give up 1 gallon of gasoline (or anything) today for just 1 gallon in the future. Another, and probably most important, factor is the productivity of capital—even if you don't die during the period in question, you could be using the nonconsumed income to earn more income.[1]

The rate of interest, then, reflects: (1) convenience of earlier availability, (2) preference for assured consumption over contingent consumption, and (3) ability to use income to increase total output. *Any* society—capitalist, communist, advanced, primitive, industrial, agrarian, democratic, totalitarian—in which these elements are present will have a *positive rate of*

---

[1] The "productivity of capital" will be discussed later in Chapter 22.

*interest*—that is, a rate greater than zero. Some of these societies have an official dogma which denies or conceals this fact—but it is, nevertheless, present in all of them.

So far, we have shown that (1) earlier availability has a value, as an implication of the postulate that more is preferred to less; (2) this higher value of earlier availability, expressible as a percentage of the present value of a future good, is called the "interest rate"; and finally (3) the interest rate applies to *all* goods as well as to money.

Methods of Expressing or Measuring
Rate of Interest

There are several ways to express or measure the rate of interest; all are really the same thing in different guises.

1. Suppose you can lend 90 cents today and get $1 a year later. We say that the rate of interest is 11 percent, because 90 cents today "grew" into $1, or required a repayment of 11 percent more than was initially lent. "If I lend 90 cents today, I can get back $1 in a year—I get 11 percent interest per year." Or, "I can today purchase for 90 cents a $1 payment deferred one year." Or, "Since I pay the 90 cents (lend it) for your promissory note as evidence of the right to a deferred payment of $1, I have bought today for 90 cents your promissory note for $1 to be paid a year hence." That promissory note may say that you will pay me 90 cents plus 11 percent interest per year, or simply that you will pay me $1 in a year with no explicit reference to interest. That makes no difference—except possibly in the eyes of the law, which is sometimes blind to certain economic facts of life. But the total repayment is composed of repayment of the money loaned, plus interest.

This way of interpreting the rate of interest is

$$p_1 (1 + r) = A,$$

which is to say that the present payment, $p_1$, will grow in one year at the annual rate of interest, $r$, to $A$. In our present example, 90 cents will grow at 11.1 percent to $1.

$$\$.90 (1 + .111) = \$.999 = \$1.$$

2. Suppose you give up today an amount of money, $p_1$, in return for an amount, $A$, to be received in one year; $p_1$ is the *present* price of that *future amount A*. Rearranging the equation, we get

$$\frac{(A - p_1)}{p_1} = r = \text{annual rate of interest.}$$

For example, if $A$ represents $1 to be obtained in one year, and if the present price, $p_1$, of that future dollar is 90 cents, the rate of interest works out to

$$(\$1 - \$0.90)/\$0.90 = 0.11 = 11\%.$$

This can be related to the goods one can buy with money. If the price for a gallon of gasoline available today is 30 cents, and if you could make an agreement to pay 27 cents today to get a gallon one year later (presumably selling at that time for 30 cents), then the rate of interest implied is

$$(\$.30 - \$.27)/\$.27 = 11\%.$$

Few of us ever have occasion to make this kind of arrangement, because we find it cheaper and more convenient to make commitments for money rather than for specific goods; barter is less convenient for exchanges involving the present and future just as it is less convenient for exchange of current goods. So we shall persistently use money rates of interest, even though underlying the use of money are the specific goods and services.

The rate of interest can be interpreted—in fact, defined—as the relative premium of the present price of *present* goods over the price of the same goods *deferred* a year. For example, if the present price of a gallon of gasoline to be delivered now is 30 cents, and if the present price to be paid now for a gallon of the same gasoline to be delivered a year from now is 27 cents, then the rate of interest is 11.1 percent, from the expression

$$\frac{\$.30 - \$.27}{\$.27} = .111 = 11.1\%.$$

Consider a more common illustration. Almost every week the U.S. government seeks to borrow money for short periods—say, one year. It does so by selling its promissory notes (called "Treasury bills") to pay $1,000 in one year to the buyer at a zero interest rate. Thus, no interest rate is explicitly specified. These notes are then sold to the highest bidders. Suppose the highest bidder offers only $900 for one of these notes. What is the implicit rate of interest? By what percent of $900 will the $1,000 repayment exceed the amount actually loaned (paid for the note) to the U.S. government? The $100 difference is 11.1 percent of $900. Therefore, the annual interest rate is 11.1 percent. (Actually, the price for the last several years for such notes has been around $950–960, implying an interest rate of about 4–5 percent.) Even though no interest rate is stated on the note, there is actually a positive rate as long as the present price or amount borrowed is less than the total amount to be repaid. This is a legal and orthodox arrangement; it is a convenient way to find the best possible terms at which the government can borrow.

3. The present price, $p_1$, of something deferred a year is sometimes known as a *discounted* value. The term "discounting" is suggested by the fact that, at positive rates of interest, $1 due in a year (deferred for a year) has a present value less than $1. The *lower* present price of a future amount due is the "discounted" value of the future amount due. This way of looking at the problem means simply that we solve the basic equation for $p_1$ as the key variable, in which case we get

$$p_1 = \frac{A}{(1 + r)}.$$

If $A$ is $1 and the rate of interest is 11 percent,

$$\$.90 = \frac{\$1.00}{(1 + .11)} \, .$$

So the amount deferred one year is worth 0.90 of that amount now, at 11 percent interest. Or, 90 cents, at the annual rate of interest of 11 percent will grow to $1 in one year. Or, if $1 deferred one year has a price now of 90 cents, the implied rate of interest is 11 percent. These three different ways of saying the same thing correspond to the three alternative expressions discussed in the preceding paragraphs.

All of this analysis is independent of any assumed inflation. Inflation is not necessary for interest rates or differences between prices of present and future dollars.

### Interest—The Price of Money?

The interest rate is often called the price of money. This "nickname" is misleading, for the price of $1 right now is, of course, simply $1. More accurately, the rate of interest is the price of earlier rather than later *availability*—sometimes also carelessly referred to as the price of time. The term "price of money" has become popular because people usually borrow or lend money rather than specific goods. Lenders buy future money in exchange for present money; they pay less now than the future amount to be received. That excess *future* amount (interest) is the future *price* paid for earlier money; the emphasis is on the *time* element. Rigorously speaking, interest is the price of earlier availability, rather than later availability, of rights to use goods.

To digress momentarily, our purpose in this chapter is not to see how interest rates are determined by the demand for present relative to future goods. We shall take this up later. Here we are concerned with the implications of the facts that (1) people evaluate and exchange present for *future* goods and services (that is, there *is* a rate of interest); and (2) future goods are less valuable now than the same amount of goods and services available now (that is, the rate of interest is *positive*).

We observe in the real world that people lend money only if they can get a positive rate of interest in one form or another. There is little need to present formal evidence here that a positive interest rate does exist in the real world. Just try to borrow money at a zero rate of interest! True, in some areas and in some times, there have been laws against "usury"—another word for interest. The Catholic Church long considered interest as improper, unjust, and unsanctioned. Similarly, Communist doctrine regards interest as a capitalist tool of exploitation (although *recent* Communist economists have "rediscovered" the presence and role of the interest rate). And when William the Conqueror ruled England, interest was illegal—except if collected by Jews—a convenience to William, who allowed Jews to live in England so that people (especially William and his nobles) could borrow from them. It is impossible to give a satisfactory economic reason for the Christian and Communist opposition to interest—when one understands that interest is merely a manifestation of individuals' preferences for earlier rather than later availability. We can only conjecture that perhaps the stricture against interest reflects the Church doctrine that people *should not* be the way they are; they *should* be neutral as between earlier and later availability. Why did the Communists object to this fact of life? Perhaps its facade of objection is a carry-over of Marxian confusions about economic fundamentals. Now, they really do recognize interest, if you judge by their actions rather than their words. The Russian government borrows money and pays a premium, and its investment policy recognizes the advantage of early over later availability. Instead of the term "interest rate," Russia uses "efficiency index," which, when you consider it, does seem like a better name.

**The Farther in the Future, the Lower the Present Value**

The *more distant* the deferred service (or income, or goods), the *lower* its present price. A dollar deferred two years is worth less today than a dollar deferred one year, if the rate of interest is positive. At an interest rate of 6 percent, the current price of $1 deferred a year is 94 cents—the amount that will grow at 6 percent in one year to $1. This is given by the formula

$$p_1 = \frac{A}{(1+r)} = \frac{\$1.00}{(1+.06)} = \$.943.$$

To get the present price for $1 deferred *two* years, simply repeat the above operation. If $1 deferred one year from now is now worth 94 cents, then deferring the dollar an additional year again reduces its present value by the same proportion. For two years, this is .943 × .943 = .890. A dollar due in two years is worth 89 cents today.

This same relationship can be expressed by noting that at 6 percent per year 89 cents will grow in one year to 94 cents, and then in the second year the 94 cents will grow to exactly $1. This can be expressed in the form

$$p_2(1+r)(1+r) = A,$$

where $p_2$ represents the amount now that will grow at the 6 percent annual rate of interest to $1, the amount $A$, at the end of the two-year period. Solving for $p_2$, we get

$$p_2 = \frac{A}{(1+r)(1+r)} = \frac{A}{(1+r)^2} = \frac{\$1.00}{(1.06)^2} = \$.890.$$

Two years' discounting is measured by the factor $1/(1+.06)^2 = .890$; three years of discounting is obtained by multiplying the future amount due in three years by $1/(1.06)^3 = .839$. The present value of $1 deferred $t$ years from today is obtained by use of the factor $1/(1.06)^t$. Multiplying the amount due at the end of $t$ years by this present-value factor gives the present value (or present price, or discounted value) of the deferred amount, $A$, due in $t$ years. A set of these present-value factors is given in Table 13–1 for various rates of interest and years of deferment. The present-value factor decreases as $t$ is larger; the farther into the future the amount due is deferred, the lower is its *present* value. This is in no way dependent upon an assumption of inflation of prices.

Table 13–1
Present Value of a Future $1: What a Dollar at End of Specified Future Year
Is Worth Today

| Year | 3% | 4% | 5% | 6% | 7% | 8% | 10% | 12% | 15% | 20% | Year |
|---|---|---|---|---|---|---|---|---|---|---|---|
| 1 | .971 | .962 | .952 | .943 | .935 | .926 | .909 | .893 | .870 | .833 | 1 |
| 2 | .943 | .925 | .907 | .890 | .873 | .857 | .826 | .797 | .756 | .694 | 2 |
| 3 | .915 | .890 | .864 | .839 | .816 | .794 | .751 | .711 | .658 | .578 | 3 |
| 4 | .889 | .855 | .823 | .792 | .763 | .735 | .683 | .636 | .572 | .482 | 4 |
| 5 | .863 | .823 | .784 | .747 | .713 | .681 | .620 | .567 | .497 | .402 | 5 |
| 6 | .838 | .790 | .746 | .705 | .666 | .630 | .564 | .507 | .432 | .335 | 6 |
| 7 | .813 | .760 | .711 | .665 | .623 | .583 | .513 | .452 | .376 | .279 | 7 |
| 8 | .789 | .731 | .677 | .627 | .582 | .540 | .466 | .404 | .326 | .233 | 8 |
| 9 | .766 | .703 | .645 | .591 | .544 | .500 | .424 | .360 | .284 | .194 | 9 |
| 10 | .744 | .676 | .614 | .558 | .508 | .463 | .385 | .322 | .247 | .162 | 10 |
| 11 | .722 | .650 | .585 | .526 | .475 | .429 | .350 | .287 | .215 | .134 | 11 |
| 12 | .701 | .625 | .557 | .497 | .444 | .397 | .318 | .257 | .187 | .112 | 12 |
| 13 | .681 | .601 | .530 | .468 | .415 | .368 | .289 | .229 | .162 | .0935 | 13 |
| 14 | .661 | .577 | .505 | .442 | .388 | .340 | .263 | .204 | .141 | .0779 | 14 |
| 15 | .642 | .555 | .481 | .417 | .362 | .315 | .239 | .183 | .122 | .0649 | 15 |
| 16 | .623 | .534 | .458 | .393 | .339 | .292 | .217 | .163 | .107 | .0541 | 16 |
| 17 | .605 | .513 | .436 | .371 | .317 | .270 | .197 | .146 | .093 | .0451 | 17 |
| 18 | .587 | .494 | .416 | .350 | .296 | .250 | .179 | .130 | .0808 | .0376 | 18 |
| 19 | .570 | .475 | .396 | .330 | .277 | .232 | .163 | .116 | .0703 | .0313 | 19 |
| 20 | .554 | .456 | .377 | .311 | .258 | .215 | .148 | .104 | .0611 | .0261 | 20 |
| 25 | .478 | .375 | .295 | .232 | .184 | .146 | .0923 | .0588 | .0304 | .0105 | 25 |
| 30 | .412 | .308 | .231 | .174 | .131 | .0994 | .0573 | .0334 | .0151 | .00421 | 30 |
| 40 | .307 | .208 | .142 | .0972 | .067 | .0460 | .0221 | .0107 | .00373 | .000680 | 40 |
| 50 | .228 | .141 | .087 | .0543 | .034 | .0213 | .00852 | .00346 | .000922 | .000109 | 50 |

Each column lists how much a dollar received at the end of various years in the future is worth today. For example, at 6 percent a dollar to be received ten years hence is equivalent in value to $.558 now. In other words, $.558 invested now at 6 percent, with interest compounded annually, would grow to $1.00 in ten years. Note that $1.00 to be received at the end of fifty years is, at 6 percent, worth today just about a nickel. And at 10 percent it is worth only about .8 of one cent, which is to say that 8 mills (.8 of a cent) invested now would grow, at 10 percent interest compounded annually, to $1.00 in fifty years. Similarly $1,000 in fifty years is worth today $8.52, and $10,000 is worth today $85—all at 10 percent rate of growth. *Forty* years from now (when you are about 65) $10,000 would cost you now, at 10 percent rate of growth per year, about $221. (See the entry in the column headed 10 percent and in the row for forty years.) Why not make that investment? Formula for entry in table is $1/(1 + r)^t$. (No inflation is involved in this table.)

Instead of deriving present values of future amounts, we can derive for any annual rate of interest the future amount that will be exchangeable for any present value. How much will $1 paid now purchase if the future amount is due in one year, or in two years, or in three years? At 15 percent per year, $1 will be worth $1.15 in one year. And at 15 percent for the next year, that $1.15 will in turn grow to $1.32. Hence, $1 today is the present price or value of $1.32 in two years. In terms of our formula, this can be expressed

$$p_2(1 + r)(1 + r) = A ,$$
$$\$1(1.15)(1.15) = \$1(1.32) = \$1.32 .$$

If the future amount is deferred three years, the term (1.15) enters three times, and if deferred $t$ years, it enters $t$ times. For three years, the quantity (1.15) is multiplied together three times, denoted $(1.15)^3$, and equals 1.52. Therefore, in three years $1 will grow to $1.52. In general, the formula is

$$p_t(1 + r)^t = A$$

for any present payment, $p_t$, that is paid for an amount $A$ available $t$ years later. The multiplicative factor $(1 + r)^t$ is called the *future-value* (or *amount*) *factor*. Values of this future-amount factor for different combinations of $t$ and $r$ are given in Table 13–2. For example, at 6 percent in five years, the future-amount factor is 1.34, which means that a present payment of $1 will buy, or grow to, the future amount $1.34 at the end of five years. Notice that the entries in Table 13–2 are simply the reciprocals of the entries in Table 13–1.

If there is a sequence of amounts due at future times, we can find a present value for this series of amounts. Just as we add up the costs of individual items in a market basket of groceries, we add up the present values of each of the future amounts due. That sum is the present value of the whole series of amounts due at various future dates.

This series might be compared with an oil well that each year on December 31 spurts out one gallon of oil that sells for $1. To simplify the problem, let's first suppose that the series of dollars (spurts of oil) continues for only two years. If the interest rate is 6 percent, the present value of $1 deferred one year is 94 cents (see Table 13–1, column of .06 rate of interest for one year); and the present value of $1 due in two years is 89.0 cents (see the same

Table 13-2
Compound Amount of $1: Amount to Which $1 Now Will Grow by
End of Specified Year at Compounded Interest

| Year | 3% | 4% | 5% | 6% | 7% | 8% | 10% | 12% | 15% | 20% | Year |
|---|---|---|---|---|---|---|---|---|---|---|---|
| 1 | 1.03 | 1.04 | 1.05 | 1.06 | 1.07 | 1.08 | 1.10 | 1.12 | 1.15 | 1.20 | 1 |
| 2 | 1.06 | 1.08 | 1.10 | 1.12 | 1.14 | 1.17 | 1.21 | 1.25 | 1.32 | 1.44 | 2 |
| 3 | 1.09 | 1.12 | 1.16 | 1.19 | 1.23 | 1.26 | 1.33 | 1.40 | 1.52 | 1.73 | 3 |
| 4 | 1.13 | 1.17 | 1.22 | 1.26 | 1.31 | 1.36 | 1.46 | 1.57 | 1.74 | 2.07 | 4 |
| 5 | 1.16 | 1.22 | 1.28 | 1.34 | 1.40 | 1.47 | 1.61 | 1.76 | 2.01 | 2.49 | 5 |
| 6 | 1.19 | 1.27 | 1.34 | 1.41 | 1.50 | 1.59 | 1.77 | 1.97 | 2.31 | 2.99 | 6 |
| 7 | 1.23 | 1.32 | 1.41 | 1.50 | 1.61 | 1.71 | 1.94 | 2.21 | 2.66 | 3.58 | 7 |
| 8 | 1.27 | 1.37 | 1.48 | 1.59 | 1.72 | 1.85 | 2.14 | 2.48 | 3.05 | 4.30 | 8 |
| 9 | 1.30 | 1.42 | 1.55 | 1.68 | 1.84 | 2.00 | 2.35 | 2.77 | 3.52 | 5.16 | 9 |
| 10 | 1.34 | 1.48 | 1.63 | 1.79 | 1.97 | 2.16 | 2.59 | 3.11 | 4.05 | 6.19 | 10 |
| 11 | 1.38 | 1.54 | 1.71 | 1.89 | 2.10 | 2.33 | 2.85 | 3.48 | 4.66 | 7.43 | 11 |
| 12 | 1.43 | 1.60 | 1.80 | 2.01 | 2.25 | 2.52 | 3.13 | 3.90 | 5.30 | 8.92 | 12 |
| 13 | 1.47 | 1.67 | 1.89 | 2.13 | 2.41 | 2.72 | 3.45 | 4.36 | 6.10 | 10.7 | 13 |
| 14 | 1.51 | 1.73 | 1.98 | 2.26 | 2.58 | 2.94 | 3.79 | 4.89 | 7.00 | 12.8 | 14 |
| 15 | 1.56 | 1.80 | 2.08 | 2.39 | 2.76 | 3.17 | 4.17 | 5.47 | 8.13 | 15.4 | 15 |
| 16 | 1.60 | 1.87 | 2.18 | 2.54 | 2.95 | 3.43 | 4.59 | 6.13 | 9.40 | 18.5 | 16 |
| 17 | 1.65 | 1.95 | 2.29 | 2.69 | 3.16 | 3.70 | 5.05 | 6.87 | 10.6 | 22.2 | 17 |
| 18 | 1.70 | 2.03 | 2.41 | 2.85 | 3.38 | 4.00 | 5.55 | 7.70 | 12.5 | 26.6 | 18 |
| 19 | 1.75 | 2.11 | 2.53 | 3.02 | 3.62 | 4.32 | 6.11 | 8.61 | 14.0 | 31.9 | 19 |
| 20 | 1.81 | 2.19 | 2.65 | 3.20 | 3.87 | 4.66 | 6.72 | 9.65 | 16.1 | 38.3 | 20 |
| 25 | 2.09 | 2.67 | 3.39 | 4.29 | 5.43 | 6.85 | 10.8 | 17.0 | 32.9 | 95.4 | 25 |
| 30 | 2.43 | 3.24 | 4.32 | 5.74 | 7.61 | 10.0 | 17.4 | 30.0 | 66.2 | 237 | 30 |
| 40 | 3.26 | 4.80 | 7.04 | 10.3 | 15.0 | 21.7 | 45.3 | 93.1 | 267.0 | 1470 | 40 |
| 50 | 4.38 | 7.11 | 11.5 | 18.4 | 29.5 | 46.9 | 117 | 289 | 1080 | 9100 | 50 |

This table shows to what amounts $1.00 invested now will grow at the end of various years, at different rates of growth compounded annually. For example, $1.00 invested now will grow in thirty years to $5.74 at 6 percent, In other words, $5.74 due thirty years hence is worth now exactly $1.00 at a 6 percent rate of interest per year. If you invest $100 now at 10 percent, you will have $1,740 in thirty years. Isn't that worth it? The entries in this table are the reciprocals of the entries in Table 13–1; that is, they are the entries of Table 13–1 divided into 1. You really don't "need" this extra table, but having it saves some calculations. Formula for entries in table is $1(1 + i)^t$.

table, same column, but now read the entry for year 2). The sum of the present capital values of both amounts due, the one in one year and the other in two years, is the sum of 94.3 cents and 89.0 cents, which is $1.83. To say that the rate of interest is 6 percent per year is equivalent to saying that you can exchange in the market $1.83 today for the right to receive $1 in one year *and* another dollar in two years.

Suppose the sequence is to last three years, with three $1 receipts. The aggregate present value is augmented by the present value of the dollar due in the third year. At a 6 percent rate of interest, this extra dollar has a present value of 83.9 cents (see Table 13–1). Therefore, the present value of the three-year series is $2.67 (given in Table 13–3). We have noted that this present value of a series of amounts due is called the *capital value* of the future receipts. Capital value is the current *price* of the rights to the stream (series) of receipts.

Some technical jargon will be convenient for subsequent analyses. The sequence of future amounts due is called an *annuity*, a word that suggest *annual* amounts. A two-year sequence is a two-year annuity. The term "annuity" denotes the series of annual amounts for a specified number of years. A person who has purchased the right to a stream of future annuities or amounts due—for example, his pension benefits—is sometimes called an *annuitant*.

How about a four-year annuity? The fourth year's $1 has a present value of 79.2 cents,which, when added to the present value of a three-year annuity of $1 a year, gives $3.46. A five-year annuity would have a present value of

Table 13–3
Present Value of Annuity of $1, Received at End of Each Year

| Year | 3% | 4% | 5% | 6% | 7% | 8% | 10% | 12% | 15% | 20% | Year |
|------|------|------|------|------|------|------|------|------|------|------|------|
| 1 | 0.971 | 0.960 | 0.952 | 0.943 | 0.935 | 0.926 | 0.909 | 0.890 | 0.870 | 0.833 | 1 |
| 2 | 1.91 | 1.89 | 1.86 | 1.83 | 1.81 | 1.78 | 1.73 | 1.69 | 1.63 | 1.53 | 2 |
| 3 | 2.83 | 2.78 | 2.72 | 2.67 | 2.62 | 2.58 | 2.48 | 2.40 | 2.28 | 2.11 | 3 |
| 4 | 3.72 | 3.63 | 3.55 | 3.46 | 3.39 | 3.31 | 3.16 | 3.04 | 2.86 | 2.59 | 4 |
| 5 | 4.58 | 4.45 | 4.33 | 4.21 | 4.10 | 3.99 | 3.79 | 3.60 | 3.35 | 2.99 | 5 |
| 6 | 5.42 | 5.24 | 5.08 | 4.91 | 4.77 | 4.62 | 4.35 | 4.11 | 3.78 | 3.33 | 6 |
| 7 | 6.23 | 6.00 | 5.79 | 5.58 | 5.39 | 5.21 | 4.86 | 4.56 | 4.16 | 3.60 | 7 |
| 8 | 7.02 | 6.73 | 6.46 | 6.20 | 5.97 | 5.75 | 5.33 | 4.97 | 4.49 | 3.84 | 8 |
| 9 | 7.79 | 7.44 | 7.11 | 6.80 | 6.52 | 6.25 | 5.75 | 5.33 | 4.78 | 4.03 | 9 |
| 10 | 8.53 | 8.11 | 7.72 | 7.36 | 7.02 | 6.71 | 6.14 | 5.65 | 5.02 | 4.19 | 10 |
| 11 | 9.25 | 8.76 | 8.31 | 7.88 | 7.50 | 7.14 | 6.49 | 5.94 | 5.23 | 4.33 | 11 |
| 12 | 9.95 | 9.39 | 8.86 | 8.38 | 7.94 | 7.54 | 6.81 | 6.19 | 5.41 | 4.44 | 12 |
| 13 | 10.6 | 9.99 | 9.39 | 8.85 | 8.36 | 7.90 | 7.10 | 6.42 | 5.65 | 4.53 | 13 |
| 14 | 11.3 | 10.6 | 9.90 | 9.29 | 8.75 | 8.24 | 7.36 | 6.63 | 5.76 | 4.61 | 14 |
| 15 | 11.9 | 11.1 | 10.4 | 9.71 | 9.11 | 8.56 | 7.60 | 6.81 | 5.87 | 4.68 | 15 |
| 16 | 12.6 | 11.6 | 10.8 | 10.1 | 9.45 | 8.85 | 7.82 | 6.97 | 5.96 | 4.73 | 16 |
| 17 | 13.2 | 12.2 | 11.3 | 10.4 | 9.76 | 9.12 | 8.02 | 7.12 | 6.03 | 4.77 | 17 |
| 18 | 13.8 | 12.7 | 11.7 | 10.8 | 10.1 | 9.37 | 8.20 | 7.25 | 6.10 | 4.81 | 18 |
| 19 | 14.3 | 13.1 | 12.1 | 11.1 | 10.3 | 9.60 | 8.36 | 7.37 | 6.17 | 4.84 | 19 |
| 20 | 14.9 | 13.6 | 12.5 | 11.4 | 10.6 | 9.82 | 8.51 | 7.47 | 6.23 | 4.87 | 20 |
| 25 | 17.4 | 15.6 | 14.1 | 12.8 | 11.7 | 10.7 | 9.08 | 7.84 | 6.46 | 4.95 | 25 |
| 30 | 19.6 | 17.3 | 15.4 | 13.8 | 12.4 | 11.3 | 9.43 | 8.06 | 6.57 | 4.98 | 30 |
| 40 | 23.1 | 19.8 | 17.2 | 15.0 | 13.3 | 11.9 | 9.78 | 8.24 | 6.64 | 5.00 | 40 |
| 50 | 25.7 | 21.5 | 18.3 | 15.8 | 13.8 | 12.2 | 9.91 | 8.25 | 6.66 | 5.00 | 50 |

An annuity is a sequence of annual amounts received at the end of each year. This table shows with each entry how much it takes today to buy an annuity of $1 a year at the rates of interest indicated. For example, an annuity of $1 a year for twenty years at 6 percent interest could be purchased today with $11.40. This amount would, if invested at 6 percent, be sufficient to yield some interest which, along with some depletion of the principal in each year, would enable a payout of exactly $1 a year for twenty years, at which time the fund would be completely depleted. And $1,000 a year for twenty years would, at 6 percent compounded annually, cost today $11,400, which is obviously 1,000 times as much as for an annuity of just $1. Formula for entry is $[1 - (1 + i)^n]/i$.

$4.21, because the dollar received at the end of the fifth year is now worth 74.7 cents. Proceed to the end of ten years, and you will find that the present capital value of a ten-year annuity of $1 each year is $7.36.

If we extended the series to twenty years (still with $1 at the end of each year) at 6 percent per year, the present capital value would increase to $11.40. Notice that the *present* value of the *last half* of that series (the ten amounts due in the eleventh through the twentieth years) is only $4.04 (= 11.40 − 7.36). At a 6 percent interest rate, $4.04 *today* will buy you $1 a year for ten years, beginning at the end of the eleventh year from now.

Table 13–1 gives the present value of each separate future payment in the annuity. For convenience, Table 13–3 gives the present value of annuities of various lengths, where the payment *at the end* of each year is $1. Looking at that table under the 6 percent interest rate, you will find that the present capital values for the *sum* of the discounted amounts due in the preceding examples are the entries in the rows for one, two, three, four, five, ten, and twenty years. Look at the entry for two years at 6 percent. It is the sum of .943 and .890, based on the data of Table 13–1. For an annuity lasting fifty years, the entry is $15.8—which says that a fifty-year annuity of $1 per year, with the first payment coming at the end of one year, has a present capital value of only $15.80 (at 6 percent).

Even an annuity that lasted forever (called a *perpetuity*), or for as long as you and your heirs desire, would have a finite capital value—namely, $16.67.

A second thought will remove the mystery from the fact that an infinitely long series of $1 amounts due yearly has a finite (limited) price today. To get a perpetual series of payments of $1 every year, all one has to do is keep $16.67 on deposit in a bank, if he can get 6 percent per year. Every year the interest payment of $1 can be taken out, and this can be done forever. In effect you pay $16.67 today to purchase an infinitely long sequence. But you can also see that the first fifty years of receipts (a fifty-year annuity) has a present value of $15.80. Hence, the remaining infinitely long series of $1 receipts, beginning fifty years from now, is worth today only about 87 cents. Distant events have small present values!

Table 13–4 gives the annual annuity payments one could purchase with one dollar now. (The entries are reciprocals of the entries in Table 13–3.) Thus $1 *now* will buy $.149 annually at the end of each of ten years (at 8 percent interest).

### Illustrative Applications of Capitalization Principles

1. *Discount or credit*? Two salesmen want to sell you a car with an official "list" price of $2,000. Salesman *A* offers it for $1,900. Salesman *B* sticks with the official price, but he will let you pay him that full amount one year hence. Which offer is "cheaper," "less costly"—that is, will reduce your wealth least? It depends upon the rate of interest, which we shall suppose is

Table 13-4
Uniform Annual Payments Provided at End of Each Year for Annuities
of Various Lengths, per $1 of Present Value

| Year | 3% | 4% | 5% | 6% | 7% | 8% | 10% | 12% | 15% | 20% | Year |
|------|------|------|------|------|------|------|------|------|------|------|------|
| 1 | 1.03 | 1.04 | 1.05 | 1.06 | 1.07 | 1.08 | 1.10 | 1.12 | 1.15 | 1.20 | 1 |
| 2 | .524 | .529 | .538 | .546 | .552 | .562 | .578 | .592 | .613 | .654 | 2 |
| 3 | .353 | .360 | .368 | .375 | .381 | .388 | .403 | .417 | .439 | .474 | 3 |
| 4 | .269 | .275 | .282 | .289 | .295 | .302 | .316 | .329 | .350 | .386 | 4 |
| 5 | .218 | .225 | .231 | .238 | .244 | .251 | .267 | .278 | .299 | .334 | 5 |
| 6 | .185 | .191 | .197 | .204 | .210 | .216 | .230 | .243 | .265 | .300 | 6 |
| 7 | .161 | .167 | .173 | .179 | .186 | .192 | .206 | .219 | .240 | .278 | 7 |
| 8 | .142 | .149 | .155 | .161 | .168 | .174 | .188 | .201 | .223 | .260 | 8 |
| 9 | .128 | .134 | .141 | .147 | .153 | .160 | .174 | .188 | .209 | .248 | 9 |
| 10 | .117 | .123 | .130 | .136 | .142 | .149 | .163 | .177 | .199 | .239 | 10 |
| 11 | .108 | .114 | .120 | .127 | .133 | .140 | .154 | .168 | .191 | .231 | 11 |
| 12 | .101 | .106 | .113 | .119 | .126 | .133 | .147 | .162 | .185 | .225 | 12 |
| 13 | .0943 | .100 | .107 | .113 | .120 | .127 | .141 | .156 | .177 | .221 | 13 |
| 14 | .0885 | .0943 | .101 | .108 | .114 | .121 | .136 | .151 | .174 | .217 | 14 |
| 15 | .0840 | .0901 | .0982 | .103 | .110 | .117 | .132 | .147 | .170 | .214 | 15 |
| 16 | .0794 | .0862 | .0926 | .0990 | .106 | .113 | .128 | .143 | .168 | .211 | 16 |
| 17 | .0758 | .0819 | .0885 | .0961 | .102 | .110 | .125 | .140 | .166 | .210 | 17 |
| 18 | .0725 | .0787 | .0855 | .0925 | .0990 | .107 | .122 | .138 | .164 | .208 | 18 |
| 19 | .0699 | .0763 | .0826 | .0901 | .0971 | .104 | .120 | .136 | .162 | .207 | 19 |
| 20 | .0671 | .0735 | .0800 | .0877 | .0943 | .102 | .118 | .134 | .161 | .205 | 20 |
| 25 | .0575 | .0641 | .0709 | .0781 | .0855 | .0935 | .110 | .128 | .155 | .202 | 25 |
| 30 | .0510 | .0578 | .0649 | .0724 | .0806 | .0885 | .106 | .124 | .152 | .201 | 30 |
| 40 | .0433 | .0505 | .0581 | .0666 | .0752 | .0840 | .102 | .121 | .151 | .200 | 40 |
| 50 | .0389 | .0465 | .0546 | .0632 | .0725 | .0820 | .101 | .120 | .150 | .200 | 50 |

An annuity is a sequence of constant annual amounts beginning one year hence, for a specified number of years. The entries in the table give the possible annuities of various lengths, for various interest rates, which have a present value of $1. For example, for $1 present value or cost, at 6 percent interest, one can receive an annuity for *one* year of $1.06, or of 54.6 cents for each of two years, or 37.5 cents for each of three years, or 28.9 cents for each of four years.

Another way to use the data is to treat annuities as *payments*. For example, a debt of $1 can be paid off, at 6 percent interest, with $1.06 in one year, or 54.6 cents for two years, or 28.9 cents annually for four years, or 10.2 cents annually for twenty years.

10 percent per year. To pay salesman *A* costs $1,900 now. To pay salesman *B* takes $2,000 one year hence, which at 10 percent is equivalent to $1,818 now. Why? Because $1,818 is the present price or present value (to the nearest dollar) that will grow at 10 percent to $2,000 in one year. By lending (investing) $1,818 now at 10 percent per year, you will have $2,000 with which to pay salesman *B* at the end of the year. Where did those figures come from? See Table 13-1 for the present values of future amounts. At 10 percent, an amount deferred one year is worth now .909 of that deferred amount; therefore .909 of $2,000 is $1.818, the present capital value of $2,000 deferred one year, at 10 percent per year. Salesman *B* costs you now $82 less than *A* does. If you buy from *B*, you have $82 more current wealth left.

Anotner way to grasp this is to consider what you could have done if you had, instead of buying from $A$, put his requested amount of $1,900 to work at 10 percent per year. At the end of the year you would have $1,900(1.1) = $2,090. Out of that future amount you could pay salesman $B$ and have $90 left over for other "goodies." That future amount of $90 is another measure of how much cheaper salesman $B$'s offer is. In present-value measure, $B$ is cheaper by $1,900 − $1,818 = $82, which, expressed as a future amount one year hence, is equivalent to the *future* $90 difference ($2,090 - 2,000). As we know from Table 13–2, at a 10 percent rate of interest, $82 now is equivalent to $90 one year from now. $82 now will grow in one year at 10 percent to $90.[2]

But suppose the rate of interest were 4 percent. The present value of $2,000 deferred one year is $1,924, which is larger than the $1,900 asked by salesman $A$. If you buy from salesman $A$ you will save $24 in current wealth. Clearly the cheaper option depends upon the rate of interest. Buy from salesman $A$. If you haven't got the amount of money now, you can borrow it at 4 percent (after all, we assumed a 4 percent rate of interest in this problem). Borrow the $1,900 now and at the end of the year pay back $1,900 plus 4 percent of $1,900, which is $76. The payment at the end of the year will be precisely $1,976, which in wealth a year hence is $24 less than $2,000.[3]

2. *The risk of expropriation.* You own a new building that you are renting out with an annual receipt of $1,000 after allowing for all expenses of maintenance, insurance, and taxes. At a 10 percent rate of interest that house will, by definition, have a present value or price of $10,000. (Can you see why? With maintenance paid for, as it is, the building will last indefinitely and if it brings in a net of $1,000 for an indefinitely long time, it is like a perpetuity.) But speaking realistically, suppose the building is in a South American country, and you learn it is about to be nationalized with a present payment to you of $4,000. How much would it be worth to you to bribe the government officials to delay the confiscation for eight years during which time you will continue to maintain the building and pay the same expenses as before—if you were naive enough to trust them? (See Table 13–3 for entry under 10 percent rate of interest for eight years. That figure of 5.33 is the present value of an annuity of 1.00 per year for eight years. For $1,000 per year that gives $5,330, to three-figure accuracy. You might risk up to $1,330 trying to delay the confiscation eight years.)

---

[2] If we use greater accuracy in our computations the $1,818 would be $1,818.1818. The present-value difference is $81.8181, and 10 percent of that is $8.1818, which, added to $81.1818, gives $89.9999.

[3] How is it that we got the same saving, $24, in both present and future values? The measure in future values must be larger. What went wrong? Not enough computational accuracy! If we had used more significant digits, the difference would have shown up. Thus the .962 in Table 13–1 under 4 percent for one year is more accurately .9615. Multiplying this by $2,000 gives $1,923 (instead of $1,924). This saving of $23 (not $24) in *present-value measure of wealth is equivalent to $24 in terms of next year's wealth—a difference of 4 percent. Check!*

3. *Honor thy father and mother.* Your parents, having reached age 70 with a small fortune of $50,000, plan to live on that fund. They want to use it up at a rate that permits them to draw out a fixed amount each year for fifteen years. After that, if they are still alive, you will shoulder your moral responsibility. How much can they spend each year for fifteen years? Rephrased, the question is the following: "What fifteen-year annuity has a present value of $50,000?" If you can invest the fund at 10 percent, the answer is in Table 13–3 in the column headed 10 percent. The entry in the fifteen-year line is 7.60. That is the present capital value of a fifteen-year $1 annuity. Since there is now $50,000 in the fund, $50,000/7.60 = $6,570 is the amount of each annual payment for the next fifteen years. (This is an approximation, since $6,570 is really the amount that could be spent at the *end* of each of fifteen years, not during each year, but the difference is slight.)

If they want to use up the fund in ten years, they can get $8,140 (= $50,000/6.14) at the end of each year. If they invest at 4 percent, they will get a fifteen-year annuity of $4,500 (= $50,000/11.1).

Do not be astonished by earning rates around 10 to 15 percent. The stock market gave 12 to 15 percent per year (based on *any* thirty-year period taken from the twentieth century, even *after* allowing for inflation). For some thirty-year periods, the market did much better. For some five- to ten-year episodes, it gave less or a great deal more. This average of the performance of all listed stocks is higher than one can get by lending money in bonds, if one is willing to accept a *variable* annuity with an average of 10 to 15 percent. In bonds and other securities in which no variation in year-to-year receipts is to be allowed, the steady-state rate of yield is about 5 to 6 percent.

4. *The low interest rate gimmick.* If I were trying to sell you a machine that gives $100 at the end of each year for the next thirty years, would I use a high or a low rate of interest to express its present value? If I used 10 percent, it would work out to $942, as can be seen from the data provided in Table 13–3. (Be sure you check this calculation. A purpose of these examples is to give you facility in using the tables.) At 3 percent, it would work out to $1,960. (Again, be sure to check this.) If the machine were priced at $1,500, I would be tempted to speak in terms of the low rate of interest, for then it would appear to be a profitable purchase.

Always be on the alert to detect incentives to use a "biasing" rate of interest. For example, advocates of the California Feather River water project, an immense state-financed endeavor to supply additional water to Southern California, held it to be an excellent investment—as it may be at interest rates of about 2 percent. But if the rate of interest is higher, as it is, the resources would be more valuable if used for other things in the meantime and the project were postponed for about twenty years. In the public pre-election debate, virtually no publicity was given to the question of the appropriate interest rate. The project is now being built.

5. *Eat your cake and have it too.* Consider a more personal application. When you enter some colleges you can borrow money (say $1,000) toward tuition and expenses without paying any interest at all for eight years. Should

you borrow? You could put the money in a savings account for at least 4 percent per year. Each year you can draw out the $40 interest and throw a big party. At the end of eight years, you can draw out the $1,000, plus the last year's interest; repay the $1,000; and have $40 for a last party.

Another way to look at this is to see that you are being given free a $40 eight-year annuity beginning in one year. Even at so low a rate as 4 percent, the present value is $40 × 6.73 = $269.20. (See Table 13–3.) The possibility of borrowing $1,000 at *zero* interest for eight years is equivalent to a gift of $269.20 upon entrance to college. Any parent who fails to encourage his children to borrow for their college education is throwing away a gift.

Question: How many college students who get interest-free or low-interest loans thereby enable parents to withhold money from college expenses and divert it to personal uses? It is no answer to say that no parent *intends* to act that way. The fact that he is *enabled* to do so is sufficient. In blunt language, a loan at a rate of interest below the market rate is a gift of the amount of interest saving. You can see why low-interest government loans are so eagerly sought by people who at the same time claim they do not get government support.

6. *It's "only" 3 percent a year.* Suppose the price level were to creep upward at the rate of 3 percent per year. Today a Coke costs 10 cents. If the price of Cokes moved up with the general price level, what would they sell for in thirty years? At 3 percent per year a present amount would grow to 2.43 times as large an amount in thirty years. (See Table 13–2 thirty-year entry in column for 3 percent.) Cokes would sell for about 25 cents. In forty years, when you are retired, they would sell for almost 40 cents. (See same table, forty-year entry.)

7. *The whole is less than the growth of its parts.* We give now another practical problem that will probably face everyone at one time or another. After ten years of working for an employer, you decide to transfer to a new job. Your old employer reminds you that for the past ten years he has contributed (that is, he has diverted from your wages) $1,000 each year to an account for your retirement (a fringe benefit), and you have contributed the same amount each year. The fund was invested at 4 percent during that time; the total value of the account now stands at $24,000. Two options are open. (1) You may leave both contributions in that fund until retirement in thirty years when you will get the future value of this amount now credited to your account at 4 percent per year interest. (2) Your other possibility is to take out the present value of "your" contributions, which is $12,000 (one half of the present value of $24,000). You can do as you wish with the money you take out, but the other half will be lost as far as you are concerned. In other words, you can give up $12,000 today for the sake of getting now the other $12,000, with which you may do as you like. Otherwise, you must wait thirty years more to get the accumulated value (at 4 percent interest) of the entire fund. Which shall you choose?

One of the issues upon which the answer depends is the rate which you can get on your own funds. Suppose you believe that you can get 10 percent per year. Should you sacrifice half of $24,000 now for the opportunity to get 10 percent on the other $12,000 rather than 4 percent on $24,000 for thirty years?

$12,000 invested at 10 percent will be worth $208,800 in thirty more years. (See Table 13–2, 10 percent column, thirty years.) If you leave your money in the fund at 4 percent, the $24,000 fund will have grown to only $77,700 in thirty years. (See Table 13–2, 4 percent, thirty years.) Shocked?

Only if you failed to earn over 6.7 percent would your own $12,000 fund have been smaller at the end of thirty years than the whole $24,000 fund at 4 percent. The interesting fact is that today most pension investment funds credit the accounts with barely 4 percent a year, while the rate of return available on the stock market just by random investing, including interest and profits, was nearly 15 percent a year, for *any* thirty-year period you care to pick in this century.

But suppose you had just twenty years before retiring. Would it pay you to take out your own contribution? Look in Table 13–2 (10 percent column for twenty years). The amount to which $1 will grow is $6.72. And at 4 percent the dollars in the fund will grow in twenty years to $2.19. Each of your own dollars at 10 percent will grow to *more* than twice the amount that the amount credited to you in the fund will grow at 4 percent. Even for twenty years a 10 percent growth rate will overtake the slower (4 percent) growing fund that is initially twice as large. What rate of interest is the rate that makes the two funds grow to the same amount in twenty years? (Answer: about 7.5 percent for your half, if the total pension fund accumulates interest at 4 percent.)

8. *"But I wouldn't have saved if I weren't forced to."* Finally, look at Social Security. Under social security an employee and his employer *must* both pay out of the employee's wages 4.2 percent of the first $6,600 received each year. That is 8.4 percent each year, or $554 annually. At age 65 the employee may retire and receive about $3,000 annually for the rest of his or his widow's life (whoever lives longer). But suppose beginning at age 25 you set that same amount $554) aside yourself. (The fact that half of social security is set aside by the employer does not change the fact that it is taken out of the employee's wage—by the employer rather than by the employee himself.) To what amount would $554 invested annually accumulate at the end of forty years? At 8 percent per year (a *very modest* rate of return for investments in the stock market) you would have accumulated an amount of $143,000! You could then eat that up at a rate of $14,568 per year for the next twenty years, which is certainly a lot more than you are going to get from social security, no matter how you figure your likely returns from social security. (Incidentally, at 10 percent, which is still *below* the stock-market average of the past seventy years, you would accumulate about $245,000, which would give you over $25,000 annually for twenty years. We have ignored the income tax you would have to pay—but that would, when applied to the 10 percent growth, bring results close to those for the 8 percent rate.)

Why the great disparity between social security and what you can do privately? Social security (as well as most private insurance companies) credits you with barely 4 percent. At that rate you would accumulate a fund of about $53,000, which would yield an annuity of $3,870 for twenty years. Again note that social security payments promise some life insurance if you should die before age 65 and medical insurance afterwards, but both could be bought on an individual basis and still leave you far ahead. The essential difference arises from the difference in the credited growth rate.

## Wealth, Income, Consumption, Saving, Profits

We are now in a position to give rigorous statements relating wealth, income, interest, profits, losses, consumption, saving, and investment.

*Wealth.* Wealth is the current stock of economic goods. The measure of wealth is the sum of the values of those goods, each unit of each good being valued at the market price. With 100 units of goods, each selling today for $1, wealth is $100.

*Income.* If wealth is put to maximum foreseeable valued use, the wealth value in exactly one year hence will, we shall suppose, have increased to $110. Wealth is 10 percent larger at the end of a year. The rate of interest, which is here the rate of growth of wealth, is 10 percent per year. It follows that during that year people could have consumed $10 worth of goods while still keeping the original wealth of $100. That rate of consumption is predictable from the current wealth and rate of interest. This predicted (by the market) realizable rate of increase in wealth is *income* available from the wealth of the economy. A person can consume his gain in wealth (or sell it and spend the proceeds) and still end the year with exactly the same amount he started with, provided he consumes only at the same rate that his wealth grows. *Income* is defined as the maximum predicted rate of growth in wealth (that is, rate at which wealth can be consumed and still leave the owner with an unreduced wealth).[4]

If wealth is $100 and the rate of interest is 10 percent, then annual income is $10 per year. Income is equal to wealth times the rate of interest: $I = W \times r$, where $r$ is the rate of interest, $W$ is wealth, and $I$ is income. Wealth, the rate of interest, and income are locked together. If any two are known, the other can be determined.

*Savings.* Why did we say "predicted" realizable rate of increase in wealth when defining income? Because there are two different ways for wealth to increase. The first is through *saving* part of income. *Saving* (investing) can occur only at a rate that does not exceed the flow of goods and services

---

[4]The effect of inflation can easily be allowed without upsetting this definition of income.

(income). Hence, at 10 percent interest, a good selling for $100 today can yield goods and services during the year which, if saved, would bring the total wealth to $110 in one year.[5] By buying that good today for $100, you are buying the claim to the predicted $110 in one year. So wealth can be increased by not consuming current income—that is, by saving (investing).

*Profits.* A second way wealth can increase is through *revision in beliefs*, expectations, or anticipations about future yields—that is through a change in values of those goods. The change may occur because people increase their expectations of yields, physical growth, or demand. In other words, present values can change *unpredictably.* Present beliefs about future yields or values of services from current goods can change for an enormous variety of reasons: earthquakes, fire, fashions, population migrations, inventions, and so on. As knowledge about those factors or events become surer, current values of goods change to reflect that revised demand for current goods. These unforeseen value changes (which are *profits* or *losses*) reflect changes in knowledge and demands, changes that were not formerly fully anticipated.

If your wealth today is $100, and unexpectedly good news develops about future yields *or* about demands for the services of the goods you own, market prices of the goods will rise, and your wealth will increase to, say, $120. (The interest rate we shall suppose is 10 percent.) Your increase of $20 of wealth may occur in only two days. Your unpredicted (by the market) $20 increase in wealth is a *profit* (the interest or income accumulation in two days at 10 percent annual interest is miniscule). In those two days you realized a profit of $20. Your income *flow* has increased by $2 per year—from $10 to $12 annually. The $20 increase in wealth will give you $2 more income *per year*. Your income flow is now $12, instead of $10 per year. Do not confuse the measure of profit with the increased flow of income.

It is tempting to say that you must have decided also to *save* the $20 increase in wealth rather than to consume it. However, this would be inconsistent with our definition of the term "saving." There is no need to do any saving to get that $20 profit, any more than there is a need to save every day all of one's wealth in order not to consume it. Saving, as defined, is not simply nonconsumption; it is a special kind of nonconsumption. It is nonconsumption of *income*. The nonconsumption of wealth is not an act of saving. In sum, if a person consumes none of his income, he saves all of his income, and he can't possibly save more than that. If he consumes all of his income, he saves nothing. And if he consumes more than his income and thereby destroys part of his wealth, he is said to be dissaving. Wealth *can* increase without saving only if there are profits.

---

[5]More accurately, if the income flows in at a constant rate all during the year, then the saving during the year will itself be yielding an income during the rest of the year. Allowing for this instantaneous compounding of interest, the wealth at year's end would be about $111.

Capital Values, Property,
and Care of Wealth

Anticipations of future events affect prices of assets, even without any other changes in the current situation. It is sufficient that expectations change. In the stock exchange these revisions are made especially apparent, for the price of a share of common stock—a share of ownership in a business corporation—is interpreted as the capitalized present worth of the expected future net receipts. A firm may have negative net receipts this year; but if it is expected to have positive net receipts thereafter, its stock price now reflects that future flow. If it is suddenly expected that *higher* taxes will be placed on cars, the capital value of General Motors stock will drop now, imposing a loss of wealth on the *current* owners.

Do not miss the implication. Both private-property rights and capital-goods markets, in which ownership of assets can be bought and sold, are essential institutional foundations of the capitalist system. If either is suppressed, the system will lead to actions that appear to be "wasteful or shortsighted," especially in the maintenance of and investment in durable goods with future yields. A houseowner will maintain and repair the house even though the repairs do not give him better housing now. The market price anticipates lower subsequent maintenance expenditures consequent to present repairs. The houseowner may, in fact, sacrifice some current heating and lighting to save money for that repair and maintenance. If, instead, the owner had spent the money for current services—such as a warmer, brighter house—the value of the house would have fallen.

This suggests that a renter-tenant who is responsible for maintenance and repair would divert less funds from current heat and light to maintain and improve the premises than would an owner. However, the owner is not blind to this "biased" tenant behavior and, therefore, takes some precautionary countermeasures. The contractual agreement will provide penalties for carelessness by the tenant in maintaining premises.

Another illustration of the differences in effects of various types of property rights is provided by the modern business firm. The owner is influenced by all effects—present and future—that change the wealth of his firm. Future developments will be capitalized more into the ownership value of the firm than onto the current employees, who will be motivated more by what happens now and less by what happens to the firm in the more distant future. To direct employees' actions more toward the total range of effects, two kinds of pay systems are sometimes annexed to the wage system. One is a stock-option scheme, in which employees have rights to buy shares of stock at pre-assigned values. Because the long-run effects of their actions will be capitalized in the present value of the shares of stock, employees will pay more heed to the long-run effects than they would without the stock-option scheme. Another scheme—called "profit sharing," in which employees share the annual "earnings" of the firm—misses the mark because "earnings" do not measure the true profits of the firm. The true profits are the changes in the capital value of the business revealed by the price of the common stock. Instead, "earnings" are computed more in terms of current net receipts, with inadequate attention to expenditures that are inherently investments in the future. The computed current "earnings" are less responsive to the longer-run implications of present events and fail to call as much attention to the wealth-changing factors. Of the two, the stock-option plan is more effective in encouraging decisions according to the wealth-maximizing criterion, because employees with stock options share in the capitalization process, in which future consequences of present actions are capitalized into their present wealth as co-owners.

## Human Capital

Capital values apply to people as well as to nonhuman goods. However, we see and measure profits and wealth of a *non*human type much more easily and clearly, because inanimate goods are bought and sold. A person normally sells only his current services as they are performed. Yet, each person represents a quantity of wealth—a future flow of services. Although there is no market sale of "free" people by which that value can be observed, measured, or exchanged for other forms of wealth, there are other indicators of human wealth.

One measure of human wealth is life insurance. People earning only $10,000 per year may take out insurance for $50,000 to insure themselves against a loss of future wealth, from death or disability. The amount of insurance a person buys is highly correlated with his human wealth.

If a person could literally sell his future services now, he could convert his income to other forms of wealth. As it is, he must keep his wealth tied up in the form of his own labor services. This is a disadvantage for "free" people. They must continue to bear the risks of unforeseen developments that may change the value of their human wealth—whether they want to bear that risk or not.

Occasionally, however, people do manage to sell some rights to their future labor services. Classic examples are athletes who receive "bonuses" for signing with some ball team to play exclusively for that team. Nearly half a million dollars was paid to a college athlete, J. Namath, for the exclusive ownership of his future football services. He sold the risk on his future services to the person who now "owns" them. Mr. Namath has sold some of his liberties. He can no longer switch to another football team without first buying back his rights from the present owner of his services. Other athletes (probably thousands) have received bonuses for their future playing services. That they will also receive annual salaries does not affect the fact that they have sold their future services. The salary is an inducement to continue to perform services.

Long-term contracts without advance bonuses are similar devices. Star entertainers make exclusive service contracts for many years at specified minimum salaries. Although the employee cannot be forced to render specific performance, he cannot legally work for anyone else, and if he neglects his present job, he can be sued for damages. These contracts help the employee to exchange his long-run service value for wealth in other forms. Long-term contracts enable the employee to borrow *larger* amounts of money now with which to buy a house and other present goods. Without the ability to borrow against future wages, most people would indeed be more restricted in their time-phased consumption patterns. Their wealth (future services) would not be so readily exchangeable for current services.

Borrowing has advantages that its critics often fail to see. These advantages may best be explained in terms of one group of people who find it extremely difficult, even today, to borrow against their human wealth—college students. If students could offer lenders iron-clad rights to collect parts of their future earnings, many people would be more willing to make loans to them. After all, a young man now entering college represents a wealth on the average of about $100,000–$150,000. When the average man asks his best girl to marry him, he is offering her at least $50,000 in wealth. If that seems large, compute the present value (at say, 8 percent) of an annual stream of wages of about $10,000 for the next forty years—which is a rough approximation to the average for college graduates.

If, after a few years of work, your earnings prove to be much higher than anyone expected, your wealth will jump—except that you won't see it recorded in some marketplace. Will you call that unexpected increase "profits"? You should. If you had formed a business firm to sell your services, the firm would have become much more valuable. Its profit is your earnings capitalized into the present wealth measure. But almost no one goes through that formality; so we confusingly do not speak of profits to labor—only to owners of inanimate goods. And if you should unexpectedly learn that your current job will end in six months, your wealth at this very moment will have fallen, even though there is no market to register the fact. You will not wait until your wages fall before you readjust your consumption. You will adjust it immediately. Your behavior will reflect that loss of wealth.

Since human capital has no market-revealed capital value, as it would if people were bought and sold, the concept of human wealth and income to labor is difficult to measure. Consequently, "income" to labor is typically considered to be the current rate of earnings. For income-tax purposes current earnings are treated as "income." The various connotations and interpretations of the word "income" are troublesome if one does not guess the correct one. Occasionally, "measured current income" is used in economics to refer to this *current-earnings* rate, while "permanent" or "equalized" income refers to some long-run life-time average of earnings, as a sort of proxy flow measure of human wealth. Sometimes current "measured" income is called "transitory" income, because it may fluctuate temporarily around some long-run average trend—the so-called "permanent" averaged income. A change in permanent income would result from some unforseen change that induced one to revise his beliefs about that long-term average.

Not every fluctuation in measured income is unexpected, hence not every change in measured income induces a change in "permanent" income.

## Summary

1    Capital goods can be used at more than one moment in time. Present prices, or capital values, exist for and reflect beliefs about a sequence or series of future services. By means of present capital values, different future sequences of future amounts can be made easily comparable.

2    Earlier availability is more valuable than later availability—that is, the rate of interest is positive. The rate of interest is: (a) a measure of the relationship between present amounts of a good and the amounts of future goods for which they can be traded; (b) a measure of the maximal rate of growth of wealth; (c) a measure of the price of earlier availability of a good; and (d) the time premium paid for borrowed wealth.

3    Failing to allow for interest—that is, assuming a zero rate of interest—will produce misleading cost figures. The higher the rate of interest, the lower is the present price of any future service.

4    $P(1 + r)^t = A$ summarizes the relationship among $r$, $P$, $A$, and $t$.

5    Income is the predicted maximum rate of consumption that can be maintained without reducing wealth. Income is numerically equal to the product of wealth and the rate of interest. Saving and investment are both defined as the unconsumed portion of income.

6    Profit (or loss) is the unpredicted (by the market) change in wealth.

7    Under the influence of a capital market with private property, decisions will be affected by the fact that future consequences of present decisions are capitalized in wealth.

8    People have wealth values, but they are not readily measured in the marketplace, because people are not bought and sold.

## Questions

1    You invest $350 today. At the end of one year, you get back $370. What is the implied or effective rate of interest?

2    To how much will $250 grow at 7 percent compounded annually in three years?

3    At the end of a year you will get $220. At 10 percent interest rate, what is the present amount that will grow to that amount? In other words, what is the present value of $220 deferred one year, at 10 percent?

4    What is the present value of $2,500 due in five years at 4 percent?

5    In what sense is interest the price of money? In what sense is it not the price of money?

6    What present amount is equivalent to $1,000 paid at the end of each of the next three years, at 6 percent interest?

7    If you can borrow money from college at a zero interest rate for six years, and if you borrow $1,000 now, what is the present value of the "gift" to you, at 5 percent rate of interest? (Hint: Each year you earn $50 interest by investing that money now at 5 percent. What is the present value of that six-year annuity of $50?) Which would you rather have—an outright gift of $250 or that loan?

8    Your wealth today is $1,000. At 10 percent interest rate, what is your income?

9    If your income from nonbusiness wealth is $500 a year, what is your wealth, at a 10 percent interest rate?

10    Your wealth today is $1,000. You can expect, at 5 percent interest, what perpetuity rate of income per year?

11    If (in question 10) you spend all your income, what will your wealth be?

12    If you consume none of your income for two years, what will be your wealth at the end of two years, if it is $1,000 now with 5 percent interest?

13    If you announce today that you intend to save all your income for the next year, what will happen to the value of your wealth now? In one year?

14    If you announce that you are going to consume all your income during the coming year, what will happen to your wealth now? What will it be in one year?

15    You borrow $1,000 today and agree to pay the loan in five annual equal installments at 6 percent interest rate. Using Table 13–3, determine amount of each payment, the first due in one year.

16    You buy a house by borrowing the full price of the house, $20,000. Your annual installments in repaying the loan are $1,754 for twenty years at 6 percent. (Do you agree?)
a. At the end of the first year, how much of the house's value is yours—what is your equity? (Hint: On $20,000, the interest for one year at 6 percent is $1,200. You paid $1,754 at the end of the first year.)

b. At the end of the second year, what is your equity?

c. At the end of twenty years, assuming the house is still worth $20,000, what is your equity?

**17** You are a building contractor. The rate of interest rises.

a. What happens to the value of buildings that you may build?

b. What do you suppose the effect will be on your business?

18 If the value of your buildings or common stock should fall, how can you tell whether there has been a rise in the rate of interest or a fall in anticipated future net receipts? (Hint: Look at the bond market. How will this help give an answer?)

**19** You own a building worth $10,000. You receive word that the value of your building has fallen to $5,000. One possibility is that the interest rate has risen to twice its former level. A second possibility is that the building has been damaged by a fire. In either event your wealth is now $5,000. Do you care which factor caused a decrease in your wealth? Why?

20 Mr. *A* has an income of $10,000 per year. At Christmas his rich uncle gives him $5,000 in cash.

a. What is his income during that year?

b. Is the $5,000 gift a part of his income?

c. How much is his annual rate of income increased as a result of the gift of $5,000 (at interest rates of 10 percent)?

21 Which do you think will have a bigger influence in revising your consumption rate over the future—an unexpected gift of $1,000 or an unexpected salary increase of $50 per month? (Hint: What is the present value of each at, say, 6 percent per year?)

# Costs and Output Programs

In Chapters 10 through 12, the *measure* of cost was deceptively simple. In Chapter 13 we explained what was meant by wealth and capital values—concepts that are necessary because goods are durable. In this chapter after explaining why current *expenditures* on durable goods are not costs, we shall (1) describe various means of measuring costs, and (2) give some propositions relating costs to the various dimensions of an output program. As we shall see, an output program has several steps in its execution; each step involves a cost. Unless one is very clear what each step is, he will associate incorrect costs with proposed actions. To avoid this error, we distinguish among several steps in the sequence of an output program and among several alternative actions that can be taken at any moment. To each there is a separate cost. This variety of actions can bog us down in a variety of costs that can be confusing to the beginning student. We suggest that you not try to retain each one in mind as you proceed. Instead, look for the meaning of each as it is presented and see how it is computed. Only a few will be used in our subsequent analysis, but these few can be more precisely understood if the closely related or partially overlapping variants are initially distinguished. Read pages 287–293 to see how costs are computed for some steps in an output program. Then in pages 294–311 we shall discuss how the size or dimensions of an output program affect the costs of the entire program.

## Costs of Acquisition, Continuing Possession, and Operating

Normally, we speak of the purchase price as the cost—when the resale price is typically zero, as for bread, shoes, or socks. But for many long-lived capital goods, the resale price is far from zero. With an ordinary new car, it may be 85 to 90 percent of the initial purchase price. If you buy a car for $2,000 and then immediately resell it for $2,000, the cost was zero. If you had resold it for $1,800, the cost you incurred would have been $200. The longer you keep possession of the car, the less will be the resale value. That subsequent depreciation in resale value is the cost of *continuing* possession, whereas the initial, immediate turn-around, purchase-resale price differential is a cost of *acquisition*. To make the example concrete, suppose the initial purchase price is $2,000, with an immediate resale value of $1,800, and with a subsequent $1-a-day depreciation in resale value. (1) The acquisition cost is $200, the difference between price and current resale value. (2) The cost of continuing possession of the car is $1 per day. The cost of *acquiring* ownership of a car and *keeping* it for one week is $207.[1] (3) The cost of driving it 1,000 miles in a week, assuming the operation costs are 6 cents a mile, is $60. The total costs thereby incurred are $60 for the gasoline, $7 for the depreciation—a total of $67 for *operating and continuing possession* of the car. On the other

[1] The cost of keeping it for another week—*given* that I have already acquired it—is $7.

hand, if I do not yet have the car, the total cost of *acquiring, continuing possession, and operating it for one week* would be $267.

*Fixed and variable costs.* You might think these costs would normally be called (1) acquisition (or entry) cost, (2) continued possession cost, and (3) operating cost. But conventionally they have been called almost everything except those names. Sometimes, (1) is called "fixed" (or "sunk") cost, to suggest that once you acquire the item this cost is "fixed" upon you and irrevocable. For *any subsequent* decision this "cost" is totally irrelevant and can be forgotten. When "fixed" is applied to this first cost, the term "variable" is applied to the *sum* of (2) and (3) costs, in the sense that you could vary them by *shutting down and selling out* or varying the output plan.[2]

Before we go to a detailed explanation of why the preceding distinctions are made, and how costs depend upon output, a few subsidiary points should be noted. First, do not confuse all expenditure with cost. Expenditure may be an exchange of one form of wealth for another—usually money for non-money goods. *Cost* of an *action* is the associated *reduction* in *total wealth*. Second, a cost of $200 *incurred now* by some action now does not mean that one must reduce his *consumption* now. He may continue to consume at the same rate, deferring the reduced consumption till later. And there is nothing wrong or irrational with deferring the consumption sacrifice. Many young people do this by buying on installment plans. Third, to incur a cost does not mean one is worse off. When you buy the car and lose, say $200 in wealth, it means only that you could not now go back (by a market exchange) to your original set of resources. But if you knew that the cost of acquiring the car was going to be $200 (difference between the purchase and the immediate resale price) we presume you decided that having the car was worth that cost, and also worth the sacrifice of other services you could have had instead.

## Example of Cost Calculation of a Specific Output Program

### Acquisition Cost

You are thinking about buying a Ford car, which has a purchase price of $2,000. Table 14–1 (top half) lists all the pertinent expenditure data, which we shall explain. The immediate resale value is $1,800. If you kept the car for two years (without using it) the resale value at the end of two years would be $1,400. If you use the car at the rate of, say, 10,000 miles of travel per year, the resale value will be only $1,300 in two years. What is the cost of acquiring the car? It is $200, the difference between the price and the *immediate* resale value. Once the car is acquired, this is a "fixed" or "sunk" cost.

[2]Sometimes, as if to confuse things, the term "fixed" cost is used to refer to the first two costs, with variable referring to just the third one.

Given that the car is acquired, what is the cost of just continuing its possession for two years? It is the difference in the value of the car now and the *present value* of its resale value in two years. Do not subtract $1,400 from $1,800! They are values as of *different* dates. If you learned your lesson well in Chapter 13, you will know that the two figures must be compared in contemporaneous values. Therefore, convert the $1,400 for two years hence to a present value. At 10 percent rate of interest, the present value of $1,400, deferred *two* years, is .826 × $1,400 = $1,156.40 (use Table 13–1). Subtracting this from $1,800 gives $643.60 as the cost of two years' *continuing* possession, *given* that the car has already been acquired. The cost of acquiring *and* continuing possession for two years is $2,000–$1,156.40 = $843.60. $643.60 is the depreciation, the present-value measure of the predictable reduction in the resale value of the car.[3]

Because we want to add more realism, we assume taxes and insurance must be paid if the car is possessed. At the *beginning* of each year $100 is due for the year's tax and insurance, whether or not the car is operated. Converting these two payments to present values gives $100 + (.909) $100 = $190.90, the present value of taxes and insurance if the car is possessed for two years. The cost of two years' continuing possession, *given that the car is already acquired*, is $643.60 + $190.90 = $834.50. The cost of *acquiring* and *keeping* (but not using) the car for two years is ($200 + $643.60 + $190.90) = $1,034.50.

But you are not managing a museum of old cars; you will want to use the Ford. Other outlays, listed in Table 14–1, will be made for repairs, gasoline, etc., and will be paid at the *end* of each year, as if they accumulated on a credit card. (Note that we call them expenditures and outlays—not costs.) Since we cannot properly add outlays now to outlays a year later, without adjusting for interest, we convert all outlays to present values. They sum to $561.80.[4] (See Table 14–1.) The resale value of the car will depreciate more if the car is used. We assume it will decrease to $1,300 at the end of two years rather than to the "non-use" $1,400. The extra depreciation over the two-year interval is $100, which has a present value of $82.60 (at 10 percent rate of interest). Adding this $82.60 to $561.80 gives $644.40 as the present value measure of costs of operations.

---

[3] Depreciation differs from obsolescence in that obsolescence is the reduction in value in excess of that predicted. At the end of this chapter is a section explaining this in more detail. Although, in strict rigor, depreciation is the *present value* of the implied decrease in wealth, $643.60, it is very common practice to subtract $1,400 from $1,800 and call the difference, $400, depreciation. Of course, this understates the true depreciation, $643.60; it doesn't allow for differences in *times* of values.

[4] ($300 × .909) + ($350 × .826) = $561.80.

$644.40 is the cost that could be avoided if operations were stopped (but the car were kept). Depending upon the actual use of the car the figure of $644.40 would vary. (We assumed 10,000 miles per year.) You can see why this figure is sometimes called the *variable* cost. It is the cost that will depend on the actually performed service. The other cost of $1,034.50 is independent of the mileage performed, and is therefore also commonly called "fixed" (which gives us a second concept of a "fixed" cost). The sum of $644.40 and $1,034.50 is $1,678.90, the total cost in capital value measure, for acquisition, continued possession, and provision of 20,000 miles of service in two years. As we shall see later, these distinctions are important for answering such questions as (1) whether to enter the business and (2) deciding, once one has entered the business, whether to get out of business if receipts fall short of expectations or to shut down temporarily until conditions improve.

We now have the following classification of costs for the two-year, 20,000-mile output program:

Cost of acquisition, possession, and operation = $1,678.90 or 8.39 cents/mile.
($200) + ($834.50) + ($644.40)

Cost of operation = $   644.40 or 3.22 cents/mile.
Cost of possession and operation = $1,478.90 or 7.39 cents/mile.

Each of these costs has several different names and keeping them all straight is a tedious task. We list their most common names:

Acquisition cost ($200): fixed; sunk.
Possession cost ($834.50): overhead.
Operation cost ($644.40): direct; operating; out of pocket.
Possession plus operation cost ($1,478.90): short-run total; variable.

Especially ambiguous, as we shall see, are the terms "fixed" and "variable," which are used in several conceptual senses. The above list of names is not exhaustive. You will simply have to deduce from the context what specific cost is meant if you hear one of these, or some other term, used. Or else ask the user.

### Per-Unit-of-Service Measures of Costs

Costs can be expressed per units of output, in particular as costs per mile of service. For the two-year, 20,000 mile program, we simply divide the total costs by 20,000 miles to get the average (per mile) cost. The results are in the extreme right column of Table 14–2: $1,678.90/20,000 = $.0839, a little more than 8 cents per mile. You can cover that cost with revenue if you rent your car for 8.39 cents per mile—but you must *collect the receipts in advance*. If you wait until the mileage occurs, interest should be included, since the measure used for cost is a *present*-value measure. If you were to be paid by credit-card at the end of each year, how much should you demand from the renter of the car? Or, in the words of Chapter 13, "What uniform two-year annuity (payments at the end of a first year and a second year) will have a present value of $1,678.90?" Using Table 13–3, we get (at 10 percent) $969, due at the end of each of the two years (9.69 cents per mile paid when transport service is provided).[5]

Table 14–1
Expenditures and Costs for Acquisition, Possession, and
Operation of Car for Two Years

EXPENDITURES

|  | Now | End of First Year | End of Second Year | Present Value |
|---|---|---|---|---|
| Purchase price | $2,000 | — | — | $2,000 |
| Resale Value |  |  |  |  |
| Not driven | (1,800) | — | 1,400 | 1,156.40 |
| Driven 20,000 miles | — | — | 1,300 | 1,073.80 |
| Tax and insurance | 100 | 100 | — | 190.90 |
| Gas, tires, repairs | — | 300 | 350 | 561.80 |

COSTS

1. Acquisition:

$2,000
−1,800
_____
$200

2. Possession for two years; zero mileage—that is, without operation.

| Current resale | $1,800 |
| Final resale | −1,156.40 |
| Depreciation | 643.60 |
| Tax and insurance | 190.90 |
| Possession for two years | $834.50 |

Acquisition and continued possession without operation: $1,034.50

3. Operation (20,000 miles in two years)

| (Extra depreciation | $1,156.40 |
| because of mileage) | 1,073.80 |
|  | 82.60 |
| Gasoline, oil, tires, etc. | 561.80 |
| Operation | $644.40 |

Total costs of acquisition, possession, and operation $1,678.90

[5] Since the receipts are to be spread over a two-year period, with interest at 10 percent each year, the payment due at time of mileage is delayed on the average about 1.5 years. At 10 percent per year, that is about 15 percent interest per 1.5 years. As expected, 9.69 cents is about 15 percent larger than 8.39 cents. Hereafter, to simplify computations, we shall express all costs, whether for the total program or a unit of mileage basis, in terms of the present-value measure.

The average *present* value cost of 8.39 cents per mile can be partitioned into operating (variable) costs and a remainder (which does not depend upon the mileage) here called the continuing possession or "fixed" cost. $644.40/20,000 = 3.22 cents per mile, the per-mile average *direct operating*, or variable, costs—excluding the initial acquisition *and* subsequent continued possession costs. The per-mile "fixed" possession cost is ($1,678.90 − $644.40)/20,000 or 5.17 cents. (Remember, this is merely the fixed cost spread over the 20,000 miles. The greater the mileage provided in those two years, the lower will be the per-mile average measure of that "fixed" cost.)

Let us compute one more average cost. What is the cost of the program minus *only* the initial acquisition cost? Costs of continued possession (that is, ensuing depreciation) are not excluded as they were in the preceding paragraph. If the already acquired car is kept and used for 20,000 miles in two years, $1,478.90 more costs will be incurred. On a per-mile basis over 20,000 miles that is 7.39 cents per mile, excluding only the initial acquisition cost. This is an "average variable" cost.

Table 14–2
Total Cost (Present Capital Value) Dependence on Volume or
Miles of Service (at Rate of 10,000 Miles per Year)

| Distance (Miles) | Total Cost | Incremental Cost | Average Cost |
|---|---|---|---|
| 5,000 | $  750 | $750 | $.150 |
| 10,000 | 1,100 | 350 | .110 |
| 15,000 | 1,400 | 300 | .093 |
| 20,000 | 1,679 | 279 | .084 |
| 25,000 | 1,940 | 261 | .078 |
| 30,000 | 2,200 | 260 | .074 |
| 35,000 | 2,420 | 220 | .067 |
| 40,000 | 2,600 | 180 | .065 |
| 45,000 | 2,760 | 160 | .061 |
| 50,000 | 2,900 | 140 | .058 |

Costs Relevant to Various Decisions

Long-Run Entry Cost

What is the minimum amount of revenue in present-value measure that you must receive to make it worthwhile to produce the output program—20,000 miles of service over a two-year interval? The answer is $1,678.90 or 8.39 cents per mile. You would not consider entering this business unless you expected at least 8.39 cents per mile for the rent of your car. That is called the *long-run* minimum per-mile cost of that complete program.

Suppose that *after* acquiring the car and entering the business you find the rental price is less than 8.39 cents per mile, say 8 cents. What should you do? You can quit by selling your equipment; you can continue to keep it without renting it out; or you can continue to rent it out for the available 8 cents per mile. The yet to be incurred cost of continuing to provide the service, once the car is acquired, is $1,478.90/20,000 miles or 7.39 cents per mile. This is called the *short period* (i.e., after entry) total cost per mile for 20,000 miles. Any price *over* that would induce you to continue in business with your acquired car and provide the service for the 20,000 miles of service. True, you would not stay in business for long, but once the car has been acquired, the relevant costs now are those yet to be incurred. By renting at anything over 7.39 cents you are more than covering any new costs, at least for the next two years. Hence, your loss of initial entry is being partly offset to the extent that you get anything more than 7.39 cents per mile, until you must replace equipment, at which time you would stop production.

*"Shut-down" level of costs.*    Suppose the rental price fell below 7.39 cents. Should you immediately shut down and sell out? Or should you shut down temporarily and await the return to better times? That depends on whether or not you think the lower price is a temporary "short-period" fall. If the fall below 7.39 cents is "permanent," shut down immediately.

If the price falls below 7.39 cents but not as low as 3.22 cents (direct operating costs) per mile for what you think will not be too long a period, continue to operate. At least you will cover your short-period *operating* costs with something left to apply toward the overhead costs of continuing possession. Any price over 3.22 cents is sufficient to induce you to continue to operate at the same rate with the existing equipment for a while at least, even though your full costs (prior to entry) were correctly estimated at 8.39 cents per mile. And though your costs, once you have acquired the car, are 7.39 cents per mile for each of the 20,000 miles in this program, you should operate if price falls, *temporarily*, even to 3.22 cents per mile. You "should" do that if you are to maximize your wealth (by minimizing your loss).[6]

[6] As a matter of fact, if price fell below 3.22 cents per mile, it might also pay to continue to operate temporarily. If the service is provided at a slower rate than at 10,000 miles per year, the costs will be lower. If we anticipate the principles to be explained in the next sections, it can be shown that the costs per mile of service would be as low as 2 cents for a lower rate of output, given the existing equipment. Operating less intensely means slightly lower direct operating costs so that the costs can be shaved down to as low as, say, 2 cents per mile for temporary operation.

"Size" of Output Programs and Costs

Obviously, costs will depend upon the size of the contemplated output program. There are several components of "size" of an output program. One is the total *volume*, or amount, of the good to be produced. A second is the *rate*, or speed, at which that volume is produced once it is under way. Finally, there are the *dates* of the output (for example, dates it is to be started and completed). In making refrigerators, the manufacturer can plan a volume of 150,000 refrigerators at the rate of 15,000 per month (for ten months), with the first completed item to appear six months from the date of decision to produce. The *volume* is 150,000 items, the *rate* is 15,000 per month, and the *date* is six to sixteen months hence. In the rest of this chapter, we will discuss how these three components of "size" affect cost.

### Cost Effect of Volume

A larger volume of output (mileage or distance, in our current example) for some given initial date and constant rate of output will cost more than a smaller volume of output. More resources are required to produce more. In our automobile example, the mileage is the volume. If the mileage is to be 40,000 miles in *four* years rather than 20,000 in two years (constant *rate* of 10,000 miles per year), the total cost will be greater. But although the volume (40,000 miles) is twice as large, the total cost will not necessarily be doubled. *Generally the cost increase will be less than in proportion to the increase in the volume* (keeping the *rate* unchanged). This is our first cost proposition.

In our illustrative problem, with miles of service as the volume dimension, we would have used a different kind of car for a planned mileage of 20,000 miles in two years than for 100,000 in ten years. It might be cheaper to use two cars sequentially for the 100,000-mile case than to use one car. Or for very small distances, renting a car from some auto dealer may be the cheapest procedure. In any case, the relevant cost is based on the *cheapest* cost method of obtaining the volume contemplated. Figure 14–1 shows the costs of various mileage programs for each of several different techniques of producing taxi services. The vertical scale measures the present value of the costs of an output program, while the horizontal scale measures the volume of output (in this case, mileage), given some rate and initial date of service. Each technique portrayed (except *A*) is most efficient at some particular range of mileage. Specify the particular mileage, and the most efficient technique is determined. An envelope curve tracing the lowest of the specialized equipment curves at each output indicates the lowest cost of achieving each of the alternative output programs (here differing in mileage but *all for the same rate* of 10,000 miles per year).

The costs of Table 14–2 are taken from that envelope curve of lowest costs for different output programs. Our example, for which we showed the costs in Table 14–1, is one of the points on that lower envelope—the point for

20,000 miles of service, at 10,000 miles per year, with a cost of $1,679. As Table 14–2 shows, when the planned *volume* is increased (by steps of 5,000 miles), cost increases–by *diminishing* increments called the incremental costs for 5,000 mile increments. The average cost per planned mile decreases for larger volumes. This is an implication of our first cost proposition, and is called *economies of mass production.*

*Increasing total costs and decreasing average and marginal cost of larger volume.* The envelope cost curve in Figure 14–1 ascends for larger volumes. Larger volume programs are more costly. How much more costly a one-unit increase in volume makes a program is indicated by the *slope* of the total cost line. This slope represents the marginal cost of unit increases in volume of output programs. (Marginal cost is always positive: larger volumes cost more.) Marginal cost decreases with larger volume.

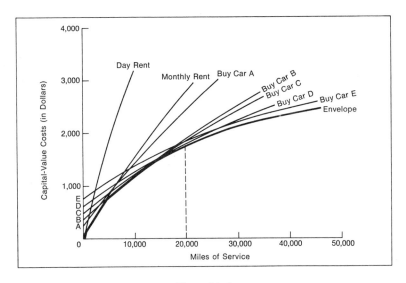

Figure 14–1
Total Cost as Function of Miles of Service at Constant Rate of 10,000
Miles per Year

Each line shows what costs would be for a given type of equipment if used for various possible amounts of service. Lower envelope indicates lowest cost for each amount of service if produced with equipment most economical for that level of service. For very small mileage, renting a car by the day is cheaper than buying and using car *E*, which is most economical for larger mileages. The fact that the envelope curve lies below *E* indicates that some unspecified *F* and *G* are even more economical at larger quantities.

The way in which the total cost changes with changes in the projected volume can be made clearer by another graph. In Figure 14–2, the *height* of the curve *MC* measures the *addition* to total cost for unit increases in volume. This is a graph of the "marginal cost of volume." If the curve were a straight horizontal line, it would mean that a unit increase in the volume raises total cost by a constant amount. But a *downward*-sloping line indicates that unit increments of volume can be produced at decreasing increments to total cost.

The *average* cost per unit of volume of different programs is also shown. For larger volumes the cost per unit decreases, possibly to some ultimate lowest value. This is, as said earlier, the *economy of mass* or *volume production*. The increase in volume is obtained by lengthening the run of production while holding the rate of production constant.

*Effect of different rates of output.*    The relationship between costs and output in Chapters 10 and 11 showed a *rising*, not a falling, marginal and average cost as output was increased. Can this be reconciled with the present decreasing marginal and average costs as output increases? Yes, and the answer lies in the ambiguity of the word "output." In earlier chapters we were increasing the daily *rate* or speed of output. Here, we have been increasing the *volume* while holding the daily rate constant. But we can change the rate. One can produce one thousand houses in one year or in ten years; in each case, volume is the same, but the rates differ. And one can produce one house in three months or ten in thirty months; here, the rate of production is constant, but the volumes differ.

For which goods is the *volume* effect important in reducing average and marginal cost? Mass-produced, large-volume-of-output goods, like automobiles, radios, typewriters, electric motors, refrigerators, and tires are produced at a lower cost *per unit* precisely because the volume of output is large.

If you ask a printer to print some personal letterheads, or circulars, you will be told that the price *per unit* is lower, the more you buy. Aircraft companies know that the average cost of a jet plane is cheaper if they can produce one hundred than if they produce only ten. Ford knows that the average cost of some model is lower if it produces half a million than if it produces one hundred. Polaroid cameras are cheaper to produce if several thousand are produced rather than merely a hundred. Different techniques of production are used for large outputs, and the result is a lower cost per unit.

If larger-volume production is cheaper *per unit* than small-volume production, *standardization* of products is implied. People who want individually styled or custom-built goods will face higher prices than for mass-produced goods. We should expect to see many people using the cheaper standardized goods, as they in fact do with automobiles, shirts, shoes, watches, airplanes, etc., because of the cost-reducing effect of a larger volume. A country with a large population can take greater advantage of this cost-reducing effect since it can produce in larger *volume*. This effect of a large market in reducing costs is one of the major advantages of the United States over smaller countries.

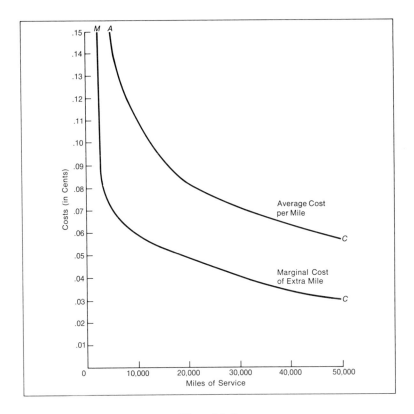

Figure 14-2
Marginal and Average Cost per Mile of Service at Constant Rate of
10,000 Miles per Year

A greater volume of output (in miles) results in a lower cost per mile. An increase
in programmed miles of services results in cost increase, but extra cost decreases
with increased mileage. These costs are valid if rate of speed of performance is not
increased; increased mileage is obtained by using equipment over longer periods of
time.

The lower per unit cost of larger volumes of output does not eliminate
the desirability of smaller volumes of output. For example, a change in
automobile models annually prevents costs from falling for that *particular*
kind of model. Then why change models every year, if that is more expensive
than keeping the same model for a larger scheduled volume? There are two
reasons: (1) The percentage decrease in average cost is related to the
*percentage* change in output volume; therefore, the cost reductions are very
small for increases of an already very large volume. A 10,000-unit increase
over 100,000 is only a 10 percent increase, whereas it is a 100 percent
increase over 10,000. (2) Tastes change, new ideas occur, improvements in
technique must be incorporated if a producer is to continue to have a
profitable business.

*Why average costs fall with larger volume.*    The larger volume (with constant rate) results in decreasing marginal and average costs per unit of volume for possibly two reasons: (1) variety of techniques and (2) learning by doing.

(1) *Variety of Techniques.* One unit can be made either by hand or by some complicated machine and assembly technique. Suppose the latter is more expensive for making only *one* unit of the product. Then "hand" methods will be used. We certainly could make 1,000 units by hand at just about 1,000 times the cost for one. But if the machine method will do it at less than 1,000 times the cost, it will pay to use the machine. If we now recognize that it is impossible to divide some complicated machines into miniatures that would produce just one item at 1/1,000 the total cost, we can see that what can be used economically for larger volume may not be economical for small volume. On the other hand, what is possible with small volumes can be repeated (at the same *rate*) to get the bigger volume. We can replicate the economic techniques for small volumes, but we can't miniaturize or subdivide in the opposite direction. Thus, if any new technique results in lower costs for some volume, there is not necessarily a way to use this technique at lower volumes too.

A case in point is the "initial setup" cost. For a large volume, this can be very large; if that same technique were used for only a small output, the costs would be catastrophically high. Therefore, large initial or investment cost will be observed only with large volumes. An example is the transport of oil from wells to refineries. If the well owner believes the well will produce about 100,000 gallons before exhaustion, he might ship the oil by truck—shipping, say, 1,000 gallons a day for one hundred days. But if he thinks he will get 1,000,000 gallons, at the same rate of 1,000 per day, he can ship either by truck or pipeline. Suppose the pipeline is cheaper if it is used for 1,000 days (at the rate of 1,000 gallons per day) but more expensive than a truck if it is used for one hundred days. Depending upon the volume (not the rate) of oil to be transported, the selected method of production will be different, with the larger volume having less cost per gallon transported.

(2) *Learning.* The other general explanation of reduced unit costs with larger volume is called the "learning" factor. Improvement by experience is evident in managerial functions, production scheduling, job layouts, material-flow control, on-the-job learning, and physical skills. The rate of learning may be greatest at first and then reach a plateau; but, in any event, the larger the volume of output, the more opportunity for learning and hence the lower the unit costs of larger outputs.

*Exceptions to the average cost-reducing effect of larger volume: exhaustion of raw materials.*    Not for every good does a larger volume yield lower unit costs. Sometimes as a larger volume is contemplated, more cheaply available raw materials are used up, and resort must be had to more expensive ores and raw materials. For example, the production of oil is now characterized by deeper drilling, in more remote areas. Fortunately, however, technological progress and growth of our wealth have more than offset that exhaustion of easily available raw materials—because men were induced to use the easily available materials first. Had they instead been worried about "conservation," they would have used resources at a lower rate, with the result that income would have been lower; and hence not so much could have been devoted to investment, technology, and research.

The advance in technology and supply of capital goods has meant that, despite the relative decrease in existing amounts of some raw materials (iron ore, coal, wood), many goods are producible at lower costs than formerly, when "cheaper" sources but poorer technology and less wealth were available. Perhaps man has been lucky in the race between technological knowledge and depletion of natural resources, but, whatever the reason, the fact remains that technology and growth of capital from saving and investment have more than offset the increased difficulty of obtaining some raw materials and have increased the stock of existing man-made wealth by a more than offsetting amount. It is profitable *investment*—rather than conservation of natural resources—that increases the wealth of future generations. Conservation, as we shall see more clearly later, means less *income*, not more saving.

### Speed of Production and Cost

The faster the speed at which a *given* volume must be produced, the greater the total, the average, and the marginal costs. This was illustrated in our earlier examples of a five-person, two-goods world. A larger *rate* of output of $Y$ involved a greater rate of sacrificed $X$. One might have thought that since the same volume of output is being produced, the same stock of materials will be used up, whether it be produced quickly or slowly; but, in fact, a higher rate of production involves bringing in more resources at the same time, thus requiring resort to relatively less efficient resources.[7] Furthermore, the resources insist on higher pay for overtime because the sacrifice of leisure is increased.

The cost effects of producing any given volume at higher *rates* are shown in Figure 14–3. The curves show higher costs for higher rates of output. The top curve shows the total costs of any of the volumes indicated on the horizontal scale if the rate of production is 25,000 miles per year. The lowest curve is for the low rate of 2,500 miles per year. Point $G$ indicates that at a rate of 20,000 miles per year and 40,000 miles of service (in two years) the cost is about $4,200. But 40,000 miles provided in four years at the rate of 10,000 miles per year has a cost of only about $2,600 (point $G^*$). The high-speed costs are about 10.5 cents per mile, with the low-speed costs about 6.5 cents per mile. This is an illustration of the general law that faster production (of any given volume) is more costly.

Do not be misled by the large cost reduction in the illustration. We used large changes to strongly illustrate the cost effects. It is doubtful that the

---

[7] Remember the analysis of Chapters 10 and 11 and the reason given there for the rising marginal costs of higher rates of output.

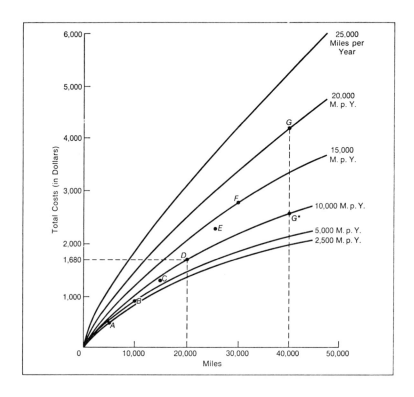

Figure 14–3
Total Cost as Function of Volume and Rate of Output

Top curve shows total costs for providing different amounts of miles of service (shown on horizontal axis) at 25,000 miles per year. Total costs of the same total number of miles of service is shown by second-highest curve if car is operated at 20,000 miles per year. Lower rate of service implies lower costs. Point G shows total costs for 40,000 miles of service provided at rate of 20,000 miles per year (requiring two years). Lower point, G*, shows total costs of 40,000 miles provided in four years at rate of only 10,000 miles per year. Points A, B, C, D, E, F, G show costs of outputs that differ in *both* speed and mileage. Point B is for twice the speed and twice the mileage as A (but for same period of production). All points are costs of output produced in same amount of time, but at faster rates and hence proportionately larger mileage in the given period of production. Point F is for 15,000 miles per year for two years and a mileage of 30,000 miles. Point D is for 10,000 miles per year for two years with mileage 20,000 miles.

numbers here are typical of the cost reductions that might result from taking more time for this particular type of output. It might be objected that taking four years could involve extra labor costs and greater obsolescence and hence greater, rather than less, costs; but this is a misinterpretation. Yet it illustrates that if one is *allowed* longer time to do something, it will not cost him more to do it–and usually it will cost less. If he wishes, he can do it as early as is most economical. By obstinately (and inefficiently) delaying his production, or starting it too early, he could incur various storage costs. But the proposition here is that allowing more time *within* which to efficiently perform some task or produce some output will result in costs that certainly are *not* higher, and most likely lower. The less time he is allowed, the less is his range of options and the less he can utilize any available cheaper means of production.

Proportionate Increases in<br>Both Rate and Volume

For many goods, a common feature of production is a joint increase—indeed, proportional increase—in *both* the rate and volume of an output program. For example, *if the length of the production run is constant*, say one year, then a higher rate for that period will also mean proportionally larger volume. An automobile manufacturer can contemplate *rates* of output from 1,000 a month to 50,000 a month for one year. If any of these rates persists for a full year, the range of volumes implied is from 12,000 to 600,000 cars. In such special cases, one can speak either of the annual rate (*lasting for a year*) or of the volume of a program, since both increase proportionally.

Higher rates of output and larger volumes both increase *total* costs, but they have opposite effects on average cost per unit of volume of output. Larger volumes reduce average costs, while higher rates raise average costs per unit of any volume produced. Which effect dominates when both the rate and the volume increase in the same proportion—that is, when the total volume is increased but is produced in the same interval of time? At first the average cost may fall as both the rate and volume of output are increased, but larger increases in the rate of output, even though accompanied by a proportionate increase in the volume, will ultimately dominate and cause higher average costs.

Figure 14–4, which is based on Figure 14–3, shows total costs of different output programs in which the volume *and* the rate of production differ in the same proportion. The numerical data are given in Table 14–3. For example, at point *A* the *volume* is 5,000 miles at a *rate* of 2,500 miles per year; the total cost is $500. At *B* the volume is 10,000 miles and the rate is 5,000 miles per year—both twice as big as at *A*. The total cost is $900, not quite twice as large. And at *G* the costs are shown for an output program with volume of 40,000 miles at the rate of 20,000 miles per year, each of which is eight times larger than for program *A*. The total cost of that bigger program is $4,200; now, the rate effect has dominated the volume effect, for costs are more than eight times as large.

The marginal cost curve, *MC*, in Figure 14–5 shows by its *height* the increase in total costs between two output programs differing by one mile of distance (volume) and 1 mile an hour of speed of production per two years. For example, the marginal cost at 20,000 miles of service is 9 cents. This means that if we were to produce 20,000 miles in two years at a rate of 10,000 miles

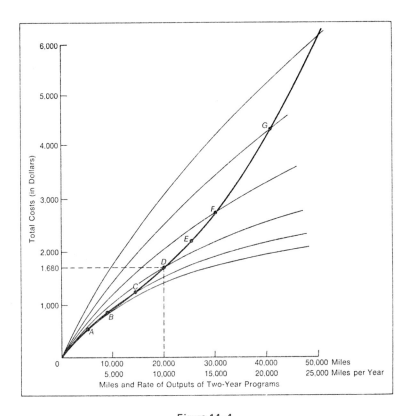

Figure 14–4
Total Costs of Two-Year Programs, with Proportional Increases in
Volume and Rate

Rising curve shows how total costs increase with *proportionate* increases in rate
and volume of output. Increase in total cost is always "positive" but increase
diminishes at first till about point C, and then increases in total cost with each
increment as output becomes greater and greater (shown by increasing slope of
line). Light lines in background are curves of Figure 14–3, where each line shows
behavior of costs for increases in mileage but at constant rate (speed) of output
during production.

per year, the total cost would be greater by 9 cents than for a program of
19,999 miles in two years (at the rate of 9,999.5 miles per year).

Converted to average cost per mile of service, these total costs are shown by
the *AC* curve in Figure 14–5 for different output programs. The total cost of
5,000 miles (at 2,500 miles per year for two years) is $500, which gives an
average cost per mile of 10 cents, shown as point *A*. The total costs of
20,000 miles in two years is $1,680, which gives a per-mile cost of 8.4 cents.
For 40,000 miles in two years the total cost is $4,200, with an average
per-mile cost of 10.5 cents. These per-unit costs are pulled down by the effect
of large volume production, but they are pushed up by the effect of higher

Table 14–3
Costs of Alternative (Two-Year) Output Programs

| Output (Miles) | Costs | | |
|---|---|---|---|
| | Total | Average | Marginal |
| A  5,000 | $  500 | 10.0 ¢ | 9.0 ¢ |
| B 10,000 | 900 | 9.0 | 7.7 |
| C 15,000 | 1,200 | 8.0 | 7.0 |
| D 20,000 | 1,680 | 8.4 | 9.0 |
| E 25,000 | 2,200 | 8.8 | 11.0 |
| F 30,000 | 2,800 | 9.3 | 13.0 |
| G 40,000 | 4,200 | 10.5 | 16.0 |

Output is miles of distance at rates of miles per year such that distance is yielded in exactly two years. Thus rate of output is equal to half the distance per year. Distance and rate increase proportionally from A through G. These data are plotted in Figures 14–3, 14–4, and 14–5. The output increase of 5,000 miles, from 5,000 to 10,000, raises total costs by $400. Dividing this increase by 5,000 miles gives 8 cents a mile—a crude approximation to the marginal cost for one mile of service in that interval. The tabled numbers are correctly computed marginal cost from more detailed information and are centered on the 5,000th mile, the 10,000th mile, etc. You could estimate the marginal costs around 30,000 miles by getting the increase in cost from 25,000 to 30,000 miles and dividing by 5,000 miles (which gives 12 cents), or by dividing the increase in costs between 30,000 and 40,000 by 10,000 miles (which gives 14 cents). The marginal cost *at* 30,000 miles is 13 cents.

rates. As a result, the average cost curve will be roughly U-shaped, with a falling segment followed by a flatter, possibly horizontal, section and ultimately rising more and more sharply.

Figure 14–5 is a very useful analytical diagram and should be thoroughly understood. Its exact shape and position reflect the particular numbers in our present automobile example. Obviously the diagram will differ for other production situations. Which features will persist? For generality, we show the curve as U-shaped—with nothing implied about the *length* of the various downward, flat, and rising segments. There may not always be a falling segment for small outputs. But a rising segment always will occur for the larger outputs (for the effect of faster speeds of production will dominate any volume effects for larger joint rates and volumes). Thus the average cost curves of all production situations have at least this one property in common: for sufficiently large outputs they will rise and rise with increasing rapidity.

The marginal cost curve always cuts through the minimum point of the average cost curve. If you remember what marginal costs are, you will see why. Marginal costs are the increment in costs for a unit increment of output. If that increment of cost is greater than the average cost of production, then increasing the output by one more will increase costs by more than the prior average. Since more is added (to the total) than the current average cost, the average cost is pulled up. Like taking another test—if your marginal score (the score on this new test) is higher than your average, it will pull up the average. And if it is lower, it will pull the average down.

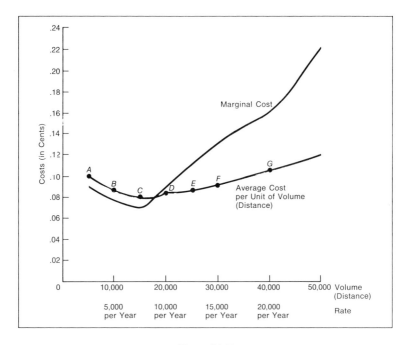

Figure 14–5
Average and Marginal Cost of Two-Year Program with Joint Volume
and Rate Increases

Total costs of Figure 14–4 have been converted to average costs per mile of
service and plotted as average cost per unit of volume (distance in miles). Points
on total cost curve of Figure 14–4 are shown here as corresponding points,
lettered *A, B, C,* etc. Notice that average costs at first fall for smaller outputs and
then begin to increase for larger outputs. Marginal cost curve shows increase in
total cost with each increase in output of one mile by increasing speed just
enough to get out one more mile in the two year period. For example, at
30,000 miles of service at rate of 15,000 miles per year, the cost per mile is shown
by point *F* and is about 9 cents per mile. But an increase in the number of miles
from 30,000 to 30,001 by increasing speed sufficiently will increase total cost
about 13 cents (depicted by height of marginal cost curve above 30,000 mile
point on horizontal axis).

While marginal cost may fall at small outputs (where volume effect dominates the speed) it will, possibly after a long flat portion, certainly rise for
larger joint speed and volume of output. This behavior is similar to the shape
of the average cost curve. If the marginal cost curve starts out from zero
output and *always* rises—the average cost curve will be below the marginal
cost curve and rising. (Can you see why? Recall the analogy of your test
scores.)

### Timing of Production: Long Run and Short Run

So far in this chapter we have seen how costs depend upon the rate and volume dimensions of a stipulated output program. Still another dimension of the program affects costs—the date or time at which the output is to be provided. "Haste makes waste" suggests the principle at work, although it would be an error to conclude that haste is never worth the price. Hasty (though not reckless) output adjustments whether made with existing equipment or with newly acquired equipment, are more expensive because revisions of equipment are more expensive the faster they are made. In other words, for a specified cost, the inputs are less variable in a shorter than in a longer interval. Turned around, this means the physical constraints are more binding for immediate adjustment.

The cost of a program beginning now will in general be greater than one beginning a year hence. Deferred output programs cost less than those initiated more hastily with existing equipment, unless the existing equipment just happens to be optimally suited to the proposed output, in which case the cost is no greater. Figure 14–6 shows two average cost curves, a short-run curve giving the costs for the output to be produced shortly and a long-run curve for production started after a longer interval. For all outputs except the one for which the existing equipment happens to be optimal, the long-run curve lies below the short-run curve.

There is a limit to how low costs can be made by deferring the output; that lower limit is called the *long-run cost*. Here we shall show just the two extreme cases, the immediate (called the short run) and the long run. Intermediate curves are for present purposes ignored.

*Carefully note that two curves do not mean there are two costs for a given program, a short-run cost and long-run cost. Rather there are two different programs, a short-run program and a long-run program, each with its own costs.*

Why utilize a long- and a short-run cost curve? Because we must allow for the fact that the responses of production to changes in demand and market price usually extend over time, and the more deferred response is usually larger and comes at a lower cost.

*Marginal costs in short and long run.* The short-run and the long-run *marginal* cost curves are shown in Figure 14–7, which is otherwise the same as Figure 14–6. These curves, you will recall, show by their height the increase in cost resulting from producing a larger output (by one mile in the two-year period). Again the short-run marginal cost rises more rapidly, which reflects the inappropriateness of existing equipment for output programs substantially different from that for which the equipment was intended.

*Short period, short run, and long run.* You may recall that we used the expression "short-period costs" on page 293. There "short period" meant a short-*lived* run of production—not a short time until production started. If we

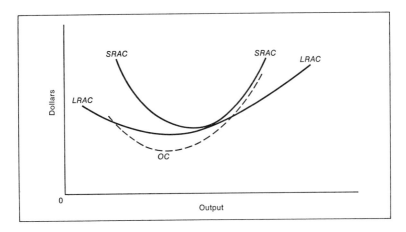

Figure 14–6
Long-Run and Short-Run Costs

Curves show average costs of long-run output program and of short-run output program, the former being the lower limit of costs achieved by deferring the output program. Output at which both curves are tangent is output for which existing equipment is optimal. For any other output, a different set of equipment would be more economical, as shown by fact that the long-run cost curve lies below the short-run cost curve for all other outputs. Curve labeled *OC* shows average per-unit operating costs with existing equipment; it excludes from *SRAC* all the costs (per unit) that would be incurred if possession were continued and if no output were produced. (See page 289.)

could create conventions, we would call one the short-period output (lasting for a short time) and the other the short-run production (beginning after a short time). But convention is too strong; often both cases are simply called the short-*run*. So from the context you must discern which is meant. A short-period output can have a cost that is lower than a short run and even less than the long run—since it is a cost of an output different not only in timing but in length of output. (Since it is short lived, we can ignore the costs of some of the activities that would have to be met if production continued for a longer interval—for example, *acquisition* costs of new equipment.)

Another convention bears noticing. Usually in elementary texts the "short run" is defined as an interval in which not all the inputs *can* be adjusted, i.e., in which one is fixed and invariant. Changes in output in the short run can, by definition, be achieved only by varying *some* (not all) of the inputs, which implies higher costs than if *all* the inputs could be adjusted. Why is this extreme, and false, assumption made, since obviously all inputs can be varied to some extent in an interval, although *all* are fixed in the immediate moment? The answer involves teaching convenience. The extreme, and simple, assumption of *a fixed* input yields about the same cost behavior as is achieved by a more accurate assumption. The implication in either case is that output changes in the short run cost more than in the long run. However, the accurate basis can be approximated in simple but extreme form as a "fixity"

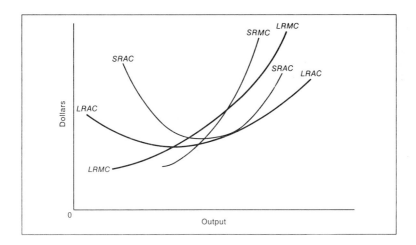

Figure 14–7
Marginal Costs of Short-Run and Long-Run Output Programs

This is the same as Figure 14–6, with marginal cost curves added (and *OC* omitted). Although short-run average costs (for a short-run program) are always larger than for a long-run program, marginal costs of short-run output program changes can be less than for long-run output changes.

of an input. While *all* inputs *can* be varied in any specified interval, the costs of varying some rates of input immediately increase so much more rapidly than for delayed variations that almost certainly they will not be varied quickly. For example, a new factory building could be constructed or purchased in a few weeks, but it would cost a lot less if done in a few months. On the other hand there is not so much difference in the costs of increasing labor or raw materials in a few weeks instead of a few months. Thus rarely will it be economical to increase all inputs in the same proportion at the same time. Factory space or equipment will usually be increased less rapidly than labor. At an extreme, as a limiting case, we may assume it won't be changed at all, i.e., is "fixed."

Hence if your instructor refers to short runs as intervals in which some inputs are fixed, remember this limiting, extreme assumption is an expository abstraction or oversimplification to avoid more complex features that may usually be ignored in elementary courses. For students who progress to more advanced work, the correct, more general interpretation must be used.

*Is it better or worse to have old equipment on hand?*    Many people believe that existing producers, because they already have purchased equipment, are faced with higher costs than newcomers who can purchase the most appropriate equipment. This is often argued as an explanation for one country's industries being more expensive than another. For example, England is said to have high costs of steel production because it still has old equipment, while Japan has new equipment—what with the destruction of the old in the war.

Not so! The relevant costs of the existing firms exclude the sunk acquisition costs. For the new firm, the acquisition costs must be faced. The older firm, for better or for worse, has already incurred those costs and can do nothing about them anymore. Thus, although the existing firms have more rapidly rising average costs, they move from a lower level of average cost because part of the costs (the acquisition or fixed costs) have already been incurred and are not costs of any subsequent action. Of course, for *sufficiently* great changes in output, their average costs would exceed the average long-run costs for newcomers. Then the existing equipment user would find it cheaper to buy new equipment, just like a newcomer (if continuing with the old is more expensive).

### Joint Products with Common Costs

*"Joint and variable" outputs.*    Production processes do not all yield only one product. Many give several *joint* products. Beef and hides are joint products of cattle. Cotton and cottonseed oil; kerosene, fuel oil, and gasoline; butter and milk—these are joint products. They are interdependent in supply; generally, more of one involves more of the other. More beef also yields more hides. More cotton yields more cottonseed oil. A higher price for one of the outputs will, by inducing a larger output, also lead to an increased output of the joint good. Thus, the supply of a good is dependent upon not only its own price, but that of other goods—especially of joint-product goods.

Yet we mustn't overdo this jointness; even for these joint products, more of one can mean less of the other. Beef and hides, although joint products, are substitutes in that there are different breeds of cattle, yielding different ratios of beef to hides. One could increase the ratio and, in fact, get more hide and less meat, by selecting different breeds and slaughtering ages. These propositions hold for gasoline, kerosene, and fuel oil—all of which are obtained by refining crude oil. Different refining methods yield different ratios of output. Cotton and cottonseed are also variable, though joint, products. Depending upon which of the joint products one is interested in, the other is often called the by-product.

*Impossibility of imputation of common costs.*    If two products are produced jointly from a "common" input, how does one allocate the costs of the common resource to each of the joint products? If, for example, hides and meat are produced from one steer, and if the feed and care of the steer is a common input or a common cost to both products, what portion is the cost of the hide and what portion is the cost of the meat? If an airplane carries passengers and freight cargo, what portion of the common costs of gasoline, labor, and facilities is assigned to each? Can a "common" cost be allocated among joint products?

Depending upon which product is treated as a residual or by-product, a different allocation of costs may be obtained. In effect, by calling one product the by-product, one is implicitly assigning all the "common costs" to the other, the "basic," product. But this, of course, is merely an arbitrary allocation, depending upon which product one calls the basic product. There is a temptation to leap to the unwarranted proposition that something must be incomplete or faulty with the analysis or with the economic system. If costs can't be allocated, how can one tell what prices to charge? How can a producer tell whether he is making a profit on each item? How can he tell how much to produce? Things seem to fall apart at the joints. In fact, however, the presence of costs which cannot be allocated uniquely to the joint products does not upset anything (except possibly some accountants—but not proper economic decision making).

*Pricing and output decisions are independent of assignment of common costs.* One purpose of prices is to allocate the existing supply of product among the competing claimants, and another is to provide revenue to induce production. But both tasks can be performed by the same market price, even if common costs cannot be allocated. The "rationing" price, as we have seen, does not depend upon how costs are apportioned; it depends upon demand and supply. What about the second function—that of inducing production of goods in the "appropriate" amounts? Again there is no necessity to allocate the common costs to the joint products. All that is necessary is a comparison of the total costs of the whole *set* of joint products with the total revenue from their sale. If the total revenue does not cover the total costs, some producers will be induced, by a loss of wealth, to stop production, leaving a smaller output and resultant higher prices of the various joint products, until the price is high enough to cover the total costs of the entire set of joint products.

Still unsolved is the question of the appropriate rates of output by those firms that are profitable. Accepting the wealth-maximizing output rate as the appropriate rate, the producer still does *not* have any use for an average cost of each joint product based on some allocation of the common costs. He requires instead a measure of *marginal* costs for each of the joint products. If he expands the output rate of any of the joint products, either singly or jointly, how much do total costs increase? If that marginal cost is observed to be less than the marginal revenue from that extra output, that output will be expanded, assuming the producer wants to increase his wealth. Otherwise, the output will be contracted. In either event, equality of the marginal cost and revenue is the wealth-maximizing clue to rate-of-output decisions. None of these decisions—pricing or output, or even combinations of inputs—depend upon separability or bookkeeping allocation of the common costs of any input shared by the joint products. This is a crucial point. Pricing and output decisions can be made even though one cannot assign portions of costs of a common production input to the products that are jointly produced. Nothing is lost, except an answer to an irrelevant, pointless question: "What is *the* cost of production of *one* of the joint products?"

To say that the question is pointless doesn't mean it won't frequently be asked. If we wonder why people should be asking such a meaningless question, we shall see that they have a different objective in mind. Essentially, they are objecting to some market price and are seeking to show that the price is not a "fair" or "appropriate" price.

### Meaning and Measure of Obsolescence

Obsolescence is the reduction in value of assets by more than the expected depreciation. Values decrease either because the demand for the asset's services has fallen more than expected or because unexpected superior methods of production have become available. For example, suppose some machine is available at a purchase price of $100 and will produce 1,000 units of $X$ before it "falls apart." Suppose further that the machine's value will decline in proportion to its use—that is, at the rate of 10 cents per unit. This means the machine depreciates at the rate of 10 cents per unit produced by the machine. Suppose also that this product has associated costs for materials and labor of 20 cents per unit, so that the total cost per unit is 30 cents. Finally, suppose that the product sells for 30 cents per unit. In this case, the receipts just cover the costs of the machine and associated materials.

Immediately after purchase of the machine, as luck would have it, a new machine is introduced for the same price. The new machine will produce 1,000 units before it falls apart, but the associated costs are only 16 cents per unit, instead of 20 cents as with the old machine; so total costs are 26 cents per unit. What will happen to the value of the old machine? Nothing—if the number of new machines is not large enough to increase the output of the good sufficiently to lower the price of the good below 30 cents per unit before the old machine can produce 1,000 units. Instead, the value (market price) of the new machine will rise to $140; and if anyone can buy one for less than $140, he will make a profit.

*The old machine will not be left idle.* It will be used until the price of the item it produces falls below 20 cents per unit. As the price of the item falls from 30 cents, under the impact of an increased supply as the new machine is more commonly used, the value of the old (and new) machines will fall. The value imputed to the old reflects the difference between the price of the item produced and the associated costs of producing the item, 20 cents. At a price of 30 cents the machine can be used for 1,000 items; therefore, the machine's value will be $100 (equal to 1,000 units times the difference between 30 cents and 20 cents). When the price of an item of product falls *to* 20 cents, that difference is wiped out; the old machine is then worthless. The machine will be retired from use if the price of its products falls *below* 20 cents. As we said, this decrease in value of the machine because of the unforeseen reduced price of the product is called obsolescence.

Only unexpected, unfavorable developments cause a "loss" to the machine owner. If buyers anticipate future developments when considering the purchase of a machine, they will offer a price low enough to avoid subsequent loss of value. If purchasers do not anticipate future developments, obsolescence (reduction in value of the asset) does not necessarily mean that the asset is idled. Instead, the reduction in value is just sufficient to permit successful competition with the newcomer. This is why today propeller airliners are still flying, despite the existence of superior jet aircraft. Not until the value of the old falls to zero will it be idled. The old item will be abandoned only when the present capital value of the reduction in operating and possession costs (or gains in revenue) of a new one (compared to an old one) exceeds the acquisition cost of a new one.

## Summary

1  Expenditures on capital goods are not costs. Costs are the reductions in wealth consequent to some action. They can be categorized by (a) acquisition of equipment, (b) continuation of possession, and (c) production.

2  Costs are not concurrent with reductions in consumption. Incurring a cost does not make a person worse off, necessarily.

3  Depreciation is the predictable reduction in resale value of assets. Obsolescence is the loss of value of equipment greater than that predicted as depreciation.

4  Decisions to enter into some output program involve "long-run" costs. Decisions to continue with production, given that production equipment has been obtained, involve "short-run" costs. Decisions to shut down immediately or to continue use of equipment until replacement depend on the direct operating costs.

5  Average per-unit costs decrease with larger volume, rate held constant. Average cost per unit increases with larger rate, volume held constant. With both rate and volume increasing in proportion, average cost per unit first falls, and then, after an interval of near constant average costs, begins to increase as a function of size of output program.

6  Reduced unit costs with larger volume imply standardization of goods.

7  Increased average costs as a function of speed of production imply that goods are not produced instantly.

8  Marginal costs ultimately increase with larger joint volume and rate programs. (They rise up through the average variable cost at the latter's minimum cost point, by logical necessity.)

9  Short-run average and marginal costs for outputs larger than that for which the existing equipment is most appropriate increase more than do long-run average costs.

10    The cost of producing any given output can be reduced by postponing the period in which the production is to occur.

11    Joint and unallocable common costs do not prevent market rationing of jointly produced goods or the determination of wealth-maximizing output combinations of the jointly produced goods.

Questions

1    "The expression 'to incur a cost' is equivalent to saying that one has committed certain acts that sacrifice an opportunity." Do you agree? If so, why? If not, why not?

2    Why are capital values used as a measure of costs?

3    Why cannot money expenditures be identified with costs?

4    A house can be purchased for $20,000. At the end of a year it could be resold for $21,000 if you had also spent $1,000 for a concrete fence, $300 for landscaping, $800 for air conditioning, and $1,200 for carpeting; otherwise, the house could have been resold for $19,000. Taxes of $300 must be paid in any event. Assume that all these expenditures—except for the taxes, which are to be paid at the end of a year—are paid at the moment you buy the house. The interest rate is 10 percent.
a. What is the cost of owning a house for one year—if you do not install fence, landscaping, airconditioning, and carpeting?
b. What is the cost of owning the house if you do install those improvements?
c. What is the year's depreciation on the house without the proposed improvements?
d. Express this cost of ownership of the improved house for one year, as a constant two-year annuity.
e. Express the cost as a perpetuity.
f. Express the cost as a five-year annuity.
g. Which of these is the correct way to express cost?

5    You operate a cleaning establishment. A new cleaning machine has a price of $5,000. You estimate its resale value at the end of the first year to be $3,000 and $1,500 at the end of the second year. The rate of interest is 10 percent.
a. What will it cost to purchase and own the machine for one year?
b. For two years?
c. What is the present value measure of the depreciation on the machine in the first year?
d. In the second year?
e. If you use the machine, you will incur expenses during the first year

of $6,000 for labor, power, and repairs; and the machine will still have a resale value of $3,000 at the end of the first year. The same expenses will be involved in the second year, and the resale value will be $1,500 at the end of the second year. Assume that all expenditures are payable at the end of the year in which they are experienced. What is the cost of having and using the machine for one year?

f. For two years?

g. What is the cost of the second year of possession and operation?

h. If, immediately after buying the machine, you should reconsider and decide to sell it, the resale value would be $4,000. What cost would the purchase of the machine "fix" upon you? This is called "fixed," "sunk," or irrecoverable cost.

i. After purchasing the machine, you can either keep it idle or use it with the attendant expenditures indicated earlier, in (e) above. As between these two alternative actions, what is the fixed cost?

j. What are the variable costs; that is, the costs incurred over and above the "fixed" costs?

6  "Don't buy your business cars. Lease them from the A and A Leasing Company. You can lease a Chevy for $60 a month. Avoid the loss of depreciation and necessity of tying up capital funds in the purchase of capital items." This is an accurate paraphrase of leasing advertising. What errors of analysis does it contain? Would the reasons given provide any advantage to a businessman? Explain why not.

7  "New business firms can underprice older firms, because the newer firms can buy the latest equipment and are not burdened with the older, less economical equipment which older firms must retire before they can economically adopt the new. This is why continued technological progress contributes to maintaining a competitive economic system." Explain the errors in both sentences.

8  Why did some airlines continue flying propeller planes long after more economical and better-performing jet-driven planes were available? Because of lack of competition among airlines?

9  Output has at least two dimensions. What two have a bearing on total costs of some output programs?

10  A firm plans to produce 2,000,000 cameras in the next six months. What is the volume and what is the rate of output?

11  If that rate is continued for one year, what will be the volume?

12  What happens to total cost of production for larger volumes of planned output?

13  What happens to total cost as the rate or speed of output is made larger, while the volume is kept constant?

14  What happens to average cost per unit of volume for larger planned volumes with unchanged rates of output?

15    What happens to average cost per unit of volume for larger rates of output with constant volume?

16    What is the behavior of marginal cost as a function of volume (for a fixed rate of output)?

17    What is the behavior of marginal cost as a function of rate of output for a fixed volume of output?

18    Are the answers to the preceding questions implied by comparative advantage and efficient means of production?

19    One of the first things an economist learns is to distinguish between total, average, and marginal cost. What are the differences?

20    If it were illegal to sell automobiles outside the state in which they were made, would cars be cheaper or more expensive in the United States? Give two reasons for your answer.

21    Why do manufacturers produce a few standardized models rather than a much larger variety of custom-made, custom-designed models?

22    Give some examples, if you can, of average costs being lower with large-volume production. Can you cite from personal memory the price history of television sets, transistor radios, surfboards, aluminum, penicillin, Polaroid cameras, ball-point pens?

23    Telephone a local printing company and ask the price for 100 letterheads on bond paper. Also get a price for 10,000 letterheads. Which has the lower cost per unit? Ask for the expected delivery date. Then ask how much it would cost to get the letterheads in half that time—even if it means setting up a night shift and overtime work. What do you expect will happen to the quoted price?

24    Ask a local building contractor to build a garage at your residence. After getting his price, see what he charges if you insist on getting it in half the promised time. Also ask how much he would charge if you want five garages. Do you predict it will be five times as much?

25    The British Aircraft Corporation manufactures a two-engined jet plane for intermediate-distance flights. Airlines are quoted a price of $2,500,000 with delivery in one year. What do you predict the price would be if you requested to have one delivered in six months? Do you think there would be any connection between the price of quicker delivery and the price you would have to pay to buy such a plane from someone who already has one—for example, from Braniff Air Lines?

26    If a business firm finds its selling price and output so related that larger output is associated with lower selling price, is this an indication that it has lower costs with larger volume or that the demand is such that more can be sold only if the price is lower?

27    Do you know of any products that have become more expensive over

the past several decades or centuries because of the exhaustion of cheaper ores or resources from which that product is obtained? (One answer is "oysters.") Is it true for copper, iron, oil, tin, diamonds, coal?

28    Give some examples of how the selected technique of production will depend upon the *volume* to be produced. For example, what about methods of producing letterheads, cookies, holes for fence posts, dresses, airplanes?

29    Give some examples of goods for which you think the selected technique of production will depend upon the *rate* at which items are produced—for fixed volume.

30    Heat and light are joint products of an electric light bulb that uses electric power at the rate of 1,000 watts. In one hour the cost of the power is 5 cents.
a. How much does the light cost? How much does the heat cost? How much do the light and the heat together cost?
b. If you were selling the heat to someone, how much would you charge him? And if, at the same time, you were selling the light to someone else, how much would you charge him?
c. Suppose that you are getting 4 cents for the light and 2 cents for the heat. You discover a new light bulb that gives more light and less heat, but this costs 6 cents per hour to operate. You can sell the extra light for 3 cents more, but you get a total of only 1 cent for the available heat. Should you use the new device? (Forget the cost of the new bulb—to simplify the arithmetic.)
d. But now the *light* buyer complains that you are charging him a total of 7 cents, which is more than enough to cover all the costs, while formerly you charged him only 4 cents, which did not cover the whole costs. He contends that the price should be lower and that the buyer of heat should pay part of the costs. What is your reply?
e. Having told him to take it or leave it, you find he leaves it! Why? (Answer: Because someone else can duplicate your service and charge him a lower price to get his business. The price will, with open markets, be cut to the point that total receipts from the joint products are just sufficient to cover the cost of production. And the total amount produced will be of such size that another joint increment would not bring in quite enough new receipts to cover the marginal cost of producing that joint increment of output.)

31    Meat, wool, and hides are joint products of sheep.
a. What assurance do you have that the prices paid for meat, for wool, and for sheepskin are just adequate to cover their cost of production?
b. What assurance do you have that meat users are not paying a disproportionate share of the common costs?

32    Your car will depreciate by $500, we shall assume, regardless of whether you use it for recreation or business, and regardless of whether

you drive it 5,000 or 10,000 miles. Each mile you drive it, you will also pay 8 cents for gasoline, oil, tires, repair, etc. (not counting the depreciation). If you drive the car 10,000 miles, the depreciation cost amounts to $500/10,000 = 5 cents per mile. If you drive it 5,000 miles, the depreciation cost is 10 cents a mile. Suppose you drive it 5,000 miles for recreation and 5,000 miles for business.

a. What is the cost for the recreation mileage, and what is the cost for the business mileage?

b. Should you allocate half of the depreciation to the recreation?

33  "The price of a new organic chemical depends on how badly it is wanted—precisely as conceived by classical economic theory, except for reversal of direction. The bigger the demand, the lower the price. A 1000-lb-per-day process operates more efficiently than a 1000-lb-per-month process—which is obvious to you but wasn't to Adam Smith. Old Adam set down the rules for our game in ignorance of elementary chemical engineering and advanced advertising." Quote from an advertisement for Eastman Kodak Co., *Scientific American*, May 1964, page 57. Explain wherein apparently even the ad writers for Eastman Kodak are doubly confused—on both the demand- and the supply-function side.

34  Gasoline price "wars" are not uncommon in cities near refineries. Why are these price changes more common near the sites of refineries? (Hint: gasoline, kerosene, fuel oil, and other distillates are obtained by refining crude oil. Although the proportions in which these joint products are yielded are not constant, it is relatively expensive to alter the proportions significantly or to store gasoline at refineries. Suppose the demand for fuel oil increases and that more crude oil is refined to meet the demand. What happens to the output of the other joint products? To their prices? Who will store the extra gasoline?)

# The Business Firm and Profits

Production is organized and controlled through the medium of the business firm. An owner or manager tells employees what to do; he decides what to produce and how and in what amounts. An analysis of the organization of production must account for business firms, employer-employee relationships, giant modern corporations, unions and banks, etc. In this chapter, we shall investigate the business firm, its reason for existence, its formal structure, and means of assessing how well it accomplishes its purposes.

As we shall show, none of the realistic business elements introduced in this chapter changes the analysis. Businesses are basically means of economizing on contractual, exchange, and communication costs. They do not constitute a different system of production control. Unless one can see through this realistic facade, he may confound means of communication and contracting with the underlying principles of control of production.

## Why Do Business Firms Exist?

Business firms are the agencies used to organize resources to produce in response to competitive market guides. In a market economy, they respond to market prices and demands and produce the kinds of products that the public deems more valuable than others that could have been produced. Every society relies on business firms; economies differ in how it is decided which firms can exist, which people will have what roles in the firm, what incentives will be used to reward and guide each member of the firm, and what signals and information will guide production.

Is the existence of a business firm really consistent with market-exchange principles outlined earlier? Why don't people in the firm individually engage in direct market exchange? If resources are directed and coordinated by prices and market exchange without conscious direction, then why are centrally directed organizations—business firms with employers and employees—in existence? Why are there "islands of conscious power in this ocean of unconscious cooperation like lumps of butter coagulating in a pail of buttermilk"?[1]

### Imperfect Foresight and Contracting

We would be at a loss for an answer, if there were no uncertainty about the future and no costs of renegotiating contracts. If we could foresee the future perfectly, we could make long-term contracts with other people, laying out once and for all the exchanges that will be made with each person. Each "employee" could be a separate business contractor who makes one long-

---

[1] D. H. Robertson, *Control of Industry* (Cambridge: Nisbet & Co., 1923), p. 85.

lived contract with what would otherwise be called his employer, agreeing to perform certain well specified services in the future in return for pay-ment—just as a house builder does for his client. There would be buyers and sellers, but no employers and employees, and no business firms—just large marketplaces. An automobile assembly line would be one large market, with each person on the assembly line buying goods from the person on his left, processing the good, and selling to the person on the right and so on down the line until the last assembler sells the completed car to the seller of the car. No employers, no employees, just independent specialists engaged in their specialities. But since contract renegotiation and record keeping costs are substantial, and since uncertainty prevents one from knowing what the buyer wants to buy now and in the indefinite future, we agree to a more flexible, less-specific performance contract. Two people agree that the first will pay the second a specific amount (wage) for the life of the contract, and the second will provide any of a range of services, leaving it to the first party to specify at each moment precisely what service he wants. The first person is called an employer and the second an employee. Calling the employer the boss is a custom derived from the fact that the "boss" specifies the particular task. One could have called the employee the boss because he orders the employer to pay him a specific sum if he wants services performed. But words are words.

### The Formal Legal Structure of Business Firms

Business firms commonly take one of three legal forms: individual proprietor-ship, partnership, or corporation. A proprietorship is owned by one person, who is also responsible for all debts of the firm to the full extent of whatever wealth he owns—that is, he has *unlimited liability*. A partnership is a joint proprietorship of two or more people, each of whom has unlimited liability for the entire firm and can individually make contracts binding the other partners. A corporation is a form of ownership usually with limited liability—that is, limited to each owner's existing financial investment in the firm. Almost always, several people share in the ownership of a corporation. One might have 30 percent of the ownership; his legal title would be evi-denced by ownership of 30 percent of the shares of "common stock"—each share denoting a minimal unit share of ownership. Corporate owners are called stockholders.

#### Features of Corporations

One might think that by mutual agreement a group of individuals could organize a corporation, issue common stock as evidence of owners' shares, and engage in business—just as one can with a proprietorship or partnership.

But historically the state has not recognized the right of people to form a corporate contract with others. In the United States, incorporation must first be authorized by state officials. In some instances, approval is pro forma; in others, substantial fees and conditions are imposed.

What are some of the distinctive features of corporations?

*Limited liability.*    Only the wealth in the corporation can be held as security or for payment of corporation debts. Other wealth of the owners cannot be legally attached for payment of liabilities in the event of bankruptcy. In England, the name of the corporation is usually followed by the abbreviation "Ltd." (Simpson, Ltd.), to indicate the corporate limited liability. Because of limited liability, lenders (creditors of the firm) may regard corporations (other things being the same) as higher risks and thus charge them higher rates of interest; but limited liability is so attractive from the investor's standpoint that corporations usually have less difficulty in collecting large sums to finance ventures.

Prior to public sale of corporation stock, approval must be received from a state regulatory agency as well as a federal agency called the Securities and Exchange Commission. To obtain that approval, the corporation must reveal about its assets and liabilities certain information that might be useful to any prudent investor. But if the regulatory commission thinks the corporation is not "strong enough," it can in some states prohibit existing owners from selling stock to other people.

*Continuity.*    Death or selling out to a new owner by any stockholder does not terminate a corporation's existence, as it does a partnership and proprietorship. Corporate continuity is achieved by the right of the owners to transfer their shares by sale, gift, or inheritance without permission of the other current owners; in a partnership, permission must first be obtained. Sales and purchases of shares of stock of many large, widely owned corporations are usually negotiated in a stock market, a formal marketplace where shares of certain corporations are publicly listed and sold by brokers. Less well-known corporation shares are sold so infrequently that they are not listed on the formal stock exchanges. These lesser-known corporation shares are bought and sold by private negotiation through a dispersed set of independent stock-brokerage agencies known as the "over-the-counter" market.

*Capital accumulation.*    Relatively large amounts of capital can be accumulated if many individuals each contribute portions of the total investment in some venture. Given limited liability, continuity, and the transferability of shares of ownership, it is not surprising that the corporate form of enterprise thrives as an institution for financing more expensive or riskier production ventures.

Because of these advantages, the corporate form of doing business manages to grow despite special burdens imposed by law. For one thing, it is taxed more heavily probably because corporation taxes do not alienate as many voters as do some other forms of taxation. Nearly one fourth of the federal tax receipts are from taxes on the corporate form of business. About 50 percent of corporate net earnings (over $25,000) is taxed away by a special tax not levied on the earnings of other forms of business.

*Ownership and control.*    Stockholders elect directors on a one-vote-per-share basis. Directors are authorized to make contracts (that is, to conduct the business) in the name of the corporation. Stockholders who own only a small portion of the shares individually have an insignificant effect on the voting outcome. In fact, in many large corporations no single owner owns a majority of stock. Hence, it is said that directors, in effect, control the wealth of the corporation (while stockholders bear the ultimate risk of changes in the value of the corporation). This kind of statement is easy to make but harder to interpret and still harder to substantiate. Is it true that only a portion or even a minority of the shareholders (the director-managers) run the corporation while the rest of the shareholders hold the bag? This has certainly been a common interpretation. However, a little thought may suggest a different interpretation. Many people want to invest wealth in ventures operated by especially skilled persons and to share in the profits. The resources they provide enable skilled managers to operate on a larger scale; in turn, the stockholders bear the value changes in those resources, freeing the managers from those risks. Whether one calls this "holding the bag" or "submitting to control of others" or "being duped by those who use your money" or "investing in resources" is largely a matter of words.

There *are* conflicts of interest within the corporate structure, but this is true for every group. The diffused ownership and the large size of the corporation raises to each stockholder the costs of policing the corporation's internal management as thoroughly and effectively as in a small proprietorship. This is similar to the case of the taxpayer, whose cost of policing government employees relative to the gain he thereby achieves is ludicrously high. However, the corporation shareholder, in contrast to a taxpayer, has a salable right in the capital value, changes in which will thrust upon him more fully the gains or losses of his employees' behavior. The relatively lower price of shares of inefficiently managed corporations serves as an inducement to replace current inefficient managers with more efficient ones. The subsequent rise in stock values gives an immediate gain to the shareholders. The advantages of the corporate form are sufficiently great to have yielded a great growth in the relative number and wealth of corporations in the past century. Neither theory nor fact supports the belief that widely dispersed stock ownership in corporations enables managers to act with small regard to stockholder interest.

### The Population of Business Firms

In sales value of output, the corporation, with approximately 65 to 75 percent of the total, is by far the dominant form in the United States. Proprietorships account for about 15 to 20 percent. But in numbers of business firms, the proportions are almost reversed. Almost half of the five million business firms are in (wholesaling and retailing) proprietorships. If we include agricultural and professional activity, the number of firms would be larger by about another five million, most of which are unincorporated proprietorships. The largest ten corporations have from 100 to 600 thousand employees each. The one hundred largest industrial corporations employ almost six million people, or about 10 percent of all employees. The top fifty each have over a billion dollars in sales annually, with assets of about the same value.[2] Often, when hearing that the size of business firms today is much larger than thirty years ago, we are tempted to conclude that it is harder to organize a new business. In fact, however, people are getting wealthier, so that organizing a $50,000 fund of capital for an initial business venture is probably easier than getting $10,000 fifty years ago. Each year for the past fifty years, new firms have been organized at a ratio of about one for each ten existing firms.

Of new firms, half die in five to ten years. Relatively large size may not *cause* or *assure* success; larger size may be a *result* of efficient operation. Bigger firms are more efficient because efficiency increases the growth rate, while the inefficient are killed off before they can grow large or get old. And small, new firms are not necessarily handicapped compared to big, old firms; newcomers *can* and do effectively compete and grow faster than bigger, older firms, but they will need phenomenal growth rates for a long time to surpass some of the giants.

A few hundred large corporations produce nearly half the total value of industrial output. But the significance of that fact is not entirely clear. General Motors buys from thousands of smaller firms; when all these products are assembled in a Chevrolet, it can be said that General Motors produced the Chevrolet; yet, thousands of firms were involved in providing parts and equipment to that giant assembly line known as General Motors. If we count only the last assembler, then we can say that General Motors "produces" 50 percent of the cars. If we count all of its suppliers, then over one thousand firms "produce" half of the cars. Does General Motors "dominate" the automobile industry in the sense of setting prices, styles, quality, and employment policies for other producers, or merely in the share of cars produced? Is General Motors less responsive to consumer demands than if there were several firms in place of one General Motors? Does General Motors' "dominance" mean that its employees are paid lower wages? Or that improvements occur less often? Or that General Motors' decisions about its production play a bigger role in affecting the economy than if there were a hundred firms replacing it? The answers to some of these questions will be suggested in the succeeding analysis. For the moment we note that the corporate form of business organization is far and away the major form and that some corporations are of enormous size.

[2] General Motors has nearly $20 billions in sales, followed by A.T.&T., Standard Oil (N.J.), Ford, General Electric, Socony Mobil, Chrysler, U.S. Steel, A. and P. Stores, and International Business Machines.

Profits and Business Firms

As mentioned earlier, business firms exist primarily as a means of increasing wealth (and thereby utility) by production and exchange. The firm sells its products and obtains receipts. If these exceed costs, the firm is said to have realized an increase in wealth—to have made a profit.

Revenues and Profits

I hope to have sales receipts or revenue from the use of a car if I operate it as a taxi for 20,000 miles in two years. The wage I would have earned at some other job is estimated at $4,000 per year. Suppose I believe I shall obtain, in the taxi business, sales of $6,500 in the first year and $5,500 in the second year, with the receipts presumed to come at the end of the year—on a credit-card system.

Collecting all estimated expenditure and receipt data in Table 15–1, where each column lists the receipts (+) and expenditures (–) as of January 1, 1970, January 1, 1971, and January 1, 1972, we estimate the aggregate profit collected over the two years as $2,450 and the *present* value (at 10 percent interest) of the business as $1,833, computed as follows.

The cost of the taxi service, *including* the foregone wages, is $8,619—the present value of the two annual $4,000 outlays ($6,940) added to the $1,679 present-value cost of owning and using the car. The present value of the sales receipts, or revenue for each year ($6,500 and $5,500), is $10,452, which exceeds the cost by $1,833 ($10,452 – $8,619). My wealth will be $1,833 larger if I buy and operate the taxi service for the next two years than if I work for wages of $4,000 per year. My *profits* in the taxi business will be $1,833.

We can clarify the deeper meaning of these results by assuming that on the first day of operating the taxi, business is so good that people perceive what a splendid idea I had. Suppose, for reasons we shall investigate later, it will be two years before other people enter competition sufficiently to eliminate subsequent net earnings. But anyone who wants to enter the business immediately can buy the business from me. The total resources in the business the day of opening consist of the car and the prepaid tax and insurance for the rest of the first year; these total $2,100. The present value of all the assets of the business is now $3,933, which is equal to the capital value of profits ($1,833) plus the initial investment. I invested $2,100 and I find my wealth is now $3,933, a profit of $1,833.

If I had incorporated the taxi company and held stock in it, the stock price would have risen. For example, if I had issued 100 shares of stock for the $2,100 to raise the money to buy a car and pay the first year's tax and insurance, the value of each share initially would have been $21. Now, upon perception of what the future promises, the price of the stock rises to $39.33, for a profit of $18.33 per share.

Table 15-1
Receipts and Expenditures of Taxi Business

|  | 1/1/1970 | 1/1/1971 | 1/1/1972 |
|---|---|---|---|
| Purchase of car | -$2,000 | | |
| Tax, insurance | -    100 | -$   100 | |
| Operating and repair | | -    300 | -$   350 |
| Wages and salary | | -  4,000 | -  4,000 |
| Receipts | | +  6,500 | +  5,500 |
| Sale of car | | | +  1,300 |
| Net receipts | -$2,100 | +$2,100 | +$2,450 |
| Present-value factor (10%) | (1.000) | (.909) | (.826) |
| Profit (capital value) $1,833 = | -$2,100 | +$1,909 | +$2,024 |

Expenditures in each year (assumed to be payable at end of each year) are indicated as negative numbers; receipts are indicated by positive numbers. Net expenditures (or receipts) are converted to a present value at 10 percent annual rate of interest by multiplying by discount factor shown in parentheses in next to last line. Sequence of expenditures shown here produces a receipt sequence whose present value exceeds that of the expenditures by $1,833—the profit of this venture.

*"Paper profits?"* When the higher market value is revealed, my wealth is higher. I have at that moment realized a profit. Although people often call this profit a "paper profit" because I have not yet "cashed" it, it *is* a genuine increase in my wealth. The only question is whether to convert the form of the greater wealth into other assets or whether to keep it in the present form of business assets.

Alternative Measures of Profits:
Wealth or Income Changes

Measuring profit as an unforeseen change in wealth is perhaps not as common as measuring profit as a change in the income stream. The wealth increase of $1,833, the profit, can be reinterpreted as an increase in the flow of income. Thus a wealth increase of $1,833 is equivalent (at 10 percent interest) to an increase of $183 in annual income. One could say his profits (in income terms) are $183 a year in perpetuity, meaning that income is larger by that amount for every year than it otherwise would have been.

Business firms usually report profit as an increase in the income stream during the production program, rather than as either a change in wealth in capital-value units or a perpetuity flow. Business firms use the expression "net earnings" or "net income" as the estimated change of income. In our taxi example, the firm might report as profits $1,531 in the first year and $531 in the second year—a two-year annuity. This is computed as follows.

The cost of providing the car service is $1,679, which, converted to a two-year annuity, is equivalent to $969 each year (at 10 percent rate of interest).

To that $969 we must add the labor costs of $4,000 each year, giving an annual *rate* of cost of $4,969 per year in which the service is a uniform 10,000 miles annually. The receipts in the first year from the taxi business (shown in Table 15-1) are $6,500 and $5,500 in the second, giving net earnings over costs of $1,531 in the first year and $531 in the second. These are the net "earnings." Incidentally, you should be able to verify that the present value of the two-year stream of net "earnings" is (at 10 percent interest) equal to $1,833, our wealth measure of profit.

We now have three ways to express or measure profits: (1) a capital-value *wealth*-change measure ($1,833);[3] (2) an increase in *perpetuity income* flow ($183 per year); and (3) a net earnings flow *during the production program*, varying with the sales value of service provided in each year ($1,531 and $531). All three have the same present value at 10 percent interest and are merely different ways to express the same phenomenon—an increase in a person's wealth.

Of these three gages of wealth changes, only the capital-value (wealth) measure is directly measurable in the market. The current price of any resource is the measure of its present value. Therefore, if upon opening a taxi business I were to solicit bids for its sale, the price I could get would be a measure of the wealth value of profits. If other people now appreciate the possibilities and estimate them consistently with our data, the market value of the business will have jumped by $1,833.

Business accountants would report, as the profits and net earnings of each period, the amounts of $1,531 and $531, if the events materialized as predicted and if they reckon $4,000 each year as the implicit wages of my own time—as we did in our numerical calculations. However, accountants do not always enter a cost item for the time of the owner. Failing that, the accountant's reported "net earnings" (*not* counting my implicit wages in costs) would be reported as $5,531 and $4,531. This differs from what we call profit because it includes a foreseeable imputed value of my labor services.

*Accounting records of earnings:*    Business accounting records are designed to keep a clear record of the company's financial activities, such as the amounts of money spent or committed to future payment, and the goods and services obtained in exchange. A record is kept of actual expenditures and receipts, but *not* of all the foreseen and predictable receipts and expenditures. More accurately, although all past expenditures and receipts are accounted for, only *some* of the future commitments for expenditure and foreseeable future receipts are included in the accounts. Noncontractual future receipts or expenditures are excluded. To see why accountants have been led to exclude noncontractual *prospects* of future receipts and expenditures from their valuation processes and data, consider the following example.

---

[3] Tax authorities usually call this a "capital gain or loss," when it is converted to cash by a sale.

Starting with $31,000, I buy some land and oil drilling equipment and pay wages during the year to the drill workers. Suppose in six months we strike oil. What should our accountant do? Should he record the present value of the oil, which as yet is an unknown amount, uncaptured and unsold? If the market offers me $100,000 for that oil land, then, whether or not I sell, my wealth has increased to $100,000 plus the resale value of the drilling equipment, which we shall assume is now $6,000 (down $4,000 from its initial price of $10,000). My wealth totals to $106,000 and since I have no liabilities, my wealth gain, my profit, is $75,000. ($106,000 − $31,000.)

The accounting records say we *lost* $24,000 during the year! (We used up $4,000 of oil-well equipment and $20,000 for wages and related services and have sold no oil.) Why is the accountant unwilling to record a value on the amount to be received from the future oil sales? Because it is not yet a legally obligated future receipt.

If the oil reservoir is to be valued, he could say that we spent $24,000 to find it. This $24,000 is the "book" value of the oil reservoir. As long as we know the convention, we can ignore it when deciding what we think the company is worth. But if we didn't know the convention, we might think the $24,000 represented an estimate of what the oil field is worth on the market. The alternative accounting convention is that of not recording any value at all, or a formal $1, until there is a clear-cut market for that asset, in which its value can be and *has been* measured by actual sales.

The zero or $1 value procedure is adopted frequently when the asset is not a physical tangible thing but an idea, design, patent, new product, trademark, or personality. A reliable product built the name "Kodak" so much that the name "Kodak" serves as a symbol of reliability, thereby attracting sales. How should that asset, the name "Kodak," be valued? At the advertising costs? At zero? Or at some estimated value? Convention prefers the zero value, false though that figure may be.

Earlier, we commented that the accountant usually ignores the implicit $4,000 annual wages that I, as owner, could have earned if I did not operate the taxi business. You can now see why the accountant does so. How would anyone know that the accountant is reporting an unbiased estimate rather than a figure to make the net earnings look good or bad as suits his whim?

Regardless of what the accountant does, *we* must not take his final figure for "profits or net earnings" to be a measure of the actual change in value of wealth. We must recognize that the prospect of future sales is an integral part of the value of a good. The local grocer has absolutely no assurance or guarantee that he will sell any goods next year. No retailer or manufacturer has any warranty that the public will continue to buy his product. He has no contract or commitment with consumers in which consumers bind themselves to future purchases. And yet we can be "sure" that sales will occur. To be "sure" means only that we are prepared to "bet" on it. I am prepared to bet that the local grocer will have lots of sales next year, and I am prepared to back my bet by *buying* some share of ownership (common stock) in that grocery. I pay for (bet on) the *prospect* of successful future operations. In fact, the value of almost *every* good rests on a present bet about *prospects*.

The present price or value rarely rests on a contract for future sales. About the only commodity for which there is legal commitment of that nature is a debt contract (bond) or money which can be so used for the legal payment of debts.

*Profits are unpredictable increases.*    A principal point of this discussion is that the wealth value of a business depends upon the expectations of the future, not simply on how much was paid in the past to create the particular assets. One reason that reports by business firms of annual net earnings or profits are so important is that they serve as an indicator of the extent to which earlier forecasts are being fulfilled. For example, business firms with rapid growth rates, like International Business Machines and Xerox, have a present price of their stock (wealth) that is nearly one hundred times greater than the annual reported net earnings. The average of most firms is about ten to twenty times current earnings. The market expects the future net earnings to increase rapidly, and the high present price of the stock relative to *current* net earnings reflects that future growth expectation. Those future net earnings are capitalized into current values of assets—that is, stock prices. Other companies (for example, U.S. Steel) have prices for their common stocks only five to fifteen times as great as current annual net earnings. If the reported net earnings for IBM in any year should merely equal the prior year's, instead of being 10 to 25 percent higher, the price of IBM stock will fall. If earnings fail to increase, expectations are disappointed and revised downward. On the other hand, if the net earnings of U.S. Steel are reported as unchanged from a prior year, the price of U.S. Steel stock will not fall—that is, the expectation that U.S. Steel does *not* have substantial growth facing it will not be upset. Evidence for these statements of fact is available from the behavior of stock-market prices.

These examples provide a good opportunity to explain another much misunderstood term, "watered" stock. Suppose that on the day I started my taxi business with the $2,100 investment, I offered to sell you one of the one hundred shares of stock in the company for $30. At first, you might think I was selling you something worth only $21. You might say I was selling you a share at an inflated value or that the stock was "watered." In fact, however, the share of taxi stock is worth more than $30, if the foresight we have is accurate. For this reason, investors often pay more for a share of stock than the costs of the resources in the business. What they are buying is part of the higher value of those resources—the profits. As long as you can get a share of my taxi stock for less than $39.33, you will have made a profit, too—assuming we have forecast future events accurately.

### Fundamental Sources of Profits

Because foresight is imperfect, unforeseen changes in market values will inevitably occur; profits and losses will be realized. Profits and losses occur in all economic systems. A change from a capitalistic to a communist or socialist or feudal society will not even hide them. It will only change the determination of who bears the profits and losses. Only if uncertainty is eliminated will the situation be different; and in all probability no earthly revolution will remove uncertainty.

It is convenient for subsequent analysis to group the sources of uncertainty into two polar classes: extraneous, uncontrollable events and deliberate innovative activity by resource owners.

*Extraneous events.*   Changes in demand serve as an excellent example of extraneous, uncontrollable events. For example, the value and usefulness of a dress or suit of clothes falls because of changes in styles. You may think a dress will still keep the wearer as neat, warm, and modest as ever, but the dress simply does not give all the usefulness it formerly did. It no longer gives a feeling of stylishness, attractiveness, or sense of belonging. And neither you nor I can say that these are irrelevant, superficial attributes that shouldn't count. The simple fact is that they do.

Some of us may think that "basic" values really do not change; we may think that people so concerned with style are extravagant and that the prices of their clothes, for example, bear little relationship to "real" values. We have every right to *say* that, but we should realize that we are saying we know better than other people what the properly desired things are in this world and, therefore, the market values that reflect *their* preferences are not proper values. And if people shift their preferences unpredictably, values will change unpredictably, with profits or losses as the result.

*Innovative activity.*   The other source of profits or losses is deliberate innovative activity, in which owners try to use resources in ways not heretofore evaluated by the community. Their hope, ambition, gamble, or speculation is that their wealth will be more highly valued by the market after innovation. Anyone who seeks to do this must have some control over some resources, the value changes in which will accrue to him. While he is the owner, *any change* in value of resources, regardless of the cause, will have to be borne by him, at least according to laws of ownership and responsibility in a private-property economy.

If I increase the value of a house by painting it, so that the new house value is equal to the former value plus that of the paint and labor, then the change in value is merely the sum of the former values of a changed set of goods. But if the value of some newly combined set of resources is greater than the sum of their former values, there is a profit, an *unexpected increase in value*.

Deliberate innovative activity can lead to profits. For this reason it is often said that the prospects of profits serve as a motivating force for innovative activity. Yet one man's innovation and resultant profits may cause a loss to another man. For example, the invention of the automobile reduced the value of buggy whips, and the innovation of television reduced the value of theater buildings. The loss in value of the theater building is more than offset by the gain from television. But the theater owner who bears that loss, if he is not somehow compensated, is no better off than if a fire damaged the theater. When losses are the result of improvement elsewhere, is the bearer of this loss compensated, even if in principle it were possible to do so? As we shall see, in every social and economic system the answer is "No." Still another question is whether or not one should try to compensate him; but that is a question of normative policy, and we shall postpone it.

### Profits, Ownership, and Management

Although he may hire a manager to run his business, the owner still owns the resources and still bears profits or losses. The owner may seem to be passive, abiding by the manager's decisions and advice; yet the so-called "passive" owner is the one who has decided to permit this use of his resources. And even though the manager makes all the decisions after the owner decides to submit his wealth to the venture, and even though the manager seems to be doing all the work, the owner still bears the wealth consequences.

If an owner operates his business as his own manager, he counts wages for his labor services. Some owner-managers make the mistake of combining into one total their wages of management and their profit—calling the whole thing "profit" or calling it all "wages." In the earlier taxi example, in which profit was $1,833, wages for driving the cab (and let us assume also for managing the firm) were $4,000. The former is profit, a value change in wealth; the latter is annual wages or payment for labor services. To call them both either profit or management wages would be to mix two different economic concepts. However, in the language of the layman, you will often find this confusing practice. You will, in each instance, simply have to reinterpret the situation for yourself, if you want to keep your analysis consistent.

### Profits of Labor

A distinction between profits and wages of management, or between profits and wages in general, does not mean that labor or personal service is not a source of wealth to a person. Wages are payments or receipts going to a person for his personal services, while "rent" is the name for the payment to the owner of inanimate goods. Both a flow of wages and of rentals has present values (wealth), reflecting anticipated future receipts. The present value of my flow of future wages may be $200,000. If I have an accident and fracture my skull, I will suffer a reduced prospective future series of receipts; and the present value of my wages will fall, say, to $150,000. The accident will cost me $50,000.

We see and measure profit of nonhuman wealth more clearly because inanimate goods can be bought and sold, whereas a person does not sell himself; he sells only the current services as they are performed. If he could literally sell his future services now, he could convert (or "cash in") his profit to other forms of wealth. But he cannot, and so he must keep more of his wealth in the form of his labor services. Even though there is no marketplace where a person can sell his future services now, he *can* borrow now against his future wages as we saw in Chapter 13.

In a sense, all profits—or values—are values of people rather than of inanimate goods. Goods are valuable only because of the way in which people use them. People with superior talents know how to use resources to make them more valuable. If, for example, General Motors hires a superior designer to design a car of greater value, the increased value shows up as a profit to General Motors. But if we keep our analysis correct, we must recognize that the designer was obtained for a salary less than his worth proved to be to GM. No one *knew*, in advance, just how valuable his services would be. GM had to accept the initially uncertain value of his services. GM's ability to hire him for less than his ultimately revealed worth reflected differences in opinion about that worth among General Motors, other potential employers, and the employee himself. GM cannot continue to purchase his services at less than they are revealed to be worth unless *all* other potential employers remain ignorant of his ability—and he will not let his ability stay hidden. The high value of his services will accrue to him as other employers bid for his work, driving up his wages and raising costs to all who thereafter use him.

None of this means that GM or any other employer makes profits by paying less for resources than they are worth. What resources are paid is what the rest of the market thinks they are worth *at the time* they are bought or hired. Always, too little is bet on the winner and too much on the losers. If anyone makes a profit, it follows, by definition, that the earlier value placed on the resource was too low. And losses result from earlier overvaluation.

### Profits, Losses, and Insurance

To avoid the risks of "losses" from physical damage (fire, flood, etc.) or theft, people "insure." Thereby, they modify the pattern of risks and incidence of losses. By joint voluntary insurance, people share losses by spreading them over the group, in the form of premium or insurance fees paid by each member. Out of these fees, compensation is paid to those who suffer the contingent misfortune. This pooling of risk of losses does not necessarily reduce the total losses. It spreads them over the insurees, as each one pays a fee for the insurance. The aggregate of the fees is (hopefully) enough to cover the losses incurred. In general, the insurance converts the risk of a possible large loss into the certainty of a small loss—the payment of the premium for the insurance.

Even though, as a condition of getting insurance, the insuring group may require that the insured take special precautions, the remaining precautionary incentives are reduced. Without insurance, we may devote more resources and care and anxiety to protection than with it. Nevertheless, even if total losses are greater with insurance than without (as they may well be), the savings in resource use and anxiety may be of greater value than the increase in losses.

Some losses are not insurable. For example, insurance by a retailer against bad business or loss of customers would mean (if such insurance were somehow available) that the retailer could try less hard to provide consumers with desirable products—relying on the insurance company to indemnify him for his laziness. The resultant claims for indemnifying the insurees against the "losses" will exceed the amount of wealth that the insurance company can get from voluntary insurees as premiums for insurance. For this reason, insurance on business failure because of loss of customers, or on crop failures for farmers, or on unemployment is not actuarily sound.

There are many other uninsurable hazards. For example, it seems you can't get insurance against having your oil well dry up, or *not* finding gold on your land, or having other people's tastes and demands shift against your services or goods, or against divorce, or against dull children, or against marital infidelity. And yet in a sense you can insure against some of these events. The risk of your oil well's drying up unexpectedly can be transferred to someone else. Just sell the asset to him and hold money. When you sell your oil-well land, you get the present value of that land as judged by other people on an expectational basis (weighing odds that it will dry up against odds that it won't). If the oil well does dry up, the buyer bears the loss.

In this way—by choosing not to hold certain goods—you can escape the hazards of loss of those goods (and chance of profit). In a private-property system, those losses or profits are imposed on the person who is the owner of the particular goods.

This redistribution of risks of loss is a form of insurance and is available in a private-property system, in which people can exchange ownership and choose which risks to bear. By shifting private-property rights to various goods and buying one kind of good rather than another, people can obtain "insurance" against certain kinds of risks and losses. More precisely, private property is not insurance in the sense that one takes a small but sure loss (premium) in order to avoid a large contingent loss; rather, it is a selective, discretionary, risk-bearing institution.

A rental arrangement is also a risk-shifting system. By renting a house on a month-to-month basis, instead of owning one, you can "own" only one month's value of the house and thereby avoid having so much of your wealth in a particular house. A renter will not suffer the entire loss of value of a house if its value changes. By renting those goods a person wants to use, he can diversify his ownership of goods or he can concentrate on one good, independently of his consumption patterns.

It is worth noting that in some countries farmers cannot sell the land they "own." They can use it for themselves or sell the crop for their own wealth, but they cannot sell the land or borrow against it as security. (If they could borrow against the land, they would borrow its current value and then let the lender take the land when they refuse to repay the loan—thus circumventing the intended ban on sale of the land.) This is a modified form of private-property rights, but it does not provide the extent of risk sharing and re-allocation that is provided by a system of full private-property rights. Obviously, the incentive to improve the land is weakened, since the risks of value changes cannot be shifted to those most willing to bear the risks of changes in the value of the land. A person who "owns" land under these restricted conditions will invest more of his wealth in forms of property with more transferable property rights. An implication of this analysis is. that people in backward countries (i.e., with these incomplete property rights) are less willing to invest in land.

Attitudes toward various systems of property rights should, in part, be based on attitudes toward the *way* they determine the distribution of profits and losses. Since profits and losses occur regardless of the form of property rights, the issue is not whether one is for or against profits and losses but whether one is for or against this or that system of distributing them over various people. Who shall bear the joy of profits and the despair of losses? Laws might be passed to impose losses on brunettes and profits upon blondes, by an appropriate system of taxes. Profits and losses could be owned by people as a whole, with each person's use rights determined by a lottery or his taxes or by his standing in line, as it is with public parks and rights to hunt deer in some states.

Profits and losses could be assigned by the political decision system, in which case the assignments will depend on one's power of affecting political decisions. Socialism is an example of this form of profit-and-loss risk-bearing system. Part of the issue between a capitalist and a socialist system is over the kind of risk-bearing mechanism or institution used. Under the capitalist private-property system, those who decide about the use of resources are more likely to be the ones to bear the effects of resulting value changes. As a result, under the private-property system the resources are more likely to be used where the profit potential is highest. But proponents of socialism believe that market values should not be so influential in determining resource uses and that individuals should not be able to specialize in bearing various kinds of risks.

### Profits, Monopoly Rents, and Changes in Monopoly Rights

Not every occurrence of profits reflects a transfer of resources from lower-valued to higher-valued uses. Suppose I managed to have a law passed preventing other people from producing goods that compete with mine. The reduced supply from a reduced number of competitors will raise the price of my goods, giving me a profit. This kind of profit can be created by the levying of special taxes on my competitors; for example, interstate tariffs on goods produced in other states that compete with mine in domestic sales.

The profit that results when greater restraint is placed on competitors' access to the market is called a "monopoly rent"—*monopoly* because of the legal restriction on market access—*rent* because it is not allowed to induce an increase in supply.

The legal-monopoly restriction on entry will raise the market valuation of assets already in the protected industry. The restriction prevents more resources from being transferred to higher-valued uses sufficiently to bring values down to costs. The result, from the consumers' point of view, is the same as would occur if costs were higher than they really are. The "privileged" or "licensed" resources earn their owners a higher value, while the excluded resources receive a lower value.

How much of the current value of a resource is "monopoly rent"? This is an interesting, important, but unanswered question. We have some estimates and evidence on tobacco acreage, ranging up to $3,000 for an acre of land on which tobacco can be grown and sold in the market without a special tax. This is nearly 50 percent of the total value of that acre of land. In New York City the monopoly rent of one taxi is over $20,000. In California the monopoly rent of a liquor license ranges from $10,000 to $40,000. In most states the present value of banks, insurance companies, airlines, and all public utilities reflects a monopoly rent of various amounts, depending upon the extent to which entry is restricted. Value also depends on the extent to which the monopoly rent is taxed away by the government, or prices are kept down by law so that the legal monopolists cannot realize the maximum market value of their monopoly situation.

We must be careful not to confuse monopolists in this situation with price-searchers, who are also called "monopolists" in the technical economic literature. Both are called monopolists because both face negative-sloping demand curves for their products. Almost all retailers and manufacturers, large and small, are "monopolists" in this technical sense because they face a negative-sloped demand curve for their products. We have in this book used the name "price-searchers" for such sellers who operate in *open* markets, where there are no restraints on entry. The reason for calling them "price-searchers" rather than "monopolists" is to avoid confusion between open and closed markets. There is nothing about price-searchers' markets to suggest monopoly rents resulting from protected competition. In a price-searchers' market, anyone can make a new kind of cornflake, and anyone can open another drugstore, but the fact that they will be facing negatively sloped demand curves for their products does not mean they can produce the product profitably. Anyone can be a monopolist with respect to some unique resource; but if the demand for the services of that unique resource is not high enough, he will have no wealth advantage. It is easy to identify many firms that are losing wealth despite a negatively sloping demand curve for their services. Yet folklore about the American economy would have us believe that the price-searcher firms make most of the profits.

Where does the myth arise? Probably from two sources. One is the failure to distinguish between the two types of monopoly. The second is the failure to distinguish between large and small firms, and even here the confusion is compounded by the notion that big firms make bigger profits because they are big, rather than that firms making big profits will become big firms. Being big is in itself no assurance of a higher probability of making profits. That, at least, is what economic theory indicates, and the evidence is consistent. It is easy to think that one can refute this evidence by pointing out a big firm like General Motors, which has earned profits in the capital-value sense during many years (and had losses during many years in that same sense). But some very large firms have lost wealth in many years (Chrysler, Ward's), and some very small firms have had spectacular growth (Litton, Scientific Data

Systems, Holiday Inns, Xerox, Control Data). The total evidence falls into the predicted pattern—namely, the probability that any firm will in the next interval of time experience a profit (unforeseen capital-value gain in its wealth) is the same for big and small firms, for price-takers and price-searchers, and even whether the resources of the firm have free or restricted access to the market. All the foreseeable events have been capitalized into the present valuations; only the unforeseen ones remain to be revealed. There is no way of knowing which firms will experience the new unpredictable favorable events.

The idea that it is possible to know which firm or class of firms is more likely to earn profits is self-defeating. If they were detectable in advance, then it would pay to buy the firms immediately, thus pushing up their values *now*. Consequently, any statement about which class of firms will in the future experience unusual wealth increases, as profits, is a statement with which the general public (and especially the wealth-holding portion of it) is in disagreement. It is in disagreement because the statement implies that there is today a class of firms whose assets or resources (stock prices) are systematically undervalued. If you know of that class, you have a good road to profits for yourself; but beware, for you are betting against the judgment of the rest of the community.

Other Definitions of Profits

*Difference between wholesale and retail price.*    "Profits" to the ordinary businessman do not always correspond exactly to "profits" as defined here, since no one has a copyright on the term "profit." The term is used for a wide variety of relationships between expenditures and receipts. Sometimes the difference between the price which a retailer pays for goods and the price at which he sells is called "profit." More normally, that difference is called "markup," as an indication of how much above the purchase price the selling price must be if all the other attendant costs are to be met. To ignore those other costs is to forget about space, shelter, management, sales clerks, inventory for display and immediate delivery, record-keeping, safeguarding, insurance, advertising, taxes, light, heat, fixtures, breakage, pilferage, packaging, returns, employee training, and many other costly activities. "Overhead costs" commonly refers to some of those costs. Some ignorantly say that a markup of 100 percent (of the wholesale purchase price, or 50 percent of the retail price) represents a profit of 100 percent—if he sells at that price. Even U.S. congressional reports have said so.

*Profits before taxes.*    Another error is to omit taxes as a cost and calculate "profits before taxes"—although allowing for all other costs. Remarkably, this concept was used by a government agency apparently unaware of its implications, for when it was initially presented no reference was made to profits *after* taxes. Does it not suggest that taxes are really not a part of costs—that they are payments for no service? It is difficult to believe that the government agency would want to suggest that taxes are merely tribute collected from those obtaining profits. One would hardly be more surprised if a labor union published a graph of "profits before wages" as if to assert, falsely, that wages are not a part of costs.

*Expected current losses.*   If you examine the annual reports of business firms, you will find assertions like: "We have started production on a very promising new product and are currently operating at a loss, but we expect that in a year we shall be covering costs and making profits." If that statement were taken literally, one would wonder why they hadn't waited until next year to start operations. In our terms what was meant is: "At the present time the rate of receipts is less than current expenditures, but the present outlays will bring larger future receipts that exceed future outlays. We believe the new product will promise a net flow of actual receipts in the future that will increase our wealth. In fact, the investing public is now of the same opinion, and that is why the market value of our shares of common stock has increased during the current year, so we have really had a profit. Hooray!"

*The quick pay-off period.*   "It takes three years for us to recover our investment before we can start making a profit." This type of statement, implying some "payout" or "cost-recovery" period, means merely that money outlays exceed the money receipts during the first three years and that only in the fourth year do total receipts begin to overtake the total expenditures. But who cares; the important thing is that the *present wealth value* of the receipts should exceed that of the outlays. To worry or be concerned about the length of that period is to be worried about whether or not the expected or hoped-for receipts will really materialize. The virtue of a short "payout" or "recovery" period is that it reduces the time one has to wait to find out whether the new venture really does as well as hoped.

## Summary

1    Business firms are groups of people jointly seeking to increase their wealth by producing goods and services for consumption by other people.

2    Within a firm the managers direct the activities of other people; there is no immediate market for exchange of services.

3    The most desirable specific future services are uncertain, and repeated recontracting for services is costly. The result is single contracts specifying general classes of services to be provided at a constant price—the wage. This is known as an employer-employee contract.

4    Large stocks of capital equipment typically found in business firms are not the essential distinctive characteristic of firms, nor is the form of ownership or risk bearing.

5     A proprietorship has one owner responsible for all liabilities to the full extent of his wealth—that is, he has unlimited liability. Partnerships have more than one owner, each of whom is authorized to act for the partnership, and each of whom has unlimited liability. Corporations can have several or many owners, each with no liability; ownership is divided into "shares," with decisions and contacts being made for the corporation by elected officers. Corporations, in contrast to proprietorships and partnerships, have continued life in the event of the death of an owner or of transfer of ownership.

6     Formation of corporation usually requires, by law, authorization from the state. Limited liability of a corporation facilitates large investment ventures. The corporate form enables investors to specialize in the skills of managers and directors; there is separation of management and ownership. The largest business firms are corporations. Corporations account for over two-thirds of the total value of market output, but they comprise only about one-fifth the total numbers of business enterprises.

7     Close to 1,000,000 business ventures are opened each year; about half do not survive three years.

8     Profits, the unforeseen changes in wealth, can be re-expressed as equivalent-valued annual flows, as they almost always are. Attempts to prorate the profit over the output stream usually are expressed as "net earnings" of the period. Profits, once they occur as an increased value of assets, are capitalized into higher costs of subsequent operations. All assets, human and nonhuman, obtain profits (or losses), but the existence of a market for selling the assets facilitates measurement of the profits (or losses).

9     Insurance, a pooling of risks and sharing of profits or losses, does not in itself change the total of profits or losses.

10     Private property enables risk re-allocation and specialization in risk bearing.

11     Closing or restricting markets enables incumbents (with access to the market) to obtain a larger market value for the services of their assets. This increase is monopoly rent.

12     The term "profits" is commonly used to cover many other concepts distinct from "profits" in economics.

Questions

1     The purpose of this question is to explain how to interpret business financial statements. Most business firms periodically (commonly every

three or six months and annually) issue financial reports of their activities and current status. Reproduced below is a slightly modified (for teaching purposes) balance sheet reported for the United Nuclear Corporation for March 31, 1966. A balance sheet presents a listing and valuation, according to the company's books, of its assets, liabilities, and ownership structure. Assets, as we know, are the property rights owned and used by this corporation. The net (of liabilities) rights of the owners to these assets are called proprietorship, capital, equity, or net worth. If there were no outsiders with legal claims against the assets, the net worth of the ownership would be equal to the total assets. However, there are always claims held by other people against a business; these claims are called liabilities. The basic identity is

$$\text{Assets} - \text{Liabilities} = \text{Equity},$$

which can be rewritten

$$\text{Assets} = \text{Liabilities} + \text{Equity}.$$

The firm's situation is then presented in the form of a balance sheet, with items classified as assets, liabilities, and equity. What do these items mean?

UNITED NUCLEAR CORPORATION
Balance Sheet, March 31, 1966
(in Thousands of Dollars)

| Assets | | Liabilities | |
|---|---|---|---|
| *Current* | | *Current* | |
| Cash | $ 3,115 | Accounts payable | $ 2,803 |
| Receivables | 3,599 | Notes payable | 6,317 |
| Reserve for bad debts | −100 | Accrued liabilities | 4,052 |
| Unbilled costs | 3,018 | Current liabilities | 13,172 |
| Inventories | 21,494 | | |
| Prepaid expenses | 500 | | |
| Current assets | 31,626 | *Long-Term* | |
| | | Long-term debt | 22,957 |
| | | Minority interest | 5,248 |
| *Long-Term* | | Long-Term liabilities | 28,205 |
| Investments | 779 | | |
| Government contracts | 2,887 | *Equity* | |
| Plant and Equipment | 46,884 | Preferred, convertible | |
| Less reserve for | | stock, 10,000 | |
| depreciation | −4,615 | shares (5%, $100) | 1,000 |
| Goodwill | 75 | Common stock ($.20 | |
| Long-term assets | 46,010 | par) 4,496,792 is- | |
| | | sued | 899 |
| | | Capital surplus | 23,211 |
| | | Retained earnings | 11,149 |
| | | | 36,259 |
| Total assets | $77,636 | Liability + equity | $77,636 |

## ASSETS

*Cash.* This is the amount of money held, including bank accounts.

*Receivables.* This records the amount of sales yet to be paid for by customers for the company's products. These are the charge accounts or credit extended to customers allowing them, usually, thirty days to pay.

*Reserve for bad debts.* Very likely some customers will fail to pay their debts when due. To express this fact and to estimate the expected amount of receivables that will become "bad," the accountants subtract an amount called a "Reserve for bad debts" or "Doubtful accounts." This is called a "reserve" because it expresses a "reservation" or "qualification" about the value of the receivables. Reserves in accounting statements do *not* represent collections of money or particular assets that have been reserved (in the sense of set aside) for some particular purpose. This balance sheet later shows "Reserves for depreciation," which is a way of expressing a reservation about the value of the assets. It represents the total depreciation so far accumulated; it is *not* a fund set aside for new equipment to replace the depreciation. As used in bookkeeping, the word *reserve* almost never denotes a setting aside or actual reserving of assets. It is almost always used to express explicitly a reservation or adjustment in the stated value of some asset or liability.

*Unbilled costs.* The corporation is making nuclear reactors to custom order; and, as a reactor is gradually completed, the corporation records the incurred costs as claims accruing against the customer, for which a bill will be submitted upon completion and delivery to the customer.

*Inventories.* The corporation also refines uranium ores. This is the value of the ore it has removed from its mines and has not yet sold, plus any other unsold products.

*Prepaid expenses.* The corporation has paid in advance for some goods and services yet to be delivered. These are rights against other people who have contracted to deliver goods and services for which the corporation has already paid. This is an asset. For example, when you prepay a magazine subscription, you would record that asset as a prepaid expense in your personal balance sheet.

*Investments.* The corporation has purchased stock in another company or some U.S. bonds. Usually, the particular investment is identified in information that accompanies the balance sheet.

*Plant and equipment.* This is the amount *paid* for the physical property—mines, mills, etc.—of the corporation. Sometimes this is recorded as the "cost of replacing" it, especially if there have been drastic changes in costs of this equipment since purchase.

*Reserve for depreciation.* The property, plant, and equipment have been used and partly worn out. An estimate of the portion of the plant so consumed is called "depreciation." Subtracting depreciation from the initial price gives the "book" value. (See above: Reserve for bad debts.)

*Goodwill.* Patents and trademarks are often given some conservative estimate of value and called goodwill. Sometimes the success of a company is attributed to certain intangibles. This may be recorded as a goodwill item. Usually the *recorded* value is not significantly large, because it is so uncertain.

## LIABILITIES

Liabilities are conventionally divided into current and long-term liabilities, with the former usually representing claims that must be paid within a year.

*Accounts payable.* The corporation has purchased goods and equipment for which it must yet pay. The amount still due is recorded.

*Notes payable.* The corporation has borrowed for a short period of time, and the amount due is shown. This item may also include the amounts of long-term debt that will fall due within a year.

*Accrued liabilities.* At the present moment (the end of the month), the corporation has accrued obligations to pay taxes or wages at some near future date. For example, if wages are paid on the fifteenth of the month, then at the end of the month it will owe about half a month's wages, to be paid in two weeks.

*Long-term debt.* The corporation has issued bonds to borrow money. In the present instance, these will run until about 1975 before falling due.

*Minority interest.* The corporation is the primary owner of a subsidiary company, the entire value of which has been recorded among the assets. However, since United Nuclear Corporation is not the sole owner, it has recorded here the ownership rights of the other owners of this subsidiary mining company. Usually every balance sheet has an appended list of footnotes or additional information giving further details. In this case the report happens to tell us in a footnote that the subsidiary company which has a recorded value of about $14,700,000 is all included in United Nuclear's reported property, plant, and equipment ($46,884,000) on the asset side. $5,248,000 of that belongs to other people—the subsidiary company's other owners, the *minority interest*. This recorded minority interest offsets part of the value shown on the asset side. In other words, of the total recorded value of the subsidiary company, $5,500,000 is the share of the other owners.

## EQUITY

Many firms include more than just equity under the heading of Equity. Some, as this one does, include also a special form of debt, "preferred convertible stock." We shall first explain what that is and then explain the way the pure *equity* is presented.

The first item shown is *Preferred, convertible stock.* "Preferred stock" is a fancy name for what is simply a debt of the company. It is called preferred stock because the holders of that stock have a claim against the company that is prior to that of the common stock holders. This might have been called bonds of $100 denominations paying 5 percent per year—except that preferred stock often differs from a bond in that if the $5 is not paid, the preferred stockholder cannot institute legal foreclosure proceedings against the company. He simply has preference to the earnings, if any, for payment of interest before any dividends can be paid to the common stockholders—that is, the owners. Sometimes the preferred stock is "cumulative," which means that the arrears of unpaid dividends (or interest, if you will) accumulate, and until they are paid, the common stock holders cannot take any dividends. And, as in the present instance, the preferred stock may be "convertible," which means that the preferred stockholder has the option to exchange (convert) it into common stock at a preset exchange rate. In the present instance, the exchange rate is ten common for one preferred stock (information usually given in a footnote to the balance sheet). Thus if the present preferred convertible stock has a par of $100 with 5 percent, it pays $5 preferred dividends each year (if earned) and may be converted to ten shares of common stock.

A person who buys a share of preferred convertible stock for $100 has some hope the common stock will rise above $10 a share; by converting to ten shares he will then have more than $100. As the price of a common share approaches $10 in the stock market, the selling price of preferred convertible stock will rise above $100, reflecting both the current price and the present values of further future rises in the common stock price. A purchaser of *convertible* preferred common stock is in fact a partial common stock holder or owner. A purchaser of nonconvertible preferred stock is simply a creditor of the company.

Finally, some preferred stock is "callable"; that is, the company has the option to pay it off prior to its due date. A $100 callable preferred stock will usually be callable at some price slightly above $100, but the premium diminishes as the due date approaches. The owner of a "callable, convertible, cumulative, preferred stock" (of $100 par value, at 5 percent, convertible at $10, and callable at $105 within five years) will collect $5 a year dividends, if earned; he may be offered $105 for the stock (which he must take unless he decides to convert); he can convert it to ten shares of common stock (since ten shares of common at $10 per share will equal the $100 par value of the convertible preferred share). As you can see, all sorts of terms are possible in a "preferred stock."

The remaining three items show the equity proper, which usually is expressed in three parts: *common stock, additional paid-in capital,* and *retained earnings* (sometimes the last two are combined and called simply *capital surplus*). We already know that equity, by definition, equals the difference between assets and liabilities (including preferred stock as a liability). In the present instance, if we subtract the liabilities from the assets ($77,636,000 − $42,377,000), we get $36,259,000, which is the *book value* of the common stockholders' equity. How was it attained? Initially there was paid in to the company when the stock was issued, $24,110,000, (= $23,211,000 + $899,000). The figure is recorded for legal and tax purposes as $899,000 as the *initial par value* and $23,211,000 as the *additional amount paid* originally for that stock. This division is of no economic significance and reflects some technically legal quirks. We mention it here to avoid any impression that the par value reflects some true economic value.

What has happened to that $24,000,000? It has been spent (along with proceeds of loans) for property, wages, equipment, etc., and at the moment the results of that management activity are shown as assets on one side and as incurred obligations on the other.

*Retained earnings.* The corporation has kept some net earnings in the company in the form of new equipment and facilities. This amounts to $11,149,000 according to the accountant's book-recorded values and prices. The corporation may have paid out some dividends to common stockholders, but we can't tell from the balance-sheet data. (Retained earnings are often called *earned surplus*.)

Such is what the historical records of the United Nuclear Corporation indicate. If we divide the recorded *book value* of the ownership, $36,259,000 (= 23,211,000 + 11,149,000 + 899,000), by the 4,496,792 shares outstanding, it comes to about $7.80 a share.

It is tempting to conclude that a share of common stock is worth $8; but don't yield to that temptation, or else you are rejecting everything you have learned in this book, and especially in Chapter 13. Why? Because the figures in the balance sheet's asset column are the historical outlays for the equipment (adjusted for wear and tear). They do not tell us what the company will be able to do in the future. How do we know that the uranium mine—which *cost*, say, $1,000,000 to find and mine—is not going to yield $100,000,000 in receipts, or maybe nothing?

None of this is revealed by the balance sheet's asset records—unless the corporation directors decide to make a prognosis of that future receipt stream, discount it into a present value, and record it under "goodwill" or "profits." But they usually don't do this, simply because they know how unreliable that is. Instead, they issue a report of operations and events along with their balance sheets. For example, United Nuclear Corporation reported in its 1963 annual report: "The outlook for widespread civilian and military use of nuclear energy for both power and propulsion improved greatly during the past year. The capability of the industry in the free world countries, based on presently known ore-reserve information, is estimated to be about 20,000 tons annually. This in the face of a projected annual amount demanded during the early 1970s of 40,000 tons, excluding military purchases." But the directors did not foresee that within a year the decision on a proposal to build another nuclear-powered airplane carrier would be negative. All the directors could do was report what was then known and make some clearly labeled forecasts, which other people can accept, reject, or revise at their volition.

Try to guess the purchase price of a share of common stock in United Nuclear Corporation in April 1966. Probably not less than $8, although maybe the mines are depleted, in which case the stock is not worth what it *cost* to dig holes in the ground. But if the mines are rich, beyond the cost of discovering, mining, and refining the uranium concentrate, the stock may have been worth more than $8. As it happened, the stock was selling for about $20 a share at that time—more than twice the cost of the assets (net of liabilities). Some would say the stock was "watered," because clearly the price is far above the cost of those assets. (And so, of course, is the price of an early Picasso above the "cost" of the canvas, paint, and labor.) That does not mean that the company will not in fact obtain a future net receipt stream whose present value is far in excess of an $8 book figure. In fact, the owners expected it to earn a stream of net earnings with a present capital value of about $20 a share.

At the time that annual balance sheet was published, the corporation also reported the results of its operations during the preceding year, on an *income statement* chronicling its operating activities. A share could be purchased at the time of this report for about $20. The reported earnings were only 31 cents a share per year, hardly a competitive return—only about 1.5 percent per year.

### UNITED NUCLEAR CORPORATION
#### Income Statement, Year Ended March 31, 1966

| | | |
|---|---:|---:|
| Sales | | $50,587,000 |
| Costs and expenses | | |
| Costs of goods sold (labor, materials, power) | $35,440,000 | |
| Depreciation of equipment (wear and tear and depletion of ore) | 6,524,000 | |
| Selling and administrative costs | 3,066,000 | |
| Interest on debt | 1,727,000 | 46,757,000 |
| Operating net income | | 3,830,000 |
| Share belonging to minority interest | | −2,707,000 |
| Other income (gains from sale of assets) | | 255,000 |
| Federal income tax (No provision was made for federal income tax because the company has substantial deductible losses from prior years which may be carried forward to the current year to offset taxable current income) | | |
| Net earnings | | $ 1,378,000 |
| Earnings per share of common stock | | $.31 |

a. What do you think owners' beliefs must be about the future earnings?

b. If reported earnings in the next few years stay at about the current rate, what do you think will happen to the price of the stock?

c. Look up the price of this stock now. Get its latest interim reports of earnings and latest balance sheet from *Moody's Manuals of Industrials* at your library or any local stockbroker's office.

2    "A corporation owned by one person is the same as a proprietorship." Do you agree? If so, why? If not, why not?

3    "Continuity of a corporation means that if any or all of the current owners of the corporation die, the corporation continues as a unit of ownership." Do you agree?

4    Why is the corporation the dominant form of ownership of very large conglomerations of wealth?

5    Is it a disadvantage of the corporation that not every stockholder can make the controlling decisions? That the control is dispersed? That some people who own less than half of the corporation can make controlling decisions?

6    "Very few corporations lose wealth, and still fewer go broke." Do you agree? What evidence can you cite?

7    "The employer is called the boss because he is able to tell people what to do." Evaluate.

8    "Business firms exist because some people do not have enough wealth to own the capital equipment and machinery with which they can work more efficiently." Evaluate.

9    A friend of yours, a brilliant engineer and administrator, is operating a business. You propose to bet on his success and offer him some money to expand his operations. A corporation is formed allotting you 40 and him 60 percent of the common stock. You invest $30,000. This is often described as separation of ownership from control, since he now has the majority controlling vote. Would you ever be willing to invest wealth in such a fashion—that is, give up control while retaining ownership in certain property rights? Why?

10    Suppose you operate a cleaning establishment and expect to obtain $8,000 revenue from use of a new cleaning machine during the first year. (Assume you receive all of it by the end of the first year.) Also you expect to receive $15,000 during the second year. (Again assume all revenue is received by the end of that year.) Assume the costs are the same as for the cleaning machine in question 5 of Chapter 14. For convenience, all the data are summarized in the following schedule:

| | Beginning of 1st Year | End of 1st Year | End of 2nd Year |
|---|---|---|---|
| Purchase | $5,000 | 0 | 0 |
| Expenses | 0 | $6,000 | $ 6,000 |
| Resale | 0 | 0 | 1,500 |
| Receipts | 0 | 8,000 | 15,000 |
| Net Receipts | _____ | _____ | _____ |
| Present Values | _____ + | _____ + | _____ = _____ (Profit) |

a. What is the profit implied by your expectations?

b. Suppose that within a month after you have installed the machine, other people form expectations consistent with yours; however, despite their efforts to open similar cleaning establishments, your revenue forecast will still be accurate (since it was in part based on anticipations that other people would soon copy your techniques). At that time the capital value of your business will be revised upward with a profit of $5,491. When do you realize that profit?

11   A criticism of the modern corporation is that the management or directors, by virtue of their central position, are able to collect proxies (rights to cast votes of stockholders) from the other stockholders; and as a result the management is in a powerful position and cannot be easily dislodged. It has been said that "the typical small stockholder can do nothing about changing management and that under ordinary circumstances management can count on remaining in office; and often the proxy battle is fought to determine which minority group shall control." Take the assertions as being correct.

a. Does it follow that stability of management in "ordinary circumstances" reveals some kind of weakness of stockholders?

b. Does it follow that a typical small stockholder "should" be able to turn out management?

c. If a minority group succeeds in getting a majority of stock votes, does this mean that a minority controls or that a majority controls through the medium of a minority group? Is this to be interpreted in the same way that political parties consisting of a group of organized politicians have elections to see which minority group shall control the government? Why or why not?

12   a. In analyzing the behavior of corporation management and directors, why is it pertinent to distinguish among nonprofit or publicly regulated, profit-limited corporations on the one hand, and private-property, for-profit business corporations on the other?

b. Which do you think would be more marked by self-perpetuating management and stockholder lethargy? Why?

c. Which do you think would show more discrimination in employment practices according to race and religion? Why?

13    Joseph Thagworthy has a stable of race horses and a breeding farm. The two, although operated as a business, lose him over $50,000 annually. Yet he continues year after year because he enjoys the activity more than if he spent a similar sum for travel or conventional types of consumption activities.
a. Would it be correct to say that he is maximizing his wealth in that business?
b. Would it be correct to say he is maximizing his utility?
c. Do you think an increase in the losses would induce an increase in that kind of activity? What does economic theory postulate about that?

14    "Under a socialist system, profits and losses are eliminated." Comment.

15    "Private property permits selective, discretionary risk bearing." Comment.

16    Contrast socialism and private property as means of distributing risks of profits and losses.

17    What is the relationship between the right to buy and sell and the distribution of profits and losses?

18    For what events is the distribution of risk the same in socialist and capitalist systems? (Hint: How about divorce, cancer, baldness, homeliness, having only female children, being left-handed?)

19    Our laws and customs reflect the assignments of risk bearing. A person who owns land as private property must bear the consequences of changes in the value of that land if people move away or no longer value that location so highly. Similarly, if he catches cold or breaks his leg or becomes hard of hearing and can no longer earn so large an income, he must bear the consequences.
a. Would you advocate that people bear the wealth losses to their private property regardless of cause (aside from legal recourse to violators of property rights)?
b. Would you want a homeowner to bear the consequences of a meteorite's falling on his house? Fire from using gasoline in the house? Flood damage to houses near rivers? Income loss from cancer? Blindness?
c. Whom do you think should bear the loss if the individual does not?
d. Why would you draw the line differently in different cases? What is the criterion you used?
e. In each case, do you think people's behavior would be affected according to the risk bearing involved?
f. Would you allow people to agree to take on certain risks in exchange for not bearing other risks, if two people could make a mutually agreeable partition and exchange of such risks? How would that differ from a system of private-property rights?

20    "It is better to buy from a firm that is losing money than from one that

is making a profit, because the former firm is charging too low a price while the latter is charging more than costs." Evaluate.

21    On July 15, 1964 Chrysler Corporation president announced that earnings for the past quarter year (April–June) were up 20 percent over the preceding quarter and 50 percent over the similar quarter a year before. At the beginning of the quarter reported on April 1, the price of Chrysler common stock was $70. On June 30 it was $65, and on the day this news was reported the stock *fell* from $65 to $60 because investors expected an even bigger earning. Did the owners of the company have any profits during the quarter from April 1 to June 30? Two years later (1966) the price had fallen to $40. Did Chrysler have profits over that two-year period? Did the owners? Is there any difference between profits to Chrysler and profits to Chrysler owners? What is its price now?

**22**    You buy some stock for $100. A month later it has risen to a high of $150. Another month later it is down to $125. Have you had a profit or a loss?

23    A young college teacher hits upon a sparkling teaching style and is rewarded with a higher salary. Has he had a profit? Explain.

24    An actress, after years in the movies, suddenly hits it big and obtains an enormously larger salary. Has she a profit? Three months later she begins to get fat, and in a year her contracts are canceled. Has she experienced a loss in any sense different from that suffered by Ford when it introduced the Edsel?

25    Estimate the present value of your future earnings. Project your earnings until age 65. Then obtain the present value of that projection, using a 10 percent rate of interest. Can you promise your fiancee that you are now worth over $200,000?

26    "Paper profits and losses are not real profits or losses." Do you agree? If so, why? If not, why not?

**27**    "I bought some stock at $70 a share. It has fallen to $55, but I'm going to hold it until it rises to $70 so I can avoid taking a loss." What is wrong with that reasoning—even assuming that the stock price does shortly thereafter rise to $75?

28    A liquor-retailing license in California recently was sold for over $40,000. The seller was the person who initially got the license from the state at a cost of $6,000. Did the subsequent buyer get a profit in the form of a monopoly rent? Did the initial licensee get a profit in the form of a monopoly rent?

**29**    a. Which of the following represent some wealth based on monopoly rents? TV station in Texas, United Air Lines, General Motors, teamsters in Teamsters' Union, General Electric Company, American Telephone and Telegraph Company, Frank Sinatra, beet-sugar farm land owners, local electric company, Aluminum Company of America, savings and loan banks, professional baseball teams.

b. In each case in which you think wealth based on monopoly rent is present, how would you test for its presence? And how would you measure the amount of monopoly rent?

c. In each case where you think it is present, who gets it?

30    International Business Machines common stock sells at a price one hundred times as great as the accountants' reported current annual earnings. The stock of Allegheny Ludlum Corporation, a steel producer, sells at about ten times its accountants' reported "earnings." Assume that the same accounting principles are used in each firm. What do you think will happen to the price of each firm's stock if in the next reporting period each firm reports earnings that are *unchanged* from the preceding period? Explain.

31    Suppose it were true that rich people got rich exclusively from profits. Suppose further that those who received the profits were no smarter, no more foresighted, no nicer, no harder working, no more productive than other people. Does this mean that their profits are "undeserved" and that the rich people perform no service? Would you advocate taxing away those profits? Why or why not?

# 16

**Production by Firms in Price-Takers' Open Markets**

Business firms have two roles: (1) a *purposive* role to increase the wealth of the members of the firm and (2) a resultant *functional* role to produce goods in response to market demands. The purpose—wealth increases for the members of the business firm—has the effect (function) of relating the production of the firm to the *market* demand. To see how this occurs, we will consider market demands and production in a *price-takers'* market in this chapter, and in price-searchers' markets in the next chapter. In each case, open markets are assumed. In the next chapter, we will study production responses in restricted-entry markets.

## Influence of Demand Changes on Output

A change in demand could mean a change in (1) the *rate* at which the demanders wish to consume or (2) the total *volume* the community demands. For example, an electric-power company may place an order for 120 generators to be delivered at the monthly rate of five for twenty-four months; shortly thereafter it may modify that decision and increase its demand by ordering sixty more to be delivered in a third year at the same rate of five per month. Only the *volume* of demand, not the rate, has increased. At the other extreme, the buyer may increase his *rate* demand from 120 in two years to 120 in one year. Or he may increase his demand for *both* rate and volume—from five per month for two years, to ten per month for two years. We will clarify cost principles by examining a *joint, proportional increase in both rate and volume* over a given period.[1]

We shall not conduct a sequence of analyses, each designed to tell what happens one day, one week, one month, one year, and so on, after an initial disturbance. Instead, for convenience of exposition, the analysis of the supply reaction will first be in terms of the response of *existing* firms. Then, adjustments in the number of firms are introduced.

## Costs and Output Programs

Initially, we shall assume that each producer knows the costs of his possible programs, that he is already in business with acquired equipment, and that the characteristic relationship between costs and production is shown in Table 16–1. These are the "short-run" costs of various outputs, given that his equipment is that most appropriate for an output of eight or nine units per

---

[1] In our earlier discussion of production problems, we could, without causing confusion, treat the increase as an increase in the demand for either the volume or rate or both. But now that production can be changed in at least rate and volume, with different effects on costs, the kind of demand change will have to be made explicit.

year. If the firm planned *initially* for one of the other possible outputs, it would have selected other equipment and then the costs of these other outputs would differ from those shown in Table 16–1. But as it is, the costs shown here are those that the firm faces given that it now has the equipment that it does.

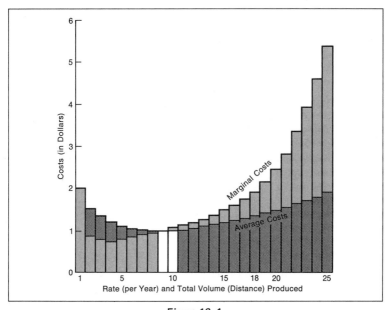

Figure 16–1
Marginal, Average Total, and Average Variable Cost for Alternative
Output Programs for One Year

This chart plots the data in columns 3, 4, and 5 from Table 16–1. It shows that, with sufficiently large rates of output, marginal costs increase and so do average costs. Average-variable-cost curve is below average total cost by an amount exactly equal to the average acquisition cost (per unit of output). Supply response of this price-taker firm at any market price is given by the output at which the marginal cost rises to the market price (for any price greater than the lowest average variable cost—in this case 85 cents). Output will not continue indefinitely by this firm if price stays below 99 cents.

Two short-run average costs are given: average *total* costs (*including* a fixed, sunk cost of $1) per unit of output (column 4), and the average *variable* costs (excluding that sunk cost) per unit of output (column 5). The remaining columns give demand, revenue, and profit data. This producer is selling in a price-takers' market and can sell all he cares to sell at the going market price of $1.10 per unit. For each output the excess of total revenue over total cost is given in column 8. The excess of total revenue over variable cost would be exactly $1 larger for each output (that is, by the $1 of sunk cost).

Which output maximizes the firm's wealth—that is, gives the greatest profit? At a price of $1.10 the wealth-maximizing output is ten units (or eleven). Total costs are $10. Total revenue is $11. Profit is $1. At all other outputs the profits are smaller, as you can see by looking at column 8.

Table 16–1
Costs of One Year's Output (Indicated Rate per Year and Volume for One Year)

| (1) | (2) | (3) | (4) | (5) | (6) | (7) | (8) | (9) | (10) | (11) |
|---|---|---|---|---|---|---|---|---|---|---|
| 1 | $ 2.00 | $2.00 | $2.00 | $1.00 | $ 1.10 | $1.10 | $ −.90 | $2.00 | $ 2.00 | $ .00 |
| 2 | 2.90 | .90 | 1.45 | .95 | 2.20 | 1.10 | −.70 | 2.00 | 4.00 | 1.10 |
| 3 | 3.70 | .80 | 1.23 | .90 | 3.30 | 1.10 | −.40 | 2.00 | 6.00 | 2.30 |
| 4 | 4.45 | .75 | 1.11 | .86 | 4.40 | 1.10 | −.05 | 2.00 | 8.00 | 3.55 |
| 5 | 5.25 | .80 | 1.05 | .85 | 5.50 | 1.10 | +.25 | 2.00 | 10.00 | 4.75 |
| 6 | 6.10 | .85 | 1.02 | .85 | 6.60 | 1.10 | +.50 | 2.00 | 12.00 | 5.90 |
| 7 | 7.00 | .90 | 1.00 | .86 | 7.70 | 1.10 | +.70 | 2.00 | 14.00 | 7.00 |
| 8 | 7.95 | .95 | .99 | .87 | 8.80 | 1.10 | +.85 | 2.00 | 16.00 | 8.05 |
| 9 | 8.95 | 1.00 | .99 | .88 | 9.90 | 1.10 | +.95 | 2.00 | 18.00 | 9.05 |
| 10 | 10.00 | 1.05 | 1.00 | .90 | 11.00 | 1.10 | +1.00* | 2.00 | 20.00 | 10.00 |
| 11 | 11.10 | 1.10 | 1.01 | .92 | 12.10 | 1.10 | +1.00* | 2.00 | 22.00 | 10.80 |
| 12 | 12.25 | 1.15 | 1.02 | .94 | 13.20 | 1.10 | +.95 | 2.00 | 24.00 | 11.75 |
| 13 | 13.50 | 1.25 | 1.04 | .96 | 14.30 | 1.10 | +.80 | 2.00 | 26.00 | 12.50 |
| 14 | 14.85 | 1.35 | 1.06 | .99 | 15.40 | 1.10 | +.65 | 2.00 | 28.00 | 13.15 |
| 15 | 16.30 | 1.45 | 1.09 | 1.02 | 16.50 | 1.10 | +.20 | 2.00 | 30.00 | 13.70 |
| 16 | 17.85 | 1.55 | 1.12 | 1.05 | 17.60 | 1.10 | −.25 | 2.00 | 32.00 | 14.15 |
| 17 | 19.55 | 1.70 | 1.15 | 1.09 | 18.70 | 1.10 | −.85 | 2.00 | 34.00 | 14.45 |
| 18 | 21.45 | 1.90 | 1.19 | 1.13 | 19.80 | 1.10 | −1.65 | 2.00 | 36.00 | 14.55* |
| 19 | 23.55 | 2.10 | 1.23 | 1.18 | 20.90 | 1.10 | −2.65 | 2.00 | 38.00 | 14.45 |
| 20 | 25.95 | 2.40 | 1.29 | 1.25 | 22.00 | 1.10 | −3.95 | 2.00 | 40.00 | 14.05 |
| 21 | 28.75 | 2.80 | 1.37 | 1.32 | 23.10 | 1.10 | −5.65 | 2.00 | 42.00 | 13.25 |
| 22 | 32.05 | 3.30 | 1.46 | 1.41 | 24.20 | 1.10 | −7.85 | 2.00 | 44.00 | 11.95 |
| 23 | 35.95 | 3.90 | 1.56 | 1.52 | 25.30 | 1.10 | −10.65 | 2.00 | 46.00 | 10.05 |
| 24 | 40.55 | 4.60 | 1.69 | 1.65 | 26.40 | 1.10 | −14.15 | 2.00 | 48.00 | 7.45 |
| 25 | 46.00 | 5.45 | 1.83 | 1.80 | 27.50 | 1.10 | −18.50 | 2.00 | 50.00 | 4.00 |

(1) Annual rate *and* volume.
(2) Capital value measure of total cost of which $1 is sunk acquisition cost.
(3) Marginal cost (for one-unit increment in annual rate *and* volume of output).
(4) Cost per unit of *volume* of output.
(5) Variable cost per unit of output.
(6) Total receipts before demand increase.
(7) Marginal receipts (at price of $1.10).
(8) Profits (at price of $1.10).
(9) Marginal receipts (at price of $2).
(10) Total receipts (at price of $2).
(11) Profits (at price of $2).
    *Maximum-profit programs.

The characteristic cost conditions can be portrayed more usefully, for subsequent analysis, by the cost *curves* in Figure 16–2. The bars in Figure 16–1 are replaced by the curves. Notice their characteristic shape. They *may* fall at first, *may* have a near-flat portion (possibly over a large range of outputs), and ultimately for larger outputs certainly *will* rise, at a rate that increases until an upper limit to the productive capacity is approached (cost increase becomes practically infinite). Nothing more should be inferred from the particular shapes of the curves.

Three cost curves are drawn. One is the average *total* short-run costs per unit of output, *including* the past fixed, sunk cost that this firm would have to cover if it were to be said *in retrospect* that the decision to buy the particular equipment *and produce* had been profitable. The dashed curve, the average short-run *variable* cost, shows the cost per unit of output *after* the firm is *already in business with acquired equipment.* As it continues to produce at any rate, its cost situation will change. The variable-cost curve will shift toward (and ultimately become) a long-run planning cost curve, which shows for each possible output the per-unit costs of production with new equipment that is optimal (least costly) for that particular output. The curve labeled *LRAC* in Figure 14–6 on page 306 is a long-run average-cost curve. The average *variable* cost curve will shift to and become the total average-cost curve, in the long run.

Although the meaning of these curves has already been explained in detail in Chapter 14, for assurance and ready familiarity the student is urged to relate each curve to the appropriate column of Table 16–1.

### Wealth-Maximizing Output

On Figure 16–2 (the tops of the bars of Figure 16–1 have been replaced by smooth lines) the horizontal line labeled $AR = MR$ is the demand line facing the producer. He can sell at $1.10 as many as he cares to: the line extends out far beyond his production at that cost. He would sell none if he raised *his* price. If the *market* price were higher, say, $2, the demand line for this producer would be at a height of $2 and extend beyond his production capability at that cost.

We now can develop the power of this diagrammatic approach by answering the question, "What determines the output program?" First, the higher the market price, the larger is the output that maximizes his wealth. That wealth-maximizing output is the output at which the rising marginal-cost curve intersects the demand line. At any smaller output, an increase of output would augment receipts more than it would total costs. In economic jargon, for any smaller output program the forsaken marginal revenue (given by the horizontal price line) exceeds the marginal cost; at all larger outputs, marginal costs exceed marginal revenue. It is solely to ascertain the maximum wealth output that we draw the marginal-cost curve and the marginal-revenue line (coinciding with the demand line for every seller in a *price-takers'* market).

But, it may validly be objected, we don't know any producer's actual cost curves, so how can we tell what his wealth-maximizing output program really is? We can't. But our purpose is not to tell each producer what to do. Instead, our purpose is to characterize his *output response to demand changes.* The powerful and important generalization suggested by the graphic analysis is that a higher price (from a higher demand) induces a larger output. The *supply curve* of a *price-taker* producer is given by his *marginal-cost curve*. That curve is a "supply curve" because it identifies for each price the output that the producer would provide. The higher the price, the greater his output.

### Continue to Produce or Shut Down?

Now we shall see why we showed total average costs (including entry acquisition costs) and also variable average costs. For each firm, there is a lower limiting price below which it will stop production. That lower limit is the lowest average *variable* (i.e., yet to be incurred) cost of all possible contemplated continued outputs. We show this by the dashed line on Figure 16–2.

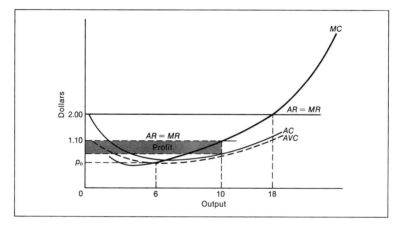

Figure 16–2
Cost and Demand Facing Price-Taker

At price of $2, wealth-maximizing output is eighteen units, which exceeds wealth-maximizing output (eleven units) when price is lower ($1.10). Output would cease if price fell below $P_0$ and was expected to stay below $P_0$. Dotted curve is short-run average variable cost, $AVC$. Light area below $2 demand line (average revenue equals marginal revenue) and above dashed line (average cost at output of eighteen units) is a measure of profits. It equals (price minus average cost) multiplied by output, that is, ($2 − $1.19 ) × 18 = $14.58.

The portion of the marginal-cost curve above where it intersects the average-variable-cost curve (and it must intersect at the minimum average-variable-cost by logic of defined relationship between the two) indicates the supply schedule of contemplated outputs at each possible price. While price is below the average *total* cost, the producer will say he is losing money—meaning that his past (regretted) decision to enter the business lost him wealth. He will continue temporarily to produce even at that low price, since he will not lose as much as he would if he shut down. So long as he operates at any price over the minimum average *variable* cost, this excess will make his loss that much less. Ultimately, his equipment will be run down. But he will not incur new acquisition or substantial repair cost, because at the low price the projected receipts would cover only the subsequent variable costs, not new acquisition (or repair) costs. So he quits production.

We can summarize with a second generalization: Price can be less than the average total cost (including *past sunk* cost) without causing a producer immediately to stop production. Nothing like this was implied in our production examples of Chapters 10–12. Hence, to make the theory more valid we had to introduce a new element—the existence of durable capital goods for which the initial purchase price and immediate resale price differ. Or in general terms, once you make or buy capital goods you can't *at zero cost* unmake or sell them. Production is not reversible. In Chapters 10–12 we assumed, invalidly, that Mr. *C* could switch back and forth between production of *X* and *Y* at *no* switching or equipment-revision costs, but we have now incorporated that cost and adjusted our analysis.

## Market Supply: Aggregated Output of All Firms

The preceding discussion concentrated on the output adjustment of one firm. However, the market supply of a good is provided by many firms—which make up an *industry*. The proposition that an increased demand induces a larger output from a *firm* is easily converted into an *industry* proposition: The higher the price, the greater the output supplied. *For each price, the sum of the outputs of all firms is the industry output.* The schedule of prices and associated outputs is the industry supply schedule.

To illustrate, *marginal-cost* data like those of Table 16–1 are shown in Figure 16–3 as a smooth line labeled $MC_A$, for Firm *A*. Also in that figure is the marginal-cost schedule $(MC_B)$ for Firm *B*, which produces less at any given price. The total output of this industry, here illustrated for *just* these two firms (as if these were only two of the many firms in an industry) is obtained by *adding the output (horizontal distance) of each firm's marginal-cost curve at any specified price above the lowest average-variable-cost output for each firm.* The summed curve, *SS*, is the industry supply curve. The *price-takers'* industry supply curve is the sum of the marginal-cost curves above each firm's minimum average variable cost. If the price were $2, the maximum-wealth production programs of Firms *A* and *B* would be $X_A$ and $X_B$. At prices below $1.30, Firm *B* would shut down, while *A* would not shut down *immediately* unless price were as low as 85 cents. These lower limits are their respective lowest average variable costs.

Figure 16–4 gives the same information as Figure 16–3, with the addition of a market demand curve, *DD*, which intersects the *industry* supply curve at the price of $2. According to the price-determination process outlined earlier, the price will be $2. The portions of the total output produced by Firms $A$ and $B$ are indicated by the distances $OX_a$ and $OX_b$. In earlier chapters, we saw how price rationed the existing stock among the competing claimants; here we see that price also affects the production by each firm. Price allocates in the sense that it both rations existing output and assigns production.

This demand and supply "intersection" price is the price at which each producer can sell all he wants to produce at that price, and each consumer can buy all he demands at that price. It is an *equilibrium* or *equilibrating* price. Price is in "equilibrium" because price has moved to the level necessary to make the amount demanded equal the amount of production evoked by that price. A higher price would reduce the amount demanded to less than the larger amount of production induced by that higher price; a lower price would mean that the amount demanded exceeds the amount produced.

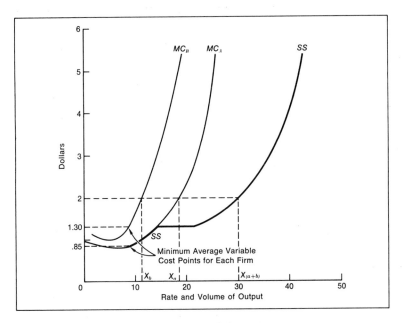

Figure 16–3
Marginal-Cost Curves Are Bases of Supply of Industry under
Price-Takers' Market Conditions

Marginal-cost curves of two firms, above the minimum average costs (variable in short run, or total costs for long run) are summed horizontally to get output of industry—here shown as just two firms. At any specified market price, the output of the industry is shown by the marginal cost. Main implication is that higher price induces larger output, because at any price each firm will maximize its wealth if it produces that output at which its *marginal cost equals market price*. Firm can sell all of the output it cares to produce without affecting the price in the market.

If demand increases (that is, if the demand schedule, *DD*, shifts to the right in Figure 16–4 to $D_1D_1$), price will be bid up—in the absence of effective laws, customs, or conventions preventing price changes. The higher price induces producers to increase output—as indicated by the *SS* curve, which shows larger output at higher prices (and marginal costs). Conversely, a reduced demand would, under the stipulated conditions, yield lower prices and thereby a reduced output.

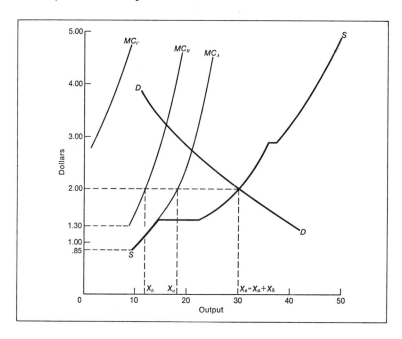

Figure 16–4
Demand and Supply and Output Determination in Price-Takers'
Markets

As market demand increases, new firms are attracted by higher prices and wealth prospects. At a price of approximately $3, Firm *C* will be able to produce profitably. Supply of output by industry shows increased output with higher price because of (1) increased output by each firm which increases output to point where marginal costs equal price and (2) increased number of firms as price rises above minimum average costs of new potential firms.

When demand and, hence, price change, not all firms change output by the same extent, because the *slopes* of their marginal-cost curves differ. For some firms the marginal-cost curves are steep and for some they are flat for a given change in output. As price rises in response to increases in demand, the former firms will not increase their output as much as the latter ones. By the same token, if price should fall in response to demand decreases, some firms will shut down before others do, the earlier ones being those with higher minimum average variable costs—*not* those that are poorer or have less money on hand. Whether rich or poor, each firm shuts down not when wealth is exhausted but when continued operation at low prices would *reduce* wealth even more than shutting down.

## Supply Response by Entry of New Firms: Long-Run Response

If price rises, new producers will be attracted. Firms that produce *only* when price and demand are high are typically higher-cost firms; they cannot survive unless price is high. This fact is not indicated by their marginal costs (for every firm adjusts its output until the marginal costs have increased to the higher price) but is instead indicated by their average costs. Many will be regarded as "marginal," "fringe" firms; for if demand falls, the lower price will induce them to shut down. Potential firms on the "margin" will appear if demand and price rise sufficiently. If demand stays high, these firms become recognized as "established" firms, and in turn look on still higher-cost firms as constituting the new fringe of marginal, unreliable firms.

This is portrayed graphically in Figure 16-4 by the marginal-cost curve of Firm *C*, a high-cost firm in the sense that the lowest price at which it will enter production is higher than for the other two firms shown.

A homely and easily observable example is that of parking-lot operators near a stadium. For big crowds, the parking fees are higher, and there are more high-cost parking lots available as local residents sell parking space in their driveways and yards. These "fly-by-night," fringe, temporary operators are disliked by the "established" operators. They appear when demand and price are high; prices are lower than if they did not appear.

However, the experienced student may note that established firms often do not raise their prices when demand increases temporarily—the fringe sellers seize the opportunity to sell at the higher prices. How do the fringe operators, who do not hesitate to take a higher price, contribute to *lower* prices—if they are the ones who in fact charge the higher price? There are two answers. Remember that "price" or consumer cost includes more than the monetary payment. People who cannot park in the "standard" lots overflow to surrounding areas. The price they must then pay is "walking farther." The cost imposed on the patrons of parking farther away and walking is greater than the parking fee of the fringe operators. How do we know? Simply because some people do prefer to pay more and walk less. Without the services of the fringe operators, the costs (pecuniary and nonpecuniary) imposed on patrons would be even higher—especially on those who do not get to park in the standard established parking lots.

When demand for building or farm products increases, the number of contractors and builders increases, and the number of farmers increases. In Washington, D.C., hundreds of people with full-time jobs elsewhere become taxi operators during "rush" hours. Steel mills operate some blast furnaces only during peak demands. Barber shops have chairs that are "idle" most, but *not* all of the time. The chairs represent high-cost, rather than excessive, capacity. Some firms use second and third shifts when demand warrants it, even though they are higher-cost ways of production. Later, if demand falls, the lower price makes it impossible to maintain so high a rate of production and still cover costs. Therefore, all firms reduce output and some begin to withdraw from that business. The resources formerly used there regretfully and complainingly revert to their next-best sources of income (which served as a measure of their costs).

### "Sick" Industries

Another useful application of economic analysis is provided by the study of what are commonly called "sick" industries—"sick" because they allegedly have an "excessive" number of firms; "excessive" because most of the firms do such a small volume of business that most of them lose wealth. And as rapidly as old ones lose out and leave, new ones enter—only to experience a similar fate. There seems to be no long-run adjustment that restores the industry to a profitable or at least a nonloss balance. The more commonly cited examples of "sick" industries are retail groceries, bars, restaurants, night clubs, coal mines, gasoline stations, textile manufacturers, and farming.

People who make this argument usually point to long-term declining demand, foolish gambling, overestimation of one's ability, plain ignorance, or the low cost of entering the business. But upon closer study these explanations fall to the ground. In the first place, all firms in an industry could be losing wealth when demand is falling unexpectedly. But to call this a sickness is to confuse the cure with the malady. There is nothing "sick" about a decreasing demand. In the second place, all firms could be losing wealth if the business has a sufficiently large amount of nonpecuniary satisfaction, as is said to be the case for horse racing or novel writing or acting or owning baseball clubs. One man grows orchids and makes money and considers it a business; another grows orchids and loses money but regards it as a hobby or consumption activity. Everyone could lose money in some business if the fun of the business operation were great enough to be worth the losses. These considerations help to explain why some industries or occupations always run at a loss and seem never to reach a long-run adjustment to profitable operations.

But there is a more basic consideration. In some industries the profits may be large for only a few winners, with the rest of the members losing money. In acting, writing, painting, and sports only a few seem to make a big success while the vast majority never make enough to justify the effort. Nothing in economic analysis says that an industry in which only a few make vast fortunes should not have a vast number of "failures." These failures (or is it more accurate to call them nonsuccesses?) entered in the hope that they might join the favored few, and they often remain despite years of frustration and disappointment.

There is the contention that an industry is sick because it has excess capacity that is almost never fully utilized (for example, barber shops and service stations). Only a naive observer would believe they should be constantly "fully" utilized. Customers do not come in unchanging rates and amounts. Some barber shops have chairs or barbers that are not utilized most of the time; but when demand hits its peaks, they are utilized, and it is precisely the peak demand that is served by this "apparent" overcapacity. How would you like to live in a community in which there were just enough barbers to cut everyone's hair if the barbers were always "fully" employed? Would you like to have to plan your purchases on some schedule that allowed you no opportunity to adjust to unexpected events? Would anyone argue that Palm Desert or Palm Beach has too many hotel rooms because most of them are empty during the summer and that there are too many ski resorts because they are idle most of the time, or that there are too many churches because all of them are empty almost all the time? If you think there are too many service stations, would you be prepared to let me assert that the one you happen to buy from is the one that should be abolished? Does Sak's Fifth Avenue have too many salesgirls because many or most of them are "idle" most of the time? Would you say two-bathroom houses are uneconomic because neither bathroom is fully utilized at all times? To ask any of these questions is to answer them all.

## Resource Valuation as a
## Director of Resource Uses

Equilibrium in the number of firms and in the industry's production means that the price is at the minimum total cost per unit of output of the firm whose minimum per-unit cost is the highest of any in this industry. An incentive for new firms to enter would then reflect the belief that the new firm would have lower costs than existing firms, not that price had risen so as to attract new firms. If all firms had the same cost conditions as in Table 16–1, the price would be 99 cents at the long-run equilibrium. In fact, of course, not all firms have identical costs. Nevertheless, in an equilibrium, prices of *productive resources* used by each firm will have been changed so as to make *every* firm's minimum average cost of production equal to the market price of the output. How will this occur?

If we tie the lessons of the preceding chapter on costs and profits to this chapter, we can see the elements of the process. When market demands change unpredictably (for example, for sports cars, compacts, mini-skirts, natural shoulders, wigs, polyunsaturated fats), prices of goods used to produce those consumer goods also change. Or the prices may be revised because someone discovers how to use resources in "better" ways than foreseen. In either event, the earlier value placed on resources proves erroneous. Producers see opportunities to revise the allocation of their resources to achieve a higher aggregate wealth. Anyone who ignores the new valuations sacrifices the gain or takes a loss of wealth. This higher productive value will increase the demand for the responsible resources. The revised demand for still other resources used in the production of these resources will, in turn, revise the values imputed to the other resources in a lengthening chain of repercussions.

The increased value (profit) of their use results in an *imputation* of that value into higher prices of the responsible productive goods. The profit has been amalgamated into higher costs. The revised greater costs are reflections of the higher use values. It is not a contradiction that a profit (a gain in wealth) leads to an increase in cost. Profits are unforeseen gains in wealth, and the higher value of output of the resources mean that costs of their use are greater once their higher value of output is seen. To say that profits imply higher costs of subsequent production is to say both that the output is of greater value and that the cost of getting it is higher. These increases are the two sides of the imputed "profit."

As an example of this imputation process, suppose I discover oil on my land. I can then sell the land with the oil rights to you and convert my wealth (including the profit) to cash. You will certainly count what you paid for the land and oil rights (and that includes my profit) in your costs of *subsequent* operation. Even if I had not sold my land and oil rights, *I* must count the cost of subsequent operation at the same high figure that *you* would. The costs of use are higher than before the increased value of the resources was recognized, and the costs do not depend upon *who* uses them. If these resources are used in any other way, the value will be less than their costs. The value which is actually ultimately realized may depend upon who uses them, but the present cost of using them does not.

The imputation process means that any firm that puts resources to higher-valued uses than any other firm will have to revise the value of those resources. This revaluation appears to the owner of those resources as a profit and to the user (whether or not he is also the owner) as a higher cost of *use*. Profits and losses not only reveal unforeseen *changes* in value of particular resources but also *direct* those resources to their higher-valued uses (as judged ultimately by the consumers' market).[2] The quicker and less constrained the revaluation of assets and recalculation of costs, the more quickly will resources be directed in accord with highest-valued uses, whatever may be the value criterion used for this purpose.

The redirection of resources in response to a change in demand extends through a long chain of substitutions. If, for example, as a result of an increased demand, more wheat is to be produced, resources must be released

[2] In Chapter 11, we defined the cost of a given use of resources by one person as the highest *alternative* sacrificed value of output of those resources, seeming to exclude the value of their *present* use. But we now see that a more general conception of costs consists of imputing to a given resource a market value which reflects its highest possible value in *any* line of activity, including the present one. Costs of resources in a particular occupation stem not only from *alternative uses*, but also from alternative *users*. Even if my land is good only for oil production (i.e., it has no alternative uses) it still has a value, which must be taken into account, because other people are willing to bid for it.

from production of some other goods. Resources are transferred into wheat production as their owners seek greater wealth. Land transferred to wheat is taken from oats, corn, and building sites, and thus their supply will fall and their price increase. Other land will then be used for corn and oats—land formerly used for, say, cotton, barley, grazing land, parks, and potential housing or industrial sites. Not only land but also labor and other resources are diverted to wheat. Some laborers who would otherwise work as barbers, carpenters, or gasoline-station attendants devote more time to wheat production. And their places are partly filled by resources from still other occupations. The long chain of substitutions and shifting of resources is so broad and extensive that each one of the many effects on output of other final consumers' goods may be so slight as to be hardly noticeable over the perturbation of the many other everyday events. For this reason we are sometimes misled into thinking that some more of a good can be produced without producing less of some other.

In sum, if any firm has people or resources that enable it to produce at lower average cost than other firms, the value of that special resource or people will be bid up as other firms compete for its use. Its price will rise until at that higher value it no longer yields a lower cost to the firm. The firm now using that resource must reckon with that higher cost.

Consequence of Basing Output<br>on Wealth Maximizing

According to the data in Table 16–1, although the wealth-maximizing industry output program at a market price of $2 is eighteen units, this producer could produce twenty-five and still make a profit. But in the interests of his own wealth, he does not. There is a temptation to call this restriction socially wasteful, because there appears to be underproduction of this particular product. However, although the price does exceed *average* costs, it does not exceed *marginal* costs. Consequently, if this producer were to expand his output beyond eighteen units, he would use resources worth more than $2 (that is what marginal costs measure), and he would be selling to people who value the extra output at only $2—which is *less* than the costs of the extra output. A larger output would *not* be preferred by consumers. Therefore, the price-taking producer, by holding his output rate to eighteen units per year in order to maximize his wealth, is not "underproducing," even though he could produce more without wiping out all his profit.

Ironically, this implication of wealth-maximizing producers with free access to a price-takers' market was developed by socialists. Socialists asked what "should" be the output, and when they used the criterion that resources should provide the greatest value as judged by individual consumers and producers, they noticed the implication that a private-property system of wealth maximizers with free access to a price-takers' market gave precisely that result. Everyone was embarrassed—the socialists because this provided an "argument" for capitalism and the capitalists because, much as they would have liked this "justification" of their activity, not all of them could validly claim to be selling in open markets or even defending open markets. Although some discussion and argumentation about each system hinges on this kind of criterion of productive and allocative efficiency, there are other important considerations: "freedom," culture, and social behavior, which we shall not discuss here.

## Adjustments without Full Information

With market-revealed values of goods, there is no necessity for anyone to have *full* information about all possible costs of various programs in order for a higher demand and price to induce a greater output in a price-takers' market. There are forces inducing a larger output if demand increases—and a smaller output if demand decreases—in a private-property, open-market economy. We examine some of them now.

In the first place, many producers do keep records and compile data with which to estimate their own costs. They have data to increase the probability of being near the wealth-maximizing output. They know that when demand rises and takes price up with it, an expanded output becomes more profitable. If their output had been less than the wealth-maximizing amount, the incentive to an increased output is now even stronger. If the output had been too large, the incentive is again to increase it; but, at the same time, the wealth-maximizing output also increases, whether or not each producer knows exactly what that output is. All the forces are now stronger for a larger output.

Second, even for those who may not compute costs in an endeavor to find the wealth-maximizing output, the increase in demand means that the set of profitable output programs is larger than formerly. Even if every firm picked outputs at random, those that picked larger outputs would be more profitable than those that picked smaller output programs. The observed or revealed profits will be greater for the producers of the larger outputs. Imitation of more profitable producers will expand output.

Third, a powerful force toward the wealth-maximizing output is the competitive actions of people. If the demand for wheat should increase, a corn farmer will more probably shift his land into wheat production. This would *not* be done by exhortations or appeals invoking the national or social interest. The prospect of greater personal wealth can be realized either by changing production in the greater wealth direction or by renting or selling his farm land and resources to others who will. Prices of productive resources reflect valuations not merely by owners but by other people, who offer to buy or rent the resources. When other people think the use value of a piece of land has risen in response to higher demands for its potential products, the owner can capture the present capital value of that future product. The important point is that resources are transferred to higher-valued uses as people seek greater wealth—if the resources are salable as private property. Information about values and costs is brought to bear even on those who are inclined to disregard changes in use values.

## Timing of Supply Responses

Not all producers make the inevitable output adjustments at the same time. Some find it economical to delay the adjustment and say to the more immediate or earlier-date producer, "Anything you can do, I can do better—if I do it later or in less haste." This deferred output is often referred to as a "longer-run" output—in the sense that the run of time prior to the output is longer.

That costs of later action are lower is a direct implication of the fundamental cost proposition that higher rates of production are more expensive. Immediate action requires a higher rate of use of existing resources. Overtime, premium delivery prices, greater use of higher-cost resources to hasten output are only a few of the cost-increasing factors involved. However, to defer indefinitely in order to get lower costs will also defer and reduce the value of the output. Therefore, we shall assume some lower limit of costs, below which they will not be reduced by any practical deferment. These lowest-cost, or long-run output, programs represent the ultimate adjustment of inputs.

## Summary of Output Response

The production and market-price effects of an increase in demand can be generalized in summary form. Starting at an initial full-equilibrium price and output position, the rate of output can be instantly increased only at very high costs; with time the output rate can be increased more cheaply. This relationship of costs to time of output can be suggested graphically, by two supply curves: one for the early reaction, and one for the later extreme limiting output rate for any given cost. Figure 16–5 shows a "before-and-after" situation. Demand, at $D_1$ with price at $p_1$, has increased to $D_2$. As it did, price rose and then fell along a path suggested by the dotted line as the larger output was forthcoming—to the long-run equilibrium at $p_n$. We cannot indicate the exact course of the price. All that can be deduced is that, depending upon how much and how rapidly the demand increases, price will move up toward the long-run equilibrium at $p_n$, as the output adjustment takes place.

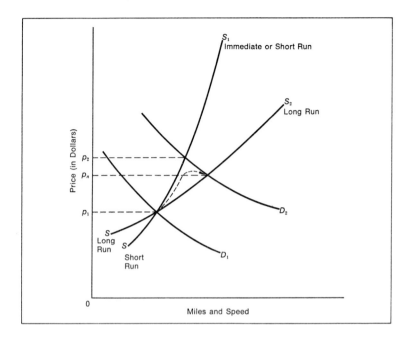

Figure 16–5
Supply Curves for Various Adjustment Dates for Various Outputs

Starting at the initial equilibrium situation, with price $p_1$, as demand increases, its intersection with supply will slide along $S_1$, the intermediate, or short-run, supply, which shows increased production from existing firms. In time, new firms will be attracted or new productive equipment will be installed by incumbent firms and outputs will be indicated by long-run supply curve, $S_2$. Short-run supply curve is summation of incumbent firms' marginal-cost curves. Long-run supply curve is sum of amounts firms (including new firms with new equipment) could produce at each price without losses.

The *ultimate* long-run equilibrium cost of production toward which open-market forces tend is one in which birth and death rates of firms in the industry are pushed toward equality. By definition, the long-run equilibrium involves an equality of price and minimum average costs and stable output in terms of industry output and number of firms. There will always be some firms expanding and others contracting (for example, the owner is aging, the firm has lost its special abilities, population is shifting). Therefore, stable output implies no *net* changes in output.

Illustrative Analysis:  Effects of a Tax

Uses of resources and outputs of consumer goods are affected by many factors other than changes in demand. Conditions of production, or supply of productive resources may change. One factor that especially lends itself to instructive analysis is the imposition of a tax on the production or purchase of some good.

*Tax on all producers in industry.* Suppose that the manufacturers of, say, playing cards are taxed 50 cents for each deck produced. This tax increases each firm's marginal costs by 50 cents at every output, and it adds 50 cents to the average cost of each deck. Summing the new higher marginal-cost curves over all the firms of the industry yields a smaller supply curve, as illustrated in Figure 16–6. Before the tax, the price was 75 cents. Each firm, now operating on a higher marginal-cost curve, will be induced to reduce its output *at the initial price* from $X_1$ to $X_2$ in Figure 16–6. The reduced output offered on the market will push up price, which will induce each firm to restore *part* of the output—back to $X_3$. Our first conclusion is that the higher tax raised costs but price rose only *because the supply decreased*. The effect on price is

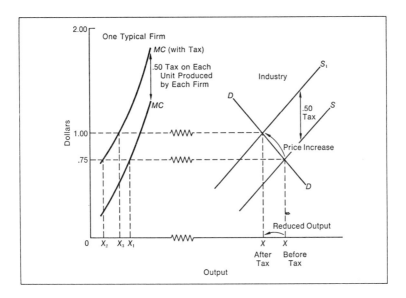

Figure 16–6
Price and Output Effect of Tax on Each Unit Produced or Sold

Tax is levied on output of playing cards of all firms in industry. Supply curve shifts upward to incorporate taxes of 50 cents per unit. This reduces output at the old price and the price moves up to $1. Higher price results from the smaller supply function. Unless tax affects supply curve, price cannot be affected. Price rises by less than tax because, at smaller output, marginal and average costs are lower. Part of tax is revealed as a higher price to consumer and a smaller rate of consumption; another part is reflected in reduced wealth value of resources used in production. Tax is borne by consumers and by owners of capital goods and labor services used in this industry.

through the effect on supply, and only because the higher tax decreased the supply did the price rise.

The price is increased by less than the tax on each deck—namely, by 25 cents (to $1 from 75 cents). Part of the tax cost is avoided by reducing the rate of output, so that the output is at a lower point on the marginal-cost curve. But this also means that part of the resources used in producing playing cards is no longer as valuable to the firm. This decrease in resource worth reflects the lower price of the final product, the playing cards, after deduction of the tax that must be paid. Thus, we see that the total tax receipts (tax per deck times number now produced) are accounted for, in part, by a higher price to consumers and in part by a lower value of resources used by manufacturers of the taxed good. If someone says that taxes are ultimately borne by the consumer, we can see the error in that statement. Instead, *part* of the tax is borne by consumers in the form of higher prices and part is borne by the owners of the resources, whose wealth fell at the time the tax was announced. Be careful not to confuse the effect on the wealth of those who own resources useful in card production at the time the tax is announced with that of those who purchase those resources afterward. New buyers will make offers that reflect the lower capital value of the future receipts *net* of the taxes that must be paid for as long as the tax exists, which we assume is for "many" years. This imposes the wealth loss on the owners of resources at the time of the announcement of the tax.

But this is not the end of the adjustment. In the long run the stock of resources devoted to card making will be reduced, and the output will be smaller than the immediate or short-run response, as can be seen in Figure 16–7. The longer-run adjustment in price and output includes the adjustment in the stock of all the resources in all the firms making cards. When this final adjustment is achieved, the price of cards will be high enough so that the price net of tax will cover the cost of *replacing* the smaller stock of resources. The reduction in output of cards is not a measure of the total output consequences of the tax; some resources that would have produced cards are now directed to other goods. But these other goods are less valuable, in the opinion of consumers, than that of the "unproduced" cards. We know this because, without the tax, the cards were preferred; that is why they were formerly being produced. However, there are two further considerations. First, it is sometimes argued that taxes are imposed on goods that *should* not be produced so extensively. Thus, some people argue for taxes on alcoholic drinks, gambling, night clubs, and tobacco. Second, it is alleged, the tax proceeds are spent by the government for goods that are "more important." Educators and parents commonly advocate taxes on cigarettes, alcohol, etc., in order to permit more educational expenditure—facilitated by resources released from card production.

This analysis of the response of price, output, and wealth to a tax is very similar to that for a change in the price, unaccompanied by any change of productive power, of some resource used in making cards.

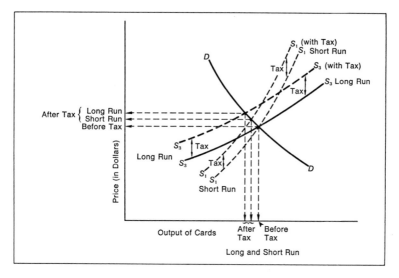

Figure 16-7
Price and Output Effects, Long- and Short-Run, of a Per-Unit
Tax on Playing Cards

The longer the amount of time allowed after a tax increase the greater the effect on the amount supplied at any price—and the flatter the supply curve (reflecting withdrawal of resources from the industry). The demand curve in the diagram represents both the long and the short run. But if we remember that long-run demand response is more elastic, the demand appropriate for the long-run supply will be flatter than the one for the short-run supply. Draw in a new demand curve with a flatter slope (intersecting the demand curve shown at the pre-tax price and pre-tax output point), and you will see the effect on the new long-run output and price. The output must be smaller, and the price must be lower than that shown in the present diagram as the long-run after-tax price. It might even be lower than the after-tax short-run price, if adjustment in the amount demanded in the long run at a higher price is sufficiently large. In any event, tax results in higher price to consumers, smaller rate of card consumption, and reduced wealth to owners of productive resources used in card production.

*Tax on one firm only.*   Suppose the tax had been levied on *just one* producer. His wealth-maximizing output rate would be smaller. Could *he* therefore raise his price? No. Without a similar tax on the other producers, the supply curve of the industry does not shift by a perceptible amount. In this case, *his* output and wealth fall more than if the tax had been levied against all producers. And he has no way to recoup part of his wealth by a higher price. If he tried to raise price, all his buyers would simply shift to other sellers, who provide perfect substitutes.

Summary

1    Increased demands and higher prices induce larger outputs. The supply
relationship between price and output of each firm is given by a firm's
marginal-cost curve above the minimum average variable (for the short-
run) costs for existing firms. For new firms it is the portion above the
minimum per-unit total costs.

2    A firm's wealth-maximizing output is that output at which marginal
cost is equal to marginal revenue—which is the average revenue or price
at which a price-taker can sell in the open market.

3    Firms will continue temporarily to produce even if price does not cover
the total costs including the fixed acquisition cost, which is a sunk,
irrelevant cost. Producing at a loss means that the decision to enter or
acquire the equipment for production was a wealth-losing decision, but
if production is nevertheless continued temporarily, the loss will be
minimized. When the *minimum* per-unit variable cost is pushed above
price as higher maintenance or replacement cost occurs, the firm will
shut down.

4    An industry is the collection of firms producing a particular good. The
industry short-run supply curve (which excludes new firms) in a price-
takers' open market is the sum of the amounts given by each firm's
marginal-cost curve at the market price—that is, those portions of each
firm's marginal cost curve above its minimum per-unit variable cost.

5    The long-run supply curve (reflecting entry and acquisition of new
productive equipment) is the portion of marginal cost above the minimum per-unit total cost. The long-run industry supply curve is the more
elastic curve.

6    Entry of new firms occurs not only when new enterprises seek to
replace or compete with other firms by producing at a lower per-unit
cost, but also when price rises in response to demand increases.

7    Healthy industries that have a high turnover of firms are sometimes
mislabeled "sick" industries.

8    Profits of production are imputed, by revised market prices, back to the
responsible productive resources. In this way costs of subsequent use of
the resources are revised to reflect higher value of the resources. Thereafter, returns to producers just cover the new adjusted revalued costs.

9    Unless resources are directed toward their highest-valued known uses as
indicated by market-revealed values, the owner will not maximize his
wealth. Wealth-maximizing use of resources to determine outputs is
economically "efficient." Full information on possible uses of all goods
and resources is not necessary for efficient resource use.

10    A tax on units produced reduces the output of the taxed good (releasing resources for use elsewhere). The tax results in (a) wealth decrements to the productive resource owners at the time of the tax and (b) wealth decrements to consumers of the product who now pay a somewhat higher price for the taxed good.

11    All the responses and actions analyzed in this chapter were those of price-takers in open markets. To think that people let open-market forces operate without attempts to interfere or restrain the open-market adjustment process would be naive. Many producers or owners of goods, faced with unpleasant losses of wealth, will seek to prevent the open-market forces from operating. Why they do so has been amply suggested in earlier chapters. How such restrictions or closures of the market can be brought about, and some of the effects, will be the subject of Chapters 18 and 19.

Questions

1    Do the data in Table 16–1 yield constant costs for the firm?

2    What is the wealth-maximizing output program if the selling price is $1.50? What is the profit? What is the wealth-maximizing output program if the price is $5?

3    Explain why part of the marginal-cost schedule (that is, for outputs at which marginal costs are at least equal to the average, or variable, costs) is the supply schedule of the firm in a price-takers' market. What is the supply curve for the firm in Table 16–1?

4    A producer with the costs given in Table 16–1 could produce *more* than twenty units at a price of $2.50, but he would be penalized with reduced profits.
a. In what sense is it good that he does not produce more?
b. In what sense is it bad that he does not produce more?

5    You are a public employee operating a publicly owned golf course, or swimming pool, or taxi service, or gun factory; and you have the costs indicated by the data of Table 16–1. Furthermore, you are selling the product in a price-takers' market.
a. At a price of $1.80 you choose to produce not seventeen units but about twenty-five units. Why do we predict you would produce about twenty-five units? (Hint: How do the rewards and punishment meted out to you as an operator of a nonprivate-property firm, depend on, or vary with, the selected output program? Compare this with a privately owned business.)
b. Suppose that you are *told* to maximize the profits. Would you? Why?

6    If, in some industry, there were 100 firms exactly like the one whose cost data are given in Table 16–1, what would be the supply schedule—assuming a price-takers' market? Plot that industry's (100 firms) supply curve on graph paper.

7    The following describes the state of market demand in the price-takers' market for the hundred firms assumed in the preceding question.

Demand Schedule

| Price | Quantity | | Price | Quantity | | Price | Quantity |
|---|---|---|---|---|---|---|---|
| $5.00 | 450 | | 2.80 | 810 | | 1.40 | 1,400 |
| 4.50 | 500 | | 2.60 | 850 | | 1.20 | 1,700 |
| 4.00 | 560 | | 2.40 | 900 | | 1.00 | 2,100 |
| 3.75 | 610 | | 2.20 | 950 | | .90 | 2,400 |
| 3.50 | 660 | | 2.00 | 1,000 | | .80 | 2,800 |
| 3.25 | 710 | | 1.80 | 1,100 | | .70 | 3,300 |
| 3.00 | 770 | | 1.60 | 1,200 | | .60 | 3,900 |

a. Draw this demand curve on the diagram of the preceding question.
b. What will be the equilibrium price?
c. What will be the rate of output at that price?
d. At that price what will be observed in the market?
e. To each seller what will appear to be the shape of the demand curve of his products?
f. If price is somehow kept from that equilibrium, what will be observed in the marketplace?
g. At the equilibrium price of the current problem, will new firms be attracted into producing this good?
h. Would the attraction be more pronounced and more effective if the demand were twice as great, with the supply schedule being what it is? Explain why.
i. If new firms can enter this business, each one having the same cost conditions as firms already in the business, to what value will the market price move? (Hint: You must first determine the long-run supply curve, including entry of new firms, in order to get the answer.)
j. When plotted on graph paper, what kind of shape or position will the new supply curve have relative to the older one?
k. As new firms enter, what will happen to the output of the existing firms?
l. What will be the total long-run equilibrium rate of output? (You should be able to read the answer from the chart you have graphed or compute it from the tabled data.)
m. Will all the firms that enter survive in the business? Why?
n. If all the new firms are not identical, in that some have higher minimum average costs, to what level will the long-run equilibrium price move?

o. What will happen to the costs of the firms whose minimum average costs were lower? (Hint: What happens to the profits of those lower-cost firms?)

8    Is there a short-run cost and long-run cost for a given output program, or are there two different contemplated output programs, each with its own cost?

9    "Marginal costs serve as a guide as to how much of a good to produce, while average costs help indicate whether to produce the good at all." Explain.

10    The process whereby secret information is revealed by the stock market is exemplified by the following episode: On March 7, 1954, the *New York Times* reported a test in which a new bomb of enormous force had been exploded on March 1, 1954. On March 31, 1954, Atomic Energy Commissioner Strauss reported publicly for the first time the nature of the new bomb and its dependence on lithium. Weeks prior to his announcement, the price of the stock of Lithium Corporation of America, one of the producers of lithium, increased substantially. How is this rise in price consistent with the fact that everyone connected with the corporation and the test really kept the secret?

11    A tax of 1 cent is levied on each pound of peanuts grown by farmers.
a. What effect will this have on the output of peanuts?
b. How will it induce that effect?
c. What will happen to the price of peanuts?
d. Will the land on which peanuts are grown fall in value—in view of the facts (i) that peanuts are grown from plants that must be seeded every year, and (ii) that the land can be used for other crops?
e. What will happen to the value of *existing* machines used for harvesting, shelling, roasting, packaging, and crushing peanuts? Why?
f. Explain why these changes in value will not be permanent even though the tax is permanent.
g. Does the temporary drop in value mean that the wealth-reduction effect of the tax is only temporary? Why or why not?
h. The proceeds of the peanuts tax is used to finance purchases of this book for free distribution to college students. Who is paying for the books so distributed? (The answer is *not* that those who lost wealth from the revised valuation of existing resources are paying for books. That loss of wealth is not offset as a gain to anyone else.)
i. Who gains what as a result of the tax and expenditure of the proceeds?

12    Suppose that the tax in the preceding problem is levied against only *one* producer of peanuts.
a. What will happen to the price of peanuts?
b. To the output?
c. To the wealth of the various peanut producers?
d. Whose wealth will be affected by this tax?

13 Stradivarius violins are rated as about the best in the world. Yet there is evidence that at the time they were built (1700) other violin makers were making even more costly violins. Those more costly violins did not, at that time, sell for as much as the Stradivarius violins, nor do they even today sell for as much. How can you reconcile this with the statement that prices depend upon, or are affected by, costs? Were the Stradivarius violins really less costly?

14 The average cost of the resources used in producing $X$ is $5, where cost is interpreted as the highest sacrificed use value. On the other hand, if these resources were to be used elsewhere, their sacrificed value of output here, $6, is their cost. What will make these two different "costs" of the same resources converge to the same value?

15 "The free-enterprise, capitalist system is a system of consumer sovereignty. Consumer preferences determine what shall be produced and how much shall be produced." Evaluate.

Production and Pricing in Price-Searchers' Open Markets

Unlike price-takers, price-searchers administer or set prices via various pricing strategies, advertise their goods, and hold inventories. We have already shown how a negatively sloped demand for its product would require a firm to search for the wealth-maximizing price instead of finding it almost ready-made in the market. U.S. Steel announces prices of its steel; Scripto Pen states its selling price for pens. The local restaurant, druggist, and grocer set their prices. Each could set a higher price without losing all its sales, and each could have set a lower price to increase the amount demanded (not to increase the demand schedule). It might seem, therefore, that each could set price arbitrarily, without regard to market demand and production conditions. Yet price-searchers cannot survive with *any* price; and some prices will yield bigger wealth than others. Which price will make the most profits for the business, and how can it be found? What restrictions are placed on price by the conditions and costs of production?

## Two Types of Monopolies

Price-searchers are often called monopolists because the seller has the power to change price. But, to avoid analytic error, we must draw a distinction between two different situations, both of which are commonly called monopolistic: *closed* monopoly and *open* monopoly.

### Closed Monopoly

Historically, monopoly referred to sellers who, by government authority, were granted exclusive access to the market. In this sense, monopoly is the reverse of open markets. *Closed* monopolists are sellers who are protected from open-market competition of the other sellers. Examples of closed monopolies are medical doctors and surgeons; telephone, gas, electric, and water companies; airlines; taxi services in almost every major city; retail liquor stores; teamsters' and longshoremen's unions; many trade unions (though probably not most); and lawyers. In some of these cases, new sellers can enter only by permission of some government agency; in others, those already in the profession have power to determine who shall be allowed to enter the market. Thus, closed markets are those with restrictions on who may enter, not just markets in which authorities completely prohibit entry of new sellers.

### Open Monopoly

*Any seller facing a negatively sloped demand curve is called a monopolist*, or as we prefer to call him, *a price-searcher*. He will be called an open-monopolist or open price-searcher if entry to the market is open to all potential sellers.

An open price-searchers' market sometimes is said to have "monopolistic competition." The term "monopolistic" concentrates attention on the uniqueness or single-seller aspect of a differentiated product, and "competition" emphasizes the context of open markets. In the remainder of this chapter we shall study only open markets with price-searchers—that is, open monopolies.

Price and Output for Price-Searchers
in Open Markets with Full
Knowledge of Demand and Cost

If a price-searcher had full knowledge of the demand for his product and of costs of alternative output programs, he could easily ascertain his maximum-wealth price and production program. To illustrate this, we shall assume the contemplated output program is for one year, and that an increase in the output rate implies also a proportionate increase in the planned volume with already acquired equipment.

The *costs* of alternative output programs (different annual rates and planned volumes for one year) are assumed to be those given in Table 16–1 (page 352) and graphed here in Figure 17–1. The average costs and the marginal costs are graphed as smoothed curves and labeled $AC$ and $MC$. The demand conditions given in Table 17–1 are portrayed in Figure 17–2 as the demand curve (average revenue) and the marginal-revenue curve, labeled respectively $DD$ and $MR$. The output program that maximizes the firm's wealth is the program of fourteen units. These can be sold at a price of $2.70, with total average cost of $1.06. The profit is $22.95. If a larger output (for instance, fifteen units) were to be sold, the price would have to be lower ($2.60), and the average cost would be greater ($1.09, compared to $1.06). However—since the marginal revenue at fifteen units is $1.20, which is less than the marginal cost, $1.55—the extra sale is not enough to compensate for the reduced gain on each unit sold. Therefore, since marginal revenue falls below marginal cost beyond fourteen units, the output program of fourteen units is the profit-maximizing output.

The seller could, instead, have set some other price if he were prepared to bear the consequences. At a price of $1.60 he will sell twenty-five units and lose $5. At a price of $3 he can sell eleven units, but he will gain only $21.90, compared to $22.95 at a price of $2.70. His market demand and cost conditions, along with the desire for more wealth, constrain him toward the price of $2.70.

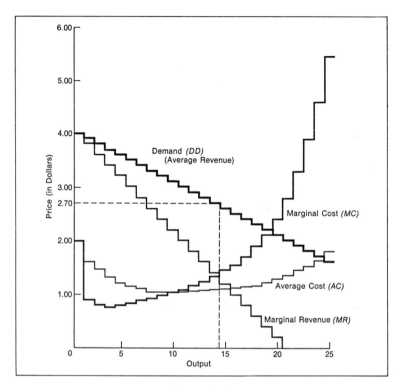

Figure 17–1
Demand and Cost Conditions for Price-Searcher, and
Profit-Maximizing Output and Price

A price-searcher, faced with the demand function, *DD*, (also known as the average-revenue function) will find his profit-maximizing output at the output at which marginal revenue falls to equality with the rising marginal-cost curve. At any output less than fourteen, an increase in output would increase revenue (marginal revenue) more than it would increase cost (marginal cost). At any output larger than fourteen, the extra output would increase costs more than revenue. If price is set at $2.70, the firm would be able to sell fourteen units, though it would be happy to sell more units if they were demanded—at least out to twenty-one units. But if it did find itself selling more than fourteen at a price of $2.70, would it continue with that price of $2.70? Why not?

The Search for Wealth-Maximizing Price
and Output with Incomplete Information

*If* businessmen did have knowledge of the demand curve facing them, and *if* they knew what it would be in the future, and *if* they knew their cost

Table 17–1
Demand for Price-Searchers' Product

| Price | Quantity Purchased in One Year | Total Revenue | Marginal Revenue |
|---|---|---|---|
| $4.00 | 1 | $ 4.00 | $4.00 |
| 3.90 | 2 | 7.80 | 3.80 |
| 3.80 | 3 | 11.40 | 3.60 |
| 3.70 | 4 | 14.80 | 3.40 |
| 3.60 | 5 | 18.00 | 3.20 |
| 3.50 | 6 | 21.00 | 3.00 |
| 3.40 | 7 | 23.80 | 2.80 |
| 3.30 | 8 | 26.40 | 2.60 |
| 3.20 | 9 | 28.80 | 2.40 |
| 3.10 | 10 | 31.00 | 2.20 |
| 3.00 | 11 | 33.00 | 2.00 |
| 2.90 | 12 | 34.80 | 1.80 |
| 2.80 | 13 | 36.40 | 1.60 |
| 2.70 | 14 | 37.80 | 1.40 |
| 2.60 | 15 | 39.00 | 1.20 |
| 2.50 | 16 | 40.00 | 1.00 |
| 2.40 | 17 | 40.80 | .80 |
| 2.30 | 18 | 41.40 | .60 |
| 2.20 | 19 | 41.80 | .40 |
| 2.10 | 20 | 42.00 | .20 |
| 2.00 | 21 | 42.00 | .00 |
| 1.90 | 22 | 41.80 | −.20 |
| 1.80 | 23 | 41.40 | −.40 |
| 1.70 | 24 | 40.80 | −.60 |
| 1.60 | 25 | 40.00 | −.80 |
| 1.50 | 26 | 39.00 | −1.00 |
| 1.40 | 27 | 37.80 | −1.20 |
| 1.30 | 28 | 36.40 | −1.40 |
| 1.20 | 29 | 34.80 | −1.60 |

conditions for various possible output programs, then the preceding analysis would be sufficient to show how people shift resources toward wealth-maximizing points.

In fact, however, the search for the price-output programs of greater wealth is done *without* perfect foresight and without cost or demand data as explicit as those in our numerical examples. People may know all the laws of economics; they may know that an increased demand indicates greater wealth for higher-price–larger-output programs. But how do they know which demand, if any, has really increased and how much? Perhaps an observed increase in sales is merely a transient, random fluctuation. How do business-men know when they are charging the wealth-maximizing price?

With complete information, it is a trivial task to find the wealth-maximizing price. With incomplete information, the businessman's task is practically impossible. But the task of the economist or student of economic affairs is slightly different; his is to predict the direction in which specified changes in

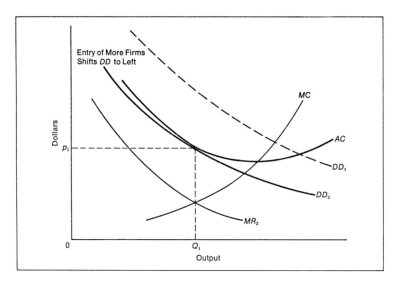

Figure 17–2
Zero-Profit Equilibrium for Price-Searcher

Entry of new firms reduces demand for each firm until price is at zero-profit situation. The new lower demand function, $DD_2$, is just tangent to average-cost curve. $DD_1$ is the old demand curve (prior to entry of new firms) with which this firm had positive profits. Under new demand function, there is no output at which the firm can make profits. At every output other than $Q_1$, it will lose wealth. (Marginal revenue for old curve $DD_2$ is not shown).

demand and cost conditions will modify the wealth-maximizing price-output programs. The economist can postulate changes in these external conditions; and then, with his principles of demand and cost conditions, he can deduce the direction in which the new wealth-maximizing price-output programs are shifted. But that is not all the economist should do; he should also show how businessmen, even in a state of incomplete knowledge about demand and cost conditions, are induced by changes in demand and cost conditions to adjust their price-output programs in the directions indicated by economic theory.

To see how output responds to market demand and cost conditions, we replace the fiction of free and full knowledge with partial ignorance—which is *not* to be identified with stupidity or irrationality. The price-searcher must feel like a gambler at the racetrack; there is *a* horse that will provide his biggest returns if he bets on it, but *which* one is it? If you told him to bet on the *winning* horse, he would say, "What good does it do to formalize a rule for maximizing my wealth if I do not know what to do to implement the rule?" Of course, the seller would like to announce a price that is his wealth-maximizing price. But what price is it?

Consider the problem faced by an airplane company. It has just designed a plane which it believes will make a good replacement for the DC–7—the Douglas four-engine piston-prop plane that was the backbone of the airplane industry. What price should it announce, and what scale of production should it plan? This is precisely the kind of question faced by Douglas when it started to make the DC–8 jet, and by Boeing with its 707, and by Convair with its 880. Only Boeing guessed sufficiently well to get a profit. How close it was to the profit-maximizing price, no one will ever know. The demand curve for the Boeing 707 did lie above the cost curve for a region that Boeing managed to find, whereas if the demand curve for Douglas and Convair commercial jets ever did lie above their cost curves, they weren't able to find out. If they had known where it was before they decided to produce, they would have saved the stockholders scores of millions of dollars. Apparently Douglas was luckier with its DC–9—a two-engine tail-jet short-range plane.

Similarly Ford, when deciding to produce the Edsel, clearly misjudged the location of the demand curve for Edsel cars—to the loss of millions. It guessed right with the Mustang. Packard Bell Electronics also badly misjudged—not on the demand curve for an important electrical item which it offered to produce for the government—but on the costs. Philco Electronics produced a "futuristic model" television set in 1960, for which the directors estimated the demand curve was above the average-cost curve at the planned output program. They were wrong—but they didn't find out until they had lost considerable wealth. Chrysler designed an automobile in 1958 for which the demand curve was under the average-cost curve. Chrysler lost millions, and this was evidenced by the decrease in the value of its stock during that year. We could list thousands of such failures.

But it is not only the giants who demonstrate uncertainty, ignorance, and fallibility. A corner restaurant must decide what prices to set and types of food to offer, and what volume to plan for. And the same goes for the local gasoline-station operator, the drug store, grocery store, discount house, automobile repair shop, as well as for General Motors, U.S. Steel, General Electric, and Du Pont. All are in the same boat. We don't hear much about those who lose wealth. Success breeds fame; failure, obscurity. No glamour publications are called *Death*, or *Misfortune*.

Let us now see how changes in demand for existing goods are revealed to existing producers and how their production programs are revised.

Buyers shop sporadically and accumulate goods for subsequent consumption. Sellers know that there is a difference between transient fluctuations in sales and fundamental changes in demand (where a fundamental change can be considered as a change in the average around which the sales rates fluctuate). Perhaps they could handle these transient fluctuations by letting price rise or fall at each instant so as to balance out demand with existing supply, much as stock-market prices match momentary demand and supply. However, *it will pay sellers to maintain an inventory of buffer stocks to meet these transient fluctuations in daily market demands rather than to try to produce to order instantly*. Inventories make the *momentary* supply schedule a horizontal line at the selling price, out to the limits of the existing inventory. However, it is only for the transient demand fluctuations that inventories serve as a buffer stock. Should demand increase, a continuing sales-rate increase would deplete inventories and induce higher replacement rates to accommodate the continuing larger rates of sales.[1]

The higher rate of production will raise marginal costs of production, and a higher price will have to be available. The higher price will be maintainable because of the increased demand. The sequence of effects from increased demand to inventory depletion, to replenishment of inventories by higher rates of production, and to higher costs and then prices can be identical with that explained in Chapter 6, when we traced the effects of a demand increase on the price of meat.[2]

Prices in price-takers' markets change more frequently within a narrow range than do those of price-searchers' markets. But prices in price-searchers' markets are not necessarily less adaptive to changed market conditions than are prices in price-takers' markets. Because of inventory availability, price-searchers will provide amounts wanted by demanders during transient fluctuations without having to change price. This kind of stability is not a reflection of price rigidity or power of seller to control price. It reflects instead the horizontal momentary supply out of inventory in the current market.

If demand falls, the theory and the evidence are that the price falls, as well as purchases and consumption. In other words, the preceding adjustment process is applicable to decreases in demand. *Changes* in demand and cost conditions are effective in inducing output changes even though firms do not know the precise demand and cost conditions or the new wealth-maximizing output and price program. A trial-and-error search process will induce convergence toward that wealth-maximizing program. The farther the actual output program is from the optimal, the smaller are profits or the greater are losses—both of which will increase the probability of the firm's changing its tactics or quitting production.

Entry of the New Firms and New Capacity
in Response to Demand Changes

The preceding analysis has concentrated on the price and output response of firms already in this "industry." Output of particular goods expands with higher demand, both because existing producers increase output and because new firms enter into production.

Increased wealth of an existing firm cannot be concealed. Its expansion is visible. If the firm enlarges, if the owners drive more expensive cars and their homes become more expensive, you have telltale indicators. Employees of

---

[1] Recall Chapter 6, pages 105–107.

[2] If the larger output is larger in *volume* as well as rate, and *if* unit costs fall sufficiently with larger volume, then prices, which may first have risen before output increase, will again fall, possibly to lower levels than originally. In any event, the increased demand is translated into an increased output.

competing firms know who is doing well. In various ways, the word gets around. As a result, other firms try to copy this firm. Perhaps employees leave and organize their own company, taking part of the company's "know how"; for example, hundreds of firms have been created by former employees of the earliest electronic-computer companies.

Other firms will find it profitable to shift production toward closer substitutes for the good whose demand has increased. If the production of steel, Cokes, Fords, or Arrow shirts becomes more profitable, other producers will produce close, if not perfect, substitutes and reduce the profits of the first producer as some customers switch part of their purchases to other products and sellers. Goods are substitutable in one degree or another, and a rise in demand for steel can be attenuated by an increased use of wood or brick. Or an increased demand for a certain kind of Ford will within a year bring similar models from General Motors, Chrysler, American Motors, or foreign producers.

The same two competitive open-market pressures that were described for price-takers in the preceding chapter operate on price-searchers: (1) Other producers will enter the market for this and related goods. (2) These other producers will bid away the resources. Assemblers, supervisors, designers, production engineers, salesmen, managers, and research staff will find competitors making offers for their services. The cost of keeping resources rises. Even the cost of having the owner stay in his business must be valued at a higher figure; the more others are willing to offer for his services, the higher are the costs he must impute to continuing in his own business.

The resulting zero-profit situation is shown graphically in Figure 17–1. The demand curve is tangent to the average-cost curve. A larger or a smaller output would result in costs that exceeded price per unit. There is no incentive for more firms with similar cost situations to enter the business.

If demand falls, the analysis is reversed. A reduced demand implies a lower price and output. The value imputed to resources used to produce that product falls as prices and output are reduced. Resources devoted to this particular good will be shifted to other activities, where they can earn more. Existing producers will reduce output, and in time some will leave the industry.

By selective differential survival, growth, and imitation by competitors, the population of business firms converges toward the maximum-wealth output and price programs. Add to these factors the activities of "raiders" who think they know how to run a business better than the present owner and offer to buy the firm. The new owner pays less than he thinks he can earn with the firm, while the old owner gets more than he thinks he could earn. The resources are shifted toward higher-valued uses—if these forecasts or conjectures are correct. If not, the new buyer discovers his error and can sell out, but only by bearing the loss. The more accurate forecasts (of the old owner) *yield* higher gains and enable the higher-valued uses to displace less appropriate uses of resources.

The simple facts stated in the preceding paragraphs are full of heartbreak.

When demand falls for any good, some people find their current services no longer so valuable. They cannot keep their jobs at the current rate of pay. Wage cuts or movements to new jobs are indicated. Business owners experience losses in the value of their plant and equipment.

The fundamental institutional features of the adjustment process are private property and open markets, not price-takers' and price-searchers' markets. In both market situations, the resource owners bear the wealth changes and are induced to make revisions in the uses to which the resources are put. In a nonprivate-property system, there is less specialization and less voluntary choice of resources; and resource use is less influenced by people's relative valuations of various goods. The influence is reduced because each person's own wealth is less correlated with the market value of resources. In the last section of this chapter, we shall explore this influence of market values more extensively.

Response of Producers
to Anticipated Demand

Some consumers believe that they can buy only what open-monopolist price-searchers decide to offer them. To some producers, the opposite seems to be true. Although both contain truths, neither of these positions is correct. The first reason we will discuss is that no one (including the people themselves) knows exactly what people will want to buy.

The Problems of Anticipating Demand

Some demands are revealed only by the appearance on the market of new goods. The development of transistor radios found a ready market demand although consumers had not expressed a desire for the radios. How many of us who now have stereo records "demanded" them before 1955? New products, varieties, and methods of satisfying consumers are continuously being tested for market demand: power steering, automatic transmissions, television, instant coffee, supermarkets, frozen foods, credit cards, electric wrist watches, cordless electric shavers, no-iron fabrics, synthetic fibers, stretch clothes, coin-operated dry-cleaning machines, water-based paints, zippers, etc. In what sense did these represent a response to demand? The hope of increasing wealth provoked someone to invest some of his wealth into producing some new item to test the market demand. The assurance of profit need not be demonstrated in advance. It is enough that there are venturesome, greedy, optimistic individuals willing to use some of their wealth to produce new goods for which they hope demand will be great enough to yield them profits. Consumers may not give birth to new goods, but they decide which shall survive.

An especially common example of businessmen anticipating market demand for as-yet-unproduced goods is the speculative builder and land developer. Potential apartment renters and house buyers usually do not urge the construction of buildings. Yet businessmen build in the expectation that the public does demand these new goods. If the builder is correct, he will make a profit; if not, a loss. In some cities suburban land developers are criticized as interested only in a quick dollar—a true charge. To whose demand are they responding by their efforts to buy the land and construct houses and apartments? The people living far away in other areas who will move to the area; even unborn generations are counted. If you were to ask some of those "unseen" people if they now demand those new buildings, they might deny it. Yet some of them will be moving into the area and will be demanders. Fundamentally, the foreseen demand of those unidentified people drives up the land values and induces speculators to bid resources away from other uses. The current market values (capital values) reveal that the land would be more valuable if used for the development. The present value of the land is the capitalized value of that latent future demand as judged by the land-owners and speculators.

The market will induce the land to be developed in ways for which its value in that use is higher, if the owner has a right to the gains in capital value of the land. Without those rights, the land developer will not respond so fully to the desires of the future. Another way to attenuate responses to capitalized values is to transfer the decision from the market context to nonmarket criteria—voting, for example. If the issue is settled by number of votes, then only those now qualified to vote will be counted. One speculator representing hundreds of future dwellers has only one vote. Current land owners of already developed sites and owners of existing homes and apartments will be likely to vote against an increase in the supply of the type of goods they own. Their wealth would be affected. Some (but not all) zoning ordinances are intended to prevent such market-induced change in resource uses in order to protect the wealth of owners of some existing sites and buildings.

The point to be emphasized is that market values expressed by speculative developers reflect demands of many people not visibly present. If gains in wealth cannot be obtained by speculative development, the future and latent demands will be less heeded.

### Reactions of Price-Searchers to New Product

Another example of the way in which market valuations operate is provided by the introduction of a new product by a new producer. With price-takers' markets, any one new producer is so small a part of the total that his effects on others' prices are too small to be detected. But for price-searchers the effects are large enough to be noticed. Consequently, the injured competitors, who lose customers and revenue, will be able to bring this loss of wealth to the attention of the new producer by offering to pay for the elimination of his competition. They could, in principle, offer the new producer an amount up to the measure of the damage done them, or they can and do offer this amount to the customers not to buy the new product—by lowering prices to customers of the old product. Will the competitors succeed? If the losses that would be imposed on the old producers by the entry of the new product exceed potential gains to the new producer, the old injured producers would successfully keep out the new product. If the gain conferred by the new product is greater than the losses to the competitors, the new product cannot be eliminated, either by price cuts to customers or by paying the new producer not to produce.

### Product Interdependence

Is it true that some goods aren't produced because they must be used jointly with some other as-yet-unproduced good? Congress, with the support of the President, enacted a law requiring every producer of television sets to sell *only* sets that can receive all 83 television channels, from channel 2 to 84. Presumably that law was passed because there was not enough incentive to make all-channel sets, and until sets were made to receive all 83 channels there would be insufficient incentive to telecast on the higher-channel stations. A "vicious circle" was alleged and apparently believed in Congress. What are the analytical implications and empirical evidence about this "vicious circle"?

Historical facts do not support it. Automobile production did not wait for gasoline stations. Did movie makers not make movies until theaters were built? Did radios wait for radio stations? Did FM receivers fail to be developed because they required transmitters to send FM first? In fact, they developed despite laws restricting FM broadcasting. Did stereo records await stereo record players? Did FM multiplex stereo programs and FM multiplex stereo receivers "bottleneck" each other? Did automobile repair shops and automobiles "bottleneck" each other? Did frozen foods and freezers for home use "bottleneck" each other? Did color television require a law compelling all manufacturers of television sets to include color capabilities?

The examples of FM radio and color television provide direct refutations of the presumed necessity for a law compelling UHF television receivers. No law required radio manufacturers to make only FM-AM combination radios. They could make any kind. As the design technology improved in the 1950s, FM sets became easier to tune and keep tuned, cheaper, and more reliable. The public demand was evident. In color television, on the contrary, for a long time the Federal Communications Commission *prohibited* color broadcasts until it could decide on the "best" kind of color system. And when it decided, it chose wrong. Fortunately, the Korean war forestalled production until the superiority of the better system became more obvious. Color television did not require a law compelling producers to sell only television sets with color capability.

What happened to the alleged vicious circle of new-product interdependence? It never was there in the first place. Perhaps a better question is, "Why should anyone have expected a blockage of development of joint products if the economic analysis given in the preceding chapters is valid?" Specialization of production is the rule in an economy in which exchange and access to the market are permitted. Specialization implies reliance on other people to produce jointly used products as they seek opportunities to increase their wealth. The search for greater wealth correlates the production of jointly used products. Only if one forgets the incentives and exchange opportunities in a market place will he fail to see the coordinated activity of other people. A visitor from Mars might contend that the real world is a much too complicated place for a capitalistic system to operate. He would be surprised that exchange prices and narrow specialization in a private-property context are capable of organizing a society as complex and productive as those he would see in Western countries. The strongest evidence that can be cited for the validity of economic theory is precisely the observed events. At the most rudimentary level, the theory implies that jointly used products will be produced "independently" even though each "assumes" the presence of the other. Specialization does not imply lack of coordination, nor does it imply that joint-product profit opportunities will be ignored. In fact, it implies that jointly used goods will be more effectively produced if specialization *is* permitted rather than if one person or firm must do the whole task.

In truth, the vicious-circle bottleneck among jointly used products is a delusion arising from the belief that output must be carried out on a large scale initially, that people are unwilling to invest now in anticipation of future receipts, *implying that present capital values are irrelevant.* These suppositions are disproved by events in the real world.

### Desirability of Directing Output by Wealth-Maximization for Price-Searchers

This discussion of the impact of capital values is not a defense of private property and open markets. In *some* communist and socialist states, market-revealed values are regarded as undesirable guides to productive-resource uses; hence, maximizing market-value wealth is considered undesirable. However, some socialist states are increasing the role of markets for consumers goods as rationing agencies and as sources of signals as to what to produce. (But incentive to follow those market signals is weaker without private property.) Every society to one degree or another reduces the power of open-market values to direct resources. Examples are provided by all goods whose production or distribution is in any way controlled outside of the market place: education, socialized medical care, radio and television, drugs, roadways, and many more.

A charge of inefficiency is commonly made against a system that allows wealth-maximizing to be a controlling force in price-searchers' markets. You may recall that price-searchers can distort production by not carrying output or sales to the point at which marginal cost equals price.[3] They will produce, instead, to the point at which marginal cost equals marginal revenue. Hence, it is concluded that a price-searcher's wealth-maximizing outputs are inefficient in that the output mix is one which could be revised so as to benefit some people by more than the loss to others.[4]

## Some Confusions about
## Price-Searchers' Markets

### Arbitrary Administration of Prices

A modern myth has grown up around the "facts of life" in price-searchers' markets—the facts that their prices fluctuate less than those of price-takers' markets, the prices of individual firms change at about the same time, and the largest firm usually acts as a price leader. These facts have been used to support the myth that dominant firms *arbitrarily* administer or set prices.[5] Therefore, it is alleged, unless price-searchers administer their prices with responsible, enlightened self-restraint, government must intervene to protect the public interest. For example, it has been said that U.S. Steel, General Motors, and large drug companies set the prices of their products by arbitrary

[3]See Chapter 11.

[4]But recent advances in economic theory indicate that the implication of inefficiency applies more to the *closed-market* monopoly and less to the open-market monopoly. In both cases, the demand function related price to quantity of output for a *given, unchanged* good. But, and this is the crux, if the producer or seller can change the product—by redesigning it, advertising, having several models, and varying his services—then the marginal cost and the marginal revenue are the changes in costs and revenues for quality as well as quantity. In this case, the relationships we perceive among price, marginal revenue, and marginal cost must include the effects of other variables. The two-dimensional (price and quantity) diagrams are not analytically powerful enough for that expanded problem. Suffice it to say that the more powerful analysis recognizing these other variables does not imply that efficiency is necessarily thwarted by open-monopoly price-searchers seeking to maximize their wealth.
Do not be distressed if the supporting logic of the preceding paragraph is not entirely clear. It would take us substantially beyond the appropriate limits of an elementary course to justify the preceding assertions.

[5]"Folklore and mythology" is admittedly name-calling and simply is a way of indicating which theory you think best explains observed economic events. There are people who regard the economic analysis presented here as mythology and folklore. What is the truth? As we said at the beginning, that must be judged in the light of both the logical consistency of the whole theory and the conformity of empirical facts with its implications. We believe the evidence provides overwhelming support for the economic theory we present.

administrative decision. Such sellers do, indeed, set their prices. They do not find or take them in the market the way wheat sellers do. The Aluminum Company of America announces its price of aluminum; R.C.A. sets the price of its radios and television sets.

*Price-setting versus equilibrium-price search.* What does such price-setting reflect? Simply each seller's search for the wealth-maximizing price.[6] But everyone does this, the lettuce farmer, the laborer, and the steel company. It's just easier to find that price in some price-takers' markets.[7] The lettuce farmer "sets" his price at the level that will maximize his wealth. All lettuce farmers in the area, for a given quality of lettuce, will find that their price is the same. Each one *could* have sold his product at a *lower* price. But his selfish disregard of "public interest" made him "set" the price at which his wealth would be greatest—the highest price possible. At a higher price he would sell none. He has a wide range of prices he can set, from zero up to the highest price at which he can sell any. This highest possible price is determined by the market and the total supply of competitors (including other commodities).

How different is the situation for the "price-searcher," who "sets" his price? His optimal price, the one that maximizes his wealth, also depends upon the demand and supply conditions. Neither self-restraint nor concern for interests of other people keeps him from raising prices. It is the effect on his wealth that restrains him; higher prices may lower his next receipts.

That same motive dominates price in *every* market. The poorest common laborer or retail clerk or employee *could* charge a lower price and be poorer; but because he, too, is greedy and wants more wealth for himself, he charges whatever price will give him the maximum of income. Thus, Du Pont "sets" *a* price of nylon. It does *not* charge the highest possible price at which it could sell *any* of its output; it seeks the wealth-maximizing price appropriate to (but not readily disclosed by) the market. The price it sets is the one it hopes is wealth maximizing. It cannot discover this price as easily as the price-taker can; it has to resort to trial and error, never being sure it has found it. Because of this exploratory charging of prices above or below the "best" price, some people think that Du Pont, U. S. Steel, or other sellers have "market power" to *set* or *administer* any price they please in a monopolistic, noncompetitive sense.

Whether sellers are described as "setting" prices or merely searching for the best (wealth maximizing) price in the market is all a matter of semantics. Call them "monopolist-administered prices" if you want to make the seller look like a powerful, selfish, noncompeting, economic royalist. Call them "market-revealed, market-demand-and-supply-determined prices" if you wish to de-emphasize individual motivation for more wealth. *All* prices in all markets are administered in the sense that each person decides at which price

---

[6]To avoid the impression that we are assuming businessmen have no goals other than maximum wealth, reread page 365.

[7]But not in all, as we shall see when looking at the market for labor, for example.

he shall sell (in the light of market demand). But the parenthetical phrase reminds us that the profitability of prices depends upon consumers' demand and the prices and costs of production of all other goods.

*Absence of aggressive price competition.*    Another naive idea is that an industry of a very few sellers, an oligopoly, is characterized by an absence of "aggressive" price competition. Although it is never made clear what is meant by "aggressive" price competition, the context of such assertions suggests that any one seller is aware that if he cuts price, others will quickly match his price, and everyone's profits will take a beating. So instead the sellers probably get together and agree to hold prices at some "reasonable" level.

The argument confuses a price in common with competitors on the one hand and the level of the common price of the few oligopolists. The maintenance of a common price may mean simply that it is not profitable to try to charge a lower price (nor a higher one!) than others are charging—just as a price-taker would find. That price could already be so low that it could not be lower with survival. Collusive behavior is not so simple as it may seem at first sight, as we shall discover in the next chapter.

### Profits and Concentration

Associated with the preceding misconception is another to the effect that the more an industry is concentrated in a few firms, the larger the profit rates. Thus, if the industry has (say) over 90 percent of sales in four firms, the profits will be larger than if the four firms had only 20 percent. The evidence does not support that common contention nor does economic analysis. How do such beliefs develop? Some industries with a few firms are observed to be more profitable than some with a large number of firms . . . a conclusion is suggested.[8] But if all industries are examined, the evidence so far collected does not support the conclusion.[9]

*Price-searchers and price increases.*    You may some day hear that price-searcher firms restrict or limit output *in order to increase prices.* If the price-searcher were interested in *raising* price, he could always raise it *still* higher and sell less until he sells just one unit—or none at all. But his total profits or wealth would be reduced. What he does is restrict his output to match the sales at prices that maximize his wealth. So, of course, do all firms. And the prices and sales of firms are interdependent. They watch each other closely and, like dogs chasing a rabbit, move together, even in those cases where there is no leader, simply because they seek the same quarry.

[8] In the photocopy business, Xerox has made enormous profits and continues to do so. It and a couple of other "copiers" have a very large share of the market. They have a large share because they have developed superior products. Unusually superior products can explain several cases of high concentration and large profits.

[9] J. S. Bain, "Relation of the Profit Rate to Industry Concentration," *Quarterly Journal of Economics*, August 1951, pp. 297–304. G. J. Stigler, *Capital and the Rates of Return to Manufacturing Industries*. Princeton, N.J.: Princeton University Press, 1963.

*Justifiable price changes.*    Compounding the confusion about price-searchers are the excuses and utterances of price-searchers who seek to justify their actions, as if they had the power to raise prices *and* get more wealth whenever they thought they had a "justifiable" reason—justifiable in the eyes of public opinion rather than in the market-demand and cost conditions. Instructive in this respect is the U.S. Steel price-rise episode of 1962.

Roger Blough, board chairman of the United States Steel Corporation, announced an increase in prices, asserting that costs were higher and that more income was needed to finance new investment. In the first place, the *use* he intended to make of the increased wealth (if the price rise increased it) is irrelevant to the *ability* to get it. Whether Mr. Blough wanted a fancier office or new steel mills has nothing to do with the ability of U.S. Steel to get more wealth by raising prices. In the second place, the fact that costs had risen does not mean that he could thereby raise prices and get a higher income. If that were true, he could let costs mount without limit and simply raise prices to cover them. What he could have said correctly is that costs of *all* steel producers were rising so that the wealth-maximizing price had changed, and U.S. Steel, in the interest of maximizing its wealth, intended to move to that new price.

At the time he announced higher prices, Mr. Blough realized that unless other companies also raised their prices and, also as a result, *had greater profits* (than if they did not raise them), the new equilibrium price was really not higher. Some other companies concluded that higher prices would not give them greater wealth, simply because market conditions of demand and costs had not changed in that direction. They did not follow the lead of U.S. Steel. The fact that the same firm is almost always the first to make a change and that others almost always follow does not mean that the leader dictates prices to other firms, nor does it imply some tacit agreement not to compete with prices. It can attest to the lead firm's greater acuity and knowledge of market conditions. Other firms watch its behavior and then follow, thereby avoiding the costs of maintaining a research staff. If the price change turns out to be a money loser, then "follower" firms will return to the original prices. They are the leaders in that return movement.[10]

*Price rigidity.*    Evidence refutes the charges that price-searchers administer prices regardless of demand and supply—or that the more concentrated is the output of an industry in a few large firms, the more inflexible the price. The number or size of firms in an industry has no statistical connection with the frequency or magnitude of price change. Yet to this day, some Congressional

---

[10] In 1963, a year later, the price of steel was raised immediately after the U.S. Tariff Commission announced it would open hearings to decide whether to impose higher taxes on imports of foreign steel—and to impose them retroactively on all prior imports at prices deemed too low. That simple announcement immediately induced foreigners to reduce shipments to the United States. For some government officials to protest the rise in the market price of steel would have been somewhat awkward, since other government officials had granted domestic steel producers closed monopoly protection from continued foreign imports.

committees are misled by the myth that administered prices are set and kept rigid in industries characterized by high degrees of concentration of output in a few firms. Also it is asserted that output fluctuates more in those rigid-price industries than where prices are not so administered. The myth lives on and on, sometimes buttressed with the same errors of statistical methods applied to more recent data.

What are the data so naively interpreted? Initially, price data were collected for goods like automobiles. The price of automobiles was reported to be stable and invariant because the list—or recommended—price announced by the automobile companies stayed unchanged throughout the year. One of the first things a person learns in shopping for a car is that the list price is the selling price only at the beginning of the new-car season. Immediately thereafter, the salesmen's pencils are sharpened for "special" deals, which are offered to everyone who says he is going to shop around.

Despite overwhelming evidence that list prices are not the prices at which all purchases occur, prices taken from catalogues and price lists are often collected and reported as *the* prices. For example, the catalogue prices of varieties of steel do not change for many months. Yet the actual transaction price at which steel is sold does vary. Discounts for cash vary; speed of delivery and special services vary from week to week; quantity discounts are common. A steel purchase is a complex transaction. Extensive studies of actual contract prices of steel show that the actual prices are highly variable from week to week, despite constant quoted prices. Furthermore, even if one firm's actual prices were its list prices, one would have to observe *all* the firms all the time to know what was happening to actual sales.

The current assessment of the price-rigidity allegation has been summarized characteristically by a president of the American Economic Association:

> Economists have long struggled to find a rational explanation for prolonged price rigidity, which is in general as inadvisable for profit-maximizing monopolists as it is impossible for "price-taker" industries. Putting aside minor or special circumstances (the cost of a price change; the procedural delays in cartel or public regulation), they have failed to discover any such explanation. It appears that the real world has been equally remiss in supplying the phenomena they were seeking to explain.[11]

### Excessive Advertising

Price-takers do not advertise their prices or the quality of their products since they can sell all they have available at the current price. Nor would advertising by any seller enable him to get a higher price, for other sellers of the identical product in the same market would provide the increased amount demanded. On the other hand, price-searchers are faced with limited sales at

[11] George J. Stigler, "Administered Prices and Oligopolistic Inflation," *The Journal of Business of the University of Chicago*, Vol. 35, No. 1 (January 1962), p. 8.

existing prices; each is eager to sell more at the current price but will not find it profitable to cut price to sell more. Advertising his product will inform some potential customers of his existence and goods. Information about possible sources of goods is a scarce resource, as anyone knows who enters a strange town and wonders about accommodations and restaurants. Often we forget this when we see advertising that tells *us* nothing we didn't already know. We may say that advertising annoys bystanders who have no interest in the advertised product. In this situation we should ask: How does a seller know which thousand persons are most likely to buy? He doesn't. So he advertises to a group of people, hoping to reach those currently interested in his type of product. The advertiser would be delighted to advertise in selective ways not noticed by people who would not possibly be interested in the product. But that is more expensive and uses more resources than some methods of general advertising. Much criticism of advertising reflects failure to take account of the lack of ability (1) to identify in advance each potential buyer and (2) to advertise in ways that will be noticed only by them. If we knew who was going to have flat tires at which times, repair cars would be at the spot ready to give service, and that would be less expensive than carrying around fifth tires. The fire-escape sign is useless on many nights, but should the light be turned off on nights when there will be no fire? Similarly, in school are we not taught several things that some of us will never use again later? Was there a waste of resources in that act of "indiscriminate" teaching? In exactly the same sense, some advertising is "wasteful"—which means only that if we all knew more, we could save resources.

One form of advertising brings forth probably more criticism than any other—that on radio and TV. Economic theory has something to say about that. The amount of advertising on radio and television is the result of the way in which radio and television are paid for. Movie theaters do not show commercials the way television does, because the patron pays directly and thus rewards or punishes producers and guides the producers' future actions. Pay television (which is illegal in most areas) could give the viewer some control over the programs shown. One can readily imagine the programs in movie theaters if patrons could come in free of charge. Programs appealing to a smaller group would be less common because a minority could not concentrate its "dollar votes" on preferred programs; diversity of preferences yields to majority tastes. If newspapers could not be sold, they would have even more advertising, as is evidenced by the ratio of advertising to news in neighborhood throw-away newspapers. The criticism of advertising on television is a criticism of the system of paying for television and radio programs.

Perhaps, next to radio and TV advertising, billboard and roadside advertising seems to run a close second as an object of criticism. But it is not necessarily advertising *per se* that is objected to; rather it is the thrusting of that advertising upon people in places and circumstances in ways they dislike. The blocking or destruction of scenic views is a prime example. There are two basic reasons for that destruction. First the scenic view is not owned by anyone, not even the landowner from whose property the view can be had; there is less reward for anyone to take action individually to preserve that view than there is for normally salable or negotiable goods. Second, even if an owner could be assigned, there is a very great cost of negotiating with all the people who might in some way destroy or alter that view. The technical problems have been too complex for man to have discovered how to bring that "good" into the rubric of resources controllable by normal operation of the property system. Failing some such system or imposed control, scenic goods, like the apples on the public tree, will be rapidly consumed.

Another complaint is about the uninformative, duplicative, competitive advertising. Camel advertises, and in self-defense Chesterfield has to advertise. The net effect is alleged to yield no gain except to the advertising people. Is there any other interpretation? The charge implies that customers buy one brand rather than another simply because of that uninformative advertising. When I see people being influenced by inane, tasteless, or substantially empty advertising, I am tempted to regard that advertising as wasteful or harmful. However, if I took a less authoritarian attitude, with more recognition of differences in tastes, I might be willing to entertain the possibility that customers prefer—perhaps for reasons which they have never articulated—the cigarette that advertises to one that does not.

Finally, we consider the situation regarded as the clearest use of wasteful advertising: the customer is supposed to be uninformed, and, as a result, the advertiser deliberately *misleads* him. But it is dishonesty that is bad, not advertising. We should not condemn advertising for dishonesty any more than political speeches. People are dishonest in daily conversation, in part, by being excessively tactful. As far as dishonesty is concerned, is it as fruitful in advertising as in private conversation? Open advertisements can be seen by competitors, and dishonest statements will more surely be refuted in open advertisements.

For fear that advertising will mislead people, it is sometimes proposed that authorities censor it—that is, decide what is permissible advertising. We already engage in much censorship. We expose our children to censored ideas when we control by authority what public schools teach them. The continuity of a culture requires that it pass on to the younger generations its customs, taboos, and habits. However, this censorship applies to children, and all parents have a large say in it. We censor our children's channels of communication because they are children—and this brings the crux of advertising content control to the fore. Are we to extend the concept to adults? Each of us may differ in our judgment. We may not like the way others behave when exposed to ideas and persuasive thoughts. But authoritarian control of advertising content is censorship of ideas; of that there is no dispute. The only dispute is whether it is good or bad.

Summary

1   Inventories, price-setting activity, and advertising are explainable by price-searchers' markets.

2   Price-searchers are monopolists in the technical sense of facing negatively sloping demand functions with respect to price.

3   Transient, fluctuating-demand functions imply inventories for price-searchers.

4   Price-searchers seek the price and output at which marginal cost equals marginal revenue, rather than price.

5   Price-searching pricing activity can be explained without collusion.

6   Open-market monopolies have no artificial or arbitrary restrictions on access to the market; closed-monopolist markets are those with restricted or closed access.

7   Production responds to anticipated demands of potential customers via speculative production for market, capital-value gains.

8   Advertising is a form of communication. Like communication at every level—personal, political, social—it contains dishonesty, exaggeration, and ulterior motives. That it contains less of these than any other communication is a defensible proposition. "Excessive" advertising may reflect its use as a rationing device for some goods distributed at a lower than market-clearing price (as with radio and TV and throw-away newspapers).

Questions

1   "If some firms producing $X$ have unsold output potential that they would like to use to produce more $X$ at current selling prices, if only the market demand were great enough, then the good $X$ is not being sold in a price-takers' market." Explain why that conclusion can be drawn.

2   The difference (for pricing and output behavior) between price-takers' and price-searchers' markets can be characterized by a difference in the demand curve facing each seller. Describe the difference in the demand curve.

3   Market closures need not result in price-searchers' markets, especially if the existing number of sellers is very large. Can you identify or suggest cases where market entry is restricted and yet a price-takers' market exists? (Hint: How about agriculture—wheat, tobacco, milk producers? Teachers?)

4    Tentatively classify the following, on the basis of your present information, as (a) price-takers, (b) closed monopolists, or (c) open monopolists. (Remember, market closure does not necessarily convert a
price-takers' to a price-searchers' market.)

Electric company                    Prescription pharmacist
City bus line                       U.S. Steel Corporation
Airline                             Lettuce grower
General Motors Corporation          Electrician
Corner drug store                   Elizabeth Taylor

5    Is it possible for an economy to be one in which everyone is a closed
monopolist and a price-taker, and yet everyone is poorer than if there
were no restrictions on the open market? Explain.

6    a. Can you suggest some good for which the differences among various
brands are insignificant? (Hint: Sugar, flour, aspirin, tires, dog foods,
bread, milk, soap, corn flakes, cigarettes, canned peaches, banks at
which you can have a checking account, beer.)
b. Obviously you will not agree that *all* these are examples of goods
whose brands are of insignificant differences. Are any? If so, does this
mean that when you buy this kind of good, you purchase at random
without regard to brand?
c. If not, what do you mean by an insignificant difference?
d. What makes you prefer one brand over another at the same price?
e. Can you name any good and two of its brands for which you believe
no one in his right mind could have a "good" reason for preferring one
over the other?

7    "General Electric announces a new 11-inch, 12-pound portable television for $99.50." "Parker '45' Pens are sold at an announced price of
$5." "Sunbeam appliances are sold at retail prices set by the manu-
facturer." Explain why the above statements do not imply price setting
by the seller. That is, explain why the prices were not all three times as
high as they are.

8    Does U.S. Steel have the power to raise the price of steel? Does it have
power to raise the price of steel in order to make more profits?

9    Higher costs have induced a firm to reduce output and raise price.
a. Is this to be interpreted as an example of the power of the price-
searcher to raise price?
b. If your answer is "No," how do you reconcile your answer with the
Council of Economic Advisers, who regarded the attempt of the Aluminum Company of America to raise its prices as an "unjustified" use of
the power to set prices?

10   In France, Italy, Spain, Hong Kong, and New York individual bargaining over the price of a good is commonplace.
a. Would you prefer that custom to the more common one in the
United States of not bargaining?

b. But on second thought, can you name three goods that are commonly purchased in the United States by bargaining?

c. How would you explain the simultaneous presence of two different customs?

11    You are collecting data for a cost-of-living survey. For each of the cases below, which "price" would you report as *the* price? Why?
"List price, $125. Special discount to $90!"
"35¢ box of Kleenex for 29¢."
"One cent sale. First for $1. Second for 1¢."

12    When collecting prices for your cost-of-living survey, you discover that not all customers can buy a good advertised on sale because the limited stock was sold out in the first hour. Continuing with your cost-of-living survey, in New York City the rents are controlled; but at the controlled rents apartments are not available to many who would pay the legal price. Would you use that legal price as the cost of housing? Why?

13    Change the data in Table 17–1 as follows: From every indicated "quantity purchased" at each price, subtract 6. If the new number is negative, simply call it zero.
a. Recompute the total and marginal revenue.
b. What is the new wealth-maximizing output for this producer?

14    Suppose a $5 tax is levied on your business—an annual license tax of a flat $5 regardless of how much you produce. Use the cost (only) data of Table 16–1 and revenue data of Table 17–1 to answer the following questions.
a. What will be your price and output?
b. What is the amount of your profits?
c. Suppose a $25 tax is levied. What will be your new price and output?

15    Again using the data of Tables 16–1 and 17–1, suppose that your costs of production are changed by a rise in the cost of materials or labor so that at every output your costs are 30 cents greater per unit of output.
a. What will this do to the marginal-cost schedule?
b. What will be your new wealth-maximizing price and output?
c. What are your profits now?

16    As a superior student you provide a tutoring service. The higher the price you decide to charge, the fewer the hours of work you get.
a. Are you a price-taker or a price-searcher?
b. Assume that your time, when you are not tutoring, is worth an equivalent of $2 an hour. The daily demand for your tutor services is not perfectly predictable; it varies at "random" around a mean rate of daily demand which depends on the price you can charge. If, at the price you charge, you find that all your available time is always used, and there are occasional applicants whom you must reject because you

are fully booked up, do you think you are charging the wealth-maximizing price? Explain.

c. If you are charging a price at which you occasionally have idle time, are you charging too low a price?

d. Given a fluctuating demand, how can you be sure that you have charged the "right" price?

**17**   You are constructing an apartment building. You can build one with many units and have vacancies sometimes, or you can build a smaller unit and have a no-vacancy sign all the time.

a. If the latter behavior is profitable, can the procedure of having vacancies sometimes be even more profitable?

b. Would you interpret an average vacancy rate on apartments of 5 or 10 percent as evidence that they are oversupplied, overpriced, or neither?

**18**   "Advertising by savings banks is wasteful. It doesn't induce any more saving. All it does is attract depositors away from one bank and to another. Since all banks are guaranteed and regulated, there is no difference among the banks. Hence, advertising that merely attracts depositors away from other banks does not a whit of good." Do you agree? If so, why? If not, why not?

19   "Much advertising is deceitful, dishonest, misleading, fraudulent, and disingenuous. Therefore, it should be subjected to government regulation." If you accept that conclusion, would you accept the same conclusion for daily conversation, political talks, lovers' pleadings—which are subject to the same charges? Explain why or why not.

**20**   Is it true that for some products you prefer one brand over the other if both have the same price, but if there is any price difference between them you will take the lower-priced one?

a. If this is true for some goods, does it suggest something about the basis for or "strength" of your preference?

b. Would you say that you "discriminate" among brands?

c. Is that "justifiable" discrimination?

21   Are there any products that are not being produced today because complementary, jointly used products are not being produced, so that each is waiting for more of the other—with a resultant underproduction of both items?

**22**   A year after the steel-price hassle of 1962, the federal government, in response to complaints from domestic steel producers about low-priced imported foreign steel, initiated hearings to determine whether foreign imports were being provided at less than the foreign costs—with nothing explicit as to what is meant by costs. The hearing determined that imported steel was being sold at prices below cost (below whose cost?), so taxes were imposed on the imported steel. Within a month, the domestic steel companies began raising the price of steel, in a discreet manner, with only lip-service complaint from politicians.

**a.** Do you think it likely that the higher prices proved to be more profitable?

**b.** Why did the government at one time object to higher prices of steel and then within a year take action to reduce the imports of steel, thereby enabling a higher domestic price?

23    In what sense can the marginal-cost curve of a price-searcher be considered a supply curve?

# Sellers' Tactics for Changing Market Conditions

Whether they be employees, business owners, or politicians, people do not always passively submit to open-market competition. They seek to close the market to competitors in three general ways: (1) predatory action against rivals, (2) collusive action with rivals, and (3) statutory legal closures of the market to actual or potential rivals.

In this chapter we shall investigate how these objectives can be achieved.

## Methods for Changing Market Competition

### Predatory Tactics

It is often said that if a firm can destroy its rivals, it can realize larger profits. And so, sales below cost are often regarded as a predatory tactic to bankrupt rivals. But there is another purpose of sales "below cost" (that is, below average operating costs). A firm can sell below cost to inform potential customers of its existence and product quality. A low price on well-known, repetitively purchased goods is designed to attract customers and enable the new store to penetrate the market. It is an investment, just like many other activities that involve greater cost than the *current* rate of receipts. The action is not designed to eliminate existing sellers so that the store can later set the price above current competitive levels. Therefore, it cannot be considered predatory.

The attempt to impose losses on competitors in order to achieve a monopoly position with subsequent "above-competitive" prices is a predatory action. A case frequently cited as a predatory action involved Rockefeller's Standard Oil Company in the nineteenth century when Standard's low prices in selected local markets were interpreted as devices to bankrupt smaller refiners. Would this be an intelligent tactic—that is, wealth-maximizing—even if no law prohibited it? Both the predator and prey lose wealth. The bigger firm with more sales will take a bigger absolute loss. The smaller firms can often shut down production of that item and wait out the return to higher prices, letting the predator take the greater losses. But whether or not the prey can take that action, it still is clear that below-cost selling, as a predatory tactic is not as smart as it is alleged to be.[1]

If a firm were to gain by driving a competitor to bankruptcy, the prey's productive assets must be retired from production. Bankruptcy does not *destroy* productive resources; they go to someone else, who probably acquired them at a sufficiently low cost to make their continued use profitable. The aggressor, who has been suffering losses to impose losses, would have to continue his predatory tactics as long as required to wear out the

---

[1] Warning: What appears to be a predatory policy is often in reality something entirely different. It can be competition by more efficient lower-cost producers. Or when demand falls, producers who cut prices may appear to be "predators" when they are merely adjusting to the new situation by trying to minimize their wealth losses (maximize their wealth at the lower attainable levels).

other resources, and this would mean larger losses for the predator too. Even if the predator were wealthier, it does not follow that he would find it sensible to bear greater losses. Careful study of the Standard Oil example has revealed no evidence of predatory tactics, although there was substantial evidence that Standard had bought rivals at a handsome price and retired the productive capacity.[2]

Collusion

It is not clear that businessmen should ever resort to predatory action as a means to monopoly wealth. The predator must take some losses that could have been avoided by joint action. Predatory action is less profitable than an agreement between the parties to cooperate, even by merger or covert agreement. However, the attempt to remove market competition does not eliminate competition. It shifts its form or locale—in the case of collusion, to the conference table, where the competitive issue is the division of the gain—by no means an easy one to resolve. Let's see what problems beset that attempt to collude successfully.

The potential gain from effective collusion, or avoidance of open-market competition, can easily be seen from our earlier water-demand example of Chapter 7, page 131, which you should review. You may recall that the individual competitive price would have been $1, but if the firms selling the product could agree to charge a price of $6 per gallon, the total income for the whole group would be larger. Achieving that control over the market and the sources of supply is an extremely difficult task.

Whether open or covert, an effective collusion—sometimes called a "cartel"—is faced with a formidable series of hazards, even in the absence of legal prohibitions:

1. Who are your competitors? If you were trying to organize doctors, what would you do about interns, chiropractors, registered nurses, druggists, dentists, and drug companies? All of them are substitutes in one form or another for some medical service. If doctors raise their fees, some people will ask more aid of their druggists and use self-prescribed drugs. Or suppose you are a steel producer. What would you do about aluminum, brass, plastics, wood, paper, and concrete? They are all substitutes. Would your "collusive" group be able to raise steel prices without intolerable losses of sales to nonsteel products? And what about firms that make their own steel? If you collude and raise prices, they will sell some of their steel output to other steel users; their steel production becomes more profitable, and thereby a new producer appears to take away your sales.

2. Suppose, however, that you decide to include only the steel companies and not those who produce aluminum or other substitutes. Of the more than one hundred companies producing steel in the United States, ten produce 90 percent of all the steel, so you plan to get just the big ten together. The rest will not be important enough to upset your plan too quickly, you hope.

[2]See J. McGee, "Predatory Price Cutting: The Standard Oil (N.J.) Case," *Journal of Law and Economics*, 1958, p. 137.

You tell the companies all they have to do is follow your price. But not all ten will agree that the price you set is the best. What is best for some will not be best for others. It depends on each firm's cost-output relationship, elasticity of demand, and growth prospects. Lower prices are more advantageous to lower-cost firms than to higher-cost, smaller output firms. Resolving this issue is not easy.

3. Each member is alert to the potential gains from secret cheating or from competition in ways not yet prohibited by the cartel. For example, a firm could vary its delivery, credit, trial, and refund privileges. Detecting *all* forms of competition is prohibitively expensive. The airlines have a regulatory agency and a cartel, but competition in beauty and personality of airline hostesses, in types of planes, and in fringe benefits to passengers has yet to be controlled.

The probability of secret price-setting is related to product and market characteristics. Secret price-cutting to a large buyer is more profitable than cutting price to a small buyer, considering the risk of detection. If all the colluding members *pooled* their output, sold it through a central sales agency, and split the proceeds, secret price-cutting could be controlled. However, how does one determine what share of sales goes to each member? The younger, growing firms want an *increasing* share. An alternative to "pooling" all output for sales via a central agency is to assign each buyer to one seller. This would reduce the incentive for price cutting (though not entirely, for by cutting prices, you would enable your buyers to undersell their competitors and in this way indirectly undermine your fellow conspirators).

An especially common case of collusion (in *open* markets) is that of sales to the government via sealed bids; a sealed-bid buyer is a "sitting-duck" for collusive sellers.[3] The government solicits bids from several sellers and opens them all at one time. Usually, the lowest bid wins. No rebidding is allowed (in sharp contrast to the purchase of a car by a private party who solicits bids from various sellers *and* giving each a chance to undercut the others). Therefore, the incentive for sellers to engage in collusion is stronger, because the buyer is less able to play one seller against the other. Furthermore, if any colluding sellers do not bid as agreed, the others will find out immediately since all bids are revealed. It does not seem accidental that almost all of the cases of established effective collusion have been on sales to government agencies or government-regulated public utilities.[4]

---

[3] Sealed bids are often used by government agencies—for example, schools, regulated public utilities, and federal agencies.

[4] An alternative explanation of the observed predominance of cases of collusion against the government is that the government is more willing to take cases to court, and hence reveal the collusion, whereas a private firm is less willing to resort to court costs. This sounds like a good alternative explanation if we forget that the greater facility of legal prosecution by the government should serve to inhibit attempts to collude against the government.

The notorious electrical-equipment case of 1962 involved sales to *sealed-bid* governmental agencies. Subsequent accusations of collusion against sellers of meat, flour, water pipe, steel, office furniture, cement, milk, banking services have all involved sealed bids to government.

4. Another problem is that not all competitors (actual or potential) can be induced to join: excluded firms are delighted at the opportunity to capture customers who shy from the higher price. These firms will grow in size and wealth—at the expense of the colluding members. The fraction of sales remaining with the colluding group becomes smaller and smaller.

5. The economic costs of quick creation of new facilities may dissuade new potential competitors from quickly entering the business. This delay in entry would appear to make at least short-lived effective collusion more likely; but there is another side to this coin. If expensive facilities are involved, the colluders will suffer a loss of their own large investment if new entrants do appear—an effect that will continue after the effectiveness of the collusion has ended.

Such are some of the inherent contradictions, obstacles, and hazards to *effective* collusion. We emphasize *effective* because many exploratory attempts to collude simply never come to fruition. Proposals are discussed, agreements are reached only to be dashed on the hard realities just mentioned.

Simultaneity of price action or "dominance" by one firm is not evidence *for or against* the existence of *effective* collusive agreements. The number of sellers and the coordinated price-search process, whether it be simultaneous or lagging behind some apparent "price leader," are also irrelevant. What is good evidence? The use of an *enforcement* technique. If costs are being incurred to enforce concurrence in competitors' actions, there is strong evidence that an *effective* collusion exists—one effective enough to make it worth the costs of enforcement. Restrictions on new entry to the market and penalties for noncompliance with the terms of the collusion are effective enforcement devices. Self-regulation or *legal* self-policing by members of an industry provides a weapon of enforcement. Members who do not comply can be denied the right to do business because licenses or special privileges can be revoked for "unethical" behavior. The privileges include access to special information or research, exemption from special taxes, the right to do business with the government or avoid strikes by unions.

A strong conclusion suggested by the foregoing considerations is that an effective collusion will be associated with some organization in which membership is essential if one is to stay in business. The organization can be one that obtains special privileges (government subsidies, tax favors, pooling of patent rights) or simply one in which membership is a qualification for doing business. Any member who does not conform to conditions of the collusion will be expelled from the organization, and thus legally excluded from the market. For example, the American Medical Association gives its members sufficiently great special privileges (for example, access to surgical hospitals) to enforce observance of its strictures against certain types of competition. Similarly, business firms in Germany prior to World War II were compelled by law to belong to Chambers of Commerce as a condition of the right to engage in business. Obviously member firms could enforce the strictures against types of market competition by expelling any firms that violated conditions and excluding them from the market! It is no wonder that Germany was typified by many collusive cartels.

A merger superficially appears to be an ideal vehicle for collusive action. Simply merge with your rivals into one big firm and thereby control output so as to get a bigger profit, which can be divided among the merged firms. Again there is the problem of who pays how much to whom. But even supposing this difficult problem can be resolved and a merger arranged, will it be worth the costs? Most firms make more than one kind of product. Is it worth merging with rivals for *one* of these products at the cost of losing productive efficiency in the others? Your superiority in other lines of products is dissipated in the merger. If one seeks increased wealth from several products, the span of firms that must be included is enormous.

So far we have ignored a very important handicap of merger. *New firms* with additional productive capacity will enter if existing firms merge and hoist prices above the competitive level. These entrants can be very damaging indeed. The merging firms may make a dollar more per year for say four years, but with new firms attracted the later results will be a smaller earning than otherwise. A dollar gain for four years, with a subsequent income that is 60 cents smaller than if there had been no merger, literally constitutes a *loss* of *present wealth*. The present value of one dollar a year for four years is $3.46 (at 6 percent), but the present value of 60 cents a year for ten years thereafter (the loss) is $3.50, a net *loss* in present wealth.[5]

Probably only a small fraction of mergers have the monopoly situation as an objective or consequence. Many are profitable, because they provide a more efficient combination of resources; others profit because of superior new management of firms that had been operated inefficiently. Mergers and take-overs of other kinds—by stock purchases, exchange of stock, or direct purchases of assets—often represent competition among managers and entrepreneurs in using productive resources. No outsider knows the purpose of a merger or how successfully the purpose is served. On this subject there is much conjecture but very little reliable evidence. It suffices for present purposes to know that mergers represent avenues to several different objectives.

### Ethics or Desirability of Collusion

Collusions raise an ethical issue. Insofar as they are voluntary, with no compulsion placed on outsiders who do not want to join, what ethical precepts, if

---

[5] The 60 cent per-year perpetuity has a present value of .792 × $4.42, because the stream is deferred four years (which accounts for the .792 factor) while the ten-year annuity of 60 cents has a capital value of $4.42. Check our calculations and reasoning by refreshing yourself on the capital-values principles (Chapter 13). These principles will come in handy for solving practical problems long after you have left college.

any, do they violate? Why prohibit collusions?[6] If firms do collude effectively to raise prices and reduce output, they do not differ from any
price-searcher, who, faced with a negatively sloped demand curve, charges the
wealth-maximizing price. For example, Bob Hope, Arnold Palmer, and
Natalie Wood hire agents to sell their services. Each could hire several agents,
who would compete with each other. Each of Hope's agents would look only
at the amount of services *he* could sell. He would cut the proffered price of
Hope's services below the offer of Hope's other agents, driving down Hope's
income. To avoid this, Hope hires *one* agent and prevents "ruinous" competition among sellers of his services. No one seems to complain. Similarly, why
should one complain if the diamond mines are owned by one person who acts
in the same way? Is it that, in the one case, diamonds will be produced in
smaller amount? But so would Natalie Wood performances. In each case,
from the point of view of the rest of us, a natural talent is not "fully" used.
In the Wood case, it is even worse, since the talent ages, whereas diamonds do
not.

The fundamental ethical question is whether the rest of the public should
require by *law* that Wood or Hope or Palmer perform more frequently.
Economics gives no judgment about this. The case against effective collusion
comes down to the same point raised in connection with price-searchers'
markets—"inefficiency" (misdirection) in the allocation of resource uses.[7]
Granted for the sake of the argument that there is misdirection, a proposal to
prevent voluntary pooling of private wealth is denial of private-property
rights. The criterion of "misdirected" or inefficient use of resources is itself
dependent on the normative premise that individuals should have the right to
make choices about use of goods. If we accept a criterion of efficiency relying
on open market revelation of values we cannot logically deny full contracting
rights to achieve "efficiency," which is meaningful only for private-property
rights.[8] Yet that is what a refusal to allow mergers amounts to. Of course,
you may feel that private property and individual choice are not desirable;
but we hope you make that judgment only in awareness of what their absence
implies.

[6]If there is something bad about collusion, is there not also something bad whenever
people voluntarily pool their private wealth to form a corporation that is big enough to
affect the market price by its offerings of some good? Every corporation and partnership
uses jointly owned resources in wealth-maximizing ways. Why is effective collusive agreement among several businesses different from merger or new creation of a large business?
It isn't. Then why have we devoted the past several pages to a discussion of inter-firm
collusion, as if it were different from the formation of a corporation or partnership? To
show the obstacles to any group's controlling of market behavior, either by collusion or
by buying up firms until only one firm is left—*in the absence* of legal compulsions
requiring producers to join a collusion as a condition of access to the market.

[7]See pages 131–132.

[8]Individual freedom of choice is the ultimate test of value or "proper" direction of
resource use in *this* efficiency criterion. This will be evident if you recall that the
measure of value is derived from "individual preference" as revealed in choice of use or
exchange of goods.

The Law on Collusive Practices

As we have seen, potent forces are working against the successful attainment of extra wealth *via* collusive sellers' arrangements. Nevertheless, we cannot say that *all* collusions are unsuccessful. The success of collusion in the absence of prohibitory laws is said to be proved by the frequency of cartels and collusive agreements in European nations. However, where successful collusions have been carefully investigated, it has been found that special laws, favors, tax exemptions, or government controls have enabled colluding groups to "police" recalcitrant members and keep out new producers.

There are laws in the United States against collusion and other actions that are considered to be "restraints on competition." The Sherman Antitrust Act, passed in 1890, prohibited "monopolizing" and "combinations or conspiracies to restrain" trade. Since it did not define "monopoly" or "restraint of trade," the act, as enforced, depends upon ad hoc arguments in individual law suits against companies. At the turn of the century, the Standard Oil Trust, the U.S. Sugar Trust, and the American Tobacco Trust were prosecuted by the U.S. government's antitrust division and were split into smaller companies. It is still a moot point whether these "trusts" did charge higher prices than would have been charged by a larger number of smaller firms and, if they did, whether or not the power to do so was a result of laws denying other competitors the right to enter the market. In any event, the Sherman Antitrust law is intended to dissuade further growth of some firms. For example, in 1961 the Du Pont Company was compelled to divest itself of ownership of a substantial portion of General Motors. Bethlehem and Youngstown steel companies were dissuaded from merging when told by the antitrust division of the Justice Department that the proposed merger would be prosecuted in court as a violation of the Sherman Act. More recently, the Brown Shoe Company was forced by court order to divest itself of ownership of a former competitor. All of these were results of judicial opinion or belief that these mergers "tended to reduce" competition. In fact, the judicial interpretation is even stronger; it is now sufficient to show that competition "might probably" be reduced. No great understanding of economics is required to perceive that the law is ambiguous, vague, and subject to individual interpretation, preference, and opinion. As early as 1914 confusion had reached the stage that the U.S. Supreme Court could seriously declare that only "unreasonable" restraints of trade were illegal.

In a futile effort to achieve greater precision in concepts, the Clayton Act of 1914 prohibited both "price discrimination" and mergers "reducing competition" (but exempted labor unions from antimonopoly laws). As we have already seen, price discrimination sometimes increases the efficiency of resource use. Mergers can enhance the competitive status of some firms in the market.

Complaints by some businessmen against their competitors' behavior resulted in passage in 1914 of the Federal Trade Commission Act, which created a commission with power to investigate any business activities alleged to be in violation of various laws, and to dissuade firms from "unfair practices" by issuing "cease and desist" orders. These orders prohibit further violations but do not penalize for past "unfair practices." What is and is not an unfair practice often cannot be determined in advance by the businessman.

In 1938 the Wheeler-Lea Act authorized the Federal Trade Commission to prohibit still other "unfair practices"—those "unfair" to the consumer, such as false advertising. For example, it is illegal to artificially color margarine without saying so on the label (but it is permissible to artificially color butter without so labelling it). Such exceptions are sometimes authorized by legislation that is not always obviously consistent.

During the Depression of the 1930s many (still existing) laws were passed to prohibit price cutting: in fact many encouraged sellers to get together and raise prices, with penalties on those who did not comply. Legislation passed at that time to prevent what was regarded as ruinous competition has done much to thwart open-market competitive forces.

*Protection* of *or* from *competition?* One of the principal "undesired" effects of business regulation is that it opens the door to protection *from* open-market competition. It is easy to confuse protection *of* competition with protection *from* open-market competition. For example, the Federal Trade Commission relies heavily on complaints of one business against another in deciding which actions to investigate. Complainants will try to protect their wealth from market competition rather than to preserve open-market competition. They complain of "unfair," "de-stabilizing," "disorderly," and "cutthroat" competition—which can mean that one's competitors are more successfully catering to buyers' preferences in open markets. A competitor whose costs are lower or who is willing to provide the service for less is selling below costs—your costs. Therefore, you contend that he is driving you out of business and "tending to reduce" competition.

### Collusion by Employees

A common successful collusion is that of some sellers of labor. If the employees of a firm or industry form a collusion to agree not to offer their services at less than some wage, they face the usual obstacles of successful collusions. They may strike in order to enforce their collusion. The right to strike and to strike effectively is currently an accepted part of our economic and legal institutions. A strike is an attempt to prevent *other sellers of labor* from offering their services at rates (or working conditions) lower than those sought by the striking employees. Access to the labor market by any other sellers of labor is restrained by the "peaceful" *threat* of violence to the person or property of would-be strikebreakers, including any striker who might be tempted to cheat on the agreement. The market is closed. While the laws do not authorize strikers to physically restrain workers from crossing a picket line, crossing the line incites retaliation. Therefore, to avoid violence at the strikers' picket line, anyone who tries to cross a picket line and thereby provokes violence may be jailed along with the strikers for contribution to a disturbance of the peace. Both the strikebreaker and striker are declared guilty. In few areas will the police sweep aside the strikers and permit strike-breakers free access to the market for work (at lower terms than those sought by the strikers), for that usually leads to violence.

If the preceding sentences seem antilabor, the reader is injecting his own interpretation. They are no more critical or disapproving than the statement that hydrogen is lighter than nitrogen. They do not say that employees ought not to engage in strikes. They do differ from common folklore in their explicit recognition of a fact which strikers sensibly prefer not to publicize; after all, threat of violence is generally disapproved by the public.

That the union acquires legal "closed-monopoly" power when allowed to strike is widely recognized. Our courts decreed this in 1914 when unions were specifically exempted from the Sherman Antitrust law. The Norris-LaGuardia Act of 1932 legalized group picketing and boycotts. The Wagner Act of 1935 required employers to deal with unions and made it legal for employees to form or join the union of their (majority) choice. And the National Labor Relations Board was created to enforce the conditions of those acts.

If you think the preceding analysis is incredulous, ask yourself: Is there any reason why the people who seek to collude or to eliminate competitors should be only, for example, businessmen, doctors, teachers, radio and television station owners, rather than ordinary employees like teamsters, carpenters, auto assemblers, retail clerks, or dock workers? What one can do, others can try. If one group can ethically rely on legal tax-supported violence via laws (the state police power), it should not be surprising that others resort to some private violence to deny access to the market.

## Charging What the Open (or Closed) Market Will Bear

Sellers accused of charging "too high" a price usually reply that they are merely charging what the traffic will bear, just like every other seller, whether he is a gardener, filling station operator, electrician, auto seller, doctor, or teacher. The doctor says he charges what the traffic will bear—that is, in accord with what his patients can afford. The television manufacturer charges the price he thinks will maximize his wealth. But there is a big difference. One is selling in a closed market, the other in an open market. If you can legislate away your competitors, the price will be different than if the market is open to them. Unions that can, like the doctors or airlines, prevent others from competing for their jobs say they are only charging what the market will bear, just as any other seller does. Is their contention correct? Yes, for sellers in closed markets like doctors, airlines, taxis, and musicians. No, for those competing in open-market competition, like TV repairmen, retail clerks, automobile assemblers, and auto makers. Do not forget the difference between closed and open markets.

### Legal Restraints against Open-Market Competition

From time immemorial rights to sell goods have been restricted. Foreigners, and even residents of neighboring towns, have commonly been proscribed from selling in domestic markets. Today residents of one state cannot always freely sell their goods or services in some other state within the United States (doctors, lawyers, or musicians to name but a few). On the buying side, some people are excluded from the market or restricted as buyers (children for tobacco and alcohol, and adults for medicines).

First, we must distinguish between restrictions on sellers' access to markets and the high investment costs of production. Some goods are best produced with large amounts of capital equipment, without any interference in the market process. By restrictions on access to the market we mean restrictions and costs imposed on people (consumers or producers) as a condition of engaging in exchange of goods. Examples are special taxes imposed as a condition of doing business in the market; requirements that the sellers pass qualifying examinations; special apprenticeship and training laws; legally imposed maximum (or minimum) prices; tariffs that prohibit or tax goods that foreigners would like to sell in our markets; prohibition of sales on certain days or hours; prohibition of sale of certain kinds of goods; necessity of having a certain race, creed, or residence as a condition of buying or selling.

Actually markets run the range from completely open to completely closed. For some markets or goods, the aspiring seller must first pass an examination about his knowledge of how to make or sell the good he proposes to sell (doctors, lawyers, dentists, morticians, architects, hairdressers); or he must have had some official education in a particular trade (teachers, barbers, butchers); or he must have acquired some experience as a trainee (apprenticeship as a carpenter, electrician, plumber); or his good must be certified as safe and appropriate for sale (drugs, foods, milk, stocks and bonds); or he must meet government criteria on appropriateness of the service (liquor stores, banks, TV and radio stations, gas and electric companies, airlines, railroads, taxis).[9] In some cases, a tax must be paid as a condition of entry. Sometimes these are so heavy as to be prohibitive; very nominal entry taxes are really payments for government service.

Certainly, completely closed markets are not the only alternative to completely open markets. Few, if any, markets are permanently closed to all aspiring entrants, and few are completely open to all. Nevertheless, we shall refer to open-market and closed-market conditions, hoping you will always remember that it is a matter of degree.

#### Trademarks and Trade Names

Anyone can enter the market with his own goods under his own trademark. But trademarks and trade names cannot be copied. Even though I were to

---

[9] The cases cited are illustrative. They vary among cities, states, and countries.

manufacture an item physically identical to Morton salt or Bayer aspirin, I could not legally sell it if I inscribed on it their trademark. Trademark laws prevent someone from trying to pretend a product is made by someone else. Some countries do not recognize trademarks and trade names, and they do not prohibit imitation of trademarks, just as we do not prohibit imitation of the good itself. However, trademarks and trade names are included in the spectrum of property rights in the United States.

### Patents and Copyrights

Patents and copyrights are grants of exclusive rights, in a closed monopoly, to sell certain goods or ideas.[10] A patent is what a statutory *monopoly* used to be called. The principle of Polaroid film is patented; this means that the inventor has exclusive rights to it and can license others to produce and sell that film. The patent is given for a period of years, usually seventeen, and is occasionally renewable for another seventeen years. Patents and copyrights are intended to induce people to discover and reveal useful techniques and knowledge—if a person invents a way to kill flies, show three-dimensional television, or cure the common cold, everyone else could quickly use the idea without paying him anything. Even though many people try to invent or do research without that incentive, the prospect of a gain will attract more people and resources into such activity.

We should not be surprised that the patent holder charges for the use of his idea. The purpose of the patent or copyright was to reward him for ideas. But the price he charges restricts the use of the idea. He may—like a price-searcher—withhold it from some useful applications, so that he can charge a price that will increase his wealth. Having given a patent as a monopoly right, we should not be surprised when the patent holder uses that closed right like a *monopolist*.[11]

What is the right amount of reward and inducement for an invention? One might conjecture that the right amount should not exceed the "value" of the resources the invention saves or the gain it gives society. If an invention reduces the costs of production by $1,000,000, then presumably the inventor should be paid something. But who knows how much? And who is to pay the inventor? Because these questions are impossible to answer, society grants a patent whereby the inventor gains, and the beneficiaries, those who use the idea, pay for it. The absence of a clear-cut criterion for "proper" inducement leaves room for considerable dispute about how long a patent should be protected and what kind of pricing and use of the patent should be allowed.

Several misapprehensions exist about uses and effects of patents.

*Suppression of new ideas.* Sometimes an inventor discovers a new idea that will make obsolete what he currently owns. If I owned a pay-television

---

[10] Patents do not prevent other people from using some idea or device if they use it for themselves and not to produce something for *sale* to other people; only commercial use is forbidden. Also notice that ideas are "public goods."

[11] See pages 128–132.

system using wires from station to home and then discovered a means to eliminate the wires, would I use the wireless system? Or would I suppress the wireless system because it would destroy the value of my wire system? What I would do depends upon the relative costs. Since the wires are already installed, their ("variable") cost of continued use is low (until they must be replaced). If it would cost me less to produce and install the new equipment than to pay the costs of using the old system, I would immediately abandon the old system. Otherwise I would not use the new system until the old wires had to be replaced or repaired. This delay in introducing a new idea is sometimes regarded as "unjustified," but instead, in fact, it may reflect the efficiency of using up existing equipment first.

Modern folklore has a legend that gasoline producers have discovered a new kind of fuel or carburetor that would enormously reduce the demand for gasoline. In order to protect their wealth, they withhold the device from use. What are the facts? If the invention were not patented, then a person who knew about it could take a new job with other people and manufacture the device and make an enormous fortune—more than the existing companies would find it worth their while to pay him in order to induce him not to sell the secret. And if the device or idea were patented, it would be public knowledge; but there is no patented evidence or record of any such device.

*Nonpatentable research and development.*    Much research and development is carried on without the incentive of patents or copyrights. Most businessmen who develop new ideas have to rely on being first and being able to make enough profit before competitors come in. For example, the supermarket, the double-pump arrangement in gasoline service stations, drive-in banks, colored soaps, open-all-night stores, discount houses, and a host of other business innovations contribute to cost reductions or quality improvements. Yet they are not subject to copyright or patent. There is no generally accepted, objective rule as to what range of exploratory activity should or should not be given the special protection of patent and copyright monopolies.

The collusive pricing tactics employed by some drug firms are feasible because of patents for new drugs. Congressmen frequently complain about prices of patented drugs. The crucial issues are: How much reward should the patent holder be allowed? What methods of monopolistic pricing *should* he be allowed? Multipart pricing? Fixed fee? All-or-none pricing? Uniform price to all licensees? No clear-cut answer is obtainable from economic analysis. Actual practice finds all sorts of combinations. When you see them, some legal monopoly is probably the basis for enabling that kind of pricing.

*Alleged extension of patent monopoly to other goods.*    We cite one example of "price discrimination" related to the *use* of some patents or copyrights, wherein the licensees of a patent pay different prices for the right to use the patented idea. This pricing tactic has been interpreted by the courts as an attempt to extend one's monopoly (in the patented item) to other kinds of items. For example, the International Business Machines Corporation, which owned the patent to punched-card computer machinery, required users of its machines to buy the *cards* from IBM only. Another example is provided by Christian Dior, who gives retailers the right to sell his dress "creations" (which he can copyright) *only* if they also agree to buy handkerchiefs from him. It might appear that IBM is trying to extend its monopoly into the paper-card areas. Yet there is another interpretation that is more consistent with economic theory and fits the facts more closely.

Recall our water monopolist in Chapter 7 who sells water at the wealth-maximizing *uniform* price.[12] There were two other pricing policies he could have used, under certain circumstances, to get more wealth with less waste of water. In one case, a person buying a certain amount at one price could then have purchased more at a lower price.[13]

The IBM company, as patentee—assuming that it faces a negatively sloping demand curve and that *no one else can legally enter the market*—would like to use a multipart pricing system to get all the wealth it can from its machines, which are rented to customers, not sold. However, to use multi-part, discriminatory pricing with *many* different buyers, IBM would have to know each buyer's demand curve and set *different* rates for each renter of business-machine equipment.

How can IBM detect each renter's demand curve and charge appropriate fees to each user? The number of *cards* the customer uses is related to his demand for the use of the machine. IBM could simply count the cards used and charge a fee for the machines based on that number—say, one cent per card per day. A big user of cards would be charged a higher rent than a smaller user of cards. In effect, that was the system IBM used. It charged a higher price for the purchase of cards than the customer would have to pay if he could have bought the cards from someone else. If a user could buy cards from some other source, IBM would lose its measure of demand and its method for collecting. Therefore, IBM insisted that, as a condition of using the machines, the renter had to use IBM-made cards (even though their price was higher). If any machine jammed and IBM-made cards were not being used at the time, the renter would be charged the repair costs. By guaranteeing to service and maintain the machines under the rental scheme, IBM could also check to see that its cards were being used. Thus, insistence on tie-in of IBM cards to be bought at higher than competitive price was not intended to *extend* IBM's machine monopoly into the card area. Instead, the tie-in of cards enabled IBM to use the cards as a meter device and to prevent its customers from

---

[12] See pages 132–137.

[13] Ideally, we saw how he was charged a price of $10 for the first unit, with the right then to buy a second one at $9; and then, *given* that he agrees to buy a second one for $9, he is allowed to buy one more at $8, and so on down until he can buy a tenth one at $1 for that tenth unit. In this way, the water seller collected $55 for the ten units of water, whereas the best he could have gotten with a uniform, constant price per unit—take all you want at that price—was only $30 (having sold six) with four being left unsold. This multipart pricing (wherein the "price" changes for each possible amount) has the "advantage" that inefficiency in use is eliminated. Nothing is wasted. There is no misdirection of resources. And it also gives the water seller a bigger wealth, leaving the consumer with minimal gain from exchange. This kind of "ideal" or complete discrimination is certainly not achievable.

renting machines to other users at lower prices than acceptable to IBM. This discriminatory-pricing arrangement has the "desirable" effect of more fully utilizing resources, as in the water case; the so-called "inefficiency" of price-searchers' markets in resource allocation is reduced. Of the total gain from exchange, most is retained by IBM, with less going to the renter.

Federal and state governments and the courts have attacked these tie-in and restrictive arrangements, alleging that they represent attempts to enlarge the range of goods monopolized or restrict competition. However, economic analysis implies that they are really devices to (1) measure each customer's demand conditions to determine and (2) collect the discriminatory price or fee that will enable IBM to obtain more of the value of the patented item.

Other examples of tie-in sales and restrictive conditions of licensing are: cans tied to use of can-closing machinery; staples to stapling machines; mimeograph supplies to mimeograph machines; repair parts to automobiles; toilet paper to dispensers; rivets to riveting machines; steel strapping to wrapping machines.

### Price Discrimination?

One must be careful to state precisely what is meant by discriminatory pricing in any given circumstances. For example, the Robinson-Patman law of 1938 prohibits "price discrimination" where it will tend "to create a monopoly, lessen competition, or injure competitors." One thing we should know by now is that the words "discrimination, monopoly, competition, competitors" are loaded with many possible meanings. We should not be surprised that the confusion created by this law has provided lawyers with higher incomes and business firms with extra costs and uncertainty as to what they can do legally.

One of the classic examples of "discriminatory" prices is that in which a railroad charged more to ship goods from New York to Denver than from New York to San Francisco. Naturally, this seems "unjustly discriminatory" against people in Denver. Why did those rates exist? The railroads from New York to San Francisco compete with transport by water via the Panama Canal. There was no low-cost competition to Denver. It is wrong to assume that rates to Denver were set high in order to permit the lower rates to San Francisco. The crucial conditions were: (1) the two services jointly had to realize sufficient proceeds to cover total costs; and (2) no matter what the Denver rates were, the rates to San Francisco had to be low enough to compete with the water route.

The prices set for rail services to San Francisco and Denver are market-rationing rates, and must meet competition of other sources of services. It seems "unjust" to charge more to Denver, since it certainly costs more to ship to San Francisco by rail than to Denver. But this statement implies that the price must be such as to collect a prorated portion of total costs. And that is a fallacy. Price rations the existing supply, *and* hopefully it provides revenue to induce the output. The idea that, for joint products, each one's price "should" cover some equal pro-rata portion of total costs is the source of the confusion.

The fact that it costs more to ship goods by rail to San Francisco than to Denver from New York neither *justifies* nor *permits* a higher price for rail shipments to San Francisco. What one can get for what he produces depends not upon what it costs, but upon what the supply will sell for when confronted with market demand. The supply of available transport to San Francisco was much larger than that to Denver at any given price.

The source of the "discrimination" is that San Francisco is located on an excellent harbor with cheap sources of transportation, whereas Denver is located in a landlocked area to which transportation is more expensive. To correct this "injustice," the law has compelled the railroads to charge no more to Denver than to San Francisco. So, rather than raise the San Francisco rate, the railroads lowered the rate to Denver. Had Denver been the major terminal of most of the freight, the rate would not have been cut. Instead, the San Francisco rate would have been raised, since the railroads would prefer to lose that smaller service income rather than the large Denver-service revenue. In that event, fares would still have been "equal," with San Francisco suffering in the cause of "equality."

Sometimes, joint products that seem to cost the same sell for very different prices. For example, daytime demand for long-distance telephone service is higher than at night. Yet the costs of the physical facilities primarily do not change; there is no way to allocate the common-facility costs to night and to day service, except in some arbitrary way. There is no point in doing so. Given the fact that the facilities exist, the phone company charges a lower night rate simply because the demand is smaller at night. If the night demand were stronger, the night rates would be higher than the day rates. The relative level of rates depends upon the relative demands which must be rationed by a price.

Is it "fair" to the day people that night workers should be able to make long-distance calls more cheaply? That theaters should charge less for matinees than for evening performances? That paintings involving the same costs should sell for different prices? That beautiful girls should get higher salaries than homelier girls, even if both spend the same amount in trying to be more beautiful? All these "disparities" arise because of some differences in the demand for the good or service, reflecting differences in availability and convenience or, in the eyes of the demander, in quality.

The person paying a higher price wishes he, too, could buy in the lower-priced market. Then why doesn't he shift to the lower-priced market? Because the lower-priced market is not worth all the sacrifices he must make in order to do so (like moving to San Francisco from Denver or working nights rather than days in order to save on long-distance calls or learning to ignore superficial beauty).

There is nothing in economic analysis that permits any propositions about what is fair or not fair. In fact the words "fair," "just," or "reasonable" have no objective content—Aristotle, Aquinas, the Council of Christian Churches, the President of the United States, or anyone else to the contrary notwithstanding. Except, possibly, "The fair price is what I think it should be."

## Protection of Consumers

### Standards of Sanitation

Laws prohibit sale of foods that the Federal Food and Drug employees deem unfit for human consumption. Foods manufactured under conditions deemed insufficiently sanitary can be banned. Surely no one should object. Consumers rely on a government agency to enforce some standard of cleanliness; time and resources are saved for them by reducing private costs of collecting information for each buyer. But on reflection, there are some "costs" of this law. Some consumers prefer the right to buy cheaper goods (for example, imported dates), even though they are produced in less sanitary conditions (cleanliness is not a costless "good"). This right may seem silly for anyone to want—if costs are ignored. But consider the fact that the Food and Drug Administration refused to allow the sale of a cheap, high-protein, biologically sterile food made in powdered form, because the Food and Drug employees said it is a filthy food—being made from *whole* fish. Yet people eat whole oysters, sardines (except for heads), shrimps; pigs and chickens are converters of garbage, insects, and worms. The point is that people who make decisions to restrict certain items do not necessarily have the same preferences as those for whom they are thought to be acting. It may be captious to emphasize that such constraints have their "costs," but we believe these costs are too often overlooked or ignored by proponents of restrictive or protective legislation. No one can object to cleanliness, if the *degree* of it is not "excessive" in view of the costs. But a high-priced barbershop that uses a new protective apron for *every* customer will find itself underpriced by one that reuses the apron with a new piece of paper around each customer's neck. The higher-priced shop would do well to insist on higher standards of cleanliness as a means of keeping out lower-cost competitors. Clearly, a requirement that all sellers maintain at least the same high standards is a restriction on those buyers who prefer less sanitary, but cheaper, service—usually the poorer people. Insisting on higher quality means *fewer* more expensive higher-quality goods rather than more, cheaper lower-quality goods. Which is better for the poor and/or for the rich?

### Quality Protection

Until about 1950, margarine could not be sold in some states—ostensibly because it was considered a "low-quality" substitute for butter. And in many areas it could not be sold except as a *white* spread—even though butter is sometimes artificially colored and flavored. The publicly espoused rationale was that margarine is inferior and consumers would be misled. In fact, however, the laws protected milk producers from new market competition—as is evidenced by the fact that major milk-producing states had the strongest bans on margarine. Even mayonnaise was at one time similarly protected from competition from the "inferior" (and cheaper) substitute, salad dressing.

Building codes in every city control the materials that can be used in buildings. One result is that obsolete methods are preserved; the codes are not revised often enough. New York City's building code was unchanged for over thirty years after the 1930s. The rapid development of mobile trailer homes can be explained partly by the fact that they are not covered by building codes. Now, under pressures from the conventional housing industry, codes are being expanded to include mobile homes.

When television sets were first built, manufacturers who used expensive, high-quality materials and techniques proposed to prohibit lower-quality television sets. If the law had passed, the current inferior, cheaper sets would not be available. Speakers would be larger. Picture quality would be better. Tuning would be easier, repairs less frequent. But over-all, the set would cost more. The highest-quality sets manufactured are so expensive that only a few are produced.

Bad goods drive out the good. Cheap champagne drives out good champagne. Cheap music drives out good. So go the complaints that arouse people to "save" others from inferiority by prohibiting inferior items. A less costly item usually is inferior, in the same sense that cotton is inferior to silk, a Ford to a Rolls-Royce, Macy's to Dior's. But the lower cost more than offsets the lower quality, in the opinion of the buyer. Everyone prefers higher quality to lower quality *at the same price*. But when quality *and price* are lowered, we can no longer say that bad drives out good. Instead, the better drives out the worse—when both price and quality are taken into account. Often, a seller may seek laws prohibiting consumers from buying lower-quality goods so that he will not be undersold by lower-cost competitors—whose products may be as good or worse but whose price is enough lower to make them preferred items, just as Volkswagens are worse cars than Porsches, Fords worse than Lincolns, and Sam's Cafe worse than the Hilton Escoffier Room.

The medical profession restricts entry to the market for medical aid by state licensing laws administered by the licensed doctors. This is supposed to assure the public of higher-quality medical attention, given the current state of medical knowledge. If a law permitted the sale of only Rolls-Royces, Cadillacs, and Lincolns, we could certainly say we had the best-*quality* automobile service in the world—and the most pedestrians. The medical profession emphasizes that it has brought the United States the highest-quality medical care. But the same cannot be said for the quantity. Without laws restricting entry to the profession, there would be many more doctors of a lower quality. It can be contended that there would be *fewer* deaths if lower-quality *and* hence more mediocre medical aid were available, because at the present time even worse substitutes are used—nurses, druggists, books, self-medication, faith-healers, friends, hearsay, phone calls instead of personal inspection, not to mention *no* medical attention at all.

It is hard to separate sincerity and duplicity in this desire to protect other people. For example, would you regard the remainder of this paragraph as sincere? Economists have not been able to obtain licensing and compulsory certification similar to doctors. Like health, wealth can be ruined by carelessness. If a person breaks his leg, it can be reset. If he breaks his budget, it can't be reset by anyone. The loss is permanent. Wealth, like health, must be protected from personal ignorance. If a person wants to invest $1,000 in some business, how can he be sure that it is a safe investment? If he loses, not only he but his family suffers. Therefore, before making *any* investment every person ought to be required to consult a licensed, certified economist, who will prescribe how wealth should be invested. He can then take the prescription to the stockbroker. Without this safeguard millions of people every day make foolish investments and irrevocably lose their wealth and harm their families. Many people follow the advice of economic quacks—stockbrokers, politicians, friends, and tip sheets. They overinvest in houses without consulting economists, who could prevent their going too far into debt or buying in the wrong area or taking the wrong job or the wrong kind of insurance.[14]

### Protection of Employees, Morals, and Service Standards

Laws prohibiting sales during evenings and Sundays ostensibly are to protect the health of employees, the morals of the community, and the quality of the service. Sunday selling diverts people from rest and violates the Sabbath. The United States Supreme Court says so. However, the facts are that although stores may be open twenty-four hours every day, the employees don't work twenty-four hours. Sunday and evening buying is a convenience to many shoppers. Of course, consumers *could* do all their shopping between 9 and 5 on weekdays. They *could* do it between 3 and 7 on Monday, Wednesday, and Friday only. Any store able to reduce costs enough by such hours could survive with the business it managed to get from consumers who prefer the lower prices at those days and hours. But there aren't enough people with such preferences, for those hours are exceptional. These laws are often supported by employers rather than by employees. In particular, conventional

---

[14] Or are there signs of progress? In 1964, the Securities and Exchange Commission issued a report evaluating the securities and stock-market dealers' practices. In the covering letter written by Mr. Cary, the chairman of the committee, is the following prescient passage: "Under existing Federal law there is a right of free access and unlimited entry into the securities business for anyone, regardless of qualifications, except those excluded on the basis of prior securities violations. The steady growth in the very numbers of investors and participants, according to the report, has made this concept obsolete. Neither the industry nor the Government nor the investing public can afford the burden of policemen at every transaction: the gateway to the industry (that is, entry into the securities dealers' business) is the point where Government and industry should look first for the solution." And it also said: "Greater emphasis should be given by the Securities and Exchange Commission and the exchanges and associations of security dealers to the concept of suitability of particular securities for particular customers."

retail stores are aided by a ban on evening and Sunday shopping. Because conventional retail stores provide more labor service relative to capital than the evening-Sunday discount houses, the extra hours add more to total labor costs for conventional retail department stores.

### Protection of Consumer from Unethical Sellers

Commonest of all attempts to restrict entry to the market in the name of consumer welfare are those aimed at "unethical" operators who promise a spectacular bargain, special prices, etc. These competitors take business from the established, better-quality, higher-cost, more reliable sellers. Surely, no one could object to the elimination of such "unreliable" sellers. One who buys his new car from the old, well-established dealer who is a pillar of the local chamber of commerce can be surer that any squeaks, defects, scratches will be given less slow attention than if he buys from the fast-dealing seller on the edge of town who sells at 10 percent less but can't be counted on to give such service. Yet the 10-percent-lower price may be worth more than the assurance of that "free" service. Laws prohibiting "bargains" provide protection to the unwary, but they impose costs on those who prefer the lower-quality bargains; the cost is the lost opportunity for a buyer to have more of other goods by accepting a lower level of quality or a greater degree of risk.

The time spent in acquiring information about purchases costs more for a rich person with high earnings per hour than for a poor person. Hence a rich person is more likely to take his custom to high-quality sellers. Forcing lower-quality sellers out of business by law would hit the poor more severely, since the poor find it cheaper to shop around and compare various sellers for the best buys than to rely on the high-quality seller.

### Advertising Restrictions

Although a person may have a legal right to enter the market, any obstacle to providing information about himself or his offers will protect those sellers already in the market, about whom buyers are better informed. Advertising is primarily a means of informing potential buyers of the presence of a seller and of his goods. To appreciate advertising, imagine trying to shop in a community with no signs proclaiming one's business, with no directories of locations of firms, and with no idea where sellers are located. After we learn about some sellers, most of us assume that their advertising is of no further use. But to strangers it is valuable—as one learns if he travels in a foreign country and cannot read the advertisements; his sense of ignorance about opportunities is made profoundly clear.

The flow of information from sellers to buyers is important, even though frequently ignored. How should General Motors act with respect to advertising if it wanted to restrain the growth of American Motors (makers of Rambler) or Volkswagen? One way would be to prohibit advertising. Since

GM is already well known, a reduction of advertising would make it more difficult for newcomers to call attention to their presence and offerings. And since the newcomer often has to demonstrate and establish the quality of his service, a prohibition on price cutting would be especially helpful to GM. Price cuts are a way for competitors to attract customers to try new products. A ban on advertising would make it more difficult for a new seller to announce his presence, availability, and lower price. Holiday Inns, a nationally known motel firm, is advantaged by bans on highway advertising. It is interesting to note that the American Medical Association prohibits advertising. Examine the yellow pages of the telephone directory and compare the advertising of various professions. Whatever business you may enter as a young man, would you regard restrictions on advertising as helpful to your ability to attract customers?

The foregoing discussion of laws designed to protect the welfare of other people by restricting entry to the market has been negatively critical. Our judgment is that most people are sufficiently exposed to the well-publicized protective effects of such laws; therefore, we have intentionally emphasized some of the "shadow costs" to provide a more complete understanding.

### Protection of Producers

#### Orderly Markets

The "orderly-market" argument asserts that unless an industry is controlled so as to ensure adequate prices and profits during hard times, some firms will go out of business, and when demand increases there will not be enough firms to take care of the higher demand. Prices and output will swing like an unstable pendulum. Thus, for highly seasonal products like milk (peak supply comes in June and the low point in November), it is argued that prices must be stabilized to ensure an adequate supply at all seasons. Presumably, if price fluctuated from troughs in June to peaks in November, the farmers would be driven out in June and wouldn't be available in November to provide adequate milk. The contention also is that when demand is good and prices are high, fly-by-night producers will enter and "skim the cream," only to leave when prices and demand fall. The "responsible," year-around producers will not survive. Therefore, controls should be placed on entry so that irresponsible short-term producers cannot undermine the long-term stability of the industry.

Can the reader spot the holes in these arguments? For one thing, all the arguments fail to recognize that the amount demanded depends upon price. Any supply is "adequate" if the price is high enough. Any supply is "inadequate" if the price is low enough. For goods with seasonal swings in *production*, a *stable* price over the year implies too large an output at peak periods and too low a supply at low-output months—unless storage costs are low enough that the output can be stored from peak-production to low-production months and thereby allow relative price uniformity. When seasonal variation of prices over a year is a predictable phenomenon, no business person will be pushed out of business by low prices in peak periods if he recognizes the seasonality phenomenon. Retail stores do about half their business in the Christmas season, but they are not pushed out of business by the summer low-sales months—just as stores are not pushed out of business by low sales on Sunday. Yet the milk industry has obtained strong control over entry to the market by alleging that seasonality requires controls in order to assure "adequate" supplies at all seasons—with a uniform year-round price despite prohibitively high storage costs. The storage is achieved by maintaining enough cows for periods of low production (per cow) and too many for the rest of the time. Instead of letting the price fall in peak-production periods, the milk in excess of the amount wanted as fresh milk at that high price is diverted into cheese, ice cream, and processed foods. Essentially, what is achieved is a higher income for the milk producers, *less* fresh milk over the year, but more ice cream and cheese, and a prohibition on entry by new farmers who would provide more milk at the peak period when prices are maintained at levels above cost.

The fluctuation argument is also carried over into business fluctuations of a nonseasonal nature. In depressions, the elimination of some producers from some industries is alleged to mean that "when prosperity returns there won't be enough producers to ensure an adequate supply. Therefore, producers must be protected during bad times to ensure their survival into good times. Furthermore, during good times too many new firms might enter the business, so that, when demand falls off, all firms will lose money. So many might be eliminated that, when demand increases, the supply will not be adequate. The excessive number of entrants will dilute profits so that some firms will not be able to earn enough to carry them over the subsequent harder times. As a result, there will be extreme variations in output."

This argument is full of internal inconsistencies. On the one hand, it says that too few firms will survive the depression, so that the *prosperity* output will be too small because of too few firms. But on the other hand, it alleges that too many new firms will enter during prosperity. Both of these things can't be true. We cannot avoid the suspicion that the "orderly market" argument seeks to deny free access to the markets by competitors simply to keep wealth and production more "orderly" for incumbent producers. The "orderly-market" rationale has an almost unlimited number of manifestations. Farm price-support laws, for example, control entry of new producers to the market. Farm marketing boards for grapes, peaches, cantaloupes, oranges, and lemons, to name a few, control the salable output of those crops in the interest of greater wealth for the producers, but in the name of orderly competition. Domestic sugar producers have been able to pass a law permitting political control of sugar imports, so that the domestic sugar price will be high enough to increase the market value of resources in the domestic sugar industry. We shall investigate one example in considerable detail—that of agricultural production.

First let's see what happens when the demand for wheat falls. Rather than take their losses and reduce output, distressed wheat producers resort to political procedures they would not normally condone in others. But now "times are not normal," "this is a special case," and besides, "everyone else does it." Their political action has been so successful that much has been said in solemn terms about the "great farm-surplus" problem. Most of these statements ignore the first fundamental law of demand: more will be consumed at a lower price, and less at a higher price. The simple fact of the matter is that prices of many farm goods have, by law, been kept above the market-clearing level; as a result, the public has demanded less than the amount available. There is no truth whatever to the popular allegation that farm production exceeds demand, for demand is not a fixed amount. The amount demanded varies with price—a fact possibly embarrassing or tedious to the reader, but one it is necessary to repeat again and again. The American public (not to count the enormous foreign population) would happily consume all the current farm output if prices of those "surplus" farm goods were not kept up by political controls. The genesis of the farm problem is the *relative* decline in demands for food. A consequent decline in price would be normal—if the output were to be purchased and consumed. Rather than submit to the reduced wealth resulting from decreases in demand for their products, the farmers sought to force the consumer to pay a higher price. But when prices were kept above free-market levels (by devices we shall investigate in a moment), the amount demanded was reduced and the amount produced was increased. Hence the so-called "surplus." This unwillingness to submit to the market discipline is not unique to the farmers. The "surplus" problem arises because the farmers have successfully obtained sufficient political power to escape some of the market's discipline.

If these seem like words of condemnation, reread them; there is no suggestion of impropriety by the farmers. We examine the agricultural case simply because it is a particularly instructive example of efforts to protect wealth from the effects of open access to the market.

*Holding crop off the market.*     Another example is provided by lemon growers, who first sought to keep up prices by voluntarily withholding part of their output from the market. Their hopes were thwarted by the refusal of some producers to reduce output, for it would pay any grower to stay out of the agreement and sell *all* his crop at the higher price while the other producers reduced their offerings. Furthermore, some superior producers preferred not to join because they could make more wealth for themselves if there were no such agreement at all than if there were an effective one. How can they and other producers be induced to join? Perhaps they can be accused of standing in the way of those who are "voluntarily" willing to reduce output and threatened with private violence.

The threat of violence, however, is not as reliable as a law—if it can be passed. The lemon growers, along with many other groups, were able to get laws passed to compel joint action. The industry calls this "self-policing." In 1941, a law was enacted permitting a majority of the lemon growers to compel *all* lemon growers to withhold part of their crop from the market. Any grower who refused to do so could not legally sell *any* fresh lemons in the American market. Thus, police power was used instead of threat of private violence.

Still, as we know, even 100 percent membership does not solve all the problems facing the sellers. How much of each producer's output is to be sold? Who is to get the lion's share of the sales? Whatever the share, how can the group know that the quota assigned to each producer is observed and that not more than that quota is sold by a producer? One way to police the "pro-rata quota" scheme is to have a central sales agency through which all lemons are sold. That is known as "pooling" the sales. It determined what part of each producer's output could be sold as fresh fruit in domestic markets and what part would be sold as concentrates or flavorings in domestic and foreign markets. Domestic fresh-lemon prices were raised. But to keep fresh-fruit prices high, the proportion of lemons authorized for sale had to be steadily reduced over the years—from 90 percent of the crop in 1942, when the sales-control scheme went into effect, until now, when over half of the crop is barred from the fresh-fruit market.

Diverting unsold output of fresh fruit to other markets resulted in lower prices for other lemon products than would have prevailed. Without the scheme, there would have been fewer, but more efficient, producers and a lower price of fresh lemons. In effect, fresh-lemon consumers are subsidizing the output of frozen juices and concentrates. The success in raising prices and incomes to lemon growers has induced a larger output by each grower and attracted new growers into production.

*Subsidized production.*     There are still more weapons in the political arsenal that producers can exploit in the interest of their wealth. Why not pass laws forcing the market to buy *all* that is produced at the proposed high price? For example, let the government buy (out of taxes) whatever part of the crop the consumers refuse to buy voluntarily in the market. This kind of law, which denies *consumers* the right of withdrawal from markets, has been passed for producers of wheat, cotton, tobacco, peanuts, rice, and corn, and it is proposed for more.

We exaggerate slightly. The government, *or* the taxpayers, do not *buy* the unsold crop. They only *lend* money to the farmer, using the crop as security. However, if the farmers don't repay the loan, the government keeps the unsold crop—which is, after all, no different from selling the crop to the government. The farmer is thus assured of a minimum price, but the maximum is open. Unfortunately for appearances, since the government is usually left holding the deteriorating "surplus" product, there will be *visible* signs that this storage scheme is wasteful. In 1965, the total accumulated crops in government-held stocks had cost the taxpayers over $5,500,000,000, including an annual cost of about $1,000,000,000 to keep them stored.

*Production controls.*    An alternative scheme is to produce only as much as can be sold at the desired price.[15]  If that is done successfully, there will be no "surplus." This kind of crop control, if effective, is very tidy and solves the problem in the sense that there will be no "surplus" around to embarrass anyone and no low price to the producers.

One way to obtain effective crop controls or "self-policing management" is to assure each producer who agrees to reduce acreage of a particular crop by at least 20 percent (obviously he will pick the poorest 20 percent of his land) that he will be guaranteed a sale at the "parity" price for all he produces of that crop, and that he will even be paid something for the released land if he keeps it idle—a payment called a "conservation" payment. Those who do not agree to restrict their acreage probably will not be able to sell what they produce at the market price. In fact, in the case of tobacco a prohibitive tax of 75 percent of the value is levied on such production.

To get such a program into effect requires a majority vote of the current producers—which usually is not so easy as it may seem. Under this acreage-control scheme, efficiency in production will *not* be the criterion for deciding which land will be licensed for tobacco (or whatever crop is being "protected"). One procedure is simply to require all existing producers to eliminate the same percentage of land. But percentage of what total amount of land used by each producer? The amount he planned to use this year? Or the amount he used last year? Or five, ten, or twenty years ago? This comical question is indeed a serious one. Acreage in any product is always changing. New areas develop. Cotton production has swept westward to more efficient lands—in the San Joaquin Valley of California, where cotton can be produced at a lower average cost than in the southeastern United States. In no small part, it is because of this new cheaper source that cotton prices have fallen; the older, higher-cost producers are using the government taxing power to help protect them from the new competitors, who are often hurt by the crop-control plan, as we shall see.

Open-market forces toward efficiency are modified because the use of land is affected by a political voting process. The selection of acreage is partly removed from the marketplace—*because* of the desire to avoid its efficiency criterion and its adverse effect on inefficient producers. Therefore, the government authorizes someone (government employees or industry representatives) to decide on the land allocation. The decision must induce a voting majority of the growers to accede, else the whole acreage-reduction scheme will be jeopardized. In cotton growing, the most efficient lands are in the western United States, and the farms are larger. Therefore, the more efficient producers are outnumbered. A proposal to cut back the use of older, less efficient lands before that of the newer ones is obviously not acceptable to a majority. A proposal to cut everyone back by the same percentage is used instead. But it is ingeniously effective in reducing the newer, more efficient acreage by a bigger percentage than the old. How? Suppose you decide to cut all acreage back to 75 percent of former use. Should it be 75 percent of last year? The farther back into the past one goes for his base, the greater the cut

[15] "Parity" price is the common euphemism for the "desired" price.

for the newly expanding areas. And conversely for older areas that are *declining*. Anticipating this kind of restriction, the newer, more efficient, expanding producers will vote against the scheme because, while they will get a higher price, it is on such a greatly reduced output that they would have smaller wealth than if they were permitted to produce more for sale at lower prices. The votes of cotton landowners for acreage-restriction schemes fall off dramatically as one moves into the more efficient western lands.[16]

Acreage control, combined with a guaranteed high price of output, promotes large increases in use of fertilizer and other jointly productive resources. Production becomes more intensive, and the output per acre skyrockets. Acreage must be cut back more than appeared necessary at first sight, because farming becomes "surprisingly productive."

Acreage controls have been most effectively and rigorously used in tobacco production. Acres that are licensed as tobacco-growing lands are carefully marked and policed. The type of output control used in tobacco production has been publicly extolled by recent Presidents as very successful and deserving application to other crops. In tobacco, the control is via *licensing* to grow tobacco on *specific* plots of land and to sell the crop on the free market. Unlicensed producers must pay a prohibitive 75 percent tax on the value of the output. No one could afford to produce without a "license"—unless tobacco growing were a hobby. Since the licenses are for so few acres, the untaxed output is small enough to yield a high price. There is no tobacco surplus because the price goes to whatever level will clear the market of the *licensed* (untaxed) output.

## Public Utilities

If larger rates (and volume) of some good can be produced by a firm with ever decreasing costs *per unit*, the firm is a decreasing-cost firm. Two such firms producing identical goods could not reach an equilibrium situation. One could expand more and eliminate the others. In view of the impossibility of more than one firm's being profitable, two is one too many. But if there is only one, that firm may be able to set prices above free-entry costs for a long time. Either resources are wasted because too many are in the industry, or there is just one firm, which will be able to charge monopoly prices. That, in

---

[16] We interject an ironic and humorous note. Although we have been calling the western lands more efficient, some of these lands are more efficient only because the costs of irrigation are not borne by the farm landowners who use that water. Some of the water is provided to the farmers by federal irrigation projects at prices substantially below the costs—the difference being made up by taxes on the rest of the country. Thus, we see farmers in southeastern United States paying taxes to enable water to be sold to cotton growers in the western desert areas at less than cost in order to compete with the cotton from the southeast. And to protect themselves from the consequent lower prices, they appeal for more taxes on the city consumers to finance "loans on unsold cotton"; finally, they appeal for federal regulations restricting production of cotton on those very same western lands for which they have paid taxes to help irrigate at less than cost.

essence, is the reasoning behind government regulation of a single authorized firm in this industry—often called a public utility.

But that analysis is incomplete. While it may be true that only one firm should be producing, nothing implies that there cannot be competition among many applicants for that right to produce. The lowest annual bidder, in terms of prices to be charged the public, could be granted a franchise. Several other techniques have been proposed for permitting competition among potential producers, even though one producer only is allowed to produce. But none has been used extensively. Instead, the political processes of control have usually endorsed the following: (1) Only one firm is allowed to produce for the market, all others being prohibited by law; that is, a legal, closed monopoly is created. (2) The monopoly firm is subjected to political regulation of the profits it can keep, the prices it can charge, the amount and kind of service it is to provide, the costs it can incur, and many other details. If the utility fails to make money, the private owners must bear the losses. The owners may then sell out at a loss to new buyers who expect to do better; or the service will come to an end (railroad passenger service, street cars) or it will be subsidized by taxes (city bus lines, subways, local airlines) or operated by government.

Examples of public utilities are electric, gas, water, sewage, telephone, railroad, and airline companies. Other products that are sometimes monopolized by law, but not because of the decreasing-cost technicality, are sometimes called public utilities (taxi, radio, television, and municipal garbage-collection services).

The creation of a legal, closed monopoly for a decreasing-cost product imposes some costs on consumers. Prohibiting new entrants does not so fully encourage new products or lower-cost methods of production. It is not that the incumbent firm refuses to use known lower-cost techniques; rather, the incumbent firm does not know everything. Others, with different ideas about how to produce, are blocked out. The incumbent is dilatory in introducing known lower-cost innovations—not because it is a monopolist but because its *profits are limited* by the regulatory commission. Cost-reducing devices would be introduced if the firm could garner the profits; however, if the firm is already making its maximum allowable profits, incentives to reduce costs are blunted. Members of the regulatory commission will not force the firm to introduce new techniques to bring about lower prices; they cannot capture the net gain of lower costs, so they, too, will be less motivated. It's not that regulators are indolent or lazy; it is just that the incentives in the form of rewards for instituting cost-reduction techniques are lower than for those in open markets, where customers can shop among competitors.[17]

---

[17] Recall the discussion (on page 405) of the likelihood of successful collusions against governments. The same analysis is applicable here in the case of sales to public utilities, since they are "profit limited" and regulated by the government. Because of the restricted incentives or rewards available to public utilities, collusion among sellers of items bought by public utilities is more viable. In fact, and as an illustration of this implication, the 1960 indictment of the major electric-power-equipment companies involved collusion of items sold almost exclusively to public utilities and governments.

In summary, the public-utility regulatory commission avoids the "waste" of duplicate facilities by several competitors where only one can survive; and it negates the possibility that an excessively high price might be charged by the one legal monopolist. But the other side of the coin is that the restriction against new entrants reduces the opportunity and incentive to use lower-cost methods of production and improvements in service and quality. The net effect on *prices and quality* cannot be discerned from analytical comparison, and the empirical factual evidence also is not conclusive, but what evidence is available from electric, gas, taxi, and airline services suggests that prices are not lower or service better in *regulated* public utilities.

### Whose "Utility" in Public Utilities?

An especially instructive and important example of the incentives for and consequences of regulatory agencies is provided by the history of regulation of the railroads. A long list of pricing "abuses" presaged the creation in 1887 of the Interstate Commerce Commission to regulate the railroads in the interests of the consumer. What was the basic problem? Prior to 1880 open-market entry had resulted in the overbuilding of railroads. Not only had railroad investors been too optimistic, but many states gave railroads land, the power of eminent domain (legal power to acquire land for rights-of-way), and tax exemptions. (Eventually there were seven tracks between Omaha and Chicago.) The high costs of creating a railroad and the relatively low variable (operating) costs (relative to the total costs of having created the railroad) enabled the railroads to cut prices far below the total average costs (including the sunk costs). Rather than shut down if price did not cover "full" costs, some dropped prices to average variable costs of continued operation of existing equipment. The railroads sought to prevent price-cutting that was self-destructive or involved secret price discounts. Shippers who paid more were at a cost disadvantage. They demanded the government prohibit secret price cuts. Even the railroads wanted to avoid it as a group.

If the government had done nothing, the lower prices of rail service even without secret price cuts would have continued for a long time, until some rails and equipment wore out and only the more economic railroads survived. The law of 1887 requiring that railroads charge "just and reasonable" rates and publicly post their rates enabled railroads to do what they had sought to do by collusion—to prevent individually advantageous, but mutually disadvantageous price-cutting.

The Interstate Commerce Commission became the vehicle facilitating the maintenance of an effective cartel. Although only three years later (1890) the Sherman Antitrust Act declared all collusive (cartel) activity illegal, the railroads with the aid of the Interstate Commerce Commission continued to act effectively as a collusive cartel until 1948. In that long interim the railroads had legal backup in setting prices (much as if General Motors, Ford, and

Chrysler were told it was illegal for them to sell their cars for less than prices jointly agreed to by themselves). In 1920 the Interstate Commerce Commission acquired the power to set prices and to *control entry* into the railroad business, thus securing the railroads' wealth position even more firmly. Unfortunately for the railroads, new forms of transportation, which developed under the umbrella of high prices for rail service and the "monopolistic service" of railroads, managed to take away many railroad customers. This led to insistence that the new competitors also be regulated. The conflict of interest among the forms of transportation is still being fought within the Interstate Commerce Commission, the Congress, and to some extent in the market.

The Commission now is authorized to approve rates charged by highway transport, waterways, pipelines, and telephone and communication companies. If companies want to change service or routes of services, they must obtain permission from the commission. Its extensive authority is used primarily for policing rather than for administering details. Additional federal regulatory commissions deal with other public utilities. The airlines are controlled by the Civil Aeronautics Board, which allocates routes and authorizes rates, types of service, mergers, etc. The Federal Communications Commission controls radio- and television-station ownership. The proposition that open-market competition is feasible for these activities is challenged by the existence of these regulatory commissions. In fact, all these regulatory boards were set up because Congress reflected the belief that open-market competition was inappropriate for providing such services.

### Monopoly Rents: Creation and Disposition

In all the preceding cases wherein legal barriers were placed on market access, the effect, and often the purpose, was to increase the wealth of those who were first in the market. This increase of wealth is called *monopoly rent*. Here monopoly refers to *closed* monopoly only. The term *rent* is used to describe wealth in excess of that which would be normal in an open market.

Closed-monopoly rent is achieved by *restricting* the transference of resources, so that a difference between value of product and costs is created. Closed-monopoly rent is not achieved by transferring resources from lower- to higher-valued uses but, rather, by restrictions on that transfer. The value difference that is created or preserved beyond what it would have been in the absence of such legal restriction is the monopoly rent. The more effective the restriction on access to markets, the greater that monopoly rent.

What happens to the monopoly rent that results from the agricultural crop-control scheme? It goes to the *landowners* who owned the land at the time the scheme was first revealed. The value of the particular land on which the authorization, or license, to grow tobacco is granted is the value of the crop after all other costs of production (labor, equipment, fertilizer, insecticides, management, taxes, etc.) are subtracted. Suppose that net revenue is $400 an acre for each crop year. Recall from the earlier capital-value analysis that if it has an income of $400 per year, the licensed land would have a value of about $4,000 if the interest rate were about 10 per cent. Taking that as a simple assumption, suppose that land of the same kind, without the "license" has a value of $1,000. This difference of $3,000 is the capital-value measure of the monopoly rent resulting from the acreage-licensing scheme in tobacco.[18] As the licensing scheme is revealed, the favored acre rises in value, and anyone who then owns it captures the higher income. He can sell the land (with the "license" for exemption from the crop tax) and use the wealth for other kinds of consumption (vacations in Florida); he can keep the land and the annual higher-income stream; he can rent the land out for the higher annual value.

A *new* purchaser gets no monopoly-rent *gain* since he pays a higher price to get the land. The high monopoly-rent income from tobacco production is equal to a normal competitive return on *his* $4,000 purchase price. The person whose wealth increased by the amount of the monopoly rent is the owner at the time the controls were announced.

If the license to grow an acre of untaxed tobacco could be sold separately from an acre of land, it would be profitable and more efficient to have the landowners of less efficient lands transfer their licenses, acre for acre, to the more efficient lands. Just as each landowner will use the most efficient of his acres for tobacco growing, withdrawing first from his less efficient lands, so it will be profitable and efficient for less efficient landowners to sell licenses to owners of more efficient lands. A bigger crop, or a lesser-cost crop, could be grown; and the owners of more efficient lands would compete among themselves to buy the licenses from the owners of less efficient lands. The owners of the less efficient lands could sell the "bare" license rather than the land itself and capture some of the value of the crop which could be grown on the more efficient lands. Regardless of who captures that monopoly-rent gain, the total costs of the produced tobacco would be lower if transfers to better land were legal. This general increase in achieved level of efficiency is not permitted under the law. Why? The total tobacco output would be larger for the same cost of production, and that would involve a lower selling price. An appropriate further restriction of licensed acreage could offset that increase in yield per acre. Some political observers have suggested that the outright sale of these bare licenses would expose the monopoly rents provided to the tobacco landowners—just as they would be exposed in the sale of bare liquor-store licenses, taxi franchises, and radio and television station licenses.

The effects of the tobacco price-support program—widely regarded as politically "good" because there is no "surplus"—are (1) reduction of consumption compared to what it would have been had the price been allowed to reflect a free-market demand and supply, (2) wealth gains in the form of monopoly rent to those who are able to get their land licensed, (3) political protection of the wealth of tobacco landowners (as distinct from tobacco growers), (4)

---

[18] These are realistic values.

reduced level of efficiency, (5) reduced range of choice of occupation for producers.

As we saw in Chapter 3, there are ways to make the monopolist pay for his monopoly rent. In some cases, the monopolist must pay a price to get that legal monopoly right. Outright bribes, political contributions, higher taxes as a payment for monopoly rights, costs of public-relations men and lawyers to obtain "rights, licenses, franchises, or authorization" are sometimes large enough to match the monopoly rent. If there were restrictions on entry into some business, so that in each year only selected people were admitted, candidates for admission would be prepared to spend money to obtain admission rights. They would each seek to buy whatever qualities the candidate believes the authorities will use in their criterion of admission. For example, a young man setting out to enter the medical profession might find that by the time he had paid the "costs" of being admitted to practice, he would be so old that the high but short-lived income he eventually gets has a capital value, as seen from date of application to medical school, no greater than the average of all college students. In other words, the monopoly rent is consumed by these entry "fees."

In California and many other states, liquor licenses—right to sell bottled liquors at retail—have sold for over $40,000. Tobacco-growing rights are worth about $3,000 an acre. Cotton allotments are worth over $500 per acre—if we judge by the prices paid in certain illegal transfers in Texas in 1962. In many areas milk farmers must have a license to produce and sell milk. Entry into the savings-and-loan bank business in many states is subject to approval of state officials. The value of permission to open a bank has exceeded $50,000 in California, as evidenced and measured by the immediate rise in price of stock of groups obtaining permission. Radio and television stations are "requested" to provide free coverage of political campaigns, especially at the national level, for the major parties. They are also required to broadcast the kinds of programs that the federal-government authorities think they should broadcast. (Notice the contrast with newspapers, which do not have to apply for a license. They act in ways that radio and television cannot.) Part of the "monopoly rent" to radio and television is extracted from the station owners, not necessarily in the form of money payments, but by the kinds of programs that the authorities prefer.

Most public utilities pay higher taxes than other businesses of similar size; these transfer part of their monopoly rent to the government. Employees of public utilities get larger wages or more secure jobs or easier jobs than similar employees in open-market firms. The extra payment to employees is a sharing of the monopoly rent. Thus we see that the owners of a closed monopoly cannot count on capturing all the monopoly rent for themselves. The political processes that can give the monopoly rent can also take it away in one form or another. People will compete for the right to be that "monopolist"; they will pay up to the value of that monopoly rent in order to get it.

Summary

1   Reduction of market competition by elimination of rivals or by collusion is potentially profitable.

2   We have been unable to show that predatory tactics are profitable, because they impose losses on both contending parties and give no assurance that elimination of one would allow higher prices or larger profits—because of potential entry of new firms.

3   Effective collusion is difficult because rivals find it hard to reach agreement, police the agreement, and keep out new entrants who would be attracted by the higher profit potential.

4   Immediate increases in receipts may not be large enough to offset effect of new entrants who will lower the future receipts, thereby lowering *current wealth*.

5   Mergers do not appear to be an important means of achieving collusive action to change market conditions. Rather, many allow efficient managers to take over less efficient firms or provide certain economies of joint production, none of which involves raising prices as a consequence of the merger.

6   Sealed-bid purchases by government agencies encourage collusion, because they make enforcement of secret agreements easy.

7   The argument against collusion is essentially the argument against monopoly inefficiency (explained in Chapter 12).

8   Under the Sherman Act, the Antitrust division of the Department of Justice and the Federal Trade Commission are supposed to prevent "monopolizing tactics" and "unfair" trade practices. Whether these laws have on net protected competitive markets or hindered them is not clear, and the evidence for or against either position is extremely weak.

9   Some labor unions represent effective collusions by sellers (of labor) to raise wages above the competitive level. Wage cutting and entry is in those cases reduced (though not entirely eliminated) by union-shop contracts.

10   Restrictions on access to the market occur for several, sometimes conflicting, reasons: (a) encouragement of invention; (b) protection to consumers, by saving them each from incurring costs of discerning undesirable features of goods; (c) to prevent uneconomic duplication of resources, as with *some* public utilities; (d) to protect existing producers from products of other potential producers. While the first three

are generally, though not universally, applauded, each serves as a facade for the fourth motive. Therein lies the source of objection to many governmental and political controls over people who would buy and sell in the open market. Political authorities can create monopoly-rent wealth through closed, legal monopolies. The ability of governmental authority to affect the allocation of economic resources induces competition for political power.

11   Some market controls are ostensibly intended to protect consumers from their gullibility and sanguineness; others are intended to lower individual information-collection costs. This latter objective implies governmental licensing for "approved" sellers, but *not* exclusion from the market for non-licensed sellers.

12   Some market-entry restrictions are designed primarily to protect existing sellers from competition of new and existing sellers. Almost every agricultural crop-market or production control does this. Although advertising restrictions are intended to protect the buyer from gullibility, they also protect existing producers from new competitors by raising the costs of entry to the market.

13   Closing the markets to new entrants, or to any sellers who would sell below an "approved" price initially provides a closed-monopoly rent to the producer. Hence, many of the crop price-support laws intended to help the poor farmers give a greater gain to the larger, richer landowner.

14   Public utilities are closed monopolies, regulated by the political process, presumably because the product is produced at decreasing cost and more than one seller would be wasteful. That regulated monopoly is superior in its over-all results (introduction of new processes and goods, reductions of price, reliability of service) to unregulated open monopoly is open to serious question.

Questions

1   Suppose there are ten identical producers of the good being sold in the market characterized by the demand schedule given here. Each producer has *zero* costs of production for twenty units; he can produce no more.

a. If all are selling in a price-takers' market, what is the price and output?
b. If all sellers could reach an effective agreement to restrict output and raise price, what price should they select?
c. What will be each seller's output and revenue?
d. How much would each seller gain by the effective agreement?

Demand Schedule

Dollar Value of Daily Revenue

| Price | Quantity Demanded Daily | Total | Increment | Marginal (for Unit Increase in Quantity) |
|---|---|---|---|---|
| $2.00 | 0 | 0 | 0 | 0 |
| 1.75 | 3.5 | $ 6.13 | $ 6.13 | 1.75 |
| 1.50 | 14.2 | 21.30 | 15.17 | 1.41 |
| 1.40 | 20.4 | 28.56 | 7.26 | 1.17 |
| 1.30 | 27.7 | 36.01 | 7.45 | 1.02 |
| 1.20 | 36.24 | 43.48 | 7.47 | .87 |
| 1.10 | 45.97 | 50.57 | 7.08 | .72 |
| 1.00 | 56.52 | 56.52 | 5.95 | .56 |
| .95 | 62.25 | 59.14 | 2.62 | .46 |
| .90 | 68.39 | 61.55 | 2.41 | .41 |
| .85 | 74.65 | 63.45 | 1.90 | .30 |
| .80 | 81.36 | 65.09 | 1.64 | .24 |
| .75 | 88.17 | 66.13 | 1.04 | .15 |
| .70 | 95.45 | 66.82 | .69 | .09 |
| .67 | 100.00 | 67.00 | .18 | .03 |
| .65 | 103.00 | 66.95 | −.05 | −.02 |
| .60 | 110.67 | 66.40 | −.43 | −.05 |
| .55 | 118.60 | 65.23 | −1.17 | −.15 |
| .50 | 127.01 | 63.51 | −1.72 | −.18 |
| .45 | 135.72 | 61.07 | −2.44 | −.28 |
| .40 | 144.48 | 57.79 | −3.28 | −.37 |
| .35 | 153.76 | 53.81 | −3.98 | −.43 |
| .30 | 163.07 | 48.92 | −4.98 | −.53 |
| .25 | 172.92 | 43.23 | −5.69 | −.58 |
| .20 | 182.79 | 37.16 | −6.07 | −.61 |
| .15 | 193.21 | 28.98 | −8.18 | −.78 |
| .10 | 203.92 | 20.39 | −8.59 | −.81 |
| .05 | 214.62 | 10.70 | −9.69 | −.91 |

   e. How much (money) would it be worth to each seller to seek means of reaching and enforcing that effective agreement?
   f. How much would you gain if you as *one* seller succeeded in staying outside the agreement or in secretly breaking it while all others raised the price and reduced their output?

2   Ten concrete-block companies in a certain community were accused by the city attorney of colluding to restrain output and fix the prices of concrete blocks. The accusation stated that the ten producers accounted for 85 percent of the output of concrete blocks in the community. Which do you think was meant by "colluding": Meeting and talking in an effort to reach an agreement? Or reaching an agreement? Or those ten firms restricting output and raising prices? Or all firms raising prices?

3   Assume that all existing firms producing a commodity were successfully and effectively to collude to restrict output and raise prices.

a. What open-market forces would operate to obstruct the effectiveness of the collusion?

b. How can those forces be restrained from operating? Illustrate in the context of the behavior of lemon growers, wheat producers, tobacco growers, longshoremen, carpenters, doctors, retail liquor stores, and steel producers.

c. What devices are used in each instance to keep the supply below the open-market supply?

d. Are these regarded as "proper"?

4    The first case prosecuted under the federal laws against collusion to raise prices involved steel pipe sold to the U.S. government. More recently, an electrical-equipment industry's collusion, which sent some business leaders to jail, was also against the government. What explanations are there for the fact that a majority of prosecuted proven cases involve collusion against the government?

5    As determined by Congressional action, radio and television networks are not required to give "equal-time" rights to any political parties other than the Republican and Democratic parties.

a. Would you consider this a collusion by the two major political parties against the many smaller political parties? Explain.

b. Why are newspapers not required to give equal-space rights to the two major political parties? (Hint: The answer is *not* that radio space is limited or a natural resource that "belongs to the people.")

6    The National and the American Baseball Leagues are two separate leagues of ten teams each. Teams are owned by different people. To prevent competition among team owners for *new* players, a draft (similar to that used in the football and basketball leagues) has been adopted, wherein each newcomer from a high school is assigned to a particular team. Under this agreement, or assignment, no other team owner will be allowed to sign that newcomer. Once a player signs a contract, he cannot change "employers" at his own volition; but the employer can trade or sell him to another team owner.

a. Who benefits from this arrangement? Who suffers?

b. Why does this system exist in sports and nowhere else?

7    Almost every team in the two baseball leagues is subsidized by the city governments, which provide stadium facilities. If new leagues cannot be assured of access to those facilities, will this have any effect on the income of the existing teams?

8    What is the difference between collusion, cooperation, and competition? How would you define collusion between two people so as to exclude partnerships and corporate joint ownership from the concept of collusion? Why is collusion considered undesirable?

9    European coal producers pool their sales through a central agency.

a. Why is that essential for an effective policing of the collusion agreement among the producers?

b. Why haven't some coal producers stayed out of the agreement and taken advantage of the opportunity to sell more coal at the price maintained by the "cartel," as it is called?

10    Why, despite so much political campaigning against "monopolies," do politicians create closed markets or closed monopolies?

11    The judicial council of the American Medical Association recommended that it be considered unethical for a doctor to own a drug store in the area in which he practices medicine. It also recommended similarly for ophthalmologists who dispense eyeglasses for a profit. "Any arrangement by which the physician profits from the remedy he prescribes is unethical," in the opinion of the council.

a. Who do you think would benefit if this recommendation were adopted by the American Medical Association and made effective?

b. If it is unethical for a surgeon to profit from the remedy he prescribes, should any surgeon diagnosing a patient be allowed to perform the recommended operation?

c. Should a building contractor be allowed to have any interest in a lumber company? Should any teacher be allowed to use his own textbook? Should a doctor be allowed to own a hospital? Or own an undertaking business?

d. As a patient, would you prefer to deal with doctors who are prohibited from ownership of drug stores? How would this help you or hurt you?

12    Diagnose and explain the various features reported in the following news story: "An attractive brunette seated in a rear row gave an excited whoop when her name was called Wednesday during a drawing at the County Building. She had good reason to be elated. For $6,000 she had picked up an on-sale liquor license with a market value of about $9,500. She was one of 54 persons who had applied for the 25 new on-sale licenses to be issued in the county this year by the Alcoholic Beverage Control Board. A drawing was used to determine who would get the new on-sale licenses, which permit sale of drinks on the premises. An applicant must have had a premise available and must operate the business for two years before he can sell the license."

13    Suppose you could live in a society in which trademarks were not protected by law and anyone could imitate the trademark.

a. As a consumer, would you prefer to live in that world or in one where trademarks were exclusively reserved for a particular manufacturer as part of his property? Why?

b. As a producer, which would you prefer?

14    You invent a photocopy machine. You know that the average cost of making the machine is $1,000 and that its operating costs are 1 cent

each time the machine is used. You could sell the machine for, say, $2,000, letting users pay the 1-cent operating costs. On the other hand, if you can discriminate among customers, and charge some a higher price than others, you can make still more money. In order to make discriminatory pricing effective, you must not sell machines to the users, for they could then resell them from the "low-priced" to the "higher-priced" customers, and undermine your attempt to get more revenue. Suppose, however, you rent the machine to each user at a uniform fee but charge 3 cents each time the machine makes a photocopy.

a. Would that achieve your purpose? Explain.

b. Selling at different prices is illegal; 3¢ per copy is legal. Why?

c. Is this kind of "discrimination" good?

15    Charles Pfizer Company, the patent holder of the drug tetracycline, used in various forms as a general antibiotic (Aureomycin is an example), has licensed other firms to produce and sell the drug. In doing so, it has set certain conditions as to price and amounts for each licensed producer. This practice has been attacked by the Federal Trade Commission as "illegal." The patent holder does not have to license other firms at all. Under the patent terms, it could be the only producer of the drug.

a. As a potential consumer of drugs, which arrangement would you prefer to exist?

b. Do you think this kind of licensing would explain why this drug is sold for a lower price in foreign countries than in the United States?

c. Is that kind of price discrimination bad? Why?

16    Milk delivery is sometimes called inefficient because when several firms deliver milk to homes, there is duplication of delivery trucks and labor.

a. For standard items such as milk, would you prefer to live in a community with one centralized delivery service controlled by a regulatory commission to ensure low prices and adequate quality, or in one where anyone who wants to deliver milk can enter the market? Why?

b. Apply your analysis of the preceding problem to the case of garbage collecting. Would you feel differently about that?

c. How about mail service? Newspapers? Electric power?

d. If your answers differ, what factor makes you change your preference?

17    European countries import inspected frozen fresh meat from Argentina. But the United States limits imports of fresh meat, because some other countries have hoof and mouth disease (a rapidly spreading disease that kills cattle, although it does not endanger human life). Whom does the import limitation benefit and whom does it hurt? How?

18    The stock exchanges, with the sanction of the U.S. Securities and Exchange Commission, occasionally prohibit (suspend) all trading in

a certain common stock, especially when some spectacular news about that company suddenly is heard. For example, if the president of a corporation is sued for fraud by some government agency, with a consequent rush of sell orders by common stockholders, the exchange suspends trading to permit time for the full news to be digested and to prevent wild swings in the price of stock. The defense of the suspension is that it protects some stockholders from selling in panic at the developing, but as yet unsubstantiated and unweighed news. These sellers would later find the price had recovered—that they had sold at exceptionally low transient prices.

Does that reasoning—as a defense of suspension of trading of the stock—convince you that it would be better for you to be in a situation in which the exchange could stop trading in common stocks you happened to own? In making your decision, consider the risk that the news will turn out to be accurate and the swing will not be temporary. Consider also the effect on the new potential buyers who are restrained from buying. (Incidentally, trading can always go on elsewhere than in the formal exchange markets—whether or not the exchange suspends its trading.)

19  Gasoline price "wars" have induced many gasoline-station owners to propose a regulatory agency to establish orderly marketing conditions in gasoline markets. Also, they propose that no service station be allowed to charge a price less than costs, and further that no new stations be opened unless the convenience and necessity of the area warrants more stations.
a. Who would benefit and who would be hurt by these proposals, if carried out?
b. If the proposals were carried out, how should the commission decide who got to open a new service station?
c. What would be your preference about this kind of regulation if you were a Negro, immigrant, or young gasoline-station operator?

20  Read the first quotation in footnote 14, page 420.
a. Why has the growth in numbers of investors made open markets for security dealers and for investors an obsolete concept?
b. If you were a Negro, a Jew, or an immigrant, would you find this development to your advantage? Why?

21  Refer to the last passage in footnote 14, page 420.
a. Restate the proposition of that passage in terms analogous to the control of medication by prescriptions from doctors.
b. Do you think economists should campaign for laws to prohibit any person from buying a security, land, or a house without a prescription from an economist certifying the suitability of that particular purchase by the particular person involved? Why or why not?

22  It is probably safe to say that a majority of the faculty at any college

contends that students are not competent to judge the quality of the instruction in various courses and hence should not be relied upon as evaluators of instructor competence.

a. What do you think?

b. At the same time, it is probably safe to say that a majority of the faculty thinks its students have come to that college because the students can tell good colleges from bad. Do you see any inconsistency in this pair of beliefs? Explain.

23    When seeking a replacement for a retiring member of a regulatory board, President Johnson said that he wanted a strong man of action to help strengthen the board, because he had noted that even the regulated industry didn't like weak regulatory boards. Why do you suppose the regulated industry likes a strong regulatory board? (Hint: Who is regulated for whose benefit?)

24    Texas, which has the legal right to subdivide itself into seven states, surprises us by doing so. One of the new states, Texaseven, with no college in its boundaries, decides to give to every high-school student a four-year annual grant of $1,500 to be applied to education costs at the college of his choice anywhere in the world.

a. Would you consider that new state to have the finest or the worst educational system in the world?

b. Why is that method not used more widely, despite its temporary wide use immediately after World War II as an aid to veterans?

c. Why is it opposed by the officials of most state universities?

25    The U.S. Postal system is a monopoly. No one else may institute a competitive system of transporting personal messages for pay.

a. Why do you think it has remained a monopoly?

b. The prices charged are uniform despite vast differences in costs of service to different patrons. Why is this kind of discriminatory pricing practiced for mail but not for food, clothes, or dancing lessons?

26    a. Do you know of any instances where inferior goods have driven out superior goods?

b. Would any of the following be such cases: compact versus larger cars; margarine versus butter; salad dressing versus mayonnaise; blended versus straight whiskey; plastic cartons versus milk bottles; frozen versus fresh orange juice; ready-made versus custom clothes; office versus home visits of the doctor. Would you consider any of these to be unfortunate developments? Why?

27    Why do union officials object to admitting that their power rests on a closed monopoly, while at the same time opposing any legislation that would destroy that monopoly power? Answer the same question when applied to the American Medical Association.

28    a. Why will a person who has salable property rights in an enterprise for which he is making decisions be more influenced by the longer-run

effects of his decisions than if he did not have salable property rights in the enterprise?

**b.** Does this difference in type of property right induce a systematic difference in the kinds of decisions made by government employees, as contrasted to employees of a privately owned enterprise—even if both are engaged in the same kind of activity (production of power)? Explain why the influence of the salable capital value of property rights will or will not make a difference in decisions.

**29**   "Capitalism encourages deceitful advertising, dishonesty, and faithlessness." Do you agree? If so, why? If not, why not?

30   Tickets for the Baseball World Series are chronically underpriced. Why? (Hint: Proceeds of the first four games go to the players while the proceeds of the remaining games, if any, go to all the teams in the leagues. Season ticket holders get priority rights to the World Series tickets. Why?)

# Derived Demand for Productive Resources

Until now our interest concentrated on the first two of the following five tasks: (1) allocating consumption goods among competing claimants, (2) determining how much of each good to produce, (3) deciding how goods shall be produced, (4) selecting the producers of each, and (5) determining incomes of each person. The first two tasks were investigated via a market in which consumers bought goods from business firms. Now we study the last three questions. Again the focus will be on a market between business firms and households—this time, the householders selling productive services to business firms.

We can portray a relationship among these two markets, households and business firms, and between goods and money by the circular-flow diagram of Figure 19–1. The top half represents consumers' goods markets, with money flowing from householders to business firms (left to right) and consumers' goods going in the opposite direction. In the bottom half, money flows from business firms to householders (right to left), while services go in the opposite direction. The bottom half represents the producers' goods market, the market in which households earn income by selling their various productive services.

We have already analyzed the influence of householders' demand on the supply of goods from producers—the top half of the circle. We shall now see how the market system determines which productive goods are used to make which consumers' goods; this is the question the business firm will be solving in expressing its demands for productive services. We shall also be seeing how incomes of people are determined, since the prices and quantities of services they sell determine their income.

The logic of the analysis contains no circularity. Instead, it is a simultaneous determination of interdependent outputs of various goods—like the simultaneous solution of a set of equations. Not surprisingly, the analysis will be based on demand for and supply of productive services. In this chapter, we investigate the general conditions of *derived demand* for productive resources, derived from the value of the consumer goods these services help to produce.

## What Does a Person Produce?

If two or more resources are jointly or simultaneously used as productive "inputs," how much is produced by each? If I mow a lawn *with* a lawn mower, how much did I produce, and how much did the mower produce? If three people jointly move a box, how much did each person move? With jointly used productive resources, it is impossible to measure or even define how much of the product is produced by any one of the jointly used inputs.

This question of "what it produces" is a "red herring." You have heard that in the communist society each will be paid according to what he deserves or needs, not according to what he produces. Whatever its emotional worth, that statement is analytically meaningless. And if it is said of the capitalist system

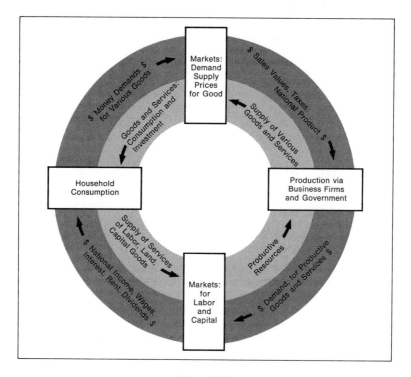

Figure 19–1

This chart relates the aggregate flows of goods and incomes with some of the institutions and problems of economics. Chapters 3–9 discussed allocation of existing goods (the upper left quarter of the circle). And Chapters 10–18 covered the amounts of goods produced (upper right portion). Methods of determining how goods shall be produced and by whom and for whom (the bottom half of the circle) are discussed in Chapters 19–23. These chapters will also cover determination of individual incomes and wealth. For each case, in the capitalist market system, the communications and controls are channeled via market prices and incomes. This book will not systematically analyze fluctuations in the total flow of services and values "around the whole economy." These are problems of aggregate employment and national-income fluctuations. The other half of the introductory course will do that.

that people are paid according to their product, that, too, is a meaningless statement. Instead of asking whether some input gets what it produces, we ask, "What determines what it gets—that is, its price?"

### Labor and Capital as Standard Names of Inputs

To explain how input prices and quantities are determined, we will work with just two kinds of inputs, even though there really is an infinite variety. We shall call them simply "labor" and "capital," identifying them in more detail whenever circumstances warrant. We should warn against a common misinterpretation: capital does not mean "nonhuman" goods. It is easy to get that impression when you hear about substituting capital for labor. At any one job location, we do substitute machines for labor. But fundamentally, one person's service is substituted for another's. Labor was used earlier to make a computer that will *later* yield output jointly with its operator (labor). The producers of the computer are replacing those who were replaced "by the computer." Those who are replaced see only the electronic computer and think that machines are displacing people.

To simplify matters, why aren't the machine producers called indirect or "offsite" labor? The answer is that the earlier labor services that produce the machinery are paid in advance of all its ultimate future services. Those earlier laborers are paid when they produce the machine; the people who pay them must wait for future payments as the machine is used. And so the people who pay earlier are called "capitalists" or investors. The machine is called capital or a capital good. The labor working later *with* the machine is said to be working with capital.

Although we shall investigate capital and capital goods more fully in Chapter 22, we should note here that people are capital—human capital. You students are investing in increasing your productive talents and knowledge. At graduation, you are akin to a machine that has just been completed. You are a capital good in that you represent a capability of yielding services *now and in the future*.

In the remainder of this chapter we shall elaborate a few simple propositions: (1) There are an unlimited variety of techniques by which any output may be produced. (2) Of these, some are technologically efficient. (3) Of all the technologically efficient ways, one is economically efficient, i.e., has lowest cost. (4) The lower the relative price of an input, the greater the amount demanded and used in the economically efficient technique. (5) The demand for a productive input depends upon the amounts of other inputs jointly available and their prices. (6) Substitution among productive inputs occurs not only by varying the productive technique but also by varying the output mixture. (7) The response in amount demanded of a productive input when price is changed is greater in the longer run.

## Variety of Productive Techniques and the Law of Variable Proportions

*Alternative techniques exist for producing every good.* One technique differs from another in using different proportions of productive inputs. One may use more water and less cooling equipment; another, fewer laborers and more equipment. One technique may use more electric power, while another uses more hand power. Houses can be built with varying combinations of power tools, pre-cut lumber, on-the-site assembly, and common-laborer assistants. In the operation of a grocery store, the variety of available techniques is enormous. You can hire fewer butchers, if you have them devote their time only to cutting while women clerks sell the cuts of meat to customers. The butchers can be provided with power cutting equipment and elaborate facilities, or these can be eliminated by using more butchers. At the checking stand an expert cash-register operator can concentrate on checking items purchased by the customer, with an automatic machine to deliver "change" to the customer, plus a moving belt to convey the groceries past the checker to a high-school boy who bags and boxes the groceries for the customer. Alternatively, the grocer could use more clerks and less equipment and still sell the same amount of groceries at the same rate.

*There are an unlimited variety of ways of doing something.* This often escapes our notice simply because we usually see very similar ways used in our own neighborhood of experience. But if you travel to other countries or regions and look for these differences, you will see them. The alert businessman watches competitors and other producers; he studies trade journals for ways to improve his operation. Equipment salesmen tell him of different ways of doing things and seek to show how their ways are better. Employees and labor-union representatives suggest that things are done differently in other firms. Business consultants and employees from other firms are hired to facilitate copying different techniques. A fundamental pervasive property of the "production function"—*the variety of combinations of inputs that can be used to produce a product*—is illustrated by the data in Table 19–1. The table shows the amounts of outputs and different alternative combinations of two inputs, labor and capital—each considered to be a homogeneous resource.

### Technological Efficiency

Table 19–1 reveals that there are several ways to produce, say, 277 units of $X$. It can be done using $5C$ and $2L$, or $4C$ and $3L$, or $3C$ and $5L$. Other combinations are available if $C$ and $L$ are divisible; thus, something between $3C$ and $4C$ along with $4L$, or about $4.5C$ and $4.5L$, will produce $277X$. All these combinations are *technologically* efficient; that is, it is impossible to produce more than $277X$ with those inputs. If there were no substitutability among inputs, only one combination of $L$ and $C$ could produce $277X$. However, there always is more than one technologically efficient way to produce any specified output. Which of the many technologically efficient processes is the *economically* efficient one?

### Economic Efficiency

Is the best process the simplest, the newest, the most reliable, or the most commonly used? Or is it the technique with large expenditures now but small ones later? Or one that maximizes the output per unit of labor? Or per unit

Table 19-1
Production of X as Function of Inputs of L and C

Output of X

| | | | | | | |
|---|---|---|---|---|---|---|
| | 6 | 246 | 304 | 340 | 372 | 395 | 416 |
| | 5 | 224 | 277 | 310 | 340 | 360 | 376 |
| Inputs | 4 | 200 | 246 | 277 | 302 | 321 | 333 |
| of | | | | | | | |
| Capital | 3 | 171 | 210 | 237 | 259 | 277 | 285 |
| | 2 | 141 | 172 | 194 | 214 | 228 | 234 |
| | 1 | 100 | 121 | 138 | 152 | 162 | 165 |
| | | 1 | 2 | 3 | 4 | 5 | 6 |

Inputs of Labor

For any combination of inputs of capital and of labor indicated along the left-hand and bottom sides, the entry in the table gives the total output of X. For example, for four units of capital and three units of labor, output is 277 of X. Note that 277 of X can also be obtained with three inputs of capital combined with five of labor.

of raw materials purchased? (Which raw material?) Or per unit of power used? Or per unit of floor space in the factory? Actually, none of these is encouraged by the capitalist market system.[1]

Society will penalize you for using an inappropriate criterion. But what is the appropriate criterion? The answer depends *in part* upon the economic system used. In a capitalistic, open-market system, users of productive resources are most rewarded if they achieve the highest known market value of the output obtainable with those resources. The farther one is from that goal, the more can other people bid away those resources and put them to higher-valued uses to increase their wealth. Open-market competition by other people for resources will make it expensive to persist in using resources inefficiently. You will lose command over productive resources, which will be diverted to users more successful at discerning wealth-maximizing techniques of production. Your personal desire for more wealth rather than less will "force" you to choose the higher-valued, or lower-cost, techniques. Whether you judge that to be a desirable solution depends upon your evaluation of the social, cultural, and economic consequences. At any rate, it is an *accurate* explanation of the incentive system that operates in the private-property *open*-market economy.

[1]From one point of view, the question of the appropriate combination of inputs may seem pointless. After all, at any moment there is a certain amount of each productive resource in the community and hence a given over-all ratio of inputs. With full use of resources the community can't help but use the resources in that given ratio. That is true for the community *as a whole*, but consistent with that over-all total ratio of inputs is an unlimited set of different sub-combinations of use by the producers of various goods. The question is not, then, to select the average ratio for the economy, but the *specific allocation* for each of the many members of the community competing for those resources. Upon what criterion shall it be decided for *each* person, and resource, how much to allocate to *each* productive task?

Returning to our numerical example, we know that there are different technologically efficient ways to produce at a daily rate of 277 units of $X$. Table 19–2 shows three (if we, for simplicity of computation, look only at the ways involving whole number units of input): five units of capital and two units of labor; or four units of capital and three units of labor; or three units of capital and five of labor. All are equally efficient in a *technological* sense, but only one is *economically* efficient. Which one? That is, which one will give 277 units of $X$ per day and the highest-valued bundle of other goods. Or in other words, which one is the cheapest-cost method? It depends upon the prices of labor and capital. Suppose that a unit of capital costs $35 and a unit of labor costs $30. Then, the lowest-cost, or economically efficient, method is with four capital and three labor. The cost is $(4 \times \$35) + (3 \times \$30)$ = $230. The costs for the other combinations at these prices are shown in the middle column of Table 19–2.

This table also shows the costs of production at other input prices. Suppose the price of capital were higher (say, $45) and the price of labor lower ($15). Now which of these techniques, all equally efficient technologically, is the economically efficient one—that is, the lowest-cost technique? Recomputing costs gives the results entered in the right-hand column of Table 19–2. The economically efficient combination has moved to one with more labor and less capital. This is not surprising, since capital is now more expensive, while labor is cheaper.

Conversely, if the price of labor had increased to $50 and the price of capital had fallen to $30, the costs would be those given in the first column in Table 19–2. This shifts the economic technique to five capital and two labor. As would be expected, the lower price of capital moves the efficient technique to a combination with more capital relative to labor.

### The Law of Diminishing Marginal Returns

Won't a different (than 277) total output rate make the producer's wealth even larger? And how will that new output affect the input combination selected? To answer this, we look at the *marginal-productivity function* of each input. This is a relationship between the *increase* in output consequent to a *unit increase* in one of the inputs. The relationship obeys the *law of diminishing marginal returns*. This law states: "As any rate of input is increased by unit amounts, the marginal rate of output, although possibly increasing at first to a maximum (called the point of diminishing marginal returns) *will* thereafter *decrease*." Note that it is the *marginal* increase in rate of output and not the *total* output that decreases. This law holds for the *rate* of production.

Table 19–2
Costs of Producing at Rate of 277 Units of X at Different Prices and
Input Combinations of Capital and Labor

|  | | Prices | | |  |
|---|---|---|---|---|---|
| Capital | | $30 | $35 | $45 | |
| | Labor | $50 | $30 | $15 | |
| 5 | 2 | $250* | $235 | $225 | |
| 4 | 3 | 270 | 230* | 255 | Costs |
| 3 | 5 | 340 | 255 | 210* | |

(The "Rate of Inputs" label appears to the left of the 5/4/3 capital rows.)

At $30 for a unit of capital and $50 for a unit of labor, 277 units of X can be produced at varying costs depending upon the input combinations shown. With five capital and two labor, shown in first row, cost is $250; for four capital and three labor, cost is $270; and it is $340 for three capital and five labor. Minimum cost combinations of capital and labor for producing 277X depend upon prices of labor and capital. For example, at $45 per capital and $15 per labor, minimum cost combination is three capital and five labor, compared with minimum cost combination of four capital and three labor at $35 per capital and $30 per labor. As price of capital is raised (from $30 to $45) and price of labor is lowered, the minimum cost combination of inputs have less capital and more labor. (Minimum cost combinations are indicated by asterisks.)

Consider the output data in Table 19–1 along one horizontal row; for example, the row with three units of capital shows outputs of 171, 210, 237, 259, 277, and 285 as the input of *labor* increases from one to six units. Each *unit increase* of labor used jointly with the fixed amount of capital yields a higher rate of output. The daily output rate increases from 171 to 210 (an *increase* of 39) as a second unit of labor is applied to three units of capital. The *increment* of output with the third unit of labor is 27 units of X (237 − 210). The *increment* of output for the fourth unit of labor added is 22 units of X. The *increments* in total output are shown in Table 19–3, which must be read along the horizontal *rows*; each *row* is for a fixed amount of capital. The *increments* in output rate with one more unit of labor (capital held constant) are called *marginal* products of labor.

A graph of the diminishing marginal products of labor, for capital fixed at three units, is shown in Figure 19–2. Also shown (with dashed lines) is the diminishing marginal product of labor, for capital fixed at four units.

Two cautioning remarks against misinterpretations are warranted. First, these increments are obtained by the use of a one unit larger rate of input of labor daily with the same amount of capital. In adjusting to this larger rate of input of labor, one can rearrange the capital so that it is most effectively used with the larger amount of labor.

The second remark concerns the meaning of "product." When four units of labor and three of capital are used, the total product is 259 units of X. How much of that is due to the capital and how much to the labor? The marginal-product concept does not answer the question of "how much a unit of input produces." According to Table 19–3, the marginal product of four units of

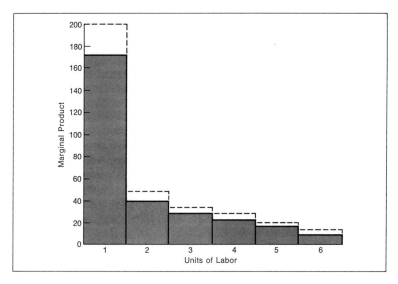

Figure 19–2

Marginal products of labor with three units of capital (solid line) and with four units of capital (dashed line). Heights of each bar are entries shown in Table 19–3. Diminishing heights portray diminishing marginal productivity of inputs.

Table 19–3
Increments in Output Rate for Unit Increments of Labor with Various Fixed Amounts of Capital

Marginal Products of Labor

|          |   | 1   | 2  | 3  | 4  | 5  | 6  |      |
|----------|---|-----|----|----|----|----|----|------|
|          | 6 | 246 | 58 | 36 | 32 | 23 | 19 | .... |
| Fixed    | 5 | 224 | 53 | 33 | 30 | 20 | 16 | .... |
| Amounts  | 4 | 200 | 46 | 31 | 25 | 19 | 12 | .... |
| of       | 3 | 171 | 39 | 27 | 22 | 18 | 8  | .... |
| Capital  | 2 | 141 | 31 | 22 | 20 | 14 | 6  | .... |
|          | 1 | 100 | 21 | 17 | 14 | 10 | 3  | .... |
|          |   | 1   | 2  | 3  | 4  | 5  | 6  | .... |

Rates of Inputs of Labor

Read this table horizontally along a row. For a stipulated amount of capital, say one unit, as inputs of labor are increased, the *marginal products of labor diminish* from 100, to 21, to 17, etc. Entries in this table are the differences between total output entries in Table 19–1, along a *horizontal row* of that table. (You can construct a table for the marginal products of capital by taking differences along a vertical column of Table 19–1.)

labor (as compared to three units of labor), when used jointly with three units of capital, is twenty-two units of $X$. Twenty-two units of $X$ are not produced by the fourth unit of labor. Instead, that is the increase in the total product when four units of labor are used instead of three units, along with three units of capital. If a basketball team used six men instead of five, would the sixth man say that *he* produced the larger score? Each can validly claim that six of them produce more than do five, by the amounts of the marginal product for six people. Instead of referring to the marginal product *of the sixth worker*, then, we should speak of the marginal product of labor when the number of workers is six.

The marginal products are smaller at larger amounts of input (*with other inputs fixed in amounts*). The productive process is adjusted to take full advantage of greater amounts of $L$; but each increment in $L$ yields *diminishing* increments in output. Table 19–3 illustrates the law of *diminishing marginal* productivity; the data given are all beyond the point of diminishing marginal returns.

Capital can just as well be treated as the variable input. Again, the law of diminishing marginal returns will hold; that law holds for every productive resource.

Interpretations of the Law
of Diminishing Returns

What use would be made of resources if there were increasing, not diminishing, marginal productivity? With a small plot of the best soil, a farmer could, by adding successive increments of labor to that soil, obtain successively larger increments of output until he was able to feed the world and do so with less labor than if he used some other soil also. He would put no labor on any other equally fertile soil since the marginal product would not be as large there—given *increasing* or non-decreasing marginal productivity of labor on the initial soil. And certainly he would not apply any resources to inferior soil. All labor in production of wheat would be concentrated on one small piece of the best land. But in fact we see inferior land being used. Farmers do so because they get a larger increment of product than if they applied that extra labor and resources to the superior land, which already has some labor and resources applied to it. The greater amount of labor applied to the superior land has moved the farmer down the diminishing marginal-productivity curve of labor to where the marginal product is no greater than that obtained by applying a unit of labor to the less intensively used, inferior land. Thus, labor is applied in varying degrees to *all* types of land, not merely to the best, with more on the best land (acre for acre). This is the kind of allocation of resources implied by the presence of diminishing productivity. And this holds for all types of resources. In sum, we see all grades of resources being used, with superior resources used more intensively (that is, with relatively more of other resources)—a phenomenon we would not expect to observe if increasing marginal returns prevailed.[2]

### The Demand for Productive Resources

*The demand for an input is a negative function of its price. That is, the lower its price the greater the amount of that input demanded.* This is the main point of this section. The basis for the demand relationship between price of input and the amount demanded in any use relies on a *substitution* effect, wherein more of the lower-priced input is used, and less of the more expensive, *without changing the total output.* We are now prepared to examine the effect of a lower price of an input in lowering production costs and increasing production by an increased employment of the lower-priced input.

A reduced input price will reduce the cost of an input below its marginal product for the amount then employed. The available potential excess of marginal product over the cost of an added unit of input would increase the wealth of the producer hiring another unit of input. A rule is suggested: "Increase the amount of a productive input to the point at which its marginal value-product is brought down to the cost of one more unit of that input." In other words, "Employ that quantity of an input at which its marginal value-product is equal to its price. Do this for all the inputs."

Since inputs are used jointly, and the marginal product schedule (for example, as shown in Figure 19–2) of each kind of input will depend upon how much of the other inputs are also used with it, the amount of labor and of capital (using the simple, two-input classification) employed in production will depend upon (a) the price of each, (b) the price of the product. Everything depends upon everything else. A simple expression summarizes some of that relationship. "In a wealth-maximizing situation, the amount of an input used will be that at which its marginal value-product (the physical marginal

---

[2] Recognition of *intensive* margins, at which the marginal products of an input are equated by varying the allocation of the input, is important because it generalizes the earlier simplified analysis of production (in Chapter 10), which was based on only one unit of each of several different qualities of productive inputs. That chapter explained only the assignment of different *kinds* or qualities of resources on the oversimplified principle that each input had a constant marginal product no matter how much it was used to produce Y rather than X. That assumption appeared as the constant marginal cost of producing X by one of the people, A, B, etc., regardless of how much Y the person produced. There we had decreasing marginal products (or increasing marginal costs) only by bringing in inferior producers, after first utilizing the lower-cost producers of Y. However, the present law says that there is a diminishing marginal product for applications of increasing amounts of each input as it is used more intensively with any specified amount of other resources. Therefore, now, for efficient production, an input should be increased wherever its marginal product exceeds its marginal product in other directions of use (where it should be decreased). We can thereby apply our analysis to the assignments of *ámounts* of different, but homogeneous, inputs, as well as to assignments of different kinds of inputs.

product times the price of a unit of the product) is made equal to the price of the input." In symbolic, abbreviated form for labor, $L$:

$$(P) \times (MPL) = P_L,$$

where $P$ is the price of the product, $MPL$ is the marginal product of labor, and $P_L$ is the price of labor.

The same holds true for capital:

$$(P) \times (MPC) = P_C,$$

and for any kind of input.

These conditions are met (1) if the selected output level is produced in the cheapest way, and (2) if that output is the most valuable one as judged by market demands. Generally speaking, this means the marginal value-product derived from an extra dollar's worth of each and every input is equal to a dollar; another dollar's worth of input would give less than a dollar's worth of output.

Much of the preceding discussion can be summarized by a graph of the *demand for an input* (Figure 19–3). The amounts of the input are assumed divisible, and the curve portrays the relationship between the price of the productive input and the amount that would be demanded for production. The negative relationship between price and the amount demanded conforms to the fundamental law of demand for any good. The position of the demand

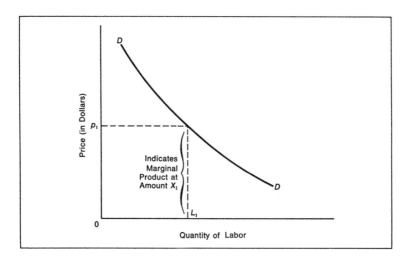

Figure 19–3
Demand Curves for Inputs as the Marginal Productivities

At amount of good $X_1$, the marginal product to the buyer is shown by the height of the curve *DD*. At price $p_1$, the amount $X_1$ would be bought, at which the marketable marginal product obtained by the employer from using $X$ is equal to the price of $X$. At any larger amount than $X$, the marketable marginal product would be less than price $p_1$, and wealth of employer would be decreased.

curve will depend upon the amounts of other inputs that it is most profitable to use jointly with this input—in other words upon the costs of other inputs. This recalls the earlier discussion of the demand curve for butter and for margarine wherein the *demand* (the schedule—not just the amount demanded at some price) depended upon the price of margarine.

At any specified price of inputs the amount of the input demanded will be given by the demand function. Since the height of demand for any input reflects the marginal productivity of that good at each different amount of the good, the intersection of a horizontal price line with a demand curve gives the amount of the input employed and also shows an equality between the price and the marginal productivity of the input for the amount that it is most profitable to employ.

### Position of Derived Demand Function

Not only is the market demand for a resource a negative function of its price, but its position depends upon the quantity (and hence price) of other jointly used inputs that it is profitable to use. In Table 19–3, the marginal value-product of labor depends upon which row you read. The more capital (the upper rows), the greater the marginal products of labor. A larger amount of capital causes a higher demand for labor. The two resources are said to be *complementary*. The opposite effect could have occurred: larger amounts of capital might have caused small marginal products for labor. They then are called *substitutes*. Unfortunately, this is very misleading terminology. The two inputs are substitutes for each other even though they are complements in the sense just indicated. One can always use more labor and less capital. The term "substitutes" has two different meanings: (1) It is possible to produce some specified rate of output with less of one input and more of another. (2) More of one input causes a *lower* marginal product for the existing amount of the *other* resource. It is in the former sense that the term "substitutable" is ordinarily used. A more precise term for the second effect would be "negative cross-marginal productivity," suggesting that the effect of increasing one resource "crosses over" to another resource and lowers its marginal product. In Table 19–1, there is positive cross-marginal productivity, and negative *self*-marginal productivity (called the law of *diminishing* marginal returns).

We cannot tell in advance whether, in the interaction between two joint inputs, an increase in the amount of one will raise or lower the marginal productivity of the other. But whatever the effect on the marginal productivity, the implied demand schedule for any input retains its negative slope with respect to its own price.

It is most important to realize that the marginal product of any worker is a function not merely of his own talents and education but also of the quality and quantity of other goods with which he can work jointly. To "work jointly" does not mean merely to work hand in hand with other goods, as a carpenter works with a hammer, a seamstress with a needle, or a driver with a truck. It means also to work within the environment provided by the equipment and resources of the whole economy. The transportation system, power costs, the education and technology of other workers, the effectiveness of the market in facilitating specialization and exchange, the amount of theft, the extent to which contracts are honored—all these are examples of "joint cooperative resources." Take all the carpenters in any small city in the United States to India, Morocco, Brazil, or Indonesia. The wages they would get are lower simply because there is less jointly available "capital." A richer country with lots of capital equipment and stable, market-facilitating institutions is a better place for a given amount of labor. While the productivity of the American carpenters would be less in other countries than in the United States, the productivity would be greater than for natives of those countries—a reflection of the greater education of the Americans.

### Inter-firm Input Substitution

The demand relationship between the price of an input and the rate of its use is dependent upon more than the purposive adjustment of each producer. Even if no producer were to shift toward a more efficient input combination, each would experience a change in his wealth. Those firms nearer the new, more efficient combination will have a greater increase in their wealth than will those firms whose input techniques are now less efficient. The economic efficiency of any utilized technique is changed by the shift in relative prices of inputs. Profits and losses will change as a result of the revised price structure, with bigger rewards going to the possibly inadvertently lucky firms that happened to have the input combination nearest the most appropriate. Less favored firms with less efficient techniques will experience bigger losses or smaller profits and will soon be dominated by the more rapid growth and proliferation of the more efficient combinations.

The changing environment *adopts* the more appropriate existing techniques by rewarding them with greater profits and growth—whether or not the individual producers themselves *adapt* to the new price situation. Productive techniques of the more successful firms will be copied. The imitating firm, emulating the successful firm, may not know the marginal productivities of various inputs. All it knows is what techniques succeeded best. Not even the initially successful firm has to know the marginal products. All it has to do is be nearest the "right" combination. Whether it got there by calculating marginal productivities via an extensive research and testing program, with the help of astrologers, by consulting economists, or by sheer luck is irrelevant. The fact of being there is sufficient.

Competition among firms with different productive techniques is a selective discriminating survival force, just as is purposive, knowledgeable discrimination by one producer among alternative available production techniques. To the extent that individuals are allowed to offer their wares in an open market, inter-firm market competition adds its force to the intra-firm selectivity of production techniques in generating and strengthening the observed demand relationship between price and rate of use of inputs.

Input Substitution via Output Substitution

There is still another route by which the lower price of an input relative to other input prices increases its employment. Even if there were no substitution between jointly used inputs for a given product, the lower price of some input leads to lower costs of those goods it is used to produce. Consumer goods that use more of the now relatively cheaper inputs will be relatively less costly, and their sales or profits will increase. Therefore, substitution among inputs also occurs via substitution by consumers among the final, produced goods. If the price of plastics falls relative to glass, the supply schedule of plastic containers increases relative to that of glass bottles; the price of plastic containers falls; the consumer buys more plastic containers; and plastics are thereby substituted for glass. This effect, operating through the consumer's substitution of different consumer goods, is called *inter-product* substitution.

Speed of Substitution and Adjustment<br/>of Production Techniques

*Making* substitutions and *changing* the rates of employment of inputs are costly activities. One doesn't change a production technique by a wave of his hand. He must learn of new ways, administer his decisions, rearrange the inputs, and schedule the arrival of the new inputs to ensure efficient coordination. In other words, the amount of substitution carried out in response to a new price situation depends upon these adjustment costs and upon how much time has elapsed since the price change. The longer the time, the more substitution or revision of employment of inputs will have taken place. In terms of demand schedules, the demand response for an input is more elastic with respect to a price change, the longer the time since the price change. And it can be portrayed graphically by showing different demand curves for different times after the price changes from that level at which the curves are all shown intersecting each other—as in Figure 4–3 (page 71).

The relatively inelastic demand for an input in the *immediate* period, when changes can be made only at relatively high adjustment costs, sometimes misleads people into thinking that the price change has no effect on the amount demanded. But in the ensuing days, or weeks, the adjustments can be made at a more economic pace. Since they are made after a substantial interval, the changes often are not identified as consequences of the price change. Of course, the employer need not announce to the inputs that he no longer will buy so much of their services because their price is too high. He simply says that his sales aren't big enough to warrant their employment.

For example, we cite the rise in wages of Chicago elevator boys. Formerly, wages were $1 to $1.25 an hour. There was then imposed a minimum wage of $2.40 an hour for operators in downtown (not suburban) Chicago buildings. Owners of some apartment and business buildings then found it profitable to use automatic elevators, which annually cost about $8,000. With two shifts of operators, the higher wage cost of $2.40 per hour raised the cost of manually operated elevators to about $10,000 per year. Clearly, it paid the owner to "automate." This process took several months. When the elevator operators were discharged several months later, after having been paid $2.40 an hour for the intervening time, they were not likely to have believed that it was a result of the higher wage, since that was "initiated" a long time ago. They blamed it on "automation." This is not to say that all introduction of automatic equipment is a response to higher wages (as we shall see in the next chapters), nor does it imply that higher than open-market wages are "wrong" or "bad." Nothing in economics establishes "badness" or "goodness."

### Pricing of Productive Resources

If the price of an input is not set by administrative fiat, decree, law, or inviolate custom, employers will be able legally to bid higher or lower prices in the open market for inputs, according to whether they want more or less inputs than they can get at the present price. If at its present price there are not enough inputs of $L$ available to bring its marginal product down to that price, some employers will find it profitable to bid a higher price for more inputs of $L$, rather than leave their demand unsatisfied. The higher price will restrict the amount of that input demanded. The higher price will attract inputs from other uses, which raises the price they must be offered in order to be kept at former tasks. In this way, the prices paid for this resource by buyers in various industries are correlated and kept together. The differences in prices that will not be competitively erased reflect nonpecuniary offers by buyers—better working conditions or more pleasant and congenial employers.

### Generality of Marginal-Productivity Theory

Before summarizing the analysis of this chapter, a few comments may be helpful.

1. *Is total product sufficient?* The payment for a unit of a productive input is its price. If we multiply the number of employed units by the marginal product, which also equals its price in equilibrium, we get the income to that resource. For example, suppose that in Table 19–1 we were employing three units of labor and one unit of capital, because the price of labor was $17 while the price of capital was $138. We now compute the total payments to capital and labor from our firm. Three units of labor at $17 each is $51 while the one unit of capital gets $138. The total payments to the productive resources are $51 + $138 = $189, an amount that *exceeds* the total value of

the output produced, $138. How can a producer continue in this situation? How could a whole economy pay a wage equal to marginal product if that would exceed the total output? Has something gone wrong with our theory? How can inputs be paid more than the total product? This is not impossible, for awhile at least. What it means is that the employer of these productive inputs must make up the difference out of his past accumulated wealth. And this is not something he can do indefinitely.

Abandoned will be the "loss-resulting" production. Resources will be released from that business and that product. As a result the input prices are pushed down and output prices increased. Other employers who were just breaking even or losing money will now be able to get profits or break even by employing the released resources. The situation is saved. No inconsistency is inherent in the open-market equilibrium.

2. *Abstractions and validity*. The present analysis does not require the assumption that there be sets of different but internally homogeneous and infinitely divisible resources. They can all be discrete, different items; interpolation such as we used in our example might be impossible; equality between the marginal value-product and prices may not be achievable. Instead of equality of marginal value-product and price, an *in*equality condition suffices; inputs will be employed up to the point beyond which the marginal value-product of the input would be smaller than the marginal cost of the input.

An economist, Senator Paul H. Douglas (Illinois), once wrote a book entitled *The Theory of Wages*, in which he examined in great detail many assumptions commonly used in marginal-productivity principles of the demand for productive resources. He showed conclusively that many of the assumptions were oversimplifications of reality. Many readers concluded that a theory built on those assumptions must therefore be false in all its implications about observable events. Do not fall into that error. Every theory abstracts from details and considerations, many of which it is not seeking to explain. All theories make redundant, overly strong assumptions for ease of logical analysis. They assume away certain idiosyncrasies in the interest of concentrating on other phenomena. For example, a theory relating caloric intake to body weight can assume, as a means of abstracting from tangential detail, that all people are alike (for a given age and sex); then certain consequences are implied if caloric intake is increased. It is doubtful that you would challenge the validity of that implication by challenging the validity of the assumption that people are alike or the assumption that when caloric intake is increased, no other events impinge on the individuals—such as their getting sick or other coincident causes. Actually the complexities could be included; but then the theory would be cumbersome in having to use more complex methods of notation, logic, mathematics, etc., in deriving and expressing its results. (And there is an opposite error. Do not presume that one theory is better than another simply because it is more detailed in its premises, assumptions, and number of variables considered in its premises.)

3. *Pecuniary and nonpecuniary productivity and "discrimination."* Is the marginal-productivity principle *of demand* applicable only to capitalist economies? No, the marginal-productivity theory of demand is valid in every

economy. In the capitalist economy, the increase in wealth belongs to an identifiable *private* owner, or *private* group of owners. If, however, a property holder were not able to keep the profits (or did not have to pay the losses) of his business, he would more heavily weight other sources affecting his utility. He would be more disposed to employ pretty girls if he weren't able to retain the profits of hiring lower-cost labor that was equally productive of pecuniary value of marketable goods. If the economic rules of surviving in business only mildly punish people for not increasing wealth when possible, and if the business owners cannot keep the profits, then neither they nor their employed agents will be influenced by the sources of profits but instead will look more toward the nonmonetary, nonmarketable sources of utility. This, it should be noticed, is implied by the *generalized* marginal-productivity theory of demand. (See Figure 19–4.) The lower the price of any source of utility, the more it will be used. Marketable wealth is only one source of utility.

To prohibit or make it more difficult for one to keep and use his profits raises the cost of increasing his wealth. The costs of other sources of personal utility are then *relatively* lower than before. Now that the costs of obtaining

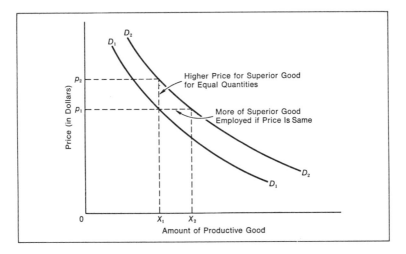

Figure 19–4
Demand for Inputs with the Marginal Productivities *Including* Marketable and Nonmarketable Marginal Products to Buyers

Curve $D_2$ shows demand for inputs that will do all that the inputs demanded according to line $D_1$ can do *plus* provide more desirable nonmarketable benefits to the demander. A beautiful secretary has a greater demand for her presence (as a secretary *and* a pleasing person) than an ugly one. The price paid for productive inputs reflects both the marketable productivity of the input plus the nonmarketable attributes as sources of utility to the buyer. Moral: Remember that nonpecuniary sources of utility are present in many inputs for productive use, as they are for consumption goods.

pecuniary benefits are higher and the nonpecuniary are lower, one will increase his purchase of goods that are more heavily loaded with non-pecuniary sources of utility—good looks, racial and religious characteristics, friends, prestige, relaxation, etc. Nonpecuniary discrimination is cheaper and will be more common. Production will be less closely oriented to market demands and values. Market prices are also less likely to be high enough to clear the market—for reasons discussed in Chapter 9. The marginal-productivity principle still stands, as long as one incorporates the various ways of "producing" utility—one of which is wealth.

Our investigation of the selection of productive techniques and uses of productive resources is incomplete in that the *supply conditions of produc-tive resources* were not investigated. The supply of laborers, who are not produced by business firms nor bought and sold like slaves, merits special investigation—something we shall try to provide in the next two chapters.

## The Circle Closed

Price determination of productive goods and rates of employment enables determination of the wealth of their owners. From given wealth and prefer-ence patterns of people, affecting their market demands for consumers' goods, we have gone via derived demands for inputs to the prices of resources and hence to income and wealth of those who provide or own the resources. Prices and outputs of consumers' goods, the wealth of individuals, and the allocation of productive goods have been analyzed primarily in the context of a market-exchange, private-property system—although we have occasionally considered these questions under other systems. If access to an open market is restricted, or if limitations are imposed on permissible bids or offers, the extent of adjustment of output to consumers' market demands is reduced; the efficient allocation of inputs is weakened, and the wealth of owners of productive goods is made less dependent upon satisfaction of consumers' market-revealed preferences.

Nothing in this analysis implies that such attenuation of efficiency in production or composition of output is undesirable. That depends upon whether or not one prefers the economic, cultural, and political implications of a free-market, private-property exchange system. Those who dislike that system (because they think they could achieve what they regard as a better way of life with a differently weighted mix of types of competition for resolving conflicts of interests in the presence of scarcity) will try to reduce the scope of that system. For example, people with certain kinds of personali-ties may find "vote-getting," political competition more favorable to them than market competition. They will prefer political competition and will expect to gain from extension of this realm of government activity. Socialists express that preference and intent. Some capitalists express a different prefer-ence; and yet some seek government limitation on their market competitors.

By this stage of this book, it should be obvious that although some of the differences in cultural, political, and economic consequences of various economic systems are discernible with the aid of economic theory, economic theory cannot evaluate their propriety.

Summary

1    Substitutability among all productive inputs is pervasive.

2    Efficient, wealth-maximizing producers reveal a market-demand curve for inputs that is inversely related to the price of each input. The inverse (or negative) relationship with price of the input results from (a) substitutability among inputs, (b) diminishing marginal value-productivity (which reflects both a decreasing marginal physical product and a lower price of the output as more is sold), (c) substitution by consumers among outputs.

3    A longer-period demand for inputs is more elastic. The effect of a price change will be less pronounced immediately than with the passing of some time.

4    An increased supply of any resource in the market implies a lower price, which induces a shift to techniques employing more of that now lower-priced input. The technique of production is revised toward more use of the now more plentiful and cheaper input—all without central direction or planning—provided, of course, that producers are not constrained by law to use inputs in proportions other than those which they choose in the light of market prices (that is, to the extent that there is open-market competition).

5    Since the income (or wealth) of any productive resource is determined by its selling price, the incomes of owners of various productive goods, be they labor or nonlabor forms of services, are determined in a free market by the forces of demand and supply. The demand for resources reflects their marginal productivities in highest-valued uses. For this reason, this analysis is often erroneously called the marginal-productivity theory of *pricing* of productive resources. More accurately, it is the marginal-productivity theory of demand for productive resources.

6    The marginal-productivity basis for demand applies to all types of economies. Economies based on different systems of property rights differ in the costs imposed on various types of decisions. This does not destroy the validity of the marginal-productivity theory of demand—whether it be demand for consumer goods or for pecuniary or nonpecuniary productive resources, in a capitalist or in a socialist economy. Nor does it have any bearing on how prices are set. They may

be set by decree or custom. But the theory is invalid as an explanation of rates of use of inputs if the allocations are also controlled by decree or custom.

Questions

1   Why is economic efficiency a more general test than technical efficiency?

2   There are two kinds of economic efficiency—one of cost minimization and one of profit maximization.
a. In what sense is profit maximization a more general criterion of efficiency?
b. In what sense could it be considered a less desirable criterion?

3   A jet plane can fly across the United States three hours faster than a propeller plane. Which is the more efficient?

4   In Iowa the yield of wheat is 30 bushels per acre; in Washington it is 50 bushels per acre. Which is better?

5   Jet engines are given an efficiency rating according to the thrust generated per pound of engine weight. Explain why that is an inadequate measure of efficiency.

6   Steers can be bred with such superb qualities that they will sell for about 50 percent more per pound than the standard steers raised for meat. Which type should the farmer raise? Give the answer in terms of technological versus economic efficiency.

7   A high-fidelity stereo sound system is called efficient if it uses a low amount of electric power per decibel of sound generated. Why is that technical efficiency not an adequate efficiency criterion for choosing among sound systems, even if the quality of the sound were the same?

8   A water-storage dam is to be built, and engineers, asked for advice, propose a dam and attest to its efficiency.
a. If they attest to its technical efficiency, does that still leave open the question of its economic efficiency? For example, if the value of the water stored is less than the cost of impounding and distributing it, is the dam, though it may be technically efficient, an economically efficient one?
b. This problem extends the notion of economic efficiency beyond the selection of the cheapest way of doing something. Economic efficiency is extended to include what?

9   The United States Federal Communication Commission says rights to use the radio-frequency spectrum should be assigned to permit maximum usage.

**a.** Explain why that statement as it stands is meaningless and useless.

**b.** Would it have been meaningful to say rights should be assigned to achieve efficient use? What would be the criterion of efficiency?

10    After adding 100 to all the output data in Table 19–1, recompute the marginal products of labor and the marginal products of capital. (This is not as hard and long a problem as it may at first seem.)

11    In Table 19–2, the data are *values* of output, where, for simplicity, each physical unit was assumed to be salable for $1. Suppose instead that the output can be sold for $2 each.

**a.** Recompute the "marginal value-products" for labor and for capital.

**b.** What is the effect of a rise in price of the product on the marginal-value productivity of inputs?

12    Use the data of Table 19–1 to answer the following questions:

**a.** Defining efficient production as the lowest-cost methods of production, which method is the efficient method for producing 277 units of $X$ if the price of labor is $60 and if the price of capital is $70?

**b.** If the price of capital is $20 per unit and if labor is $10 per unit, which is the efficient way to produce 228 units of $X$: with 2 capital and 5 labor or with 5.1 capital and 1 labor?

**c.** Which is cheaper (that is, efficient) if the prices are $2 and $1 respectively?

**d.** $60 and $30 respectively?

**e.** So long as the prices bear the same ratios to each other, will the same method remain the cheaper method?

13    The law of diminishing returns is a law of diminishing *marginal* returns. What is the difference between diminishing *total* returns and diminishing *marginal* returns?

14    **a.** In Table 19–3, is the law of diminishing marginal returns illustrated by the decreasing values as one reads a row from left to right, or as one reads a column from bottom to top?

**b.** Explain the meaning of each method of reading the table.

**c.** Is Table 19–4 interpreted in the same direction? Why not?

15    "Chicago, August 10, 1962. A federal judge blocked today the firing of thousands of workers on the nation's railroads pending final court ruling on the legality of the drastic economy. Prior to the decision five unions representing the men were ready to order a nationwide walkout. Today's U.S. District Court action, technically, granted the unions a court order barring the railroads from applying new work rules pending a union appeal to the U.S. Circuit Court of Appeals. Judge Perry said, 'I have preserved and protected the right of appeal,' adding that he felt an interim decision affecting both jobs and capital must be resolved in favor of jobs and men." In what sense can it be contended instead that the issue is one between jobs *and jobs*, rather than between jobs and capital?

**16**    Who is substituted for whom when a firm uses one typist, an electric typewriter, and a copying machine rather than two typists and two nonelectric typewriters? This is called a substitution of capital for labor. Why is that misleading?

**17**    "The advent of the one-man bus involved more capital equipment: an automatically operated coin box and a door-control device—to name two of the capital goods that replaced the conductor."
**a.** Is this a case of capital replacing labor? Where?
**b.** Is it a case of labor replacing labor? Where?
**c.** Is it a case of no substitution for labor at all, but instead a job revision with a greater total output? Where?

18    "Invention and the lower cost of power in the home have replaced the domestic servant by capital equipment. Without that machinery more people would be working in homes as 'servants.' But the replacement of domestic employees by capital has not led to the replacement of labor. The released labor is used elsewhere."
a. Can you suggest where?
b. What other goods are more plentiful because of the advent of domestic machinery?
c. Who was aided and who was hurt by the use of the vacuum cleaner, washing machine, water heater, forced-air furnace, garbage disposal, automatic oven, electric mixer, and refrigerator?

**19**    The electric refrigerator replaced the iceman with capital. By eliminating (making other means cheaper) the job of the iceman, was the total number of jobs reduced? Explain.

20    "Automation does not mean there will be more people than jobs available. It does not mean fewer jobs for unskilled people—in fact a person can be less skilled if all he has to do is punch buttons, pull triggers, and turn steering wheels, compared to driving a team of horses, shooting a bow and arrow, or wielding a chisel." Do you agree? If so, why? If not, why not?

**21**    You operate a factory and discover that some resource used obtains *increasing* marginal returns.
a. What would you do?
b. Does this suggest that we will never find any firm using an amount of resources involving increasing marginal returns?

**22**    "A molecule of sugar is composed of a fixed ratio of atoms of hydrogen, carbon, and oxygen; it follows that there is no substitutability of inputs in the manufacture of sugar."
a. Do you agree? Why?
b. Is the reasoning in the preceding question applicable to every other kind of good that can be manufactured—whether or not the good is composed of a fixed ratio of components? For example, is the reason-

ing applicable to making gasoline, running a railroad, operating a bus, building a house, or selling groceries?

23 "Even if only one combination of productive inputs could be used to produce some good, there would still be substitution among productive resources in response to changes in their prices." Explain what that substitution is and how it would be induced.

24 According to the analyses developed in this chapter, resources will be employed in open markets in amounts at which marginal value-product is not less than price. That also determines their earnings (price times the number of units employed).
a. What ensures that the total earnings will not exceed the value of the total output?
b. Who makes up the difference if payments exceed the value of output?
c. If the payments are less than the total value of output, who gets the difference?
d. In each case, what forces revise payments toward equality with value of output?

25 "If the ratio of the prices of two resources differs from the ratio of their marginal products for the amount being employed, a change in the amounts employed can increase the total output without any increase in costs, or can reduce costs without reducing output." Explain why.

26 "If the ratio of the price of resource $A$ to the price of resource $B$ exceeds the ratio of the marginal value-products of $A$ to $B$, it will be efficient to decrease the employment of $A$ relative to $B$." Explain why.

27 "If a firm uses resources efficiently, a change in their prices will induce a change in the relative amounts employed." What will induce that change—some directive from a central planning agency, the social consciousness of the employer, or what?

28 Adjustments in the amount of resources used so as to equate the *absolute* prices of each resource with its marginal value productivity imply more than does the equality of the *ratios* of prices to the ratios of marginal productivities. What is the stronger implication?

29 Suppose you operate a publicly owned factory in which profits cannot be retained.
a. What would be your criterion of resource use in production?
b. What would induce you to act in accord with that criterion?
c. Would you have any incentive to adjust the use of resources to preserve the equality of the ratios of prices and marginal productivities—that is, to minimize the cost of the output? Explain.

30 "In a socialist state it is difficult for the state to own the producers' goods that are involved in artistic creativity—the human brain and

body. Consequently musicians, artists, authors, and poets will be more able to behave in deviant, unorthodox, non-nationalistic ways than those whose earnings are more dependent upon state-owned resources—machines, factories, land, etc. In a capitalistic system this difference would not be present."

a. What premises underlie the propositions?

b. Would your preference for one system over another be influenced by the validity of those propositions? Why?

31    In Russia and China, two socialist states in which most producers' goods (goods with which you can earn a living) are owned by the government, targets are assigned to factories in terms of the total value of the output (not profits) they are supposed to produce. Plant managers are told to accomplish and overfulfill targets as much as possible. Prices are set by law.

a. Is it desirable to have these targets overfulfilled?

b. Is it more desirable to state a target in terms of total value of output or in terms of profits? What are the differences in performance that will be induced?

c. Which criterion is more likely to provide a more effective incentive for the manager?

32    Assume that you are a member of a minority group in some country and have reason to doubt that your private-property rights would be enforced and respected in that community.

a. In what forms of capital would you invest?

b. What kinds of skills (as forms of accumulations of wealth) would you encourage for your children?

c. Do you know of any evidence of such actual behavior by minority groups?

33    When Defense Secretary McNamara recommended against building nuclear rather than oil-fueled airplane carriers because the nuclear system was more expensive, Congressman Pastore of New Jersey is reported to have said that if we had looked at economics we would never have shifted from wooden sailing ships to steel, oil-fueled ships. Whatever the congressman may have said, is the asserted remark correct? Explain.

# 20

Wages, Employment, and Unemployment in Open Markets

"Labor is not a commodity" is a battle cry of some labor groups. Whatever its propaganda and romantic value, the assertion is misleading. Labor service is bought and sold daily, because that is a convenient way to obtain the advantages of specialization and exchange.

What *is* different about labor is the general prohibition against buying and selling *people*: however, human *services* are bought and sold. For example, when you work for someone, you sell him your physical and intellectual labor.[1] In some countries, slavery still exists; people are bought and sold by other people—or are "owned" by governments. Slaves do not have private-property rights in themselves or their services. Even where no one is a slave, private property in one's own labor is restricted if he is prohibited by law from exchanging his services for goods or money with any other person at mutually satisfactory terms, or if he cannot migrate to another area to sell his labor services there. A few hundred years ago, Englishmen could not work where they pleased, for whom they pleased, on whatever terms they found mutually agreeable. Nor was entry into occupations unrestricted. And this is true today in many countries in varying degree, even in the United States. For example, even if you were willing to buy, I could not legally sell psychiatric, medical, or dental services to you. Laws often dictate qualifications, permissible wages, hours of work per day, and working conditions; other terms, although mutually agreeable between employer and employee, are not legal. These restrictions on market competition and sale of labor do not prevent labor from being a marketable commodity.

Furthermore, the fact that labor services involve personalities and social relationships does not preclude market forces, though they do affect contracting and negotiating procedures. But before exploring that, we shall concentrate on the factors affecting wages and allocations of labor services via market competition—using again the analytic concepts of market demand and supply.

Economic analysis denies that, in the absence of legal protection for labor, employers would grind wages down to the minimum survival level. An analogy will suggest why. Why are rents on land not ground down by renters to zero? The demands by those who would use the land bid up the rents. Simple supply and demand are in operation. And so it is with labor. The alternative uses and values to which labor could be put are determined by all who compete for it. Potential employers, faced with the available supply, bid

[1] Fortunately, the ban against selling all one's future services for a single advance payment, as he could sell other things, does not prevent a person from converting some of his future earnings into present wealth values. If he has just obtained a higher salary, he can borrow more money now to buy a house and car and repay out of the greater future income. In this way, he has exchanged part of his future earnings and obtained goods. Without the right to borrow or to mortgage wealth as security or to buy on the installment plan, laborers would be at a greater disadvantage in adjusting consumption to present wealth value of future earnings.

wages to whatever level enables them to get an amount of labor that can be put to profitable use. That may be a very high level, if labor is relatively scarce given its productivity function. The price of labor, like that of every other good, depends upon demand and supply forces.

## Demand for Labor

The basis of demand for any productive input was investigated in the preceding chapter, where we saw that market demand reflects the anticipated marginal value-product of that input and that the marginal value-product depends upon the amount of other jointly used inputs. The lower the price of the input, the greater the amount that will be demanded—this holds for labor services as well as for all other productive inputs. In this chapter we shall explore the supply of labor and then put demand and supply together to see what can be said about wage rates and the allocation of labor to various jobs.

## Supply of Labor

The labor force is, in the United States, usually the adult male population and part of the female population. Males of about 14 or over are usually considered to be members of the labor force, even though some of them are in school. If we were a poorer country, youths of an even younger age would enter the work force.

America's wealth has been increasing, and so has its population. Over the years, part of the increase in wealth has been utilized to support a larger population. More recently, cheaper techniques of birth control seem to have destroyed the old generalization that poorer people have larger families, at least in the United States. At the present time, with adjustments for level of education of the parents, their wealth, and agricultural versus city status, the evidence is that higher education and higher wealth are associated with *higher* net reproduction rates. Agricultural areas (after adjustment for education and wealth) have a higher reproduction rate. Whether that relationship will change in some systematic way is still a question with no answer.

If wages and incomes affect supply of labor, we ought to observe labor moving from lower-wage areas to higher-wage areas. And we do. Nationwide, the movement of people during the decade 1950—1960 was predominantly to areas with high income; gains in the total population of various counties through migration occurred only in the counties with median family incomes (in 1959) of $6,000 or more, while all county groups with lower incomes had migration losses in both male and female and white and nonwhite populations. The counties with lowest median family incomes (under $5,000) had a net loss of over 28 percent of their population. Those in the $6,000 to $7,500 median family income group gained 11 percent. The migration was greater for younger people.[2] No doubt, labor is attracted by higher wages and repelled from the lower-wage areas.

### Wage Rates, Wealth, and Labor Force

As wealth increases, what is the effect on the proportion of the population seeking work? In considering this question, be sure to distinguish between attained wealth and the rate of pay per hour. The first, attained wealth, may imply a reduction in the proportion of the population working; the second, pay per hour, may induce a larger proportion (given some level of wealth) to work. The desire to work more at a higher wage rate—thereby substituting wealth for leisure—is countered by the greater wealth a person has at higher wage rates. Increased wealth increases the demand for leisure. The "substitution" effect of higher wages runs against the "wealth" effect.

In graphic form, a supply curve of hours of labor offered by a person would look like Figure 20–1. At the wage $W_2$ per hour, the maximum number of hours of work per week would be offered. The wealth effect and the wage-rate effect are working against each other. At wages above $W_2$ the wealth effect on the demand for more leisure is strong enough to more than offset the higher wage-rate effect. The supply schedule is backward bending. But the implication is *not* that less than 60 units of labor will be available if wages are higher than $W_2$. To see why, we must reckon with two kinds of supply curves. One indicates the number of hours of labor offered at each wage rate, *in a situation where the employee (or seller) can choose how many hours* he will sell at that wage rate. A different supply curve shows the wage that must be offered to induce the employee to work a specified number of hours.

Suppose an employee prefers to work not over 60 hours a week if he gets $2.50 per hour (which is $150 per week). Suppose also that he would prefer to reduce the hours to 54 if wages were $3 per hour ($162 per week). That reduction implies the backward-bending supply, where the employee can choose the number of hours. However, an employer might decide to offer what he had to pay in order to induce laborers to work *at least 66* hours every week. Suppose he offered $198 for a 66-hour week *if and only if* they worked 66 hours per week. By successively raising the offer for *a stated amount of time*, he could get more labor. This supply curve *facing an employer* involves higher wages for more labor (despite the other backward bending curve). A wage of $198 for a 66-hour week is equivalent to $2.50 per hour for the first 60 hours, *plus, $8 per hour for the next six hours*; no

---

[2] Data reported by Gladys K. Bowles and James D. Tarver, "The Composition of New Migration among Counties in the United States, 1950–1960." *Agricultural Economics Research*, U.S. Dept. of Agriculture, January 1966.

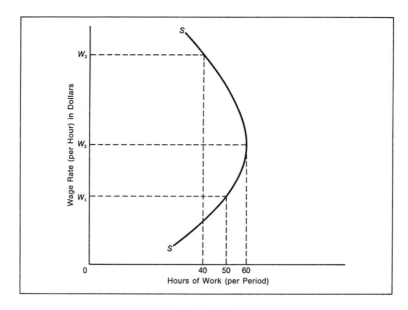

Figure 20–1
Supply Curve of Hours of Labor

wonder the laborers are willing to work six more hours. Higher overtime wage rates can be used to counter the backward-bending supply curve of labor where the laborer is offered a set wage rate per hour and allowed to choose the number of hours. If you recall the discussion of "all-or-none" pricing by the monopolist seller of water, you will see the similarity; the *buyer* offers a fixed payment on the condition that at least a specified number of hours is sold to him. Although in this example the employer makes the special offer to get more labor, the employee could have told the employer that he would work if and only if the employer would pay at least $198 for a work week of 66 hours. Who happens to think of the arrangement and first suggests it is irrelevant.[3]

Employers can obtain greater amounts of labor, therefore, by offering higher wages. This supply-of-labor curve is positively sloped with respect to wages, throughout its range, despite the backward-bending type of supply schedule (where a laborer is given the sole control of choosing how many hours to work). This supply curve indicates how much must be paid to induce specified amounts of work; the relationship between offers of work and total (or even hourly average) wage is "positive." The amount of labor supplied at any given wage will be larger if the job is safer, more pleasant, steadier, with

---

[3] In May 1964, nearly 30 percent of all jobholders worked over 40 hours, most of the overtime on weekends. One in three of these received overtime premium pay. Service-industry workers dominate the over-40-hours workers, but of those getting premiums for overtime, most were in manufacturing. Source: *U.S. Monthly Labor Review,* September 1965.

more congenial atmosphere; and if the talent involved is more common, cheaper to develop, and easier to display and demonstrate to employers.

### Open-Market Wage Rates

Demand-and-supply analysis of *open*-market determination of wages and employment is similar in principle to that for any other good. Underlying is the assumption that people are free agents and can quit or change jobs when they wish, and that at least some will change jobs when knowledge of more attractive openings is available. Employees who entertain offers or look for opportunities elsewhere also permit their current employers to make a counter-bid.

An employer, then, if he is to retain his employees, must be prepared to match offers of other employers. The employer who detects competing wage rates and matches them (through periodic wage and salary reviews and raises), without forcing his employees to seek offers and then ask for a raise, will have to pay no higher wages than if he waited for each employee to initiate negotiations. Job comparison is costly for employees; so the employer who takes the initiative in anticipating or matching market offers will find more employees willing to work for him than for one who tries to impose all the costs of job comparison on employees.

Because many employers periodically review wages and give raises without an employee's obtaining a competing offer, it is sometimes alleged that wages are not set by market competition, so that instead, wages are adjusted simply because it is conventional or proper to do so or because of some internal employee pressure. But market competition *is* present; the employer is meeting it by "rehiring" or keeping his existing employees from going elsewhere, as they would if he did not provide competitive wages. It is instructive to consider an example in which the supply of labor changes.

Suppose that the labor force in an occupation *decreases* because some laborers go to other jobs or communities. The smaller remaining supply will result in a rise in wage rates. Employers who lose employees will prefer to bid up wages to replace some of the employees, rather than continue with unfilled jobs (and less wealth). Competition among employers for employees will pull up wages. Not all employees must move to get higher wages. Present employers will bid up wages to retain employees; otherwise they will lose workers and suffer some loss of business. And if employers do raise wages, they will demand fewer workers than at the old lower wages. In this way, the amount now demanded will have been made equal to the smaller amount available.

The higher wage rate, consequent to the reduced supply, will induce substitution of some other types of labor or productive inputs, according to the principles explained in the preceding chapter. For example, higher wages for fewer carpenters will induce more standardization of types of woodwork, because standardization involves less carpentering service. The number of wood-paneled walls will decrease, and there will be more plaster and glass windows, with steel and aluminum window frames. There are thousands of ways to reduce the amount of carpenters' services by using other goods.


Wage Differences


We have been investigating open-market wages as if everyone were equal in ability and personal characteristics. But people are not equal, and it is time that we examined some of the factors that make for differences in wages among occupations and among people within an occupation.

Some sense of proportion of differences in wages can easily be obtained from available data. First, however, Table 20–1 presents the distribution of the labor force by types of work. The largest category in 1963 was machine operatives, constituting about 18 percent of the work force. The fastest-growing category is that of professional and technical workers, followed closely by clerical workers, with farm labor showing the greatest decline over the past several decades.

Table 20–1
Percentage Distribution of Civilian Employees in
Various Tasks, 1963, Subclassified by Color

| Major Occupation Group | Nonwhite | White |
|---|---|---|
| Professional, technical | 6 | 13 |
| Farmers and farm managers | 3 | 4 |
| Managers, proprietors | 3 | 11 |
| Clerical | 7 | 16 |
| Sales | 2 | 7 |
| Craftsmen | 6 | 14 |
| Machine operatives | 20 | 18 |
| Private-household services | 15 | 2 |
| Service workers, except household | 15 | 9 |
| Farm laborers | 5 | 3 |
| Laborers, nonfarm | 13 | 4 |

Source: U.S. Department of Labor, *Monthly Bulletin of Labor Statistics,* 1963.

Table 20–2 presents estimates of annual wages of nonsupervisory employees in various industries in 1963. These are the *averages* of actual earnings, not the full-time equivalents. If people work on the average only about two-thirds of a full year in personal services work (as is the case), their full-time annual equivalent wages would be 50 percent larger.

An average wage does not indicate the *range* of wages in a given occupation. A substantial range of annual earnings is illustrated in Table 20–3 for department stores, groceries, automobile dealers, and gasoline service stations. The range shown there is basically dependent upon the differences in hours of

Table 20–2
Average of Annual Wages of Nonsupervisory
Employees by Selected Industries, 1967

| | |
|---|---|
| Personal services | $3,200 |
| Retail stores | 3,500 |
| Apparel | 3,600 |
| Textiles | 4,300 |
| Assembly (toys, sporting goods, jewelry) | 4,600 |
| Furniture | 4,800 |
| Lumber | 4,800 |
| Electrical | 5,600 |
| All manufacturing | 5,700 |
| Local bus | 5,800 |
| Chemical | 6,400 |
| Mining | 6,800 |
| Contract construction | 7,700 |
| Petroleum refining | 7,700 |
| Bituminous coal | 7,800 |
| College teachers (9 months) | 7,800 |
| Motor vehicles | 7,800 |

Source: U.S. Department of Labor, *Monthly Bulletin of Labor Statistics*, 1968.

work per week. Note, however, that the earnings of automobile salesmen, who are primarily on a commission earnings basis, do not conform as closely to hours of work.

Do not conclude that the range of wages in an occupation reflects just hours of work. Table 20–4 illustrates a range of wages reflecting incentive and skill, in this case for women sewing-machine operators in New York City. About 10 percent earn over $3.50 an hour, and almost 10 percent earn less than $1.50 an hour on a piecework pay system.

Table 20–3
Percentage Distribution of Average Weekly Earnings of Nonsupervisory
Employees in Selected Lines of Retail Business, 1961, by Hours

| Hours per Week | Dept. Stores | | Groceries | | Motorcar Sales | | Service Stations | |
|---|---|---|---|---|---|---|---|---|
| | Percent of Employees | $ | Percent of Employees | $ | Percent of Employees | $ | Percent of Employees | $ |
| 1–14 | 8 | 12 | 9 | 12 | 1 | 14 | 8 | 11 |
| 15–34 | 21 | 32 | 26 | 33 | 4 | 47 | 20 | 29 |
| 35–39 | 13 | 53 | 6 | 59 | 4 | 76 | 3 | 49 |
| 40 | 43 | 67 | 25 | 83 | 16 | 100 | 11 | 61 |
| 41–48 | 13 | 73 | 23 | 78 | 45 | 100 | 18 | 70 |
| Over 48 | 2 | 86 | 12 | 76 | 30 | 93 | 40 | 70 |

Source: U.S. Department of Labor, *Monthly Bulletin of Labor Statistics,* 1963.

Table 20–4
Percent Distribution of Incentive, Piecework Wages per Hour for
Women Sewing-Machine Operators in New York City, 1963

| Hourly Average Wage | Percent of Employees |
|---|---|
| Under $1.50 | 8 |
| $1.50 and under $2.00 | 24 |
| $2.00 and under $2.50 | 25 |
| $2.50 and under $3.00 | 20 |
| $3.00 and under $3.50 | 11 |
| $3.50 and under $4.00 | 6 |
| $4.00 and over | 3 |

Source: U.S. Department of Labor, *Monthly Bulletin of Labor Statistics*, 1963.

Even the size of the firm is a factor that affects wages. Larger firms pay more on the average than smaller ones. Employees may prefer small firms and therefore obtain higher wages in large firms as a pecuniary offset to the nonpecuniary advantages in a small firm. Or possibly the large firm employs a higher general quality of labor. In retail trade, the average hourly earnings in 1963 for nonsupervisory employees were $1.74 for firms of over $1,000,000 in annual sales, $1.40 for firms with less than $250,000 in annual sales.

Table 20–5 shows the distribution of hourly wage rates of nonsupervisory employees in retail trade in 1963, subclassified by geographical areas. Thus, the 1963 percentage of employees earning less than $1.25, the 1963 legal minimum-wage rate, was 29 percent in the Northeast, 57 percent in the South, and 17 percent in the West. This does not mean that the West is more law abiding; the minimum-wage law exempted many employees in several trades. However, the variation reflects productivity of employees, type of industry, and cost of living.

Table 20–5
Hourly Wage Rates of Nonsupervisory Employees in
Retail Trade, 1963, Cumulative in Regions

Percent of Employees by Regions

| Wage Rates | Northeast | South | North Central | West |
|---|---|---|---|---|
| Under $ .75 | 1% | 13% | 3% | 1% |
| "       1.00 | 3 | 31 | 12 | 3 |
| "       1.25 | 29 | 57 | 34 | 17 |
| "       1.50 | 49 | 72 | 54 | 35 |
| "       2.00 | 74 | 88 | 77 | 60 |
| "       2.50 | 88 | 94 | 89 | 77 |
| Average | $1.74 | $1.32 | $1.65 | $2.00 |

Eating and drinking places excluded. Source: U.S. Department of Labor, *Monthly Bulletin of Labor Statistics*, 1963.

*Relative demand and supply.*    If the talent to be a first-class musician were very widely available and the talent (strong back) to be a ditchdigger were relatively rare, some ditchdiggers would get a higher salary than fine musicians. The larger the supply, with given demand, the lower the wages; and for an equal amount of labor, the higher the demand, the higher the wages. For example, with exactly ten window washers and ten doctors in a town of 5,000 people, the wages of doctors would be higher. The marginal product of a tenth doctor would probably be greater than of a tenth window washer. If the number of doctors were increased enough, their wages would fall below those of window washers.

Wages of window washers are lower than those of lawyers because the supply of lawyers is small enough *relative to its demand* to maintain a higher wage. And it is smaller because of the relative scarcity of the kind of talent that is wanted in lawyers as compared to window washers. Consequently, given the demand, wage differentials reflect the relative differences in supply of acceptable talent, resulting from heredity and training. If an extra dollar's worth of education and training increases a person's estimated productivity, it will pay him to buy the education, whether it be for a brain surgeon or for a cotton picker. The amount of training (investment in human capital) responds to its marginal cost relative to the increase it provides in productivity.

Suppose a person could borrow now against the clearly perceived higher future earnings he will be able to have as a result of education. Then a poor man, by borrowing against his prospective future earnings, could buy education as readily as a rich one. Notice, we do not say that the opportunity to buy education will equalize wealth among all people, but that all would have the opportunity to exploit their potential talents by borrowing against their future, clearly perceived potential increase in earning power.

But, in fact, not everyone who wants to exploit his educational opportunities in this way can do so—for at least two reasons: (1) The future is uncertain. If I wanted to borrow $10,000 to buy an education, lenders would check into the evidence and form judgments of whether the education really would enhance my earning power and repayment probability. What will happen if the future earnings aren't as big as I expected? Will I repay and be poorer than if I had not borrowed so much money, or will I plead bankruptcy, or undue duress, when my creditor demands payment? (2) A large part of one's academic education is obtained before he reaches 21. Our legal system and courts will not enforce rigorously debts incurred before the age of 21. And since the courts are not inclined to enforce repayment out of earnings it is no wonder lenders are wary of educational loans to young people.

*Specific versus general on-the-job training.*    College students are apt to overlook the very large amount of on-the-job training provided in business firms. Apprenticeships are only one form of such education. Professional football and baseball players learn during their first couple of years of professional play. In fact, they are probably paid more in the initial years than their services are worth. Why? Your instructor learned a lot in his first few years.

Was he paid more than he was worth in those first years? It depends upon whether the on-the-job education is useful for just that one *specific* employer or whether it is useful in *general* for other employers. *Specific* training is useful only to the current employer, who will get the benefits of the worker's higher productivity. Hence, the employer is willing to pay for it, if the employee is not likely to quit as soon as he is trained and go to work elsewhere. The military service "gives" on-the-job training and some of it is useful for general civilian life. As you can expect, wages paid during training will be lower if the employee develops *general* abilities he can sell to *other* employers.

Employees with heavy specific training are less likely to quit and are less likely to be laid off or fired in the event of a decrease in demand than untrained or generally trained employees. One implication of this is that we would expect to find more of the untrained in the group of people who more frequently change jobs and go through a period of unemployment while evaluating alternative job options.

*Risk-bearing differentials.*    Some people are more willing to try new applications or techniques, giving up relatively sure prospective wages in the hope of getting a higher wage. An architect who gives up a secure job designing conventional buildings and risks coming up with desirable new designs may end up very much richer or poorer. Some choose the risk of ending up poorer for the prospect of being richer. In this sense, they prefer to have had the chance to be rich even though they may fail. And their choices produce a wide spread of *realized* life-time earnings.

We note that wage differences *within* many occupations are greater than among averages of occupations. The spread of actors' incomes is much greater than the difference between the *averages* of doctors' and actors' incomes. Better a fine actor than an average doctor. Better a fine ball player than an average lawyer.

### Salary Differences Depend on Associated Wealth

Some people have been paid over a million dollars in one year for their personal services. Are talents and abilities of people as dispersed or varied as the earnings? Is there some force making personal earnings more different than the "inherent" abilities or skills? It has been argued as follows: "The president of General Products receives $500,000 a year. When he retires, someone now getting far less will take his place and will get that high salary. Surely the high salary is a function of the *position* rather than of some differences in abilities." But be careful to remember your economic principles. The marginal productivity of any resource or input affects its price, and as we saw in the preceding chapter the associated amount of capital affects his marginal productivity. To see what differences in ability imply, when associated with different amounts of wealth, consider two managers, one with ability to make correct decisions 5 percent more of the time than the other. Roughly speaking, that 5 percent superiority is worth about $50,000 in a $1,000,000 business, but only about $5,000 in a $100,000 business. The larger business will gain more with the superior man than would the small company. On the other hand two common labor employees that differed by 5 percent in their ability would not be making decisions that affect the total wealth as much as those of the top executives, and so the difference in their talents would not be so magnified. This implies that the nonmanagerial skills will be paid about the same in *large and small* companies, whereas the salaries of top management will be correlated with the size of the company. This is in fact what happens. Notice that the explanation provided here is not that the big companies have more wealth and therefore the manager can get more. Rather it is that the bigger the company the greater is the marginal productivity difference between the managerial skills of any two potential managers.

### Wage Differences and Nonpecuniary Factors

Employment conditions differ in nonpecuniary respects: employer personality, size of firm, safety, prestige, climate, type of work, location, congeniality of fellow workers. The higher pay offered to offset nonpecuniary disadvantages is called an "equalizing" wage difference; it helps equate labor's total rewards in different working conditions. These conditions can persist indefinitely if the cost of getting rid of them exceeds the "equalizing" difference in wages. For example, people may be willing to work in the heat only at premium wages; if the premium is less than the cost of air conditioning, hot work will continue.

Nonpecuniary productivity of *employees* differs also. Better looking, more courteous, pleasant, uncomplaining, cooperative, and congenial employees provide employers with nonpecuniary sources of utility. Both the pecuniary and nonpecuniary products affect the employer. Therefore, an employer also discriminates among potential employees with respect to nonpecuniary attributes. If two stenographers have equal pecuniary productivity, but one is more beautiful, pleasant, well dressed, with a better-modulated voice, then, at equal wages, she would be preferred. Her nonpecuniary qualities, in addition to the pecuniary productivity, will enable her to get a higher wage than the inferior (in a nonpecuniary sense) stenographer. The higher wage to the superior stenographer is the same thing as lower pay for inferior people. And that lower pay enables inferior people to get jobs. "Equalizing wage differences," then, provide employment opportunities for inferior employees, just as equalizing wage differences induce people to work in inferior environmental conditions. However, although people recognize differences among employers in working conditions and environment as valid reasons for employees' discrimination in choice of employers, they resent such actions by employers on the basis of personal characteristics of employees. Federal laws declare employ*er* discrimination illegal, while employ*ees* may legally discriminate.

Preferences and discrimination are revealed by "compensating" or "equalizing" wage and price differences, if markets are open to all types. Poor paintings sell for less than superb paintings; otherwise, the poor paintings would not be sold. Because Chevrolets sell for less than Cadillacs, Chevrolets can survive in competition against Cadillacs. At the same price, fewer would want Chevies.

Less attractive and homely people can offset their weaker appeal to other people to whom they desire to sell services by charging a lower price than that charged by beautiful people. You buy round steak rather than filet mignon only because the price of round steak is sufficiently lower, thus compensating you for the inferior tenderness and flavor of round steak, even though the food value of the two is the same.

People have preferences, and discrimination will occur *either* in wages paid or in extent and kinds of employment. At the same wage rate, the less preferred people will get less employment in good jobs. At lower wage rates, they can get more employment. But the less preferred will *not* receive *both* the same wage and the same amount or kind of employment—for the same reason that high-quality goods get a higher price or women of 35 get fewer jobs in a chorus line than girls of 25. The *customers* are discriminating. So is an employer, even though he may be the only one who sees some of the employees. He discriminates among people in order to maintain morale, productivity, and cooperation of employees—that is, to satisfy the nontechnical aspects of employment. This interest in personal attributes explains why employees and employers both place so much reliance on personal channels of recruitment and job finding. It also helps to explain some marketing procedures for labor.

The preceding set of factors affecting wages and wage differences did not include unions. We shall analyze their effect in the next chapter. For the present, we inquire into their structure, history, and main economic activities.

### Labor Unions

"The high standard of wages of the American worker is a result of a strong labor-union movement." Would that it were true. The path to higher income for all workers in poor countries would be open. Organize labor unions and strike for higher wages. However, neither economic reasoning nor factual evidence supports that prescription. It is the high marginal-productivity schedule of labor that explains high wages and employment levels. If a community has abundant natural resources and capital equipment, high educational levels, skilled workers, and a system for organizing productive activity, then the marginal productivity of the existing supply of labor will be higher. The foundation of high wages and large incomes is there and no place else. What the spread of unions can do in that respect is help that system organize diverse talents more efficiently by smoothing grievance procedures, providing increased information about job opportunities, helping workers improve their skills, and providing facilities for joint purchases.

By no means are these trivial objectives. Anyone working in a large corpora-- tion under foremen knows that a disinterested and not easily intimidated agent to handle grievances helps working conditions. Unions can also provide very valuable and hard-to-get information about alternative jobs. Joint purchases of insurance or joint provision of loan services via credit unions are efficient, in that the union credit agency knows the member's work record and has a relatively quick means of assessing his credit worthiness and prospects of job and income continuance. These objectives deserve emphasis because some people think the only purpose of a union is to enable employees to strike effectively. That is, of course, the union's basic source of strength in improving wages and working conditions of *some union members* beyond those determined by open-market competition.

Labor unions enable employees to coordinate their actions and more directly influence the employer's behavior by affecting the markets in which he buys labor or sells his products. Unions also are effective in influencing legislation. Labor unions have existed for a long time, often despite their being held illegal as "criminal conspiracies." However, in 1842 the Massachusetts Supreme Court rendered a precedent-setting decision in *Commonwealth v. Hunt*, declaring unions to be legal activities of employees. Presently in the United States about 16,000,000 employees (20-25 percent of the labor force) are members of unions. Union membership is charted in Figure 20-2 along with the total civilian labor force. The *fraction* of the civilian labor force belonging to unions has fluctuated, as shown in Figure 20-3. The rise

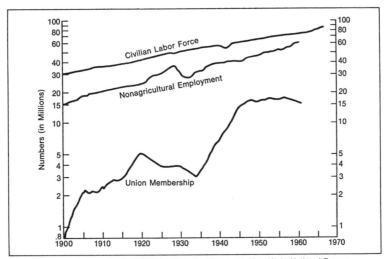

Source: L. Troy, *Trade Union Membership, 1897-1962* (New York: National Bureau of Economic Research, 1965).

Figure 20-2
Civilian Labor Force, Employees in Nonagricultural
Establishments, and Trade Union Membership, 1900-1962

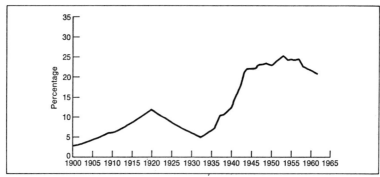

Source: L. Troy, *Trade Union Membership, 1897–1962* (New York: National Bureau
of Economic Research, 1965).

Figure 20–3
Extent of Union Membership of the Civilian Labor Force

during the late 1930s has been attributed in large part to legislation passed at
that time compelling employers to recognize and negotiate with union agents
for groups of their employees, if a majority of the employees in those groups
voted for a union (the Wagner Act of 1935).

In some industries, virtually every employee is a union member (musicians,
longshoremen, transport workers, construction workers) and in others, nearly
none (chemists, typists, economists, farm workers). The fraction of union
members is larger in the northern and western states than in the southern
states. A few of the largest unions contain most of the members. For
example, the ten largest contain almost half the total. (Teamsters with
1,500,000, Steel Workers with over 1,000,000, and on through Auto
Workers, Hod Carriers, and Garment Workers, down to the Textile Workers
with about 200,000.)

*National* unions are amalgamations of chartered "locals" to which
employees belong. Although the national organization, or federation, has a
constitution, the "local" usually has the basic power to apply membership
rules and contract approval. For example, national federation constitutions
assert that membership is open to all, regardless of race or creed, but the
actual admission standards are determined by the local members, with much
discrimination, especially in craft unions. Some craft unions have separate
union locals for Negroes (e.g., musicians).

Craft union members are all skilled in the same craft; industrial union
members all work in one industry regardless of particular skills. For example,
the carpenters' union is a craft union, whereas the steel workers' union is an
industrial union containing members with various skills. Most national craft
unions are associated in a national *federation*, American Federation of Labor
(AFL), while the Congress of Industrial Organizations (CIO) comprises
mostly industrial unions. A few national unions (teamsters and coal miners)
belong to neither. The AFL and the CIO have a top-level joint council called
the "AFL-CIO." One of its purposes is to define jurisdiction of the different
national unions in order to reduce inter-union rivalry about, for example,

whether an electrical fixture is to be installed by a carpenter or an electrical worker.

Local unions have officers (usually elected by the local membership) to maintain and expand coverage of union membership over more employers, to negotiate new contract terms, and to administer the routine affairs (pension funds, shop grievances). A "shop steward" is a union member and employee of the firm in which he helps to avoid or settle workers' grievances, much as an agent acts as an intermediary between two contracting parties. Safety rules, working hours, vacation interpretation, "goofing" on the job—these are a few of the perennial sources of misunderstanding and dispute that a shop steward can help to alleviate. The costs of union activity are financed by union membership initiation fees and monthly dues. Some initiation fees are hundreds of dollars, with monthly dues usually under $10.

Unions are recognized as the *sole* bargaining agent for a specified type of employee in any firm, if a majority of the voting employees so prefer under procedures established by the National Labor Relations Law, as administered by the National Labor Relations Board (NLRB). At the present time (and probably for many years in the future) one of the major disputes among employers, unions, and the NLRB concerns the Board's scope of authority.

A less ambiguous situation is the scope of requirement for membership in unions. Some employers have *closed shops* meaning that only union members can *apply* for and retain jobs. Some have *union shops*, in which all employees must become union members or at least pay union fees, if they are to retain a job for more than one month (they need not be members when applying for a job). Open shops do not require union membership in any respect.[4]

In addition to modifying the negotiatory techniques for the sale of labor services, unions use methods of imposing severe costs on employers to induce agreement to union demands. A *boycott* is a *concerted* refusal by union members to buy the products of the employer being boycotted. Sometimes, other firms that do business with the boycotted firm will also be boycotted—a *secondary boycott*. The *strike*, which has proved to be a stronger weapon, consists of two parts: (1) incumbent employees stop work for their existing employer, *and* (2) other laborers are prevented from competing for those jobs on terms inferior to those sought by the striking incumbents. Without the ability to prevent other applicants from negotiating for these jobs, the strike would merely be a mass resignation. In fact, the union *as we know it today* would be practically destroyed. Since the strike involves closing the market to some sellers of labor, it is commonly associated with means of preventing those other people from entering the market. Initially violence or, later, its threat is required. We shall examine this in more detail in the next chapter, which deals with market restrictions for labor services.

[4] Current federal legislation (Section 14B of the Taft-Hartley Act) permits a state to prohibit union shops. This is called the "right-to-work" law, somewhat misleadingly. This law is under violent attack from unions, and almost every year attempts are made to repeal it in Congress by prohibiting any state from requiring open shops in all places of employment. About twenty states prohibit union and closed shops.

Effect of Technological Progress<br>on Job Allocation and Wages

Although viewed with alarm and fought by various labor groups, automation (which has been progressing since man first learned to wield a stick) is a major source of increased wealth, new and easier jobs, and higher real incomes, and a larger population. The plow drawn by horses (rather than people) was a great technological advance. What happened to the displaced people who lost their jobs in front of the plow? They turned to what were formerly less important tasks like collecting wood and building stone fences. And when the tractor replaced the horse and several plowmen, what did the workers do? They went to work producing more of other things. With the advent of the new machines labor services became less valuable in the old jobs than in jobs to which the workers then turned (and which formerly were too costly). Today, after millenniums of technological progress people still worry about the mechanical, self-controlled machine because it induces labor re-allocation. And that is a valid reason for concern, though not of the kind most commonly talked about—that is, a lack of jobs.

Invention and Job Re-allocation

It is tempting to say that automation or technological progress creates new jobs. But that really is an irrelevant contention, despite overwhelming talk to the contrary. To see why, suppose that *no* new jobs were created by new inventions. Some workers must now turn to jobs which formerly were left unfilled or unperformed because the cost of filling them was too high. That is, the sacrificed output would have been more valuable than that to be had from the unfilled jobs. But now the formerly unperformed jobs or unavailable output can be produced by those whose services are less valuable in the old jobs. Therefore, whether or not the new invention or technique creates new jobs or increases the demand for workers in that new industry, there still will be plenty of jobs—in fact, more than can *ever* be filled. There are not too few jobs, but *too many* jobs! The problem is deciding which jobs or tasks to perform and which jobs to leave unperformed. That is the persisting problem of labor allocation. Inventions, automation, and progress do not eliminate it. The more rapid the pace of invention the more attention the problem requires. But it is *not* a problem of too few jobs, as many writers contend.

The underlying cause of concern is that people whose services in their current jobs are outcompeted by new methods must shift to new jobs—presumably to jobs that pay less than the current jobs formerly did. We must therefore distinguish among three groups of people. (1) Some people get higher wages because they are able to work with the new techniques or because they are demanded to produce the new equipment. Some people shifted from radio and movies to the manufacture of television programs and equipment and earned larger incomes. They benefit doubly; they gain from the higher income and from the lower prices of the increased output of goods. (2) Some people do not experience any perceptible impact on the value of their jobs or on their working conditions. They benefit from the lower prices of goods now produced in larger amounts or more cheaply, and they suffer no loss of income. (3) Some people find their old jobs being displaced by the new techniques. They must transfer to new jobs that pay less. This class can be further classified in three sub-categories:(a) Some nevertheless were better off on net, after considering the gains of their being able to use television as a consumer. (b) Of the remainder who did not reap a gain even after considering all the effects of this particular innovation, some were nevertheless better off than if they had been able to keep their old income but had to forsake *all* new progress since television. They gained through the general dispersal of improvements via lower prices and quality improvements to consumers—despite their income loss. (c) Some employees and owners of equipment suffered such severe reductions in demand for their services that, even after taking into account the gains from television and from all other technological improvements during the rest of their lives, they were still worse off. This category is more characteristic of older people than younger.

Obviously it is preferable to be a member of group 1. But the group in which a person finds himself depends upon the characteristics of new inventions and techniques. All of us fall in group 2 with respect to most inventions. Clearly we will resist inventions that place us in category 3; and we will complain and will be noticed more often than those in groups 1 and 2.

As yet, economic theory has been unable to tell in advance for any invention how many people (let alone which ones) will fall in each class. Even afterward it is often impossible to tell, because other changes impinge on the situation and obscure the effects of each earlier change. For example, did the invention of the typewriter increase or decrease the demand for secretaries? Demand may have increased enough so that more people obtain jobs as typists than formerly obtained jobs as scriveners and at higher wages, to boot. The discovery of oil may have attracted labor from coal mines into oil-well drilling, refining, and pipeline work, so that the wages of coal miners increased despite the effect of oil on the demand for coal. New inventions not only affect the schedule of marginal value-productivity of workers in the affected jobs; they can also attract workers away from other jobs, thus raising wages elsewhere. Spectacular examples are the railroad and the automobile. They substantially lowered the costs of transport; as a result, the amount of transport services increased, as did the demand for workers to provide materials for transportation. Yet even that involved a job shift. The old canalmen, livery-stable operators, and buggy-whip makers shifted to better-paying jobs in the new transportation industry before they were no longer demanded in their old jobs. It is true that the new machines sometimes reduce the cost of products so much that the increased amount demanded raises the demand for labor in that job; consequently, wages are raised.

Employees whose present wages or jobs are threatened have argued that the whole community ought, out of the net gain, to compensate re-allocated workers for their loss. This is a logically airtight possibility *in principle*, because the increased value of output exceeds the losses of the displaced factors. However, one difficulty is that innovations are so extensive that it is impossible to identify each and to determine who loses how much. How would we know how much to pay a person who claims to be displaced by the introduction of electronic computers? How could we be sure that he has not taken some easy, low-paying job—in the expectation that he will be given a payment large enough to make up the difference? Only *if* people's incentives were not changed by the compensation principle, and *if* there were *no* costs in discovering who gained or lost how much, would that compensation system be feasible.

Nevertheless, compensation is not ignored in our social policy. Today people pay taxes for a program to retrain and to relocate workers. This aid is proposed, however, not only for those whose incomes are cut by competition from new, more productive equipment, but for any laborer who lives in an area where there is general decline in demand for services—whatever the reason.[5] A displaced worker in a prosperous *area* is not eligible.

A more fundamental difficulty with the compensation proposal is that not only labor but also existing capital goods lose productive value as they are outcompeted by new innovations. If one compensates labor, he should, in simple justice, also compensate owners of nonhuman assets. But if compensation is paid *out of taxes* for every change in value resulting from innovation, the *owners* of productive resources, human and nonhuman, do not bear the risks of unforeseeable future consequences; instead, the general public becomes the risk bearer according to the tax load. The compensation principle via taxes conflicts with a basic purpose of a private-property capitalist society: to enable people to specialize in risk bearing—to escape common bearing of all risks of future values of all resources. If I don't want to bear the risks of the future value of some building, I simply choose not to be an owner of it; in that way I neither capture any gain nor suffer any loss of value. I let other people own the item. If I wish to bear the risk, I can buy a share of ownership in it or in like resources. Risk bearing is selective and adjustable. Suppose I were to agree to bear all the losses of value of my services, whatever the cause, and in exchange I obtain the right to keep whatever gains might occur in the value of my resources. That kind of agreement is implicitly made by a private-property owner. The compensation-by-taxing principle denies his making that agreement with the rest of society.

---

[5] The Trade Expansion Act of 1962 gives the President additional powers to negotiate for tariff reduction and provides for "trade adjustment assistance" for both business firms (through technical assistance, loans, tax relief) and workers (through special unemployment benefits, retraining, loans for moving to jobs in different communities) when injury from increased imports can be demonstrated.

Adjustment to Innovation

The shift from a job where demand has fallen to a new job is a poignant problem of human adjustment to circumstances. A move to a new area, a new job, a lower standard of living, and new colleagues and social circles can be a traumatic experience, especially for older people. Economic analysis may be scientific, impersonal, and unemotional, but the subjects are people with emotions and desires. Even if, in the overwhelming majority of cases, the job displacement caused by new innovations in technology shifted people to better and higher-paying jobs, the hardship for some is not avoided. These hardship cases are the ones most likely to be remembered.

Some adults never outgrow childhood fantasy; they believe scarcity is a result of some plot or failure to exploit our allegedly unlimited production potential. Technological advance has raised the over-all level of productivity of human labor to very high real earnings and real output. More people are alive today (probably about one in ten of all those who have ever lived to maturity) because we are not trying to survive with the technology of 1870 or 1770 or 1570. More are alive because they have knowledge and capital for a high marginal product. But there is no prospect that man will have all his wants fulfilled, with no jobs any longer worth doing. Until that unforeseeable day he must allocate his productive energies to the most valuable jobs—an allocation that will be persistently changing with new inventions, resources, and demands. And until that day we shall see some people resisting the effects of those changes. Those experiencing a reduced market value of output of their current jobs (because others are outcompeting them in the market) can and will resort to nonmarket-competitive behavior to try to offset market competition. Political competitive power may be directed toward changing the results of, or restricting, market competition. It is a very safe prediction that whenever one's wealth is being competed away in the market by new inventions, changing tastes, or new products, his attempts to restrict that market competition will increase.

The Magnitude of Employment
and Unemployment

In the United States, over 80,000,000 people had gainful employment of one kind or another in 1966. More than 55,000,000 worked full time and 25,000,000 worked part time. Approximately 10,000,000 changed jobs or took new jobs during the year. Every month approximately one in twenty employees quit, was laid off, or terminated a job for some reason; the same proportion took new jobs or returned to an old job. In this process, over 15,000,000 reported themselves as unemployed at some time during the year, although at any one time the number of unemployed averaged about 4,000,000. Of those 15,000,000, some 2,000,000 were unemployed all through the year; 1,000,000, from one to three months; and a little less than 3,000,000, from four months to more than six months. Over 5,000,000 had at least two spells of unemployment, the total time of which is the basis of their classification in the above categories. There is a persistent and extensive flow of people from job to job and between jobs and unemployment, along with constant reassessment of old jobs and consideration of possible new occupations. Such unemployment of people and resources—and even widespread and prolonged unemployment—can be made consistent with the economic analysis presented in earlier chapters. (Review pages 153–157.)

An analysis of unemployment must first consider the meaning of unemployment (of labor and of goods)—a term often applied indiscriminately to very different phenomena, not all of which are to be avoided.

### Some Sources and Kinds of Unemployment

One kind of unemployment is the excess of some resource, caused by a restraint on access to the market. For example, it is erroneous to call people "unemployable" because the value of their services is less than some maintained minimum wage. They are employable; but they are not employed because of the constraints placed on their employment in an open market at terms that are mutually acceptable to buyer and seller. A similar group of "unemployed" are excluded from particular jobs because of apprenticeship or licensing laws. These people call themselves unemployed "electricians," "meat cutters," "projectionists," or "bricklayers" while taking less-desired jobs elsewhere on a temporary basis. If there are prices and wages below which sales and employment are illegal, some people will be prevented from selling their services at prices acceptable to buyers. If the wage rate is legally set at a minimum of $1, some less productive people who could do something worth, say, 80 cents, cannot be employed at that wage. We present a more detailed discussion of this in the next chapter. Suffice it to note that some of these people will constitute members of the "unemployed" until they shift to "independent" owner-operator status. How many people are in this situation is not known.[6]

Another class of the "unemployed" are those who entered employment when demand for their services was high enough to warrant the higher wages that attracted them. For example, some housewives work during seasonally high demands at certain types of labor—in fruit-packing houses or dress shops during the Christmas season. The rest of the year, they prefer not to work at the lower available wages. People working in jobs that involve short-lived projects, like movies, plays, or construction, are commonly found in the ranks of the unemployed between projects—again, especially if they have qualified for unemployment benefits.

[6] It is believed that this group is comprised primarily of the very young, the uneducated, Negroes, and women.

Sometimes it is asserted that there are not enough jobs available. This assertion is simply unacceptable if reality is to be recognized. Jobs are always available, but the wage offer may be unacceptably low in view of alternative job prospects or leisure. To ask a former steel-mill employee to work at 50 cents an hour as a gardener, handy-man, farm hand, clerk, or machine-tool operator is "ridiculous"—which means only that the steel-mill employee deems it preferable not to work at those jobs for those wages, perhaps because he believes he can get a better job by continued exploration of other job options. In other words, he believes the time spent seeking information is worth more than 50 cents an hour.

There are also people who would be happy to continue at their *old* job *at the old wage* if *that* job were still available. But they will refuse to accept a wage cut sufficient to keep them at work in their former jobs, because they believe (sometimes correctly) that other job opportunities exist at approximately the same wages—or certainly at better terms than now available in the old job. After all, those other opportunities are what kept their wages up to the level at which they were in their recent jobs. Employees will therefore explore and compare these other opportunities—as long as the expected cost of discovering them is less than the loss of wealth from accepting a wage cut in the previous job.

When demand for a product falls, if the productive inputs immediately shifted to other tasks, there would be no unemployment and no "idle" resources. But such shifts are not possible at zero costs, because of the costs of finding the various buyers and sellers and bringing them together, so that each can realize his best trading opportunities. And this, as discussed earlier in pages 153–157, will explain a wide class of unemployment.

*Frictional unemployment.*    Although it may seem paradoxical, "unemployment" is consistent with efficiency. Consider the costs that would be imposed on you if you were *never* allowed to be unemployed regardless of changing demand and supply conditions. Suppose you were dissatisfied with your present job and wanted another. You could not quit and spend a week or a month looking for a new one, because you would then be "unemployed." It is unlikely that you could find the *best* alternative job with an instant search of no cost or while working at the old job in order to avoid "unemployment." The activity in question is not *job* seeking, it is *job-information* seeking. Many jobs are available, but information is being sought about still other jobs in the belief that the other jobs may be superior. The currently known jobs do not pay enough to induce a person to stop looking for *better* job opportunities.

If an employer should experience a decrease in demand, so that he wants to employ fewer employees at the existing wage, he will drop employees. This is equivalent to the case in which a renter terminates his renting and leaves the apartment empty. Like the apartment owner, the employee now has the option of cutting his wages immediately by a relatively large amount to get a job quickly, or he can invest in a hunt for information about various alternative jobs. Like the apartment owner, he will not accept a cut in wages to whatever level is necessary to find another employer immediately. And if he believes that the sacrifices and costs he incurs in the search yield a greater increase in the present value of his wealth, then he will engage in some information hunting, an activity called job hunting.

A transparent example of such activity is provided by new college graduates who spend much time and other resources investigating alternative potential employers. No student knows everything about each potential employer, nor does each employer know everything about each potential college graduate. Wage offers differ among employers, in part reflecting nonpecuniary features that are in turn evaluated differently by various people. Offers obtained by college graduates for the "same" kind of work will differ by 5 to 10 percent of the average offer. Accepting the first offer reduces the probability of getting the highest-paid job and lowers one's *wealth* (present value of his future earnings) compared to what it would be if he took longer to find more offers. The more firms that are contacted, the greater will be the probability of finding higher wage offers or better jobs. The greater the difference among potential wage offers and working conditions, the greater the amount of search that it would be profitable to perform.

A person should search for and explore other wage offers until the expected marginal gain (in present value of anticipated future income) equals the incremental cost of continued search. The increment of *gain* from *extra* search time diminishes the longer the time devoted to information collecting. Hence, there is a limit to the length of search. Although very few persons may make detailed calculations, their observed behavior conforms to this explanation.

Search by employees (and employers also) would eliminate all dispersion among offers *if* there were unchanging conditions of demand and supply and tastes of employers and employees. The greater the rate of change of tastes and demands, the greater the differences among worker talents and employer's working conditions; and the greater the costs of movement, the greater will be the dispersion among job opportunities and the greater the gain in wealth by more extended search. Employment agencies, which specialize in obtaining and disseminating this kind of information, give concrete evidence of the cost of information.

A person engaged in this process of acquiring information for better jobs is said to be "frictionally unemployed." Frictional unemployment is applicable to labor, houses, capital goods, or any good whatsoever. It is the efficient way to adjust to unpredictable demand and supply changes. It might be called "frictional *use*" because the resources are being used to *overcome* "frictions" in the operation of an economic system.

Another facet of the frictional process is the presence of "unfilled" jobs. Some employers would like more employees, and, if information and transfer costs were zero, they would instantly hire the right people at the appropriate wage. But filling jobs immediately is more expensive in that it will take a higher wage to get the right person immediately; or, if the employer takes the first available person, he will have a smaller probability of getting the "best" person.

Structural Demand and Aggregate
Demand Decreases

We explained why people and resources will become idle in the face of a fall in demand. However, there are two distinct kinds of demand decreases. One is *structural demand*, and the other is *aggregate demand decreases*. They may occur simultaneously.

Structural Shifts

Structural *shifts* in relative demands for labor cause unemployment. Aggregate money demand over all goods may be steady or rising, but the demands for some goods fall while demands for others increase.[7] New techniques often change the relative values of each type of labor in various uses, and people whose services fall in value must either accept lower wages or shift to other jobs. Some people do not have any other skill that would enable them to maintain their old wage, so they may accept the lower wage. Others who are upset by the changing patterns of consumer tastes or changing technology initiate a job-evaluation search (unemployment) rather than accept the lower wage.

An increase in supplies of new young labor, as at the beginning of each summer, introduces a shift in relative supplies. Again, the job evaluation process (as well as the potential employee comparison and evaluation by employers) yields the phenomenon known as unemployment.

Structural unemployment, based on *relative* demand or supply shifts, implies a shift in relative wages, incomes, and wealth of people. The sensible expectation of discerning a job that will avoid a wage cut initiates and extends the unemployment episode. Some people never find another job paying an acceptable wage. Old people whose services are outcompeted by new techniques may find it not worthwhile to incur moving costs to a new job for only a few remaining years. Unquestionably, jobs exist and are available, but at wages many regard as unacceptably low—as discussed earlier in this chapter.

Shifts in relative demands and supplies may constitute a major portion of what we call frictional unemployment—although we are not sure about that. If these shifts in demands for various skills are complicated by minimum-wage laws or other restrictions, then the least-skilled labor (young, Negro, women, uneducated) will find employment opportunities closed off.

Fluctuations in Aggregate Demand

The unemployment of labor explainable by the information costs associated with changing (relative, but not *general*) demands for various products, chang-

---

[7]Costs of acquiring information about alternative job operations and of moving, as explained in the preceding sections, are present in each case.

ing tastes, new products, etc., seems to run about 2 to 4 percent of the labor force. However, at times the rate of unemployment (as evidenced by data taken from people eligible for unemployment pay or who report in labor force surveys that they are "out of work and seeking work") rises to substantially higher levels. In what we commonly call recessions, the rate runs between 5 percent and 10 percent. In the deep depression of the 1930s, it is believed to have reached 20 to 25 percent. But if the preceding analysis is valid, why should it ever go as high as 5 percent?

Possibly the demands for various goods shift so rapidly and greatly that many people have to shift jobs, and job information activity increases accordingly. In fact, relative demand shifts do occur on a significant scale and contribute to unemployment. However, evidence suggests that the factor responsible for the large increases in unemployment is a general decrease in demand for most (though not all) goods without an offsetting increase in demands for other goods. Some industries are expanding and some are contracting; sometimes more are contracting than expanding. For example, Table 20–6 shows the *directions* of month-to-month changes in the value of new orders in manufacturing establishments over a representative interval. In the monthly change from June to July of 1966, new orders increased in six industries and decreased in eleven. Further, as one looks across the columns, each industry shows noticeable fluctuations. For example, iron and steel showed ten increases and nine decreases in the nineteen-month interval.

Within each industry a similar variety of behavior among firms comprising that industry would also be observable.

A more extensive index of the diffusion of productive activity is shown in Figure 20–4. The rate of *employment* is the variable whose *expansion* in thirty different industries is plotted. The percentage of those thirty industries experiencing an expansion in any given month is indicated by the height of the curve. The curve fluctuates up and down, rarely reaching 100 percent or zero. In other words, not all industries are expanding at the same time, nor are all contracting at the same time. The curve usually oscillates within the limits of about 20 to 80 percent. *Industrial production* in various industries shows the same general pattern of diffusion of expansions and contractions.

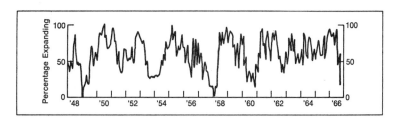

Figure 20–4
Percentage of Employment-Expanding Industries

This graph is based on thirty industries and month-to-month changes. Source: U.S. Department of Commerce, *Business Cycle Developments*, August 1966.

Table 20-6
Direction of Change in Value of Manufacturers'
New Orders, Selected Industries

One-Month Spans

| Industry | 1965 | | | | | | | | | | | | 1966 | | | | | | |
|---|---|---|---|---|---|---|---|---|---|---|---|---|---|---|---|---|---|---|---|
| | Dec–Jan | Jan–Feb | Feb–Mar | Mar–Apr | Apr–May | May–June | June–July | July–Aug | Aug–Sep | Sep–Oct | Oct–Nov | Nov–Dec | Dec–Jan | Jan–Feb | Feb–Mar | Mar–Apr | Apr–May | May–June | June–July |
| Percent rising (36 industries) | 59 | 39 | 64 | 50 | 44 | 58 | 60 | 42 | 61 | 61 | 56 | 76 | 31 | 50 | 85 | 42 | 50 | 49 | 47 |
| Iron and steel | + | + | − | − | − | + | + | − | − | + | + | + | − | + | − | − | + | − | + |
| Primary nonferrous metals | + | + | + | + | + | + | − | + | − | + | + | + | + | + | + | − | + | − | + |
| Other primary metals | + | − | + | − | + | + | 0 | − | − | + | − | + | + | − | + | + | − | + | − |
| Electrical generator apparatus | − | − | 0 | − | − | + | + | + | − | + | − | + | − | + | − | + | + | − | − |
| Radio, television, and equipment | + | − | + | + | − | + | − | − | − | + | + | + | + | − | + | + | + | − | − |
| Other electrical equipment | − | + | − | − | − | + | + | − | + | + | − | + | − | + | + | − | + | + | + |
| Motor vehicles | + | + | + | − | − | + | + | − | − | + | − | − | − | + | + | − | + | + | − |
| Motor vehicle parts | − | − | + | − | + | − | + | − | + | − | − | − | + | − | − | + | + | − | − |
| Aircraft | + | + | − | + | − | + | − | + | + | − | − | + | + | − | + | − | − | + | − |
| Stone, clay, and glass products | − | + | − | + | − | − | + | − | + | − | + | + | − | − | + | − | − | + | − |
| Metalworking machinery | + | − | + | − | − | + | + | + | − | − | + | + | + | − | + | − | − | + | − |
| Special industrial machinery | − | − | + | + | − | + | − | + | − | − | − | + | − | − | + | + | + | − | − |
| General industrial machinery | + | − | + | + | − | − | + | + | − | + | − | + | − | − | + | + | − | − | + |
| Engines and turbines | + | + | − | − | + | + | − | + | − | + | + | − | + | − | + | − | + | − | − |
| Agricultural implements | − | + | − | − | + | + | − | + | + | + | + | + | − | + | 0 | − | − | + | − |
| Household appliances | + | + | − | + | − | − | + | − | + | + | − | + | − | + | + | + | − | − | + |
| Fabricated metal products | + | + | − | + | − | + | + | − | + | + | + | + | − | + | + | − | + | 0 | + |

+ = rising; 0 = unchanged; − = falling. Series components are seasonally adjusted.
Source: U.S. Department of Commerce, Bureau of Census, *Business Cycle Developments,*
August 1966.

As one would expect, when the curve runs along the bottom—most industries experiencing a contraction—a recession is indicated. When the curve runs along on the upper side, the period is called a recovery or prosperity.

If the line in Figure 20–4 were steady at about 50 percent, it would mean a relatively steady state of demand, with offsetting shifts occurring among various goods. However, the diffusion index fluctuates over a wide span, suggesting that the growths and declines in various industries are not reacting to shifts of demand from product to product—by a large number of independent random deviations. Instead, an upward swing seems to indicate that most industries are expanding more than enough to offset contractions elsewhere; and at other times total demand summed over all goods seems to be decreasing. Fluctuations in *aggregate demand* for the products of various industries seem to be correlated rather than independent or mutually offsetting.

Fluctuations in employment and production are closely correlated with what are known as prosperities and depressions. In fact, depressions and prosperity are practically definable by total output and employment. Figure 20–5 shows an index of industrial production from 1948 through 1966, while Figures 20–6 and 20–7 show the number of employed and the percentage of unemployment since 1948. It is evident that in the periods 1949, 1954, 1958, and 1961 there were minor recessions.

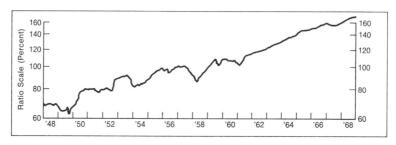

Figure 20–5
Industrial Production

Index is based on physical volume, adjusted for seasonal variation, 1957 = 100.
Source: Board of Governors of the Federal Reserve System, *Monthly Bulletin*.

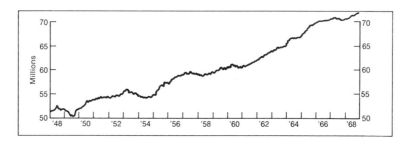

Figure 20–6
Total Nonagricultural Employment

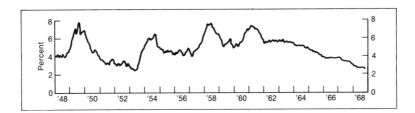

Figure 20–7
Unemployment Percentage (Nonagricultural Employees)

When there is a decrease in *general* demand that people do not realize is a *general* decrease, many refuse to lower their prices in existing jobs. They suppose that they could get about the same wage elsewhere, but they will be unable to do so. They discover how obsolete or false their beliefs are only in the course of the information acquiring, and it takes a good deal of information to detect the *generally* lower state of demand. For example, when sellers see a low set of offers from a sample of potential buyers, the lower observed offers will at first appear as unrepresentative, and for a time it will be expected that better opportunities will shortly be found. It takes *additional* acquisition of information to discover that the *general* state of demand and opportunities has indeed declined. The period of unemployment or information-acquisition, will be extended and beset with disappointment.

Unemployment resulting from a general demand decrease will increase as the general demand continues to decrease. The situation can continue for several months or years if it is not simply a once-and-for-all drop. Beliefs about opportunities elsewhere become obsolete and must be *continuously revised downward* with new information. Acquisition and comprehension of information lag behind the event, so a continuing fall in general demand is more costly to detect. Prolonged search for the best of the available opportunities is implied by a declining general demand. The maximal wage offers with continued sampling fail to rise gradually as they should with extended search in a stabilized demand situation. The searcher must learn to lower still further his conception of acceptable offers. His conception of an acceptable wage offer lags behind (because of his incomplete information) the actually available best offers, so an indefinite length of continued inspection of available jobs persists.[8] If the decline in aggregate demand would stop,

[8]The word "lag" may be misinterpreted. It does not refer to some "stickiness" or "inflexibility" of wage rates behind prices of other goods. We here assume that there is nothing to prevent any worker from immediately adjusting his offer price as low as he wants to; no custom or convention denies him perfect, instant flexibility. What we mean by lag is that his *conception* of what price he can get lags behind the facts; the cost of getting information makes his *state of knowledge* lag behind the actual equilibrating price which would restore employment. It is an *informational* lag. He chooses not to reduce the price of his services because he thinks the equilibrating price is higher than it actually is; or if it actually is as high as he thinks, the costs of search, and hence use of time, introduce a time delay between the old and the new job. The lag must be understood to mean the time it takes a person to discern that the equilibrating price has fallen

unemployment would begin to be reduced. If the decline were to terminate and be replaced by an increase, unemployment would end even sooner. Much unemployment could be avoided by economic policies that prevent general decreases in demand. Some of the most severe decreases in general demand have been an unwitting result of extraordinarily inept and ignorant monetary policy. We have in mind the great contraction from 1929 to 1933. But that story is covered in the other half of introductory courses.

Some unemployment is an inherent part of an open-market system of exchange, in which people are entitled to select their work and produce at their own volition at open-market prices rather than being tied to jobs as serfs or assigned them by dictators. In the military, everyone always has *a* job. However, it is not clear that this is more efficient or preferable to an "idle" search for other *better* jobs. Authorities will always regard an "idle" person as inefficient, since *they* know something he could do that is useful in the absolute sense, if not the most useful. If less attention is paid to seeking over-all efficient assignments of workers, it is easier to keep everyone busy. Concealing or avoiding unemployment by arbitrary work assignments is called "disguised unemployment."

We can categorize the factors affecting the *extent* of unemployment as: (1) the nature of the costs governing production of information and adjustments in job allocation and transfer; (2) income available during the search and transfer (relief or unemployment benefits); (3) the frequency and magnitude of relative demand shifts; (4) the frequency of changes of supply of various kinds of skills and talents; (5) the extent and frequency of declines in aggregate demand.

The explanation of unemployment suggests that after a decrease in demand with its increase in unemployment, there will be a gradual swing back to full employment. The implication is that the size of the downswing or recession determines the size of the following recovery. In other words, the analysis rests on inherent market forces pushing toward full employment. We should therefore expect to observe a complete recovery, with full employment after some depression. The bigger the recession, the greater the recovery. However, the reverse is *not* true—that the extent of the prior rise to new highs of output and employment sets the stage for some commensurate increase in unemployment. The degree of recovery is neither a random variable, being higher or lower according to some accident of fate without some built

relative to his conception of the equilibrating price. There is nothing in this lag about a difference between the wages currently being paid and the price of other goods. It could be that for *every* kind of good, labor or non-human, there is unemployment, so the sellers of each type of unemployed good manifest the same lag of their own conception of their equilibrating price to the actual equilibrating price. All prices of labor and of other goods still employed and sold may be moving in exact proportion, while the unemployed in each category are lagging in their conception of the new wage or price they must accept to adjust to the new discerned (with a lag) equilibrating price.

This suggests that more homogeneous goods sold in a single market with cheaply accessible information about the equilibrating price (as, say, in the stock and commodity markets) should display practically no "lag" and no "unemployment." And the facts support that.

in forces toward full employment, nor is the increase in unemployment during recession correlated with a preceding "boom." As implied by economic analysis, recoveries are correlated with preceding depressions; but depressions are not correlated with the preceding recoveries or booms. Whatever the extent of some downswing, the economic system contains forces pushing output and employment back to full employment. It is the downward "shocks" that produce unemployment, not some inherent "what-goes-up-must-come-down" explanation. The bigger the downward "shock," the bigger the later upward recovery sweep. There is a powerful force toward full employment.

### Dispassionate Analysis and Compassionate Policy

Those who have lost their former higher-paying jobs in a recession or depression see a world of reduced opportunities. It seems that there are *no* jobs, certainly not of the kind they had been performing. To point out that there are other jobs, although not of the kind each person thinks it intelligent to accept, is not to say that people are foolish for not taking those jobs or that they deserve to suffer if they do not take those jobs. Nor does an understanding of the reasons for massive unemployment constitute an excuse for it. Quite the contrary. It is not true that the rate of recovery from a recession is some natural rate that should not be affected by deliberate fiscal and monetary actions. Unfortunately, however, there are many well-intended but ill-conceived proposals to alleviate or avoid unemployment. Sometimes the proposals *intended* to reduce unemployment or help the lot of the unemployed actually will bring undesirable consequences.

### Determination of Aggregate Demand

What makes aggregate demand fluctuate instead of being constant with shifts from one product to another offsetting each other? What ties the demand for the products of various industries together? There is a connection among them. Expansions in one industry or sector set up forces for expansion in other sectors. Specialization in production means that some firms buy their inputs from other firms. Thus, an increased output of final goods in one industry will increase the inputs bought from supplier industries. For example, an increased demand for cars will increase the demand for steel and a whole host of other services, with some consequent feedback on the demand for cars. The web spreads throughout the economy. That several sectors expand and contract in close step should not be surprising. But this does not explain the fact of relatively large fluctuations in these mutually interrelated industries. Although correlated, why should they experience such large persisting swings in general demand for the aggregate of their products? It is to these general questions—the interconnection and the size and duration of fluctuations in output and employment in general in the economy—that the other half of the introductory course is devoted.

Summary

1    Labor service is a commodity, subject to the laws of demand and of supply like any other commodity.

2    The demand for labor is a negative function of the wage rate paid for labor. The supply function for labor services is one in which larger amounts of labor can be obtained by offering a higher payment for more services.

3    Differences in wage rates, like differences in prices of various goods, reflect relative demands and supplies of various kinds of labor. *Qualitative* differences in people's productive talents yield differences in relative supplies of those talents and hence in the wages paid. Differences in supplies of various talents reflect inequality in amounts of various *natural* talents, *costs* of training and developing talents, and *willingness* of suppliers of labor to engage in various kinds of work.

4    Differences in *monetary* wages sufficient to compensate for nonmonetary features of various jobs or of personal traits of employers or employees are called equalizing differences. These differences are sometimes called discriminatory wage differences, in that they discriminate or compensate for differences in the *nonmonetary* attributes of the job and the employer and employees.

5    Much education of people for productive work is on-the-job training. Some wage differences reflect compensation for on-the-job education, since the employee is willing to pay for this by accepting a lower wage. Employees receiving specific training do not thereby receive lower-than-competitive wages; instead they receive wages larger than their current marginal productivity to the employer and later receive wages less than their marginal productivity to this one employer.

6    Union membership increased from about 5 percent of the work force in the 1930s to about 20 percent at the end of World War II and has remained practically unchanged since then.

7    Unions affect the structure and procedure of wage and job negotiation. Wages will be affected insofar as the supply of labor is changed by modified conditions of labor entry to the labor markets. The union shop, the closed shop, strikes, control of entry to the union—all are

means to affect the labor supply conditions for employers. Underlying all factors is the power to strike, without which the union would be a relatively ineffective instrument for influencing labor supply conditions.

8　Technological progress (currently called automation) does not reduce the number of work opportunities. It reduces the value of some jobs and induces people to shift to others formerly too expensive to perform—or formerly left unperformed because of lower value relative to other performed tasks. Not everyone gains from every technological advance. Some gain with higher demand for their services in the new activity. Some gain by lower costs of improved services from the new activity. Some owners of productive goods (labor as well as physical goods) lose wealth by being displaced to new tasks not paying as much as they formerly earned.

9　Compensation to people hurt by technological progress is in principle feasible, but because of exorbitant costs of determining accurately who is hurt and how much, either crude approximations are made by tax-financed compensation schemes or the risks of such effects are distributed via ownership arrangements.

10　Most public discussion of automation and technological advance suggests a "lump-of-labor" fallacy: that there is only so much work to be done, and that every task more efficiently performed with less labor means just so much less worthwhile work is thereby left to be performed. This is identical to saying that currently society could produce all the goods and services it desires, so that any released effort has no other productive uses—an obviously false proposition.

11　Contrary to what would be implied in a free-information-and-no-cost-of-quicker-adjustment world, reductions in demand do not imply that prices will be immediately reduced to market-clearing levels with sustained total employment and use of all productive resources. Instead, unemployment and idle productive resources are implied as modes of adjustment to changing demand and supply conditions.

12　Unemployment is not a sign that there are no jobs or work worth doing. It is, rather, a job-relocation process that involves search over other job opportunities to find the *best* one.

13　Unemployment occurs for several reasons: (a) Restraints on markets (such as minimum-wage laws) that prevent some people from working at wages that reflect their marginal productivity. They shift to "noncovered" jobs or become self-employed "contractors." (b) Restraints on people working at some job without a license or authorization (such as union membership or apprenticeship regulations). (c) The fact that some workers are willing to work only during seasonal peak demands when wages are high. (d) Shifting of relative demands or supplies that induce job shifting. This is called structural unemployment. (e) Falling *general* demand that requires reduced wages and prices. This is called "aggregate demand deficiency" unemployment. (f) Resources often appear to be idle, or "unemployed," in order to economize on the costs of physical readjustments to unpredictable fluctuations in demand.

14    Unemployment of resources can be reduced by reducing the extent to which *general* demands fall. General demand decreases are a major source of the severe unemployment characteristic of depressions.

15    Major general decreases in money demands for goods and services reflect "malfunctions" in the monetary and economic institutions, rather than decreases in general wants in any real sense.

## Questions

1    Minors are not "free" individuals; for example, they cannot own property (a guardian oversees them) and they cannot make legally binding contracts. Their legal status is not far removed from temporary slavery. Because of the conflict of interest between parents and minors, such legal restrictions as compulsory education and prohibition of child employment (both of which are nineteenth-century developments) are imposed to increase the probability that the parent will make decisions of the kind the minor would presumably make if he were "of age and sensible." Is there an alternative and not necessarily incompatible force at work that would bring about an increase in academic education and a decrease in child employment even if no laws had been passed?

2    A 20-year-old with an earning expectancy of forty-five years (beginning at $3,000 per year and increasing annually at the rate of 6 percent to about $13,000 per year at the end of twenty years and then holding constant thereafter to retirement at 65) has a present capital value of his future earnings of about $100,000 at 6 percent rate of interest. If he expects continued salary increases after age 40, his present value will be even greater. It has been estimated, on the basis of projections of wage earnings of college graduates, that the "time-of-graduation capital value" of a college graduate's future income is on the average about $150,000 at 6 percent rate of interest. This means that if he could sell his future wages (and not affect his willingness to work!), he could "sell" himself for approximately $150,000 at graduation. A woman who marries him gets ownership of half his wages; by marrying him she "purchases" a wealth of about $75,000. Is there any other way "in effect" to sell off those future earnings? What method do most people use to spend now some of that capital value?

3    "Overtime premium wages are a device to restrain employers from working employees overtime." "Overtime premium wages are means whereby employers induce employees to work overtime more than they otherwise would." Which of these two propositions is correct? Explain.

4    "The birth rate is controlled by custom and emotion, not by economic calculations. Certainly, it is not reasonable to expect more children, the wealthier the parents." Yet the fact is that in communities with relatively widespread knowledge of contraceptive methods, there is a positive correlation between number of children and wealth of parents (after allowing for other factors like education, occupation, and location). For purposes of testing the above propositions, would you define "number of children" as number of pregnancies, of live births, of children surviving to age 1 month, or to 1 year, or to 6 years, or what?

5    Assume that wage rates of gardeners were to double, despite an unchanged demand.
a. Would people go on hiring the same amount of gardener services and pay more?
b. What would happen to gardens?
c. What substitution for gardeners would occur?
d. Where or from whom could you learn about the available substitution techniques?

6    "The higher the wage rate, the higher the wages." Explain the error in this statement.

7    "Different workers receive different wages because the workers are different, the jobs are different, and workers can't move to other jobs easily." On the other hand, "Workers are different but get the same pay in many jobs; many different jobs pay the same wages; and it is just as 'easy' to move across the country as it is to move next door." Obviously one of these quoted statements is either wrong or ambiguous. Rewrite it to make it correct.

8    "The population of Arizona is increasing at a record rate. Special effort must be made to create new jobs to provide employment for the increased labor force." Explain why this is wrong.

9    "Automation is destroying 300,000 jobs a month." Accepting this as a fact, explain why it does not mean that anyone will be left without a job.

10    "Automation, like any change in demand or supply of labor, leads to changes in jobs and wage rates—not to increased unemployables." Explain.

11    "A substantial number of relatively unskilled persons reported that they cannot find work. At the same time, there are many unfilled jobs

for relatively skilled people. Apparently, the problem is that there are more unskilled people than unskilled jobs." What is wrong with the reasoning?

12    "My doctor charges me a high fee because he has to cover the high cost of his education and equipment. On the other hand, my golfing teacher also charges me a high fee, even though his education is practically absent." Is either one cheating or fooling me? Explain.

**13**    "Elizabeth Taylor was paid over $5,000,000 for making the film *Cleopatra*. Yet Audrey Hepburn could have taken her place for, say, $1,000,000. There must be something wrong with the movie industry. Certainly, Taylor is not worth that much more to 20th Century-Fox than Hepburn would be." Explain, using marginal-productivity theory, how it can be sensible to pay Taylor that much, even though Hepburn might have been available for one-fifth as much.

14    "The presidents of some big corporations are paid as much as $500,000 in one year. All they do is make the kinds of decisions that are made in thousands of other companies by much lower-paid people who are as intelligent, but who just haven't had a chance to get those fancy jobs and who aren't as well known or don't have the reputation. Clearly, salaries are based more on past experience, reputation, and pull. Therefore, marginal productivity—which is an academic, unrealistic abstraction of an imaginary world—is useless at best and false at worst." Explain why the last sentence is not implied by the preceding sentences.

15    In deciding who is an unemployed person, would you consider the following:
a. Is he now working for someone else as an employee? If his answer is "yes," would you classify him as unemployed or as employed?
b. He answers "Yes" to the preceding question, but answers "No" to the question "Is your current job your usual kind of work?" He reports that he is working at a service station, while looking for a job as a lathe operator. Would you change the classification?
c. Next he is asked, "Are you willing to take an available job as a lathe operator at a wage of $2 an hour?" He answers, "No, I used to work for $6 an hour and I'm an experienced operator, not a novice." Is your classification of him still the same? Why?
d. If you do not call him unemployed in the preceding question, then how can you call anyone unemployed; for there are always jobs available at some sufficiently low wage—a wage he would call "ridiculous," "un-American," or "below standard"?

**16**    The usual criterion of an unemployed person is "not employed by someone else and actively looking for a job." It says nothing about the range of jobs or wages he refuses to consider. What do you think the criterion implicitly assumes to avoid being completely useless?

17    In feudal England there was no unemployment—only work and leisure. Employment for wages was rare. Even rarer were market-negotiated wages. But the rise of the commercial system introduced markets for labor services and induced peasants to break away from their feudal ties and to sacrifice their feudal security for the hazards of private contractual employment and unemployment. By the sixteenth century employment for money wages was well established (but maximum permissible wage rates were set by government, and potential employers were exhorted not to offer more and were punished if caught).

a. What devices do you think developed as a means of circumventing the maximum-wage restrictions?

b. Why would the government impose *maximum* limits to wages whereas today *minimum* limits are commonly imposed?

18    America was founded partly on "slavery" of white men. In colonial days immigrants "indentured" themselves, pledging to work for the benefit of a master for seven (or some specified number of) years if the master would finance their way to America. Today, this is illegal.

a. Why?

b. Who gains and who loses if such contracts are prohibited?

19    "In the open market, wages are driven down to the subsistence level." That is the iron law of wages. What is meant by "the subsistence level"?

20    "A man who loses his job through no fault of his own should not have to bear the losses of unemployment. The government must see to it that he does not." This is a quotation from a campaign speech of a major candidate for governor of California.

a. Is the candidate proposing that there be no unemployment or that anyone not currently employed should be given an income equivalent to what he was formerly getting?

b. How can either of these be accomplished?

21    Is a person who loses his job through no fault of his own also unemployed thereafter through no fault of his own? Explain.

22    In what sense does the range of wealth and income of people reflect their own preferences?

23    Why are the wages of the top managers of large companies generally higher than those of small companies? The answer is not that the larger companies have a greater ability to pay because they are richer (they do not pay more for their buildings or subordinate employees).

24    A tape-recording machine displaces a telephone-answering girl. Who or what has displaced whom? Explain why the displacement of labor by capital reflects a displacement of labor by labor.

25    On the average, the cost increment of each extra job investigated increases. Also, on the average, the gain in wages from another job investigated diminishes. If these two propositions are true, then what

must be the relation between the increment of gain and the increment of cost in order to conclude that it will pay to take the first job investigated?

26   Employment agencies charge about 50–60 percent of one month's salary for their services for jobs paying about $400 per month. For jobs paying about $800, the fee is one month's salary. If this is paid to the employment agency by the employer, does it mean the employer bears the costs? Do you think this fee is too large? Why?

27   a. What different kinds of unemployment (with respect to why unemployment exists) do you think it is relevant to distinguish?
b. Why?

28   Suppose the daily sales of each of fifty firms are determined by a process simulated by the turn of a roulette wheel with numbers from 0 through 30. Further, suppose that the firm will on the next day seek to hire as many employees as the sales of the preceding day. Thus, if sales are 20 on the first day, the firm will seek to hire twenty people on the second day—given the wages of $25 per person per day. If there were fifty firms, the average number of employed people would be $50 \times 15 = 750$.
a. Would that employment rate stay constant day after day despite the independent additive random process for determining the number of employees demanded at that wage rate?
b. If those who were laid off by one employer took a day to select a new job, would there always be some unemployed?
c. Would there always be some unfilled vacancies?
d. Would these be equal to each other?
e. What would happen to the number of job seekers and to the number of vacancies if the top five numbers on the roulette wheels were erased?
f. What would happen if all the numbers had been increased by 5?
g. The change from day to day in the totals of the fifty firms, with an unchanged roulette wheel, and the change from day to day when the roulette wheel is changed are two different kinds of changes. Which is consistent with the independent additive random fluctuations?
h. Which would correspond to a correlated decrease in general aggregate market demand for goods?
i. What could cause a general aggregate decrease?
j. How quickly do you think a person would detect a general demand change?
k. What does all this have to do with the real world?

29   "Unemployment is a wonderful privilege. Without it we would all be slaves to tyrants."
a. Can you interpret this "ridiculous" statement so as to make it not ridiculous. (Hint: There is no unemployment in the military. There is reputed to be none in Russia. Distinguish among the factors that shift demands, those that make job information costly, and the losses of

wealth consequent to those demand shifts and costliness of job information.)

b. Would you prefer to live in a community in which unemployment is forbidden? Why? (Later we shall analyze ways of reducing unemployment without forbidding it.)

30    Is the analysis of this chapter consistent with the fact that unemployment among Negroes has become higher than among whites? Does it explain the level of employment at "full employment" or the massive changes in the unemployment rate?

31    When requesting a Congressional investigation into the methods, charges, and quality of services of private employment agencies, Mr. Abel, president of the United Steelworkers of America said, "A man or woman should not have to pay—often a large sum—for the privilege of obtaining a job." He also asserted that society and government had an obligation to make it possible for "every willing and able individual to work at or near his highest skill." Evaluate those remarks in the light of economic analysis.

# 21

## Labor Market Restrictions

As we have seen, buyers and sellers in markets often seek to restrict other people from the market as competitors. And the buyers and sellers of labor services are no exception. Now labor markets will be analyzed in an effort to detect the constraints that work to change wages from the open-market levels.

## Employee-Employer Bargaining Power

First, we explore a fallacious idea. Restrictions on the open market are often advocated as a means of protecting the employee from the superior bargaining power of the employer. Proponents of such restrictions usually say that individual workers have limited bargaining power and hence are helpless against the powerful employer. An employee, acting alone, can readily be replaced if he asks for higher pay; his alternatives are limited. Employees are urged to unite in group action to prevent the employer from playing one against the other. To further protect the laborer minimum-wage, fair-employment, and working-condition laws are proposed.

Whatever one's impression about the deserts of employees relative to employers, the fact is that the price *anyone* can get is limited by the offers made to him by potential buyers. General Motors is also limited. What, for example, limits its ability to keep wages down? The answer is that if General Motors offers less pay than other employers, it will get fewer employees. Any employee can get a salary that is at least as high as his services are worth to some other employer.

The authors are employees of the state of California. Any time we feel like it, we can quit and take jobs elsewhere. That is what "forces" the state to pay as much as it does. That it is willing to do so means that our services are worth at least that much to the purchaser. What "bargaining power" may mean, therefore, is simply the highest salary one can get from *other* jobs. If that is a great deal less than he is now getting, the employee will be reluctant to press for higher wages and may even accept some impositions rather than quit. It may be said that the employer who loses an employee loses only one employee while the employee who loses his job loses his entire source of income. In fact, the employee does not lose his entire source of income; he loses the premium he was getting in his former job over the next best alternative adjusted for moving and job-exploration costs. Of course, if the employee quits, his losses can be greater than those imposed on the employer; but such a comparison is totally irrelevant. Employers hire employees because the employer gains by doing so, not because the employee gains less or gains more.

Do not mistake the purpose of the preceding remarks. They are not anti-labor, antiemployer, or antiunion; they are anticonfusion.

Restrictions on Open Markets for Labor

Minimum-Wage Laws

Minimum-wage laws prohibit employment at less than some stated wage per hour. Currently the minimum legal wage rates vary among the several states that have such laws. Federal law specifies currently that the minimum wage shall be $1.60 an hour.[1] The implication is that a minimum wage rate above the current market rate will reduce employment. At the minimum legal wage rate the quantity of labor demanded will be less than the quantity of labor services supplied—if the minimum wage is above the open-market wage level.[2]

[1] Current federal minimum wage law specifies $1.60 per hour as the minimum. Several exceptions are permitted. Among the major ones are motion-picture theater workers, highly seasonal amusement area workers, employees in small firms (less than $500,000 in annual sales), restaurant employees receiving a substantial portion of their income in tips, agricultural employees who would have a lower minimum ($1.00) and employees of educational institutions, and summer work by college students. It is a challenging problem to explain why these exceptions are granted if the effects of the law are desirable.

[2] Except possibly in a "monopsonistic" market, in which the employer is such a significant part of the total demand that to increase employees he must offer higher wages for new *and* old employees. The graph shows a rising labor-supply curve, *WW*, to the firm. The marginal-wage-cost curve *MWC*, the height of which shows the increase in the *total wage bill* for one more employee, lies above the average-wage curve, *WW*, because the higher wage for the new employee must also be paid to all the employees. The intersection of the demand curve, *DD*, with the marginal-cost-of-labor curve, *MWC*, indicates the wealth-maximizing employment, $E_0$, at which the wages paid each person is $W_0$, indicated by the average wage curve, *WW*. To hire one more employee would increase total costs by the height of the *MWC* curve but would yield a marginal product indicated by the demand curve, *DD*.

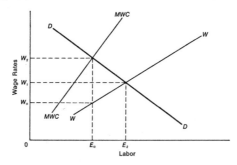

If now a minimum uniform wage is imposed at $W_1$, the employer would be able to hire as many employees as he wished at a *constant* wage rate out to the intersection of the horizontal line $W_1$ with the curve *WW*. Each extra employee (out to that limit) would increase his total wage bill only by the wages paid that new employee; it would not increase the wages paid those already being employed by this firm. The marginal cost of more labor is therefore *equal* to the constant average uniform wage already paid each employee. It would pay the employer to hire employees out to where the horizontal wage line, $W_1$, intersected the demand for labor curve, *DD*. In the illustrated case, this employment rate at the higher constant wage $W_1$ is greater than with a rising wage for successive employees (which higher wage must also be paid to existing employees). Both

Some of those who cannot get jobs because of prohibitions on their seeking work at lower wages than those being paid incumbent workers, can and do resort to working as private, independent contractors to their former employer, taking a lower income by means of a low contract price rather than a reduced wage rate. For example, a person seeking a job as a taxi or a truck driver, at the stipulated rate of, say, $100 a week, could rent a vehicle from his employer and drive as an independent subcontractor, or independent driver. He can cut his wages below $100 by renting the taxi from his "employer" for a weekly fee of, say, $20 a week *above* the free-market car rentals (a sort of secret rebate).

Why do we have minimum-wage laws if they mean lower income to some workers? Because those who retain their jobs get higher incomes, and this is usually the majority (depending upon the elasticity of demand for that kind of labor). *If* they were formerly earning so little as to qualify for supplementary welfare payments, the number of supplementary payments will be reduced. In effect, the taxes used to pay for the welfare are now collected and distributed via the higher prices of the goods being produced. Although the minimum wage law may, if the above conditions are correct, have the effect of reducing the *number* of people on relief, it increases the *extent* of relief to those pushed into lower-paying alternatives. We wish we knew who are most likely to be disemployed. It has been contended that a majority of that group would be Negroes and teenagers because of the relatively large proportion who have not acquired sufficient training to have sufficiently high productivity. If so, then our minimum wage law strikes hardest at the poorest Negroes and teenagers.[3]

### Immigration Restrictions

Laborers can seek to limit entry into their market via immigration laws; this has been done in the United States since the mid-nineteenth century. While it is "impolitic" to admit a desire to create barriers against competition from one's fellow "Americans," it is ancient practice to bar entry to "foreigners."

---

the wage rate and the employment rate are made greater by imposing a *uniform*, constant wage.

So far so good. But there are three, often overlooked, factors to consider. First, the higher wage rate will raise total costs of operation for the firms; output will be reduced as price must be raised and, with that, employment will be reduced. Second, employers faced with a rising supply curve for labor are often able to confine the higher wage only to the new employee: the old employee has no better option in any event, whether or not the new employee is hired; special fringe benefits or job classifications permit differential pricing without requiring uniform wages for all employees. Third, it is an empirical fact that extremely few employers are large enough relative to the market from which they draw labor to have significant long-time effects on wages by individually varying their rates of employment. Over a longer period, the flow of workers from other employers and areas makes this case of little significance.

[3] To the extent this is true, it follows that since the minimum wage laws are not very effective for household help, a large portion of which is provided by Negro women, the law hits harder at Negro men than women, thereby making more difficult the task of preserving a strong paternal family head.

Also many *products* of foreign workers have been excluded; the use of "pauper labor" abroad has been a persistent (but fallacious) argument of American high-tariff proponents (both employers and employees).

Equal Pay for Equal Work

Wage differences exist among different occupations and even within the same occupation. In some instances, the differences reflect nonpecuniary factors. There are equalizing or compensating differences in wages. As we shall see, compensating differences are not always welcomed. One of the classic methods of trying to eliminate them is to advocate "equal pay for equal work"—on the presumption that equal work is easy to identify and that nonpecuniary differences among services of employees or employers should not count.

*Proponents of imposed wage uniformities.*    Almost all employees seem to dislike wage differences based upon nonpecuniary differences—"equalizing differences." The "inferior" person dislikes being paid less for the "same" work, even though the wage difference enables him to offset his nonpecuniary "disadvantage." The source of his lower income is not the equalizing wage difference but other people's preferences about the traits that prompt it.

"Superior" people complain about the equalizing difference because it allows "inferior" people to compete for jobs that would otherwise have yielded a still higher wage to superior people. In many jobs where both men and women might do equally well in a pecuniary sense, men usually are hired because of employer preference for male employees. But that preference is in part overcome with lower-wage competition by women. Rather than try to prohibit women from access to these jobs in order to preserve the jobs for men, the men will advocate "equal pay for equal work"—at, of course, the wages now being paid to the men. Men can profess to be doing this for the benefit of women. Whatever the motivation, the effect is to protect men's jobs by reducing opportunity for women to replace men by taking a lower salary.

This analysis extends even to geographical differences in pay. Wages for the same kind of labor are lower in the South than in the North. Also, wages are lower in Puerto Rico than in the United States. How can a northern employee protect his wage level from the competition of lower-wage southern labor? And how can a laborer in the United States protect his job (and higher wage rate) from Puerto Rican labor? One device would be to advocate "equal pay for equal work" in the United States, *including* Puerto Rico, by legislating minimum wages higher than the prevailing level in the South and Puerto Rico. It should come as no surprise to learn that in the United States support for minimum-wage laws comes primarily from northerners who profess to be trying to help the poorer southern laborers.

*Opponents of imposed wage uniformities.*    Who can object to equal pay for equal work? First, it is opposed by some people who are less productive in a *nonpecuniary sense* and who understand that their source of market power lies in their accepting a compensating wage difference. Second, employers and their customers might object; but if they do, they will be confessing to a "greedy" desire for more wealth as well as confessing to "prejudice" and discrimination in hiring. A third objection to these laws is that they interfere with freedom of voluntary contract.

### Fair-Employment Laws

If a uniform or minimum-wage law is effective in raising wages, discrimination will be transferred from wage rates to employee types. Fewer "inferior" people will get jobs. Therefore, pressure mounts for "fair-employment laws," prohibiting employers from choosing employees on the basis of any criterion ruled unethical—usually race, creed, age, and sex. These laws probably reduce the extent of observable discrimination among employers. But they are incredibly difficult to enforce. How can one tell whether an employer is hiring as many workers he and his customers consider "inferior" as he would if he really didn't think them "inferior"? Furthermore, the employer will be even more reluctant to observe the spirit of the law when he knows it will be more difficult to fire those whose services are unsatisfactory.

Fair-employment laws impose burdens on some employees. If a class of people want to work together, they are forbidden to do so by the fair-employment laws. If Armenians prefer to work with Armenians, or Catholics with Catholics, or a Negro with Negroes, or a Mormon with Mormons, these laws make that illegal, for the employer would be susceptible to legal prosecution for "discrimination."

### The Strike as a Basis of Union Power

It is a tribute to the intelligence and economic acumen of union leaders that they fought hard for the right to use the strike and that they insist the right to strike effectively is crucial to a strong and effective union. It is a tribute to their political skill that they concealed their real purposes behind the facade of "equating bargaining power" as a means of protecting the standard of "labor's" wages in America. It would not be a tribute to the intelligence of the reader to let that distinction pass unnoticed. Therefore, we shall apply economic analysis to the role of the union in affecting wages and employment allocation.

*Legislation concerning unions and strikes.* In England and in France, since the French Revolution, labor or trade unions were prohibited as "conspiracies" to modify market negotiations. They threatened violence against other laborers who undercut their desired higher wages. Although the threat of violence via the strike was basically what anticonspiracy laws aimed to stop, they tried to do it by abolishing the right to form a union—which is a very different thing from a strike. To unite voluntarily is defined as a right of free men, in most concepts of freedom. Hence, the anticonspiracy laws were opposed both by employees who have their eyes on the right to strike and by people who had their eyes on the ideal of freedom. By 1830, the English anticonspiracy laws had been repealed *and* the right to strike tacitly granted—with the forlorn hope that no violence or coercion would ensue.

The right to strike has had its subsequent ups and downs. At times, it was prohibited as an interference with a nonstriker's freedom of access to labor markets. Even when legalized, it has sometimes been tolerated only if strikers did not interfere with nonunion people who continued to work at less than the wages demanded by the strikers. Violence was almost inevitable if nonunion employees tried to cross the picket line. Police have at times permitted pickets to block entry and have refused to help nonunion employees cross the line, because that would mean a breach of the peace. At other times they have protected the nonstrikers.

Today some countries (Russia and Spain, to name but two) prohibit strikes; anyone can quit his job, or the whole group can quit. In other countries, tolerance ranges from legal restrictions against any interference with nonstriking employees and job seekers to legal support of the strikers by preventing strike breakers from working.

Congress, in the Clayton Act of 1914, intended to restrict judiciary power to use antimonopoly laws and "restraint-of-trade" injunctions against certain types of union activities, including the strike. In 1932, the Norris-LaGuardia Act more effectively restricted the judiciary's power to prevent unions from engaging in strikes, picketing, and certain types of boycotts. But subsequently, the Taft-Hartley Act of 1947 permitted the President to prohibit any strike that would create what he considers to be a "national emergency." Section 14-b of that act permitted states to ban union shops. Approximately twenty states have passed such so-called "right-to-work" (without joining a union) laws. Such laws do not, in logic, necessarily increase the workers' freedom or range of choice. For example, if some employer and all his employees want to have a union shop, the state "right-to-work" law would prevent it. On the other hand, one group of employees cannot force other employees to join a union if the employer or his other employees do not want a union shop.

*Compulsory arbitration.*   To prevent strikes or settle grievances the employer and union, if unable to resolve a dispute, sometimes hire an outsider to suggest terms that might be mutually acceptable, though neither party necessarily agrees to accept the terms. The outside mediator may be a private specialist, a government employee, or a disinterested person such as a university president. Presently, no law requires employers and unions to submit disputes to an arbitrator for a binding settlement, but about 90 percent of labor contracts provide for arbitration of grievances.

Some people favor compulsory arbitration by a governmental agency. Whether the results would be more like those that would prevail in a situation with open markets for labor or would result in greater market restriction is impossible to say. Often is it thought that wage and work conditions can be most sensibly determined by the "ability" of an employer to pay—as judged by his income, the cost of living, or the change in productivity. None of these proposed forms of arbitration would reproduce the free market's wage and work conditions. But, of course, that is precisely what the union is trying to avoid by its threat to strike.

### Maintenance of Effective Strike Power

Unions lose power as fewer of the existing employees join the union, for they may refuse to join in a strike. A way of overcoming this latent weakness is to insist on a "union shop," wherein all employees must become union members. Furthermore, all employees with a given skill should belong to the same union. If two unions represented, say, musicians, the two groups would try to dominate each other; and the employer could play one against the other—just as he lets one employee bid against another in the free market, and also just as each employee lets one potential employer bid against the other in a free market. The single bargaining agent and the union shop then become the "silent" rallying cry for unions.

Once the power to strike effectively is sanctioned, better working conditions can be sought for *some* members of the striking unions—better than if other people were free to compete in the same market. Higher wages, shorter hours, better working conditions, and increased job security are ways in which *some* union members can increase their wealth and utility.

However, the fact that union bargaining is associated with increases in wages is not conclusive evidence that it achieves higher wages than are obtained in a free market. Suppose, for instance, that a wage contract were signed two years ago for specified wage rates, and since that time wages in general have risen by 15 percent. The employer is ready to grant a pay raise of 15 percent. In fact, he may be eager to do so in order to retain, as well as improve, his work force in the face of better wages elsewhere. Union officials, however, might demand a 20 percent increase. After a ritual of negotiation and bargaining, the terms come out to be 15 percent; and the union claims it has raised wages. However, neither the employer nor the union sets the wage rate; instead, both accept, adopt, or adjust to wages in the free market—the employer offering that amount because he must in order to get employees, and the union negotiators accepting it unless they are prepared to face a loss of job opportunities from this employer. In the absence of a union, the wages would have risen anyway—maybe even earlier, since employer and employee had to wait for a formal union-contract negotiation.

Some people say that under present conditions the power of a union to strike effectively is tantamount to closing the market to competition, and that therefore the concept of free collective bargaining is misleading in the sense that it does not permit society a choice among alternative sources of production; nonunion labor is excluded and labor markets are restricted. Given the reduction of the competitive market, compulsory arbitration is viewed as a replacement of one form of closed market control by another form of closed market control—compulsory arbitration.

### Unions and Wage Rates

Have unions affected wages and working conditions? Certainly they have affected working conditions, insofar as a union bargaining agent will help settle grievances more efficiently than the industrial-relations officer for the company. As for wages, possibly a vast majority of people would assert that unions are necessary if wages are to be kept at a "reasonable" level, and that unions have succeeded in raising wages.

Surveys indicate a large difference in effects among unions. Some unions have been able to raise wage rates substantially above the open-market level (though not necessarily able to maintain the difference for more than a few years). Many appear to have had no effect on wage rates. The best estimates are that the effect of unionism on the average wage of union workers compared with the average wage of nonunion workers has been at least 10 percent, and probably not over 15 percent.[4] Some unions have had much greater effect—for example the wages of coal miners were estimated to be about 50 percent higher. Probably in the 1920s when unions were less widespread they may have increased wages as much as 20 percent. There is some evidence that after World War II the unions' effect diminished.

### How to Raise Wage Rates

How can unions raise wage rates? Our economic analysis (graphed in Figure 21–1), suggests three ways: (1) raise demand; (2) reduce supply; (3) raise wage rates directly.

1. While there have been a few cases of unions seeking to show employers how to use labor more efficiently and raise demand through lower prices, there is little evidence of extensive significant success.

2. Supply may be reduced by restricting entry to the labor market. As a result of a reduced supply in the market, wages are raised by competitive bidding among employers.

3. Wages may be arbitrarily raised as a result of strike threat, leaving the employer and union with the task of rationing out the jobs among applicants at the higher wage.

Some unions use one and some use all tactics. The coal miners used the last, and then had the problem of deciding which miners got the available jobs. The displaced had to take jobs which they formerly refused to accept.

Restricting entry to the labor market is a method used effectively by seamen, barbers, plumbers, teachers, electricians, projectionists, teamsters, linotypers, and butchers, to name a few.

When unions are effective in controlling market competition so as to put wages higher than they would be in a free market, who gains and who loses?

---

[4]See H. G. Lewis, *Unions and Relative Wages in the United States* (Chicago: University of Chicago Press, 1963).

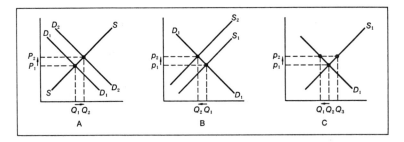

Figure 21-1
Alternative Means of Affecting Wage Rates and Employment

Panel A shows that an increase in demand will increase wage rates from $p_1$ to $p_2$ and employment from $Q_1$ to $Q_2$. Panel B shows that a decrease in supply will increase wage rates but not employment. Problem is how to exclude some people from the market, in order to reduce supply. Immigration restrictions, licensing, entry qualifications are some of the means utilized. Since those to be excluded will oppose restrictions, it's clever to reduce supply by restricting potential new entrants to this labor market. Panel C shows that an arbitrarily higher negotiated wage rate without a change in demand or supply will leave a group of displaced workers whose presence may be sufficiently strong to restrain possibility of pushing up wage rates. Problem is how to prevent new entrants and displaced workers from undercutting the agreed-upon wage rate. Jobs can be rationed or shared by spreading reduced work over all members, as the musicians' union does.

Usually it is claimed that the gains come out of the employers' profits. But, according to economic analysis, the consequences are spread more widely. Some employers who cannot survive at the new higher costs sell their assets at correspondingly lower prices or take a write-down in the value of their assets. Output diminishes until supply is small enough to raise prices to cover the higher wage costs, or a growing industry does not grow quite so much. People who would have been employed had wages not been raised work elsewhere with smaller incomes. Output of products of the higher-wage labor is smaller, and output of other goods is larger. The labor transferred to the other good would have produced a greater value of output in the first good if all labor could compete freely for highest-valued markets.

Nonwage Rationing of Employment

When any group succeeds in getting a higher wage than the open-market level, the number of qualified job applicants will, by definition of an open market, exceed the number of jobs available at that wage rate.[5] The jobs must be rationed on some nonwage criterion. This task is thrust on the union and the employer. A common procedure is to use probationary union members for temporary and seasonal jobs; when demand falls, they will be the first to go.

[5] See footnote 2, page 508.

The use of apprentices and probationary members, whatever its other purposes, serves as an employment-rationing device protecting senior members. If the reduction in employment is particularly severe, so that some "seniority" men also are without jobs, explicit work sharing is likely to emerge, with limitations on the number of hours a week any one person can have. Compulsory attendance at frequent union meetings as a condition of good standing will help to reduce "excessive membership," because the hope of getting a job is less of an incentive to payment of dues and attendance at meetings than is keeping a present job. In time, some of the "hopefuls" will drop out, thus reducing explicit unemployment in this union.

Jobs may be rationed through restriction of union entry (through larger initiation fees and more rigid standards: color, age, personality, sex, education, experience, probationary membership periods). Unethical job-seeking conduct prejudicial to the senior employed members of the union (whether it be the American Medical Association, the American Bar Association, the teamsters, or the longshoremen) can warrant expulsions; thus, advertising or price cutting is unethical conduct. Probationary membership periods also help to inculcate a sense of "proper" conduct and to weed out those who are prone to violate the standards. They also restrict entry into the union. One publicized complementary reason for these restrictions is protection of the employer and consumer from shoddy work.

Pervasive and creative of social conflict is the control of entry to occupations on the basis of color. Today, a person who wants to become a carpenter, plumber, electrician, studio projectionist, mason, plasterer, to name only a few examples, cannot enter the occupation of his choice merely by joining the union. He must first obtain admission to the union as an apprentice. In some instances, he must first be nominated by three members in good standing, in the fashion of entry to a country club. Negroes have long been excluded from many unions. Even though a union charter states there is to be no discrimination, some criterion must be used to ration entrants as long as entry is not open to all who wish to join and work at existing wages.

Recent Negro demonstrations and replies by union officials have elicited irrefutable evidence of union discrimination by color. Union officials have promised to try to change the situation; but substantial changes probably cannot be made quickly. Union locals make their own decisions about admissions; and, as long as union membership is limited, discrimination is necessary in deciding who shall be admitted. The only question is what form of competition shall be weighted in granting membership—which returns us to the earlier discussion of principles of rationing when open-market pecuniary offers are not allowed as a competitive device to every potential employee and employer.

If the union is strong enough, it can impose work rules, known as "featherbedding," whereby an employer must employ laborers whether or not he wants them. Teachers decry the use of television; hod carriers once refused to carry premixed concrete; typesetters require newspapers to set duplicate type if preset type forms are submitted by advertisers; building codes specify unnecessarily expensive labor-using techniques; standby local musicians must be hired when visiting touring orchestras perform locally. All are legal, and all rest on the monopoly power deriving from the power to strike effectively. The railroads have had perhaps the most publicized featherbedding provisions; and this should not be surprising, because the railroads were themselves in a *legal* monopoly position. The companies had a protected income. In effect, higher wages were paid out of the monopoly-rent potential. However, the growth of competition from trucks and airplanes has bankrupt several railroads. Threatened with complete loss of wealth, the railroad owners won court prohibition against the unions striking for such featherbedding contracts.

### Monopoly-Rent Acquisition and Disposition

Restriction on entry into the union may be so severe that death, retirement, and normal attrition will reduce the membership. Entry might be completely closed for years (as with longshoremen's unions). If unions can maintain the restriction on entry, employers will bid up the wages of the union workers.

Limited membership in the union with higher than free-market wage rates permits "unusual" behavior. If the union agent or officer can keep wages *down*, the available workers must be rationed to the competing employers—who, at the repressed (although above free-market) wage, want more workers than are available. If the wage rate would have been $5 an hour under the contrived scarcity, and if the agent can hold the wages to $4 an hour, then the employer would be prepared to pay an additional $1 per hour per worker to get more employees, perhaps to the person responsible for assigning workers to various jobs. The union agent can demand or accept payments from the favored employer. In effect, the cost is just as high to the employer, but it is paid not entirely in the form of wages to the workers. Reluctant employers can be penalized by not getting many employees.

Trustee controls typically imposed on banks have not been applied as strongly to union officers. An especially notorious form of monopoly reward to the union officers (for example, Teamsters Union officers) comes as a result of their management of union funds for pensions, health, and recreation. These funds are invested and used to buy insurance policies. Frequently the officers make loans at lower than normal rates of interest; the borrower pays the difference to the union officers in the form of special salaries, commissions, or favors.

Considerations of equity and morality of the "sharing" by union officials are not simple. The union organizers can say that they developed, directed, organized, and accomplished the closed-market monopoly for the union. Why shouldn't they be rewarded with larger salaries, expense accounts, vacation resorts, and homes than the union members, who really had little to do with the development of the organization—in fact, no more than the employees of a successful businessman who builds a great enterprise? Economics gives no ethical criteria by which to judge this. It merely "explains."

*Utilization of closed-monopoly power.* Employers are quick to exploit opportunities inherent in the contrived labor monopoly. Some employers will propose to pay the union a special reward if it will withhold workers from competitor firms. If the output of competitors is reduced, the favored firm will be able to command higher prices for its services. (James Hoffa, the Teamster Union president, used this tactic.) The increased profit, or "monopoly rent" (obtained by restricting market access to competitors), can be shared among the owners of the protected firm, its workers, and even the union members, if adequate payment is made to the union. This form of agreement is known as a "sweetheart" contract. Whether it is first suggested by the employer or by the union official is immaterial; nor is it important whether the union officials or members get the monopoly rent.

*Difficulty of maintaining long-lasting monopoly rent.* The right to exclude competitors from the market does not give one unbridled economic power. Competition facing a union carpenter, for example, cannot be excluded merely by prohibiting nonunion carpenters from offering services to *his* employer. Other employers will hire nonunion carpenters and sell their products at lower prices. Even if all carpenters joined forces and forced all employers of carpenters to hire only the members of the carpenters' union, product competition in the market would be effective. Plaster, steel, cement, glass, and other building materials can partially displace carpenters. Even doctors' attempts to raise fees are partly restrained by the availability of brand or proprietary drugs, advice of friends, Christian Science, do-it-yourself care, faith healers, etc. As any organization—be it a business firm, union, or professional group—acquires greater power to restrict competitors from the market and thus make effective the higher prices it wants for its services, the rest of the society is more likely to object to such use of power. Whether it is objecting primarily to the higher prices or to the denial of freedom of others to compete in the market or to the interference with production during strikes is an open question.

Some people object to the interference with the right of individuals to seek jobs in the open market. They believe that the participation in voluntary market transactions should not be prevented by anyone, let alone one's direct competitors. These critics do not object to unions as voluntary associations of employees for collective negotiation with employers, but they do object to the strike as a coercive method of controlling access to the market. It is not clear whether these critics are aware to what extent a union would lose power if strikes were prohibited. Unions could still exist and negotiate with employers, but their power to get working conditions above the free-market level, by preventing access to the market for jobs, would be reduced. When the President of the United States says that unions are basic institutions in a free society, the relevant question is still to be faced: "With what kinds of power over access to the market for jobs?" And on that issue reasonable, "humanitarian" men differ.

What is the difference between a labor union that keeps nonunion workers from working at wages less than those sought by the union, and a medical profession which prevents a free market for medical services? The differences are that the medical profession has *more successfully* defended its actions not in the name of higher wages, but in the name of higher quality of medical service. That it also enables doctors to get higher wages is obvious, and presumably not irrelevant. The second difference is that the medical profession does not have to rely on strikes and intimidation against competitors who would sell services at "substandard" prices; instead, it has obtained a licensing law, and, rather than strike against any seller or buyer of "substandard" service at "substandard" wages, it merely telephones the government to send a policeman and restrain the competitor. If labor unions could get laws passed prohibiting the sale of workers' services by anyone except a "licensed" (union) person, then, by controlling the licensing, the union could keep the supply small and wages higher.

Until the union can call upon the state to enforce the exclusion of nonunion members from the particular job market, the union will probably continue with its procedure of threats and intimidation of nonunion members. Were the public police force available, gangsters and hoodlums—the specialists in intimidation—would be of less value. Then union officials would all be as free of the "undesirable elements" and as respectable as are the officers of medical and legal associations and public utilities.

*Union monopoly versus employer monopoly.*    Union monopoly power is often said to be necessary to match the monopoly power of industry. This is a superficially plausible, but invalid, generalization. Consider the steel industry, which is often called a "monopoly." The steel industry is a group of independently owned firms—just as a union is a group of independent workers. The firms are "price-searchers"; consequently, their process of search for the wealth-maximizing price contains all the facade of "price-setting and administering," though, as we have seen, open-market demand and supply conditions control the price that will maximize wealth of the sellers. The union is also a "price-searcher"; for it, too, is desirous of seeking wage rates that will give its employed members a higher income. Yet there is a fundamental difference in that access to the market is open to existing and to new steel companies. Under the law only *one* union can exist for any class of employees. Other unions may try to take its place, but only *one* is permitted to exist as the "exclusive" bargaining agent. In this one crucial difference lies the error of thinking that a group of price-searching employers who have joined together for negotiation with the union constitutes a "monopoly," which requires a countervailing union monopoly. Not even for purposes of negotiating with a common "antagonist" is it possible for the steel companies to avoid open-market competition. The industry simply is not a closed monopoly. It is an open monopoly. This bilateral-monopoly-bargaining thesis is empty unless the employer is a closed monopoly.

*Public utilities are closed monopolies.*    When faced with union strikes, public utilities can, *at first*, more easily accede to union demands since they can draw on monopoly-rent power. The regulatory commission can allow the public utility to raise its rate to offset higher wage costs. True, sales will be smaller with higher rates, but the wealth of the utility will not necessarily suffer, since the rates initially were below the wealth-maximizing level. The monopoly rent derived *via* the public utility's protected position is transferred to the utility employees.

Closed Monopsony: Buyers Close a
Market to Other Buyers

Monopsony is analogous to monopoly, except that it describes the *buyer's* side of the market. Its derivation is "single buyer." The preceding discussion in this chapter focused on means whereby labor *sellers* (employees) sought to close the market to their competitors. And in Chapter 18 the cases of collusion all involved sellers. But sellers are not alone in their efforts to restrict market competition. The buyers, particularly employers as buyers of labor, are anxious to close the market to other employers of labor in an effort to keep wages low. They have had some spectacular successes, many of which have not been recognized for what they are. Some of the successes have been regarded as socially desirable. The most public attention is often drawn to the relatively ineffective cases of attempts to lower wages below open market rates.

For example, when asked to name cases in which employers "ganged up" on employees, people usually talk about "yellow-dog" contracts and "sweatshop operators," "child-labor" employers, and "company stores." A "yellow-dog" employment contract was one in which the employee had to agree not to enter a union. Sweatshops were businesses that paid low wages. (But lower than what? If lower than paid by other employers, why didn't the employees work elsewhere where wages were higher?) Child labor is not very productive labor and will therefore get less. However much we may decry it, the fact remains that it does not consist of paying people less than they are worth as employees. This of course does not imply that child labor is good. The general objection is that since children have such low productivity they ought to be in school learning how to be more productive. But a hundred or so years ago, the productivity of children was not that much below unskilled adult labor to make child labor so relatively unrewarding. Child labor reflects a very poor society, relative to modern standards. The decrease in child labor in the past fifty years in the United States has been almost entirely a consequence of the shift from agricultural to industrial employment. The rate of child labor on farms has not decreased much. It's the decline in the amount of agricultural labor relative to non-agricultural employment that has produced the overall decrease in child labor in the population as a whole.

Company stores were owned by the employer, who paid his employees in credit good only for purchases at a company store. The prices in the company stores were higher than elsewhere so the employee got a lower real wage. But why would an employee work at such places if the net wage was lower than that available elsewhere? Why wouldn't the employer simply pay lower wages and abandon this inefficient, more expensive roundabout means of paying lower wages. Were both employers and employees stupid? The answer is simple. The *employee* knew what he was doing. He was cutting a *legal* minimum wage rate. For example, if the minimum payable wage is $1.60 an hour and if the open market wage is $1.00 for this type of labor, the laborer, rather than go unemployed, could agree to work for $1.60 on the condition that he spend his earnings at the company store, where he would pay high prices. In effect, he would net only about $1.00 an hour. Such was the reason for the payment of wages via credit at company stores. As those minimum wage laws gradually were abandoned and as wages in the open market gradually rose above the obsolete minimum wages, the company store wage system was abandoned.

We turn now to some cases of very effective collusive action by *employers* in restricting wages to below open-market levels by closing the market to other employers. We call them important because they affect *over half* the young men in the entire labor force of the United States!

### Hospital Interns

All the states require licensing by the American Medical Association or its members before a person is admitted to medical practice. Membership in a medical association is required if a doctor is to realize the greater income available from practice in a first-class hospital (other than at a medical school). Now suppose that the association were to restrain the hospitals from paying more than $400 a month for interns, whereas with open competition among hospitals the rate would be higher—say, $600 a month. Any hospital that violated the agreement could be punished by having its "class-A" certification withdrawn. The power to *enforce* the price agreement is now established. The gains from secret violation are small relative to the possible punishment, and violators will very likely be detected.

The hazards and obstacles have been conquered. All the buyers (class-A hospitals) of this service (interns) are forced into the agreement. The organization (the American Medical Association) wielding the power to enforce the price collusion was formed not simply to keep interns' wages down, but for other more valuable purposes, so that denial of membership as a doctor or surgeon means a greater loss of wealth than can be gained by violating the intern wage agreement. Persuasion of recalcitrants or secret violators to stop violations is made effective by the laws giving the organization control of certification of hospitals and licensing of doctors *and* of even allocating the interns to hospitals (since the wage is not high enough to ration out the supply).

One conclusion stands out: It is sufficient to get the power of the *law* on the side of the collusive organization so that persons who do not agree to abide by the price collusion can be *legally* prohibited from buying any of the "service" at any price. Without this *legal* constraint, secret violators could go their way, independently taking advantage of the price agreement by paying slightly more than the already low price and getting a larger share.

### College Football Players and the NCAA

An effective collusion is that of colleges to hold down wages of college football players. Not long after intercollegiate football became a substantial source of income to colleges, the best football players received money inducements—hereafter called "wages" in our discussion. Some college administrators opposed all money payments to athletes, because that was professionalism. They believed amateurism had some inherent virtue or that a professional would attend college only to play football. Other administrators, with an eye on the football income, were dismayed that the wage competition among schools was raising costs.

It is easy to see there was a strong inducement for college administrators to curtail wages for the student football players. An agreement among the colleges to pay no wages was reached through the agency of the National Collegiate Athletic Association (NCAA). Not surprisingly, this collusion was violated as colleges switched to athletic fellowships, free room and board, travel to college, sinecures, jobs for relatives, free clothes, etc. These methods of competition were also curtailed under an agreement permitting wages up to $2 an hour; for not all colleges could be induced to refrain from making offers. At identical low offers, the most distinguished colleges would get the best football players. With identical money offers, the incentive was stronger for the less distinguished colleges *in metropolitan areas* (with large potential gate receipts) to resort to covert offers, and they did so—as evidenced by the frequency with which their violations were detected and punished. Choosing from hundreds of examples, two California colleges, U.C.L.A. and U.S.C., were caught violating the NCAA code. They were assessed $100,000 fines and prohibited from playing in post-season (the most profitable) Bowl games. Even the tennis, basketball, track, and baseball teams—members of which had received no "unethical" payments—also were banned from national tournaments.

Why did the colleges agree to pay fines and accept the punishment? How could the collusion to restrict wages survive in the face of the great advantages of "cheating," especially when colleges that stayed outside the agreement could offer just slightly higher wages than the rest were maintaining? After all, if television and radio networks tried to suppress performers' wages, other networks could profitably be organized to take advantage of the reduced wages. Somehow newcomers must be induced to agree to the terms of the collusive agreement as a condition of operating at all. The National Professional Football League tried to keep wages low but soon found itself faced with two other leagues that wouldn't abide by its pay scales. Similarly, the National Baseball League was faced with a new American League. Or, to put the question in analytic terms, what rewards of membership in the collusion are greater than the advantages obtainable by not belonging, so that the

threat of membership cancellation can be effective in enforcing the agreement—on the assumption that violations can be detected without prohibitive
detection costs. (The various athletic conferences—all members of the
collusion—hired private detectives and investigators to spy on recruiting
activities of students, coaches, and alumni.)

The answer lies in the fact that all the colleges belonged to the National
Collegiate Athletic Association or to related associations, which supervised
the rules of the games. The NCAA not only is the supreme authority in
assessing fines and punishment, but, more important, it indicated that any
college violating the athletic "code" could find its academic accreditation
threatened. Any college placed on probation or expelled would find it much
more expensive to recruit faculty, and students would be dissuaded from
attending. Even Phi Beta Kappa refused to authorize chapters at colleges that
gave "disproportionate" amounts of money to athletic scholarships, regardless of the academic qualities of the college. The survival of the college could
be threatened.

But we can't stop here. Why don't some colleges that want to hire football
players form their own accreditation group? Why does the present accreditation group have so much power that it can prevent formation of new colleges
with their own accreditation system? A very important reason is that colleges
do not operate on a self-supporting basis. The profits from football are not
enough to offset the losses from the low tuition fees at state or endowed
colleges. A new college could not expect to survive from football profits if it
had to charge competitive tuition to students. No new school could get
subsidies from the state or major philanthropic foundations without recognition by the present accreditation group—which is powerful in influencing the
government and the foundations. We have finally arrived at the source of the
value of membership in the NCAA and related organizations: subsidized
education. Since the value of the subsidy exceeds the potential football
profits, and since control over the subsidy lies partly in the hands of the
NCAA, the wrath of the NCAA can mean some college's life or death. We
emphasize that the NCAA was not created to restrict pay of football players.
It was set up for other purposes, but once its greater value for these other
purposes could be denied to a nonmember, it became an enforcement agency
against certain kinds of competition.

### Employers' Collusion for Professional Athletes

College athletics is small stuff compared to professional sports. Until the rise
of the American Football League as a competitor to the National Football
League, wages paid football players were trivial. In fact the National Football
League draft did not permit its team owners to bid against each other for
players. Players were simply "drafted," and they had to play for whatever
team wanted them.

With the rise of the vigorous American League to compete against the older
National Football League, football players began to get their open-market
price, which sometimes approached $1,000,000 for an outstanding athlete.

For many years the two professional baseball leagues had a compact not to bid against each other for baseball players. That cozy arrangement was possible because entry of a new league was extraordinarily difficult. If a new league arose, any player who signed with it was permanently banned from the two older leagues. Clearly no young player would want to throw away his future prospects. Yet even with all that collusive power, the teams, under enormous incentive to get the better players, managed to offer side rewards to players, and thereby the system of bonuses developed. More recently the baseball teams have returned to a *draft* system whereby the teams do not compete with each other in signing up new players.

There are (as of 1968) two professional basketball leagues competing for basketball players. With the advent of the second league basketball salaries for new players have increased substantially.

### Military Draft

We have saved the most spectacular and "notorious" "collusion by buyers" for the climax—that of the military draft. The United States obtains the bulk of its enlisted men by a "draft." A draftee must work at wages set by Congress—unless he wants to lose valuable citizenship rights. Why does the United States require that young men work at less than market wages, when there is no law that requires them to work as policemen, firemen, astronauts, garbage collectors, generals, admirals, or politicians at less than the open-market competitive wage. It is not true that mercenaries, or volunteers, are less able or less reliable. Nor is it true that "we" save money this way. It lowers *only* the *explicitly* revealed money payments, which is merely a way of saying that we tax young people *in kind*, just as the old French kings drafted labor to build their palaces and roads. And that tax is not included in the money payments of our defense budget. The wrong measure of cost is looked at, since not all the services pass through the market and are costed in money terms. Under the draft, those who do not bear the tax in *kind* are those who are not drafted—the old, the smarter, the "physically handsome" who marry early and have children, and the women. One wonders if that is the intended basis for distributing our defense load.

The fact is that the true costs of the draft are *greater* than if the military forces were obtained without a draft, via explicit money taxes on all who should bear the burden of defense. Without the draft, all who serve would be obtained by market *money* bids for their services—just as airplanes, missiles, munitions and officers and politicians, policemen, firemen, and teachers are obtained. Not only would the true costs of the draft then be revealed but they would literally be *reduced* for any specified military capability. Remember what happened in our five-man economy if the wrong people were drafted into producing the various goods. The total possible output became smaller. And so it is with the draft. The explicit monetary tax bill could be larger than it is now, but the real cost would be smaller.

If the cost of the military were measured by the budgeted expenditures, as it more fully would be without a forced draft, the military would have to pay more attention to the true costs of assignments and to means of providing services. Drastic shifts in combinations of inputs would occur, according to the principles outlined in Chapter 19. At the most obvious level, there would be more reliance on civilian employees to provide food and routine services. Custodial and sanitation work around military camps would be provided by labor cheaper than that of strong young men of greater value as soldiers. Less training in various trades would be given by the military. The turnover rate and new enlistee training costs would be much lower. In short, lower-cost methods would be forced into the open and the true cost thereby reduced. Nothing herein implies that we would have to shift to foreign mercenaries to fight our wars. And claims that it is a person's duty to defend his country are beside the point. (Is it not a "duty" to pay taxes?) The question is what is the best way to defend one's country. Everyone has an obligation to defend his country: but it does not follow that the obligation is to pay the tax *in kind*, which is what those who claim an obligation from *young men only* are really contending. Specialization in achieving military capability is just as sensible as it is for achieving our food, clothing, and domestic police protection.

If the military personnel were obtained by open-market competition, even the explicit money tax bill might *not* be larger. Recent studies made by the Defense department suggest that higher wages would attract more efficient labor, would reduce enlistee training and replacement costs, and would also induce military leaders to substitute more efficient forms of capital for labor. But the military people strongly resist methods that would force them to change their way of life and modify their methods. They are not accustomed to principles of efficient allocation of labor—that is, a market-price system. Under the revised system they would have to give more heed to total costs. Any change of life is difficult, especially if it results only in more efficient methods and provides no gain for those who must revise their way of life. And most politicians find it impossible to believe that the superficial costs they are concerned with—total *budgeted* costs—would be smaller.

Finally, lest it be thought the draft of military personnel is an unfortunate necessity and that the military is somehow so different that our economic theory doesn't apply, let it be noted that the Civil War Army of the North, in which we used a far greater proportion of our young men than in any subsequent war and in which the men fought with unexcelled valor, was *not* a draft army. It was purchased in the open market in the following way: men were "drafted" but every "draftee" had the right to hire someone to take his place, usually done by paying that other person a lump sum. In effect, the draft was a means of *assigning the tax* among the young men; once taxed, one could either pay the amount necessary to buy a substitute or he could work it out in the Army. The point is that those who served did so in the cold calculation of the amount of the tax and of the market value of services. Only the tax was imposed by the draft, not the decision as to who would serve in the military.

Summary

1     Bargaining power is a vacuous concept of little analytical substance.

2     Minimum-wage laws raise wages for some employees, while displaced employees must shift to lower-paying jobs not covered by the laws, or become unemployed. Beneficiaries are those who retain their jobs at the higher wage; higher-paid employees face less competition from services of the lower-cost labor.

3     Immigration restrictions limit labor supply and keep wages higher.

4     Equal-pay-for-equal-work laws help keep "inferior" producers (non-monetary sense) from higher-paid jobs. Equalizing wage differences are prohibited.

5     Fair-employment laws make it illegal for an employer to choose employees on the basis of age, sex, color, race, religion (but do not prohibit employee's choice of employer according to these criteria).

6     The strike is a concerted action by a group of employees to prevent other people from working in specified jobs at wages less than demanded by the strikers. The union's right to strike effectively and close markets to competitors is protected by law and exempted from antimonopoly or unfair-trade laws.

7     Compulsory arbitration would prohibit some strikes and force an employer and a union to agree to terms set by government agencies.

8     The effect of unions on over-all wages is not definitely known. Estimates are that unions on the average have raised wages of their members about 5 to 15 percent above those of nonunion labor.

9     To the extent wages are set above the open-market clearing level, non-pecuniary productivity more strongly influences job allocation. People strong in desired features are not easily underbid by the people who are poorer in personal traits. "Discrimination" increases.

10    Wages set above the open-market clearing level yield a monopoly rent. Union leaders find their control over that rent enhanced to the extent that fringe benefits are utilized.

11    Union closed-market power appears "undesirable" because of the way it is enforced—usually by threatened or actual violence. Other professions with closed markets appear socially correct because laws authorize closing of markets with police force.

12    To the extent unions can close the market to competing labor the union is a closed monopolist. If the employer cannot close the market to *his* competitors he may be an open monopolist. The powers of the two types of monopolies are different.

13    Collusions among buyers have been most effective in the market for special types of labor.

14    The military draft, one of the most effective collusions against sellers, leads to inefficiency and a biased measure of the true cost of the military. It is an implicit tax on young, able-bodied, less educated males.

Questions

1    You are an immigrant. Would you prefer laws insisting on equal pay for equal work, minimum-wage laws, apprentice laws, or strong unions that have been effective in raising wages above the open-market level? Explain.

2    The federal government is taxing and paying for job retraining for those who lose a job.
a. Do you think it should provide an apartment-renovation service for people whose apartments become vacant?
b. What is the difference between the two forms of aid?
c. Why would you support one and not the other, if you would?

3    "Long ago we stated the reason for labor organizations. We said that they were organized out of the necessities of the situation; that a single employee was helpless in dealing with an employer; that he was dependent ordinarily on his daily wage for the maintenance of himself and family; that if the employer refused to pay him the wages that he thought fair, he was nevertheless unable to leave the employer and resist arbitrary and unfair treatment; that a union was essential to give laborers opportunity to deal on an equality with their employer." (Charles Evans Hughes, Chief Justice, Supreme Court of the United States, from the decision in the case of the *United States v. Jones and Laughlin*, 1937.) Evaluate the above propositions for their meaning.

4    "In a society where there has not been an adjustment of wages to the savings of time afforded by the use of new techniques, and where such savings may result in an over-supply of labor, an agreement among laborers to prevent such conditions has a lawful labor objective." (Decision by Superior Court Judge Martin Caughlin, San Bernardino, California, in case of *Orange Belt Chapter of Painting and Decorating Contractors v. AFL-CIO Painters District Council 48*, July 1958.) Suppose the introduction of spray and roller painting methods reduced the amount of man hours in painting a house to 50 percent of its former level.
a. Does the above decision mean that wages should be doubled? Or that the laborers can force the houseowner to hire as many hours of labor with the new technique as with the old?

**b.** What does it mean?

5    As a beginning lawyer, would you benefit if fees for the following were set by the bar association: drawing up someone's will, serving as an executor of an estate, arranging for a divorce?

6    As a summer-job-seeking college student, are your chances of getting a job increased or decreased if the wages you can get in a cannery, summer resort, factory, etc., are set by a union comprised of current full-time employees? Why?

7    As a college-aged baby sitter, would you benefit if an association of baby sitters were organized and a minimum wage of $1.50 an hour enforced? Why?

8    "A man's labor is perishable. If he isn't employed, he loses forever that potential earning. Therefore, labor has a special disadvantage compared to nonhuman goods, which can be stored and used later." Is that correct? (Hint: Suppose labor were storable. What do you suppose would be the effect?)

9    "The higher the legally constrained minimum-wage rate, the greater the amount of unemployment of unskilled workers." Is this correct? Explain.

10    A representative of the Congress of Racial Equality advocated raising the minimum legal wage to $2 an hour in order to help Negroes get higher wages.
a. Would Negroes benefit from a higher minimum wage?
b. Would it reduce or increase discriminatory hiring?

11    A law is passed requiring each employer to provide hospitalization and premature retirement benefits for his employees who have "heart attacks."
a. Who will benefit by such a law?
b. Who will be hurt?
c. Who will pay the costs? (In answering, first consider the same questions if a law were passed requiring employers to pay for all the housing costs of redhaired employees. Explain why if you were a redhead you would be smart to dye your hair black. Similarly, if you had a heart condition, why would you try to keep it a secret? Does the employer pay for these services—in the sense that his wealth is lower as a consequence of the law? If he doesn't, who does?)

12    Some employment contracts provide the employee with the following: paid time off for jury duty, funerals of relatives, voting, sickness, and vacations; free parking space and work clothes; retirement; two weeks' severance pay; seniority rights over new employees; no discharge for union activities; no discharge if job is displaced by new machinery.
a. Suppose you were to offer to work for some employer who did not

give any of these provisions and who insisted on the right to fire or discharge you at any time for any reason whatsoever. Would you consider working for him at the same take-home pay as for the other employer?

b. Would the employer be willing to pay you a higher take-home salary for an employment contract without all those provisions listed earlier?

c. In the light of your answers to the preceding questions, who do you think pays for those fringe benefits listed earlier?

13    The National Teachers Federation, a teachers' union, advocates as a basic proposition a single salary scale—wherein every teacher, regardless of specialty, gets the same salary in his first year of teaching, with salary thereafter tied strictly to years of service. Who would benefit and who would suffer if that were made universal: Men or women? Negroes or whites? Superior or inferior teachers? Mathematics or physical-education teachers?

14    If in some town the minimum wage rate for taxi-driver employees were raised to $5 an hour, what would happen to the ratio of cabs driven by the owners to cabs driven by employees of cab owners? Why?

15    "If an enterprise cannot survive except by paying wages of 75 cents or $1 an hour, I am perfectly willing for it to go out of business. I do not believe that such an enterprise is worth saving at that price. It does more harm than good, socially and economically. It is not an asset; it is a liability. So if this kind of business is killed by a minimum wage of $1.25, I for one will not be sorry." (George Meany, Hearings before Subcommittee on Labor Standards, 86th Congress, 2nd Session, 1960, p. 36 of Part 1 of printed hearings.)

a. How does this statement differ from one that says, "Any person who cannot produce a product worth at least $1.25 an hour should not be allowed to work as an employee"?

b. Explain why Meany did not suggest that a business that paid wages of $5 an hour was an even greater liability to the community?

16    "Technically speaking, any labor union is a monopoly in the limited sense that it eliminates competition between workingmen for the available jobs in a particular plant or industry. After all, all unions are combinations of workingmen to increase, by concerted economic action, their wages, i.e., the price at which the employer will be able to purchase their labor." (Arthur Goldberg, Justice, Supreme Court of the United States, and formerly Secretary of the Department of Labor and counsel for the United Steelworkers; quoted from *AFL-CIO: Labor United*, New York, McGraw-Hill, 1956, p. 157.) Why did he write "*technically speaking*" and "in the *limited* sense"? Is there some other mode of speaking and is there an unlimited sense of monopoly? Does a monopoly (closed or open?) eliminate competition? What does it eliminate and how?

17    "The strike is an attempt to deny some people the ability to sell their services at open-market prices." Explain why this is a true statement. For which people?

**18**    "The union that utilizes or threatens to use the strike is a closed monopoly." If true, does that make unions bad?

19    A union strikes against some employer. The strike is unsuccessful if the employer is able to get sufficient other laborers. In order to prevent his successful operation with these other workers, the union initiates a "boycott," urging the public not to buy this employer's products. If that maneuver is successful, the employer will lose sales and close down, unless he is willing to hire only the union men at the wage they request. Thus, boycotts prevent the employer from profitably employing other workers than those on strike. Sometimes the union will also engage in a secondary strike—against anyone who buys that employer's products. Whether the union is refusing to work for the employer, picketing the employer as a means of urging customers to boycott products made by nonstrikers, or using secondary strikes against any producer who buys this employer's products, the tactics are designed to remove from the open market one particular group of people. Who? Explain.

**20**    In strike or labor-dispute negotiations, the government sometimes appoints an investigating panel composed of representatives from the union, the employers, and the consuming public. Which especially affected group is *not* represented on these panels? Can you explain why?

21    You are the leader of a strong, closed union that has obtained wages above the open-market rate for the union supply of employees.
a. At next contract negotiations, at which it is clear a still higher wage can be obtained in view of increased demand or reduced union supply relative to demand, what incentives are there for you, the union officer, to seek to get that higher wage not in the form of higher explicit money wages for the union members but instead in the form of fringe benefits—such as retirement pensions, medical insurance, vacation resorts, workers' uniforms—which are dispensed and controlled by the union?
b. Would a greater portion of the "wage" being diverted to the control of the union leaders increase the utility of the union leaders? How?
c. Does the income tax on *money* income also produce a "bias" toward nonmonetary fringe benefits?

**22**    Construct the analogue to the preceding problem for a situation in which the state, instead of paying money to students and letting them buy their education, pays the money to the schools and lets them give the education to the students. Does financing schools directly rather than giving money to students to spend for schooling increase the "utility" of school administrators and faculty relative to the students? Which schools? Which faculty members?

**23** "The steelworkers' union and the U.S. Steel Corporation are both monopolies." In terms of the closed and open monopoly distinction, is that correct?

**24** You work for a television manufacturer as a welder, and two unions contend for recognition as the sole bargaining unit for welders. One, a "craft" union, would be composed only of welders; the other, an "industrial" union, would admit all employees who work for television manufacturers.
a. In which type of union do you think you will be able more effectively to raise your wages by imposing apprenticeship conditions and other devices to restrict the number of people who can seek jobs in competition with you?
b. Which union do you think will be more able to impose a wage-rate increase upon the employer without first restricting union membership? Explain why.

**25** The National Association for the Advancement of Colored People contends that the building-trade craft unions (among others) discriminate against Negroes. The national-headquarter officials of each union reply that the local unions in each city are autonomous and determine membership. The charter provides that there will be no discrimination. The unions reply variously that no qualified Negroes have applied, that a new member must be nominated by three members in good standing, that they do have some Negroes, that they use a quota system to ensure that all groups are equally represented, and that the present time, when even the white members are unemployed, is not a feasible time to increase entry rates. Given that the craft union has the power to determine who and how many may join the union, some system of choice is necessary—if the number is to be restricted in order to maintain wages above the open-market level.
a. What criteria for selection do you think should be used and declared defensible? Explain why.
b. Would you recommend a quota system? Why?

**26** "Plumbers' and steamfitters' union local 2 of New York has no Negroes, and 80–95 percent of the members are the sons of existing or former members." News story from *New York Times*, August 2, 1963. What explanation can you offer for this?

**27** a. Labor groups were strong advocates of raising barriers to immigration in the nineteenth century. Employers objected. Why?
b. Labor groups were less enthusiastic for tariffs (taxes on imported goods), but some employers were in favor of them. Why?
c. In what sense do immigration barriers and tariffs make the people of the United States closed monopolists against the rest of the world?

d. Would you therefore advocate abolition of tariffs and immigration restrictions? Why?

28    Walter Reuther, head of the auto workers' union, contends that automobile producers should lower their prices to benefit the public.

a. Why does he not propose that the current tax (tariff) of 12 percent on importation of foreign cars be abolished as a means on increasing domestic supply?

b. Why do you think Reuther wants lower prices for products produced by members of his union?

29    Some employers welcome the growth of powerful unions that will be able to raise wages and control number of employees admitted to the union. Why? In answering, show why some employers would be hurt by the elimination of effective unions (even ignoring the conflict in trying to eliminate the union).

**30**    Laws have been passed designed to prohibit employers from discriminating among potential employees according to race, religion, and, in some instances, age. Why are there no laws prohibiting employees from similarly discriminating among employers for whom they choose to work?

31    "Any craft union that has to resort to the strike to get higher wages is not being operated efficiently. It should instead concentrate on control of apprenticeship rules and admissions in order to assure high-quality, reliable, skilled union members. And it will incidentally thereby achieve its higher wages in a peaceful, democratic way." Explain what the speaker, a highly successful union leader, meant.

32    Is the analysis of this chapter consistent with the fact of high unemployment rates among Negroes in the North? What is the explanation for high unemployment among male Negroes, Puerto Ricans, and Mexicans? (Do not answer "low education," "prejudice," or "immobility" since all of those would imply lower wages, not higher unemployment.)

33    "The National and American Football Leagues have finally gotten together and agreed to have a common draft of college players. The draft will eliminate those utterly ridiculous $600,000 bonuses that were paid to untried muscular meatballs from the college campuses. The peace pact will also put a stop to the alarming movement to tamper with the legal property of other clubs (i.e., bid players away from other leagues). The peace pact is welcome. If the cost is high, a continuation of the warfare would have been costlier." (Sportswriter Arthur Daley, *New York Times*, June 9, 1966.)

"Pete Gogolak, the star American Football League placekicker, said today he thought player salaries would not suffer because of the merger of the two leagues. He said, 'The new players who stood to get big bonuses because of the competition between the two leagues may get hurt, but I think the salaries of the other, older players will remain high.' Gogolak had played out his option with the American League Buffalo Bills and then signed with National League Giants at a salary believed to be $32,000." (News item from *New York Times*, June 9, 1966.)

"The common draft, now agreed to by the two leagues, will drastically cut bonus payments and should appease the colleges who have railed against the in-season solicitation and premature signing of college players attributable to the scramble for talent." (Sportswriter J. M. Sheehan, *New York Times*, June 9, 1966.)

a. To which two of the three writers just quoted would you give a flunking grade in economics. Explain why.

b. If General Electric, Westinghouse, and other electrical companies could get together and have a common draft of graduating engineers, would engineers' salaries suffer? Why?

c. If General Electric, Westinghouse, and other electrical companies could get together and have a common draft of college students at a salary of $100 a month and could compel chosen students to work for them or face jail and loss of citizenship, do you think the draft would be regarded as defensible and in the social interest? Reconcile your answer with the existence of the Air Force, Army, and Navy common draft.

**34**   "An official Defense Department study reported that the elimination of the draft by raising wages to enlistees would cost about $5–$15 billions annually. Therefore the Defense Department in view of that prohibitive cost is recommending continuance of the draft." (News item from *New York Times*, June 1966.)

a. Explain why the first sentence is an incorrect assertion.

b. Would you be willing to assert that raising wages to abolish the draft would *reduce* costs? Why?

35   Minimum wage laws prevent relatively untrained people, especially teenagers and Negroes, from getting jobs. To overcome this the federal government is going to subsidize employers for hiring these less trained people. The rationale is that the workers hired at the minimum legal wage, though not that productive, will learn on the job and in time become productive enough to warrant that wage. In the meantime, the employer, receiving a subsidy of an amount equal to the difference between the worker's productivity and the wage paid the worker, is providing on-the-job education. Show how this amounts to facilitating a privately operated educational system, with choice by students of the private "school" they will attend.

# Interest, Saving, and Investing

Ever since man's fall from grace in the garden of Eden he has wanted more wealth. He has found he can have more by consuming less. How much wealth he will get with his savings depends on the opportunities for converting present income to wealth. Wealth and capital goods include more than inanimate machinery, buildings, fertile land, sheltered harbors, rivers, and good climate. *People* are wealth, too; skills, talents, knowledge, initiative, manners, and customs are part of our capital. To know that the total stock of nonhuman wealth of the United States is about $3,000,000,000,000 is to know the value of just part of our wealth. Because people do not sell themselves like capital goods, even though they sell their services, market valuations of the wealth of people, as productive resources, are not readily available. Another segment of wealth is the stability of our government, reliability of the judicial process, and certainty of property rights. All have evolved from centuries of testing and adaptation and the past endeavors of man. Again, since these services are not marketed, we have no directly observable market values for them.

We spoke of "labor" and "capital" in Chapter 19 as generalized categories of resources. A better classification might have been human and nonhuman resources. People are capital goods. A person is an asset capable of producing future services, and his productive ability results partly from past investment in his training. Every student sacrifices current consumption for more production power (wealth). The knowledge and skills he acquires become embodied in him. A parent can spend current income for his child's education, or he can build a business for him. Either increases the child's capital goods.

The accumulation of wealth in any form is not a happenstance. We turn now to the many factors and forces upon which it depends. Whatever the form in which capital is accumulated, what incentives and economic controls determine the rate of profitable investment (growth of wealth)? First we should see how current income (flow of services) can be converted to wealth (stock of productive resources).

## Means of Converting Current Income into Wealth

A person can save (invest) in several ways. (1) He can *lend* current income for rights to future income (wealth). (2) He can buy fewer perishable goods and more durable goods. Neither of these changes the social totals. What one person gets, someone else gives up. But the third method does change the social total: (3) He can direct current output to *producing* goods that are more efficient for future income than for near-term, present consumption—which is to say he *invests* in making "capital goods." Houses, steel buildings, automobiles, lathes, bridges are usually considered "capital goods," while lettuce, fresh meat, pianos, shoes, and most commodities that are consumed are called "consumer goods." "Consumer goods" are bought by individuals for *nonwealth-augmenting* purposes. It is apparent that a capital good can be a consumers good to one person and a wealth-producing good to another; for example, the pianist uses a piano to increase his wealth and another uses a piano for private pleasure. For some, a house is a consumers good, for others it is a source of monetary income.

### 1. Lending or Borrowing: Bond Markets

Anyone can lend part of today's income for more future income. The lender usually gets a promissory note or a bond as evidence of his claim to future income. He has sold current income for more (future) income.

The borrower may use the funds either to finance current consumption, perhaps a vacation, or to buy capital goods. Saving and lending do not necessarily result in a larger production of wealth; they may result in consumption through a transfer of current income from one person to another. A positive rate of interest will exist if the portion of current income supplied to borrowers is less than the amount demanded at a zero interest rate—which is certainly the case in any normal society. (An "abnormal" one could be one in which the wealth of the world was expected to be reduced next year by some catastrophe.)

### 2. Buying and Selling Capital Goods

Anyone can convert current income to some wealth for himself by using part of his income to buy existing capital goods from someone else. Since we must buy and sell existing goods from each other, these exchanges do not change the social stock of resources.

Because people's circumstances are always changing, there is a constant buying and selling of capital goods. A person saves part of his income and buys some capital goods; at other times he sells some of his wealth for money to buy current consumption—that is, he dissaves. The parents of most college students saved and then sold assets to finance a college education. They may have accumulated wealth by saving money (which is a kind of a capital good) and then exchanged that for bonds or stocks or for a house, building, or land.

The continuing re-allocation of capital goods, money, and current services occurs in the retail markets (money is traded for consumption goods), bond markets (claims to future amounts of money are traded for money now), stock markets (claims to capital goods are traded for money now), and real estate markets (land and buildings are traded for money). All of these markets facilitate the accumulation of capital goods, because the easy revision of asset holdings by exchange will make a person more willing to accumulate any one kind of wealth. If I could never trade a house once I had built it, I would be less likely to build one. Furthermore, prices in these markets reveal information about the relative values of producing various kinds of goods. The principles explained in the example of exchange between the Cuban and Hungarian and the exchange among the five people in our toy economy of Chapter 4 apply here too.

*The interdependence of lending (bond) and the capital-goods (stock market) prices.* Suppose the explicit interest rate in the *lending* market were 5 percent. Suppose also that in the stock market, some stock, expected to yield $10 a year for the indefinite future, were priced at $333, a yield of 3 percent. If you sold the stock and lent $333 at 5 percent in the loan market, you could get $16.65 a year instead of $10. The offer of this stock would lower its price (thereby raising the implicit yield rate in the capital-goods markets); and lending the money in the bond market would lower the explicit rate in the lending market. This "arbitrage" between markets by selling in one and lending (buying bonds) in another brings the yield rates nearer together.

Similar adjustments take place between countries. (1) The higher-interest-rate economy will borrow from the lower-interest-rate economy—as when the United States lends to South Americans. (2) The South American country will sell some of its future-service-yielding goods to the lower-interest-rate country in exchange for current-consumption-yielding goods or resources.

Most changes in prices of common stocks reflect something other than a change in the interest rate. All companies have an uncertain future. For some, things get better and for others worse. The change in fortunes is reflected in changes in stock prices. It is not easy to separate the factors causing deterioration in future income prospects from those causing a rise in the interest rate. Although the two are different in principle, they show their effects in similar ways—reduced prices of stocks. We usually, therefore, study the differences by looking at bond markets, where the future payments are less variable and subject only to the possibility of default. If stock and bond prices fall at the same time, a rise in interest rates is probably the cause. If stock prices fall while bond prices stay steady or rise, the cause is likely to be a deterioration in future income prospects, rather than a rise in the interest rate. The "quality" of the capital goods represented by the common stocks is deteriorating. Regardless of the reason for a drop in stock prices, the effect on capital-goods production is quick.

### 3. Saving and Investing by Production

Production of wealth by diverting present income from current consumption occurs in many ways. We convert fresh milk to cheese, apples to cider, pork to bacon, grain to whiskey, grapes to wine, olives to olive oil. The various goods produced differ in the length of time they can yield service. We can choose steel or wood, concrete or blacktop roads, diamond or metal-tipped record needles, pipelines or trucks.

Be careful of possible confusion. Saving means not consuming all of one's income. This can occur in different ways. We can save or invest in several *forms*—by not consuming all currently produced consumption goods or by devoting part of present income *production* to producers' goods instead of consumers' goods. Hopefully the production of capital goods will be the amount that the public at large wishes to accumulate—a desire that will be revealed by their expenditure patterns. If they exactly match, then saving takes the form entirely of the accumulation of producers' capital goods. If they do not match, serious consequences may follow for the subsequent rate of production of such goods and for employment, depending upon the process of bringing demand and supply into equilibrium. This phenomenon will in part be covered in the other half of the introductory course. Here we lay the groundwork for that analysis.

## Net Productivity of Investment

For a dollar of current consumption sacrificed, more than a dollar of income is often obtainable in the future. That *net* increase is called the *net marginal productivity of investment.* Plant a seed today and next year have more than one seed. This net productivity of investment is "economic" productivity. Profitable investment, directly or indirectly, converts energy, or material, to more desired forms. Capital goods usually require the intermediate step of making a tool or a good that is used later to produce consumption services; this is often called a "roundabout," or "indirect" method of production. Although we are accustomed to seeing future output increased by use of capital goods, we sometimes erroneously conclude that all durable goods or tools are productive of more future income than their current cost. That is not true; it is easy to make durable goods that are worthless for future production. However, obviously wasteful production or investment is usually avoided, so that the capital goods we usually see are those that have proved productive.

*A measure of the net productivity.*   If we invest one unit of a good today and thereby get 1.15 units a year hence, the net gain is .15 units per year. In general for an amount, $A$, invested today, if we obtain a *year later* an amount $A(1 + g)$, we consider $g$ to be the net productivity of investment per year. This is measured in units similar to rate of interest, as an *annual rate* of growth. However, the net productivity of investment ($g$) may be greater or may be less than the interest rate.

We never know in advance what $g$ will be. But nevertheless, almost all of us make investments of one type or another—in education, buildings, cars, and business. We thereby "bet" (by sacrificing current consumption or going into debt to others who lend us current income) that the future product will be sufficiently greater than the present sacrifice; everyone who invests must gamble. His decisions are influenced in part by his estimates of the profitability of investments.

*Profitable investment.*   Profitable investments are those that pay enough in the future to make the investment worthwhile. For example, if the interest rate a year ago had been 5 percent, and you invested $1 with a current payoff of $1.10—your investment would have been profitable; it yielded at the rate of 10 percent.

A profitable investment is one that gives a *net* increase of wealth at a rate, $g$, greater than the interest rate, $i$. In the example, the future wealth value was predicted to be $1.10, with $g$ of 10 percent exceeding the 5 percent interest rate. If that $1.10 were discounted back to value at time of investment, the good into which the $1 was invested would have been immediately revalued to $1.05. A profitable investment is one that (a) immediately raises one's *wealth* by more than the investment now, or which (b) will result in a future wealth increment larger than the amount of investment compounded by the interest rate.

Now we can see how crucial uncertainty is. You may be confident that your investment will in a year result in more than the present investment cost plus the interest even though no one else believes it. One way to test your belief is to make the investment. You may find that within two months other people may become persuaded, so that they bid up the present value of your asset above your cost. That gain in value becomes profits to you. How long you must wait for the value of an investment to be revealed cannot be foretold. It all depends upon how quickly the rest of the community revises its market-expressed valuation.

Do not jump to the conclusion that it is desirable for an investor if the rest of market reacts quickly to his activity. The longer others fail to see what his activity is leading to, the more he can avoid imitative competition from other people.

*Higher rates of investment will reduce g.*    The net marginal productivity of investment, $g$, depends upon many factors. More wealth helps to increase productivity. Our legal institutions, property laws, security of peace, knowledge of laws of nature, availability of markets, and mental talents are also factors. But one that particularly affects the net marginal productivity is the *rate* of investment.

The higher the rate of investment, the lower is the net marginal productivity. Each increase in the investment rate will yield a smaller net product.

A decrease in *net marginal productivity* of investment at higher rates of current investment does *not* necessarily mean there is a shortage of ideas or ways to create more wealth. It means that less and less appropriate resources for investment are being diverted from current consumption to investment and that the old law of diminishing marginal returns is operating. The higher the current *rate* of investment, the more we resort to resources that are less efficient in investment activity. You may recall from Chapter 10 on production that the higher the rate of production of $Y$, the higher the cost. Similarly here; the cost will increase for successive increments in the rate of investment, which is a reverse way of saying that the net marginal gain will be lower at successively higher rates of current investment.

Demand for Investment: The
Profitable Rate of Investment

We can summarize some of the foregoing ideas with Figure 22–1. The investment demand curve *DD* shows, for each interest rate, the most profitable rate
of investment. It indicates the largest rate of investment that people think
(bet) they can make and get on the marginal dollar of investment, a rate of
return, *g*, that is at least equal to the interest rate. The lower the interest rate
the larger is the rate of investment that is most profitable.

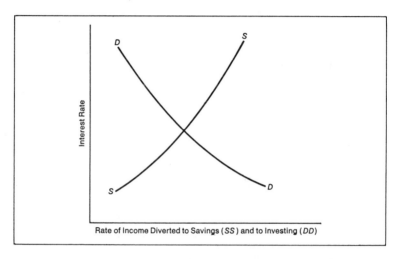

Figure 22–1

Demands for Investing and Supply of
Savings Are Related to Interest Rate

The lower the interest rate of the economy, the greater the most profitable rate of
investment, shown by the *DD* curve sloping from upper left to lower right. The
lower the interest rate, the lower the rate of saving that people are willing to
incur, illustrated by the slope of the *SS* curve. The interest rate at which the most
profitable investment rate would equal savings is brought about by adjustments in
production, relative prices, and income (not graphed).

*Lower interest rate is not merely a lower cost: it is a change in relative
prices.*    A lower interest rate should not be considered as merely a reduction
in the interest costs one pays when borrowing for some particular investment.
Many people, noticing that interest costs of borrowed funds are only a small
portion of the total investment, jump to the erroneous conclusion that
reducing the interest rate has little effect on the profitability and hence on
the rate of investment. Their reasoning ignores the fact that a lower *market*
rate of interest *means that present values of capital goods rise relative to their*

*current costs of production.* Usually, shorter-lived services are used to produce longer-lived capital goods; hence *service prices do not rise as much as capital-goods prices when interest rates fall.* A higher rate of (or quicker) investment becomes profitable for a *wider* range of capital goods.

We can illustrate this principle quite easily. Suppose a concrete building costing about $750 would yield $100 a year net of all other costs for nine years. Its *g* is about 4 percent (See Table 13–3, page 270; 7.4 × 100 = $744, a close approximation to $750, for 4 percent). Given a 5 percent interest rate in the market, the building would not be a profitable investment, for its present market *value* would be only $710. But if the interest rate were 3 percent the present value of the building would be about $780. The investment would be profitable. (Check our calculations by reference to the data of Table 13–3.) Since most people think of the interest rate as simply the rate at which they borrow or lend, *rather than also as a means of expressing current prices of capital goods relative to current service prices,* we can see why most of them would think it relatively trivial in affecting general investment activity. A failure to recognize this is often responsible for thinking that interest rates are simply the costs of borrowing.

## Savings Supply

The *SS* curve in Figure 22–1 shows the rate of current income people are *willing* to divert (save) from consumption to accumulation of wealth *if* they were offered the net rates of growth of wealth (indicated on the vertical axis). The higher the interest rate or growth of wealth offered for a unit of saving, the larger the rate of saving supplied.

The *DD* curve indicates the feasible most profitable investment rate for each market rate of interest. People might be *willing* to save at the rate of $3,000 a year *if* they could get a growth of wealth of 15 percent on the marginal dollar of saving. But no one may believe he knows how to get so high a rate of growth of wealth on the marginal dollar invested.

*Saving is—and is not—the same thing as investing.* We warn of ambiguities about the terms "saving" and "investment." Sometimes *both* terms are used to describe the *same thing*—diversion of present income from present consumption to creation of wealth. However, the terms very frequently refer to the two *different* concepts explained in the preceding paragraphs: (1) *investing* means the amount of current income, at a stated rate of interest, the community *can profitably* divert to wealth creation; (2) *saving* means the amount of current income that the community is *willing*, at an interest rate, to divert to wealth creation. Since the rates of investing and saving in these senses of the word are dependent on the interest rate, they are shown as *functions* (or curves) of the interest rate. In short, in the function *sense* savings and investment are the *willingness* and the *feasibility* concepts. *You must from the context of use decide which sense of the word is meant.*

Do not make the mistake of thinking that the distinction between the concepts of investment-demand schedule and savings-supply schedule is made *because* people who direct the investment are different from those who save. The basis for the distinction is not that they are made by different people; some people do both. However, having said this, we emphasize the importance of the fact that savings and investment decisions are in large part made by different people. Therefore, some markets or devices are required to coordinate the two—the (saving) lending and the (investing) capital-goods markets. If one or both of the functions shifts, serious repercussions can follow for the total rate of income and aggregate employment, as we suggested in the preceding chapter.

### Coordinating Investing and Saving Decisions

Every *person's* behavior is characterized by personal *DD* and *SS* curves, summarizing his investment yield beliefs and savings propensity. In Figure 22–1 the *community DD* and *SS* curves represent summations of the individual curves over all the individuals. For the community as a whole, the interest rate is pushed toward that equilibrium at which the amount of income that people believe they can invest profitably is equated to the savings (that they are willing to provide). But it would be a mistake to think this adjustment occurs in a special market for savings and investment, as such.

There is no market for "savings" or "investment." Instead, those activities are guided in the lending and borrowing markets, the capital-goods markets, and in markets for production activity. It is in all these markets that we observe the effects of changes in (1) beliefs about feasible, profitable investment opportunities and (2) preference patterns for present consumption relative to more wealth (savings propensities).

The response of investing and saving to changes in underlying preference patterns and productive investment possibilities can be investigated and, perhaps, better understood with a few examples.

#### A. Increase in Savings Propensity

If personal preferences should change toward a greater desire for future income, or to more wealth relative to present consumption, this would imply an increase in the supply of saving out of current income, a shift in the *SS* curve to the right. (1) This would be manifested in markets by an increase in the supply of loanable funds. An increased willingness to save implies, in part, an increased demand for bonds—that is, claims to future income. An increased demand for bonds raises the price of bonds, which means that the interest rate is lowered in the bond market. That change in price, or interest rate, allocates the increased savings over the competing claimants—the same old rationing problem investigated in earlier chapters. (2) Prices of existing assets will rise. Prices of steel and concrete buildings will rise relative to those of wood. Young, rapidly growing trees or animals will rise in value relative to older and slower-growing ones. Since a yearling steer grows at a faster percentage rate than an old steer, every pound of a yearling represents a greater increase of future beef than does that of older, slower-growing steers. The demand (and price) of yearlings will rise relative to steers; the price of veal will rise relative to that of beef. Less veal will be consumed.

We can express these events in terms of interest rates. Recall that in the analysis of capital values and interest rates (Chapter 13), we said that a rise in the price of long-lived goods relative to the price of short-lived goods (steel buildings relative to wooden ones) means the implicit interest rate has fallen. In fact, a change in the relative present values *is* a change in the interest rate in the capital-goods markets. For example, suppose the community initially places the value of $710 on each of two goods, one yielding $100 in each of nine years and the other yielding $200 annually for four years. This implies a 5 percent interest rate, which you can (and should!) check by using the data in Table 13–3. If the community's preference changes in favor of longer annuities, the nine-year annuity will be increased in value more than will the four-year annuity. If the present value of the nine-year $100-per-year sequence rises to $779 and the four-year stream to $743 (both up from $710), the interest rate will be 3 percent, down from 5 percent. (Check this, too!) Note also that production of the longer-lived goods will now be relatively more profitable.

### B. Increase in Productivity of Investment

Suppose there is an increase in the perceived *possibilities* of producing wealth profitably relative to its current costs. New inventions are useful in enabling us to get more future income. Cheaper refrigeration, more durable and rust-resisting metals are examples of ways to create more future consumption per doller of present income diverted from consumption. They will induce more investment.

The *DD* curve (of Figure 22–1) shifts to the right. The interest rate increases. In the lending and borrowing markets this appears as an increased demand to borrow current income—in the form of money. In terms of the demand and supply of bonds, the supply of bonds increases. The price of bonds falls—that is, the interest rate rises, facilitating rationing among the competing demanders of the presently available savings offered on the loan market. Failing a rise in the interest rate, more nonprice rationing would occur. The allocation would be more heavily influenced by nonmarketable wealth-exchange offers—something we shall again investigate later in the context of specific lending markets.

### C. Increased Stock of Capital Goods

What would happen if there were an increase in the stock of capital goods, possibly by a gift from a foreign country or by the accumulation of capital goods over the years? Don't jump to the conclusion that the interest rate will be lower just because the increased stock of capital goods means an increase in the potential future income. Once the increase in wealth is realized, present income is higher too. A larger stock of capital goods, once realized, provides an increase in the *present and future* income. If the increase in wealth is heavily weighted by goods yielding greater future-service relative to the present, the interest rate would be higher than otherwise. Why? With a larger ratio of future consumption, relative to present, people are willing to pay more future income for present-consumption rights. The analogy of the person who learns he will in the future have more income than formerly expected is apt; he immediately borrows against his future. On the other hand, a reduced proportion of future, relative to present, consumption potentialities may be inherent in the increased stock of capital goods. The interest rate would be reduced. (Why?) Thus, we do not know whether a country that is rich in capital goods will have a higher or lower interest rate than if it were poorer.

Effect of the Quantity of Money versus
Effect of *Increasing* the Quantity of Money

Often it is said that the larger the quantity of money the lower the interest rate and the larger the rate of investment. However, a larger quantity of money would mean higher prices of wages and goods, land and stocks. If all prices double, everyone's wealth doubles and people will demand twice as many bonds to hold. The demand would push up bond prices—except that the supply of bonds will also increase, so that the net effect on bond prices and interest rates will be nil. There will be twice as much debt and twice as much wealth in money terms—but no change in interest rates or in real quantities.

But there are interim effects, as we shall see later. There may be long-run effects too, resulting from *increasing* the quantity of money, in particular from the *way the new money is created and spent*, not from the fact of having more money in the economy. To see why, suppose that new money were created by a legal counterfeiter who proceeded to spend it on wine, women, and song—with the result that there was an interim increase in the demand and prices for wine, women, and song, without effect on interest rates. But suppose our fellow had used his new money to buy bonds. That would immediately push up the price of bonds, or, if you prefer, lower the interest rate. (Later new bonds would be sold, but so long as he continued to hold the bonds or new ones when the old ones were redeemed, the interest rate would be lower than it otherwise would have been, even after allowing for the increase of more bonds.) That creator of the money is a member of the community and he has shifted the *community's demand for future* income relative to present income by his expenditures.

It so happens that the usual process of legally increasing the quantity of money by our banking system is almost always associated with the purchase of bonds and promissory notes. Money creation is *institutionally* associated with an increase in the demand for bonds or promissory notes. The money creators, in effect, *lend* the new money, and so long as they continue to hold debts (as they will while that money is in existence), the interest rate will be lower than otherwise. You can see that the low interest results not from creating and issuing money but from the purpose for which that new money is *initially spent*. The increase in the quantity of money and its initial expenditure increases the relative demand for bonds. This is why you will frequently read that increased money leads to lower interest rates—but only because of the institutional way in which the money is created and first spent for bonds.

### Prospects of Reduced Future Yields

Let's take a more difficult case. Suppose beliefs about future yields of existing producible assets were to deteriorate; the *DD* schedule shifts to the left. Those who first develop this belief will sell their common stocks or capital goods to others before the belief is confirmed by ensuing events. Their efforts to sell will depress stock prices (hereafter including prices of capital goods such as buildings and land). People will switch to assets whose future yields are not expected to deteriorate so much, for example, bonds or money. This will lower interest rates in the bond markets (raise bond prices). Lower stock prices make investment less profitable, so investment will be reduced.

The process is not very pleasant. Investment workers (and others) must shift to new jobs. Reduced employment means lower incomes which, in turn, make prospects look even worse as savings are reduced. So *both* the *DD* and the *SS* curves shift to the left, because both are affected by the wealth, or income, change. Firms, caught in the squeeze of falling asset prices, and reduced income, and the necessity of paying off debts will seek to borrow money to refinance their debts and tide them over the "adjustment." As the interest rate in the loan markets is pushed up, stock prices keep falling. (Why?)

The point of this example is to show that the determination of the interest rate pervades every market and exchange. Nor can a shift in the demand schedule for investment necessarily be treated as something that will not also shift the savings-supply schedule. Events that can change the demand for investment and for capital goods or for more wealth have broad ramifications, which are not confined to one small market. The events cannot be compared with a change in the demand for tires, wheat, or some other particular good. The interest rate reflects the relative demands for *all* types of goods capable of rendering services in the future. And since rights to present and future income can be traded in many ways in many markets, the interest rate will be implicit or manifest in many markets.

*Why the loanable funds market is a key market.* Since almost all exchange occurs via the medium of money rather than between goods directly, people seek to revise the time profile of their income or consumption streams not by trading this good now for that good later, but by trading money now for money later. Hence, we can expect almost all revisions in investment prospects and savings willingness to affect borrowing and lending markets. That is why the factors affecting the rates of interest and investment are often analyzed in terms of the demand and supply for loanable funds.

### The Meanings of the Interest Rate

If you reread this chapter you will note that the expression *interest rate* is identified with several different concepts. First is the net rate of increase in wealth from a dollar more of investment, also called the net marginal productivity of investment. Second is a personal subjective valuation of present consumption rights, measured in terms of the amount of future income that is equivalent to one dollar of consumption. Third is a market rate of return on loans, called a rate of interest on bonds, or promissory notes. If this third rate is greater than the second, people will give up more present consumption (save more). If the second is less than the first, investment will increase. Fourth, there is an implicit interest rate in the relationship between present prices of capital goods and their future income streams. All these rates—(1) the net marginal productivity of investment, (2) personal valuation of future income relative to current consumption, (3) return on bonds or loans, and (4) the interest rate implicit in relative prices of capital goods—are brought into equality by switching activity among the various markets and goods. When all are equal, the common value is the interest rate. If any are not equal, then adjustments will be induced in the various markets, pushing them all toward equality. Since the most easily perceived and measured rate is the rate in the market for secure bonds, we usually refer, loosely, to the rate in that market as the interest rate.

You will note the interest rate is referred to variously as the price of "current consumption," the price of "savings," the price of "loans," the "rate of time-preference," and the price of "money." It is, as we have seen, a measure of all these things.

### Money and Real Rate of Interest

This is a good place to explain the difference between the *money* rate and the *real* interest rate.

If the price level were expected to be twice as high next year as it is now, how much interest *in money* would you pay next year for a loan today, if the interest rate were 10 percent in money units for a stable price level? The amounts of $100 today and $200 next year will be equivalent in buying power at their respective times. A *real* interest rate of 10 percent would require that $220 be repaid next year for a loan of $100 now. This would require a *money* interest rate of 120 percent per year. On the other hand, if the price level were expected to be *halved*, an interest rate of –45 percent for a one-year loan would be equivalent to a 10 percent stable-money interest rate.[1] All of our previous discussion of the interest rate has been based on the assumption that the money-price level is stable. If it is not, and *if* the rate at which the price level is going to change is *foreseen*, then the money rate of interest on money loans will be higher, to give the lender the rate (real) that would have existed if there were no change in the price level.

Summary

1    Wealth consists of all goods, human and nonhuman. Some have readily measurable market values and some do not. Many of our institutions, such as laws, customs, and systems of property rights, are fundamental components of our social wealth.

2    Saving is the nonconsumption of current income. Investing and saving, under one popular definition of these two terms, are identical concepts.

3    Investment and saving are different concepts when used in the demand- and supply-schedule sense: saving represents the rate at which current income will be *willingly* diverted from current consumption to accumulation of wealth. That willing saving rate is a function of the interest rate. Investment is the current income that *can be profitably* diverted from consumption at a given rate of interest. In these senses, saving is a positive function of the interest rate, while investment is a negative function. The investment schedule is often called the demand for savings, while the savings schedule is called the supply of savings.

4    An individual may save and accumulate wealth by trading his current saving for someone else's goods—wherein the other person thereby dissaves—with no change in the social total. A person can save and lend to someone else who thereby consumes more than his income and dissaves—again leaving the social total unchanged. A person may save and accumulate a larger total stock of wealth by production, rather than by exchange with someone else; the social total will increase.

5    Capital goods render (marketable) services in the future. A fall in the price of capital goods, *relative* to consumer goods prices, *is* a rise in the interest rate.

[1] The relationship between the "real" interest rate, $r$, in money units for a stable price level, and the actual market interest rate, $R$, in money units, if the price level is *known* to be changing at the rate of $p$ percent a year, is: $R = (1 + r)(1 + p) - 1$.

6   The interest rate is manifest in several markets: the lending and borrowing market, the capital-goods market, and production-activity market. All are interdependent; arbitrage among them will bring each to a common interest rate.

7   The net marginal productivity of investment is the net rate of increase of wealth per marginal unit of investment. The net marginal productivity of investment is a decreasing function of the rate of investment.

8   A lower interest rate affects investment demand (in the sense of available profitable rates of investment) more than merely by lowering the interest costs on a loan. *The relationship of prices of capital and consumers goods—short-lived and longer-lived—changes.*

9   Saving and investing are equated not in a single market for saving and investment but in the loans markets, the capital-goods markets, and the production-activity market—all loosely called the saving-investment markets.

10   An increase in preference for distant income relative to present implies more current savings, an increase in the saving-supply schedule, and a lower rate of interest with more investment. An increase in investment demand consequent to an increase in perceived profitable investment opportunities results in a higher rate of investment and a higher interest rate.

11   Since both the supply and the demand schedules are explicit functions of the interest rate, it is tempting to think that the interest rate changes to equate the rate of investing with the rate of saving. But both saving and investing are dependent upon other variables also (wealth, income, expectations about the future), and these other variables also change to equate saving with investing.

12   An increased stock of wealth has effects on the rate of interest and rate of investment, depending upon the particular attributes of the increased stock of wealth.

13   *Increasing* the quantity of money affects the interest rate because of the ways the increase is first spent. But the quantity of money will not in itself affect the interest rate; however, the price level is changed.

14   Our institutional mode of creating money is such that the increased money is spent in acquiring bonds; hence, the typical result is that increasing the quantity of money leads to lower interest rates during the increase.

15   The interest rate reflects the net marginal productivity of investment, the personal value of present consumption relative to wealth or future income (often called one's time preference), the rate of return on loans, and the relative prices of capital goods and consumers goods.

16    The money interest rate is the real interest rate adjusted for the changes in the price level.

1    A farmer who dries grapes to convert them to raisins is investing. Why is this investing, since it merely changes one form of consumption good to another form of consumption good?

2    Instead of playing bridge, a man works around the house painting and refinishing the walls. Explain why this is a form of investment.

3    Changes in the rate of interest are detectable in the changes in the structure of relative prices of various types of goods.
a. If the price of raisins (relative to grapes), of prunes (relative to plums), of whiskey (relative to corn), of cider (relative to apples) should rise, would that mean a change in the rate of interest? In what direction?
b. What effect would that have on the profitability of producing raisins, prunes, whiskey, etc?
c. Ultimately, what effect would the revised production have on the relative values (for example, of raisins and grapes)? What effect would that have on the rate of interest?

4    Suppose the world were going to last for just two years and you have wealth of $100.
a. If the interest rate is zero, what is the income available in each of the next two years?
b. If the interest rate is 10 percent, what is the income of each period (again assuming a two-year life to the world)?
c. If the interest rate is 10 percent but the world is going to last for an indefinitely long period, what is the maximum annual maintainable rate of consumption?
d. If the interest rate is 5 percent, what is the rate of income—assuming wealth is $100 ?
e. If your wealth unexpectedly increases from $100 to $120, what happens to income (with an interest rate of 5 percent)?
f. What was the amount of your profit when that wealth increase occurred?

5    Goods differ in their rate of yield of consumption services, or in their "durability." Pine lumber naturally deteriorates more rapidly than redwood. If demand for future consumption rights should *rise relative* to present consumption rights, would pine or redwood experience the greater rise in present price? Show why this is expressible as a fall in the

rate of interest. (Hint: The interest rate is the exchange rate between present and future consumption rights.)

**6** **a.** "If savings is defined as an increase in wealth and if investment is defined as an increase in wealth, then savings by definition is always equal to investment; for it is merely the same thing looked at from the point of view of two different people." Correct or incorrect?
**b.** Since the preceding statement is correct, how is it possible to speak of equilibrating the rate of investment and the rate of savings?

**7** Define the demand for investment; define the supply of savings and do so in such a way that the two are not synonymous.

**8** "The most important fact about saving and investment is that they are done by different people and for different reasons."
**a.** Is that why savings must be equilibrated to investment via a demand for investment and a supply for savings function? Why not?
**b.** Suppose that everyone who invested had to do his own saving and could not lend or borrow or buy capital goods from other people. Would that destroy the principles of demand-and-supply analysis for growth of wealth? Why?

**9** If a person saves all his increase in wealth, how much does he save?

**10** By giving up $100 of present income for $105 of consumption rights available in one year, a person gets what rate of interest per year?

**11** The interest rate is 10 percent per year. A person uses $100 of current wealth to make his wealth grow to $105 at the end of a year.
**a.** Has he maximized his wealth?
**b.** In what sense has he not even maintained his wealth, despite the fact that he has $105 at the end of the year compared to $100 at the beginning. (Hint: When his wealth was $100 at the beginning of the year, with an interest rate of 10 percent, how much could he consume during the year and still end up with $100? Could he not have consumed any amount up to $5 and still ended up with $105?)

**12** You are a visitor in some underdeveloped country in which all lending and borrowing are effectively prohibited.
**a.** Is there a rate of interest?
**b.** If so, where could you get data to compute it?
**c.** How could you tell when it changes?

**13** "Roundabout, more capitalistic methods of production are always more productive than direct methods using less capital equipment. Therefore, any country that wants to develop should start increasing the amount of capital goods it has." Evaluate.

**14** A man plants a seed for a tree. Assume for simplicity that there are no subsequent expenses. The tree, if cut and converted to lumber at the end of any of the ages indicated in the table below, will yield lumber worth the amount indicated in the second column. The third column gives the *present* value of that future potential lumber, at 10 percent rate of interest. Some of the entries are not presented.

| (1) Age | (2) Lumber Value | (3) Present Capital Value of Lumber | (4) Present Value of Costs | (5) Profit If Cut at Age Indicated |
|------|------|------|------|------|
| 0  | $ 0   | $ 0   | $5.00 | $–5.00 |
| 5  | 1     | 0.62  | 5.70  | –5.08 |
| 10 | 4     | 1.54  | 6.20  | –4.66 |
| 15 | 11    | 2.63  | 6.50  | –3.87 |
| 20 | 25.0  | ——    | 6.60  | —— |
| 25 | 60.0  | 5.54  | 6.80  | –1.26 |
| 30 | 140.0 | ——    | 6.82  | —— |
| 35 | 260.0 | ——    | 6.95  | —— |
| 40 | 450.0 | 10.00 | 6.96  | +3.04 |
| 45 | 650.0 | ——    | 6.97  | —— |
| 50 | 800.0 | 6.80  | 6.98  | –0.18 |

a. Compute the missing values and find the age at which the tree should be cut to provide the maximum *present* value of that tree.

b. What is that maximum present value?

c. How much is a newly planted tree worth?

d. Suppose now that the rent for the land on which the seed is planted is 50 cents per year. Suppose that, in addition to that cost, there are other costs—spraying, watering, fire protection, taxes—to be paid over the years. The present value of those future costs for various lengths of time is indicated in column 4. Column 5 gives the present value net of these costs. Compute the missing data for that column.

e. Suppose that the value of the tree rises relative to current lumber prices. What would this imply about the rate of interest?

f. If no one owned the tree, and it could be cut by anyone who wanted to use the lumber, when would it be cut?

15 Some whiskies improve with age. The following table lists the consumption value of a barrel of whiskey at various ages. For example, if the whiskey is removed from its aging vat and sold now to consumers for current consumption, it will sell for $100. If sold in ten years, it will fetch $250 for *consumption*.

a. How much will the vat of whiskey be worth right now (at 10 percent) if it is to be held until the end of the second year before being bottled and sold?

b. For what length of time should one expect to keep the whiskey in the vat for a maximum present value? (Hint: How much is it worth paying for the whiskey now if it is to be held for five years? For ten years?)

c. If no one owned the vat of whiskey, how long would it remain unconsumed?

d. Suppose it were owned but could not be sold: how long would it be kept before consumption?

| Consumption Date | Consumption Value | Consumption Date | Consumption Value |
|---|---|---|---|
| Now | $100 | | |
| 1 year | 120 | 6 | 205 |
| 2 | 140 | 7 | 220 |
| 3 | 160 | 8 | 230 |
| 4 | 175 | 9 | 240 |
| 5 | 190 | 10 | 250 |

16    "When interest rates rise, the profitability of constructing buildings falls relative to other kinds of productive activity." Why?

17    "A rise in the profitability of constructing houses and buildings tends to push up the rate of interest." Why? Reconcile this statement with the preceding one. (Do so in terms of shifting demand or supply curves and movements along a curve.)

18    In a certain country the only productive goods are "rabbits." Either the rabbits are eaten, or the rabbits increase at the rate of 20 percent per year.
a. If there are 1,000,000 rabbits in the community at the first of the year, what is the income of the community (measuring the income in rabbit units)?
b. What will be the rate of interest in that community?
c. What is the maximum possible growth rate of the wealth of that country?

19    If the rate of interest is 10 percent in the New York bond markets and 5 percent in the Boston bond market, describe the adjustments you think will ensue.

20    Someone discovers how to reduce refrigeration costs to almost zero, and tells everyone about it.
a. What will this new improved technology do to the rate of interest?
b. What price shifts are implied?

21    The propositions on costs in Chapter 14 imply that the demand curve for investment is negatively sloped with respect to the rate of interest—that is, that higher *rates* of investment will be less profitable. Why is this implied by the earlier propositions on behavior of costs?

22    "Debtors are exploited by creditors, because a person who has to borrow is usually in distress and is willing to pay a very high price to get the loan. Unless laws were passed controlling the rate of interest, debtors would be forced to pay unreasonable rates of interest." Is the analysis correct? Explain why.

23    If you received a gift of $10,000 in cash, in what forms would you hold your wealth? Suppose you decided to convert it to some intermediate

kind of claim or goods (like bonds and savings-bank deposits) before finally holding more stocks and personal or business goods directly? Trace out the sequence of effects on the interest rate if you follow the sequence suggested in the preceding sentence.

24    The following is a quotation from the *Scientific American*, 1963: "Recently a number of steelmaking organizations in Western Europe and the U.S.S.R. have eliminated several costly steps in the manufacture of steel by advancing the technique known as continuous casting. U.S. steel firms, which account for about a third of the world output, were for the most part content to observe these developments. They were inhibited by a paradox of industrial supremacy: the huge sums already invested in established methods made experimentation with the new technique seem impractical. The smaller producers, whose competitive position might have been enhanced by continuous casting, could least afford to build the pilot plants."
Assume that the facts stated in the first sentence are correct. The second sentence describes the alleged behavior of U.S. steel firms in response to these facts; and the remaining sentences strive to explain that behavior. Do you agree that the last two sentences present an economically acceptable explanation of the events in the second sentence? Explain why they do not.

25    A further quote from the same article in the *Scientific American*: "The ideal time for a producer to consider the use of a continuous-casting machine is when he is building an entirely new steel mill, from melting furnace on through to milled products. In such a situation the mill can be designed around the known limitations of the continuous-casting process, and there will be no costly overlap between conventional and continuous equipment. Unfortunately, U.S. firms are not planning to build many new steel mills. Therefore, many U.S. producers are 'not ready' for continuous casting, whereas small producers in India, Venezuela, and Peru, for example, have already obtained plant designs. The producers in these countries will avoid the large cost of primary mills. If there is any solace in underdevelopment, it is this 'advantage.'"
Note that the writer did put the last word in quotation marks, as if to admit there really was no advantage as he seemed to suggest. Comment on the reasoning in the quotation; but first note whether or not the quotation says that *no* U.S. firms are now using continuous casting or merely that *not all* are; and whether *no* firms or *not all* firms plan to introduce it. In evaluating this quotation, consider: If you already have an old-model car, would you be more or less likely to buy a new-model car that *is* more economical than your "old" model?

26    The rate of interest helps to equilibrate investing and savings and the demand for borrowing and the supply of savings; it is the premium price of current consumption rights over future consumption rights; it is the price of money; and it equates the demand and supply of assets. Explain how it is all these things at once.

# 23

Growth and Distribution of Wealth

In the preceding chapter the roles of the rate of interest, savings, and investing were explained. Their effective interdependence depends upon the institutional situation within which decisions to save and invest are carried out. In this chapter we explore some institutional features and their effects.

## Specialization of Borrowers and Lenders

The loan market is a vast variety of institutions and marketplaces. Why are there so many? Again, the answer is "because of gains from exchange of specialized services." Since potential borrowers differ, specialized lenders can more cheaply channel savings to the most profitable investment activities after allowance for risks. Just as producers specialize in the products they make, so lenders will specialize in the types of borrowers and purposes of the loan.

One reason for the variety of borrowers can be illustrated by a few of the stages in making, selling, and using an automobile. A firm's employees and suppliers want to be paid so that they can consume now, but they are glad to make a car if someone else is willing to wait for the future services of the car. If the owner of the business were to finance the work, he would have to defer his consumption to the future. But he wants to specialize in production activity, not in saving. A lender finances the current production by transferring current income rights to producers in exchange for later repayment.

Automobile manufacturers borrow by selling bonds to the public and to such institutions as insurance companies that channel public savings. Producers also borrow from commercial banks to carry them over seasonally active periods. Car retailers also rely on commercial banks. In addition, they borrow from finance companies and commercial credit companies. The ordinary consumer has little occasion to deal directly with these firms. Yet, because they exist, the car dealer can carry a bigger inventory, allowing the consumer to inspect a larger variety of cars and get quicker delivery.

The typical consumer will borrow to pay for the car. He is likely to deal with a consumer credit company directly or indirectly via the car dealer, who attends to details of the loan. The consumer may borrow from a credit union at his place of work, because the credit union is relatively well acquainted with his personal situation and prospects of repayment. He may borrow directly from a neighborhood bank or from an insurance company with which he has a policy. As goods pass along the line from producer to final consumer, a series of different lenders with special knowledge about successive participants finance each stage.

Specialization occurs also in the gathering of savings from the public. Savings banks and commercial banks solicit savings deposits from savers. Insurance companies and pension funds are an especially important collection agency for savings. All of these money-market institutions lend to businessmen and home buyers, for example, and are interrelated by the interest rate via a complex chain of exchanges and flows of funds from one to another. Few of us negotiate with more than the institutions in which we deposit our savings and those from which we borrow. But scores of financial intermediaries specialize in facilitating a flow of information and funds from suppliers to demanders.

Stipulated Interest Rate and the
Implied Effective Interest Yield

We learned in Chapter 13 that there are many ways to express or measure the interest rate or yield on a loan. We know that the interest rate stipulated in the loan as, say, 6 percent per year may not be the rate *effectively* promised. For example, if at the present moment you lend $900 for a promise of $1,000 in one year for a zero interest rate stipulated in the written terms of the loan, you will in fact, if the loan is repaid when due, have realized an interest rate of ($1,000–$900)/900 = .111 or 11.1 percent per year. The implicit, effective *yield* is 11.1 percent per year at the time the loan is made (taking into account not only the stipulated rate of zero percent but also the initial present amount loaned and the amount due later). You can see that the implicit yield differs from the stipulated rate if the present price or amount actually loaned differs from the amount to be repaid (excluding the explicit interest). In general, for any *one*-year loan, the *implicit* or *effective* yield, $i$, is given by the following formula:

$$i = [(Ar + A)/P] - 1$$

where $r$ is the stipulated interest rate expressed in the loan agreement, $A$ is both the amount on which the interest is to be paid and the amount to be paid as principal when the loan is due, and $P$ is the present amount paid or loaned.

For example, suppose you buy an outstanding bond promising 5 percent interest per year on a principal amount of $1,000, due and payable in one year. The present price, or amount paid now, for that bond may be $900. The implicit yield is [($50 + $1,000)/$900] −1 = .167, or 16.7 percent per year. If the present price had been $1,000, the implicit effective yield would be 5 percent.

In referring to an interest rate, we shall usually mean the implicit effective yield rather than the rate stipulated in the loan instrument. And if the loan is paid on schedule, the implicit effective yield will be the *realized* interest rate on that loan.

*Default risk.*    Some debts have a very high assurance that the borrower will pay interest and principal promptly. Currently, U.S. government bonds are as high in quality as any available, but not because government officials are more honest or reliable than private individuals. Instead, the government can use the police to collect taxes.[1] (Also it can be shown it has the power to collect "taxes" by creating money.) Private bonds sometimes can be repaid only if the borrower is able to induce people to purchase his products. Bonds issued by private firms like General Motors, American Telephone and Telegraph, and Santa Fe Railroad are of very high quality because they are almost certain to be paid when due. Bonds of other strong firms promise an implicit yield of about 6 percent, with some running up to 10 percent. And then there is a vast range of riskier bonds that *promise* even higher yields.[2]

You will notice that we have referred to "promised yields" and not to the interest rate. Superficially, riskier bonds appear to pay a higher rate of interest. The promised yield includes a risk premium. For example, suppose a potential borrower offers to repay in one year with 5 percent interest per year, and you regard the chances of repayment as being only a half. To make that an attractive proposition, you could offer to lend him $50 for his promise to repay $105 in one year, if the stipulated interest rate is 5 percent. Under this arrangement you will get $105 with a probability of .5 and nothing with a probability of .5. *On the average* you would expect to get $52.50, which would be equivalent to 5 percent on your loan of $50. The promised yield on any *one* loan is 110 percent on a loan of $50.[3]

A test of the validity of this interpretation is provided by events in the bonds markets. If the risk premium accounts for the differences in promised yield, then when a business firm has increased earnings that improve its prospects of being able to meet its debt obligations promptly, the price of its outstanding bonds should rise. And they do.

Most of us are tempted to complain when lenders express doubts about our ability to repay. I may know I will repay a debt when due, but I cannot expect the lender to know it. Some people call the loan market imperfect because *they* cannot borrow at the same promised rate of interest as their neighbor; and some complain they cannot borrow at all. This is analogous to a seller of automobiles complaining that people are buying competitors' cars, when his are just as good. If they were just as good, he would sell his cars. But there is a difference in the eyes of the buyer.

The lender sees differences in the prospects that the borrower will repay promptly without extra costs being imposed on the lender. You should not expect a lender to tell you that your promises are too risky, especially if he can say it in a less offensive way. Thus, a banker says, in refusing to lend to you, "I'm sorry; we just don't have any funds to lend now." You should (we hope) wonder how the supply could be inadequate if the interest rate were really high enough to ration out the existing supply so that all who want to borrow can do so. Actually, however, the banker is merely being tactful—and

[1] Evidence of the importance of the ability to collect taxes is that government bonds that are repayable only from receipts of particular projects (such as toll roads) are of lower quality than "general" tax-supported bonds.

[2] For example, Chilean government 3 percent bonds can be purchased for about $400, Boston and Maine Railroad 4-1/2 percent bonds at about $500, and Estonian government 7 percent bonds for about $50. All promise to pay $1,000 at maturity.

[3] This is like reporting the yield on the *winning* ticket in a lottery.

misleading. If he were tactless and completely honest he could have said, "We think the prospect of your repaying is not high enough. *We specialize* in loans to people with better credit prospects. To lend to you, we feel that we should ask 15 percent instead of 6 percent. And then we would have to be prepared to have a staff to take care of the collection problems and other activities involved in defaulted loans. We prefer not to engage in that kind of business. You should go to other lenders who specialize in higher risks and are prepared to handle your type of defaults."

### Negotiability of Bonds

Lenders who may not want to defer consumption until a bond is repaid could sell the bond to someone else, who will act as his substitute, deferring consumption rights. The right to sell an outstanding bond to someone else is known as "negotiability." The lender would then be willing to accept lower interest for the greater "liquidity."[4] However, a borrower may prefer not to have his debts transferable. The original lender, he feels, would be more considerate and lenient in pressing for legal action in the event of difficulty in repaying a debt. Because of the agreement not to sell the bond to someone else, nonnegotiable notes usually carry a slightly higher rate of interest.

Negotiability of bonds is facilitated by the New York Bond Exchange, a formal, privately owned marketplace where the bonds of well-known, strong American corporations can be bought (and sold)—not from the corporation itself but from people who lent money to the corporation, or from those who subsequently bought the bond from the original lender.[5] A large portion of bond resales takes place elsewhere via bond brokers or dealers—much in the fashion of used-car dealers. They maintain small inventories of bonds, but they know other dealers from whom any particular bond can be bought—at a price. These security brokers are known as "over-the-counter" security dealers, since they do not operate in a formal, physically compact exchange like the New York Bond Exchange. They rely on telephones.

Because none of these bond-market transactions transfers money to the original borrower, some people erroneously think these markets serve no useful purpose to *original* borrowers or lenders. Used-bond markets are as important in the production and sale of new bonds (saving and lending) as the used-car market is for production and sale of new cars. How many people would buy cars if they could never sell them but had to keep them until they were junked? Because these markets facilitate the transfer of bonds, more

---

[4]Most of our money is in the form of commerical bank debts, debts payable on demand. Holders of this kind of debt, because it is repayable immediately *on demand* at the option of the holder, will get a lower rate of interest *per year* than on a debt payable only after some time.

[5]Reports of prices and amounts of bonds exchanged on the major organized exchanges are given in the financial pages of major newspapers and in stock brokers' offices.

people are willing to hold bonds. Negotiability of bonds also permits people to be more selective.

## Legal Restraints on Access to Loan Market

The fact of a positive interest rate has been much denied, condemned, and legally "prohibited." Even Aristotle asserted that money is "sterile," so that no interest should be paid for money loans. Interest was paid long before Aristotle and continued thereafter—despite theology, protestations, and dogma. It was paid because the borrower offered to pay it rather than not get the loan. And he had to pay it because the demand for savings was greater than the supply at a zero price. Until about the sixteenth century Christian theology "officially" condemned interest as a venal sin. Christians conveniently borrowed from Jews, whose religion placed no severe ban on interest taking. As a matter of fact, however, the Papacy itself charged a positive interest—though under the name of "fees," "gratuities," or anything but "interest" or "usury." In medieval times, lords had claims to payments from users of land. Sometimes the lord wanted to sell to the church his rights to the future rents. Suppose an annuity of rents was expected to run for at least fifty years. For what price could it be sold? A fifty-year annuity of $1 a year would be sold to the church for less than $50—because the rate of interest was positive. In buying lands, the church was charging a positive rate of interest—unless it paid a price equal to the expected *undiscounted* sum of the future annuity payments. And it never did that, so far as we know.

*Interest rate ceilings.* Economic facts of life have insidious ways of circumventing laws or decrees designed to ban them. With man's usual speedy perception, it took the church only about 1,000 years to lift the ban against interest on loans—and now the state government decrees that "unreasonably" high—usurious—rates of interest are illegal. For example, in most states any rate over 10 or 15 percent is called usurious and illegal.

Lenders who make riskier loans at a higher rate of interest in the hope of averaging an acceptable return must resort to legal fictions. For example, pawn shops lend to strangers of dubious credit at a rate of 30 percent per year—not by a "loan," but by a purchase and repurchase agreement. You sell your camera to the pawnbroker for $100 (which is less than its market value) and simultaneously obtain the right to buy it back in one year for $130. Then when, and if, you buy it back, you have paid 30 percent to cover the risk and higher costs, under the facade of a capital gain to the lender.

An effective prohibition of high interest rates would prohibit borrowers with more dubious credit from borrowing at all. It would not lower the interest rate to the riskier borrower. Legal barriers, of course, are not necessarily undesirable. That depends upon one's attitudes toward the consequences of free contracting and free access to markets for lending.

Restrictions on the access of commercial banks to the market for certain types of loans (for example, long-term business loans, second mortgages, and stock-exchange loans in excess of certain amounts) are defended as attempts to prevent a bank owner from making "too risky" loans. For their "own best interests" and the safety of their depositors' accounts, commercial bank owners are legally restricted in the kinds of loans they can make—as well as in the rates of interest they can offer to depositors or charge borrowers. However, a bank prevented from lending on certain *types* of loans can still make risky loans within the authorized class of business borrowers. A law restricting the class of borrowers to whom banks can lend does not prevent banks from competing with each other in other cost-incurring services in order to lend.

*Limits on borrowing.*    Some restrictive laws are directed at the borrowers. For example, laws control consumers' installment purchases of furniture, appliances, cars, vacations. The principle behind these laws apparently is that since some consumers go "too far" into debt, everyone should be *prohibited* from going "too far" into debt. Furthermore, although it's all right to go into debt to buy a house, to meet doctor bills, or to buy business equipment—to go into debt "merely to enjoy consumption before one has earned all the costs" is bad. Thus a generation ago there was considerable publicity and legislation about the evil of consumer installment loans. But the convenience of earlier over later consumption, and of consuming while earning, won out over the virtue of consumption in one's old age. Today, despite many laws trying to limit the rate of interest and amount of borrowing, installment buying is an accepted modern convenience—which has brought the specialized loan market to the young man as well as to the older.

Still, the U.S. government has a law that enables the Board of Governors of the Federal Reserve Banks to place limits on installment purchases. It once prohibited installment credit for more than 50 percent of the value of the item purchased. A 50 percent "down-payment requirement" is a prohibition against going into debt for more than 50 percent of the price of the item purchased. What is the purpose of this restriction? Three reasons have been advanced. First, as said earlier, it protects the consumer from "excessive" debt. A second reason is that the total amount of consumer credit is deemed too large for the "good of the economy," and must be curtailed to prevent "too rapid" an expansion of credit and "too vigorous" a growth of output of the items being purchased. A third reason alleged by *opponents* of the restriction was that the Federal Reserve Board, which is alert to the U.S. government's borrowing problems, wanted to channel more of the available savings to the government: by establishing borrowing limits for private consumers, the government was left with less competition for loans and could borrow at lower interest.

What are the effects? Do higher minimum down-payment regulations reduce the amount of installment debt? Yes. But they increase other kinds of debt.

Frustrated consumers increase or maintain mortgaged debt on their houses or land instead. The inconvenience and costs of increasing such debts often exceed the costs of installment loans. In addition, these loan restrictions have different impacts on people: the older, richer, and more informed are not restricted as much as the younger, poorer, and less informed about other sources of funds.

Individuals are prevented from "excessive" indebtedness not only as consumers but also as investors. The Federal Reserve Board can now limit the amount a person may borrow from a security dealer against the stocks and bonds he owns. Why? Not to protect him from loss of security if the stock should fall, but instead to prevent stock prices from being bid up higher—as they allegedly would be if people could buy shares with lower down payments. This power to control credit assumes the Federal Reserve Board is better able to judge what the general level of prices of stocks should be at any moment than are investors in an open market.

There are many ways to get around the debt limit. Borrow from your banker (instead of the security broker), using the stock as the pledged security. Your banker can lend more if he wants to, but not for the express purpose of buying stock. That restriction means very little, because the money you get from the banker can be used to pay some other bills, while the money you otherwise would have used to pay these bills is released for stock purchases. Money is fungible.

Most countries apply strong restrictions on access to security markets. Any person proposing to sell new bonds or new common stock who does not give out certain information or who attempts to market gleaming promises can be prevented from selling the securities via the mails or on security exchanges. If there are no controls on open-market solicitation and sale of investment securities, there will be more "suckers" in the get-rich quest. Some people will make bad investments. Established business firms will find it more difficult to borrow if new, unproved firms can compete for funds on those organized markets. Open markets do enable the market *testing* of investment options, but that requires actually making the investment. If it is believed that some people can select among investments better than can other people, and if these people can be identified in advance, then giving them power to control the kinds of investments for which funds can be solicited in the market may lead to less waste of resources.

The issue of the propriety of controls on the stock market cannot be settled by simply weighing their effects on the extent of profitable or unprofitable investments nor on the extent to which unethical security dealers are detected. It concerns also the question of whether a person ought to have a "right" to make whatever investment choice he would like to make, through whatever agency he chooses, as long as he pays for the resources used. Whether he invests foolishly or consumes too much chocolate cake is a decision he might consider his own. Who is right? It depends upon what you conceive to be the desirable basic rights of a person.

The Rate of Growth of Wealth

You will hear about high-interest-rate versus low-interest-rate policies. (The former is also called "tight-money" policy.) Low interest rates encourage a higher rate of production of capital goods. In other words, high prices of capital goods relative to prices of short-lived goods or to current consumption services, encourage a higher rate of investment (production of capital goods) by making it more profitable. The problem, however, is how to reduce interest rates. We might attempt to encourage people to want to save and lend more; if successful, that would increase the supply of lending through the loan markets and also it would increase the demand for capital goods. That alteration of preferences would lower the market rate of interest and encourage a more rapid rate of growth of wealth.

A second way to encourage more investment is to make people less fearful of theft of the wealth they accumulate. An unwillingness or inability to strengthen property rights is one of the obstacles to rapid growth in many poorer, undeveloped countries of the world. Some countries (for instance, Switzerland) have superb reputations for observing private-property rights, but some other countries (such as Brazil, Chile, Mexico, Iran, Egypt, Algeria, India, and Indonesia) have somewhat different reputations.

Third, private investment can be supplemented by tax-financed government investment, on the belief that private wealth owners refuse to invest enough in "vital" projects. One way is to tax private wealth and use the proceeds to redirect current income toward the kind of investment activity deemed more appropriate. One counter effect of this is to reduce the rate of saving out of the reduced disposable income. Furthermore, individuals, to escape the tax, will use savings more to create goods that yield more nonpecuniary income, since nonpecuniary income is rarely taxed as heavily as pecuniary income. (An example of this is evident in the United States, where homeowners are not taxed on the incomes from owning their own homes, whereas an investment in rental apartments or business tools yields a taxable money income.)

Fourth, leaving aside techniques for increasing saving and investment in general, the government may seek to increase investment in one particular kind of wealth—namely, education, research, or invention, i.e., public goods. Private investors in the discovery of new knowledge find that other people can use it at practically no cost—which reduces the incentive-reward value of the discovered knowledge to the initial discoverer. How much income should be diverted by governmental authority to research activity in the hope of discovering new principles and ideas that will enhance wealth (at a rate greater than the rate of interest)? If some investment in research seems to be wasted, the researcher can always claim that the real gains aren't perceived by the critic, that they are dispersed and not objectively measured. But the person footing the bill may just as honestly contend that the expenditure is really only consumption under the guise of research. There is as yet no generally accepted, available, objective test against which the value of more or of less research can be assessed.

Growth, Property Rights,
and Conservation

To maintain or increase our future wealth, it is often argued that we should restrict exploitation of many of our natural resources—for example, forests, fertile lands, and iron ore. But this argument fails to comprehend the meaning of capital values of resources and to recognize that "using" goods *can* mean converting them into even more valuable forms of wealth. If a tree is more valuable for the future than are the current goods that could be made with the lumber now, the present capital value of the live tree will exceed the value of the lumber in the felled tree. Consequently, the tree will not be cut now. All this would reflect the fact that capital goods made from current use of the lumber will give a smaller future income than the standing tree; otherwise, the tree would be cut. People can save and invest in trees, or they can save and invest by cutting trees and producing wealth with products made from the trees. Comparison of present values indicates which of the two will give the greater wealth. This analysis explains why it is *not* true that the private-property system tends to cut trees "too" fast. It does "conserve" them by capitalizing the future lumber values to present market values to determine whether the live tree value is greater than the felled value.

But there are circumstances in which people will be induced to cut the trees even though the live value exceeds the felled value. If no one owns a tree and the only way to capture the value of the tree is to cut it and take the wood, no one will have wealth incentives—or legal power—to preserve the tree from those who cut it now for lumber. This is why the forests in many parts of England and China were prematurely cut. They were community property—first come, first served. *Lack of ownership*, not personal greed, is responsible for this "wasteful" use of resources.

This same analysis can be applied to fish and wild game. Uncaught fish belong to no one. Everyone has an incentive to catch them, regardless of whether they may be worth more for future uses. If someone owned the fish, or had the right to prevent others from catching them, that owner would have an incentive to avoid premature or "over"-fishing. In this way, fishing would be restrained, if it is "excessive," as is claimed for tuna, seals, whales, and salmon. As a substitute for property rights in "wild animals," governments have sometimes managed to reach agreements limiting fishing in order to prevent waste. Similarly, so long as no one owns the fresh water in the United States, and so long as rights to its present *and future* uses are owned by no one, everyone has less incentive to keep the water fresh and used in its most valuable ways. First come, first served. Everyone dumps his garbage in the lake, since the loss of value of more polluted water is not thrust upon him or upon anyone with sufficient force to control pollution. But an owner would suffer that loss of value and would therefore prevent others from fouling the lake. Since most (but not all!) major lakes are not held as private property, lakes are polluted with garbage. In the absence of property rights in the water, governments must intervene (1) to take action of the kind a private owner would take as a means of preventing uneconomic wastage of the fresh water or (2) to establish property rights.

A similar threat once existed for petroleum. A form of solution was reached when subsurface oil rights were pro-rated to surface area owners. Now no one has an incentive to pump oil excessively in order to catch it and get its value, before someone else does—as with the fish or non-owned goods. (This kind of ownership is being developed for water.)

A specification of private-property rights in air is beyond our abilities. The fleeting nature of air is too great to do other than resort to nonmarket political controls.

*Conservationist contentions.*    The conservationists have three contentions. First, even if the use of trees now would give a more valuable form of wealth for the future, they contend the actual rate of saving should be larger. One way is to force people to save by not letting the goods be used for consumption. Clearly, this contention assumes that other people prefer more present consumption than that which the conservationists think desirable.

Second, conservationists argue that other people have the wrong idea about the most valuable *kinds* of goods to preserve for the future. Wildlife and natural-wilderness advocates want to close off certain areas from use as residences or as resort and ski areas. This has nothing to do with conservation or growth of *wealth*. It is instead an argument about which people will have their preferences satisfied. This is the issue with which this book started, the question of allocation of an existing stock of goods among competing claimants.

Third, an examination of the particular classes of goods that conservationists propose to conserve will reveal that many of them are goods in which private-property rights do not exist, or under the laws can be obtained only by "using" the goods. Water, beaches, and air provide examples. Water is today generally, though not universally, owned only by the person who "uses" it. Today people build aqueducts to sources of water, even though the water, if currently used, would not justify the present costs. Why build the aqueducts? The construction of the aqueduct and "using" the water now, often far in excess of currently economical amounts, is simply a (costly) way of establishing property rights to continued access to future flows of water.

The conservationists propose to control the rate of use with government planning boards. However, as we know, there is another kind of solution: to establish salable property rights in these resources, rather than to let them be claimed by the first person who makes use of the resources. Then, like the tree, they will remain untouched until their use is economic. It is not necessarily the capitalist private-property system that is responsible for what appears to be a wasteful use of resources. It is instead its absence.

Sources of Greater Wealth

The sources of greater wealth are saving and higher productivity and efficient use of human and nonhuman resources in exploiting profitable investment options. The existence of natural resources is not sufficient. Many countries (for example, a number of South American countries) are rich in natural resources but have not succeeded in exploiting them by efficiently organized or directed economic activity.

Natural resources have to be *converted* to useful form. In this country, the prairie was a forbidding area until man with the plow sweated over it. (With what incentive?) The Western areas are dry and require irrigation. New England's soil is rocky, its winters severe and summers short. Natural resources are not "free" resources. They were available to the Indians for centuries, but still the Indians were poor. Resources must be worked with skill and energy. In other words, people are a part of the natural resources. America was fortunate in being populated by a biased sample of mankind. Those who came were harassed into leaving Europe because they possessed unusual attributes. Many of the criminals who were "transported" to Georgia and Australia from England were guilty of strange crimes—disagreement with the crown, religious heresy, bankruptcy, evasion of economic restrictions on market competition in England. Murderers and thieves were more likely to receive capital punishment—which is not to assert that none of them was transported. In general, those who came were escaping regimentation; they were more self-reliant and dependent upon their energy in a community of open-market competition.

During the advance to the West, people who occupied and cleared the land could claim it as private property. They could sell it or borrow against it; they didn't have to stay on it in order to obtain the value of the income of the land they had created, as one must today in many foreign countries—for example, Mexico, Iran, Egypt, and India. They could "capitalize" and be directed by the present market value of the future consequences of their present actions. The coordinating, organizing effects of a market-directed system were relatively strong. Prices, profits, and resource mobility were influenced by open-market competition—relative to many countries today in which property rights and markets are curtailed. Suppression of open-market competition and incentives by political competition for power over prices and production and by prohibitions on market exchanges reduces the scope of specialization in achieving growth of income and wealth. Despite these disadvantages, can the political authorities provide other, offsetting advantages? A definitive answer cannot be given. Adam Smith believed that restrained access to open markets suppressed growth. But another school of opinion holds that a socialized economy can achieve a higher rate of growth by government control, rather than by leaving the rate and kind of investment to be determined by the voluntary market-coordinated decisions of individuals. Undoubtedly, a higher proportion of income can be saved by government action. The issue is whether a higher rate is desirable on those terms, and whether the higher proportion of diverted income will in fact be invested *successfully with as high a future yield*. The debate waxes hot, and the evidence is conclusive only to the adherents of each position.

### Size Distribution of Wealth and Income

Whatever the wealth of a society as a whole, the wealth and income of each person is of greater interest to him. One can view the distribution of income and wealth as if it were determined by dividing up an existing total, like dividing a cake among claimants. Or one can view the total amount of cake as a result of each individual's contribution to the total. In either case there must be a procedure for determining who gets what part of the inheritance and who gets what portion of current product. The preceding chapters have shown that economic analysis can explain who gets current product in various societies, although our predominant application was to the capitalist, market-exchange system. We know that each generation inherits from its parents a legacy. The form, total size, and division of that legacy among the heirs varies among societies. The amount a person will leave to the next generation certainly depends upon the rules of inheritance. For example, no doubt the legal right to endow one's own children—rather than the next generation at large or only the "state"—is an incentive to accumulate wealth as a legacy for one's children. Furthermore, the form of the "wealth" is affected. Parents who wish to endow their children in ways that cannot be thwarted by other people would devote more to educating children in skills, knowledge, and developed abilities, and not primarily in buildings, land, or goods. Jewish emphasis on education and development of the personal skills of their children has been called a survival trait for the Jewish group in the face of governments that confiscate Jewish wealth—an experience in which the Jews have long suffered.

### Age Distribution

Assume every person has an identical lifetime history of income, rising to a peak at about age 50 or 60 and then declining. If the population is composed of people of *different* ages, then at any moment the current incomes will be very unequal, with the younger having the smaller earnings. Yet every person could have the same life history of earnings. All are equally wealthy, when adjusted to a lifetime basis.

A source of income dispersion for people (of the same age) is differences in past savings and investment. Some people will save at an early age and invest in property, personal knowledge, and skills. At an older age they will have higher incomes than people who earlier consumed more of their income. Those who saved earlier sacrificed the pleasure of earlier consumption for the sake of more income or wealth later. (Does a person who saves a larger fraction of his income in his youth for high consumption after retirement have a greater "life utility"?) The upshot is that savings when young can lead to greater wealth (property and personal) in older age. This will increase the *old* age dispersion of reported income. But it represents a voluntary choice by each person.

Medical doctors, college teachers, and scientists with a doctoral degree have larger wealth at age 30 because they invested more during college age. If a high school graduate were to go to work and save 75 percent of his income for about seven years he too would accumulate a respectable amount by age 25.[6]

Earnings over a lifetime do not have a gradually growing pattern. Chance events make for extra-high incomes in some years and lower ones in others and this too contributes to the dispersion in the distribution of income at any one time. Business earnings (industrial, commercial, and agricultural) are especially volatile compared to earnings of employees or salaried people. There is no way to avoid this volatility, given our imperfect foresight. The question is, "Who will bear it?" We can all share it and thus spread that volatility over everyone so that it contributes to each a smaller fraction of their total earnings volatility, or we can let some people escape it more fully by inducing others to bear a larger share. This is what is involved in the specialization of asset holdings by property owners and profit receivers. Those who choose a larger fraction of risky (volatile) earnings will show a greater dispersion of later incomes. Some businessmen are very wealthy and some are poor; self-employed lawyers have a greater dispersion of incomes over their lifetimes *and* in any year at any one age than do salaried lawyers. In part, this is the result of a choice of a *chance* for more income relative to greater probability of an intermediate income.

[6] If he earns $4,000 a year for seven years (and saves $3,000 each year) he will, at 8 percent, accumulate a wealth of about $27,000 in seven years. And this would yield him an annuity thereafter for thirty years of about $2,500 a year. In other words, at the end of seven years he would have a gross income from his labor *and* his accumulated wealth of $4,000 + $2,500 = $6,500 annually, ignoring the growth in his personal labor-earning power. Will your college education do as well for you?

Obstacles exist to full exchange and specialization in risk bearing. To the extent that it is easier (cheaper) for people to negotiate exchanges of rights to various types of goods, this specialization is more effective. Investment in personal talents and skills is believed to be more difficult than in physical property. It is said that young people have a harder time borrowing for their own education than they do for housing or cars. However, in view of the subsidized college education for some young people, compared to their ability to get "free" cars, land, or buildings, it is not at all clear whether investment (at the less educated taxpayers' expense) in personal skills suffers a net handicap.

Even with initial equality of opportunity, talents, ability, and endowments (such as we have assumed so far), there are still forces for inequality of reported annual earnings.

### Market versus Nonmarket Income

Reported *money* earnings differ because people receive different portions of their earnings in nonmarketed goods (farmers versus city dwellers). Although having the same income, the money income flowing through the market may differ, thus giving another souce of difference in personal money incomes.[7]

Although possessing the same present wealth potential, some people prefer to take life easier and enjoy more leisure rather than marketable purchases. The teacher who takes an easier life, with three months absence from teaching, has a smaller money income than if he worked all year. Money incomes will differ, because the "income" is taken in different proportions of marketed goods and services.

Housewives' services are never included in income measures. Yet, if the services of a housewife were to be purchased, they would typically run from $2,000 to at least $6,000 per year. Caring for children, cooking food, shopping, caring for the home, planning purchases—all these could be provided by paid servants, governesses, and housekeepers. If that were done, an explicit market measure would be available. As it is, the income value of those activities is never included. This understates the income of poorer families by a larger proportion than it does of the richer families. A husband earning $4,000 a year would probably have services costing close to $2,000 provided by his wife. A person earning $40,000 a year would have services provided by his wife to the household at less than $20,000. Ignoring this makes money income distributions more unequal than real income distributions because it is customary to classify money income recipients as "families," or as what are known as "spending units"—a group of related people who live together and share income.

---

[7] Doctors typically provide services for other doctors at "nominal" charges. The "real" income of the patient is larger than indicated by his money income, and services provided by doctors are larger.

### Different Endowments

Although all the preceding factors are sufficient to introduce a wide dispersion of earnings as of any moment, two of the most striking factors are differences in ability and endowments. In a sense these two are the same thing, for ability is an endowment received from our parents, just as is any physical wealth. The genetic skills and talents with which they endow us are not a result of their lifetime activities—it is just "natural"; but the propertied wealth and culture they bestow on us are more dependent on their conscious action.

Be careful of one common error. It is not the *inheritance* of property wealth that contributes to dispersion or inequality of wealth. It is the prior *accumulation* of wealth at different rates that contributes to the differences in wealth holdings. The inheritance merely continues it (and provides a convenient place to tax it away). The wealth of the Crosby larynx, the Monroe body, the Koufax arm, the von Neumann brain, the Kennedy personality were not taxed as an inheritance from their parents; but the Ford, Getty, and Crosby endowment of propertied wealth to their children is heavily taxed—though not the Crosby voice in his children.

### The Poor

"The poor will always be with us, by definition." But will the distressed? Even though the bottom 20 percent of the income receivers may be enormously richer in the United States than in India, China, or Afghanistan, the concern for the local poor or distressed will not thereby disappear. First, a few of the poorest in the United States, and they are very poor and relatively few indeed, would not be much better off in absolute terms than in other, poorer countries. Second, even if our poorest were rich compared to other countries, there would still be reason to ask if the poorest here were being denied opportunities to realize their feasible and desirable potential. And even if they were achieving their full potential, some would have so low an income that the rest might be willing to do something to improve the lot of the poorest.

Undoubtedly some of the poorest (for example, the blind, crippled, feeble, and mentally weak) are incapable of producing a significantly greater income for themselves. Some with normal capacities lack the drive and responsibility to produce and save toward normal contingencies. Some were, in childhood, not given the kind of education that the rest of us received. Some are widowed, working mothers. Many of the poor are the very old, living off their wealth and relatives and reporting small incomes.[8] And our analyst will also

---

[8] A person with a life expectancy of five years and a wealth of $20,000 would report an income of about one or two thousand dollars, although he could consume at the rate of about $6,000 a year for five years.

have noticed many very young married couples (in college) with low *current* incomes.

Families whose primary source of income is from a woman or a Negro or an immigrant are more heavily represented in the poor than families with male, white, native-born family heads. The immigrant status seems to be transitory: In a few years, once the language is well learned, their representation in the poor falls off. Women and Negro heads of families show greater persistence in the poorer groups.

One's response is not the same to each of these many situations. For some we are torn with sympathy and a willingness to help. For others we withhold aid. In other words, we do not look at just the current money income and conclude that for every low-income recipient the same corrective or alleviative actions are desirable. To analyze the problems of the poor or of the very poor is to analyze a variety of very different situations.

Family responsibility for relatives is a prime means of providing aid to the poor. Probably the discrimination displayed in voluntary charitable aid reflects our judgments about the merits of each case and reflects our own attitude toward the problems of others. Social policy via government action cannot display such discrimination. When one is dispensing other people's money, extra care must be taken to ensure that the dispenser observes approved standards of discrimination. Individual judgments and opinion must be given less weight. Tax-financed activity to revise the distribution of wealth is part of our social policy. The graduated income and inheritance taxes take a larger portion from the higher incomes. But other taxes, like the sales and property tax, seem to take larger proportions from the lower income groups. A comparison of the distribution of income after taxes with that before taxes usually shows a less unequal distribution, at least in the sense that the extremes are less disparate. Unfortunately that comparison is defective because it does not allow for the distribution of government services financed by the taxes. If the services are distributed even more heavily to the richer (than are the taxes) the richer would be aided and the poor hurt. Many government services are favorable to the richer income groups. Public subsidized golf courses, better schools, parks, and roads in richer residential areas suggest that no clear answer can be given about the over-all effects of government tax and expenditure activities.

Government social welfare and poverty program activities represent deliberate attempts to ensure aid to the poorer. These programs are designed not merely to relieve the indigent by offering funds but also to foster rehabilitation, training, or increased productive ability. There are some who argue that the poor, with relatively few exceptions, are poor because they have not worked as diligently and been as careful in husbanding their income as have those who are not poor. Others have argued that the poor are poor for reasons not of their own making. "Poverty is the social by-product of a complex, highly interdependent, dynamic economy; therefore responsibility for alleviating this poverty rests primarily upon society." Both arguments, one placing blame on the individual and the other on the society, are defective. The first does not imply that nothing should be done to help even those who are so irresponsible as to be poor. The second argument is defective in that the poor existed even when society was less complex, dependent, and dynamic; furthermore everyone lives in that kind of society, so should everyone be taken care of by everyone else? Neither argument gets us very far in deciding whether or not to give aid. More germane is the issue of what kind of aid to give—in what form, how much, and under what conditions? Should we lend or give? Should the aid be in kind (housing, food, education) or is a grant of money appropriate? Should we take over their discretion and provide them with all the amenities as we do with institutionalized people?

Finally, poverty is not a result of the capitalist system. Poverty exists in socialist, communist, mercantilist, and whatever kind of system has ever existed. All have extremes. A socialist state may not have as many millionaires (in market value) as a capitalist state, but in the socialist state the relative political power of the political authority over resources is greater. It has more "political millionaires." Taking into account *market* and *political* access to and control over economic resources, there is little basis to state in which society wealth is apportioned to greater extremes.

### Evaluation

An explanation of factors causing the dispersion of incomes does not constitute a "rationalization" or an evaluation of the propriety of the dispersion. Nor should it be forgotten that the dispersion is one thing and the absolute income another. A rich society with a large dispersion or a poor one with a small one may have entirely different connotations. A rich society with a wide dispersion may still leave the lowest 10 percent with more income and wealth than the middle 10 percent in a poorer society. The collected evidence of economies like that of the United States leaves no doubt that over the decades the rise in wealth in incomes has *not* been achieved by a small fraction getting wealthier while the masses stayed poor. The upward trend has moved up the lowest 10 percent by at least the same multiple that it has the top 10 percent. But using a worldwide reference, is it true that over the past century or two the worldwide distribution has seen the bottom quarter move up in the same proportion as the top? The common impression is that it has not. But if we consider that a poorer person had a very short life expectancy a couple of centuries ago, then the increase in life length is a form of greater income and wealth that we must not overlook.

Nothing so far said denies that discrimination and inequalities of opportunities are important factors contributing to income and wealth inequalities, but they are only part of the contributing factors—which is not to suggest that since they are a "part" they can therefore be regarded as unimportant and irreducible. We know that children from the same family display an enormous variety of lifetime earnings; yet we know that income differences of children from poor families and from richer and more educated parents also exist.

We hope this discussion has provided some understanding of what policies will work in what ways toward avoiding undesirable obstacles to realization of income earning and saving potential of each person. For example, if you keep in mind the analysis of Chapter 8 on philanthropy, you will be more alert to the policies and actions that purport to benefit children but which in fact benefit the parents, with only minor effect on the children. You will also be more likely to detect policies that close markets to newcomers, the handicapped, or minority groups and therefore increase the proportion of those who must earn less than they otherwise could.

## EPILOGUE

This book has presented the choice-theoretic economic analysis of (a) the prices and exchange of goods, (b) the particular mix of goods produced, (c) the demand for and supply of productive resources, and (d) the earnings and wages of the owners and suppliers of productive resources, i.e., their wealth and income. In actuality, the outcome within each of these depends upon all the others—yet we considered one at a time, assuming the others to be fixed. We used, in short, "partial-equilibrium" analysis to comprehend each problem without studying in detail how the solution of one would depend on or change the solutions to others.

A more rigorous and advanced formulation of the entire problem would explicitly indicate all interdependencies and would solve all these artificially segregated problems jointly and simultaneously. That is known as "general-equilibrium" analysis. When one turns to the general-equilibrium problem—involving *general*-equilibrium prices and outputs in all markets jointly—he discovers that the interdependencies imply that changes in one sector will cause changes in other sectors. Suppose the prices of tires and potatoes do clear the markets for those goods—on the assumption that the incomes of tire and potato buyers are determined in an equilibrated market for their productive services. But if the demand and supply for their productive services were *not* instantly and effectively matched and cleared, their incomes would change and, in turn, change demands for potatoes and tires. Furthermore, the changed demands for these consumer goods would change the derived demand for productive resources used to produce potatoes and tires; so the income of the producers of these goods would change, affecting their demands for other goods, and so on and on.

If all markets could be *independently* cleared, regardless of what was happening in other markets, the partial equilibrium analysis would be entirely reliable and usable for study of the operation of the economic system *as a whole*. The whole would be the sum of its independent parts. But the parts are not independent, and the adjustments in each market are not achieved costlessly and instantly. What happens in one depends upon what happens in others and the convergence toward a general equilibrium situation may involve swings in income and production and fluctuations in demands for goods and services. Regardless of what any one person is doing, the whole of the economic cosmos reflects the speed and costs of ascertaining and moving toward those general equilibrating prices and outputs. Thus, recessions and booms occur in the economy as a whole.

In our exposition we implicitly assumed a monetary system that generated a supply of money in such a fashion as to avoid fluctuations in general demand and employment. Unfortunately, that is a false presumption: occasionally (e.g., during the 1930s) the authorities of the money system fail to control the money supply. We have also implicitly and gratuitously assumed that sudden, large fluctuations in the portion of wealth the public demands to hold as money, in response to shifts in the anticipated profitability of investment, were absent or effectively offset by appropriate monetary and government policy. The other portion of the complete elementary course in economics (not presented in this book) investigates these factors affecting general income and employment in an endeavor to explain monetary activities and government expenditure and taxing policy (called "fiscal" policy).

The theory of national income fluctuation (associated with J. M. Keynes) has often been misinterpreted in oversimplifications which ignore its underlying relative-price, choice-theoretic structure.[9] Such strong (incorrect) assumptions simplify the introductory analysis of current monetary and fiscal policy, but a full-blown Keynesian analysis does not make these gratuitous assumptions. While you may not in the other portion of the course observe an emphasis or heavy reliance on this relative-price, choice-theoretic foundation, do not make the mistake of thinking that the modern income determination theory rejects it or can exist without it. Whether or not the other portion of this course, as taught to you, makes such simplifying assumptions will depend on your instructor's view about the degree of simplification appropriate for the level of exposition for your course. This will vary among instructors and courses, depending upon the background and future curriculum of the students.

Summary

1    The capital market for lending and borrowing is a complex network of specialized intermediaries between savers and investors.

2    Interest yields are typically expressed inclusive of risk, so that riskier loans indicate a higher yield. The implicit interest yield on a one-year bond is $i = [(Ar + A)P] - 1$, where $r$ is the stipulated interest rate and $A$

[9] Details and justification of this statement can be found in Axel Leijonhufvud, *On Keynesian Economics and the Economics of Keynes—A Study in Monetary Theory* (New York: Oxford University Press, 1968).

is the principal amount, both due at the end of the year, and $P$ is the present price of that bond.

3    Negotiability is the legal right of the owner of a bond (creditor) to sell the bond to someone else. Bond exchanges facilitate negotiability; they also facilitate borrowing, because lenders regard negotiability of bonds as a desirable attribute.

4    Like many markets, the lending market is not entirely open and free of restrictions. Interest rates, extent of borrowing, and length of loans are commonly restricted by laws. These restrictions are supposed to protect borrowers and lenders from their own over-optimism. They do protect one class of borrowers or lenders from open-market competition of other borrowers and lenders.

5    The growth of wealth is increased if savings are cheaper (more plentiful), if property rights in wealth are more explicit and secure, and if profitable investments are more readily perceivable and exploitable by investors. Faster rate of growth of wealth is achieved not only by saving and investing more but by more profitable and effective institutions for *organizing*, coordinating, and directing productive activity.

6    Conservation, in the sense of preservation of resources in their initial form, is not necessarily a means of preserving or increasing wealth. Conversion of goods to other forms of wealth can be more productive of wealth. Incentive to conserve or convert goods to most valuable forms is aided by identifiable property rights in goods.

7    The distribution of income is partially a function of the age distribution of the population and the variations of a person's income with his age, life expectancy, investment in personal education and skills, savings, and investment in physical wealth. Hence, even if everyone had an identical earnings potential, at any moment neither incomes nor wealth would be equal.

8    Chance and imperfect foresight of conjectural events lead to choices of risk bearing that result in differences of wealth of various people. Chance effects that cannot be sold to other people result in differences in income and wealth that do not reflect a choice of risk bearing.

9    Market, pecuniary income underestimates "real income" to spending units, because of self-production by, for example, farmers and housewives.

10    Preferences for monetary wealth relative to leisure and less difficult work contribute to increased differences in monetary income.

11    Different endowments occur both in personal abilities and in physical wealth. The accumulation of wealth, not the endowment, is a source of wealth differences.

12    Differences in productive ability are magnified by the correlation between superior abilities and the amount of capital resources submitted to the direction of superior talent.

13    The distribution of wealth, reflecting past savings and investment and future earnings of different life lengths (since people are not all the same age at any moment), is more unequal than the distribution of incomes.

14    Closed or restricted markets contribute to differences in wealth by permitting some people to acquire monopoly rents (unless markets are closed to the richer people with only the poorer having access—which appears *not* to be the situation in closed or restricted markets).

Questions

1    "Five states—Arkansas, California, Oklahoma, Tennessee, and Texas—have constitutional provisions restricting the maximum contract rate of interest. All other states, except Colorado, Maine, Massachusetts, and New Hampshire, have generally statutory restrictions upon the rate of interest that may be contracted for in the absence of special statutory authorization for higher rates. The most common maximum contract rates are 6 percent and 8 percent a year, but a few states permit contract rates as high as 12 percent. Loans to corporations are generally exempt." So says the *World-Telegram Almanac* of 1962.
a. What is the difference between the "contract" rate and the rate paid?
b. Who is helped and who is hurt by these laws if they are effective?
c. Do you think they have any effect on the rate of interest?
d. What effect do they have on borrowing activity?

2    You propose to buy a house for $20,000. You have $3,000 in cash now. So you seek to borrow $17,000 from a lender at 5 percent rate of interest. We say 5 percent because the government of the state in which you live has agreed to guarantee the loan on your house since you are a veteran. The law will guarantee your loan so long as the lender will lend at not over 5 percent. Unfortunately, no one will lend to you at that rate because 6 percent is available elsewhere. But you are clever enough to find a lender who will lend to you at 5 percent, *after* you make the following proposal: If he will lend you $17,000 at 5 percent (which is, let's say, 1 percent less than the 6 percent rate he could get elsewhere—and thereby costs him $170 a year interest otherwise available; that is, 1 percent of $17,000 is $170 per year), you will buy from him insurance on the house and on your car and life. In doing this, you may

or may not realize that you could have bought the same insurance at a lower rate or more conveniently elsewhere.
a. Why do you make this agreement with him?
b. Is he being "unfair" or "unscrupulous" or "unethical"? Are you?
c. Who is aided or hurt if such tie-in agreements are prohibited?
d. Do you think they can really be totally prohibited by laws? Why?

3    Diagnose and evaluate the following news story from the *New York Times* (February 7, 1959, p. 30): "Earl B. Schwulst, chairman of the Bowery Savings Bank, said he would be greatly distressed if other savings banks moved soon to increase their dividend rate to depositors. Most New York City institutions are paying 3¼ percent. There have been some rumors that some institutions would announce soon an increase to 3½ percent. Mr. Schwulst said that the Bowery, the largest savings bank in the nation, was as well qualified as any other institution to pay the higher rate. But, he said, the Bowery would not lead the way because of a number of reasons he described as 'in the long-run interest of our depositors.' "

4    The President of the United States, to prevent a loss of gold, decides to take governmental action to increase the rate of interest. If he can successfully do this, he believes foreigners will leave gold on loan in the United States for that higher interest rate rather than take the gold home. Suppose that belief is correct and suppose the interest rate is increased.
a. What do you think the effect will be on the rate of building and housing construction? Why?
b. Will the higher interest rate affect all kinds of business activity equally? Why?
c. Why do you think the businessmen are so concerned about the policy that may be taken by the President and Congress if those officials decide to try to prevent a further outflow of gold?

5    "Havana: October 15, 1961: All renters in the towns and cities of Cuba became property (building—not land) owners this morning when the Castro government approved a long-awaited reform law. However, renters must pay the Cuban government for their newly acquired property during the next five to twenty years at the same monthly rate as their present rents. In addition, they must pay the government the taxes formerly paid by the owners. The former owners will receive a "life monthly indemnity" of from 200 to 600 pesos without regard to the amount of property they owned. Heirs will receive nothing. Any buildings now in construction will be turned over to renters selected by the government. If the owner (up to today) refuses to complete the building, the state will seize the existing building with no compensation at all. Holders of mortgages on residences and apartment houses will

receive 50 percent of the amount paid by the tenants to the state until the loan is paid, but no interest will be allowed." Why do people in many foreign countries "foolishly" hoard gold instead of using their wealth to develop the country?

6    "Where total investment is concerned, the economic system is in the lap of the gods." Do you agree? If so, why? If not, why not?

7    "Large corporations have so much of their own funds that they do not have to borrow in the capital-funds markets in order to make new investments. They are therefore immune to interest rates in the capital markets so that their investments are not screened as are those of investors seeking funds in the capital markets." Explain the error in that analysis.

8    Distinguish between conservation of specific resources and the growth of wealth. Is conservation of specific resources an efficient way to increase the productive wealth of the community?

9    Mr. A. Brimmer of the Federal Reserve Board is reported (*Time*, July 1966) as saying that the rate of investment in the United States in 1966 was too high to be sustainable and that the damper should be put on the rate of investment. Evaluate that statement in the light of the following observations:
a. Which particular investments should be reduced?
b. A dean of a law school is reputed to have told his entering students that one out of three of them would flunk. Should he therefore have reduced enrollment by 1/3?
c. Fifty percent of new firms do not survive three years. Should half of new business be prohibited from being organized?
d. What does Mr. Brimmer know that individual investors do not know which, if they knew, would induce them to change their actions or which would be good for the community at large?

10    In a public park an apple tree yields excellent apples. These may be picked by the public, but not more than one apple per person·at a time. When will apples be picked? Why?

11    If the American buffalo had been owned by someone, do you think the buffalo would now be so nearly exterminated? Why?

12    Do you think seals and whales would be faced with extinction if some person or group were able to buy, as private property, the right to catch whales and seals? Why?

13    A large lake is stocked with excellent fish, but no one owns the fish or the lake. Only by catching the fish can you acquire ownership in the fish.
a. What do you think will be the average age of fish caught as compared to the age of fish in a privately owned lake?

**b.** Which system will induce overfishing in the sense that more resources will be devoted to catching fish than the extra fish caught are worth? Why?

14    You are an unborn spirit; you are offered your choice of country in which to be born. In country *A* all land is owned by its users; absentee landlordism is forbidden by a progressive government. The land cannot be mortgaged by the owner or rented. Everyone is born with rights to use certain parcels of land and these cannot be taken away or contracted to others. In country *B*, absentee landlordism is common and legal. All land is privately owned and either used by the owner or rented to the highest-paying tenants. Land can be sold or mortgaged. Private-property rights are strictly enforced for everyone. Many people do not own land at all. Into which country will you request that you be born? Why?

15    If you were a Jew in an Arab country, or an Asian in Africa, or an Englishman in Indonesia, or an American in Argentina, or a Moslem in India, would you invest for your son in personal human capital or in physical capital? Why?

16    "Extending the three-mile limit now in force for American territorial waters out to 1,000 miles would help to conserve sea resources." Explain why. Why not extend the territorial claims out to half way across the ocean up to the territorial claims of other countries, as has been done in the North Sea for oil rights? What would that do to the doctrine of the "freedom of the seas"? What does the doctrine of freedom of the seas do to the efficient use of ocean resources?

17    If the State of Washington owned the water of the Columbia River, would that mean that Oregon could not get any of the water? Nor California? Or would Oregon and California be surer of getting water from the Columbia River? Why?

18    "Farmers' incomes are on the average lower than nonfarm income. Therefore farmers should be given special aid." If you agree, reconcile with the statement: "Teachers' incomes are on the average lower than those of businessmen. Therefore teachers should be given special aid." Why might the incomes of one group be lower without motivating a desire to help that group with special aid? Under what conditions would a lower income to some group be regarded as warranting tax-financed aid?

19    Having learned the lesson in Chapter 1 of this book on varieties of competition, you have just overthrown the existing government and established yourself as liberator of the people. If now you set out to establish conditions conducive to a growth of wealth and freedom for the people, without succumbing to the temptation to install devices that enhance your own wealth and political power instead, what kinds of laws and property rights would you enforce? Why?

20    Ask your parents what your family's income was last year, before income taxes. Then compare the answer with the data in the following table, showing the 1964 distribution of money income received by each tenth of all spending units, by lowest income in each tenth:

Lowest Income within Tenth

| Spending units | 1964 | 1960 |
|---|---|---|
| Lowest tenth | not available | |
| Second " | $ 1,600 | $ 1,500 |
| Third " | 2,850 | 2,640 |
| Fourth " | 4,050 | 3,700 |
| Fifth " | 5,200 | 4,600 |
| Sixth " | 6,320 | 5,500 |
| Seventh " | 7,500 | 6,280 |
| Eighth " | 8,860 | 7,200 |
| Ninth " | 10,680 | 8,600 |
| Highest " | 13,700 | 11,100 |

a. Probably most of the students in your class come from families in the top half. Guess what fraction of total national income goes to the lowest tenth, to the fifth tenth, and to the highest tenth.

b. Do you think the dispersion of *individual* incomes is less than for spending units? It is. Why?

c. If after-income-tax incomes were recorded instead of pretax incomes, how do you think the numbers in the above table would be changed? What would be the effect on the percentage of post-tax income available to each tenth?

d. Why is the post-tax measure of income better than the pretax as a measure of incomes to each spending unit? Explain in what respects it is a worse measure than pretax income.

Answers

Chapter 1

**1.** You are not expected to be able to answer this now. But upon finishing this course, you should be able to show why the concluding sentences are wrong. As for the first sentence, economic science has not trapped us—scarcity has.

**2.** False. It is because people are reasonable and, therefore, act in accord with their interest that there are economic problems and wars.

**3. a.** Until you know what "socially preferred" means, you cannot answer this question.
**b.** We do not know what socially preferred means. For example, does it mean that a majority prefer it, or that the most important people prefer it, or that everyone prefers it, or that the speaker thinks everyone should prefer it, or that he prefers it? Beware of any expression referring to the preference of a group.

**6. a.** Yes.
**b.** We know of no institution with dominant power of coercive violence that is not the government in any country. Government is an institution for enforcing certain admissible rules and procedures for resolving interpersonal conflicts of interest. The making and enforcement of laws and the judicial settlement of disputes are events that support the propositions. (Note that the statements say that government is *an* agency, not the only agency. For example, many social disputes are resolved by social ostracism, and by agreement to use an arbitrator.) Do not assume that government should not have that coercive monopoly.

**7.** G. Washington; F. Franco; T. Mao.

**9. a.** You should first want to know the behavioral consequences of each kind. More than that, we can't say now.
**b.** The only kind of competition made illegal by a price ceiling is that of offering more money (and all that can be bought with it) than the legal limit as means of offsetting weaknesses in other attributes in competing for goods. Fair-employment laws (prohibiting choice of employees by color, creed, or age) prohibit competition in terms of specifically offering an employer the personal attributes he may prefer. Pure food and drug laws prohibit offers of inferior food at lower prices or of new and possibly better but untested (according to government tests) foods and drugs. Private-property rights prohibit competition by violence and involuntary dispossession of goods deemed to be private property. Socialism prohibits competition in terms of offers of types of services and goods that individuals privately prefer, without having to obtain authorization of government officials for propriety of producing the services. These are merely examples of types of competition that are ruled out—not a complete chronicle, and certainly not an evaluation of the desirability of the various types.

**12. a.** Promises to raise or lower taxes (affect other people's wealth) in order to benefit those who vote for you. But the politician can't offer to sell services as a businessman can.
**b.** Will letters of recommendation help you get a better grade in this course? Does your past record influence the teacher of this course in making grades? Does wealth of parents?

c. Employees can offer to work for lower salary to get a job with favored employer in preferred town. Will this work in fraternities? How about candidate's ability to increase wealth of fraternity?

**17.** This question will be answered much later in the book and is designed to provoke a little independent thought on a term commonly used in economics.

**21.** A theory is logically valid if all its elements are *logically* consistent with each other or with some broader theory with which it is associated. It is empirically valid if its implications about observable phenomena agree with the observed phenomena. Neither implies the other.

**23.** **a.** They are different—because these all involve social, interpersonal interactions. As such, one person's behavior with respect to these characteristics or attributes will affect other people, and their response to his behavior will vary accordingly. Their response and their ability to influence his actions will depend upon whether or not there is private property—for reasons we shall see as we progress through the book. **b.** Nothing like this question to kill a discussion! (Remember, evidence does not consist of one's idiosyncratic memories or *ad hoc* examples.)

**24.** All societies use force and compulsion. The pertinent issue is what kinds of coercion and force do various economic, political, and social systems use. The capitalist system uses the force of self-interest; it is coldly impersonal in its market effects; it is a severe and unforgiving taskmaster. He who produces at a loss is forced out of business, perhaps with less compassion than under a socialist dictator, who could spread the loss over other people. More relevant than the question of which system uses less force is the question of the various kinds of forces (incentives, rewards, signals, orders, and penalties)—in terms of the resultant effects on the economic, cultural, and political behavior. For example, how are freedom of speech, job mobility, social fluidity, individual dignity, religious worship, search for the truth, etc., affected? The effects on all the various goals of a person must be considered.

Not even reference to the use of the rule of law versus the rule of arbitrary dictators is a basis for ultimate judgment. Here too the question is what law and what rules will be enforced by the ruling law: the rule of private-property rights, the rule of socialism, or some other?

Differences are implied about the kinds of opportunities or "freedoms" provided to individuals living under each system. The implications are that an open-market system gives individuals a greater range of consumption patterns or goods from which to choose. Whether it is "good" that individuals should have such a range of options to explore is a question that economic theory cannot answer. A greater range of choice can be regarded as a greater range of temptation, risk, error, regret, and deviant behavior. Just as a parent restrains his children's choices for their own good, we may prefer to restrain the choices of adults because everyone retains some childlike impulses.

Whether you wish to regard one system or the other as giving more freedom depends upon your meaning of "freedom." In one sense, freedom can include protection from the costs of resisting temptation and from making unfortunate choices; and, in another sense, freedom might include the right to bear those costs and to make those choices and explore tempting alternatives. Whatever your interpretation, the implications derived from economic theory about the factual consequences of different allocative systems will be helpful in forming a judgment.

# Chapter 2

**1.** The first statement contains no implication about any thought process. It would also apply to rocks and water obeying the law of gravity. The second statement suggests some mental calculation and choice among alternative possible actions. Neither statement has the slightest dependence on the concept of free will or independence of behavior; both are red herrings to the present problem. Economics does *not* have to assume the second statement as a basis for its theory, despite common arguments that it does.

**3.** Individuals, not abstract things called "colleges," make decisions.

**4.** The first statement means that more of one goal is achieved at the cost of having less of another. The second statement means that goals do not exclude each other.

**10.** It is.

**12. c.** Postulates 3 and 2 together.
   **d.** Yes.
   **e.** Postulate 3.
   **f.** Postulate 4.

**16. a.** Economics does not use the concept of satisfaction. It refers only to choices among available options. Remember "utility" is merely a name for an index for ordering choices.
   **b.** Ditto.

**17.** By drawing another curve above this one (or to the right of it) with similar properties (slope and curvature).

**19. a.** Yes.
   **b.** We don't know that any of them do.

**27.** *No* to all questions.

# Chapter 3

**1. a.** Between .25 and .33 meat for one unit of vegetable. Or, saying the same thing in reverse, between 3 and 4 vegetables for one unit of meat.
   **c.** Linus values vegetables higher in terms of meat than does Charlie. But Charlie values meat in terms of vegetables more than does Linus. So we could say that Linus, instead of valuing vegetables higher, values meat less than does Charlie. Implication is that values of any one good are expressed and measured in terms of some other good. Hence, both are involved in valuation, and we cannot tell which *one* is being valued; each is being valued in terms of the other.
   **e.** Consumption-substitution ratios must differ between two people, at their present situations, if exchange is to be mutually acceptable.

3. No. They do not imply what is good, bad, better, or worse. They imply what will be observed in the real world.

5. **a.** If it is supposed to mean that one area had more of some good than it wanted (could possibly use at all), the statement is dead wrong. And we can't think of anything else it might mean.

**b.** We propose that the relative supplies were different so that relative values were different—leading to mutually preferred exchange and re-allocation of goods among Mediterranean and Baltic people, á la Charlie and Linus.

8. No, it does not. It is the theory and its structure that conform to laws of logic and rationality. The predictable regularities of response of people to changes in their environment do not require they be "rational" any more than the response of water to a slope requires rationality by each molecule of water.

10. **a.** Yes. It is true for all goods.
**b.** We have yet to find one.

13. Middlemen facilitate exchange and specialization, while "do-it-yourself" is a reduction of specialization and exchange.

14. It assumes that the middleman performs no service to consumers or producers in facilitating exchange and that therefore he can be eliminated without someone else's having to perform the service in which he specialized. Eliminating the middleman is a form of do-it-yourself and as such is not necessarily more economical.

15. All are denials of open markets.

Chapter 4

1. Borrow one pair of shoes; sell the pair for four shirts; sell the four shirts for eight pairs of socks; then sell the six pairs of socks for one pair of shoes—leaving you with two pairs of socks. Repeat the operation, each time picking up a net gain of two pairs of socks.

2. *Exchange rates* among goods are prices, whether or not money be one of the goods exchanged. Prices are not bids.

3. Recognizability, portability, storability, divisibility—all of which go to make the price of the good relative to any other goods less susceptible to variation among people. Possibility of producibility would induce production until value of one unit of the money would equal cost of production—unless quantity is limited by law or controlled by government.

4. Rate of 18,250 gallons a year.

6. 70 gallons, because he will consume 140 gallons in the week rather than 70 gallons.

**7.** It is a fall in the price of candy in ice-cream units. Candy is cheaper relative to ice cream than formerly.

**9. a.** No.

   **b.** The negative functional relationship between price and amount demanded. The explicit numbers serve merely to illustrate explicitly the meaning of the negative relationship.

**13. a.** Incorrect. Ratio (ignoring the algebraic sign) is greater than one.

   **b.** Correct.

   **c.** It is conventional to call this an increase in amount demanded, not an increase in demand—which refers to a shift in the whole demand relationship.

**15.** He who purchases seven per week, for that is the same as a rate of 365 per year, and he does it at a higher price.

**20. a.** Economic theory says they would. Compare cars in countries with higher gasoline prices. How about extent to which automatic transmissions would be used?

   **b.** Increases gas use.

   **c.** Effects would be more extensive in three years than in three months.

**21.** All except last one. (Why?)

**22.** Nonsense expressions. Presumably, these terms mean only that someone wants more of something than he now has.

**23. a.** No such thing as basic need. We could use more and we could also get by with less security. It's a matter of what price we are willing to pay.

   **b.** We "need" more of everything that is not free. The amount of any economic good we choose to have is a function of its price. To say our children need more schools ignores what we propose to give up to get more schools.

   **c.** It depends upon the price, whether it is good enough to have at the price. If this says simply that more is better than less, O.K. Otherwise, it seems to deny relevance of alternatives.

**28.** If this happened with *equal* prices for slums and for high-quality spacious apartments, we would be stumped. In fact, however, we find that the prices of the high-quality dwellings are higher, which reduces the amount of the high-quality apartments demanded. Given the law of demand, we see that with a higher price of higher quality apartments, it is possible to reduce the amount people want or demand so that it does not exceed the amount available. Just why the price of slums should be so low as to induce more slums to be wanted than are available is something we shall take up later. For the moment we are interested in showing the implications of the law of demand.

**29.** What does invaluable mean? We are reminded of a caption in *Life* magazine describing a pearl necklace: "This priceless four-strand necklace is now in the possession of Mrs. Lovely, who bought it for $85,000." Rarely do we find such an incongruous juxtaposition of obvious inconsistencies. However, in fairness to those who often use the term "priceless," we suspect they usually mean that the priceless good is not reproducible. Thus, a Grecian urn or original Dufy cannot be replaced at any price if destroyed. At the same time, one should be careful not to think it can't be bought at a finite price, or that a nonreproducible item is necessarily valuable.

## Chapter 5

**1. a.** 0, 1, 2, 4, 6, 8, 9, 11, 13, 15 for prices from 10 through 1.
   **b.** 4 to $A$ and 2 to $B$.
   **c.** Shortage.
   **d.** Surplus.
   **e.** All depends upon where price is.

**3. b.** No. He values a sixth one at $5.

**5.** True.

**6.** True.

**8.** First is rate; second and third are stocks.

**12.** The "excess demand" quantities beginning at the highest price are –3, –3, –2, –2, –1, 0, +1, +2, +3, +5. Zero excess demand occurs at a price of $500. It is positive for lower prices and negative for higher prices.

**13.** If the demands of some people for housing could increase by exactly the amount the demands of other people fall, the aggregate demand to own houses will be unchanged. The former will purchase housing from the latter. In this sense, the demand to purchase has increased and the supply to sell has also increased. The price of housing would be unchanged.

**3.** You should disagree. A higher price permits a re-allocation of existing goods—a re-allocation that would not occur in the absence of higher prices. Immorality is a gratuitous judgment. That the profits to those who own the goods when prices rise are "unwarranted" is also a gratuitous judgment. The point is to note that higher prices do have a consequence—re-allocation—and that personal preferences should not blind one to that fact.

**7.** Holding down the wholesale price of cattle to the meat processors increases the spread between purchase price and selling price for the processors. The price to consumers would rise anyway because of the increased demand for meat. The wealth that would have been available to cattle growers is instead given to the cattle processors.

**8.** Both. Choice is an act of discrimination.

**9.** All.

**10.** True.

**12.** Price controls do not increase probability that lower-income groups will get more housing. They may get less (and over time with effect on production of housing, housing quality and quantity will deteriorate). Outcome depends more upon possession of nonpecuniary attributes that now play a greater weight in allocative decision.

**15.** Open-market prices would encourage (force) consumers to use other goods. Restaurant customers will take other foods, of course; but then this means households use more rice than if they too had to pay higher price. Greater revision in food habits occurs for those who eat in restaurants rather than at home. Continues apparition of "shortage."

**16.** Yes, for it does advance the argument (analysis?) to grasp the meaning of scarcity and to understand that economics says nothing about which goods ought to be allocated via the exchange-market form of competition. We leave it to you to try to figure out why the "degree of scarcity" should affect the form of competition that should determine how a scarce resource is allocated among alternative uses and users. We can't.

**17.** The belief that money or market-exchange value is the sole criterion of allocation is so widespread, deeply ingrained, and incorrect that it is worth spending some time in examining it. Money is not the only criterion; that much has already been established with our analysis. (That it ought to be or ought not to be is not the issue.) When I dine in a restaurant, I select my dinner according not only to prices but also according to what the item is. I never tell the waitress to bring me the cheapest items only. The taste, nutrition, and looks of the item are considered. Similarly, when buying a suit, I take into account the style, feel, looks, and fit, as well as the price. For national security, we don't buy the cheapest weapon regardless of what it will do, nor the most modern, expensive weapon simply because it is the most expensive or modern—but not as effective as three units of a cheaper weapon (for example, one B-70 as compared to three missiles).

Only if the options are equivalent in *all* other respects do money costs become the *sole* criterion, simply because cost is the only one that, in this case, makes any difference. On the other hand, if money costs were equal, then only the other attributes would be relevant.

Suppose that I own some land next door to where I live. Of two people who apply to buy the land, one—an ordinary man who offers $1,000; the other, a beautiful woman who offers at most only $995—I will sell to the woman. Her presence as a neighbor is worth more than $5 to me. The man could overcome his handicap if he offered $100 more. Money (exchange value) does count, but it is not the sole nor even the dominant (whatever that means) criterion.

A related criticism of the capitalist system says it relies on *market*—revealed money demands rather than intrinsic or humanitarian needs. By now there is no "need" to discuss the nonsense of "needs." But why do *market* demands count so much? The reason market demands are so effective is simply that exchange is a way to increase utility. Every person is free to reject the market demand and to exchange his wealth with "more deserving" people who offer less attractive market bids. But the market demand for exchange is heeded because people prefer to gain by exchange—not because they are perverted by capitalism or a desire for money.

If private-property rights did not exist, people would not be able to make such extensive market offers, because they would have nothing legally to buy or sell. In a university, the faculty does not have private-property rights in offices and classrooms; therefore, there is no marketplace where classrooms and offices are so easily exchanged. In a socialist system, market money demands are less effective simply because there is relatively less exchangeable property.

**18.** According to this criticism, a person is so influenced by his interest in his economic wealth that other criteria are dominated. However, the exchanging of goods does not make it difficult for anyone to be influenced by the artistic, social, humanitarian, or cultural uses to which he can put his goods and services.

Playwrights complain that the financial "backer" invokes his crass monetary standards. Artists complain that businessmen want mere display copy, not true art. The architect complains because builders do not want the artistic designs he proposes. What they really are objecting to are other people's tastes and preferences. But the issue is rarely put in so embarrassing a way.

Saying that only lowbrow products sell well seems to suggest that this is a result of the money-value system. But that system effectively reveals and enforces the "lowbrow" tastes and desires of the public. The actors and writers wish the public valued such quality more than it does. Hence, actors and artists are frustrated because other people don't want as much "quality" as the artists would like to provide at the prices they would like to get. Or putting it "selfishly," the artists must admit that the income they can get from "low-quality" work is so high that they prefer to produce low-quality plays and get a big income rather than produce high-quality plays and live with a lower income. In this case, it is also the artists' and actors' own tastes for more wealth, not merely that of the public's, that precludes quality.

## Chapter 7

1. **a.** At $2 per bushel, I could not affect price by withholding my stocks of wheat. Best price I could get is the market price of $2, whether I sell 1 or 1,000 bushels.
   **b.** No.
   **c.** Horizontal straight line.

2. **a.** Yes; 4,000 bushels; 2,000 bushels; none.
   **b.** Yes.
   **c.** No.

4. Yes. Because higher rate of sales is available without a lower price, hence increase in revenue for each higher rate is equal to the price of the unit of the higher rate.

5. Constant.

6. Yes, although in strict terms we assume that there is no rise in price as a result of withholding one's offers. This analytical classification yields implications that are for all practical purposes equivalent to those of a less extreme, discrete classification. For example, in this instance, it would not pay anyone to reduce sales for a higher price. The trivial effects are, for all intents and purposes, equivalent to no effects at all. Hence, in all the discussion it must be understood that we are using an extreme assumption simply because it makes the analysis so much easier without changing any of the pertinent implications. Marginal revenue is about 61-3/8 per share; total revenue difference is ($61,500 − $30,812.50 =) $30,687.50 for 500 shares change in sales. This is $61.37 per share.

9. **a.**

| Price | Quantity | Revenue | | |
|-------|----------|-------|----------|---------|
| | | Total | Marginal | Average |
| 20 | 2 | 40 | | 20 |
| 19 | 3 | 57 | 17 | 19 |
| 18 | 4 | 72 | 15 | 18 |
| 17 | 5 | 85 | 13 | 17 |

| | | | | |
|---|---|---|---|---|
| 16 | 6 | 96 | 11 | 16 |
| 15 | 7 | 105 | 9 | 15 |
| 14 | 8 | 112 | 7 | 14 |
| 13 | 9 | 117 | 5 | 13 |
| 12 | 10 | 120 | 3 | 12 |
| 11 | 11 | 121 | 1 | 11 |
| 10 | 12 | 120 | −1 | 10 |
| 9 | 13 | 117 | −3 | 9 |

**b.** It goes to purchasers as a lower price. For example, between a price of $18 and $19 with sales of four and three units, respectively, the marginal revenue, $15, is less than the average revenue, $18, by $3. This amount is distributed to buyers of the three units by a price that is $1 lower than formerly.
**c.** Six units.
**d.** $16.
**e.** Yes. See (f).
**f.** Having smaller profits than if price were set at $16.

10. **a.** He is searching for the wealth-maximizing price.
**b.** He is likely to find himself losing money as others enter business and reduce the price-cost spread.

12. **a.** Either $5 or $6.
**b.** $7.
**c.** None. It is the wealth-maximizing price.

14. **a.** Yes.
**b.** Two more, for a total of eight trees.
**c.** No. Remember, an eighth tree is worth at most $3. What you paid for "earlier" trees is irrelevant except insofar as it affects your remaining income and thus your demand for everything else. But this effect is spread over all your purchases, and we assume here it is a trivial amount compared to your total income.
**d.** Eight.
**e.** Yes.
**f.** Marginal price is same under each circumstance, and we adjust to price of extra units.

# Chapter 8

1. Law of demand relates purchase-rate to price. Law of demand and supply states price is at intersection of supply and demand. The former holds generally. The latter does not.

3. **a.** Yes.
**b.** Yes, and it pays not to cut rent to get an immediate occupant (because the cost of his moving soon is greater than wage cut would be worth).
**c.** No.

6. Seats are allocated first come, first served, rather than sold to worshipers—except in some churches, where a person donates a large sum and is given a special pew as a token of appreciation.

**8.** False.

**9. a.** Camp sites are not privately owned.
**b.** Less space per person.

**11.** As many as people want to use or create. No other objective test of the right number.

**12.** Depends upon extent to which you want to give parents authority to determine allocation of funds to family members.

**14.** Building and nonfaculty purposes gain and faculty also gains to extent faculty salaries are raised more than they otherwise would have been raised. Money that would be spent for faculty salary increases can be spent for other purposes.

**15. a.** $500 release of money for other purposes, plus a better education, which you deem worth $400 more than the one you otherwise would have purchased.
**b.** Parents gain a cash release of $500 (and you get an education worth $400 more to you).

**21. a.** Price of stock fell.
**c.** National and Eastern gained wealth value of the airline route. Taxpayers lost the value of those rights, which otherwise could have been kept by government when it sold those rights—as it sells timber and gas-prospecting rights on federal lands.

**23.** Tendency to price public parks and services at less than a market-clearing price is explanation. Motels, priced higher than facilities in parks, rely on the law of demand to keep amount demanded in line with facilities available.

**24.** The market-exchange system characteristic of private property (capitalism) has been the dominant institutional context of the preceding chapters. The economic theory used in the analysis is applicable to any system of competition (capitalist, communist, or what have you) for resolving conflicts of interest among people arising from the fact of scarcity. In fact, the analysis of allocation with prices at less than the free-market price is an application of economics to a socialist society in which free-market prices are not used. Think of the actual money price as being zero, or at some level below the free-market price. Then how will goods be allocated among the competing claimants? (Review Chapter 8.) The relatively greater nonpecuniary "discrimination" should come as no surprise.

Many communist systems rely on money prices and private property to ration existing stocks of some consumers' goods. In Russia, many goods are sold for money, and individuals get money income from wages and salaries—*but not* from ownership of productive physical capital goods and instruments and land. Given a person's money income, he is allowed to choose among a variety of consumption patterns by voluntary exchanges with other people via controlled (as distinct from open) market prices.

The postulates are not idiosyncratic to capitalist systems. They hold for all known societies. The laws of demand and production hold also, whether or not exchange of resources *via* a private-property exchange system is used. We illustrated the use of these laws under noncapitalist situations where private property and open markets were not the ruling institutions for the particular goods and services investigated.

What we are striving to emphasize is the distinction between economic theory and analysis on the one hand and, on the other hand, the institutional (legal and political) circumstances or conditions to which they are applied.

**25.** (c) is correct.

**28.** False; it is the consumption of the good that is referred to in the definition of a public good.

**31.** True.

**33.** Yes, this could be so. While it is not possible to know what is necessarily better, it is true that the total cost of providing parking space could be cheaper if it were not policed as carefully as a park-for-pay lot. A free lot would impose the costs on those who purchase from the persons who provide the free parking lot, but not on those who use the lot without doing any business with the providers of the parking space.

Chapter 9

**1. a.** May through September.
  **b.** May price is lower than March price, suggesting new crop is appearing. Lower prices for July suggest new crop is still being harvested and stocks are increasing, permitting higher consumption rates at lower prices.
  **c.** One or two cents a bushel—estimated by differences between futures prices during interval when no wheat is being added to stocks.

**2.** Primarily for profit.

**3.** Perishable. Increase in new supplies will be greater relative to carryovers, enabling greater increase in rate of consumption and lower prices. High storage costs (high perishability) implies lower future supplies (and larger present consumption).

**5.** Spot.

**7.** Can't tell. Do not know who have greater range of possible future positions nor what their relative probabilities are.

**8.** In the sense of having a greater range of potential future positions with greater probability of having a different wealth than now, I have the greater risk.

**10. a.** I bet on Mets and you bet on Dodgers.
  **b.** We have shared some risk and reduced range of our resultant wealths; in that sense we have reduced risk. I buy some (half) rights to your parking lot and you buy (half) rights to mine for the World Series days. Neither of us expects actually to help the other operate the parking lot. Instead, we just buy out the contracts later. He who lives in the winning team's town simply pays half his parking revenue (zero, since there are no games in his town). Each gets half the receipts regardless of which team wins the playoff game.

**12.** If we assume the price of the futures contracts falls by the same amount as the spot price, he will be able to buy back his futures contract at 35 cents per 100 pounds less than the price at which he sold it. The profit on his futures contract (ignoring contracting costs of about $30) is $175 (35 cents per 100 pounds for 50,000). This will offset his loss on the processed soybeans—if the two prices move together by exactly the same amount.

**13.** It usually protects against large losses, without giving up rights to large gains.

**16.** No. Speculation also exists where future is uncertain. Futures markets permit re-allocation of speculative burden.

**17.** You should disagree. Open futures markets reveal information for all at a lower cost. Those with superior knowledge could benefit from abolition of futures markets because they could then more readily keep their information secret.

**20.** Ask those who consider it immoral. Some people say "Selling what you haven't already got is immoral." A contractor who bids on a building at a fixed price sells what he doesn't yet have. He has sold a promise or commitment. Short sellers do the same thing.

**21. a.** We couldn't think of any method. Can you?

**22.** To $50.

**25. a.** No. It means there is less exchange and re-allocation of risks.
   **b.** Processors, growers, middlemen, and some consumers.

# Chapter 10

**1. a.** Usually production is used to refer only to activity that is not illegal. We wish we knew of a better answer. The question helps to reveal the hidden normative content of concepts which at first seem to be objective and free of ethical presuppositions.

**2. a.** 7 and .6; 6 and .8; 5 and 1; etc.
   **b.** .2 bushels soybeans for 1 bushel of oats.
   **c.** 5 bushels of oats per soybeans.
   **d.** Yes.
   **h.** Does it refer to weight, volume, value, calories? Without some rule for converting to equivalent common units, there is no way to assign meaning to question. As it is now, one has more soybeans, the other more oats.

**3. d.** 1.67 of each for Smith; 1.50 of each for Black.
   **f.** Nonsense question. (i) is 6.5 oats and 2.5 soybeans while (ii) is 3.17 of each.
   **g.** Still meaningless.
   **h.** No, for reasons we shall see later.

**4. b.** Different set.

**5. a.** Smith grows oats and Black grows soybeans.
   **b.** Switch to oats.
   **c.** If the price of oats is less than one-fifth the price of a bushel of soybeans, Smith should switch to soybeans.

**6.** (1) Production is efficient if the output of one of the possible products is maximized for stated amounts of the other products. (2) Production is efficient if an increase in output of one of the products can be achieved only by reducing the output of some other product.

**9.** Private property and observance of contracts.

**10. a.** Large.

**b.** Greater variety of relative talents and training so that differences between people's relative abilities are more common. Further, the larger market enables a person to sell more of his special output at profitable prices.

**c.** Greater concentration of time on same repeated subtasks. For example, hair-shearing for poodles only; specialists in color-TV only; architects specializing only in certain types of buildings; greater number of specialty shops.

**13.** Suggests I shall be poorer and engage more in "do-it-yourself." Reduced opportunity to trade limits extent to which gains from trade can be achieved.

## Chapter 11

**2.** Costs are not undesirable consequences of an act; they are the highest value of the forsaken output—the opportunity forsaken.

**3. a.** Highest valued.

**b.** Expressed in a common denominator or measure of value.

**c.** In general, no. Not if more than one thing could have been produced—including leisure.

**4.** Disagree. Lower cost is measure of substitution ratios between outputs, not a measure of the maximum amount of a good that can be produced.

**5.** The slope is the ratio of the change in output of one good to the implied change in the other, along an efficient possibility curve. This ratio of substitution in production possibilities is called marginal costs.

**8. a.** $B$.

**b.** $A$.

**9. a.** $C$ and $E$ produce $Y$; $A$ and $D$ produce $X$. $B$ can produce either.

**b.** Yes.

**c.** All except $A$ produce $Y$.

**d.** Yes.

**10. a.** Output of $Y$ would increase to eight units.

**b.** Appears here as increased demand for $Y$. But relatively there is no difference.

**11. a.** Rates of output, say per day—not measures of total output of $X$ and $Y$ over time.

**b.** No. It means that if demand changed at noon, 7.5 units would have been produced that morning at a rate of 15 per day.

**c.** $60Y$ and $90X$ in five days.

**14.** $A$, $B$, $C$, $D$ lose compared to what they would have been able to purchase with their income had $C$ been able to produce $Y$ and sell to $A$, $B$, and $D$. $E$ gains in wealth compared to what he would have had with open access to markets. $C$ loses wealth also. That $C$ lives on an island across the Pacific rather than on the American continent does not change effects.

**18.** No. It merely assumes that existing knowledge can be used and subjected to performance tests. Assumes no restrictions on rights to purchase or exchange knowledge. Knowledge is a valuable (economic) resource. To assume it is free is, for example, to deny that schools exist and that teachers perform a useful desired service. A substantial fraction of our wealth is devoted to gathering information of one kind or another. Do not assume that ignorance is irrational, ridiculous, or the result of inefficiency or wastefulness or deliberate lying.

**20. a.** GOODS

| $X$ | | $Y$ | |
|---|---|---|---|
| 8 | and | 0 | |
| 7 | " | 1.5 | $A$ produces 1.5 |
| 6 | " | 2.9 | $A$ produces 2.9 |
| 5 | " | 3.9 | $B$ produces $1Y$; $A$ produces $2.9Y$ (and $3X$) |
| 4 | " | 4.9 | $B$ produces $2Y$; $A$ produces $2.9Y$ (and $3X$) |
| 3 | " | 5.9 | $B$ produces $3Y$; $A$ produces $2.9Y$ (and $3X$) |
| 2 | " | 6.8 | $B$ produces $3Y$; $A$ produces $3.8Y$ |
| 1 | " | 7.5 | $B$ produces $3Y$; $A$ produces $4.5Y$ |
| 0 | " | 8 | $B$ produces $3Y$; $A$ produces $5Y$ |

Increments of $Y$ per successive units of $X$ sacrificed are 1.5, 1.4, 1.1, 1, .9, .7, .5. These diminishing increments of $Y$ for unit sacrifices of $X$ mean that marginal costs of $Y$ increase for higher rates of output of $Y$. Thus, marginal costs of $Y$ increase from $.67X$, to $.71X$, to $1X$ and on to $2X$, and then to infinite costs, since no more than $8Y$ can be produced per day.

    **b.** Mr. $A$ would be first; Mr. $B$ would be last.

    **c.** Mr. $A$ would be first.

**21. a.** Yes. Larger.

    **b.** We have assumed independent additive outputs from each person, as if they were lifting boxes separately. If they work jointly, two might do more than twice the work of each. We should then denote a team of workers as $A$, and another team as $B$. Similarly we could denote a team as a business firm, and the same principles would be applicable to firms. Joint interdependencies do not affect allocative principle but do make the exposition and analysis more complicated. At the present level of exposition, the simplification employed here is permissible.

Chapter 12

**2.** All costs of a decision are borne by the decision maker.

**4.** If you define access to sunlight as an aspect of land ownership, then it is a strengthening of private-property rights.

**6.** Nonsense. Property rights are the rights of people to do things with goods and services. They are human rights. Usually objection is made to the way a person uses his property, which means that the conflict usually is between one set of human rights and another set of human rights—not between human rights and property rights.

**12. e.** Nothing is implied about that.

**14.** The laws and regulations have an impact far beyond the cost of implementing them. For example, restricting use of markets to all but those with licenses can be considered a greater role than building a dam, which may cost more.

**15. b.** No, it shouldn't.
   **c.** In some cases damages have been awarded, but this is rare.

**17.** *A* is suing for property rights to uncongested streets. Under current law this kind of right seems not to be recognized. Presume we would rule against him. What do you say?

## Chapter 13

**1.** ($370 − $350)/$350 = .057.

**2.** $250(1 + .07)^3 = 306.25.$

**3.** Refer to Table 13–1, present value of $1. At 10 percent the present value of $1 deferred one year is now $.9091. Therefore, the present value of $220 deferred one year is $220 × .9091 = $200.

**7.** 5.075 × $50 = $253.75.

**9.** $5,000.

**11.** $1,000 and it will stay at that value.

**14.** Nothing will happen to your wealth now. And in one year it will be the same as it is now.

**15.** Annuity of five years with present value of $1,000 at 6 percent rate of interest is $1,000/4.21 = $237.53.

**17. a.** They fall relative to costs.
   **b.** Reduce profitability.

**19.** Yes. With higher rate of interest you still buy other resources equivalent to your house, but with fire you can buy only half a house or equivalent type of resource. In both cases you do suffer a loss relative to some other resources, but loss is more general in case of fire.

## Chapter 14

**1.** True, by definition.

**2.** Because they include future foreseeable sacrifices of present actions.

**4. a.** $3,000 (to nearest dollar) = 20,000 − .909 × (19,000 − 300).
   **b.** $4,482.
   **d.** Two-year annuity with present value of $4,482 is $2,591 per year.
   **f.** $1,183 per year.

**5. a.** $5,000 - (\$3,000 \times .909) = \$2,273$.
 **c.** $2,273. See answer to (a).
 **e.** $(\$6,000 \times .909)$ plus $2,273 = \$7,727$.
 **f.** $(\$6,000 \times .909)$ plus $(\$6,000 \times .909^2)$ plus $3,761 = \$14,171$.
 **g.** $f - e = \$6,444$.
 **h.** $1,000.

**6.** The renter of the car pays for the depreciation as part of his rental charges. He avoids tying up capital funds only in the sense that the leasing company is lending him the car and charging him for its rental, whereas he could have borrowed money, bought a car, and then paid rental on the borrowed money (as interest). The rise of leasing services is primarily a consequence of business tax laws too detailed to go into here. But the point is that renting or borrowing money or paying out of your already accumulated wealth doesn't change the costs at all—aside from idiosyncracies of the business tax laws.

**7.** Old firms are not burdened by old equipment. They too can switch to new goods. That they don't simply means they can compete by using old equipment, whose value is recapitalized to whatever level will enable it to continue to be used—unless its value must be zero, in which case it will certainly be retired. First sentence is typical of a very common error—an error that ignores market's valuation process of existing goods.

**9.** Rate and the total amount planned for production.

**11.** 4,000,000 units.

**12.** Cost increases less than in proportion to volume. (What did you assume about rate of output?)

**14.** It decreases.

**16.** It decreases.

**18.** Yes.

**21.** Public prefers lower cost more than greater variety of models.

**23.** Price will be greater for quick delivery of completed product.

**26.** The latter—regardless of the relationship between output and cost.

**31. a.** None. That they will not far exceed it for long is a result of open markets.
 **b.** None.

**32. a.** Impossible to divide costs between these two uses.
 **b.** Not answerable. Divide it half and half if you wish. But what difference does it make for any real problem? None.

**33.** The ad writers have mixed up rate and volume effects on costs. A greater supply—volume—implies a lower unit cost and also a lower price. Bigger volume demand yields lower price because it evokes a greater supply (in volume sense). But in the *rate* (or speed of production) sense, higher demand yields a higher price. When demand increases in both the volume demanded and the speed at which that volume is demanded, price may fall (in response to volume effect) but it will be higher than otherwise in order to increase the rate of production. What advertising can do is to affect the volume demanded, but if it also increases the rate at which the good is demanded, it leads to higher prices.

**34.** Output of other products, of which gasoline is one, increases. Since gasoline, unlike oil, must be stored in very expensive tanks, refineries induce service stations to buy more gasoline and store more in station storage tanks. These retailers, presented with lower prices, keep their tanks more nearly full—and is evidenced by retailers' increased frequency of smaller than usual orders. In other words, retail service stations keep their storage tanks more fully loaded, maintaining a higher average load during low-price periods. In turn, motorists are induced to keep their tanks more nearly full.

## Chapter 15

**3.** Yes. Also salable without permission of other owners.

**4.** Convenient way to assemble capital. No one owner has to put all his wealth in one company in order for company to be large. Easy salability of ownership also enhances attraction of investment. In other words, it is an efficient form of property risk bearing.

**5.** No to all questions.

**6.** Depends upon what you mean by "very few." Annually many corporations show decreases in the value of their common stock. Approximately 30 to 40 percent of all corporations report losses for the year, although the firms reporting losses are not always the same. Since 1916 the percentage has always been above 20 percent and has been over 50 percent in several years. For all reporting corporations the aggregate earnings (after taxes) normally run about five times that of the losses. For more details consult *Statistics of Income*: U.S. Treasury, issued annually.

**7.** The "boss" is able to tell people what to do because he pays them. Turning it around, the employee tells the boss what to do—that is, to pay the employee some money. Obviously, neither tells the other what to do. Each agrees to do something if the other will do something. If it be said an employer can fire an employee, so can an employee fire his boss by changing jobs.

**10. a.** Present value of receipts is $19,662. Subtracting present value of costs of two-year ownership and operation (from question 5f, Chapter 14), $14,171, the difference $5,491 is the imputed profit.

**11. a.** No. In ordinary circumstances we would expect stability.
    **b.** Should the typical voter or minority groups be able to turn out the governor of their state? It is precisely in order to prevent every single person from making his own will count that voting systems are utilized.
    **c.** It means a majority controls through the medium of a minority of the stockholders to whom a majority gives its votes, as the Congress represents a minority of the American public, being only some 537 people representing 200,000,000.

**12. a.** Wealth constraints are different in the two classes of cases.
    **b.** The former, because of reduced possibility of personally capturing capitalized value of improvements of new management—as can be done in private-property corporations via purchase and sale of common stock.

**15.** Sentence is correct. By selective purchase of assets of personal wealth holdings, people can vary their mixtures to suit their risk-bearing preferences.

**16.** Socialism does not permit selective, discretionary, optional selection of wealth holdings by each individual. Profits and losses are borne in accord with taxes, rights to use government resources, and powers of political office.

**17.** Former facilitates or permits the latter to be revised in accord with personal preferences.

**22.** Both—you first had a profit of $50; then, by continuing to hold that wealth, you incurred a loss of $25 during the second month. Whether or not you convert it to cash has nothing whatever to do with the fact of your change in wealth—that is, of profits or losses. Only the income-tax people use the conversion-to-money principle, for computing taxes.

**27.** A loss was realized when the stock price fell. If the price rises, the old loss is now fortunately offset by a new profit. You can't hide from losses by burying your head in the sand or by not converting your wealth from one form to another. You merely throw away options with that kind of reasoning. Don't make the logical and economic error of thinking you can escape a loss by not selling while the price is lower than it used to be, or even lower than what you paid for it. That kind of thinking does not engender strong survival traits for your wealth.

**29. a.** All. Some by patent rights, some by licensing which limits entry, some by limiting access to open markets for competitors, and one (Sinatra) by natural superiority.

**31.** They perform selective risk-bearing function, whether they know it or not. In prospecting for oil, some will lose and some may win. And some of us do not have to commit our wealth to that risky venture. Still, if we want more oil, the "lucky" investors who bear the risks relieve us of that risk. For that function they are allowed, under private-property system, to obtain profits. As for taxing them away, that depends upon your desire to have risks borne selectively, voluntarily, upon your willingness not to renege on general agreement to let lucky ones keep wealth, and upon attitudes toward differences in wealth among people.

Chapter 16

**1.** No.

**2.** Output program is 15 if price is $1.50; $6.20 profit; output program, if price is $5, is 24.

**4. a.** To produce more would involve costs that exceed the value of the extra amount produced. Resources could be used elsewhere in higher-valued uses—as reflected in their costs.

**7. b.** $1.40.
   **c.** 1,400 per year.
   **f.** Buyers or sellers who want to buy or sell more than they can at the existing price.
   **m.** Under our assumption that all firms are identical, yes; all would survive up until total output reached 2,100. If more enter, losses will occur and some will have to leave or continue to lose wealth.
   **o.** Profits will be capitalized into costs; and costs, recognizing value of all the resources used by the firm, will equal revenue.

**9.** Marginal costs along with marginal revenue indicate maximum wealth output, while average costs in relation to price indicate whether the profits are positive or negative.

**10.** Suppose only the president of the company knew the secret and also owned some shares. He would be less willing to sell at the old price and would be willing to buy more shares. In other words, his demand to hold shares increases and thus affects market demand. Certainly several people in the company knew the secret and several also owned stock in the company. Price would rise because their own demand to hold the stock had increased in the light of the secret developments.

**11. a.** Reduce the output.

**b.** At first, if output is not reduced but taxes are paid, the wealth of peanut growers will fall. Higher marginal costs indicate a lower output as the new wealth-maximizing output. Or some who formerly made profit or broke even will now have a loss and be induced to abandon or reduce peanut production.

**c.** Reduced supply, shown by shift of supply curve to left, implies higher price.

**d.** Land will fall in value only to extent it was worth more for peanut growing than for next-best use.

**h.** Peanut consumers.

**14.** Resources will be increased in production of $X$ until extra value of output of $X$ falls to $5.

**15.** Not "consumer sovereignty" but "individual sovereignty" is more accurate. Individuals make choices as consumers (buyers) and as producers (sellers). An individual expresses choices about working conditions as much as about consumption goods. If mining is unpleasant compared to cutting timber, so that individuals are more willing to work at the latter rather than the former, the amount of lumber relative to coal will be larger than if individual preferences as producers were reversed.

Because there are so many other people, each of us is usually powerless to affect output or market demand in a significant way. This does not mean we cannot choose among alternative purchases or products to produce. Nevertheless, because we cannot significantly change the range of offers made to us, each open-market producer thinks the consumer (a personification of the market) is sovereign, while the consumer erroneously thinks that producers (personification of supply) decide what consumers can have.

## Chapter 17

**2.** Price-takers' demand curve is horizontal at highest price at which seller can sell any of his product, while in price-searchers' market his demand curve is a negatively sloped function.

**5.** Yes, because extent of exchange and specialization is reduced, with consequent smaller wealth.

**7.** Price that maximizes their wealth depends on demand, not on their own desire for more wealth. Prices three times as high would, in opinion of sellers, yield smaller wealth or profits.

**11.** Sales price, if goods were available at that price at time of sale. Price means exchange prices, not hoped-for price.

**13. a.**

| | | Revenue | |
|---|---|---|---|
| Price | Quantity | Total | Marginal |
| $4.00 | 0 | 0 | 0 |
| 3.90 | 0 | 0 | 0 |
| 3.80 | 0 | 0 | 0 |
| 3.70 | 0 | 0 | 0 |
| 3.60 | 0 | 0 | 0 |
| 3.50 | 0 | 0 | 0 |
| 3.40 | 1 | 3.40 | 3.40 |
| 3.30 | 2 | 6.60 | 3.20 |
| 3.20 | 3 | 9.60 | 3.00 |
| 3.10 | 4 | 12.40 | 2.80 |
| 3.00 | 5 | 15.00 | 2.60 |
| 2.90 | 6 | 17.40 | 2.40 |
| 2.80 | 7 | 19.60 | 2.20 |
| 2.70 | 8 | 21.60 | 2.00 |
| 2.60 | 9 | 23.40 | 1.80 |
| 2.50 | 10 | 25.00 | 1.60 |

**b.** Output is 18.

**14. a.** Same as before; $2.70 price and output of 14.

**15. a.** Raise it by 30 cents.

**16. a.** Price-searcher; an open-market monopolist.

**17. a.** Yes.

**18.** Disagree. Advertising gives information about new locations of banks. Banks are not identical even though they are guaranteed and regulated. Personal terms of service, location, facilities differ. If advertising were prohibited, some people would be less informed about other alternative opportunities. To say it does *no* good is a pretty strong statement that is easily disproved.

**20. b.** Yes.
   **c.** It is, when I do it. How about you?

**22. a.** Yes.
   **b.** The government is not a monolithic agency of just one person. It often does conflicting things at the same time, in response to different pressures.

**23.** In the sense that it indicates the amounts of the good that the productive resources would be willing to provide through the intermediary of the businessman. But it does not present the supply schedule of the amounts actually forthcoming at each potential selling price of the good, because the intermediary businessman is heeding marginal revenue rather than price (average revenue).

Chapter 18

**1. a.** Slightly more than 10 cents. (Call it 10 cents for subsequent computations.)
   **b.** Between 65 and 67 cents. Call it 67 cents for subsequent computations.

**c.** Each would sell ten units at 67 cents each, for $6.70 daily.

**d.** Formerly received (10 cents $\times$ 20 units) $2 daily. Each gets $4.70 more.

**4.** Government agencies enforcing laws against collusions concentrate on collusions against government. Second, government uses system of sealed bid, publicly opened. This is ideal for preventing secret price cutting or evasion of collusion by colluding firms.

**5. a.** We don't know the answer to this question. But it shows the difficulty of deducing collusion from overt behavior.

**b.** Newspapers are privately owned and use privately owned resources. Their right to publish is not controlled by government agency.

**6. a.** Team owners are able to sign new players at lower wages, since other owners agree not to compete for these players. The team owner's problem is to pay just enough to induce the newcomer to play; he does not have to compete against other owners. The competition is transferred to that of determining the initial assignments of newcomers to each team—by giving the lowest-standing team first choice of the newcomers (high school graduates) and the next-lowest team the next choice. This is the "draft." Although this assignment system is alleged to help equalize team abilities, it does not; players are subsequently sold to other teams, at prices far in excess of that paid the newcomers. The draft is simply a device to pay players less than they would get in open markets, while the resale of the players to other teams at higher prices is a scheme of wealth redistribution among the team owners. (If the two football leagues reach an effective agreement, as seemed to be happening as this book went to press, they must beware of the Canadian Football League, which, being "left out," will be able to get new players more cheaply than otherwise.)

The better athletes suffer. Since it is impossible to know in advance precisely how good an athlete will be, the initial sign-up price will be lower to reflect that uncertainty. There is a stipulation in all contracts that wages cannot be cut "rapidly," so those who turn out to be poorer than expected will be overpaid for a substantial time. Those who turn out better than expected will be underpaid thereafter, because other team owners will not bid for their services by offering the player the higher wage, but will instead pay the team owner to get that player.

**b.** Perhaps this explains why we call these "sports" rather than "businesses." No business could do this. It is a much tougher, and still unsolved, task to explain why other businesses cannot do what sports can do. The existence of laws restricting business firms does not solve the problem.

**8.** Collusion connotes elements of deception in seeking to negotiate exchanges in the pretense that the sellers are acting as independent competitors. Buyers are misled into presuming sellers are acting independently. If buyers knew sellers were in agreement, buyers would be alerted to incentive of each seller not to bid as he otherwise would. Without element of secrecy, buyers are aware of lack of inter-seller conflict of interest—as, for example, among the two salesmen of the same firm. The pretense of competing with respect to prices and quality is designed to induce buyer to think he is already obtaining advantages of inter-seller competition.

With open collusion, such as mergers, there is no pretense. Buyers are not deceived and can then obtain offers from other independent sellers. Open agreements not to compete are not deceptive and consequently are much less effective in open markets. Partnerships being open are not deceptive, hence do not connote elements of collusion. Element of deception is undesirable.

Competition connotes elements of method of resolving who will get what of existing resources, while cooperation connotes joint action to increase total stock of wealth to be distributed. Some actions do both at the same time. Thus, exchange with specialization is both competitive and cooperative in increasing wealth as well as in allocating it.

**15. b.** Yes, because it permits discrimination among customers according to their demand.

**18.** Each can judge what is best for himself, we suppose. As for us, we would prefer formal exchanges not to shut off trading in particular securities, thereby reducing exchange opportunities. Under present system, presumption is built up that stock-exchange officials are good judges of what price changes are justified or what news ought not to be allowed to affect decisions of individual investors—a presumption which not even the stock-exchange officials will defend. Rationale for restrictive practice is that wide price swings resulting from news that turns out to be incomplete or exaggerated are often blamed on the stock market, with suggestion that stock-market officials were responsible or that they ought to have prevented such unjustified (with hindsight) swings. In fact, these wide swings are the result of incomplete information, which no one can improve on at the time. On the other hand, if the stock exchange closes trading at such uncertain times, and if the news is verified and does bring a persisting change in demand and supply conditions, the exchange can say that the new price truly reflects the situation. What this ignores is that stopping trading during those times locks existing owners into continuing ownership even though they would prefer to shed the uncertainty by selling to others who are more willing to bear it. Bad news is made more damaging for existing holders in that they cannot sell out as early at the suggestion of worsening conditions. Consequently, it is not correct to say that closing down the exchanges at the arrival of big news (assassination of president, outbreak of war), or suspension of trading in particular stocks, is a good thing.

**19. a.** Owners of high-cost stations and stations already in existence would benefit. Low-cost stations and those who might enter business are hurt.
   **b.** Your guess is as good as ours. How about men with the prettiest wives?

**20. b.** As any of these groups, we would oppose the development proposed.

**22. a.** We think students can discriminate as ably as any other group you would suggest. To the argument that students are prone to take snap, popular, "theatrical" courses, we ask, "What is bad about popular, theatrical courses if the course is nevertheless good?" To say that students select snap courses (meaning courses that are easy—not because teaching is good but because course content is trivial) is to provoke question as to why students do that. To say they are lazy is to presume that they should not be lazy or that only hard-working students should attend a class—a rather presumptive judgment. More germane is question of why students who are able and motivated to go to college should nevertheless sacrifice "good" courses for sake of an easy grade. Does it suggest something about the criteria imposed on the students by the college administrators? What?

**24. a.** The best—by definition, since the students can select from the entire world, rather than just within one state.

**26. a.** No. We know only of more economical goods driving out less economical goods. Ignoring price or costs, we can cite examples in each direction—an irrelevant exercise.

**28. a.** Longer-run consequences are, insofar as foreseen, discounted into present capital value of the enterprise and are hence borne by the present owner.

**b.** If he did not have salable rights, these effects would be borne by those who come along later. He would be more concerned with the immediate effects than if salable, and hence capitalized, values of assets under his control were his; for these current values would more fully reflect long-run effects.

**29.** That capitalist money-seeking activity cultivates deceitful advertising, false claims, and dishonesty is so serenely believed by some people that it's a shame to waken them. The fact is that dishonesty and deceit often do pay. Therefore, it is sometimes said that free and open competition in the market gives a seller an incentive to lie in order to get customers from his competitors. Yet politicians also lie and don't tell the whole truth when campaigning or making speeches. They are not more honest than commercial advertisers. The socialist governments are not distinguished for their devotion to the truth. Surely there are good grounds for doubting that capitalism is more conducive to dishonesty than other systems. Nevertheless, it is worth considering the questions "Does capitalism reward one more for cheating than does any alternative system? Is the cheater likely to be discovered in the capitalist system and punished as effectively as in a different system? Is the public more likely to be deceived?"

That everyone has an incentive to lie and cheat is not denied. But is the ability to get away with it affected by the ease of competitors' making counterclaims? The question has only to be posed to be answered. A newspaper will be more careful with the truth if it knows that other news media can challenge its veracity. Politicians are more cautious if they know opponents can challenge their statements. A witness in court is more careful with the statements of facts if he knows he is going to be cross examined by the opposition. The easier it is for all to enter the market of ideas, the more counterclaims and different interpretations of events will be offered. In open-market capitalism, the incentives to disprove the claims and to submit counterclaims are increased. That is why it is a good rule to talk to a Ford salesman if you want to detect the truth about Chevrolets, and conversely.

## Chapter 19

**1.** There are many alternative ways of doing something, all of which can be technically efficient. But, of these, only one minimizes the value of forsaken opportunities; that is the economically efficient one.

**3.** It is impossible to tell from that information. Costs are unknown.

**6.** Can't tell. This tells us nothing about cost. We presume new method is technologically or technically efficient, in that no more could be obtained as output for given amount of specified inputs. But this doesn't tell us output is worth the input.

**8. b.** To include exchange efficiency. Values of outputs are being included as judged by what people will pay in an exchange system. Thus, efficiency is broadened to include deciding what to produce, rather than merely the cheapest way to produce an arbitrary output.

**9. a.** Suppose you had one piece of paper and were told to maximize your use of that paper. What would you do? Is it clear now that the expression has no meaning or that it means anything you want it to mean? Usage is not something you maximize; for usage is not measurable in a single-dimensional sense. In international radio-communications conferences, the statement sounded good to many radio and electronic engineers working for the Federal Communications Commission and for the State Department—precisely because it lets them interpret radio uses however they wish to. It's like having your parents tell you to maximize the use of your time at college.

11. **a.** All now twice as large.
    **b.** Increases them proportionally to rise in price.

12. **a.** Three labor and 4 capital, but if we interpolate we can do still better by using a little less than 4 capital and a little more than 3 labor—but not as much as 4 labor and 3 capital, which costs more than using 3 labor and 4 capital.
    **b.** 2 capital and 5 labor.
    **c.** Same one is cheaper. Relative prices of inputs did not change.

13. Decrease in total versus decrease in increments.

15. Jobs of workers on railroad engines and jobs the displaced workers will accept elsewhere; also, jobs of workers on railroad engines and jobs of workers making equipment that will be used if railroads can revise their work rules and assignments.

17. **a.** Yes. Equipment on the bus for a laborer on the bus.
    **b.** Yes. Labor off the bus for labor on the bus.
    **c.** Yes. Total labor is re-allocated in its tasks. No labor is released from work force, since that labor is used to produce more of other goods—except to the extent that some now choose a bit more leisure (as total output is larger).

19. No. Unlimited number of jobs available; only those are filled which are highest-value jobs, given present knowledge and resources. New inventions induce labor to move to other unfilled jobs. Each time the labor moves to a less valuable job, relative to old job. But at the same time the total wealth of the community is increased. The displaced person, as explained in the text, has no assurance of realizing a net gain from the particular innovation which displaces his most profitable job opportunities; but he does gain from most other innovations that do not displace his job.

21. **a.** Increase the amount of that resource used relative to other resources.

22. **a.** Fixity of ratios of kinds of inputs in the final product says absolutely nothing about the ratios in which those inputs will be used to produce the good.

25. Explained in text on pages 452–453.

26. See text, pages 452–453.

27. The desire for greater wealth and the competition among actual and potential employers for those resources that give greater rather than less wealth.

29. **a.** Same as before: maximize utility. But, now less profit or net value of output can be retained or taken out by the owner; hence, less attention to profits as a source of utility.
    **c.** Possibly some, but not as strongly as if enterprise privately owned. Would let it depart from ratio if thereby obtained more utility from other uses of resources rather than for profits or higher pecuniary exchange value.

32. **b.** Invest in personal intellectual skills, since these are not as easy for the state to appropriate as physical wealth.

Chapter 20

**3.** Both can be correct—as explained in text.

**4.** Depends upon infant mortality rate. If half of all children died in first year, and .2 survived to age 10, and if desire for children reflects desire for "grown-up" children, and if these mortality rates were lower for higher wealth and education of parents, we would expect higher number of births for poorer parents and fewer for richer; but in number of children in family at age 10, we could find more for richer than for poorer. The point is that in comparing countries, if one uses the same definition of "children," he can be misled about effects of wealth and education and population growth.

**7.** People differ in their productive abilities, and their costs of acquiring skills. The cost of acquiring skills (costs referring to all factors that restrain one person's ability to duplicate that of another) are such that wage differentials can exist. These wage differentials will be smaller than the costs of acquiring skills that would enable lower-paid workers to do work of higher-paid people. Except for fortuitous matching of demands and supplies at wages equal in all tasks, differences in wages will persist, but they will be less than costs of acquiring skills of higher-paying jobs and/or any other transfer costs.

**8.** An unlimited number of jobs are available in a world of scarcity. If productivity in those jobs or tasks that people can perform in Arizona is not as great as elsewhere, population increase will fall off as people move elsewhere.

**9.** It means that 300,000 workers in jobs now refuse to cut wages enough to compete with new techniques in present jobs and prefer to accept jobs elsewhere at not so great a cut in wages. Of course, they prefer not to shift to a new job at all at a wage cut. Automation is revising the relative demands for labor on various jobs, lowering some and raising some. Only those that are lowered are noticed in this statement that is being evaluated. (We do not hold the number 300,000 as valid other than for purposes of discussion.)

**11.** An infinite number of "unskilled jobs" exists. Most pay less than people are willing to accept, because they can get more money elsewhere. Whatever the reason for the unemployed, it is not that there are fewer unskilled jobs than unskilled workers. (We discuss some reasons for unemployed later.)

**13.** Movie producers do believe that receipts from picture will be at least that much larger if they have Taylor rather than Hepburn. In other words, last sentence of quoted statement is challenged. Whether or not she is worth that much more is a judgment that producer has to make; and his actions reveal that if Hepburn could have been obtained for only $1,000,000, the marginal product of Taylor is, in his opinion, greater by at least $4,000,000.

Marginal product in demand for resources is reflected in estimates of what marginal product will be when the resources are employed. On what basis would you as an employer estimate product of various resources? Would you ignore past record of various people? Would you as a football coach pay no attention to high school athletic performance when recruiting athletes, or would you look only at their physical appearance? Undoubtedly there are many talented people who could do just as well—if you only knew who they were. Marginal-productivity theory does not say that marginal product of every person in every possible job is known to all people. It says instead that demand for any resources is based on employer's estimates of marginal product of any given resource to him. It also says demand is a negative function of price of resource. Whether the theory is useless or false depends upon how well its implications agree with facts of economic life (compared with other theories). On that score it is far and away the best available theory of the demand for productive resources.

**16.** A person should be able to get a job at a salary close to his last salary without a significant cost of finding such a job.

**18. a.** Induced higher rate of immigration. Perhaps labor already in U.S. wanted to restrict entry of new laborers from Europe. Ask your history teacher. (Note that today you can import a foreigner if you will guarantee him a job or guarantee that he will not be a public-welfare recipient for a year.)

**19.** We don't know.

**21.** No. He chooses not to accept best alternative job he has so far discovered and is instead looking at more jobs—which is not to say that he is lazy or deserves to be poorer.

**23.** The superiority of one manager over another in making good decisions is worth more to a bigger firm, since the value of wealth affected by his decision is greater in big than in smaller firms. Firms will bid against each other for that superior skill—up to the value of the gain to them of that superiority, or, in other words, up to the marginal productivity to the firm of the superior managers.

**28. a.** No. The sum of a random variable, summed over trials (one for each firm), will still be a random variable. Random deviations do not cancel each other exactly.
**b.** Almost certainly. Very rare that every firm would have bigger sales on following day.
**c.** Almost certainly. Very rare that every firm would experience a decrease in sales.

# Chapter 21

**3.** All the statements are empty, wrong, or irrelevant. This question is designed not as a device to evaluate unions but rather as a device to evaluate sentences written about unions. That many sentences written about unions are empty, wrong, or irrelevant in no way implies that unions are useless, wrong, or misunderstood.

**4. a.** Ask the judge.
**b.** Ditto.

**6.** Decreased. Union will set wages higher to keep only full-time employees at work, with less interest in casual, seasonal laborers.

**9.** Correct. Those who cannot provide services worth as much as the minimum-wage rate will have to work as self-employed or commission-basis employees. Thus, in saying that a higher minimum wage reduces employment, we meant employment for wages—not productive work as self-employed or commission-basis employees.

**11. a.** It will aid people who already are employed and who are going to have heart attacks and who either do not plan to shift to new jobs or who appear not prone to heart attacks.

**b.** It will make job shifting more difficult. Will hurt those who reveal a higher probability of heart attacks insofar as they want to change jobs. Will help them as long as they stay with *current* employer (with employer at time of passage of law).
**c.** All new employees will bear some of costs since heart attack is not perfectly predictable. People with record of attack will bear heaviest cost, since they will not be able to get jobs at as high a wage as formerly.

**14.** Increase. Self-employment is a way of evading wage regulation.

**15. a.** Doesn't differ except in degree to which it reveals implications of what is said.
**b.** At $5, reduction in number of employees would be too great. Self-employed do not join unions. Meany depends upon unions.

**18.** True, but not necessarily bad.

**20.** Those people who would be willing to work at open-market wages and who do not belong to unions. You explain why.

**22.** Too embarrassing for us to answer.

**23.** Yes, except for important fact that union is not open-market monopoly and U.S. Steel is. (With respect to world open markets, both are closed-market monopolists as a result of immigration laws and tariff and taxes on imports.)

**30.** We don't know. We conjecture that employee discrimination is regarded as acceptable, and would be incapable of being prohibited by any law, in any event.

**34. a.** Correct form of statement would be that it would raise the *payments* the federal government would have to record in its budget. Real costs are being paid already by those who are drafted. The income they are sacrificing is the cost and this would be reduced if the draft were eliminated and military personnel were obtained by paying adequate wages to attract men.
**b.** You should, since it will. By better assignment of people to jobs in this country—which would be a result of using adequate wages for military personnel—the total productive efficiency and output would be increased, which means that our sacrificed output would be smaller. Draft conceals costs—by making federal expenditures lower through device of compulsory service—just as police-department costs could be made to appear lower if police were drafted.

# Chapter 22

**2.** It increases the marketable pecuniary value of wealth because it increases the future available consumption.

**3. a.** Yes. A fall in the rate of interest.
**b.** Increase the profitability.
**c.** Reduce the ratio of the price of raisins to grapes. Raise interest.

**4. a.** $50 per year.
**c.** $10 per year.
**e.** Increases from $5 to $6 per year.

**6. a.** Correct.

**b.** A different definition than that given in this question is used. (See next question.)

**7.** Investment is defined as that rate of conversion (of present income) to wealth which can be profitable. The function relating these rates to the rate of interest is the investment-demand function. Saving is defined as that rate of conversion of present income to wealth that the community wants to engage in. This desired rate, or rate at which the community is willing to divert income from current income to wealth accumulation, is a function of the rate of interest (among other things); and this relationship between the saving rate and rate of interest is the supply-of-savings function.

**11. a.** No.

**b.** In the sense that he could have even more wealth if he used his wealth differently. To say the interest rate is 10 percent means he could have used his wealth to have $110 at the end of one year. If he actually made it grow to $110 (regardless of what he then consumed), he did the best expected. If instead he managed to have it grow only to $105, his poor management has cost him $5 in consumption. We can say his poor management is equivalent to a $5 consumption activity, except that we doubt he regarded the joys of poor management as a sort of consumption activity. But then again, who knows; maybe he did—by hiring pretty girls as congenial employees rather than pecuniarily efficient ones.

**13.** False. Remember, only the more productive roundabout methods are employed. Those that are less productive are shunned. Important thing is to get right kind of capital goods—not *any* capital goods.

**15. a.** $115.60.

**b.** Three years.

**18. a.** About 200,000 rabbits.

**21.** Higher rate of investment means a higher rate of production of some goods, and this implies a higher cost per unit of those goods.

**23.** Ignoring the effects arising from the adjustments of the person from whom you got the money, and looking at only your own impact, the effect of the sequence of actions would be to push down interest rates in the bond market as you purchased bonds—but later to be reversed as we sell the bonds preparatory to purchase of other goods. If we assume the money received was new money issued by the government, then, in addition to the above transient effect, the general price level would be pushed up as the demand for goods experiences a net increase. (Admittedly, $10,000 is a drop in the bucket for the whole economy, but even drops have their ripples; and sensitive devices can measure fractions of drops.)

Chapter 23

**1. a.** Contract rate refers to stated, not effective rate. See question 1 of Chapter 13.

**b.** Among those hurt are people whose credit is so poor that they are unable to borrow at these low rates. Among those helped are the better-credit borrowers, since some funds that would have gone to high-risk borrowers are now diverted to the safer borrowers with a consequent lower interest rate to them.

**7.** Corporation managers do not have to invest all funds within the corporation. They can invest in other companies; they can lend the money. So long as they consider possible alternative investments, they will use funds within the firm only if that looks more profitable, as would be the case if the funds were to be borrowed from the market.

**10.** Soon as someone thinks an apple is ripe enough to eat with more satisfaction than not eating one at all (contrasted to eating it when it is riper and better). Apples will be eaten greener than they would be if privately owned.

**13. a.** Fish will be younger and smaller, for the same reason that apples don't ripen in a public park.
  **b.** When no one owns all the fish in the lake, the extra value of fish taken will be judged by each separate fisherman according to *his* catch rather than by the total catch in the lake. Absence of property rights in fish causes competition to acquire *property rights* in fish.

**15.** Personal human capital. Less subject to expropriation. If I were absolutely sure there would be no expropriation, I would invest in nonpersonal capital; for the buyer of the services of such goods does not associate them with the owner's personal characteristics as much as he would if buying personal services.

**17.** No. Oregon and California could buy water, just as they buy lumber and canned fish from Washington. Whether state ownership and sale of *water* are more difficult than exchange among individuals is a fine debatable question, about which not enough is known to justify any statements.

**20. b.** Higher-income spending units have a larger number of individuals in the unit; spending units are defined as groups of "all persons living in the same dwelling and belonging to the same family, who pool their incomes to meet their major expenses."
  **c.** Graduated income tax is heavier proportionately on higher incomes, hence after-income-tax picture should show smaller dispersion. But many other taxes (for example, sales, gasoline) take larger proportion from lower-income groups. Best evidence seems to be that gross tax effect is to lower very largest incomes relative to lowest, thus reducing degree of dispersion, lowering proportion of total income in top tenth, and raising it in lowest—though not by spectacular amounts.
  **d.** Post-tax measure indicates income available for spending at discretion of income unit. But to look at post-tax measure exclusively is to ignore the purposes to which taxes are put. Larger taxes provide more government services and income transfers; hence, income in fullest sense to any person is not correctly measured by his post-tax income alone.

Index